The Handbook of Marriage and Marital Therapy

The Handbook of Marriage and Marital Therapy

Edited by
G. Pirooz Sholevar, M.D.
Division of Child, Adolescent and Family Psychiatry
Jefferson Medical College
Thomas Jefferson University
Philadelphia, Pennsylvania

SP MEDICAL & SCIENTIFIC BOOKS

New York

061571

SPECTRUM PUBLICATIONS, INC.
175-20 Wexford Terrace, Jamaica, N.Y. 11432

Library of Congress Cataloging in Publication Data

Main entry under title:

The handbook on marriage and marital therapy

  Includes index.
  1. Marriage counseling—Addresses, essays, lectures. 2. Family psychotherapy—Addresses, essays, lectures. I. Sholevar, G. Pirooz.
HQ10.M37333   362.8′286   80-23237
ISBN 0-89335-120-2

Contributors

Ellen Berman, M.D.
Marriage Council of Philadelphia
Philadelphia, Pennsylvania

Ivan Boszormenyi-Nagy, M.D.
Wyncote, Pennsylvania

Sandra B. Coleman, Ph.D.
Director of Research and Evaluation
Achievement through Counselling and
    Treatment
Philadelphia, Pennsylvania

Margaret Cotroneo, M.S.N., M.A.
Department of Family Psychiatry
Eastern Pennsylvania Psychiatric Institute
Philadelphia, Pennsylvania

Norman Epstein, Ph.D.
Marriage Council of Philadelphia
Philadelphia, Pennsylvania

Ilda V. Ficher, Ph.D.
Philadelphia, Pennsylvania

Lana P. Fishkin, M.D.
Bala Cynwyd, Pennsylvania

Ralph Fishkin, D.O.
Bala Cynwyd, Pennsylvania

Abraham Freedman, M.D.
Philadelphia, Pennsylvania

Alice Greenberg, Ph.D.
Rye, New York

Milton Greenberg, M.F.T.
Rye, New York

Florence Kaslow, Ph.D.
Hahnemann Medical College
Philadelphia, Pennsylvania

Michael Kerr, M.D.
Department of Psychiatry
Georgetown University Hospital
Division of Georgetown University Medical
    Center
Washington, D.C.

Barbara R. Krasner, Ph.D.
King of Prussia, Pennsylvania

Stephen B. Levine, M.D.
Assistant Professor
Department of Psychiatry
Case Western Reserve University
Cleveland, Ohio

E. James Lieberman, M.D.
Washington, D.C.

Harold Lief, M.D.
Marriage Council of Philadelphia
Philadelphia, Pennsylvania

Betty A. Magran
Clinical Psychologist
Melrose Park, Pennsylvania

Susan V. McLeer, M.D.
Medical College of Pennsylvania
Philadelphia, Pennsylvania

William R. Miller, Ph.D.
Marriage Council of Philadelphia
Philadelphia, Pennsylvania

Mirta T. Mulhare, Ph.D.
Philadelphia, Pennsylvania

Otto Pollak, J.D., Ph.D.
Bryn Mawr, Pennsylvania

Clifford Sager, M.D.
New York, New York

G. Pirooz Sholevar, M.D.
Clinical Professor and Director
Child, Adolescent, and Family Psychiatry
Jefferson Medical College
Thomas Jefferson University
Philadelphia, Pennsylvania

John C. Sonne, M.D.
Morristown, New Jersey

Geraldine Spark, M.S.W.
Elkins Park, Pennsylvania

M. Duncan Stanton, Ph.D.
Philadelphia Child Guidance Clinic
Addict and Family Project
Philadelphia, Pennsylvania

Deborah Swirsky, A.C.S.W.
Philadelphia, Pennsylvania

Carl A. Whitaker, M.D.
Professor of Psychiatry
University of Wisconsin
Madison Medical Center for Health Sciences
Madison, Wisconsin

Anne Marie Williams, Ph.D.
Marriage Council of Philadelphia
Philadelphia, Pennsylvania

Arnold H. Winicov, J.D.
Wayne, Pennsylvania

ACKNOWLEDGMENT

I wish to express my deep appreciation to Mrs. Lillian Marcovitz for her valuable and efficient editorial assistance with this manuscript. It has been a great privilege to have the benefit of her sensitive editing, as I had with *Emotional Disorders in Children and Adolescents*. I also wish to thank Paul Jay Fink, M.D., Professor and Chairman, Department of Psychiatry and Human Behavior at Jefferson Medical College for his continued support and encouragement.

Contents

PART I

Psychodynamic Theories in Marital Therapy

Chapter 1

A Model of Marital Interaction

Ellen Berman
Harold Lief
Ann Marie Williams

INTRODUCTION

For the dynamically oriented therapist, the central problem of developing a working model of marital interaction is the difficulty of integrating individual and relational theory. Interactional models, such as communications theory, behavioral theory and systems theory, present the interactional field as the frame of reference, and behavior, in the here-and-now, as the focus. Psychodynamic models present the individual as the primary frame of reference and concentrate on motivation, conflict and defense, and the relationship of the past to the present. Finding a middle ground that includes both past and present has presented problems both in theory and in practice.

A specific issue of particular interest to marital therapists flows from this central dialectic: Are a person's responses in a given situation predominantly determined by the person's internal dynamics, so that most of the behavior can be explained by focus on the individual, almost regardless of the properties of the "object"? This would produce behavior triggered by individual and presumably regressive or idiosyncratic needs. Or is behavior determined primarily by the interactional pattern in the present, so that it can only be described or explained by reference to both partners?

A related question is whether marriages are in some way different from other relationships in terms of the rules that govern them. Behavior theory and communications theory suggest that couples respond primarily to common-sense rules and to partners' behavior: e.g., clear communication is important for lasting relations; you like someone who is good to you. Psychodynamic theory suggests that one primary function for marriage is to provide space for regression and the working out of internal conflicts. Therefore, one might choose to remain with a highly critical, ungiving person because one "needs" to, and may deliberately misconstrue communication to keep the person in that role. Marriage would then be a special case, determined by more regressive needs.

In theory, most of us nonpurists tend to see past and present as synergistic. However, in the office, faced with a depressed woman who has a distant, ungiving spouse, one tends to find oneself *either* thinking of early object loss and masochism *or* perceiving the depression as one polarized half of an interactional field, with the depression being both a response and a demand. Seeing the roots in the past and the function in the present at the same time requires considerable effort and a multilevel model.

Three recently developed theories—Sager's contract theory (Sager, 1976), Dicks' model of object relations and projective identification (Dicks, 1967), and Boszormenyi-Nagy and Spark's model of family systems loyalty (Boszormenyi-Nagy and Spark, 1973)—help us keep both systems and dynamics in perspective in the treatment of marital relationships. These theories treat issues from the past as tendencies or potentials which require the properties of an intimate other, whether innate or "coerced" by the system, to produce symptoms. These models admit the possibility of motives, will, etc., and acknowledge pain (pathology, symptoms) occurring within the person, but see symptoms as tending to manifest themselves in response to a *particular* and *specific* other and to the expectations produced by a particular institution (*this* marriage to *this* person). Each sees marriage as a special type of relationship, producing a particularly intense transactional field. Heavily based in ego psychology, these models expand the field with particular focus on transactional/marital issues.

In teaching marital dynamics from a multilevel perspective, the authors are faced with the problem that each of these theories, as well as several others, contains aspects of the truth. Rather than a new conceptualization, we have proposed a model which includes a number of these theories in relation to one another.

It is a pragmatic linking of several helpful concepts in a way that permits a look at multiple issues simultaneously (to see "all sides of the elephant") while enabling us to examine specific issues separately. As an aid to visualization we have developed Figure 1.

FIGURE I
MARITAL DYNAMICS

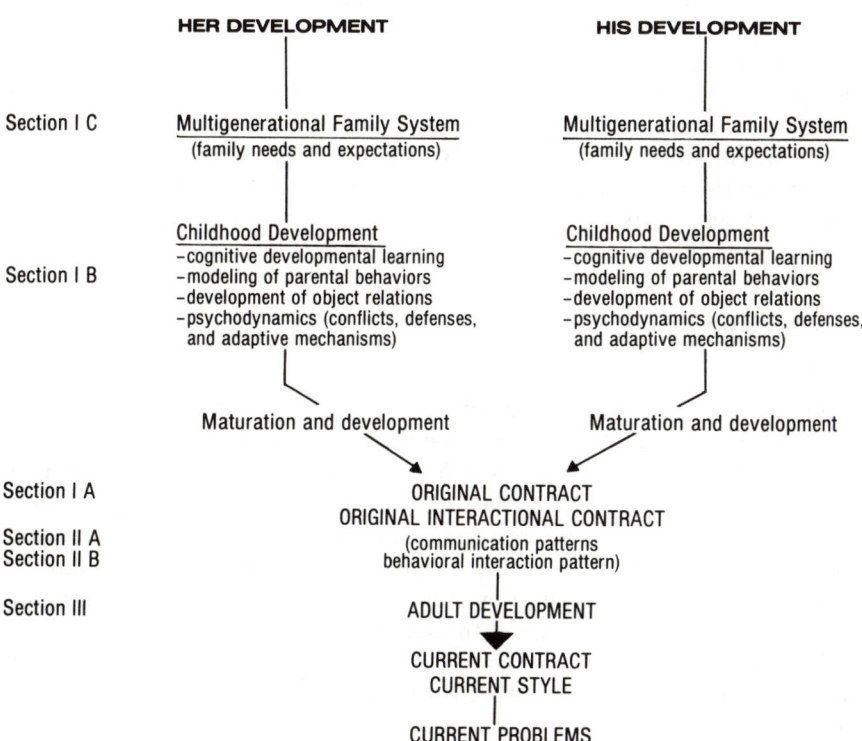

REFER TO:

HER DEVELOPMENT **HIS DEVELOPMENT**

Section I C — Multigenerational Family System / Multigenerational Family System
(family needs and expectations) / (family needs and expectations)

Section I B — Childhood Development / Childhood Development
- cognitive developmental learning
- modeling of parental behaviors
- development of object relations
- psychodynamics (conflicts, defenses, and adaptive mechanisms)

Maturation and development / Maturation and development

Section I A — ORIGINAL CONTRACT
ORIGINAL INTERACTIONAL CONTRACT
Section II A
Section II B — (communication patterns behavioral interaction pattern)

Section III — ADULT DEVELOPMENT

CURRENT CONTRACT
CURRENT STYLE

CURRENT PROBLEMS

This chapter will discuss in detail some of the theories connected by Figure 1. Information on the others is easily available.

For the purposes of this chapter, we have chosen to cover three general areas:

Section 1. The three theories we find most intriguing as ways of connecting intra- and inter-personal phenomenon: Sager's, Dicks' and Boszormenyi-Nagy and Spark's.

Section 2. Systems theory and behavioral analysis, because understanding of the basics of these theories is necessary for using them as part of our model.

Section 3. Adult development, because it is usually neglected in a discussion of marital dynamics.

Section 4. Discussion and case study. The paper concludes with a case examined from the multiple-theory perspective (as in Figure 1) and treated with a multiple-intervention approach.

It is a relief to the authors, as well as an intriguing fact of psychotherapy today, that most theoreticians are gradually coming to see systems and dynamic models as working in concert rather than as opposing ideologies. Ego psychology continues to explore transactional phenomena, systems theory has been incorporated into our psychiatry textbooks (e.g., Arieti's *American Handbook of Psychiatry* [Grinker, 1975]) and behavioral therapy is moving toward examination of cognitions, affect and unobservable reinforcers (Weiss, 1978).

Comments on Figure 1

The organizing principle of this chapter is the concept that internal processes (both conflictual and nonconflictual) affect one's present behavior and perception of the partner's behavior. These internal structures may determine the *purpose* of the behavior ("I criticize you because I want you to go away") or the *performance* of the behavior ("I criticize you because I learned from my mother's behavior that this is the way women behave"). The actual behavioral output, however, is a responsive part of the here-and-now system and is best modified through the system.

Our model, as shown in Figure 1, moves from the past to the present, examining the various events that form and modify a person's behavioral repertoire. The question of which pieces of this repertoire will be used in a particular relationship at a given time is predominantly determined by the interactional field. It is important to recognize that although they are placed in the model as "developmental issues," both projective identification and family loyalties function actively in the present.

Sager's contract theory is placed in the model at the point where the two participants join to form a relationship. The authors have a particular fondness for Sager's contract theory as an organizing principle wherein the internal percepts are translated into a particular kind of dyadic dance. Because it organizes and incorporates the other models, contract theory will be discussed in the first section of this paper.

The model then moves to the specifics of couple interaction: communications and behavior patterns at the beginning of the relationship. It then follows the changes over time in both contract and behavior, which are due to external events and internal adult development issues. Conflicts in the current contract or changes in the past-to-present contract, or both, constitute the presenting problem.

SECTION 1. THREE DYNAMICALLY BASED TRANSACTIONAL THEORIES

A. Marital-Contract Theory

Marital contract theory provides a convenient model for relating a mass of complex data from a person's past to his/her behavior in the present and for examining the formation of a dyadic system. Sager's concerns are the needs, wishes and expectations which the person brings to the marriage, which Sager describes as "the contract." Here, *contract* refers to the set of assumptions and expectations of self and partner with which each person approaches the relationship, not to a "legal," jointly agreed-on pact. Each person's individual contract is conceptualized by him or her in reciprocal terms ("If I give X, I will receive Y"), and the person behaves as if the partner had explicitly agreed to this exchange. However, since much of this contract is not shared with the partner—indeed, in the case of certain intrapsychic needs, it is not even conscious to the person making the contract—the possibilities for confusion are considerable.

Sager describes a group of expectations drawn from past learnings (both familial and cultural), within which the person chooses his/her behavior and, even more importantly, perceives and evaluates the other's behavior. The resulting contract is the abstract, or blueprint, from which will come behaviors. For example, an abstract concept such as "wives should be homemakers, husbands breadwinners" may get translated into an argument about doing the dishes.

Sager describes a three-level contract:

1. *Expectations of the marriage as an institution.* Example: "Marriage will provide financial security, children and social status."

2. *Expectations of "what I as a person need from you as a person"— intrapsychic and biologic needs.* Example: "I need sex"; "I need a certain amount of closeness"; "I need to be in charge."

3. *External foci of problems.* Example: Lifestyle, number of friends.

These contracts come from the various types of childhood development that are part of our schema. Category 1 is primarily derived from modeled behaviors (from watching parents and peers in action) as well as from cultural norms. Category 2 is developed from needs and wishes of the family of origin (see Section 1C below) and from internal, dynamically based needs. Object-relations theory (Section 1B) figures heavily in this category. Category 3 is made up of everyday behaviors and includes specific types of communication and behavioral exchange.

An important element of the individual contract is the degree to which it is shared with the partner. Sager lists three levels:

1. *Verbalized.* The person's contract is verbally stated to the other (whether or not the other agrees).

2. *Secret.* The person is aware of his contract but has not shared it, usually due to shame over the wish ("I want you to do whatever I say") or fear of the consequences ("If I tell you I don't want children, you will not marry me").

3. *Beyond Awareness.* These are preconscious or unconscious needs, such as a repressed need for nurturance in an obsessive.

The contracts a person makes are dependent on age, situation and partner. A person may form different contracts with different persons.

From these individual contracts, couples join to form a system which has its own dyadic rules, the interactional contract. This is the "how" of behavior. For example, a shared contract might be that the man is the "strong" one in the relationship. His part may be played out in a number of ways, from polite firmness to bullying. The wife's part, on the other hand, may range from gentleness to severe psychosomatic or emotional illness. The transactional contract examines reciprocal behavior and multi-person goals. In the above example, the wife's psychosomatic illness may not serve her own conscious goals, such as self-actualization, but it may serve the system's goal of maintaining stability by keeping the husband in control.

Marital *conflict*, in this model, results from incongruent or unfillable contracts. Contracts may conflict between the partners, or the person may be having an internal conflict between the conscious contract and the one beyond awareness. In addition, the contract may be unfillable by anyone (e.g., "Be perfect"), the contract may be unfillable by the particular partner (e.g., asking a schizoid person to be warm and expressive), or the person may change his/her needs over time (adult development).

The complexity of marital dynamics (and marital conflict) is due, primarily, to the level of the contract which involves the person's intrapsychic needs and which is beyond awareness. For example, we see a couple whose overt and verbalized contract includes the woman's desire for caring from the man, in return for which she will be sweet and womanly, and the man's statement that he will be strong and protective to a woman who is respectful and caring. However, her fragile self-esteem and her conflict with (and admiration for) her critical father may produce an unconscious contract that her husband be critical so he "can be a man like her father." This unconscious contract would allow her to continue to experience vicariously the original conflict with, and closeness to, her father. At a behavioral level, we see her pulling away when her husband is gentle, moving toward him when he is cruel. He, on the other hand, may also have fragile self-esteem and may respond to a woman whom he can "put down" in order to feel strong. Therefore, their verbalized contract, which requires both of them to become loving and supportive, is undermined in both cases by the unconscious contract in which distant and critical behaviors are expected. An attempt to increase his caretaking behaviors may produce resistance unless we first uncover her (and his) internal perception that kindness means he's not "really being a man."

In this couple a transactional system is initiated in which she pays attention to him when he criticizes and he supports her only when she cries helplessly. Each is then likely to continue these supposedly unwanted behaviors. The system is now self-perpetuating. If the criticism is seen as aversive, the couple can be taught to change this pattern behaviorally (e.g., she agrees to approach him lovingly whenever he is gentle). However, if at the unconscious contract level the criticism is seen as positive ("Only critical men are strong"), then nothing can be changed until her association (strong-critical) is changed.

Just as a person may change a contract with a partner over time, she/he may make a different contract with a different partner. This contract is not necessarily drawn from the whole person's personality, but is dependent on the dyadic interaction. For instance, the woman in the example above might make a contract with another man in which she is cruel and critical and he is weak. For a further discussion of this, see Section 1B, Object-Relations Theory.

Relationship to psychodynamic theory. This model is dynamically based but not oriented toward psychopathology.

Relationship to systems theory. The model includes a transactional perspective in that people are related with sets of interlocking expectations and the resulting system is based on dyadic issues.

Relationship to behavioral theory. What constitutes a reinforcer can be clarified by means of a Sager model. If a person's caretaking behavior increases in response to criticism, then either the criticism is aversive and she responds to make him decrease criticism (negative reinforcement) or the criticism itself is seen as a positive reinforcer—e.g., when he criticizes her, he is a strong, good man who is paying attention to her. Sager's model explains how an apparently aversive stimulus can be a positive reinforcer or how an apparently pleasant gesture can be interpreted as punishment, depending on the internal assumptions (the marital contract) involved in the transaction.

B. Object-Relations Theory

Objection-relations theory, especially the concept of projective identification, is an important component of the marital contract, usually occurring beyond awareness and at the level of intrapsychic needs. Object-relations theory, originally described by Fairbairn (1967) and Klein (1959), and applied to marital relationships by Dicks (1967) and others (Framo, 1970), describes the process by which conflicts that the child has with the parents are handled by introjecting the relationship and dealing with it on an intrapsychic level. The child introjects both parts of the conflict—for example, both the helpless child and the critical parent. The child may also introject *both* halves of the *parental* conflict, e.g., critical mother and passive father. In projective identification, the person, as an adult, projects on to the partner an introjected part of the self which is repressed or repudiated.

For example, using the case described in Section 1A, a woman who introjects both sides of the conflict with her father (critical father, helpless child) may repudiate the aggressive, critical component in herself and project it onto her husband. She will then interact with her partner as if he had those characteristics as a way of externalizing, while maintaining, the conflict. On the other hand, she may exhibit aggressive behavior with a weak man. This indicates her internalization of both halves of conflict and demonstrates that the nature of the relationship may elicit one or the other side of the introjected conflict.

Projective identification requires, first of all, that the person retain some identification with the projected part (otherwise she/he cannot continue the attempt to resolve the conflict). It also requires that the partner, because of his or her own needs, collude consciously or unconsciously in accepting the projection. For example, many men accept the role of logical, unemotional spouse because it fits in with their intrapsychic needs and cultural expectations. "The projection of disavowed elements onto the spouse has the effect of charging a marital relationship with conflict that has been *transposed* from the intrapsychic sphere to the interpersonal" (Zinner, 1976). Thus object-relations theory becomes a transactional frame of reference.

The polarized relationships resulting from such projections have many problems. It becomes difficult to share feelings, to "own" one's own ambivalent feelings or to produce collaborative behavior. At its extreme, people in such relationships demonstrate rigid behavior which appears sharply pathological to the observer. For example, a woman who before her marriage had competently lived alone for a number of years, proud of her total independence, marries. Her husband is seen as a strong, powerful man, like her father. She projects onto him all of her competence, allows her hidden helpless, dependent self to surface. Suddenly she is unable to drive or make a shopping list, insisting that she doesn't know why but she has "lost her nerve." Her husband objects verbally, but drives her everywhere and laughs about "my helpless little wife."

It is important to recognize the needs that such projective identification and collusion serve. First of all, they serve a defensive need—that is, one does not have to struggle with one's own ambivalent wishes. (They serve as a mechanism for continued attempts at conflict resolution.) They also serve a restorative need. They may, for example, bring back to life the individual's original object in the form of the spouse. A passive woman with an angry, assertive mother may wish to reject identification with her mother but may also need her and so bring her back in the person of her husband.

In general, such collusive relationships are tightly bonded, even if highly unpleasant, each one needing the other to carry the disavowed elements of the personality. The pain is caused by the conscious perception of the partner as oppositional, ungiving, "impossible," in spite of the unconscious collusion.

This model suggests that marriages are indeed different from other relationships. It provides a partial explanation of why a person's behavior is so often pathological or different within a marriage: only in the marriage does the person choose one polarized half of the conflict to act out while projecting the other half. It is important to recognize that most people do not project the same internal conflict equally on everyone, but only on the person with whom one allows oneself to be intimate. The intense attachments of marriage tend to elicit one's earliest conflicts in the area of object relations.

Relationship to contract theory and the overall model. Projective identification is often one part of the unconscious contract. It is an agreement expressed in "if-then" terms, developed from its origin in the initial polarized introject. It sets up internal perceptions which affect the system by interfering with communications and by programming certain kinds of behaviors.

Relationship to multigenerational family system (see Section 1C). Object-relations theory examines one mechanism by which family loyalties can be balanced using a marital partner. One can restore a lost parent. One can continue to play a family role (e.g., the fool) by projecting all of one's strength or one's anger onto one's partner. For example, a girl's role has been to "stay home with mother." She marries a mildly critical man on whom she projects her own anger and demandingness. She then responds to any criticism by calling her mother for "help," remaining loyal to her mother, who then takes care of her.

Relationship to systems and communications theory. When active (if unconscious) attempts are made to shape the other to fit the internal role models, communication can get extremely confused, since the person doing the projective identification will refuse to hear communications which do not conform to the projection. For example, a woman who states that she would like a loving, kind man, meanwhile projecting all of her disavowed aggressiveness onto her husband, will remember and acknowledge only his harsh and aggressive communications, steadfastly refusing to recognize any kind words.

Relationship to behavioral theory. Behaviorally, if the woman in the example above ignores her husband's kind behavior and responds with attention, obedience or caring only to his criticism, he may be "forced" into a set of increasingly critical behaviors (shaping by selective reinforcement). He may "collude" in producing more and more angry behavior (compliance) because of his own needs. But he may also respond in some other way, such as becoming depressed, going for therapy or getting divorced (avoidance). Although her behaviors will probably decrease his kindness, they do not *have* to increase his aggression.

The concept of collusion assumes that the person does not *have* to respond to behavioral cues in a particular way, but that the *choice* of response is determined partly by *internal* needs. Behavioral theory agrees that the person does not have to respond to cues in one predetermined way, although the role of stable internal states and traits is not assumed (that is, they may or may not exist or be necessary as constructs). Behavioral theory states that a person's response to another's behavior is a function of his or her reinforcement history, his or her response repertoire and the relative attractiveness of each option in the current cost/benefit analysis.

C. Multigenerational Family Systems

In marriage, two persons who are members of family systems join to form a marital dyad. This new system is irrevocably tied to the older ones, both through the introjected object relations of the new spouses and through the active involvement of the parent generation in day-to-day life. The totally isolated "nuclear" family is a myth; as a consequence of introjections, no family is completely isolated from its roots.

Among those examining these three, even four, generation systems are Bowen (1976), Framo (1970) and Boszormenyi-Nagy and Spark (1976). All describe complex chains of relatedness in functional families, family pathology in dysfunctional ones and how symptoms in such families may be passed down from one generation to the next. Bowen's focus is on the child (and adult) growing and moving out of the family, and he concentrates on processes which allow or disallow the differentiation of the self from the "family ego mass." Framo discusses family relatedness using the object-relations theory described in the previous section of this paper. Therapeutically, by bringing the parents into couple therapy sessions, he helps adults decrease or eliminate projections onto the spouse and deal with the conflict where it belongs, with the family of origin. He uses multigenerational-family therapy as a way of reducing spousal conflict. Boszormenyi-Nagy and Spark add a new dimension, focusing on concepts of loyalty, justice and balance of merits. They see the "major connecting tie between generations as loyalty based on the integrity of reciprocal indebtedness" (Boszormenyi-Nagy and Spark, 1976). They see parenting and "childing" as relationships in which certain things are owed—caretaking, for example, in response for love. Such concepts as loyalty and balance are multiperson considerations: one must look at the two people in relation to each other. They are also ethical and moral issues beyond pathology and personality theory. Boszormenyi-Nagy and Spark see much of the central and intense nature of family relationships as residing in this "ontic dependency," that is, the existential dependency on the "other" of one's inner family circle.

In their model families keep account ledgers of balance and imbalance—indebtedness and reciprocity. This concept does not imply a constant moment-to-moment egalitarianism. Functional families have flexible ledgers, so that one may eventually pay back what one owes at an alternate time. Only pathological families have rigid and fixed imbalances, which produce severe dysfunction. For example, a highly depressed woman acts as a martyr to her children, constantly giving of herself and allowing them to give her nothing in return. She gives up food, clothing, etc., so that they can "be happy." This produces an unchanging system of balances in which the daughter is forever in the mother's debt. She tries constantly to pay her mother back even as an adult, at the risk of ignoring her husband. She never feels that she has been able to make up for or be free of the debt to her mother. After her mother's death, she attempts to be free of the debt by giving in the same way to her daughter. Her daughter, feeling equally guilty, responds with furious anger. However, the daughter, the third generation, in spite of some attempts to separate from her mother by sexual acting-out, feels that she "owes" her mother. She remains unmarried and asks her mother to join her and her partner in a complex family business.

Spouses may try to right family imbalances through the marital partner. For example, a businessman and his wife raising children in the Depression work seven days a week, leaving little time for their children. Their child feels abandoned but loyal to her parents because "they couldn't help it." She attempts to balance her accounts by marrying a man who "should make up for my lost childhood" as a conscious, although secret, part of her contract. Severe marital stress follows his inability to do so.

One of the tasks of adulthood is rebalancing one's obligations to one's family and learning to balance old loyalties with new ones. One of the most common ways of balancing loyalty to one's parent is to become a parent, thereby giving to one's child what one has received. However, this is not a totally satisfactory solution. The grandparent generation may still demand, either in reality or in the person's fantasy, overwhelming loyalty. For example, the son of immigrant parents, who had fled their country penniless, grows up in this country, marries and has children. Both he and his parents feel that he could never make up to them for their loss of country and their total concern for his welfare. Therefore, after he marries he still sides with his parents against his wife and takes his parent's side when the parents and the wife argue. This man is unable to rebalance his old loyalties with his new ones because of his sense of fixed and inflexible indebtedness and loyalty.

Even if the couple is able to make a reasonable attempt to balance their old loyalties with their new ones, many new problems come up in the new dyad because each family has its own type of accounting system. For example, the husband in a new marriage comes from a family where one shows affection by financial giving. The wife's family does not use money as part of its accounting system but is eager to give affection and support. Does the couple owe one family more than the other? What does the couple owe each family?

The multigenerational focus is a crucial and often neglected area of marital functioning. Boszormenyi-Nagy and Spark's conceptualization is a multiperson, system-based theory. It speaks particularly to the specialness of family relationships.

Relationship to contract theory and the overall model. Loyalty and balancing of accounts are critical parts of the marital contract, as each member tries to determine what is owed to the partner versus what is owed to the family of origin.

Relationship to psychodynamic theory. This model is essentially an addition to, and elaboration of, certain aspects of psychodynamic theory. Concepts of loyalty and justice are cognitive constructs, but involved with and elaborated from a dynamic base.

Relationship to behavioral theory. Family-systems approaches provide another way of looking at the cognitive constructs that become translated into behavior. For example, the child who continues to give and give to a highly critical and ungiving parent is apparently increasing behavior in the face of punishment. However, if the child has an inner sense of unmet obligations to the parent and therefore feels guilty, he continues the behavior because it satisfies his inner accounting system. In this case his internal response (decreased guilt) serves as a negative reinforcer and maintains his behavior.

SECTION 2. SYSTEMS THEORY AND BEHAVIORAL ANALYSIS

A. Systems Theory

It is the authors' contention that systems theory itself is not in conflict with dynamic models but, rather, can incorporate them. To examine this we must first move to a discussion of its basic postulates. The concepts expressed in systems theory form the underpinning of all interactional models of behavior. In our model it describes the interactional contract.

Systems theory is usually mentioned in discussions of family theory or therapy as if its premises were widely known, and thus is seldom reviewed in any detail. It is often forgotten that "systems theory" itself is really a highly abstract set of postulates essentially derived from mathematics and physics rather than from psychology.

Systems theory offers a point of view rather than specific information about specific people. Systems theory is a set of postulates or rules describing the interaction of "objects which are mutually interdependent" (*objects* in this sense can be, for example, people or factories or chemicals). The objects in a system form a group which is not additive (five pennies in a row) but cumulative—the machines, men, copper, that are components of a mint interacting in a way to produce pennies. The interactions of the components form a transactional field that can be studied.

Systems are characterized by the following: wholeness, equifinality and relationships among objects by means of feedback loops. Watzlawick defines these terms as follows (Watzlawick, 1967):

1. *Wholeness.* "Every part of the system is so related to its fellow parts that a change in one part will cause a change in all of them and in the total system. That is, the system behaves not as a simple composite of independent elements, but coherently and as an inseparable whole."

2. *Equifinality.* "In a circular and self-modifying system, results (in the sense of alteration and state after a period of time) are not determined so much by initial conditions as by the nature of the process for the system's parameters. The same results may spring from different origins because it is the nature of the organization which is determinant."

3. *Feedback Loops.* Parts of the system relate by means of feedback loops, which are highly complex nonlinear chains of relatedness. Feedback loops are circular, with each response being determined by the one before.

In examining a system, therefore, one thinks not in terms of unidirectional cause and effect, but in terms of ongoing interactions. One can only pick an arbitrary point at which to begin the examination of the circular feedback chain. In the factory above, for example, a slowdown in production may be the result of multiple interacting events—poor machinery because of poor maintenance because the men are angry at the foreman because of old machinery. In a marital system one can also see such chains. For example, a husband and wife come in for therapy together. The husband complains that the wife nags. The wife complains that she nags only because the husband is quiet and never speaks to her. He complains that he is driven to silence by her nagging. As the wife nags, the husband becomes more passive in response to the nagging, and as he becomes more passive, she becomes angry. The question of which came first becomes academic, since both now reinforce each other. Within the system, therefore, these two people form a transactional field in relationship to each other, and their behavior is determined by feedback loops and demonstrates equifinality. Changing either's behavior *must* change the other's since they occur in relation to each other (wholeness).

Each system usually has some differentiated parts, which serve special functions in relation to one another, and some hierarchy or organization, but the important thing is that all of the parts are interrelated. In open systems, groups of objects in equilibrium with their environment have a free passage of materials between the system and its environment. If the human body is considered as a system, the internal organs form subsystems, each affected by the other. Or the man could be seen as a subsystem of a larger biological system (all humans) interacting with the environment (nature). In this way organic systems can be seen as Chinese nesting boxes, each part of a larger system.

As we shall see, what is intriguing about this model is not its simplicity but its complexity; that is, when groups of organisms are viewed in this perspective, it becomes clear that there is no unidirectional cause and effect, but that one must consider all parts of the system in their relationship to one another and take into account a hierarchy of systems. It is also fascinating to recognize that this particular set of abstract principles applies to such a wide variety of seemingly unconnected things.

What it offers is the possibility of organizing principles beyond the individual person, e.g., shared multiperson goals. For example, if the family system goal is stability, a child's behavior can be seen in the larger context of keeping the family together. A child's sickness may be functional in terms of stabilization for a family system because it allows the fighting parents to join around the child. Conversely, when the child is well, the parents' arguments may escalate toward divorce.

The abstract quality of systems theory obviously omits a number of issues. It does not discuss teleology, although it does examine a system's role in the larger system. In human psychological systems, the theory says nothing about motivation, although it says a lot about communication. It cannot say *why* a relationship begins or survives (how the components got together) or why two people may stay in a relationship, making each other miserable for years, while two other people may divorce. It only states that *as long as* the participants remain in relation to each other, they will form complex and interacting patterns which can be tracked and examined in certain specific ways.

Relationship to the overall model. Systems theory is the basic theoretical construct underlying all transactional models of behavior. It explains the functioning of the interactional contract.

Relationship to psychodynamic theory. Psychodynamic theory explores the "properties of the objects"—in this case, people. To some extent any system obviously must vary with the properties of its parts. In human systems, for example, people do not have infinite repertoires of behavior. Systems theory at the abstract level does not involve itself with the aspects of people that include motivation, value systems, personality styles, etc., except as they are properties of the objects which affect interaction. Neither, however, do psychodynamic theories suggest that feelings or behavior take place in a vacuum. All dynamically oriented models include transactions with the environment. However, there is a real difference between psychodynamic theory, in which the *majority* of the person's behavior is seen as determined by internal forces, and systems theory, which examines the behavior of the objects *in relationship to one another*, as an organic whole.

Relationship to communications theory. Systems theory assumes that in the relationships among objects the feedback loops may be of different kinds. With plants, for example, the actual interactions between the plant and soil are chemical reactions. With people, the interactions occur by means of communication—including symbols (words) and nonverbal messages. Systems theory assumes that messages have impact on the system regardless of whether the target receives them, since the sender assumes reception. Communications theory examines sending and receiving behavior. It points out that human beings as objects in a system are often "faulty senders"—that is, the "intent" may be different from the observable message sent. They may also be "faulty receivers"—that is, what is intended or sent by the sender may not be what is heard by the receiver (impact). Communications theory can be seen as a piece of systems theory which can be factored out and examined.

Relationship to behavior theory. Behavioral theory states that behaviors are produced in interaction with another, and that certain kinds of communication produce certain specific effects on the other. For example, a positive reinforcement (smile) will probably increase a behavior that precedes it. Behavioral theory, therefore, is one way of describing some of the internal transactions of a human system.

B. Behavior Analysis

Behavioral analysis is a way of describing the working of the interactional contract. Contrary to the caricature of "behavior mod," behavior analysis of dyadic interaction is dynamic rather than static: it assumes that there is more to interpersonal behavior than meets the eye. Based on operant theory and the social learning model of transactions, it incorporates the empirical observations of Skinner (see *Science and Human Behavior*, 1953) and the social-exchange theories of Homans (1950) and Thibaut and Kelley (1959). For a description of the integration of these theories with the more recently developed cognitive approach (Mahoney, 1977), see Weiss' theoretical overview (Weiss, 1978).

The major emphasis of behavior analysis is on the four basic types of behavior: two types of *reinforcement* that *increase* or maintain the likelihood of the responses they follow, and two types of *punishment* that decrease the likelihood of the responses they follow.

These four basic types of behavior are assumed to occur intermittently, frequently and either alone or in combination. They are thought to be largely, but not entirely, responsible for the waxing and waning (approach-avoid) patterns in dyadic relationships in dynamic equilibrium. Individual learning history (childhood development), biological functioning (genetic inheritance and physical health) and social environment (culture, society, neighborhood, job schedule, situation, etc.) are all assumed to have chronic impact on the individuals who comprise the couple. These variables are considered extremely important but are not generally the primary focus of behavioral analysis or intervention unless or until they impinge acutely on the behavioral system (e.g., job loss, herniated disc or visit from parents).

Increased Responses

The first type of behavior, *positive reinforcement* (often referred to as a reward), is something the person wants more of or will work to get (e.g., a salesman's commission or a good grade on an exam). When we want clients to be more pleasant with each other, we can point out and applaud (give attention and approval to) the interactions we want to encourage rather than dwelling on the problems we want to eliminate.

While we may guess that a particular response will be positive, its value can be defined only by its *impact* on the behaviors or events it *immediately follows*. For example, a husband was transfixed by a football game all afternoon, and his wife (who felt taken for granted) served him a particularly good meal *immediately* after the game. Subsequently, the special dinner increased (or maintained) the likelihood that he would watch weekend sports on TV in the future. She has accidently reinforced him for ignoring her by rewarding him with dinner. She was correct in guessing that the food would have a positive impact. However, due to bad timing, the positive impact was to increase the behavior she had wanted to decrease (his ignoring her) rather than to increase the behavior she had hoped for (his attention and affection).

The second type of behavior, *negative reinforcement*, is a difficult concept to grasp and is usually confused with punishment. Despite the connotation of "negative" as *bad* in the sense of criticism or negative feedback, negative reinforcement is a *good* thing. It involves the reduction or elimination of an unpleasant stimulus (a situation or behavior). It *increases* or maintains the response it *immediately follows*. For example, a shot of Demerol for the pain of a broken leg reduces the pain and can *increase* the likelihood of seeking medical help in the next emergency. We can be accidently reinforced for banging a fist on a TV plagued with static interference if coincidentally the static stops.

As with the husband-wife example given above, negative reinforcement can have the desired impact but on the wrong behavior. In the case above, the wife's nonverbal behavior at dinner (slumped shoulders, head bent, deep sighs) signaled the husband that her feelings were hurt. In order to escape feeling guilty and avoid a crying spell, he complimented her cooking and suggested they go see a movie together. She agreed. Removal of her sulking increased the probability of his compliments (negative reinforcement for him). Unfortunately, it cannot be forecast whether his attention to her *at that moment* (that is, when he stopped ignoring her) will also increase the likelihood of good meals or instead increase the likelihood of her dejected mannerisms, or both.

Decreased Responses

The third type of behavior is *punishment*, the presentation of an aversive stimulus or condition in order to decrease or eliminate an unwanted behavior. While punishment is often used because of its immediate impact (i.e., decreasing temporarily the behavior it follows), the short-term effects on the target behavior are usually eclipsed by the long-term effects on the giver-receiver relationship. A fourteen-year-old who is beaten for yelling back at his or her parent may be quiet then (short-term), but may run away from home to avoid future beatings (long-term).

As with both types of reinforcement, punishment may have an unexpected impact if it is not carefully timed. When a husband calls to tell his wife he will be late and she screams at him *for being late*, he apologizes on the phone. However, her punishment may decrease the likelihood of both his calling her and his working harder to get home sooner. She *intends* to decrease his lateness behavior, but instead decreases his "phone calls to wife" behavior. Furthermore, the long-term impact may be to increase his avoidance of her. More generally, we avoid those who have punished us in the past, depending on the cost/benefit ratio involved in keeping up the relationship.

The fourth type of behavior is a form of punishment which involves removing or withholding something the person wants more of (e.g., sex, money, conversation, etc.). When access to a positive stimulus is prevented (e.g., when a parent says "no TV" in response to a poor report card), the form of punishment is referred to as a *time out*. The wife, in the example above, may time-out her husband sexually for the duration of football season. Again, he may associate the punishment with her as a person ("She's frigid") rather than with the behavior of his that she was attempting to decrease ("He always takes me for granted").

One final behavior pattern is essential to our discussion because of its pervasiveness in distressed relationships. This pattern, *coercion*, is noteworthy as an attempt to change or control one's partner in that its short-term effects are rewarding for both partners while its long-term effects are devastating to the relationship. One partner demands an immediate response by haranguing, nagging or some other relatively inescapable aversive stimulus. The recipient has three options: (1) complying, (2) avoiding the situation by leaving or (3) overtly punishing the instigator (e.g., by physical abuse).

If the recipient's response is compliance with the coercive demand, the instigator gets what he or she demanded (positive reinforcement) while the recipient gets a temporary end to the nagging (negative reinforcement). For the short-term, both partners are paid off. In the long run, the instigator is seldom satisfied with the response given under duress ("He didn't really mean it, it doesn't count"). The receiver feels coerced and usually shows his or her resentment by reciprocating with punishment or a time out.

The recipient's second option, avoiding the situation by leaving, may be an effective time out to decrease the nagging. However, avoidance can be "rewarded" to the point of separation or divorce. Alternative partners may become more attractive.

The third option, the use of direct punishment, such as physical abuse, is often at great cost to the individuals and to the relationship. Again, the punisher in this case becomes aversive, and sooner or later punishment begets punishment or avoidance. In practice the best option is the most difficult—to ignore the nagging *at the time*, state clearly *later* that nagging is aversive and reward a more desirable form of "request" from the partner.

In cases of wife abuse in which "the wife doesn't seem to mind being beaten," it may turn out that a thirty-minute beating follows four weeks of being ignored and immediately precedes six weeks of "honeymoon" behavior from the repentant husband who goes to extraordinary ends "to make it up to her." The beating may signal the end of being ignored (negative reinforcement) *and* the beginning of being catered to (positive reinforcement). Again, the behavior decides the value of the behavior (taking a beating) in her individual cost/benefit analysis.

Behavior analysis would be simple enough if each of these four types of behavior occurred one at a time; however, they tend to occur in combination or concurrently. Furthermore, it is assumed that due to stimulus generalization (e.g., *any* TV sports besides football may remind the wife that she felt ignored), the triggering behavior may not appear to an outside observer to be related to the previous interaction. Also, the "schedule effects" (Skinner) may be such that because of a lean schedule of *intermittent* positive reinforcement from the husband, the wife may seem to be "masochistic" due to her repeated attempts to get her husband's attentions, apparently to no avail. He need pay her off only occasionally to maintain her behavior. An understanding of the effects of schedules (fixed versus variable, and interval versus ratio), which is critical to applied behavior analysis, is beyond the scope of this chapter (Skinner, 1953).

Behavioral Analysis of Marital Interaction

The behavioral approach assumes that the happiness derived from a long-term intimate relationship like marriage is a function of the ongoing reward/cost ratio in the male-female interactions as well as of each partner's comparison level for alternative sources of reinforcement. Depending on the time, energy and resources required by the relationship and the corresponding benefits received, the partners stay with each other or seek a less costly, more rewarding relationship elsewhere.

Behavior analysis focuses on the identification of dysfunctional patterns of interaction between partners rather than on the identification of intrapsychic conflicts of married individuals. Behavior therapy emphasizes fading out these detectable cycles of maladaptive behavior and gradually replacing them with more adaptive, more rewarding interactions. By teaching the couples to specify *which* behaviors they want more of from their partners, *how* to avoid punishment and coercion, *how* to accentuate the positives and *how* to negotiate a mutually satisfying exchange, behavior therapy works to strengthen the marital bond through successful fulfillment of the transactional contract.

Relationship to Sager and the model as a whole. Behavioral analysis is a way of looking at the details of the *interactional* contract. What each person sees as a reinforcer is determined by the terms of his or her *individual* contract (i.e., based on the reinforcement history, response repertoire and the relative attractiveness of interaction with that person at that time and place).

Relationship to psychodynamic theory. Behavioral theory, like psychodynamic theory, relies heavily on the history of the organism, including early experiences in parent-child interactions. However, the behavioral approach also emphasizes the more recent history which occurred *since* the formation of the dyad. A traumatic early event may set the stage for a dysfunctional pattern, but it is assumed that the current relationship is maintaining it by supporting old responses.

Relationship to systems theory. Systems theory states that feedback loops exist and that components of a system influence one another. Behavioral analysis is one way of examining the functioning of transactions within a human system. It specifies *how* components interact and *how* feedback loops work; it can provide us with a microanalysis of psychological systems functioning.

SECTION 3. ADULT DEVELOPMENT

Once a contract has been made between the members of the couple, what will cause them to wish to change the terms of the contract? This area is best examined through recently developed research on adult development, which suggests that certain kinds of needs and expectations in adults change over time in relatively predictable stages. If this is true, the marital contract would need periodic restructuring if the members remain together.

This particular model is not transactional but individual. The original theory, as proposed by Levinson (1978), does not describe how individual needs are translated into the relationship. We have included this subject because we feel that it is an often neglected reason for contractual changes and resulting conflicts.

Levinson's concept of the life structure and its changes is central to this construct. Life structure is defined as the "underlying pattern or design of a person's life at a given time" and includes the individual's socio-cultural matrix, aspects of the self (such as values), ego functions and the person's participation in the world. The person is viewed as an active agent creating his/her own life structure. Levinson describes stable periods of six to eight years, in which the task is to form a stable life structure, and transition periods at the end of each decade of three to five years, in which the task is to review, examine and revise it. He describes the following periods in the life structure:

22 to 40—early adulthood. Forming an initial life structure, becoming fully adult (Erikson's [1950] "intimacy vs. isolation").

1. *22 to 28.* "Getting into the adult world" and forming a provisional life structure.
2. *27 to 31.* Age 30 transition—questioning one's initial life structure.
3. *32 to 38.* "Settling in," becoming a full adult; the usual life structure includes marriage, children or occupation, but there are many functional life structures (singlehood, childlessness, etc.).

40 to 60—mid-adulthood. (Erikson's [1950] generativity versus stagnation).

1. *Age 40 transition,* which may take much of the decade: What have I done with my life?; issues of generativity, giving back to the community; life structure for the next half of life, reassessment and revision of life structure.
2. *50's transition.* Questioning one's new life structure. May not be necessary if age 40 transition has been prolonged.
3. *52 to 60.* Settling down into mid-adulthood.

60 to 80—later adulthood. (Erikson's [1950] integrity versus despair). Settling accounts with oneself, choosing a life structure for the remaining years.

1. *59 to 62.* Age 60 transition—life review: summing up, finding new life structure and goals for remaining years.
2. *70 transition.* Settling into older adulthood.
3. *70's.* "Old old," issues of declining health are usually central.

Levinson and others see the period of the forties as perhaps the most turbulent and confused, with people being at the peak of their power and also coping with their loss of youth, changing bodies and missed opportunities.

Adult-development research suggests that real change in personality can occur as one ages. Vaillant's research indicates that intrapsychic defenses change and mature (1977). Neugarten and others (1964) suggest increased passivity and interiority among men in older age groups. Certainly one's sense of time, of what is vital to one's existence and what isn't, and one's perception of oneself in the world are apt to change quite drastically over adult life (Neugarten and Datan, 1974).

Since marriage requires, among other things, at least some shared goals and some shared perceptions of the spouse's personality, needs and wishes, individual developmental changes can produce considerable marital disruption. The husband in a counterculture marriage who at age thirty decides to exchange his casual lifestyle for a high-pressure career in business is going to have real problems with his marriage regardless of the couples' communication skills. At a less extreme level, the obedient "little wife" who realizes at age forty that she has ideas and wishes of her own may begin to demand notice and consideration. This may require considerable changes from a husband who assumes he "knows what is good for the family."

Marital stress is most likely to occur at transition periods. Periods of life review often begin with a sense of vague dissatisfaction and restlessness. During the transition phase, everything may feel "out of joint"; serious questioning occurs and a need for change is often felt. The decision as to life structure can affect the marriage; for example, the husband wants to settle down, while the wife wants to get into the adult world. These are particularly stressful points for already troubled relationships because marriages that have been difficult but bearable often tend to be perceived as unbearable during a life review. There is some evidence of an increase in therapy seeking, both marital and individual (Marmor, 1975), during transition periods.

This model also has implications for people who are working on life-structure tasks in nontraditional order or who marry someone much older or younger. For example, a man in his early forties going through the mid-life transition may divorce and marry a woman twenty-three or twenty-four years old. He may be experimenting, but it is still a different kind of experimentation from the kind he experienced in late adolescence or in his early twenties. It is therefore crucial that the marital therapist examine the marital contract in terms of the age of the couple and of whether the conflicts and needs of different life stages have been a precipitant of marital conflict.

Relationship to contract theory and overall model. Adult development is a frequent reason for unilateral changes in the original contract. When these are not matched by compatible changes in the partner, conflict may result.

Relationship to psychodynamic theory. Adult-development theory suggests that conflicts and motivations derived from child development tend to be modified and change in adulthood. This broadens and amplifies psychodynamic theory.

Relationship to systems theory. Adult development discusses the "properties of the object." Although these changes are internal, they occur in the context of the system and are modified by it.

SECTION 4. DISCUSSION AND CASE STUDY

Discussion

We have seen that there are a variety of ways of organizing data that allow the historical and individual past to be linked to the transactional and behavioral present. We have examined the ways in which perceptions affect behavior and how individuals can form interlocking systems where outcome is determined by the transactional field.

A problem with a model such as ours, which is a multitheory approach, has to do with therapeutic effectiveness and ideological purity. Can an eclectic approach be organized, or is it by definition a grab-bag approach?

There is little question that in order to develop new theory, and especially to do research in the field, one must limit one's scope in order to study specific interventions. However, research indicates that no one theory has been clearly superior to others. Nonspecific factors, such as hope, are crucial to success (Frank, 1973), while the characteristics of the therapy relationship—such as having someone in the role of helper, having a place to ventilate and having a rationale for changing one's behavior—are, rather than specific therapy modalities, often the moving forces for change.

It is also true that therapists are more alike in what they do than in what they say about therapy. Most psychoanalysts find themselves in some way indirectly making behavioral suggestions, and behaviorists develop warm, empathic relationships with clients, even if they do not focus on them or deem them important.

How does a therapist choose interventions in keeping with a consistent style and philosophy while taking all aspects of the problem into account? Particularly in marriage and family therapy, there are an extraordinary number of issues to be considered.

The authors feel that a model such as ours provides a point of approach. It allows attention to be paid to both past and present, to both internal percepts and the transactional field.

The model can be used to plan an approach to therapy which pinpoints a variety of problem areas while allowing a concise formulation. It can be used to form a multiple intervention therapeutic approach or to allow the therapist, using one preferred model, to check her/himself against other points of view.

The following case describes a multi-problem dyad treated using a number of approaches at different points in time. We have organized the history using the form suggested in Figure 1 to demonstrate its use. The particular case was treated by one therapist who was trained as a psychiatrist and who tends to make frequent use of individual sessions. There are a variety of styles by which this couple could have been treated. We offer this as one example of the use of our model.

CASE STUDY

Mr. and Mrs. A are thirty-two and thirty-three years old, respectively. He is a lawyer and she is a housewife currently attending school on a part-time basis. They have two children and have been married ten years. They are attractive, well-dressed people.

Mrs. A requested treatment as an individual patient for a depression, increasing in severity over the last year, lightening slightly when she was away from the house. Her depression included somatic symptoms, such as fatigue, lack of appetite and some sleep disturbance. She was unsure whether the depression was her own problem or the result of her poor marriage, and alternately placed the blame on herself ("Maybe I'm crazy") and her husband, whom she described as distant and ungiving. Her major complaints about marriage involved "not getting what I want—neither money nor sex nor affection."

She gave a history of feeling totally neglected as a child. She is the oldest of three children born to parents who owned a small, not too secure business and who worked seven days a week. Her mother is described as a dominant and intrusive woman, her father as depressed and critical. The parental value system included education, social status and an upper-middle-class life style for the children. She states that she had no friends while growing up, and spent a good deal of time taking care of her youngest sister.

The patient's early history alone was sufficient to have easily produced a demanding and depressive personality. However, because of pervasive complaints related to her marriage, the couple was seen together and the husband also was seen alone.

Her husband turned out to be the first and adored child of quiet and controlled people. The predominant motifs of his early upbringing were "Don't make a fuss," "Be a good boy" and "Be a lawyer." A competent and take-charge professional at work, by the time he and his wife came into therapy, he had given up all authority in the house. Most of his energy was put into his work. He did not appear depressed and indeed denied feeling almost anything at all. His apparent lack of affect enraged his wife.

The couple married the summer before the husband began law school. Courtship had occurred while they were both in college. They shared a common commitment to an upper-middle-class life style and value system. Mr. A described his wife as funny and amusing. Mrs. A felt that her husband "put her up on a pedestal" and also offered her a way of leaving home. Her husband began law school immediately following the honeymoon and devoted himself totally to his studies. His wife tried to be a "good wife" but was upset by any criticism and angered by the low sexual frequency (once a week). At first she responded to this distancing by increased anxiety and then by slowly increasing depression. As the children were born, she spent most of her energies taking care of them. Her continued depression generally produced avoidance behavior in her husband. After he finished training, he began a demanding job for a firm. However, she became further depressed by his inability to rapidly pay off his law school debts so that their standard of living would increase to a high level.

For the last several years, sex occurred with decreasing frequency due to the husband's lack of interest. There was no specific sexual dysfunction. Both were, and are, orgasmic during intercourse. Mrs. A's response to sex: "It is usually good, but why not more often?" Mr. A's response to sex: "I have to do this for *her*."

Both families of origin have continued to be somewhat active within the marriage. Mrs. A is still quite close to her mother, whom she visits frequently. She responds to her mother's frequent criticism with anger and hurt; she watches carefully for signs of affection from her mother. Mr. A's parents are more tentative and less directly involved. However, he feels that they "gave up a lot so I could be a professional, and I owe it to them to be a success." Numerous holidays are spent with the maternal inlaws or both sets of inlaws. Mr. A feels that Mrs. A "neglects" him when her mother is around, and he resents his mother-in-law's intrusions. However, both spouses are committed to continuing contact with both sets of parents, in spite of the turmoil they sometimes create.

Specific conflicts occur around disciplining children, sex, spending money, family parties.

Interaction pattern. Critical comments by husband tend to produce intense upset in the wife. She is alternately hostile and demanding, and withdrawn and depressed. The depressions last two to three days, during which she generally withdraws emotionally, although she does complete household tasks. Mr. A adopts a stance of helplessness and resignation, alternating with mild complaints and occasionally an explosion over a minor issue. He tends to be most giving when she is physically ill. She becomes more upset at his withdrawal and also becomes angry when his promises to "do better" are not followed up.

The husband's attempts at giving are usually rejected. For example, his wife sent back a coat he bought her because it was "too expensive," reducing his interest in trying to find appropriate presents. The wife's attempts at giving are rejected by the husband because (1) she makes inappropriate or criticism-including attempts (e.g., making an elaborate dinner she knew he wouldn't like and being upset when he wouldn't eat it); and (2) he perceives any positive move as a demand for affection.

There are numerous ways of organizing this material. Referring to Figure 1 as a way of taking history and organizing it helps place a complex marriage in perspective and pinpoint multiple areas of intervention.

HER DEVELOPMENT	HIS DEVELOPMENT
Intergenerational Loyalties	*Intergenerational Loyalties*
Angry at parents for "not giving me a childhood," but also protective (loy-	Loyal to parental values—hard work, low affect level.

alty) because "they had to survive and they didn't know any better"; therefore, husband is to make up for lost childhood.

Loyalty to original family outweighs loyalty to husband: "If they were both in a rowboat and I had to save one, I'd save Mother."

Feels he has to pay back his parents' devotion by being a success at work.

Dynamics

Feelings of neglect produce lowered self-esteem (I am bad) and anger (I am good—the world is rotten). She vacillates between projection and introjection of hate.

Unsatisfied oral needs—produce need of but fear of closeness.

Dynamics

Nurturant, protective father produces identification with nurturant male (caretaking).

Strong punitive superego—sees self as needing to be "good" at all costs.

Object Relations

She projects onto him her image of disliked, weak father and her own introjected critical, angry impulses.

Object Relations

He projects onto her his introjected emotionality and repudiated need for nurturance.

CHILD DEVELOPMENT

Cognitive Vision of the World and Her Place in It

I deserve nice things to make up for my hurt—I am really a princess and deserve a prince.

If I am a perfect wife, I will get what I want.

Being a good wife is opposite of my mother.

All men are unloving and ungiving.

Cognitive Vision of the World and His Place in It

The world is an O.K. place.

If something goes wrong, I am responsible.

Making a spectacle of yourself is bad.

Feelings are dangerous.

Modeled Behaviors

Complaining, nagging and intrusive behavior (from mother).

Inability to accept warmth or compliments (from both parents).

Focus on money and "things as a way of showing loving" (from mother).

Modeled Behaviors

Passivity, silence and retreat in the face of strong feeling (like father).

Unwillingness to "make a fuss" (from both parents).

Unwillingness to admit to feelings (from father).

From these early learnings a *conflicted contract* is produced.

ORIGINAL
INDIVIDUAL
CONTRACTS

Hers	*His*
I will be amusing, warm and respectful. I will share your life style, have children, keep a beautiful house. In return, you will take care of me emotionally and materially.	I will be faithful to you and take care of you. I will be a lawyer and provide you with house, children, and enough money; in return, you will be warm, loving and social.

Secret

I will love you and you will put me first, put me up on a pedestal and make me feel like a princess.

I will be a perfect wife (unlike my mother). I will be sexy, open and vulnerable. In return, you will be sexy (like my father), strong (unlike my father), and intimate and loving (like my fantasy parent).   (conflict)

You will be perfect.

You will be the man my mother wanted me to marry.

You will help me get out of my house and make up for my lost childhood.

You will become rich, so we can live well (money does buy happiness).

(conflict)

(conflict)

I will be quiet and work hard.

You will allow me to work hard.

You will not demand much of me emotionally. In return I will be a good provider, a good father to our children.

Beyond Awareness

I will be loyal to my mother's values.

All men are unloving and ungiving, like my father—you will be too—thus I can keep my defenses up.

(conflict)

You will be distant and ungiving so I can feel hurt but not at fault.

You will be weak so I can side with my mother.

(conflict)

I will take care of myself because I really am alone.

Sex is frightening. You will not ask me for sex. I will not demean you by asking for it.

You will provide a burden to take care of so I can prove I am good; in return I will take care of you.

You will be the emotional one in the family.

ADULT DEVELOPMENT

Age thirty crisis produces first attempts to seek therapy.

Difficulty in feeling "settled" produces increased depression.

Increasing need for intimacy during thirties (wish to settle in).

Sense of increasing age ("time is running out") makes him more amenable to therapy.

CURRENT CONTRACT

No basic changes

CURRENT PRESENTING PROBLEM

Conflicts over: Sex (his disinterest)
Money (not enough for her)
"Communication"
In-laws
Her depression, which makes him feel helpless or depressed

Formulation 1—Dynamic, transactional level. A depressed, demanding woman with low self-esteem and rigidly negative views of the world, married to an emotionally isolated, protective male with a strong need to be a "good person." She projects onto him her self-hate and her cold, critical, distancing feelings; he projects onto her his disavowed helpless and dependent needs.

Formulation 2—The contract level. A couple conflicted both inter- and intra-personally. Conflicts occur primarily in the area of intrapsychic needs (especially dependence and distance versus closeness) at the secret or unconscious levels. Conflicts over marital expectations, developed primarily from family loyalty patterns, are also present.

Formulation 3—Behavioral systems level. She withholds positives and replaces them with demands (more sex, money, attention). He punishes her with "time outs" (withdrawal). Cycle returns to starting point when either her depressions become aversive to him and he apologizes to her or she becomes frightened by his distance and becomes warm and affectionate to him.

TREATMENT PLAN

Our model (Figure 1) determined that this couple has problems at several levels. At the *behavioral* level, poor communications techniques (due to modeling of undesirable behaviors from parents, plus frustration and anger with the partner) lead to a high frequency of punishment (both direct and time out) and coercive demands and nonacknowledgment of what would normally be positive reinforcement. Internal conflicts in each partner confound the effect of apparently positive reinforcers. For example, the wife's approach is interpreted by the husband as both pleasant (love) and aversive (desire for intimacy perceived as coercive demand).

At the *contract* level, there is a conflict between partners at the "secret" and "beyond-awareness" levels. There is also a conflict within the wife between contract levels. The conflicts lead to confusion over which behaviors each wishes increased. Strikingly, the verbal contract between the partners is not in conflict, and there are wide areas of agreement as to values, life-style issues, etc. The conflicted contracts are developed from

1. Multigenerational systems—the wife's conflict between loyalty to her family and loyalty to her husband, the wife's need to have her husband balance her parent's deficiencies.

2. Projective identification—the wife's projection of her critical and self-hating introjection onto her husband, and the husband's projection of his soft and emotional introject onto his wife.

3. Child-developmental issues—the wife's low self-esteem, from her psychodynamic conflicts and rigidly held irrational beliefs, and the husband's inability to tolerate intimacy, from both parental models and cognitive learnings. Adult-development issues were not central to the problems in this case, although they helped to precipitate entrance into therapy.

In this case it was decided that teaching specific communications techniques was necessary and that in addition, the couple needed more clarity on exactly what each wanted from the other (i.e., a reduction in conflict in the contract). The decision was made to work on both simultaneously. In couple sessions the focus was on increasing each person's acceptance of the fact that the other was attempting non-aversive or pleasant stimuli. It was necessary to have each partner examine carefully the other's behavior so that he or she could see it as pleasant and it could become a positive reinforcer. For example, the husband's compliments were consistently ignored by the wife, although she continued to insist that she wanted them desperately. Once she was able to acknowledge their existence and their intent, the compliments began actually to have some effect on her subsequent behavior. In addition, we attempted deliberate reduction of specific punishments, especially the wife's high rate of complaining behavior and the husband's withdrawal from any intimate interaction.

In individual sessions we wanted to reduce both internal and transactional contract conflict of the couple by examining their internally based "sets" in a more dynamically oriented way. This was somewhat easier with the male partner, who predominantly needed support. With rather gentle exploration, he became increasingly aware of his sense of powerlessness, his feelings both positive and negative and his wish for intimacy. He was able to withdraw his projection from his wife and experience his own need for intimacy. The woman's rather fixed cognitions and her depression at intake made her treatment more difficult. She was grimly unwilling to give up the hope that her parents themselves might someday compensate her for her lost childhood. She was, therefore, unwilling to separate from them and respond to her husband. In addition, her fear of dealing with her own self-hate made her continue to attempt to project it on her husband. As she stated clearly, "It's better him blaming me than me blaming myself." Therefore, numerous individual sessions were held. The techniques used here were primarily expressive and cognitive, with specific exploration of her feelings and of labeling inappropriate cognitions, such as a demand for perfection in herself and her husband and her insistence that any critical comment meant that both he and she were hopeless. In addition, the patient was offered specific support in the person of the therapist, whom she saw as a woman near her in age who continued to affirm that intimacy and warmth were possible. She was able slowly to withdraw from her husband her demands that he be the "bad guy."

The couple was seen over a period of many months, with a continued back-and-forth pattern to therapy as new behaviors were followed by improvement (less conflict, more warm feelings), fear of the growing intimacy and withdrawal. However, the marriage eventually stabilized at a much more supportive and comfortable level, with the couple better able to be specific about their needs and to reinforce and support each other appropriately.

Unused but certainly appropriate options in the case included:

1. Further joint exploration of contract issues
2. Short-term communications workshops
3. Bringing the family of origin of one or both partners into the session
4. Specific sexual counseling
5. Individual long-term psychodynamic psychotherapy for one or both partners.

The specific techniques used are somewhat determined by the therapist's style as well as by patient's presenting problems. Principal choices are, first, whether intervention at either the behavioral or the contract level ought to be done sequentially or concurrently and, second, what types of therapy are most appropriate to foster the person's freedom to change a conflicted contract.

Different patients may need different interventions in order to facilitate change in a conflicted contract. Some may need direct intervention with the family of origin before they can rebalance old ties. Some may need psychoanalysis in order to work out some of their conflicts, particularly those at "beyond-awareness" levels. Many marital therapists feel that a much larger proportion of the contract negotiation can be worked at in conjoint therapy. Basically, however, our model, as illustrated in Figure 1, clarifies the nature of the conflicts, enabling the therapist to keep track of the multiple dimensions of the couple's transactions, permitting him to make a more rational judgment as to the level of intervention which will be the most effective.

Notes on Figure 2

This schematic of the interactional contract demonstrates the self-perpetuating nature of the system, the relationship of the persons by means of feedback loops and the types of reinforcement used. The couple alternates

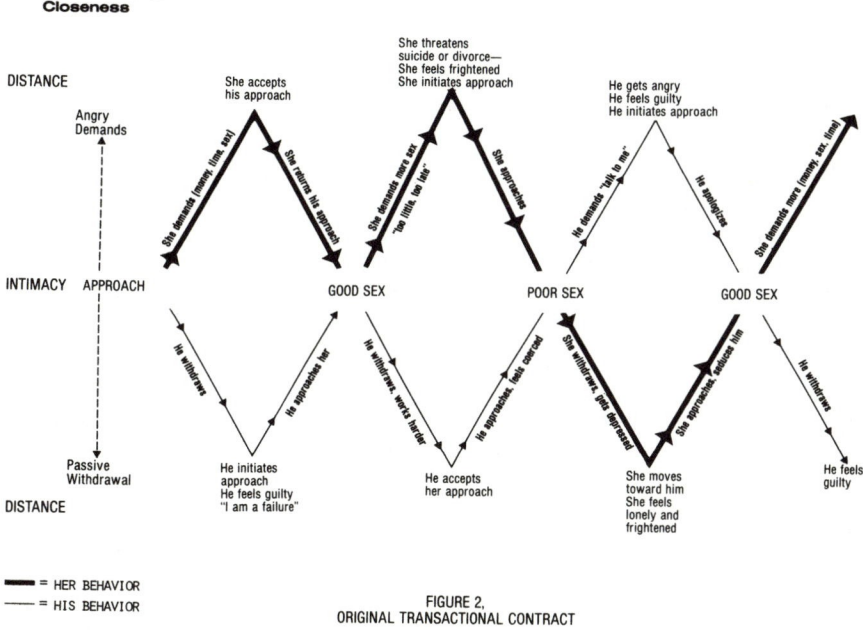

FIGURE 2,
ORIGINAL TRANSACTIONAL CONTRACT

approach-avoidance behavior. Distancing (either overt anger or withdrawal) is produced by direct punishment from the other or from a feeling that demands are not met. Approach behavior is generally initiated by the person who feels most frightened of the increasing distance. The points at which the couple is emotionally and physically closest contain elements of compliance with coercion, which has resentment as a byproduct. This produces anger and a wish not to meet further demands. In addition, the wife's initial sense that nothing is ever enough makes her feel cheated, and so the cycle starts over again.

REFERENCES

Boszormenyi-Nagy, I., and Spark, G. *Invisible loyalties*. New York: Brunner/Mazel, 1976.

Bowen, M. Family therapy and family group therapy. In D. Olson (Ed.), *Treating relationships*. Lake Mills, Iowa: Graphic Publishing, 1976, pp. 219–274.

Dicks, H. *Marital tensions*. New York: Basic Books, 1967.

Erikson, E. *Childhood and society*. New York: W.W. Norton, 1950.

Fairbairn, W.R.D. *An object relations theory of personality*. New York: Basic Books, 1967.

Framo, J. Symptoms from a family transactional viewpoint. In N. Ackerman (Ed.), *Family therapy in transition, Vol. 7, No. 4: The international psychiatry clinics*. Boston: Little, Brown, 1970.

Frank, J.D. *Persuasion and healing in psychotherapy*. Baltimore: Johns Hopkins Press, 1973.

Grinker, R. The relevance of general systems theory to psychiatry. In S. Arieti (Ed.), *American handbook of psychiatry*, Vol. 6, 2nd Ed. New York: Basic Books, 1975, pp. 251–274.

Homans, G.C. *The human group*. New York: Harcourt Brace, 1950.

Klein, M. *Our adult world and its roots in infancy*. London: Tavistock, 1959.

Levinson, D., Darrow, C., Klein, E., Levinson, M., and McKee, B. *The seasons of a man's life*. New York: Little, Brown, 1978.

Mahoney, M.J. Reflections on the cognitive learning trend in psychotherapy. *Am. Psychologist*, 1977, *32*, 5–13.

Marmor, J. *Psychiatrists and their patients: A natural study of private office practices*. Washington, D.C.: American Psychological Association, National Association for Mental Health, 1975.

Neugarten, B., and Datan, N. The middle years. In S. Arieti (Ed.), *American handbook of psychiatry*, Vol. 1, 2nd ed. New York: Basic Books, 1974, pp. 592–608.

Neugarten, B., et al. *Personality—middle and late life*. New York: Atherton, 1964.

Sager, C. *Marriage contracts and couple therapy*. New York: Brunner/Mazel, 1976.

Skinner, B.F. *Science and human behavior*. New York: Macmillan, 1953.

Thibaut, J., and Kelley, H.H. *The social psychology of groups*. New York: Wiley, 1959.

Vaillant, G. *Adaptation to life*. New York: Little, Brown, 1977.

Watzlawick, P., Brown, J., and Jackson, D. *Pragmatics of human communication*. New York: W.W. Norton, 1967.

Weiss, R.L. The conceptualization of marriage and marriage disorders from a behavioral perspective. In T.J. Paolino and B.S. McCrady (Eds.), *Marriage and Marital Therapy*. New York: Brunner/Mazel, 1978.

Zinner, N. The implications of projective identification for marital interaction. In H. Grunebaum and J. Christ (Eds.), *Contemporary marriage*. Boston: Little, Brown, 1976.

Chapter 2

Marital Contracts

Clifford J. Sager

THE PROCESS OF COUPLE THERAPY

This presentation illustrates the methods and the therapeutic approaches used in the treatment of a couple who had severe marital dysfunction but were well motivated to stay together. I have set forth, as best I can on paper, the rationale for my therapy. Therapists are constantly faced with alternatives; hence I might have done many things differently and in some instances the couple's progress might have been more rapid if I had done so. The couple was seen for ten sessions over fourteen weeks and then for five follow-up sessions over a four-year period.

Some of the theoretical concepts behind my modus operandi will be discussed first, followed by a detailed account of our therapeutic work together and my ongoing evaluations of the couple's marital system and intrapsychic dynamics that served as a guide to my interventions.

The marriage or couple-contract concept lends itself to an underlying design for organizing data to determine the dynamics of a couple relationship and for suggesting how to intervene therapeutically. The case that is described will demonstrate how the threads of the contracts concept run through the treatment of this couple as a variety of interventions are utilized.

MARRIAGE CONTRACTS

The term "marriage" or "couple contracts" is an intentional misnomer because the essence of the concept is that when two people join in a committed relationship, each has his or her own and separate understanding of what he or she expects of the relationship and the partner as well as of what each will give to the other in exchange for what each expects to receive. Most of these "terms" have not been discussed together by the partners and some remain unconscious within each. Hence in reality there are two, not one, "contracts." Each has his own private or individual "contract" that he relates to as if the other were fully aware of the terms and had agreed to them. Each mate may become angered, hurt or disappointed because he believes he has fulfilled the contract but that the other has violated the terms. This concept has been enlarged upon elsewhere.* Terms of their unilateral non-contracts may be verbalized, or the individual may be aware of terms of his contract that he elects not to make known, and there are other terms that are beyond his own awareness. Therapy, in a sense, can be regarded as working toward a single agreed-upon set of contract terms that both can subscribe to. We are more concerned, in these "contracts," with the psychological and biological needs of both mates, with their concept of what they will give to the relationship, what each will give to his mate and what each will want in exchange than we are with the commonplace difficulties of living together, as important as these are. This means not that the difficulties are to be overlooked, but that practical, tangible differences are much more readily solvable when the emotional and biological parameters are satisfied.

Essentially there are three basic theoretical systems of psychotherapy. These three are the insight-therapy theories, which include the various psychoanalytic methods—transactional analysis, Gestalt therapy and any other method that is designed to produce essential change through insight; learning-theory approaches, the most familiar form of this being behavior modification therapy; and those approaches that are based upon applications of general-systems theory. A fourth therapeutic approach is the biological, which includes the use of psychotropic drugs. The last will not be discussed here beyond stating that appropriate use of medication can play a decisive role in certain treatment programs.

Each of the three major theoretical models has given us a host of techniques that may be utilized in a number of modalities, such as group, individual, couple, family and multiple-family therapy. Most therapists employ one or more theoretical approaches and a variety of techniques as well as one or more modalities. I generally may take something from any or

---

*Sager, C.J. *Marriage Contracts and Couple Therapy—Hidden Forces in Intimate Relationships*. New York, Brunner/Mazel, 1976.

all of the major theoretical systems and, when working with couples, use conjoint couple therapy (the two mates seen together), with some individual time when that appears to be appropriate to achieve a particular objective.

In treating the Smiths, conjoint sessions were used for the most part, with an occasional splitting of the session to see each alone briefly. The presentation is designed to illustrate the particular multifaceted, flexible approach I used, dipping into a variety of techniques from each general approach that melded into a synthesized unity, albeit somewhat imperfectly. Any number of theoretical approaches, techniques or modalites could have been used instead of the ones I had. The contract concept can be useful and valuable within the framework of almost any theoretical or technique system that allows for the interplay and validity of transactional and intrapsychic factors as determinants of the quality and dynamics of a marriage. It provides a means of understanding these dual determinants and a way of using them therapeutically.

THE SMITHS

Susan Smith, 30, and Jonathan, 32, had been married 7 years and had a son of 5 and a daughter of 2 when they came for treatment. The husband voiced their complaints first in the conjoint session: "Too much bitterness, not enough satisfaction, we fight about unimportant things." From Mrs. Smith: "I wanted a strong husband, but not too strong or I would not be free. Once more, it would be like it was and still is between me and my mother. Jon isn't free enough with me and often he's more stubborn than strong. I can't play with him, he doesn't imagine enough. Sex is poor. It's not frequent and I don't have orgasms anymore. We don't have sex unless I start it."

Jon, an engineer, took a position a year ago at about two-thirds of his former salary. He enjoys his new job because it allows him to be directly in command of a large number of employees in the field rather than doing mostly paperwork, as in his previous job. Susan favored his taking this position because he would enjoy the work. She claims she doesn't care if her husband doesn't wish to climb to the top of his profession, but she is concerned about money because they are committed to a high standard of living, which necessitates that they once again accept money from her mother. Her mother, in turn, is insistent that Susan join her in her business. Susan does not want to do so because her mother has a tough and domineering stance with her, especially at work ("You are not my daughter—just another employee"). Susan is a folk-song writer and singer of moderate success who has also worked successfully and creatively in her mother's business. Her rage toward Jon was apparent as she looked at him and pointedly said that she did not mind accepting money from her mother but she would not accept her mother's control.

As I listened to their reporting and witnessed their interaction, I began to organize the data, putting it into a tentative picture of their emerging contracts, their way of dealing with their frustration and anxiety and how each maneuvered to try to get what he or she wanted.

I did not deal formally with the contracts at this first session because of the great pressure of their frustration and pain, but I did so de facto when I elected to center first on their sexual relationship. They had brought up their sexual difficulties as epitomizing much that was wrong in their marriage, both as cause and as effect. My decision to enter and to intervene in their system at this point was determined by the sharp difference in the terms of the sexual parameters of their "contracts" and by their agreement that improvement in this area was a high priority goal. Each wanted a definite style of sex from the other, each thought it had been promised, and now each was disappointed and angry because he felt the other had not fulfilled his part of the contract. From my point of view, the sexual parameters epitomized their poor communication and misunderstandings and it was reciprocally symptomatic of, as well as contributing to, the perpetuation of underlying pathology. Therefore, the sexual parameter might provide an excellent field on which to begin work toward a single contract. I felt that in this case sex could lead us rapidly to the center of their difficulties.

Susan had been uninhibited and assertive sexually: she had had sexual relations with several men before her marriage. Her husband liked to hear stories from her of the details of these experiences and would become excited by them. Susan now felt that she wanted to be sexually desired by her husband and to be excited by him and not vice versa. This desire was consistent with her romantic image of having spontaneous sexual love in a forest glade, where she would feel one with all nature and with Jon. She felt that sex should not begin in bed but was part of a total loving, warm and supportive relationship. Jon, who had also had considerable sexual experience before marrying, wanted to be sexually passive and expected her to be seductive and wanton and to initiate passionate sex with him. His wife felt guilty and repentant about her promiscuous past and felt that she should be loved as a woman and mother, not just as a sex object.

Susan presented herself in the session as a sort of flower child, yet also very much in touch with reality. She had a beautiful, fluid way of moving in and out of her ego boundaries. Jon was more pragmatic: he was set about his likes and dislikes and clearly passively aggressive in his adaptations. He had an honesty and bluntness that was very refreshing and was obviously devoted to his wife. He said that he wanted to be more giving to her but did not know how to do it her way. She wanted "to open him up more and then I will be more open," and as she said this her smile made clear the intent of her double meaning.

He talked readily about his depressed, "morbid" moods and his preoccupation with violence. He was currently in charge of developing and overseeing the installation of the security aspects of a new prison. In this first session he was able to talk about his sadistic fantasies, the pleasure he received from the idea that "his" prison would really be secure and would keep the male inmates separated from society (and women) because they had injured innocent people. Susan, on the other hand, expressed love for all mankind. She wanted to be true to herself and to be one spirit with the sky, sea and earth. Their opposing views on crime and violence and his passionate need to sequester "criminal forces" constituted the fodder for a running battle between them. He stated at one point that he enjoyed reading about violence and fantasized doing violence to those who hurt others. He recognized that this was his way of controlling his own inner violence and felt he was in good control of these feelings. The 1971 Attica prison revolt and its aftermath had left the couple at each other's throats, as he sided with "law and order" and she with the inmates as victims of the social ills that had spawned their crimes. As he put it, "I am more concerned for the victims of violence and she for the perpetrators."

I commented on their seemingly opposite views and feelings about violence and how they might be closer than they suspected, depending on whether they looked at their positions as points on an almost closed circle or as the extreme poles of a straight line. I did this not because I thought they would accept this almost-closed-circle idea but to illustrate how even the most apparently divergent viewpoints may be closer to achieving reconciliation than the protagonists realize, both philosophically and practically. He seemed to be in better touch with his primitive anger and the threat to his omnipotence than she. He sublimated his in his work and with fantasies about violence, whereas she used reaction formation as a major defense against her impulses. Actually, each was struggling differently with underlying feelings of infantile rage.

When I suggested the sexual area for initial work, they enthusiastically agreed. I instructed them to take turns at home playing out each other's sexual desires. In this way neither would be capitulating to the other, an important issue to them. To avoid an argument over whose fantasy would be acted upon first, I asked Jon to approach Susan the first time. In view of her more stubborn feelings of injury, it seemed that it would be easier if he made the first move. She then might reciprocate more easily. This was the beginning of teaching them the possibility of quid pro quo solutions to impasses.

Susan had fantasied how sensual and gratifying it would be for them to make love in a wooded area near their home. My task assignments to them were that within the next two days he should initiate and make love to her in the woods; within two days after that, she would initiate sex in the style he had fantasied, with her taking the initiative and being "wanton" and passionate while he remained passive. They both agreed and seemed delighted with these instructions. The tasks were designed to see if they could accept what they claimed they wanted and if they could give to each other. I was not concerned about their sexual functioning since it was clear there were no sexual dysfunctions. But how would they react to the opportunity to have what they claimed they wanted?

I saw them again a week later. They had made love several times, taking turns playing out fantasies, and both had enjoyed all the experiences. It had been their most peaceful week in a long time. However, all was not well, as was indicated by Susan's dream the night before the second session. She had dreamed that her pubic hair was growing very long and that Jon stuffed it into her vagina so that her vagina was completely filled and blocked. She felt somewhat depressed in the dream because she could not have sex, though these feelings were not strong. Jon reported no dreams.

When asked about his reaction to her dream, Jon said he thought it showed that she believed he wanted her not to have sex. He said, "I don't want her to make love to other men, but I certainly want her to with me. Perhaps she thought stuffing the hair was like I was putting a chastity belt on her—we have kiddingly talked jokingly about that once or twice." Susan said there was something in what he said, but she felt that he, or maybe she herself, wanted to turn off her sexuality. That idea bothered her because she had enjoyed it this week. I pointed out that it was her dream. She had had her husband stuff her vagina. Perhaps she wanted to blame him if she turned off sexually. Was she upset in any way about enjoying sex this week? She said she felt better when they had sex in the woods and when Jon was more active. I suggested that in view of all they had been expressing about control and violence, it was understandable that she might be on guard against trusting herself with her husband; yet she seemed to prefer him to be assertive.

Jon responded by stating that she had known how he was and she had seduced him by telling him about the other men she had been with and how sexually active she had been. They both knew that he was jealous but tried to control it. She said that she had been seductive at the start of their relationship, but she had changed, and now, years later, she no longer wanted to talk about her previous sexual affairs, even when he pushed her to do so. She wanted "their hearts to be open to one another," and when that happened, sex would follow naturally and easily. He interpreted this to mean that she wanted to close up her vagina to him unless she had her way. At this point he reacted with mixed feelings while she expressed adamantly that loving feelings and openness had to be evident before sex or she felt as if her vagina was closing up—"I can't even lubricate." I reviewed with them how good sex had been and suggested that the dream had brought to the surface her feelings of anxiety at their sexual success and that these feelings possibly reflected his anxiety as well. I told them they need not agree fully, but they might look at how much each had enjoyed implementing the other's fantasy, a viewpoint each had overlooked.

Feeling that to pursue sex further at the moment would be counterproductive, I drew them out about their expectations of each other's feelings toward their two children, the role assignments of the children, parenting responsibilities and so on, thus getting more contractual material without trying to push them in sensitive areas. It was apparent that Susan enjoyed mothering but wanted greater participation with the children from her husband. She included the children as central in their unit. Jon kept them somewhat at a distance, to some extent resenting their existence as an intrusion into the marital system.

We discussed the basic ideas of the marriage contract, the three levels of awareness: verbalized, conscious but not verbalized, and beyond awareness. This was done with emphasis on the exchange quality: "I do for you and expect you to do for me in return." I asked them to write out their contracts separately at home and not to discuss them together until both had finished. If they wished to read or discuss the two contracts after that, it would be fine.*

Thus, I asked this couple during the second session to write out their contracts at home and bring them in for the third session. I believed they were ready to do so and would use the opportunity constructively.

I also told them to continue to take turns initiating sex and playing out fantasies, but this time the initiator would play out his or her own fantasy. I knew that genuine progress toward a single sexual contract would be achieved when each also used part of the other's fantasy on his own initiative, so that the leadership went back and forth in the same sexual encounter without thoughts of "what is for me and what is for him?"

At the beginning of the third session, they reported that the first week's improvement in sexual activity and pleasure had not been sustained. Susan felt that her husband was merely following my instructions and did not feel the proper love for her because he acted lovingly only when he wanted sex. She saw me as her mother pulling the marionette strings and her husband as her weak father. I used this to point out that many matters in their

---

*I now find it much more effective to give the couple a reminder list that covers the most common controversial topics, and ask them to discuss these to see where they agree and disagree and which are emotionally laden. This approach moves them toward a single agreement more quickly.

relationship had to be reevaluated but that good sex and love were ready for them when they both felt willing to give as well as receive and that was up to them, not me. I interpreted her transferential designation of me as strong mother and showed her how self-defeating that was for her in this situation. Sex would have to wait for further attention or would eventually take care of itself when suspiciousness, hostility and the use of sex in their power struggle were no longer necessary.

The early focus on sex had illustrated the essence of their problems to them and indicated that remedy and satisfaction were possible if they wanted it, but that their sex problem was a sympton, not a cause, of their more general marital difficulties.

I suggested that we look at the marriage contracts together. They had not had time to discuss them together before the session, but in response to my question said they did not mind the other's learning the contents now.

SUSAN'S CONTRACT

1. *Verbalized*

Expectations
He will give me financial and emotional security—to be a sane balance wheel for me.
He will share my interests.

Receive
I will get deep satisfaction from our relationship—I will feel safe and protected.
We will work toward a common end (we're after the same rainbow's end, my Huckleberry friend).

2. *Conscious but Not Verbalized*

Give
I want to be completely at his mercy, his victim. He will make me feel. Weak women feel.
Strong women don't feel. I will put myself completely at his mercy. I will be his concubine, slave, victim.

Receive—In Exchange
He is a powerful male.
Womanly deep feelings—it is good to be dependent on this strong man; it is my realization of my deepest being as a woman. A strong man. So I will receive protection on an earthly level.

3. *Beyond Awareness*

You are a strong male, unlike my father.
I fear your strength and I want to destroy it.
I will not encourage your strengths, because you may destroy me.
I need to be the strong and independent one.
I want you dependent and weak.

JONATHAN'S CONTRACT

Conscious Verbalized

Give

1. Support you monetarily to the best of my ability.
2. Be your companion and escort socially.
3. Be faithful sexually.
4. Assist you in solving day-to-day problems.
5. Do work around the house which is heavy or unusual and which I am capable of doing.
6. Be a father figure for the children.
7. Share verbally and emotionally in shareable experiences.
8. Accommodate to your personal hang-ups and prejudices.

Take in exchange

1. You will be a good wife and mother; carry the household.
2. You will be my companion and escort socially.
3. Be sexually faithful.
4. Help relax and ease tensions after the day of work.

Conscious, Not Verbalized

Give

1. Tolerate your moodiness.

2. Will not impose on you sexually, but will be available sexually on your demand.
3. Prepared to admit I do not earn enough to support you properly.

Take In Exchange

1. Want you to be passionate and demanding of me sexually.
2. Bear with my negative personality traits.

3. Make do with my income without complaint.

Sub- or Unconscious

Give

1. Prepared to "forgive and forget" past sexual experiences, although I am jealous and feel insecure in comparison to (your) former sex partners.
2. Prepared to forego demand that you don't take money from your mother because I realize it's absolutely necessary.
3. Prepared not to pursue other women, though attracted to the idea.

Take in exchange

1. Want a wild, passionate and whore-like bedmate who will be verbal in lovemaking and accommodate to my sexual fantasies.
2. Want an adoring and verbally complimentary female who will be ego-massaging to me as both person and male.
3. Want you to be attractive and teasing to other men but never to be available to them.

These "contracts" are quite revealing, even in the way each mate headed the columns. Susan used the terms "expectations" and "receive" while Jon used "give" and "take." Both sets of terms are valid, but her terms suggest her more gentle approach, as compared to his bluntness. However, in reality she is just as firm about what she wants as he is, if not more so.

The ability to be in touch with strong contradictory desires on a deep, "beyond-awareness" level is not unusual, though, of course, if these terms were fully beyond awareness there could be no response. The existence of the category and the areas suggested in it cause many people to get in touch with vague feelings they often have not dared to examine or think about openly. This level of awareness is therefore significant and consciousness-expanding for both spouses. Usually it leads to greater understanding for both.

Susan indicated great conflict over control—wanting to be in charge and also wanting to be enslaved—and not being able to trust. She apparently related this ambivalence to her feelings toward her mother. Her desires to be a mother and a wife and to do her own work were clear and seemed to be consistent with her actual behavior. She was in good contact with her "unconscious" need to be strong and in charge. This was the cause of internal conflict for her and between them, although she also enjoyed and accepted her strength. Jon drew sharper limits and definitions about what he would and would not do.

When we first discussed the two contracts, I thought the differences were sharper and more rigid than they actually proved to be later. Jon's need for distance became clearer as time went on, but clues existed in his "share . . . shareable experiences."

The desire and determination to make their relationship work were stronger motivating forces than appeared on the surface of the contracts, and understanding and compassion for each other were greater than apparent.

The major problems seemed to be in their different life and cognitive styles—in his difficulty in openly showing love and being close, in her ambivalence about control and power, in his about closeness-distance, and in his passivity at home. Each wanted independent activity and appeared to be willing to allow it to the other—a good quid pro quo if this was to stand up in practice. His sexual desires were not antithetical to hers, provided he also gave love and sex on her terms, which involved his being less passive and making her feel more desired. The money issue and his supporting her economically and physically with the children remained important points of difference. Increasing his ability to include them in family (marriage) would be a crucial factor here.

Each lacked security in adult femininity or masculinity, and each required strong reassurance and affirmations from the other. She wanted to feel his strength, to have him master her while loving and protecting her. She wanted to see him as a strong, loving father—not a weak father or a strong mother. She was angry, partly because she felt he had the ability to give her what she wanted but was not living up to his potential to do so. She wanted him to be strong—not stubborn or defensive.

Addressing themselves to writing out their own contracts began to clarify their understanding of themselves and each other. In the therapeutic process, both had spontaneously begun to see how damaging their feelings of injury and anger were when each believed that he/she had delivered on this part of the contract but the other spouse had not done his/her part as specified in the unilateral contract.

Jon thought he gave his wife the strength, security and freedom from material concern she wanted: "I do give her all that—it's just the damm money—not that I don't want to become fully responsible financially, but I will not maintain our standard of living by doing work I do not want to do. Either we change our standard or accept money from her mother or Sue will have to work." She understood his position and claimed no anger at that, but she did want emotional support and "togetherness" from him—he should not act as if the children were hers alone. Emotionally, she felt that a man who did not make enough money for his family and expected his wife to do so was weak, like her father. She knew that if she worked for her mother, she would be successful and would eventually take over the business. She would then be wealthy but would have no respect for her husband; furthermore, she would not be doing the work she wanted to do (music). Intellectually and ideologically, she believed otherwise, but she could not alter her feelings.

Dialogue on this basic question continued. The position of each was founded on deep psychological needs. The money issue, like sex, was a symptom, not the real problem. Susan's problem with Jon arose from her ambivalence between wishing to be strong and to be weak and taken care of ("weak women feel; strong women like her mother do not feel"). Jonathan's contribution existed in his need to maintain the illusion of infantile omnipotence through his manipulation of Susan as doting-mother image.

Ambivalent feelings Susan had expressed in her contract were pointed out to her—she knew her husband was indeed a strong man, unlike her father, but she feared his strength. I asked her if she also perceived Jon at times as she did her strong, controlling mother—at once wanting to be her slave and at the same time rebelling to be free. They both agreed with this formulation and each gave a supporting anecdote. Jonathan added ruefully, "Neither of us can win that way, can we?"

I did not share with them my further speculations about their dynamics, which dealt with the crux of their struggle. He demanded reassurance, support, the love of an adoring woman. If she did not behave so as to reassure him and quell his anxiety, he would withdraw punitively and not give her what she wanted. Her contract demanded that he be strong and weak at the same time, which presented him with an impossible double bind.

Actually, her sexual withdrawal and refusal to move toward him sexually gave her a potent weapon in her struggle for power. He could not satisfy her for long because of her contradictory needs: he was to be strong and she his slave, but on the other hand to be enslaved was to be controlled by mother and required rebellion. Susan felt she could be independent only if he was weak and her slave (as her father was her mother's), but if this happened she would despise him as she did her father. She had endowed Jonathan with real and fantasied qualities of both parents. Thus, with her husband's unwitting collaboration, Susan found it easy to evoke countertransferential reactions from her husband that readily supported her own distortions and negative expectations.

Each was acting the role of a childlike partner in their interactional script. I classified them as childlike-childlike partners, or two children in search of a parent.*

Jon, for a man who considered himself a pragmatist, was surprisingly ready to cooperate in the therapeutic venture, with its demands for openness, exposure and change. Appreciating how much more difficult the therapeutic process was for him, I found myself feeling increasingly warm to and supportive of him.

From the data gathered in the first three therapeutic sessions, I began to develop the Smith's individual contracts more fully while the treatment continued. The marriage contracts, as I formulated them more elaborately and wrote them out, were developed after the fifth session, utilizing all the information available to me, including the contracts the couple had written; my evaluation of their productions, including the initial history; the dream material, their statements about each other and their parents; how they interacted in sessions, reacted to and treated each other as they reported other events. How they carried out tasks, as well as their reactions to these, all contributed additional interactional information. The contracts as formulated at this point were working hypotheses that I regard as always subject to change. They were to be a guide toward the goal of a commonly agreed-upon single contract. Compromises would have to be made between the two individuals and within each person in regard to his/her own conflicts and ambivalence. Some new contract terms would have to be created. Compromise with acceptance is one method of arriving at a common contract, while using newly created contractual terms or facets that develop during treatment or life experiences is another.

These contracts are formulated in terms of the three major parameters of

---

*These terms are from a typology of partner types and of marriage:
Sager, C.J. *Ibid*, Chaps. 6 and 7.
Sager, C.J. A Typology of Intimate Relationships. *J. Sex & Marit. Ther. 3*, 1977, pp. 83–112.

contractual terms: (1) what is expected from the marriage, (2) those terms based on biological and intrapsychic factors, and (3) the parts of the contract that reflect derivative or externalized foci of marital problems rooted in the first two areas. *In the formulation presented here, the three levels of awareness of the terms of the contract are merged, since it is the therapist's statement.* Because these two contracts are my working hypotheses, I find they are more useful when I pool the partners' information from their three levels of awareness and from all other sources. What I formulate is done within the limits of my best awareness and theoretical biases. I am able then to transmit my hypotheses, observations and therapeutic maneuvers to the couple so that they can be used constructively to move toward our common therapeutic goals. Like all psychotherapists, I am subject to blind spots, mistakes and my own values and countertransferentially determined pronouncements. I try to be aware of these and hold them to a minimum.

The following contracts, written by me, *not* Susan and Jon, follow the order of the reminder list of common contractual parameters.*

PROJECTED CONTRACTS

Susan Smith

                                Jonathan Smith

Parameters Based on Expectations of the Marriage

1. Marriage means that the center of my life and Jon's is with one another and our children. We are a unit, self-sufficient and mutually supportive. My creative career is definitely secondary to the above, yet I must have it too. I should not have to exclude one or the other if Jon will cooperate.

1. Susan and I are central. The children are secondary to us and are often an intrusion. Each of us has our work, too, which is also an important center for me. I do not know which is more important to me. If pressed, I might choose my work over Sue and the children.

2. We are the family unit—Jon, me, and the children—not his original family or mine.

2. Same as Susan, but the children are secondary. The less we have to do with our original families the better.

3. I want him to be gentle and understanding as well as firm as a father. He should be concerned and participate in caring for the children.

3. I will be a father image to my children. They must see me as strong, wise and just. I do not want to be too close or involved in daily problems with them.

4. Family life will be run democratically, and decisions about what, when and how we do things will be joint. I prefer that Jon make decisions about money and support.

4. I will take care of money and my work decisions; Sue will be in charge of family and social matters as long as I can depend on her to do what I want.

---

*Sager, C.J. *Ibid*, Append. 1.

5. Roles will be traditional. That approach makes me feel right and content. I will care for home and children; he will earn money, be my protector against outside forces I can't cope with.

6. In marriage, two people should like the same things, think similarly, share their feelings and thoughts. I feel uneasy and troubled when Jon won't accept what to me is so important (nature, spiritualism, the concept of the essential goodness of mankind, etc.) If he can't do this, I don't know if I want to try to meet him on what he wants.

7. In marriage we should be sexually available to each other. If he gives me security and love, I will then be a model wife to him. He must want me sexually and reassure me of my desirability if I am to give him what he wants.

8. I do not want to be controlled in my marriage as I was at home by my mother. If I am secure with my husband, I can flower and grow like a plant that gets the right nutrients, water and sun. I can then be free to be creative. My husband will be richly rewarded for this—I want to and will take care of the house and children (with his help), give to him sexually and make life exciting for him with my rich fantasy and imagination.

9. If I do not get what I need, I will not give him what he wants. He must be strong enough to give me what I want. I don't want to be allowed to take what I want just because he is weak. I don't want to have to be strong for us both.

10. I will compromise—he does not have to join me in most of my interests if he allows me to pursue them.

11. I do not think much about sexual fidelity. It is not the important issue—being there for another when needed is. I would be upset if my husband could

5. Same as Susan. But she should not expect me to bail her out or fight her battles with some of her far-out friends.

6. I am a private person—I share only what I want to. My likes and dislikes can differ from Sue's, and do. I am a separate person and must remain so. Sue wants me to merge with her—I won't and can't. That is definite!

7. I expect my wife always to want me sexually and to show it. My wife will be my refuge, my supporter. She will cater to my ego needs and will demonstrate how much she loves me and how sexual a man I am by her making passionate love to me while verbalizing how wonderful I am and how I turn her on.

8. My wife must understand my needs—I am special and should be catered to because I am a man and because I am me. I must control our life. I will allow her some freedom to pursue her silly friends, but this threatens me and makes me anxious.

9. If I do not get what I want, I will not give her what she wants. I must establish my authority so that it is not constantly contested.

10. I will not give her all she wants because she would engulf and change me. If she gives me what I want, I will give her as much as I can. I know compromises must be made—for example, I now agree to accept money from her mother.

11. My wife must be sexually faithful to me—I feel insecure enough about myself as it is.

12. Same as Sue. But our fantasies can be different. I cannot and will not have

not give to me sexually but could give to someone else.

12. We should be able to let our fantasies go with one another.

the same fantasies she has. That is not necessary in marriage. A couple does not have to be the same, but should fit together properly.

SUMMARY OF COMPARISON OF SPOUSES

Positive. (1). A genuine desire to stay together and make their marriage work; feelings of love for each other. (2). Both want the same general conventional marriage form with somewhat modified, similar, gender-determined roles. (3). Each may have independent activities, although she wants him to join hers. (4). Each claims to be willing to compromise and make some quid pro quos.

Negative. (1). Inclusion-exclusion of children—ratio differs markedly. (2). Jonathan is more distant and removed and sees this as a desired stance. (3). Susan claims to be more democratic, whereas he is autocratic in decision making, although I suspect that she does not cooperate until she gets her way. (4). Each wants the other to approach sex and love "unselfishly" and threatens withdrawal and anger if each does not get what he/she wants. There are genuine differences over sex. She wants demonstrations of love—for sex to be more spiritual; he wants concrete reassurance of his sexual desirability. (5). Her conflict over weak-strong is the source of much confusion and trouble and is a basic determinant of how their marital system functions. (6). She wants to be left to "do her own thing" (spiritual and humanistic movements and her music), but makes clear she really expects and wants him to approve and participate, which he refuses to do because he fears he will lose his sense of self. Susan wants him to like what she likes and to think as she thinks, which is antithetical to him. (7). She tries to be guided by a tight definition of "shoulds" and "shouldn'ts" regarding control, but she is ambivalent. (8). Both of them state clearly that each will withhold from the other if he/she does not get what he/she wants. (9). He fears being controlled, even in the fantasy area. (10). He is defensively rigid about his husbandly rights, adhering to a model that is not consistent with the reality of his life today.

At present they live in an uneasy parallel relationship, each going his/her own way and each very unhappy and puzzled about why he/she is not joined more harmoniously, since they agree on so many of the superficialities of what they want from marriage. Harmony and growth are not ascendant, as each rigidly insists on having his/her own way in the particulars of living and relating. Ambivalence on the part of both in a struggle for power that each one only half wants is a central negative force.

PARAMETERS BASED ON INTRAPSYCHIC AND BIOLOGICAL DETERMINANTS

These parameters are the most significant in determining a couple's interaction. The therapist does not necessarily need to make as complete a list as is given here for demonstration purposes. In practice, one usually selects only those problem areas and strengths that are revealed as crucial in the contracts and in the couple's behavior. It is helpful to most couples to point out the positive parts of the contract and where the contracts are symmetrical or truly complementary, as well as where disagreement or conflict exists.

Since these contracts are my working hypotheses, I include tentative intrapsychic and interactional dynamic formulations. It is not necessary for the readers to agree with my dynamic formulations. Since I can illustrate but one approach here, I have chosen the one I used in this case. The reader may substitute his own formulations based on his own theoretical and clinical approach. In this presentation, italics are used to indicate where I have included my hypotheses of intrapsychic and marital-system dynamics and comments. These illustrate how the therapist can incorporate using the marriage contracts within his own theoretical system.

SUSAN SMITH   JONATHAN SMITH

Independence-Dependence

She wants to be dependent and independent, but in different areas. This generates major conflict that she expects her husband to resolve for her. She wants to be her husband's slave and also to be free. *I do not accept her conscious formulation of this. I believe she wants a strong but loving and benevolent man who will protect and take care of her, in return for which she will give him love, sex, children and a warm family life. In turn he will further provide her with an ambience that permits her to be independent in other areas. Thus there need not be a conflict in what she wants if her husband could give it to her; it is possible and a not uncommon quid pro quo on a more mature level. The master-slave or weak-strong polarization is therefore not an accurate assessment.*

He is clear about his desire to be independent—but this is a false independence. *Basically, he requires a giving mother-wife who must fulfill his infantile need in order to make him feel good. In return he will then be a "good boy" at home and help out, share what he wants to share, be sexually faithful. A part of his contract that he cannot yet confront is that the women in his life are expected to give to him the goodies he wants while he lies back passively and is in charge.*

Activity-Passivity

She is willing to be active to bring about what she wants—active in deed as well as ideationally. In exchange for her active doing, she wants his protection and care.

He is more passive than Susan but in a very aggressive way. He states clearly what he will do and that's it. He will compromise when he realizes he will lose the war if he insists on winning every skirmish—e.g., he agrees not to protest her asking her mother for money rather than cut down on their standard of living. He reacts more than he initiates.

Closeness-Distance

She claims she wants closeness, but her tolerance for closeness is short-lived. She talks a great deal about closeness but protests too much. Closeness to her is equated with control or being controlled. She tries to bring Jonathan closer, i.e., to make him understand and to accept her style and cognitive approach. *He feels threatened by this and feel, his integrity to be violated.* However, he is more able to accept their cognitive style differences than she. *Her attempts to control through taking away his defense—distancing operations—are done in a way that relinquishes her control to him, because he is strong enough to refuse to play the game on her terms. She then takes revenge with anger and her own withdrawal.* Her closeness is often within herself—self-awareness in meditation. *On a deep level, she does not fully comprehend or empathize with Jonathan.*

He is wary of closeness, is too guarded. *Possibly he is fearful of his violent, infantile and sadistic impulses.* He will make some gestures of closeness in order to remain distant, but draws a line across which he stubbornly will not step. As Susan said, he gives her the injunction "Don't be close," which frustrates her—robs her of a powerful weapon as well as a source of genuine gratification.

Power

She is clearly conflicted about how much power she wants to have and how much is permissible for her husband in order for her to feel safe—but basically she wants power and control. She feels she cannot trust him with it. He is too alien and different. She is

He is not in conflict about power. He wants to have it, *but wants to delegate the active role to his wife so long as she does what he wants. His is a classical passive-aggressive personality syndrome. The power and control question is crucial for them.* He would want uneasy about the violence and sadism she senses. Her ambivalence contributes to their disharmony, *as it both promises and withholds the mother-wife he wants whom he then can control.* Their struggle for power is a major preoccupation between them. Both enjoyed it early in their relationship, before it led to a deterioration of their marriage. When she has power, she fears it and wants to hand it back to him—but then she can't trust him to take care of her: a terrible dilemma if one sees the alternative only in terms of her syllogism.

to exercise power as does a little boy who controls his parents. However, this tactic does not always work with Susan, and *he then becomes upset when he is forced to recognize that his omnipotence is a chimera.*

Fear of Loneliness or Abandonment

This is a moderately important determinant of her behavior—particularly fear of the loss of the strong-mother fraction of her husband. It does not appear as a prime motivating force; the entire universe is her sisterhood. *Perhaps that is her ultimate defense against loneliness and abandonment.*

He hides this fear well, but he does cave in when Susan really pulls away from him. If she maintains her distant position, he capitulates so that he can salvage the remnants of his fantasy of a blindly giving and doting mother-wife. If she threatens to leave him, he threatens that his abandonment of her will be greater, swifter and more terrible. *Thus he controls by stimulating her anxiety, not allaying it.* What could be an opportunity to move positively is turned into threat to Susan, and they escalate.

Level of Anxiety

Her level is overtly higher than his. She expresses it openly, is in touch with it, requests him to do something to relieve it for her. When he does not, she focuses her anger on him or punishes him by not giving him what he wants. *When too anxious, she fears disintegration and protects herself by withdrawing, getting in touch with mystical forces that give her poise, calm and a sense of being connected.*

His anxiety is better defended against direct awareness and expression. It can most readily be measured by his sadistic fantasies, authoritarian position and dogmatism. *Unconsciously, he is fearful of abandonment, and Susan senses this and even uses it.* Without reassurance from Susan he becomes a cold person who knows he can hurt "Mother" by withdrawing. However, this does not work too well with Susan because he cannot control her this way and she now perceives him, *when he uses this maneuver, as her weak, inef-*

fective father. At these times she then assumes the role of her strong mother—and then finds with horror that she has replicated her own parental situation. This is an unstable state that she can tolerate only briefly. She then tries to force her husband to be the strong mother-husband and take charge. But he must take charge and do as she wants! His superficial show of being the strong mother-husband for her also does not stand up, as reality comes through to her despite her desire to see him as strong. She then swings back to anger and withdrawal and running away from him to be with her friends in the spiritualist movement. Once again, in charge of herself, she returns and they square off for another round.

Consolidation of Gender Identity

Her gender identity is female—but she is confused over whether being female means being like her strong mother. She wants to feel, but the strong do not have feelings—that is weak. She still confuses being a "good female" with being Hestian, yet is conflicted by her desire to enjoy a whole gamut of activity independent from her husband. How can she be Hestian and at the same time be strong, driving and in charge? This would make her the "male" in the family, like her mother. However, if she is to be independent, she must be like her mother and have a weak husband. *But she can't carry it off—it frightens her to be strong. To be strong would mean she could challenge her mother, and that is a terrifying idea. Besides, she is a child.*

His gender identity is male—but a beautiful, loved male child, adored merely because he exists, not for anything that he gives or does. He demands she be sexually excited by his mere presence and to be actively demonstrative of her desire for him and show her wish to service him.

The possibilities of sharing and of powers shifting back and forth between them *are lost in the anxiety generated by the recognition that one's mate has the same flaws as oneself.* The problem of passing control back and forth is one of the more important for them to work out together. It is significant that gender role, control, independence, etc., all become interrelated aspects of the same overall ebb and flow within their marital system. Homosexuality is not an abhorrent idea to her, but she prefers a male sex partner. She does not experience erotic feelings toward either weak or strong women.

Characteristics of Sex Partner

She wants a partner who will be turned on by her and who will make intense spiritual and physical love with her. Unless he instigates it in a loving way, she does not want sex. It angers her that her husband does not keep his part of the bargain in the quid pro quo. She feels this is illustrative of what often occurs. Also, she feels she was wanton and "sold herself" sexually before marriage because she felt she had nothing else to offer. She does not feel that way now and resents his demands. Physically he is fine sexually for her and can turn her on when he wants to. There are no sexual dysfunctions. It is his lack of sexual initiative and assertiveness as well as his not creating a loving ambience that puts her off and makes her feel undesirable. She stated at one point, "I, too, want to be loved for the person I am, not just a hot cunt." She wants him to be more aggressive and not to be stopped by her rejection of his sexual advances. In exchange, she will become sexually giving.

His ideal sex partner resembles her picture of herself acting sexually with other men. Physically he finds her face and body beautiful and voluptuous, just what he wants. He is angered at her "refusal" to be wanton with him and to fit into his whore-in-bed fantasy. In exchange for her doing this, he would not contemplate other women and would take care of her "to the best of my ability." Again, this is an equivocal and not reassuring statement. He wants her to accept him sexually; he says he stopped taking the initiative sexually with her because she rejected him.

Acceptance of Self and Others

She basically questions her own worth as a person and as a woman. Therefore the man who accepts her must be defective too. This produces a perfect stage for the acting-out of problems based on her low self-esteem, particularly as her mate reinforces the negative attitudes she already has about herself and is very parsimonious about offering recognition for her positive contributions and attributes.

Although he assumes he is an adorable male infant, *he also fears he is not a match for a "real man," including any of her previous lovers.* This lack of acceptance of himself as an adult male contributes greatly to his need to control and structure his world so that he always appears to be in command. He is strong enough to choose the areas he wants to be "weak" in. These are not necessarily the ones she wants—e.g., she wants him to be strong in making money, in desiring her sexually, in being able to tolerate her going off by herself, in being less passive. He is strong in doing the work he wants to do, and he won his Phyrrhic victory in the sexual area, which precipitated their coming for treatment.

Cognitive Style, Energy Level, Intensity, Absorption, Enthusiasm

Susan's cognitive style is open and intuitive. She allows data to flow in and around her, and then makes a decision based on her feelings and guts. She writes her lyrics and music and lives this way. This style is markedly different from Jonathan's. She finds it difficult to accept his way and keeps trying to push him into her style. She feels hurt and alone because he won't (can't) join her in her seemingly unstructured approach. Yet, she follows logic and sees to it that the essentials are taken care of for herself and for her husband and children. She has a high energy level, intensity, absorption and enthusiasm, and expects the same from Jonathan, which he does have, but unfortunately not in the same areas as she.

Jonathan's cognitive style is very logical and precise. He is a proper engineer, surveys all situations, collects information, sifts through it and organizes it into its appropriate categories and weights, and then arrives at a practical decision in accordance with the "facts." He has learned that his wife cannot do the same, and will condescendingly tolerate her "escapist, spiritualist and humanistic activities." This difference in styles makes for communication problems. In addition, each has become impatient with the other's style and thinking. *Because they know they will not change each other's position, they tend to cut off communication and are too impatient to listen, each believing that he/she knows what the other will say.* Energy level, intensity, absorption and enthusiasm are high. He does not care much anymore about the direction of Susan's energies, so long as they are not too threatening; ultimately she does what he wants.

Parameters Reflecting Derivative or Externalized Foci of Marital Problems

These are the complaints that often bring a couple into treatment. They are usually symptoms of something more basic that is conflictual or disappointing in one or both of the other two parameters.

Communication

Susan appears to be quite open and direct in what she does and does not

Jonathan is open in what he wants in terms of events and things but is not in want, even when these are contradictory. She appears to ask for what she wants, but in reality many of her messages are not clear and often are double binding because of her ambivalence. She is in good contact with her feelings but allows negative ones to pile up and may then explode without adequate thought to the consequences. She can express love and tenderness as well as anger.

However, when she feels disappointed she does not state what she wants but expects Jonathan to know. She will give subtle signs, which are not likely to be understood or even perceived, and then finally blows up with anger when she has accumulated a series of what she considers refusals to respond on Jonathan's part.

In summary, Susan is in touch with her feelings but often does not clearly communicate what she wants.

good contact with his feelings and hence cannot express them directly. At times he expects his wife to know and to fulfill his unexpressed wishes. He finds it difficult to express love but can express anger readily. Many of his communications come through in an authoritarian and blunt way that arouses the ire of his wife. Early in their relationship, she thought this was an evidence of his strength, but she now sees it as weakness and is angered by it. His hostility is often expressed indirectly and in a subtly sadistic way that only thinly masks his underlying anger. When Susan gives her minimal signals, he does not perceive them or, if he does, usually misreads them. Instead of asking for clarification, he "guesses" what she means, usually taking the most negative interpretation available. In summary, Jonathan, in contrast to Susan, is not in good contact with his feelings but does communicate clearly what he consciously wishes to communicate.

Interests

She is an artist and interested in matters of the spirit and in her own work as well as her family life. She had expected him to be concerned with her sphere of interest and to agree with her opinions. She becomes angry and disappointed and feels unloved when he disagrees with or can't comprehend her point of view. She is not especially interested in his work because she has not found a way of seeing how it relates to her basic philosophy of life. Hence she is somewhat suspicious of his work, which makes him angrily defensive.

He is interested in himself, essentially. He wants to tell her about his work— but only those aspects that he feels enhance him. He is not interested in what she does but is willing to live and let live. She may pursue her own interests as long as he is not deprived of her wifely services. If he is, he retaliates angrily.

Life Style

All living matter is one. She wants her life to be free, spontaneous, spent with

He is closed-in, ordered, a planner. He likes some people as long as they do gentle people, music, singing, dancing, conversation, nature, and without worry about money. She is outgoing. She is willing to compromise, i.e., wants to do all of the above with Jon but will settle for his not punishing her for sharing with others if he will not join her.

not threaten his supremacy. He dislikes being close to nature, prefers motels to camping out. He is very agreeable about spending money if they have it. He goes along with her activities to some extent but is threatened as he comes to realize that the people to whom she is drawn are not like him, and he fears he may eventually lose her. He therefore tries to rein her in, which angers and depresses her and makes her pull away.

Families of Origin

Her mother is a source of problems for her and for them. Sue uses her mother as the yardstick by which all human qualities are measured, both good and bad. She regards her father as a sweet nonentity. She wants her mother out of her life. Therefore, she resents Jon "putting her" in a position of asking her mother for money because she then feels that she must pay for it with her mother.

He fears her attachment to her mother and is jealous. He regards her mother as having too much influence in their daily life. But he is partner to perpetuating the situation by either not insisting they live within his income or not making more money. He consciously made the choice to accept the situation, rationalizing that he did so for Sue and the children. His family presents no current problems to either. At times Sue resents his father's past indulgence of him and his mother's coldness and distance. His father is dead and his mother lives in another state and is not an active force in their lives except historically.

Children

They both agree that the children are primarily Susan's responsibility. She gets angry, however, resenting his distant stance with the children, which he considers providing "a proper father image." She would like him to take over more with the children when she is pressured. There are minor conflicts over child-rearing practices, but he usually abdicates to her in this area.

Money

To her, money represents power and freedom, as amply illustrated above. She becomes anxious as the realization strikes her that money is short. Rather than cut down, she takes the easy way

Money means the same things to Jonathan, but he is not overtly concerned about material matters and feels confident that financial needs will be met one way or another.

out, accepting money and therefore
control from her mother.

Values

There is nothing to add here to what has been covered above. There are
many areas of agreement in addition to some profound differences.

Friends

Friends represent independence to her.
She claims she would like to share, but
she did choose a husband who can't
share her most significant friendships.

He has few friends of his own. He is
willing to share those he does have with
her, but she finds his choices dull or
obnoxious. It is all right for her to have
her own if they do not threaten his
sexual possession of her.

Roles

She is willing to follow traditional
gender-determined roles if she gets
what she wants in return. She resents
his not fully accepting responsibilities
of his role as money-maker in exchange.

In his honesty and bluntness, he at
times appears as an exaggeration of the
dominating and yet ultimately complying husband. Roles are clearly gender-
determined for him ("I will help with
the heavy work at home, if I can"), but
he wants to define his responsibilities
and brooks no discussion about them.
His intransigence is frustrating to her.

It is clear that the derivative factors were perceived by me as well as by the
couple as secondary to the intrapsychic and interactional. Hence in therapy
we were soon able to deal directly with the latter factors. In the communication area, the clue was that Jon had difficulty in comprehending Susan's
more idealized concept of giving and loving. This may or may not have been
due to the fact that his only warm and giving parent was his father. Susan
needs to become more competent in helping him see what she means and in
communicating directly. (Because some aspects of my value system were
closer to hers than to his, I had to be alert not to make myself his competitor
or to be patronizing.) Susan almost refused to respect Jonathan in his work
area because of what she considered her humanistic values, but their values
were more similar than they realized. Jonathan felt threatened because he
couldn't be the spiritual man she wanted, and struck back out of fear of
losing her. He was puzzled by and attracted to her capacity to experience joy
and her artistic qualities, which fascinated him, confounded him and made
him feel defensively inadequate.

TOWARD THE SINGLE CONTRACT

We now began in earnest to work toward a single contract. Most of the next session was spent reviewing the marriage contracts they had written out earlier, along with my additions and comments. One would read a section of his contract, starting with the verbalized part; the other would then read the corresponding section; then we would discuss similarities, differences and sources of problems. I elaborated on conflict or cut through to the common denominators, explaining to them the differences in their cognitive styles and the significance of the disparities.

Both of the Smiths wanted to work directly on their sexual problem. I had thought earlier that we could use sex as an entry to their change system, but we were now at a temporary impasse and would not be able to go further in that area until we had dealt with some other anxiety-producing parameters. Because sex was so laden with significance and meanings that related to all these parameters, to pursue their sexual-avoidance syndrome directly as a means of changing the total relationship could not work. At this time I thought they should postpone attempts to improve the quality and quantity of their sexual expression for the sake of improving the overall marital relationship. I explained my reasoning to them.

Before again focusing on sexual expression, we would first have to soften the defensiveness and anxiety produced by other parameters. In the future, if it was necessary to do so, sex might be used in this way again or as an end in itself. Because of the uneven development of different areas in their marital system, we would need to move back and forth between these areas.

Proceeding on the basis of this concept of uneven development, the Smiths and I agreed that the major areas of difficulty for them as a system were dependence-independence, passivity-activity, inclusion-exclusion, closeness-distance, power, acceptance of self, differences in cognitive styles, and communication. With their agreement, I chose the areas of cognitive style and communication as the next ones to work with directly. I had already begun by pointing out the differences between their cognitive styles—he assembling data, sorting out, examining and arriving at a "rational choice," she more "intuitive" and dependent on feelings for making her choices. Examples were given of the differences in the way they approached problems, including those with each other, and of how this, too, affected their communication and made them impatient with each other. They each believed that just a few words would cue them to what the other thought about any issue, and that because neither could influence the other's thinking, it was useless to say more. Long ago they had arrived at a communication impasse. It was important that they accept their differences in style and try to understand each other's cognitive approach. Both styles were perfectly valid but different.

I told them I thought they complemented each other very neatly, and gave them the task of finding ways to use their differences to their common advantage. They were told to question each other carefully if one of them did not fully understand the other's point of view. Emphasis was put on communicating clearly and simply with each other, understanding and listening, and then trying to arrive at a compromise or a quid pro quo agreement without either feeling defeated in the process. This task, along with the one of using their different cognitive styles, might accomplish changes in their relationship expeditiously if it did not cause too much anxiety and consequent sabotage.

In the next session they reported having talked more openly and freely for a few days but then began a mutual withdrawal and distancing. Neither had made sexual overtures during the week. Jonathan stated he felt upset by a lack of sex. I urged him to assert himself and make his desires known. When I asked Susan how she would like him to approach her so that she would be most likely to respond warmly, her answer was definite but vague in the particulars. "I want it to come from the heart as well as the penis—you make me feel as if it's just your penis that wants me." I asked him if he knew how to translate what she said into feelings and actions. He did not. I turned to her and told her to tell him more precisely what she wanted. She now became more explicit, and he was able to comprehend and to begin to appreciate the kind of loving relationship she had in mind. For the first time he was able to hear her and she could appreciate his difficulty in not having understood her previous figures of speech.

After that session we did not meet for two weeks because Susan had impulsively gone on a weekend retreat with her spiritualist friends. On the night of the day she returned, Jonathan had the following dream:

> There is fucking in the dream. She and I return from a dance with Bob and Adele (friends who fight constantly). We pass a house and Sue says, "Many a fuck have I fucked there." We go someplace, probably home. B. and A. are still with us. I angrily ask Sue, "How many times did you fuck there?" She answers, "I'm not going to tell you." We go back and forth like that a few times and then I hit her a few hard punches in the face. Blood comes from her mouth and she says, "No tell." She's in pain and the blood is oozing out, and she then says, I'll tell you. Forty or fifty times." B. and A. disappear. I say, "See, you wasted all your cunt juice there and now there's nothing left." I then added, "The girl who will eventually take me from you won't even have to be pretty; all she'll have to do is fuck."

Jonathan's controlling passivity was demonstrated by his having told the dream to Susan for her to write down. She read it to me. In this indirect way he let her know his anger over her leaving him for three days, which he had not expressed to her before she left or afterward. The dream provided the opportunity to go into Jon's feelings of sexual rejection by Sue, his fear of her desertion, aroused by her having gone to the retreat, and his anguish, desperation and passivity about direct expression of his anger. Her going off at a time when they were working together with me and its provocative effect were dealt with too, and Sue came to realize that she had been anxious about their growing closeness and had physically, as well as emotionally, distanced herself. Her action in going to the retreat, along with his dream, made it possible to confront both Jon and Sue with their sense of inadequacy and their need for distance so as to avoid discovery as inadequate persons. His violent reaction in the dream was what she felt to be smoldering within him. It frightened and fascinated her as she toyed with provoking him enough so that he would be violent. Violence would be an impotent defeat for him— but on the other hand, did she really want him to be effective? That was one of her dilemmas that he complemented so well with his aggressive passivity. He behaved as she (neurotically) wanted, despite its frustration for her.

Jonathan's dream provided a wealth of material that could have been interpreted in a number of ways. I had elected to take from it the aspects that I thought pertained to the direction of our work at that moment. After this there was a deeper appreciation of the valid and genuine difference between their cognitive styles, of their sense of worth to each other and of the fact that they could communicate better if they wished to—for example, if she had stopped to feel her anxiety about closeness, instead of running away, and had talked about her feelings with him.

Gradually, over the next six weeks, we worked toward agreement on significant aspects of the single contract. Jonathan became more sensitive to himself and to Susan, but had further to go. She became better able to accept her own strength as well as her interdependence with her husband. He accepted the children much more, particularly after Sue stopped using them to increase his feelings of exclusion by insisting he do more with them. Her insistence had made him distance himself from them; left to his own resources, he began to include them. Consulted now in the process of making decisions that affected the children rather than just carrying out Susan's decisions, Jon showed evidence of taking the initiative in developing his own relationship with each child. When Sue showed an increasing readiness to have Jon take over more family power, he became more active in assuming it. They continued to have disagreements but were now able to discuss them more effectively and arrive at a resolution rather than invariably withdrawing or abdicating in anger.

They agreed to accept their differences on numerous issues and types of problems, and worked out several quid pro quos with me present as well as on their own. I was concerned with teaching them the process of discovering and elucidating sore spots and then arriving at their own acceptable solutions.

It was important for them to learn in their sessions that both wanted similar things—love, security, independence while being cared for too; that each could give to the other if assured he/she would not be taken over; that each wanted power to make sure their world held together, but was also fearful of having power and was only too glad to hand it over to the other if assured he/she would not be hurt. Some tasks were designed to break their impasses by developing trust, to overcome the watchful waiting and suspicious assessing and weighing of the "Who-did-what-for-whom-last?" approach. A very useful task was instructing each to be in charge for three days at a time. The strong feelings engendered by this task were then discussed in the next session. With some ups and downs, trust began to improve. Jon became more active on his three days and then became dependent, asking Susan what to do or sometimes planning activities he knew she would not like. She reciprocated in kind when it was her turn. But they were beginning to change their interactions. Therapy had to be terminated (ten sessions had been planned for) before some of the changes hoped for could be realized. Treatment was stopped with the knowledge that all was far from perfect, but that they had turned a corner and were now better equipped to identify and work on the problem areas of their contracts and to work toward a single agreement. We all realized they had a way to go on this, but they now feel equipped to proceed on their own.

Follow-up Interview

At my initiative I saw the Smiths nine months later in a lengthy follow-up interview. I was struck at once by their changed appearance. Sue had lost considerable weight and her face was composed and beautiful. She looked as if she had a new pride in her own being. Jon had lost his air of dogged defensiveness and had an ease and self-assurance he had lacked the year before. He seemed much more in charge of himself. They had had some difficult times but had continued to review their contracts and to work toward a common one. Jon was now more accepting of her spiritualist friends and no longer so threatened by them; he realized that he had a solid relationship with his wife. They discussed some of their feelings and ideas together these days. At one time during the meeting I misunderstood something Jon had said, and Sue quickly informed me of my mistake, which had conveyed a negative connotation about Jon.

A few months prior to our meeting, Sue had considered divorce, faced the alternatives and decided that life with Jonathan offered her most of what she really wanted. She now spoke lovingly about him and with understanding for him. Although she disagreed with many points, she now respected his opinions and saw validity in much of what he said. They sounded as if they finally had been listening to each other. Jon also spoke lovingly of Sue and indicated a true sense of understanding and affection for her. He said that he now realized and accepted the fact that she had periods when she had to withdraw emotionally. When she reassured him that it was not his fault, he could accept this and be there for her when she was ready to come back.

Recently Sue had lunched with her mother, who had told her she now realized her daughter was an artist, respected her for it and could understand her need to be true to herself. She would no longer try to make her daughter a business person. Apparently Sue's changes also affected her relationship with her mother, from whom she now elicited a very different response.

Sex was excellent when they had it, but some of the old problem of lack of assertion on Jonathan's part persisted. His tendency to be rigid and literal surfaced in unexpected ways, despite a general change in regard to understanding Sue and her style. Her style and her messages certainly were difficult to understand at times. For example, now that it was summer she wanted to sleep on the ground out-of-doors. She had compromised by sleeping on the floor next to their bed but had not told Jon why she had left their bed. He took her sleeping on the floor as a rejection. He did not wish to follow her to sleep on the floor if she had "moved out." Therefore they had not had sex for ten days. He was surprised when I asked Sue why she was on the floor and she said it was a compromise because she wanted to sleep outside but she knew Jon would not, so she met him halfway by sleeping on the floor in their bedroom. She had hoped that he would come to the floor and make love with her there and then get back into bed or not as he wished. Sue thought she had made an advance to him by what she had done, but she had not told Jon why she was on the floor and he had not asked her. Both felt hurt and abused by the other. As the truth of this situation unfolded during the session, it drove home to them the fact that they could not count on subliminal messages but had to tell, ask, explain openly and clearly to each other. Sue accepted her responsibility in the *pas de deux* for not having verbalized her intent. Jon accepted his for not having questioned her and moved toward her.

After our session I found myself thinking that instead of Sue lying on the floor feeling hurt and rejected after she had made such an "obvious" offer of compromise and he lying in the bed above her feeling angry and rejected, he would now come to the floor and they would make love and enjoy sex. Sometimes he goes back to bed after she falls asleep, I thought, and sometimes he stays on the floor with her all night. And then, too, on some evenings she comes into the bed first and they make love there. He also learns, in my fantasy, that her being close to nature need not exclude him. Indeed, he likes nature at times—but he never need like it as much as she; he always will remain essentially a bed-sleeper and she essentially a floor-sleeper. Often the presence of the need for touch and closeness will outweigh the need for distance. Each will realize what each now senses—that the essence of what they both want is also feared by them, but to a lesser degree, and that it is there for each of them when they are ready for it.

When I saw the Smiths again, I was to find that my optimistic musings had not fully materialized.

THE SINGLE CONTRACT

Six months after the follow-up visit, I telephoned the Smiths to arrange another follow-up session and to ask them to write out together a single contract that would include what they agreed upon as well as their differences. I would send them a reminder list * that would serve as a guide. Since they had copies of the individual contracts they had written at the start of treatment, they could refer to those if they wished to. They seemed to welcome the idea, and it was decided that when they had finished their single contract, they would mail it to me and call to make an appointment.

Four weeks later, after another call from me, I received their single contract, which had obviously been carefully and thoughtfully worked on by both of them, and the next day they called and made an appointment.

THE SMITH'S CONTRACT

The numbers correspond to the item letters of the reminder list. The in-session comments summarize our discussion and evaluation when we discussed the contract in the session.

Category 1. Expectations of the Marriage.
1. Both expect mate to be loyal, devoted and loving, but not exclusive. In session they said by "exclusive" they were not referring to sex and meant they did not need to be possessive but just to love—could allow the other time for him/herself.
2. Both agreed marriage provided support against the rest of the world. In the session their sense of closeness and being there for each other was indicated by several incidents in which they offered support to each other.
3 and 4. Both agreed that they liked solitude and that they did not see marriage as a goal in itself.
5. Both agreed marriage helped them in life's struggles but as a tool and a support, not a panacea.

---

* *Ibid.*

6. Both did not believe it was realistic that marriage should last "until death do us part."

7. Sex remains a problem area (see category 2).

8, 9 and 10. Children are desired and only they are included in their family unit.

11. Home is a refuge from the world. Husband answered "definitely yes," wife a weaker "yes." They explained that home is largely her work area and therefore not her refuge as much as it is his—she must seek a refuge from home at times.

12. Husband answers "no." He does not need marriage to give him a respected position and status in life. Wife: "A weaker yes." She wants structure in her life; she was an aimless flower child for several years and does not want chaos anymore. This is a key factor that came through for the first time—her need for her husband to help her maintain order in her life and within herself. She went on to say, "I had had lots of sex, a life of free love—it was enough of that."

13, 14 and 15. They agreed that they were an economic and social unit and that marriage served as an inspiration to work and build, etc., but that marriage was not a cover for their aggressive drives.

16. Susan: "As a lover I have been let down and I am dejected because of this." Jonathan: "Expected more settling by my wife into middle-class life style and higher sexual drive. Result: uncertainty and frustration." Both felt that the answers above served as an adequate summary and had nothing to add.

Category 2. Psychological and Biological Needs.

1. *Independence-Dependence.* Jonathan: "Set style and pattern for my-self. Feel I am too dependent on my wife physically and materially and not dependent enough spiritually." In the session he elaborated that he recognizes he is too dependent on Susan to take care of his physical needs at home, such as preparing meals, initiating recreational and cultured activities, etc. By "spiritual" he meant he has come to recognize and give credence to some of the facets of relating to people and approaching life that she has espoused, even in terms of his developing some interest in music and in the significance of spiritual values. Susan: "I set the pattern for myself; very often I feel either abandoned—'my-God-I-am-here-all-alone' feeling—or else my husband is too dependent on me and I feel put upon. This is a troublesome area." In the session they talked as if these statements were more from the past; the implication was that although still present, such problems had diminished. They cited a variety of incidents to remind each other that there had been a shift from the above, although not yet to the

ideal. Jonathan stated that they were really becoming much more interdependent in a good way, with which Susan concurred.

2. *Activity-passivity.* Jonathan: "Feel both are too passive and especially me." Susan: "I agree." In the session, much was made by Susan of Jonathan's passivity; it makes her angry with him and turns her off sexually. She does not care how active he may be at work—with her he acts like a passive child. He agreed and felt it was contrary to his nature to be otherwise. However, he said he would accept more responsibility to take the initiative at home.

3. *Closeness-distance.* Jonathan: "Expected more closeness than I am getting. Am aware of distance between us." Susan: "There is distance between us. When there is closeness it is a noticeable and pleasant occurrence. Would like it to happen more but can't force this sort of thing." In the session we went into several incidents in which Susan was responsible for distancing because of her lack of communication to Jon and her projection of her own feelings. For him, on the other hand, closeness meant being the adored child. Actually, they are now closer more often than when first seen. For example, if he wants to watch football on television, he often invites Sue to join him, which she sometimes does. She is appreciative of this change from his previous way of just peremptorily picking himself up and leaving her alone. As she has become disappointed in her spiritualist movement, she has turned more to him for closeness and support. Most of the time he has been there for her.

4 and 5. *Power; submission and domination.* There was no response to this subject. They were not ready to deal directly with all the implications of this area. When asked, they said it had been adequately covered in terms of his passivity and that each felt he or she acted quite independently and therefore shared power. He felt he submitted to her in regard to sex, but not otherwise. Conversely, she felt she was controlled by his sexual passivity and lack of help with home chores. Actually, both still abdicate power in many common areas of their interrelationship and resolve it by an uneasy assignment and assumption of traditional roles and duties. To an extent they still remain two children in search of a parent, but with a growing recognition that neither will accept the parental role and that they have to work toward a more mature interdependence with the surrender of more of their childish expectations.

6. *Abandonment and loneliness fears.* Jonathan: "These fears definitely exist and are an important source of anxiety." Jon was referring to Sue's withdrawal of affect when she would become more deeply involved with her sect. He knew he could not reach her then. He feels somewhat better since she is no longer as deeply involved, having become disillusioned with her sect's leader, who turned out not to be as strong and loving a father image as she wanted. She now turns more to Jon. He likes this but is also somewhat

apprehensive over the expectations and obligations that go with Susan's turning to him more. Susan: "I feel abandoned when the load falls on me and I feel inadequate." By "the load," Susan meant the traditional chores of housekeeping and child-rearing. She feels that in view of her support of Jon's accepting a lower-paying job that he liked and or their agreement not to accept money from her mother, she is entitled to more support in chores and child-care responsibilities when he is home. He agreed but stated that she must tell him what she wants or where she needs help and not assume he should know, because she is not sensitive (resistant?) to these needs. She recognized the need to express her wants as they occur, and not to collect a long series of injuries.

7. *Possession and control of spouse.* This item was not responded to. Each felt that in Category 1, Item 1, and under "Independence-dependence" they had been clear that neither wanted to possess, but both recognized in the session that although each "respected" the other's autonomy, autonomy was allowable only in areas of non-concern or non-threat to the other. Here again, there was no answer to a question that is a central problem area. In the session this was called to their attention with humor—a "Sure-you-don't-have-to-control-when-you're-getting-what-you-want" sort of approach.

8. *Level of anxiety.* Both responded: "Level of anxiety can get high for each. Triggered by any of the problem areas at any given time. We react to it by withdrawing from each other." Their recognition of this marks a big advance for them. It was suggested to them in the session that they be more alert to try to deal directly with the anxiety. Not feeling too upset when the other withdrew was fine, but could this wedge into helping each other be advanced further?

9. *Feelings about yourself as a man or woman.* Jonathan: "Often inadequate." He bases this on the fact that Susan does not stroke his ego and make passionate love to him very often on her own initiative. On the other hand, he recognizes that recently they have had excellent sex several times when he was loving to her; she then responded openly and freely. But he had to be active! He recognizes that he has enjoyed good sex with her, but on her terms. His sense of inadequacy, as well as Susan's, is also based on other aspects that were dealt with in the session. The similarity of their responses was pointed out and the question was left with them of how they could best help each other reevaluate him/herself. Susan: "I don't feel beautiful or lovable. I cannot abide the feeling that I am desired and loved and I find ways to deny it. For example, I feel that the lover is turning me into an object, or I cannot conceive the meaning of desire without this dimension of mystery, or I use fantasies that cause shame. The feeling of shame is painful, so I avoid sex." Although it had been talked around several times, this was her first forthright statement about feeling that she was unable to accept love. Her avoidance of sex is due, at least in part, to shame for her fantasies

and for past sexual freedom and promiscuity. Jonathan wants her to act with him as she did with others in the past, thus arousing strong shame, anxiety and antipathy in her. When she is praised for her beauty or for any other reason, she feels it must be false because she knows she is not perfect. From her childhood, she has believed perfection is required of her if she is to be loved. And now her husband loves her for what she considers a most heinous imperfection! This is an apparent contradiction with which she needs additional help. Her rejection of Jon for his passivity in turn increases his feelings of masculine inadequacy, which are already so close to the surface.

10. *Physical and personality characteristics of mate that affect your sexual reaction.* Jonathan: "I recognize that my wife is objectively attractive, but her sexual passivity and coldness turn me off. I would like a more active partner who enjoys the activity." Susan: "My husband does not turn me on because he is too absorbed with a male image, being what he thinks is masculine, macho behavior. For example, liking football is a male activity. Also, I feel he is fettered in matter, fettered in his body." By this last sentence Sue meant that Jon's body is too tight and that he cannot enter sex sufficiently with his spirit as well as his body. Other aspects of their sexuality were covered above; this area is improved but remains an irritating symbol of the conflicts within each one as well as between them.

11. *Ability to love and to accept yourself and your mate.* Jonathan: "Yes." In view of what he has just stated, this monosyllabic answer cannot be taken at face value. Susan: "No, for above reasons." (See 9 and 10.) It is quite clear that each can only partly accept himself or the other. There is a growing acceptance of each other that is not based on "I am not much, so I am not entitled to more." The latter may have been unconsciously operative for each, but if so, it is a diminishing force.

12. *How do you and your mate approach problems?* Jonathan: "Both make half-hearted attempts to tackle problems, then withdraw." Susan: Approach problems differently. Gives us something to talk about. I do agree that we make half-hearted attempts and withdraw." Jonathan often does not state his ideas and feelings—as when he did not question Susan when she was sleeping on the floor—and she expects a loving husband-father to divine her needs and feelings. She approaches problems more intuitively, he in an organized, "rational" way. Their attempts to resolve problems have remained half-hearted and they are not consistent in pursuing them to resolution; they state a position and then tend to let it rest there, yet over a period of time do change. They seem to be loathe to acknowledge positive changes and backslide somewhat when not in active treatment.

13. Both felt they had covered adequately those areas in which the mate let them down or caused trouble.

14. Both felt no *summary* was necessary as their wants and wishes to give

had been covered adequately among their other responses. However, both were much clearer about what they wanted than they were about what they would give the other!

Category 3. Derivative Problems.

1. *Communication—sending and receiving.* They agreed they had serious communication problems. In the session this was a major focus of attention because they, particularly Sue, often do not send clear messages, nor do they always listen to the message that is sent. Sue is too attuned to the latent meaning in Jon's messages; he takes her too literally. I coached them in how to practice open and clear communication.

2. *Intellectual differences.* They both agreed that these were numerous and that there are different views of what is important. Despite this statement, it was clear in the session that they now have much more common ground than they had twenty months ago. They are both highly intelligent.

3. *Energy level.* Both interpreted this question in terms of active-passive and agreed that Susan's energy level is higher than his and that she wants him to have more energy, more activity. This problem has been discussed earlier.

4. *Interests, life style.* Jonathan: "Vast differences between us." He alludes to outdoors, spiritual, cultural, etc., although the activities they had shared most recently were contrary to this flat statement. Susan: "I love to sing and dance, and we hardly ever do it." But why she does not arrange for such activities either together or by herself we did not get to in the session.

5. *Families of origin.* No problems now that peace has been made between Susan and her mother.

6. *Child-rearing.* Jonathan: "Not a problem area, since husband lets wife do most of it, which she resents, so it is somewhat of a problem area in that respect." That sums it up neatly. No separate response from Susan, which means they both agree. Like many of the other reponses, this does not mean that there is an acceptable single contractual arrangement on this issue. It is a statement of what is, and it will require work to either change it or make it acceptable to both by means of quid pro quos or in some other way.

7. *Children.* Both agree that children are not used in alliances against either parent, nor does either parent identify a particular child with spouse or self.

8. *Family or personal myth.* Both agree that there are none. I felt that there is a myth about how different each is from the other, which is a false concept in many respects. This idea was not pleasing to either of them—it had the effect of a confrontation.

9. *Money.* Both agree there is not enough to fight over, but they do have concern about the lack of it. The strong feelings about money have lessened;

they have tightened their belts. I do have some concern because they do not appear to have plans for changing the situation, a somewhat unrealistic position and perhaps somewhat irresponsible. The stress of money shortage is felt more by Susan, who is weighted down by household duties that interfere with her creative work. Therefore this, too, remains an unresolved contractual area.

10. *Sex*. Jonathan: "Wife initiates most of the time, mainly because I feel undesired and do not want to impose on her. Very low frequency in sex. No alternative sex partners. Sex is generally not pleasurable or gratifying because of above reasons." Susan: "See category 2. I feel we both want terrific romance in our lives. There is a hardness in my heart that keeps me from feeling or being a good lover. We are opening our hearts a tiny crack toward one another. I feel hopeful, as though the marriage begins again after the first seven years—at a different plateau, with some trust." As stated earlier, sex has been better than they record here, but it is still far from satisfactory. "Hardness" in Susan's heart refers to her alleged disappointment at Jon's passivity, but also to her now-revealed judgmental attitude toward herself. Note Jon's complaint and his method of attempting to manipulate Sue into taking the initiative.

11. *Values*. Jonathan: "I feel wife's values are more spiritual, romantic, religious and artistic, while mine are more worldly." Susan: "I feel husband's values are often too male-oriented, or incomprehensible, irreverent, irrelevant. On the other hand, I know his sensitivity for the underdog and the defenseless and would like him to open up more to that side of himself." Jonathan is somewhat defensively cowed by what he seems to assume to be the "better" values of his wife. Early in therapy I may have countertransferentially helped to increase this feeling, but I believe this is no longer operative. Her response, as well as his, is indicative of their moves toward understanding, even if they do not yet accept one another fully. In this single contract, as well as in the session, Susan saw many of Jon's positions as being "too male-oriented." Again a single contract is not agreed upon here, the differences are described and Susan outlines how she would like Jonathan to change.

12. *Friends*. Jonathan: "We share most. I have some of my own, individually. I have no female friends, only acquaintances." Susan: "I have friends of the opposite, as well as the same, gender." There do not seem to be serious problems in this area anymore. He is much less threatened by her friends now, especially since her disillusionment with her spiritual leader and her turning more to him.

13. *Gender-determined roles*. Jonathan: "I feel it is husband's duty to work and earn money, and wife's responsibility to keep house and rear children." Susan: "When other things are not going well, it becomes an irritation and I feel alone in marriage, but if we are strongly together, this

sharp division does not actually exist." As often happens, Jonathan sounds much more rigid and heavy-handed than he really is. Susan apparently has come to know this. This was corroborated in the session.

14. *List those areas where you feel let down.* Jonathan: "Primarily sexual area and common-interests area." Susan: "I feel let down on Jon's energy level, our lack of communications, that our interests are so different, and I am disappointed in sex life. But I don't dwell on it." This is their common refrain—except for her last sentence. Note that whenever both write different responses, Jonathan is always first. I forgot to ask why.

15. *How do you react when you have been let down?* Jonathan: "I withdraw." Susan: "I feel anger and withdraw."

16. *Other areas not mentioned.* No responses.

17. *Summary statement.* Jonathan: "See my summary at end of category 1." Actually he had not summarized and he did not elaborate further except in our discussion. Susan: "I want high energy with a lot of verbal and love give-and-take between my beloved and myself. In turn I will give high-energy level and verbal give-and-take and love give-and-take between beloved and myself. I now see my husband giving more with the children. I'd like him to initiate more activities. There are some beginnings here that I want to encourage. I want an outdoors man. In turn I will play cards."

Susan continued:

> I will give:
> I want to give receptive devotion. I want to be a nurturing adult to my children and an uplifting force to my husband and home. I want to see the possibility of my divine self, what is creative and loving in me, expressing itself.
>
> In return I will get:
> I want to get a partner with fire in his spirit, whose spirituality, good thoughts and sage advice give a fatherly life-giving character to our family. I visualize a mature father, radiating his creative power of love and warmth toward our children and affectionate caring for them.

Does she ask for more than she has a right to expect from Jonathan? Can she make compromises without being bitter? Can he insist upon open communication from her and that they accept one another on a more realistic level? I believe they have moved some in this direction. I also believe they want to continue to do so. The decisions will, of course, have to be theirs.

DISCUSSION

The single contract indicated that each knew himself better now and had fewer illusions about the other. They were very clear about where and what their problems were. They saw themselves as a couple and had made some advances in trusting each other, but sex, although better in general, still suffered from each one's being set in his own fantasy of what he/she wanted to receive before giving.

They no longer accepted money from her mother, so that financially they were in a crunch, but they felt united and pleased with themselves. However, Susan showed her resentment over the pressure on her (a large house, no help, caring for and chauffeuring children, etc.) with what she felt was too little help from Jon. She resented what she described as his "macho" position. They agreed they had many ideological and taste differences.

When they came in for the follow-up interview, I felt much better about them than when I had first read their single contract. They looked well and happy and treated each other with affection and respect. I asked them how they felt about the single contract. They said it had been difficult for them to write out because it had confronted them with themselves and they felt negative when filling it out; however, they went on to say that they had felt much better about themselves since then. They had realized that they had focused on negative things in writing up the contract and that there were actually many more positive things going on between them.

In working with their written single contract I did not go down the list item by item but stimulated discussion. In advance I had noted areas that needed to be covered or that I wished to interpret or reinforce. I started by reading Susan's response: "I feel we both want terrific romance in our lives . . . I feel hopeful, as though the marriage begins again after the first seven years—at a different plateau, with some trust." It was after I read this that Susan responded with an eloquent statement. At one point Sue reminded Jon of several good sexual experiences they had shared recently. He then reminded her of how close they had felt driving together at night through a heavy snowstorm: "We worked together like one person with four eyes." When they got home early that morning they had the best sex they had had in a long time. As the session went on, more and more positive aspects of their behavior came through, not only in what they remembered but in their interaction and tenderness to each other.

Jon pointed out how Susan accumulates frustration and bitterness toward him and then lets it come out all at one time. He made a plea for her to be more open and spontaneous with him. She then responded with the insight about why she gets upset when she is praised or told how attractive she is— not because she fears sex or to be a sex object only, but because as a child she had to be perfect. She feels imperfect and therefore inadequate. This was a whole new area for Jon; he was surprised because he had felt he was the flawed one.

Susan and Jon have moved closer together. They, with their children, have become more united as a family. They are struggling, making headway and dealing more realistically with each other and their life situation. They are now less like two children in search of a parent and realize that neither will be parent to the other. They still want that, but more as if it has become a pro forma demand—a ritual that no longer has meaning or expectation of fulfillment.

In this last session I tried to focus on giving them the tools to continue to work on their own problems by means of the single contract. They are equipped and motivated to continue to try to make changes in their problem areas. We will have another follow-up session in a year, or sooner if they request it.

Twelve months later Jon called my office with an urgent request that I see him alone; he came in the same day. Susan, he told me, had had an affair, which he discovered a month ago. She admitted it when he confronted her with his suspicions. He first felt furious and reacted by seeing, in turn, two former women friends with whom he then had sex. But "a revolution had been taking place." He and Susan were now having the best sex and overall relationship they had ever had. His reason for wanting to see me alone was that he wasn't sure whether he could or should "fully forgive her." He wanted to, realizing a big change had taken place for both of them; he was now loving to her and she to him. He was much more assertive in sex and Susan was now more responsive to him. However, Jon told me, Susan had not agreed to sever the relationship with her lover. I explored his feelings further with him. He agreed that Susan's behavior was not a put-down of him but was a symptom of their relationship and that her action had changed their behavior together for the better. During the past year Susan had returned to work in her mother's company—"somehow" her relationship with her mother had changed and Susan now felt accepted as a talented and competent adult. She was enjoying the business and was being groomed to eventually take over.

Jon agreed to ask Susan to come in together with him for an appointment the following week and to tell her he had seen me. We set up a time, subject to Susan's approval.

When they came next, they were warm and loving and there appeared to be a new bond and glow between them. I saw Susan alone after a few minutes because I had seen Jon alone previously and I wished to hear her story from her directly. She had turned, for her love relationship, to an old friend whom she felt close to but had not had a sexual relationship with previously. Susan felt he was tender, loving and understanding. She was glad to tell Jon of this relationship when confronted and was extremely pleased by his reaction. He became decisive and firm, insisted she tell him all about it. He was angry, went and saw his old girlfriend, told Susan after he had done so and later saw another. He then was able to become tender and loving to Susan. Incredulously, she found herself responding to him. Jon had demanded she stop her affair with her friend (she had told him who it was, at his insistence); she had not yet told Jon she would do so, but she told me she had already stopped seeing him. When I asked her what she intended to do, she said she was pleased by the renaissance of their love and sex and their elevation to heights they had never achieved before; but it was all very new and she thought she would tell him shortly, as she now felt more secure within herself—she was still a little angry with him but was enthralled at his newly demonstrated strength. During this past week, he had told her he had overcome his vengeful feelings over her actions and now appreciated their positive effect on both of them.

Susan now felt, too, that she appreciated better his views on many matters on which the two of them had been polarized. And Jon had been enjoying camping, music and dancing with her. He was now alive and responsible about their home; helped to care for the children and got pleasure from it.

Much had fallen into place. Despite many upheavals, they maintained communication; if one of them withdrew, he or she returned shortly to continue the dialogue.

We parted from this session with warm feelings. A sense of accomplishment was felt by the three of us, plus a feeling of awe on my part. Inwardly, I am sure, we all hoped that their new achievements and closeness would stand up. They appeared to be in love again but on a different and more secure level than previously. I expressed a caveat to them that they should not be surprised if the high did not continue but that they were now in a new ballgame that should remain very different from the old one.

Apparently, during the year that had elapsed since their last visit, the forces set in motion by our previous work and their drive to grow individually and to resolve major problems had produced sufficient changes in each so that each now could function differently. Susan appeared to have resolved her crippling ambivalence about her mother, and Jon had dropped his defensive stance about his work and his role as adult within his family. Susan's affair was probably a preconscious bit of acting-out in desperation to push through the roadblock to the maturing of their love relationship and its sexual expression. As she had expounded in an early session, Jon had opened his heart to Susan and she now could be open to him. From childlike-childlike partners they were now moving rapidly toward being adult-adult partners with an underlying romantic flavoring.

I contacted them one year later for a follow-up. This was four years and four months from when first seen, and they now had had a total of fifteen visits, plus all the conscious and unconscious work they had done at home. Both agreed that there had been a change from the idyllic height of last year's dramatic jump to a more realistic but gratifying modus vivendi.

Susan had decided with her mother that becoming a business tycoon was not for her. She had changed her job to two days a week in a limited but creative area of the business. She devoted the rest of her time to her music and being Hestian. She felt at peace and comfortable with this division. The children were happier and functioned and behaved better now that she was at home more. Jon was much more helpful at home with household tasks, child-care and improved overall relatedness with the children. Sex was usually excellent although not as frequent as last year, at the time of their renaissance. Jon's work situation was progressing well and he was about to effectuate a job change that was part of a long-range career plan.

Both agreed that Susan's "moodiness" made for problems between them. As Jon summarized, "We are two egos colliding and trying to accommodate." They had been working hard on these accommodations. Both now perceived a cyclical change in Susan's moods, which they were trying to correlate to other variables, without success. They agreed their life as a couple, as a family and individually was infinitely better than four years earlier, but they still wanted to continue to improve matters.

This last time they had appeared to be consolidating their gains. They now had a single contract that included respecting each other's differences and could be fulfilled by both. Susan and Jon have been a rewarding couple to work with. Their motivation to work toward change and to stay together had made their progress possible. Their work on their marriage and their single contract is a process that will continue. As they go through their life cycle with family-task and aging changes, new interactional and internal needs and problems will emerge, others will recede. This will require periodic reexamination of their contract and possible changes in some of its terms.

This is not the most dramatically successful case I have treated; yet I am pleased with the results, especially in view of where Sue and Jon were when they began therapy. We had done very well to have reversed a deteriorating process in the marital and family systems and the two individuals. I believe Sue and Jon and their children now have an excellent chance for a better life together.

Susan had expressed it all exquisitely in the second follow-up session, at a time when a genuine sense of hope was emerging as changes were beginning, although the road ahead still looked rocky:

"After seven years, it's like the cycle of marriage has had a beginning, a middle and an end—it's a cycle or like a spiral. At the end of seven years, we were in the death throes of that phase of it. Now it's taking off on its second spiral. There's a lot to be said about sticking with something, because if you would give up at the seven, there is a death, but there is a resurrection coming if you can just stick with it. In this resurrection everything now has a double entendre, a richer meaning, it's more interesting."

REFERENCES

Berman, E., and Lief, H. Marital therapy from a psychiatric perspective: An overview. *Am. J. Psychiat.*, 1975, 132; 583–592.

Dicks, H.V., *Marital tensions*. New York: Basic Books, 1967.

Ferber, A., and Ranz, J. How to succeed in family therapy. Set Reachable goals—Give workable tasks. In A. Ferber (Ed.), *The book of family therapy*. New York: Science House, 1972.

Goldstein, M. The uses of dreams in conjoint marital therapy. *J. Sex & Marit. Ther.*, 1974, *1*; 75–81.

Gurman, A.S., and Rice, E.C. (Eds.) *Couples in conflict*. New York: Jason Aronson, 1975.

Haley, J. *Strategies of psychotherapy*. New York: Grune and Stratton, 1963.

Lederer, W.J., and Jackson, D.D. *The mirages of marriage*. New York; W.W. Norton, 1968.

Martin, P. *A marital therapy manual*. New York: Brunner/Mazel, 1976.

Paolino, T.J., Jr., and McCrady, B.S. *Marriage and marital therapy*. New York: Brunner/Mazel, 1975.

Sager, C.J. The development of marriage therapy: An historical review. *Am. J. Orthopsychiat.*, 1965, *36*, 458–467.

Sager, C.J. Transference in conjoint treatment of married couples. *Arch. Gen. Psychiat.*, 1967, *16*, 185–193.

Sager, C.J., Gundlach, R., Kaplan, H.S., Kremer, M., Lenz, R., and Royce, J.R. The marriage contract. *Fam. Proc.*, 1967, *10*.

Sager, C.J. *Marriage contracts and couple therapy*. New York: Brunner/Mazel, 1976.

Sager, C.J. The role of sex therapy in marital therapy. *Am. J. Psychiat.*, 1976, *133*.

Stuart, R.B. Operant-interpersonal treatment of marital discord. *J. Consult. & Clin. Psychiat.*, 1969, *33*, 675–682.

Chapter 3

Self-Object Considerations in Marriage and Marital Therapy

John C. Sonne
Deborah Swirsky

INTRODUCTION

This chapter will address itself to considerations of distortions of self-object definition, which can cause difficulties in love and marriage, and will also address the treatment of these distortions in therapy. The more one studies the area of self-object definition in the treatment of marital disharmony, the more important it seems to be. Yet this study is a fairly recent development in psychiatry that has probably been retarded by a natural tendency of most of us, including our unhappy couples, to view love and marriage primarily in terms of gratification of instinctual needs or in terms of related instinctual transference distortions.* Also, self-object distortions and the struggle for personal integrity and affirmation or confirmation are often so interwoven with the need for sensual gratification that they are only dimly visible to couple and therapist alike in the midst of an emotional

---

*See Chapter 4 in this book, Sonne, J.C., "Transference Considerations in Marriage and Marital Therapy," for an exploration of this area.

melange. Although it is possible, even in the study of relational difficulties based on self-object distortions, to include them within the category of gratification of instinctual needs or related instinctual transference distortions, there is merit in defining and examining self-object considerations separately from transference considerations. Self-object transferences, if we would call them that, are not so much transferences of instinctual drives as they are transferences of the need to fill deficiencies in the sense of self or to work out incomplete development of self with another person. Self-object distortions are concerned with identity, sense of reality, affirmation and sense of self rather than with gratification in the usual sense. It is important for the therapist to be alert to the fact that blended within conspicuous instinctual transferences there are often self-object distortions as well, derivative from very early developmental experiences, although the usual description of a transference relationship implies the presence of a sense of self and object. Poetically speaking, one could say that instinctual transferences are acted out by and based upon the cast of self-object definitions, and the relative degree of transferential and self-object distortions contained within any given transaction is a product of the participants' developmental level, their instinctual conflicts and the momentary situation. While analyses of transference and self-object distortions often go hand-in-hand, there is a definite distinction between the two phenomena, and beyond recognizing the distinction between these two relational phenomena, it is particularly important in therapy not to confuse one with the other. Analysis and intervention must be pertinent to whichever process is preeminent at any given moment, and it is often necessary to dissect transactions in which both instinctual transferences and self-object distortions occur in concert.

In order to be able to work on distortions of self-object definition in love and marriage in marital therapy, it is necessary to have an understanding of the role of self-object distortions in mate selection, and an understanding of how shifts can occur in this area over time as the marriage changes to the point of entry into therapy. An understanding of the process by which a sense of self and object is acquired in the course of early developmental experiences is also a prerequisite. In addition, the therapist must have a clear self-object definition of his own, must be sensitive to nuances and clues of self-object distortions in the couple and in the couple-therapist transactions, and must develop a style and technique for intervention. This chapter will discuss these issues and illustrate their operation in two case examples.

MATE SELECTION

In voluntary mate selection, courting mates seek, more or less consciously, the fulfillment of two objectives: instinctual gratification, plus a match to affirm, exercise and develop themselves and the self of their mate. The partners find themselves motivated by a mounting feeling of happy anticipation that they will continue to experience increasing reciprocal satisfaction of a wide variety of basic human needs, plus a mutual validation and enhancement of self. As the union gels, the mates feel satisfied, affirmed, loved and loving. To them, all seems well with the world, and they happily make a conscious mating contract.

These conscious and more or less healthy processes operative in mate selection are usually accompanied by and blended with more or less unconscious and psychopathological ones. On the unconscious level, and sometimes consciously or semi-consciously, the mates seek and contract for mutual gratification of instincts which are either immature or defensively expressed, plus the joint acquisition of a presumed part of another's self to fill in for a repressed or undeveloped part of one's own self. Each mate hopes, although unconsciously in most cases, to experience reciprocity in primitive satisfaction and, through borrowed functioning, to change reciprocally feelings of incompleteness to ones of wholeness of self. Although reciprocity of satisfaction and affirmation on this part-self and neurotic basis can, indeed, temporarily provide a couple with a feeling of happiness which can mask the pathology in the marriage and blend it with the mature love present, it often affords merely a semblance of security and safety, without joy. In time, as will be described later, changes occur.

SELF-OBJECT DEVELOPMENT: BASIC CONSIDERATIONS

As the primary focus of this chapter is self-object considerations in marriage and marital therapy, a crucial concern is the origin and nature of whatever self-object distortions each mate may bring to the process of mate selection and marital functioning. The following is a brief sketch of some of the work of various authors defining the developmental stages of self-object definition beginning with early infancy. Subsequently, additional work will be presented which can expand conceptualization of self-object definition to include marital and family imagery.

Many workers have contributed to our knowledge in the area of self-object definition, notably Erikson (1950), Fairbairn (1954), Ferenczi (1913), Anna Freud (1937), Guntrip (1961), Hartman (1939), Jacobson (1964), Klein (1946), Mahler et al. (1975), Piaget (1973), Sandler and Rosenblatt (1962), Spitz (1957), Sullivan (1953) and Winnicott (1965), to name a few. Others, such as Abraham (1927/1954), Adler (1940), Arietti (1967), Balint (1952), von Bertalanffy (1967), Bowlby (1969), Brodey (1961), Buber (1955), Federn (1952), Freud (1914/1957, 1938/1964), Horney (1950), James (1890/1950), Jung (1967), Kafka (1971), Kernberg (1976), Kohler (1929), Kohut (1959/

1977), Laing (1960), Lichtenstein (1961), Loewald (1962), MacMurray (1957), Maslow (1968), Modell (1968), Nunberg (1951), Pollak (1960), Rank (1932), Reich (1933), Reusch and Bateson (1951), Rogers (1951), Rosen (1953), Sartre (1956/1966), Schachtel (1959), Schilder (1935/1950), Searles (1962), Spiegel (1959), Suzuki (1956) and Tillich (1952), have all made valuable contributions to our understanding of self-object relations in infancy and adulthood, some of which are derived from quite varying philosophical or experiential frames of reference. Mahler's descriptions of the psychological birth of the infant, plus certain concepts of Jacobson, Hartman, Erikson and Spitz, perhaps best summarize an initial exposition of early object-relations development.

In the neonatal period, the infant has only the most rudimentary awareness of itself as a separate being and functions primarily as if it were in a fused symbiotic instinctual-perceptual relationship with the mother. At about four months of age, the infant begins to undergo an extended process of separation and individuation, which Mahler and coworkers, building on the works of others mentioned above and making major use of direct longitudinal observation of developing infants, have described as a "psychological birth" composed of four discernible subphases. In the first subphase, "differentiation," from around four to eight months, there is a beginning appreciation of a sense of separateness from the mother, a smiling response of recognition, some degree of internalized self-representation of body image and, toward the end of this period, stranger anxiety and a gradual increase in the use of splitting as a defense mechanism. In the second subphase, "practicing," from around eight to eighteen months, there is further development of the sense of and capacity for independent functioning through experimental movement away from and back to the mother and, toward the end of this period, a beginning struggle to blend "good" and "bad" splits of self and others into integrated images. Jacobson has emphasized the need for the infant, through adequate mothering, to learn eventually to see the mother as *one* person who is mostly "good" but sometimes "bad." A milestone of self-object development, emphasized by Spitz, which occurs around the age of fifteen months, or near the end of the practicing subphase, is the acquisition by the infant of the capacity to say "no" with head-shaking. This audacious declarative expression of self-object definition comes about in part through an identification with the aggressor-frustrator mother and marks the beginning of symbolic thought and allocentric communication. Hartman has described this identification with the aggressor as part of the construction of the infant's secondary autonomy, a creative accomplishment coming from the autonomous, synthetic functioning of the ego. In the language of Erikson's developmental stages, the infant is cementing its sense of identity in terms of basic trust versus mistrust during the subphases of differentiation and practicing. The third subphase, "rapprochement," at eighteen to twenty-four months, is characterized by the development of the toddler's reality-testing ability, an increase in awareness of differences between self and others, desire and capacity for greater autonomy, rapprochement crises, awareness of the father and a struggle in handling ambivalent feelings. Jacobson has particularly underscored the importance of processes of identification with admired rivals, including the father, during the last two of Mahler's four subphases.

Mahler's fourth subphase, "consolidation of individuality and beginning of emotional object constancy," commences in the third year and continues beyond. There is a continuation of the process of unification of "good" and "bad" parental and self-images, with resultant subsidence of ambivalence via reality-based acceptance of "good" and "bad" aspects of self and others and the eventual internal stabilization of object representation to a level of object constancy. Also during this period, gender identification becomes solidified and there is an increased sense of affirmation and identity and an expanded capacity to love. An important conceptual overlap is Erikson's characterization of the third and fourth subphases as periods during which there is an acquisition of a sense of autonomy versus that of shame and doubt.

SELF-OBJECT DEVELOPMENT: FAMILY IMAGE AND A TRIADIC HETEROSEXUAL SENSE OF REALITY

In addition to the conceptualizations of developmental accomplishments outlined above, there are two additional concepts which can expand our understanding of self-object definition and the development of a sense of reality: the development of a family image and the development of a triadic heterosexual sense of reality.

Most of the literature on early infant development has had a predominantly dyadic orientation in research conceptualization and design, and has concerned itself with self-object considerations primarily in relation to the mother, with minimal emphasis on the role of the father. When the role of the father has been examined, especially during the period of early infancy with which we are presently concerned, it has been seen primarily as that of helping the mother and infant separate from each other, plus providing the infant with an alternate love object.

It is important to emphasize the significance not only of the infant's having another love object in the father, but of the infant's having in the father a love object of a different gender from that of the mother. The presence of the father, his entrance into the mother-child dyad and the dyad's increasing interest in and awareness of him are of particular importance in the development of the infant's gender identity. The infant discovers in the father an interesting and interested creature who thinks, feels, speaks and behaves somewhat similarly to, yet differently from, mother, and who is similar yet different in physical appearance. This is not only important in terms of the child's development of his or her own gender identity and self-image, but is of equal importance in terms of the development of the child's awareness and knowledge of the reality of the difference in genders of other people.

That the father is also interesting to and interested in the mother is an additional variable in the child's world with which he must cope. He or she watches the relationship, relates to it and is related to by it, and the parental marriage as an entity becomes a major reality, which is perceived and introjected in the process of the child's development of a sense of the self-object world. This is perhaps the child's most difficult yet necessary accomplishment, requiring simultaneously an awareness of genders and the struggle to grasp the complexities and qualities of a triangular situation (Sonne, 1972). The child must recognize the parents in the marital dyad as having a special relationship to each other, and must orient himself or herself in this triadic context. The child must actually relate to the parental dyad as an "object organism" in a fashion similar to the relationship he or she has had with the individual parent figures. In doing this, the child develops a "heterosexual sense of reality." Sonne, Speck and Jungreis (1962) have used the term "family image" to describe the intrapsychic self-object representation of this expanded reality. It includes an awareness of one's position in a triangle in which two participants have genital fulfillment and one does not. In acquiring a heterosexual sense of reality and a family image, a child engages in three simultaneous processes:

1. The development of an internal triangular representation, including the "parental dyad" as an "object organism," i.e., a "self-parent dyad" or "self-parents triad."

2. A gradually increasing identification with the roles assumed by each parent in the marital and parental processes, roles which he or she will assume or vicariously experience in later life.

3. An increasing awareness of his or her own role, separateness and lack of genital fulfillment in relation to this "dyadic object" in the context of an ongoing, creative triangular situation.

Research in the use of heterosexual cotherapy (Sonne and Lincoln, 1965, 1966) has helped to illuminate the role of the father and the role of the marriage in the development of gender identity, marital object representations and the construction of a family image. Robbins and Sadow's (1974) paper on reality-processing outlines triadic concepts which are along lines similar to those presented here, as do Binstock's (1973) beautiful paper on the two forms of intimacy and Abelin's (1971) paper on the role of the father in the separation-individuation process. An understanding of self-object definition and the development of a sense of reality is incomplete if it stops at a dyadic level and does not conceptualize a triadic level which includes the significance of parental-gender identities, the marital dyad as an object representation itself and the development of a family-image representation and a heterosexual sense of reality.

With the completion of a reasonably adequate sense of autonomy, identity, self and others, as described and expanded above, by about the third year of life, the child is ready to encounter the vicissitudes of the oedipal maelstrom. Given a reasonably adequate resolution of the oedipus complex and a reasonably stable latency, one's self-object definition, heterosexual sense of reality, gender identification and internalized triadic family image will be further refined and strengthened, and one will enter adolescence prepared for the struggle for emancipation and renunciation of childhood dependency, a process Blos (1967) has called the second individuation.

In considering all of the foregoing discussion on self-object definition, it must be borne in mind that when one defines oneself as separate from others, one is still involved with others. Also, all of these definitions are processes which are ever-evolving, creative, negentropic, metaphorical, communicative ones, and should not be seen as static or mechanical, despite the somewhat sterile-sounding terminology, such as self and object, used in these abstractions from human reality. Life has beauty and ugliness in it and, as emphasized by Schaefer (1970) in his paper "The Psychoanalytic Vision of Reality," there are comic, romantic, tragic and ironic aspects of reality which color all the above self-object conceptualizations. Furthermore, this paper's focus on self-object considerations is by no means meant to imply that numerous other intrapsychic and transactional variables are not of the utmost importance in psychic life.

MARITAL CHANGE AND ENTRY INTO THERAPY

In discussing mate selection, marital functioning, marital change and marital therapy in this and subsequent sections, the term "self-object definition" will often be used alone for the sake of brevity, without qualifiers, to include the expanded family image and other connotations outlined above.

To the degree that the process of self-object definition is impaired, one grows to adulthood more or less incomplete. Someone who has failed to master the developmental stages described has not yet integrated into a reality-based and unified context the good and bad aspects of the self-object world. "Splitting" occurs on various levels of personality functioning, for example, in terms of good and bad object perceptions, affects and thoughts, male and female differences, and parent and child differences. Reminiscent of Allport's (1955) two-valued mentality, people with self-object problems have difficulty blending, synthesizing and creatively interacting with the world. In later life such "infants grown up" do not seek or experience in relationships with others an enhancement or rejoicing of self and others. Either they seek in other people parts of unrealized self or they project onto them parts of unrealized self, or both. They often let themselves be used similarly in a socially shared psychopathological system. Denial, projection and ego splitting are prominent operative defense mechanisms. In addition, there is a real, unmet developmental need for an object relationship through which they might have a second chance to reenter the path of self-object separation with all its promise of creativity and meaningful love.

At the time of mate selection, any operative defects in self-object definition may be so indiscernible, due to ego-syntonic matching, that they are blended with and reinforce the realistic, genuine love aspects of the relationship, and the overall union can appear to be a loving one. If the realistic and genuine love in a marital relationship is of sufficient strength and magnitude, it is possible in the course of a growing marriage experience for self-object differentiation to occur and, to a degree, for unmet developmental infantile needs to be mutually met. In order for this to occur, however, the pathological, collusive bonding must be disrupted via the development in the system of the strength in one or both spouses to renounce and frustrate the previously satisfying collusion without simultaneously destroying the genuine love aspects of the relationship.

In many cases creative growth does not occur in marriage, and each spouse continues to see and relate to the other primarily in terms of split-off aspects of self, which are kept disguised and unconfronted. Pathological attraction and selection are impelled by the infantile needs of the spouses, and the partners "collude" in their unconscious or conscious shared fantasy perceptions and projections based on early impaired object relations. Usually, although there can be other patterns of idealization and denigration as well, the mates initially projectively imbue each other with the split-off good object qualities, idealizing the object and ascribing to self the negative, antilibidinal object role. These idealized and devalued images come into conflict with the reality of the spouses and life, which emerges and intrudes as time progresses. A reversal typically occurs at this point; the fragmented projective identity (Klein, 1946, Malin and Grotstein, 1966, and Stewart et al., 1975) of the spouse now shifts from one of a good object to one of a bad object; and the initial period of idealization of the other and devaluation of self is replaced by an equally unreal denigration and blaming approach to the object and an idealization of self. The marriage moves from being one of harmonious collusion to one of dissonance. Contained within the dissonance is usually a degree of healthy disinclination of one or both spouses to continue giving or borrowing inappropriate and maladaptive part-selves. This transformation to dissonance arises from a phenomenological admixture of personal growth and development, the impact of cultural influences, major family changes, such as illnesses, births, deaths, affairs, successes and misfortunes, and a potentially growth-stimulating saturation with the unpleasant marital reality which can motivate one or both spouses toward a renunciation of collusion. It is at this point of marital dissonance that one or both spouses are precipitated into seeking therapy.

In viewing difficulties in marital systems in terms of socially shared psychopathology, the authors generally tend to see spouses as being at parity in terms of self-object development. Nonetheless, an unbalancing disruption in homeostasis and collusion must occur, often involving uneven change in one spouse, in order to provide a readiness for therapy and an opening for further marital growth. There are a variety of ways in which the spouses as individuals may contribute to this creative turbulence and in which they bring their problems to therapy. Sometimes a spouse will come alone for treatment for depression or with a concern about acting-out, with little awareness that part of his or her symptomatology represents a defense against facing problems in the marriage. Underlying marital conflict based on self-object distortions may surface as symptoms are dealt with in the course of therapy. In other cases where there exists from the start an awareness of marital difficulties as part of the presenting symptomatology, one spouse may still present alone as the "identified patient," self-defined as such or sent by the other. Marital self-object issues soon emerge and become a major therapeutic concern with or without a move into conjoint marital treatment. In a third instance, both spouses may seek help together, each complaining of marital disharmony and dissatisfaction, with the possibility of one or both or neither being clinically grossly symptomatic. In many instances, neither spouse evidences a discernible clinical syndrome; rather, there are vague clusters of a variety of psychological defenses and maladaptive coping patterns operating in the marital system. Many of the conceptualizations interrelating self-object definition and marital functioning described above have been similarly expressed in recent years in the writings of Ackerman (1958), Blanck and Blanck (1968), Dicks (1967), Jackson (1967), Lidz (1963), Martin (1976), Zuk (1971), the contributors to Eisenstein's (1956) and Paolino's and McCrady's (1978) edited books and many others.

THERAPEUTIC ISSUES: THERAPIST SENSITIVITY, PERSPECTIVE, STYLE AND TECHNIQUE

In approaching a discussion of therapy centering around self-object considerations, a matter of first importance has to do with the therapist's own level of self-object awareness and functioning. It is essential that the therapist have a clear sense of self, including gender identity, a heterosexual sense of reality and an internalized family image. He should be exquisitely aware of, sensitive, empathic and responsive to the ongoing flow of self-object transactions that continuously resonate between self and others. All of us are constantly participating in social communication matrices which mutually define ourselves and the selves of those with whom we relate. A therapist needs to have a generalized personal sensitivity to these processes and a refined understanding of the nuances and subtleties of persons in relation. If not, the therapist may be blind to patient messages that attempt to distort or clarify self-object reality, many of which are metacommunicative or non-verbal. A seemingly innocuous patient remark or question may carry important meaning for the self-object level of therapist-patient relating, and therapist responses to such remarks can carry equal significance and should therefore be predicated upon a foundation of relative personal autonomy and self-object-based reflection. The patient may be attempting unwittingly to form a psychopathological dyadic alliance with the therapist to replace incomplete parts of self. By being aware of this, the therapist can choose to frustrate or gratify the patient's expectations based on what is appropriate and timely to the patient's level of self-object development. Therapist understanding in itself can paradoxically foster a blurring of self-object boundaries that is countertherapeutic to the desired development of a sense of self.

To elaborate further on some of these concepts, the therapist must be alert to the conscious and unconscious use of kinesic and linguistic cues, such as smiling, frowning, crying, voice inflection, eye contact, inappropriate masculine or feminine mannerisms, body posture, dress and dialogue-response interval, and must be aware of and have control over his or her own automatic-response tendencies. In addition to the operation of self-object variables at the microorganismic level of the therapy session, there is also an operation at a macroorganismic level which is of equal and often unrecognized importance. The formal structuring of the therapeutic experience contains implicit and explicit variables around which self-object definition can occur. The definition and evolution of this overall formal structure derive from the manner in which the therapeutic contract is begun and terminated, the manner of entry into the exit from each session, decisions of whether or not to see one spouse alone and the way in which all intermediate communications are handled in phone calls, letters, fee or insurance issues, and any area involving confidentiality. All communications from outside sources, including family members, friends, social-agency personnel, lawyers, significant peripheral persons (Sonne, 1965) and any other involved third parties must be viewed in terms of their significance for self-object definition and handled accordingly.

One of the hardest things to write about, both because of the difficulty of essential characterization and the risk of so easily being misunderstood, is how to *be* a therapist (Sonne, 1971, 1973). It is important to be neutral, at times to be opaquely silent and thoughtful, not to respond automatically, to listen, to be knowledgeable and to have a good theoretical background. It is important to know oneself. Even with all this, however, one often does not know how to act. With notable exceptions, many writers say or imply that if one listens carefully, all else will follow; they hesitate, with some wisdom and perhaps some fear of telling what they themselves actually do, to write about what a therapist does. They will often reveal bits of this in case discussions, in precepting or in offhand comments in seminars, yet still hesitate to put themselves, their actions or advice to others in print. Recovering or recovered patients can tell of some meaningful behaviors on the therapist's part which were helpful to them in therapy but which were neither explicitly part of dynamic formulations and insight nor involved explicit analysis of the instinctual transference or self-object distortions.

Bearing in mind the possibility that he or she may be being manipulated or may be acting out, it is nonetheless important, especially for the therapist of self-object distortion, to respond as appropriately as possible and show an animated interest in particular to the patient's or couple's stories in general about their experiences with the culture, friends, family and world at large. It is part of the clarification of self-object distortions for the therapist to be interested in these experiences, to respond to descriptions of people and events with agreement or disagreement, to comment about the other people's behavior when the description sounds plausible, even though he hasn't met them, or to speculate about their possible motives or likely future behavior based on a general knowledge of and perplexity about human behavior. The therapist is not only a living mirror but a cultural window as well. This is particularly important with people who have problems with self-object definition and who are testing out reality and comparing how they see the world—i.e., their *Weltanschauung*—with how the therapist sees the world. These conversations form part of the empathic, introspective, metaphorical working-out of the spouse-therapist self-object definition and the spouse-world self-object definition, and are more important here than in instinctual transference analyses, where they may even be contraindicated as overstimulating and seductive. The therapist has probably met people such as described by the patient, or at times experienced bewildering situations similar to those the patient is experiencing, and often knows the books, plays, movies or other works of art, sports or music of which the patient speaks. It is important for the therapist of self-object distortions to respond genuinely and naturally at times with remarks such as "Sure," "Of course," "Naturally," "Wow!," "Oh, oh!," "That sounds strange," "That sounds terrible," "That was thoughtful of him," "That was beautiful" or "I guess she was so depressed and jealous she wasn't able to have time for your feelings."

Sometimes a patient needs a straight yes or no, needs in fact to know what the therapist thinks or feels—for example, when asking whether the therapist thinks the patient was wrong in not letting a jealous female "friend" know of her vacation plans with her husband. The answer is no. The patient knows the answer; she needs to know what the therapist thinks. The therapist needs to be serious and reflective, yet as part of his sense of separateness, he should also have the capacity to be appropriately playful and comfortably aggressive. A nonimposing chuckle, a smile, a gasp of horror, a wince of pain, a frown, a tear not held back, a shrug can all be completely appropriate expressions of the therapist's empathic responses to the patients' descriptions of the reality of their experience with the world and the people in it. This in no way precludes analysis of self-object distortions, but can in fact facilitate examination and resolution of what are distortions and what are not. At times patients with self-object distortions are so incredibly distrustful and feel so weird about their perceptions of reality that although at other times they may be equally certain that their distortions are true, they are desperately in need of a human corroboration of the healthiness and naturalness of their perceptions and need to know that the therapist, although he, too, may be mistaken, often sees and would see just about what they saw, and feel just about what they felt. This therapist-patient process is not only therapeutic per se, it also sharpens the likelihood of the therapist's credibility enduring at times when misperceptions are being questioned. Furthermore, it creates a more open inclination of the patient to consider his or her distortions from a less alien position, one of not being wrong about everything or of having views so completely different from those of the therapist. In addition to considering the therapist's interpretations and observations, the patient uses, and the therapist offers, the therapist's self as a responsive, informative, reliable transitional human object, involved with the world, neither impotent nor omnipotent, around whom he or she can re-form, define and reorganize self; as a human object who can be used as a temporary model for trial self-identification; and as a human object who can be used as a temporary model for trial assessment of the reality of other objects in general. Kohut's (1977, p. 306) remarks are pertinent here: "Empathy is not just a useful way by which we have access to the inner life of man—the idea itself of an inner life of man, and thus of a psychology of complex mental states, is unthinkable without our ability to know via vicarious introspection—my definition of empathy (cf. Kohut, 1959, pp. 459–465)—what the inner life of man is, what we ourselves and what others think and feel."

Although many of the above considerations apply to individual as well as marital therapy, they are of particular significance in the treatment of the collusions of marital disharmony. Awareness of them can aid a therapist not only to help couples in acquiring self-object definition in the narrow sense, but to help them in the expanded sense conceptualized above toward the acquisition of a family image, a heterosexual sense of reality and the definition of the marital unit as a special dyadic organism. In order to do this, the therapist must be aware of the organismic reality of the marital dyad and not collude in any splitting processes, assuming the triangular position of an "outside" party, somewhat analogous at times to that of a parent, child or friend. The therapist does not collude in any breaching of the boundaries of the crippled marital dyad, which have already been breached and compromised historically by a blurring of generational boundaries. By taking this noncollusive position, the therapist communicates a respect for and a beginning reinforcement of the heterosexual reality and integrity of the marital dyad. All requests from one spouse for individual attention and all seductive gestures directed toward the therapist must be seen with these issues in mind. The use of a heterosexual cotherapy team (Sonne and Lincoln, 1965, 1966) can be particularly helpful in handling much of the above.

Delicacy, sensitivity and timing are all needed in therapy, for therapists, while remaining "outside" the marital dyad, must nevertheless lend their own egos in the process of helping others develop theirs. A seeming paradox is present in any therapy situation: therapists, in helping people to renounce dependency, are transiently gratifying their dependency. Sophistication and awareness on the part of the therapist are necessary lest the self-object distortions already present be reenacted rather than resolved. Though a degree of symbiosis occurs and is probably necessary therapeutically, the therapist's participation differs in character from that of the patient. The therapist has empathy and the capacity for transient and partial identifications; yet he is still separately embedded in a matrix of myriad and complex investments in self, others, including family, friends, colleagues and other patients, broadly based reality, and a knowledge of psychological processes, and has one eye turned toward eventual self-object growth and development. Although a therapist may have areas in himself which are undeveloped and can legitimately expect to grow in the therapeutic endeavor, awareness of his own needs and taking responsibility for them should preclude the kind of unconscious collusion with the patient that the patient is already participating in within the marital and probably other relationships. Although it may be crucial for the patient or couple to maintain temporarily an illusory belief in the omnipotence of the therapist or in the existence of a symbiotic relationship with the therapist, the aware therapist will, through a variety of appropriately timed moves, frustrate these illusions and help patients move out of such expectational sets. Consideration of collusive self-object distortions is especially relevant in relation to expectations for therapist alliance with one spouse against the other. Not only is timing important with regard to dealing with such often irrational and self-destructive hopes, but the question of which spouse to whom one addresses interventions becomes important. For example, if a wife presumes that the therapist concurs with a particular position of hers that is critical of her husband and the husband sees the therapist's position similarly, the therapist must decide whether to direct therapeutic inquiry and interpretation to the spouse claiming positive alliance with the therapist or to the criticized and self-critical spouse, or to both.

The tendency of one or both spouses to see and to trap marital therapists in their self-object distortion processes constitutes both a great hazard and a great opportunity for patient and therapist alike. The same truth holds here that holds for transference distortions. This distortion tendency may become manifest either through spontaneous patient expectational verbalizations about or behavior toward the therapist or patient reactions to the therapist's verbalizations or behavior. In the therapeutic process of exploration and attempted clarification of self-object distortions in the marital dyad, both of these processes, spontaneous and reactive, of spouse-therapist self-object distortion occur. Conflict arises between these distortions and the reality of the therapist, who in a mostly friendly manner declines or even is unable to conform to or confirm or affirm the patient's self-object distortions. This conflict requires a reexamination of reality and reality processing and a shared creation, mostly by the patient, of a new reality and new reality processing methods my means of a conceptual reorganization and recon-struction. How much of this creative process occurs explicitly and by conscious decision and how much occurs implicitly, metaphorically (Sonne, 1964), unconsciously and inexplicably spontaneously is debatable. In any event, it is a negentropic process which frees the patient from the regressive tyranny of prior infantile self-object distortion relational traps. Piaget's (1973) comments are pertinent here: "The conceptualized reconstruction that characterizes 'becoming conscious' may be adequate right from the start when it is not inhibited by any contradictions. But if it conflicts with some already established conceptualization, it is at first distorted and incomplete and then becomes complete little by little as new conceptual systems emerge which encompass the seeming contradictions and integrate them."

Both spouses' self-object distortions are jolted from their illusory secure communicative positions, and major shifts and processes of redefinition begin to occur when a spouse-therapist self-object distortion is clarified which is similar to that being acted out in the marriage. Even though this clarification may mainly involve one spouse, with each successful interven-tion both spouses are increasingly relieved of the burden of self-object distortion in their marriage. Individual and system energies are freed for greater autonomous functioning, reality testing and expansion of the relational potential of the marital system. Although, as mentioned, the therapist must, to a great extent, remain outside the marital dyad and not be drawn into any splitting processes in order to think freely and make credible comments, there is another hazard which can at times occur. The pathological marital collusion may be so strong and close that the couple deprives the therapist of an appropriate therapist-couple experience with them, rendering the therapist an impotent outsider and his interpretations vain. Often both collusive and extrusive processes impact on the therapist in the course of a given therapy. To be effective, the therapist must be "in" but not too far "in," and "out" but not too far "out."

There are differences in style with regard to the way in which various therapists make use of "self" in doing marital therapy. Some therapists work primarily on the self-object distortions within the marital dyad while implicitly and sometimes explicitly defining themselves as separate from it without directly utilizing and interpreting the couple's attempted distortion of them. Bowen's (1972) emphasis on the therapist's maintenance of a position of nonalignment and on the marital partners and the therapist taking "I stands" exemplifies this style. The authors' style is, in addition to the implicit use of self, to observe explicitly, interpret and clarify attempts at self-object distortion involving the therapist. Sophisticated therapists are acutely aware of the couple's inclination to impose distortions upon them and to test reality with them, whether they handle this process implicitly, metaphorically or explicitly, by an interpretation and clarification, a noninterpretative, nondefensive definition of self through action or statement, or a mixture of all these means. Whatever the therapeutic orientation and technique of the therapist, self-object issues, as discussed above, are probably a part of most marital therapies whether the therapist is consciously aware of them or not.

As mentioned earlier in the discussion of self-object definition in the expanded sense, sequential phases can be conceptualized in a person's developmental experience. When self-object distortions are resolved in therapy, it is possible to witness progressions in the therapeutic microcosm roughly analogous to those optimally occurring in childhood development. It must be emphasized that this process is not usually a neat straight-line progression, but often an irregular one, with many regressions, progressions, oscillations and interweavings at any and various times in therapy, early and late. Primarily through therapist interpretation of attempts of the spouses to act out with him or her various levels of arrested or idiosyncratic development, the spouses are able to see and give up their pathological use of each other and to reenact, reconstruct, resume and accomplish a progression through hitherto untraveled stages in the development of self-object definition. This process can open the way for more healthy and creative functioning in the marriage. The therapist interprets not only self-object distortions impinging on him or her but also, and importantly, those operative in the marital dyad. As mentioned, the likelihood of making an effective interpretation about the marital dyad is greatly enhanced subsequent to a spouse-therapist interpretation. When one or both partners see that one spouse is treating the therapist or wanting to be treated by the therapist in a way similar to that which has been occurring in the marriage, processes which were previously bewildering and confusing become less mysterious. The spouses develop a facilitating level of insight which decreases their need for and vulnerability to dyadic distortion processes and allows for continued self-object growth. In health, feelings, thinking and action are again in harmony with perceptions, as they were in earliest infancy, with the difference that perceptions are now based on an organized conceptual appreciation of and creative adaptation to physical and metaphorical reality rather than on illusion, delusion or collusion.

A final point in regard to the therapy of self-object distortions is that the therapist should be prepared for the possibility that when the spouses experience a degree of resolution of distortion, there will often, but not always, be a transitional decrease in a defensive preoccupation with or frequency of sexual intercourse, while poise and the enjoyment of other pleasures are increasing. This is in contrast to the changes in couples with instinctual transference problems with whom an increase in sensuality and sexual intercourse and a decrease in defensive interests in other pleasures often occur.

ILLUSTRATIVE CASE EXAMPLES

Two clinical examples will be presented illustrating the operation of some of the foregoing theoretical concepts and related technical considerations.

The first couple, Anne and Art, both had had difficult early relationships with their mothers. Anne had presented herself initially as the identified patient, with symptoms of depression, marital difficulties and a fear that she was going crazy. In her infancy and childhood, she had been neglected by her mother and was frequently called crazy. She developed into a clinging, indecisive, dependent person who was constantly looking for someone to take care of her. Art, in early infancy and childhood, had had attention paid to him by a demanding and needy mother. He developed as a caretaker who was unable to say no to women. As for the couple's fathers, Anne's father had been unable to establish an adequate marital dyad in his own marriage, was unable to get his own needs met, and functioned with his daughter more as a substitute mother than as a father. As for Art's father, he either left or was sent from the home when Art was an infant, leaving Art with his mother and without a father, marital model or male figure. He was unprotected from women's demands on him.

Anne acknowledged marrying Art with the conscious aim of having a father for her two-year-old son from a prior union. At the unconscious level it became apparent during therapy that she had been seeking a caretaker for herself as well as for her son, plus a mother to replace her ungiving mother and also a replacement for her mothering father. Art married Anne while consciously feeling very much in love and with an additional conscious motive of breaking free from his mother. At the unconscious level, as came out in therapy, he was reenacting taking care of his ungiving mother and also was playing the part of the father he wished he had had when he was a small boy alone with his mother.

As time went on in the marriage, Art became gradually more disinclined to play the role of caretaker. He began to denigrate Anne, calling her crazy in much the same way Anne's mother had done. He was unable to articulate his own needs. His caretaking function became mixed with increasing hostility. In time the marriage shifted to a point where Art was functioning as if he were a resentful, exploited child with mother, unable to say no or ask for what he wanted, and Anne was acting as if she were a worthless little girl with a denigrating mother. This pathological homeostasis was disrupted by two events: pregnancy and the birth of their first child, and Art's subsequent turning to other women for a sexual gratification nonexistent in the marriage.

As mentioned, Anne came in initially alone. It was possible to help her see quickly that she did indeed have conflicts of her own which were impinging upon Art, but that part of her difficulty was coming from her acting out her relationship with her mother by accepting Art's designation of her as crazy. With insight into this defense against dealing with Art, she was able to speak of his part in the marital difficulties and felt entitled to bring him into the therapy.

As might have been anticipated, Anne's initial effort at self-object distortion with the therapist involved her presenting herself as an incomplete self, crazy, bad and helpless, with the therapist assigned the role of condemning caretaker. Although this patient-therapist distortion was dealt with rather early in the therapy, her efforts at distortion of her relationship with the therapist continued to need a great deal of interpretation, as well as implicit and explicit definition of the therapist as an autonomous, caring individual in contradistinction to the assigned role. Art, in his relationship to the therapist, already having one woman, Anne, in the demanding mother/dependent child role, assigned the therapist the role of the giving, sexual woman. The therapist's declining to accept this assignment was essential in helping Art to be able to say no appropriately to the women in his life and to begin to ask what he wanted from them. With improvement in self-object definition in their marriage, both Anne and Art, as parents, were able to relate much more appropriately to and to enjoy their children as separate people.

The second couple, Bill and Barbara, came into treatment together. Bill, consciously motivated by a recognition that his increasing thoughts about having an extramarital affair were symptomatic of serious marital difficulties, chose marital therapy rather than acting out. Both partners expressed open dissatisfaction with their marital situation and wanted help, with Barbara assuming responsibility for the problems and blaming herself for Bill's unhappiness.

Both spouses described unsatisfying filial relationships with narcissistic mothers. Bill's mother repeatedly gave him the message that one should anticipate others' needs, yet made it impossible for him to anticipate hers. She was always one step ahead of him. She would spend much time anticipating what she thought were Bill's needs, but seldom, if ever, met them and often negated them if he expressed them directly. Her attitude toward Bill was reflected in a statement she made to her daughter-in-law that she was glad to have "that thing" out of her when he was born. She also described her perinatal marital reality in terms connoting that her husband was of little value to her and the child.

Bill's father was unable to satisfy the mother's demands or get his own needs met by her. He was largely ineffectual in participating in the family constellation and was ultimately unable to avoid being sent away by his wife when Bill was in the middle of his oedipal period. Bill recalled repeated rebuffs by mother of father's attempts at reconciliation, culminating in father's eventually turning to other women. Bill's developmental experience thus precluded the internalization of a healthy marital representation and family image, and he frequently said that he had no model of what family relationships should be.

Despite the early family chaos, Bill's relationship with his father did have aspects of caring and closeness in it, which helped Bill in his gender identity in latency and adolescence. He saw a great deal of his father and often worked with him, benefiting from his sense of humor, his discipline and his heterosexual strivings, even though they were limited and nonmaritally actualized.

Although Barbara's parents' marriage was more tranquil, it was characterized by mother being catered to by husband and children as well. She recalls often being told by her father that it was more important to give than to receive, a message which was reinforced by a deathbed assignment from him to her to take care of mother.

Barbara, as with Bill, was always trying to please mother, but was baffled as to exactly what she was supposed to do. Furthermore, while she felt that it was expected of her to love, she also felt that her love was of little value. Both the death of her father and her mother's insatiability led her to conclude that her love accomplished little.

Although Barbara developed similarly to Bill an excessive need to make others happy, she had the additional stress of gender-identity confusion in adolescence stemming from her father's assignment to her to take care of mother as a replacement for mother's loss of her husband.

Both Barbara and Bill had impossible childhood assignments of undefined tasks. Barbara's relationship with her father had given her a warmth, closeness and sense of value that she hadn't received from her mother, yet these very qualities, combined with the impossible assignments connected with them, produced intense conflicts for her. She felt tremendous guilt at the thought of having a closeness with father that mother did not have and much hostility toward father for betrayal by his impossible task assignments and ultimately by his death. To let herself love and be loved by another man would require her to see clearly the negative elements in her relationship with this manifestly sweet and loving father; hence she constantly protected herself from the heterosexual love she was seeking.

On the conscious level Barbara and Bill chose each other conventionally enough, meeting through mutual friends. Barbara resonated to the sensitivity she saw in Bill, his respect for her as a person and the feeling that he was someone she could trust. Bill was attracted to Barbara's gentleness and kindness and her articulate, bright and happy qualities. Each was attracted to qualities in the other which his or her own parent of the opposite sex possessed to a certain degree, seeking to recreate and simultaneously amplify and refine positive aspects of their self-object parental relationships. Over time, however, other elements in the relationship on the unconscious level became powerfully operative. In the course of therapy it became clear that Bill was acting out his need to anticipate the needs of a woman who was almost impossible to satisfy, like mother, and to give up his self to an idealized object. Although resentful at vaguely recognizing his own feelings of deprivation, he had his own difficulties with letting himself be affirmed. Barbara had a double-track distortion operative in her relationship with Bill. She projected onto him her image of her needy mother, whose caretaker her father had assigned her to be, and also an expectation that he be a replacement for her father, who had given her a significant degree of warmth. Neither spouse could be a self without threatening the other. Bill's temporary outdistancing Barbara in his initial struggle for separation and individuation and renunciation of collusion was accompanied by a great deal of rejection of Barbara, which intensified her feelings of worthlessness. She reacted by regression, increasing self-denigration and self-destructive behavior, unable to handle the requirements of this marital shift that she resolve her separation from maternal and paternal self-object distortions. Her increased dependency augmented Bill's resentment and reified his perceptions of her as a woman like his mother whose needs had to be anticipated but could never be met. This resentment increased Barbara's feelings that her love was no good for Bill, and she stopped giving. This withdrawal left Bill's irrational hostility unexposed and interfered with either spouse realizing the way Bill had of refusing to accept love even when it was given.

The initial breakthrough in therapy occurred primarily around a distorted interaction between Bill and the therapist. While Bill was discussing his relationship with his anticipating mother, he handled the therapist's understanding responses by saying in effect that he had already anticipated them and that the therapist could not have understood him so well if he had not so clearly described himself. He was able to see that he was acting as if no transaction had occurred, that he had asked for something and then not let himself receive it. This type of process had been occurring between him and Barbara for years and amounted to the preclusion of any spontaneous, empathic interaction between the two. Bill had been relating to her as he had to his mother, his behavior containing both the wish for an empathic response and the defensive blocking of this. There also was an element in this of Bill's presuming to take care of the therapist where he did not need taking care of, which Bill also did with Barbara. A great deal of distrust of women surfaced on Bill's part once he had relinquished the pseudo-caretaking role and recognized and acknowledged his blocking. Witnessing this process between Bill and the therapist and experiencing Bill's response to the interpretation of what was occurring helped Barbara to see clearly some of the forces which had been impacting upon her. Released by this, Barbara successfully proclaimed herself as her own person, refusing to continue to collude in Bill's distrustful distortions of her. She subsequently saw that she, on her part, had been to a great extent seeing her mother in Bill and had been following father's instructions to anticipate and meet mother's impossible needs. She shortly made a statement that she could give no more and that it was impossible for her to prove to Bill that she loved him unless he changed. With an opening up on Bill's part, she was nevertheless able to give more and Bill was able to receive more. Bill apologized to her for the impossible position in which he had placed her.

From this new level of achieved freedom for both spouses, it was possible for a second breakthrough to occur. Barbara came face to face with her additional distortions of both the therapist and Bill, which she had been using to protect herself from dealing with her love of and hate for her father. She realized at this point that she had been resistant to letting any other man replace her father, while simultaneously demanding that Bill do just this. The working out of these distortions in her relationship with the therapist occurred little by little over time, with a tendency to refuse to acknowledge empathy and understanding from the therapist and attempts to block his spontaneity. During the process of clarification of Barbara's self-object distortions of the therapist, Bill experienced a mixture of a loosening up of his capacity to be more fun-loving and some degree of jealousy of and identification with the therapist. This contained a healthy aspect in that it triggered in Bill an aggressive competition for his wife and an increased but more loving disinclination on his part to accept the almost impossible assignment that in this instance was impacting on him from Barbara. At this juncture, Barbara clearly acknowledged the impossible position in which she had placed Bill, apologized to him as he had done to her earlier and released him to be himself.

Subsequent to this healthy step on Barbara's part, a third major breakthrough occurred, in which Bill and Barbara began for the first time to relate, delicately but authentically, to each other as real people. At Barbara's insistence, Bill told her with genuine feeling how he felt about a certain piece of self-destructive neurotic behavior on her part. The position Bill assumed was neither that of persecutor nor rescuer or supplicant, but was rather one of a person determined and caring for himself and his wife. Bill felt frightened but real, finding himself spontaneously expressing himself in this new fashion. He was risking losing his old self and possibly risking losing the marriage. Barbara responded to Bill's move by saying that this was the first time he had ever spoken to her in this manner, that she felt very cared for and very loved. She described the experience as incredible. She said that she realized that she had been acting like her self-destructive father, testing her husband to see whether he, in contrast to her mother in her behavior with her father, cared enough about her to want her not to die. Very shortly thereafter, when Bill again resorted to his own self-destructive behavior of not letting himself be given to, Barbara was able to draw on her feelings of being loved to move easily through this temporary barrier. An ensuing development from changes in Bill and Barbara was a dramatic shift in their relation to their children, whom they began to see much more as separate from themselves. They enjoyed them more, handled discipline better, defined generational boundaries more clearly and knew more appropriately how much to give to or ask from them.

DISCUSSION AND SUMMARY

Self-object distortions arising in infancy and often perpetuated in a disordered family of origin situation can be carried into adult life and acted out in mate selection, marriage and parenting in pseudo-adult transactions. Failures in self-object development can result in a person reaching "adulthood" deficient in object constancy, self-object definition, family image and a triadic heterosexual sense of reality. Incompleted developmental tasks at various stages of separation-individuation will, over time, express themselves turbulently in a marriage which may have initially seemed to be a happy one but which was, in fact, functioning greatly on a level of unconscious collusion of self-object distortions. Under the impact of life experiences within or without the marriage which frustrate collusions or promote renunciation of collusion or which provide opportunities for higher level functioning, homeostatic self-object distortions in one or both spouses can be thrown into a state of disequilibrium and a move toward clarity of self-object definition can begin. In therapy, consequent to interpretation of therapist-spouse and spouse-spouse self-object distortions, it is possible to see the spouses separate and individuate and to move through hitherto incompleted substages of self-object development, such as differentiation, practicing and rapprochement, to the level of consolidation of individuality and the development of object constancy, and the achievement of a triadic family image and a heterosexual sense of reality. Therapist sensitivity and possession of a clear self-object definition, a triadic family image and a heterosexual sense of reality are important ingredients of the therapy. Heterosexual cotherapy is often helpful in marital therapy.

The therapy of the two couples presented illustrates that when marital homeostasis is unbalanced through a degree of relatively solid growth in one spouse, a pattern of continued growth in the couple is often begun. The other spouse may experience a degree of freeing up when released from the burden of being acted out against or may be forced to examine his or her own acting out because of the loss of a collusive ally. In addition, the other spouse may be inspired by the first spouse's growth to move into new areas of his or her own development, from which to draw further or impel the first spouse forward. Whereas formerly the spouses were cooperating in non-growth, now they are cooperating in growth. It is particularly important at moments of growth and creativity in the marriage for the therapist to appreciate the distinction between a negentropic, constructive confrontation versus an entropic, destructive one, and to see the beauty and delicacy involved in what may seem at times to be further self-object distortions but which are in fact part of the couple's shared creation of a new reality. The aware therapist enjoys their development, is available but not intrusive, has respect for the integrity of the marital dyad as an organism, as well as for the individual spouses. There is a hazard of quibbling and making trouble which can occur at these junctures if the therapist is unable to perceive and enjoy the couple's unique and separate budding relationship as they move through levels of separation, self-object definition and family-image construction to a point where they can enjoy themselves, each other and their children and can exclude the therapist. The therapist celebrates and affirms the spouses' accomplishments of autonomy and the elegance and artistry of the resump-tion of their courtship, and shows faith and trust in his or her own reality and the couple's new reality-processing ability by not wavering if subjected to a possible last-minute-test invitation to prolong therapy at the decided time of termination.

REFERENCES

Abelin, E.L. The role of the father in the separation-individuation process. In J. McDevitt and C. Settlage (Eds.), *Separation-individuation: Essays in honor of Margaret S. Mahler.* New York: International Universities Press, 1971.

Abraham, K. *Selected papers on psychoanalysis.* (D. Bryan and A. Strachey, trans.). New York: Basic Books, 1954. (Originally published 1927.)

Ackerman, N. *The psychodynamics of family life.* New York: Basic Books, 1958.

Adler, A. *The practice and theory of individual psychology,* P. Radin (Ed. and trans.). New York: Harcourt Brace, 1940.

Allport, G.W. *Becoming: Basic consideration for a psychology of personality.* New Haven: Yale Univ. Press, 1955.

Arietti, S. *The intrapsychic self: Feeling, cognition and creativity in health and mental illness.* New York: Basic Books, 1967.

Balint, M. *Primary love and psychoanalytic technique.* London: Hogarth Press, 1952.

Bertalanffy, L. von *Robots, men and minds.* New York: George Braziller, 1967.

Binstock, W.A. On the two forms of intimacy. *Am. Psychoanaly, Assoc.,* 1973, *21,* 93–107.

Blanck, R., and Blanck, G. *Marriage and personal development.* New York: Columbia Univ. Press, 1968.

Blos, P. The second individuation process of adolescence. *Psychoanaly. Study Child,* 1967, *22,* 162–186.

Bowen, M. On the differentiation of self. In J. Framo (Ed.), *Family interaction: Dialogue between family researchers and family therapists.* New York: Springer, 1972.

Bowlby, J. *Attachment and loss. Vol. I: Attachment.* New York: Basic Books, 1969.

Brodey, W.M. Image, object and narcissistic relationships. *Am. J. Orthopsychiat.,* 1961, *31,* 69–73.

Buber, M. Distance and relation. *Psychiat.,* 1955, *20,* 97–104.

Dicks, H.V. *Marital tensions: Clinical studies towards a psychological theory of interaction.* New York: Basic Books, 1967.

Erikson, E. *Childhood and Society.* New York: W.W. Norton, 1950.

Eisenstein, V.W. (Ed.) *Neurotic interaction in marriage.* New York: Basic Books, 1956.

Fairbairn, W.R.D. *An object relations theory of personality.* New York: Basic Books, 1954.

Federn, P. *Ego psychology and the psychoses.* New York: Basic Books, 1952.

Ferenczi, S. Stages in the development of the sense of reality. In *Sex in psychoanalysis.* New York: Basic Books, 1950. (Originally published 1913.)

Freud, A. *The ego and the mechanisms of defense.* New York: International Universities Press, 1966. (Originally published 1937.)

Freud, S. On narcissism: An introduction. *St. Ed., 14,* 67–102. London: Hogarth Press, 1957. (Originally published 1914.)

Freud, S. Splitting of the ego in the process of defence. *St. Ed., 23,* 139–171. London: Hogarth Press, 1964. (Originally published 1938.)

Guntrip, H.J.S. *Personality structure and human interaction.* New York: International Universities Press, 1961.

Hartman, H. *Ego psychology and the problem of adaptation.* New York: International Universities Press, 1959. (Originally published 1939.)

Horney, K. *Neurosis and human growth.* New York: W.W. Norton, 1950.

Jackson, D.D. The eternal triangle. In J. Haley and L. Hoffman (Eds.), *Techniques of family therapy.* New York: Basic Books, 1967.

Jacobson, E. *The self and the object world.* New York: International Universities Press, 1964.

James, W. *Principles of psychology.* New York: Dover, 1950. (Originally published 1890.)

Jung C.G. *The undiscovered self.* New York: Mentor Books, 1967.

Kafka, J.S. Ambiguity for individuation: A critique and reformulation of double-bind theory. *Arch. Gen. Psychiat.*, 1971, *25*, 232–239.

Kernberg, O.F. *Object relations theory and clinical psychoanalysis.* New York: Jason Aronson, 1976.

Klein, M. Notes on some schizoid mechanisms. In J. Riviere (Ed.), *Developments in psychoanalysis.* London: Hogarth Press, 1946.

Kohler, W. *Gestalt psychology.* New York: Horace Liveright, 1929.

Kohut, H. Introspection, empathy and psychoanalysis. *J. Am. Psychoanaly. Assoc.*, 1959, *7*, 459–483.

Kohut, H. *The restoration of the self.* New York: International Universities Press, 1977.

Laing, R.D. *The divided self.* London: Tavistock, 1960.

Lichtenstein, H. Identity and sexuality: A study of their interrelationships in man. *J. Am. Psychoanaly. Assoc.*, 1961, *9*, 179–260.

Lidz, T. *The Family and human adaptation.* New York: International Universities Press, 1963.

Loewald, H.W. Internalization, separation, mourning and the superego. *Psychoanaly. Quart.*, 1962, *31*, 483–504.

MacMurray, J. *The self as agent.* London: Faber and Faber, 1957.

Mahler, M.S., Pine, F., and Bergman, A. *The psychological birth of the human infant: Symbiosis and individuation.* New York: Basic Books, 1975.

Malin, A., and Grotstein, J.S. Projective identification in the therapeutic process. *Int. J. Psycho-Analy.*, 1966, *47*, 26–31.

Martin, P.A. *A marital therapy manual.* New York: Brunner/Mazel, 1976.

Maslow, A.H. *Toward a psychology of being.* New York: D. Van Nostrand, 1968.

Modell, A.H. *Object love and reality.* New York: International Universities Press, 1968.

Nunberg, H. Transference and reality. *Int. J. Psychoanaly.*, 1951, *32*, 1–9.

Paolino, T.J., Jr., and McCrady, B.S. (Eds.), *Marriage and marital therapy: Psychoanalytic, behavioral and systems theory perspectives.* New York: Brunner/Mazel, 1978.

Piaget, J. The affective unconscious and the cognitive unconscious. *J. Psychoanaly. Assoc.*, 1973, *21*, 249–261.

Pollak, O. Relationships between children in the family. In Freeman, H., LaBarre, W., Pollak, O., and von Mering, O., *Understanding family dynamics.* Pittsburgh: Family and Children's Service, 1960.

Rank, O. *Art and artist*, C.F. Atkinson (Ed. and trans.). New York: Knopf, 1932.

Reich, W. *Character analysis*, T.P. Wolfe (Ed. and trans.). New York: Farrar, Straus and Cudahy, 1949. (Originally published 1933.)

Reusch, J., and Bateson, G. *Communication: The social matrix of psychiatry.* New York: W.W. Norton, 1951.

Robbins, F.P., and Sadow, L. A developmental hypothesis of reality processing. *J. Am. Psychoanaly. Assoc.*, 1974, *22*, 344–363.

Rogers, C.R. *Client-centered therapy: Its current practice, implications and theory.* Boston: Houghton-Mifflin, 1951.

Rosen, J.N. *Direct analysis.* New York: Grune and Stratton, 1953.

Sandler, J., and Rosenblatt, B. The concept of the representational world. *Psychoanaly. Study Child*, 1962, *17*, 128–145.

Sartre, J.P. *Being and nothingness.* New York: Simon and Schuster, 1966. (Originally published 1956.)

Schachtel, E.G. *Metamorphosis.* New York: Basic Books, 1959.

Schaefer, R. The psychoanalytic vision of reality. *Int. J. Psycho-Analy.*, 1970, *51*, 279–297.

Schilder, P. *The image and appearance of the human body.* New York: International Universities Press, 1950. (Originally published 1935.)

Searles, H. The differentiation between concrete and metaphorical thinking in the recovering schizophrenic. *J. Am. Psychoanaly. Assoc.*, 1962, *10*, 22–49.

Sonne, J.C., Speck, R.V., and Jungreis, J. The absent member maneuver as a resistance in family therapy of schizophrenia. *Fam. Proc.*, 1962, *1*, 44–62.

Sonne, J.C. Metaphors and relationships. *Fam. Proc.*, 1964, *3*, 425–427.

Sonne, J.C., and Lincoln, G. Heterosexual co-therapy team experiences during family therapy. *Fam. Proc.*, 1965, *4*, 177–197.

Sonne, J.C. The role of significant peripheral persons in alloplastic resistances of schizophrenogenic families. In A.S. Friedman, I. Boszormenyi-Nagy, J.E. Jungreis, G. Lincoln, H.E. Mitchell, J.C. Sonne, R.V. Speck, and G. Spivack, *Psychotherapy for the whole family*. New York: Springer, 1965.

Sonne, J.C., and Lincoln, G. The importance of a heterosexual co-therapy relationship in the construction of a family image. In *Psychiatric Research Report 20*. American Psychiatric Association, 1966.

Sonne, J.C. Dos and don'ts of family therapy. In A.S. Friedman, J.P. Barr, I. Boszormenyi-Nagy, G. Cohen, J.E. Jungreis, G. Lincoln, J.C. Sonne, G. Spark, R.V. Speck, and O.R. Weiner, *Therapy with families of sexually acting-out girls*. New York: Springer, 1971.

Sonne, J.C. Poetry, sentimentality and family living. *Am. Poetry Rev.*, Nov.–Dec. 1972, *1*, 40.

Sonne, J.C. *A primer for family therapists*. Moorestown, N.J.: Thursday Press, 1973.

Spiegel, L.A. The self, the sense of self and perception. *Psychoanaly. Study Child*, 1959, *14*, 81–109.

Spitz, R. *No and yes: On the genesis of human communication*. New York: International Universities Press, 1957.

Stewart, R.H., Peters, T.C., Marsh, S., and Peters, M.J. An object-relations approach to psychotherapy with marital couples, families and children. *Fam. Proc.*, 1975, *14*, 161–177.

Sullivan, H.S. *The interpersonal theory of psychiatry*. New York: W.W. Norton, 1953.

Suzuki, D.T. *Zen Buddhism*. W. Barrett (Ed.), New York: Doubleday, 1956.

Tillich, P. *The courage to be*. New Haven: Yale Univ. Press, 1952.

Winnicott, D.W. Ego integration in child development. In D.W. Winnicott (Ed.), *The maturational processes and the facilitating environment*. New York: International Universities Press, 1965.

Zuk, G. *Family therapy: A triadic-based approach*. New York: Behavioral Books, 1971.

Chapter 4

Transference Considerations in Marriage and Marital Therapy

John C. Sonne

INTRODUCTION

As described in a companion piece to this chapter (Sonne and Swirsky, this volume), transference processes and self-object definition processes can be viewed as two distinct phenomena in therapy and in life in general, even though they function simultaneously in varying degrees. This chapter will discuss transference processes in marriage and marital therapy.

Transference processes as usually considered pertain to instinctual gratification, emotions, feelings, impulses, affects, lust, sensuality, movement, action or potential action. By contrast, self-object definition processes are concerned with imprinting, identity, sense of self and others, ego development, body image, gender identity, cognition, recognition, communication, concept formation, love, perception and reality sense, including a reality sense which contains a triadic heterosexual sense of reality and a family image.

A full definition of the concepts of instinctual drives and instinctual transferences connotes sensual experiences of hugging, kissing, licking, sucking, rubbing, comforting, feeding, providing and caring for self and others, as well as sexual intercourse and orgasm. It includes the wish and need for reciprocal visual, aural, olfactory, vestibular, proprioceptive and alimentary sensual stimulation, as well as mucous membrane and dermic stimulation.

Beyond questions of direct and perceived physical sensual stimulation, a consideration of the sensuality in instinctual gratification must also contain an appreciation of the sensual stimulation and gratification, consciously perceived or not, obtained from stories, works of art, relationships, symptoms, mental imagery and fantasies.

SENSUALITY, SEXUALITY AND COMMUNICATION

I will be using the term "sensuality" frequently in this paper, as well as the terms "instinctual drive," "libido" and "sexuality." Despite the fact that *sexuality* has been broadly defined in the literature to include pregenital sensual processes, it still has, especially in the English language, the connotations of genital sensuality diffused and vectored backward in time. Sexuality thus broadened adulto-morphizes infants who have not yet achieved self-object definition, and tends to characterize people with self-object difficulties as more developed than they are. It can lead to confusion about the meaning of sensual processes as they are encountered in life in general and in therapy. *Sensuality*, a more inclusive term than "sexuality," is anchored in our fundamental bodily experience of stimulation in being alive and is applicable to a wider variety of functions than sexuality. Sensuality, more naturally than sexuality, can be thought of as capable of being vectored, organized and condensed forward in time from diffuse to refined modes of operation. Sensuality includes sensory excitement and discharge, sensory stimulation and gratification, but also includes sensory perception and learning. Sense is sensual. It is through our senses that we not only achieve gratification, as in sexuality, but also, in conjunction with autonomous cognition, develop a meaningful sense of reality and self-object definition.

The term "sexuality" has so focused on the need for sensual gratification per se, and has so subsumed "sensuality," that it has obscured the function of sensuality in communication. Sexuality, a special type of sensuality, is always object-directed, even if the object is the "self," as in autoeroticism. Hence the term does not allow us room for learning about self-object development. Its overuse even interferes with our learning about sexuality, transference processes and sensuality as well by contributing to blurring the distinction between processes which are pleasurable per se and processes which may be sensual but are essentially developmental and learning processes. Sensuality has multiple functions and can subsume sexuality within it; sexuality is narrower and, although sensual, cannot subsume all the functions of sensuality within it.

In their paper "The Proprioceptive Body Image in Self-Object Differentiation: A Case of Congenital Indifference to Pain and Head-Banging," Frances and Gale (1975) present an excellent argument, including a review of supporting writings of other researchers, for the role of sensuality of all modalities, including proprioceptive sensuality, in the development of a sense of reality, self and self-object definition. Their work and that of those cited by them, plus the work of Freedman (1971, 1975), Hebb (1959), Lilly (1956), Witkin et al. (1954), Zubek (1969), Zuckerman et al. (1964) and others on the consequences of sensory deprivation in adults and children, plus the work of Friedman et al. (1968) on children with phenylketonuria, Sibinga and Friedman (1971) on children casted in early infancy and the work of Robertson (1962), Spitz (1945) and others on hospitalized children, help us to understand the importance of the function of sensuality in the service of developing and maintaining a sense of reality and self-object definition. It serves also in obtaining pleasurable sensual gratification.

Although it is beyond the scope of this paper, it should be mentioned that appropriate sensual stimulation is necessary for normal infant neurological development and the maintenance of healthy neurologic structure and functioning in adults. Riesen (1960), Zubek (1963, 1969), Rosenzweig et al. (1968) and Prescott (1971) are some of the notable contributors to the extensive literature on this subject, which deals with such issues as neuronal abnormalities, supersensitivity, insensitivity, EEG and biochemical changes consequent to sensory deprivation or immobilization. It is a challenging study to attempt to correlate various modalities, combinations and degrees of sensual stimulation and discharge, excitation and gratification with neurophysiological development and function. Jones' (1946) comments are pertinent here: "The capacity to endure the non-gratification of a wish without either reacting to the privation or renouncing the wish, holding it as it were in suspense, probably corresponds with a neurological capacity, perhaps of an electrical nature, to retain the stimulating effects of an afferent impulse without immediately discharging them in an efferent direction."

CONFUSION BETWEEN TRANSFERENCE AND SELF-OBJECT PROCESSES

A great deal of confusion relative to transference and self-object issues has come about in the literature because of the lack of clarity in the definition of terms in case reports and in the theoretical formulations derived from or applied to them. Different therapists and theoreticians may see different aspects of a case in terms of assessment of the amount or level of the self-object or psychosexual and transference elements operative. They treat the case accordingly, interpret their success or failure accordingly, and their work is usually criticized or accepted by fellow scholars and therapists more on the basis of issues of conceptual framework than on the basis of success or failure of treatment. The absence of shared live observation of phenomena inherent in the communication of most case reports puts a heavy burden on us to clearly define our terms. For example, if a therapist is working with a patient who has difficulties in the area of self-object distortion and doesn't define this as the issue but describes the case and the therapy primarily in terms of instinctual processes, instinctual transferences, symbolic realization or a corrective emotional experience, neither the case nor the therapy is accurately described. The question of acting out in response to the transference will surely be raised even though the treatment may have been appropriate for the self-object aspect of the case, which was addressed but not defined, nor was its treatment defined in clear terminology. Similarly, reporting of a case involving primarily analysis of instinctual-conflict aspects using a preponderance of self-object terminology will surely raise questions as to whether in fact a self-object problem needed to be dealt with more directly. An additional impediment to observation of phenomena and clear definition of terms derives from the preponderance of a dyadic orientation in therapy and in developmental studies over the use of the triadic orientation inherent in family studies (Sonne, Speck and Jungreis, 1962) and heterosexual co-therapy (Sonne and Lincoln, 1965, 1966).

Confusion has existed about the essence of the phenomenon of transference since the concept was first defined in *Studies of Hysteria* (Freud, 1895/1955, p. 302), *The Interpretation of Dreams* (Freud, 1900/1953, pp. 184, 200) and in the Dora case (Freud, 1905/1953, pp. 116, 118). The original definitions of the transference process—and this is true today as part of our current conceptual difficulties—used both instinctual and self-object terms, and oscillated in emphasis between the two. Naturally it is difficult, if not impossible, to describe instinctual processes in a vacuum without including their subject, aim and object. It is, however, possible to consider separately the instinctual-drive-exchange aspects versus the self-object developmental or morphological aspects of a mental process or transaction. The increasing interest in self-object study and the development of an extensive body of self-object theory lead us to a reexamination of transference and the need for a more precise definition of transference as essentially a process involving the transfer of poststructural instinctual-drive vicissitudes. Although it is obvious that optimal progression through the stages of self-object development depends on appropriate rhythmic sensual gratification and frustration during the stages of psychosexual development (Kestenberg, 1965a, 1965b, 1967) and vice versa, and that the processes of self-object development and psychosexual development are interdependent and should develop hand in hand, this is often not the case. One process may lag behind the other or be sacrificed for the other or may be misdefined as the other by the growing child, person, patient or the human environment, including theorists and therapists. Hence, there is a need for as clear a definition of terms as possible in describing these processes, even at the risk of definitions being wrong.

Some of the confusion between instinctual-transference processes and self-object processes has come about in the actual process of self-object study itself because of the heavy emphasis on libidinal instincts and instinctual defenses which saturated the studies. For example, discussion of self-object distortions occurring at the price of natural development and composed of characterological defenses against instinctual expression—as in instances described by Freud (1908/1959) in *Character and Anal Eroticism*; by Abraham (1927/1954) in his work on orality, anality and character defenses; and by Blum (1977) in his paper "The Prototype of Preoedipal Reconstruction"—are not so much descriptions of impairments of self-object definition per se as they are of characterological defenses against instinctual impulses. These defenses developed as adaptive to the intrusion into the self-object process of the gratuitous precocious or tardy environmental requirement that the child either defend itself against or comply with impulses aroused by inappropriate rhythms, volume and intensity of stimulation, gratification and rest which were out of phase with what might have been a normal progression of self-object development. Character disorders, characterological defenses and character analysis are not in the same category of phenomena as self-object definition problems, the use of terms such as "narcissistic character" notwithstanding. When the Wolf Man (Freud, 1918/1955) witnessed the primal scene in the rapprochement subphase, his endeavors at formation of self were interrupted and his energies were prematurely diverted from his necessary self-object work. His self-object development was impaired when he was in the middle of Spitz's (1957) "no," and he had to develop characterological defenses against the stimulation of a precocious wish for sensual gratification at a level of organization which he could not really comprehend and for which he was not prepared. Consequently, he developed both a self-object problem and an instinctual-transference problem. The aggression that in the rapprochement subphase usually goes into the development of self and the consolidation of a sense of autonomy and separateness was diverted to the service of seeking sensual gratification, with consequent frustration, increased hostility, fear, guilt, repression and the development of rigid character traits. The "no" of self-determination, integrity, self-respect and autonomy, akin to Spitz's (1953, 1957) "no" and the "no" described by myself (Sonne, 1979) in "Entropic Family Communication in Adolescence," is not the same as the fearful "no" used in the service of a repressive defense against the possible dangers presumed to be necessary conditions for the obtaining of sensual gratification.

Some quotes can illustrate further the heavy emphasis on libido, sexuality and sensual pleasure per se which permeated the early writings on the study of object relations. Although Abraham (1924/1954), in his pioneer paper "Origins and Growth of Object Love," lists six stages of object love, the sense of self and self-object definition through a process of separation and individuation as we are beginning to understand it today does not come through and is overshadowed by a strong emphasis on sensual gratification for pleasure per se. He states: "She was conscious neither of *affectionate feelings nor of sensual ones* towards him" (p. 483).

"Complete and unrestricted cannibalism is only possible on the basis of unrestricted narcissism. On such a level all that the individual considers is his own *desire for pleasure*" (p. 488).

"And the mere idea of putting excrement into the mouth is now the very essence of all that is disgusting. In certain illnesses we can observe a serious process of *regression* taking place in which the individual once more has as his *sexual aim* the eating of faeces" (p. 497).

In "Character-Formation on the Genital Level of the Libido" Abraham (1925/1954) writes thus: "At this point I will dwell in greater detail on a particular aspect of this process of change, since its significance for the formation of character has as yet received hardly any attention. This is the extensive alteration which takes place in the boy's attitude toward the body of persons of the opposite sex, i.e., in the first instance towards the mother. Originally her body was to him an object of mingled curiosity and fear; in other words, it aroused ambivalent feelings in him. But gradually he achieves a *libidinal cathexis* of his love-object as a whole, that is, with the inclusion of those parts of it which had formerly aroused those contrary feelings in him. If this has been activated there arises in him expressions of his *libidinal relation* to his object that are *inhibited in their aim—feelings of fondness, devotion, and so on—and these co-exist with his directly erotic desires for it.* And indeed during the boy's latency period these *'aim inhibited' sentiments predominate over his sensual feelings*" (p. 409).

These statements, despite their focus on the questions of character development and the stages of object love, are heavily weighted and colored by an emphasis on sensuality, gratification, instinctual vicissitudes, instinctual transferences, character defenses and the development and transformation of psychosexual instinctual drives and their aims. Abraham (1924/1954), struggling as we are today, acknowledges limitations in his work and leaves the way open for new knowledge: "Even at the present day we know almost as little as we did then, and we can only hope to have made an addition to our knowledge in two points, and that with every reserve" (p. 497).

A part of the discussion of identification with a love object presented by Freud (1921/1955) in *Group Psychology and the Analysis of the Ego*, even though heavily focused around sexual instincts, foreshadows and fits into the category of self-object development and definition as we think of it today. It includes a consideration of the role of aggression, imitation and empathy in identification. He mentions that identification "may arise with any new *perception* of a common quality shared with some other person who is *not an object of the sexual instinct.* The more important this common quality is, the more successful may this partial identification become, and it may thus represent the beginning of a new tie" (p. 108).

These papers are brilliant, but the blurring and confusion between self-object definition processes and instinctual vicissitude transference processes contained therein persist today and demand clarification.

The work of current researchers attempting to clarify this confusion continues to contain a blurring of terminology even when approaching more clear definition. For example, Masterson (1978), in an effort to describe the distinction among transference, working alliance and self-object distortion processes in therapy, writes: "A precondition for psychoanalysis, the therapeutic alliance forms the framework against which the fantasies, memories, and emotions evoked by the transference are measured, contrasted, and worked through. However, in psychotherapy with the borderline patient the therapeutic alliance is a goal or objective rather than a precondition" (p. 437). He said a few sentences earlier: "The therapeutic alliance can be defined as a real object relationship that is conscious and in which both patient and therapist implicitly agree and understand that they are working together to help the patient mature through gaining insight, progressive understanding and control. It is based on the capacities of the patient and the therapist to maintain a real relationship with each other as completely separate figures—whole objects with both positive and negative attributes" (p. 437).

It would seem that Masterson is separating self-object processes and transference processes. He says further that a working alliance is a necessary framework for transference and, beyond this, that establishing self-object definition is a necessary condition for the development of a working alliance. A moment later he blurs terms: "Since there is no transference in the strict whole object sense of the term, what does exist in the therapy of borderline patients? Rather than coin a new term, with all the handicaps that implies, I would qualify the term 'transference' to 'borderline transference'" (p. 437). He defines the borderline transference as consisting of "the activation and alternate projection on the therapist of the patient's primitive, split, positive and negative object relations part units" (p. 437).

The writing here perpetuates the present confusion of terminology. Masterson presents an excellent outline of self-object distortion phenomena, using a new term, "split object relations unit" (also used by Kernberg, 1976), subsequently referred to as RORU (rewarding part-unit) and WORU (withdrawing part-unit). However, he has already blurred his terms by calling these phenomena borderline transferences. He proceeds in a section on transference: "The borderline transference consists of the alternate activation and projection onto the therapist of each of the split object relations part-units." And later: "Both, however, represent forms of transference acting out—an instant replay—in which the therapist is treated not as a real object on whom infantile feelings are displaced but as if he or she actually were the infantile object" (p. 439).

After separating the phenomena of transference and self-object distortion processes and emphasizing the distinction between the two, Masterson nevertheless continues to apply the term "transference" to the distinct self-object processes he so clearly describes. He simultaneously uses newly coined terms for them, such as RORU and WORU, despite his earlier statement that he would prefer to use the term "borderline transference" than coin a new term. I submit that unless we do coin such new terms, as Klein (1946) did with the term "projective identification" and Nunberg (1951) with the term "transformance," even the old ones, such as transference, will not be clearly defined.

CONSEQUENCES OF CONFUSION OF TERMS IN LIFE AND IN THERAPY

Keeping in mind the distinction between self-object processes and instinctual processes that I am making, it is important to view sensual stimulation and gratification per se as separate from, though blended and intertwined with, whatever learning, conceptual appreciation or self-object affirmation and development may be occurring in a sensual transaction. It is particularly important for the scholar and therapist to make this separation conceptually, for patients are often confused as to which process is occurring in the main and often think it's one when it is the other. Just as a struggle for clarification of self-object definition is often hidden within a mélange of emotionality which suggests a search for pure sensual gratification, the processes and conflicts of sensual gratification are often occurring out of awareness under what appears on the surface to be a self-object struggle for knowledge of reality.

It is my thesis that the term "transference" should be used only to describe the phenomena of the vicissitudes of instinctual drives. In therapy, then, when we address ourselves to transferences, we are concerned primarily with issues of inhibition or expression of sensual stimulation and gratification for pleasure per se. To be internally consistent with this thesis, we would consider this to be so regardless of the level of self-object development, and we would assume the existence of some sense of self—formed, deformed, undeveloped or multiple, as the case may be—as forming the stage and cast of characters upon whom and by whom the instinctual-transference processes are acted out. Naturally, the mode or style of instinctual expression will be shaped and colored by a person's unique self-object definition. The concept of a "no self" is an asymptotic theoretical abstraction which does not exist either in the adult or in the infant. To speak of instinctual expression as totally unaccompanied by any sense of self or object, no matter how rudimentary or limited, would be a meaningless reduction; hence some analysis of instinctual transferences is probably always an issue, even in instances where self-object definition is the major problem. A more highly developed and complex person has an increased chance for an enhanced and exquisite experience of sensual expression because of an appreciation of the multiple aspects of self and others involved and a capacity to surrender to the glory of sensuality without fear of loss of self. Yet the same person may be vulnerable to inhibition of sensuality for the same reasons and may experience major transference difficulties.

The consequences of failing to make a distinction between self-object and instinctual-transference processes in therapy can be disastrous. To focus on instinctual-transference issues when self-object distortions are the main issue deprives the already overly emotional patient of the opportunity of perceiving the reality of the therapist as a person and of affirming his or her own sense of self. This deprivation of reality, plus the therapist's erroneous perception of the patient's message as primarily one involving sensual gratification, can lead to increased self-object distortion, lack of trust and increased emotionalism. This can lead to an intensification of the focus by the therapist on the analysis of instinctual conflicts, with more aloofness and "unreal" behavior on the therapist's part or an overly emotional response from the therapist. This state of affairs can exacerbate whatever problems of self-object definition were present originally, is unproductive and may intensify whatever instinctual-transference difficulties might be needing attention in the therapy at some other time. In contrast, to focus on reality and self-object issues, and not to deal with instinctual transferences when the issue is mainly one of conflicts around emotional expression and gratification, can be overstimulating, teasing and repressive as well as insulting. The instinctual conflicts go unanalyzed and are intensified. The relationship can deteriorate into one in which the patient loses trust in the therapist's ability to handle instinctual impulses, and can create a self-object distortion and confusion about reality which originally may not have been present.

It is important in the analysis of instinctual transferences to know when and where to do it, and this involves perceiving the distinction between self-object processes versus instinctual and transference processes as they are occurring in life in general and in therapy. Although when in harmony and functioning in concert, self-expression and instinctual expression are often indistinguishable from and mutually reinforce one another, when they are chaotically masking one another they must be delineated, analyzed and dealt with separately in order for them to reassemble and function indiscernibly in organic harmony.

WHAT IS TRANSFERENCE?

In the case of Dora, Freud (1905/1953) describes transferences: "What are transferences? They are new editions or facsimilies of the tendencies and phantasies which are aroused and made conscious during the progress of the analysis, but they have this peculiarity, which is characteristic of their species, that they replace some earlier person by the person of the physician. To put it in another way: a whole series of psychological experiences are revived, not as belonging to the past, but as applying to the person of the physician at the present time" (p. 116). He says later: "At the beginning it was clear that I was replacing her father in her imagination, which was not unlikely, in view of the difference in our ages" (p. 118).

Although the replacement and reenactment aspects of transference as mentioned above are striking, often hidden and important to discern, they do not define the fundamental essence or core meaning, significance, function of or reason for the transference process, the "false connection," as Freud (1895/1955, p. 302) originally called it. What characterizes transference, and is the essence of it, is the vicissitudes of instinctual sensual drives embodied therein. It is the transfer of affect and defenses against affect, "tendencies and phantasies which are aroused," which is the core of the process. The process in transference is a conflictual struggle to become aware of and acquire a capacity to handle instinctual sensual impulses and to find a way of obtaining eventual sensual gratification through the transitional use of a temporary replacement object around whom impulses pushing against repression can be reexperienced, integrated and rechanneled. Intrapsychically, transference is an autoplastic defensive mechanism of the ego employed to handle the anxiety associated with repressed, unconscious, instinctual drives which are pushing toward awareness. Interpsychically, the transference is a potentially liberating alloplastic expression of this defense in the interpersonal transactions.

Freud's writing and Dora's statements imply in no way that either Freud or Dora were operating on any assumption other than that they each had a sense of who they were as separate people, selves and objects and of who Dora's family and intimates were as separate people, selves and objects. The focus in the case description and therapy report was not on distortions of self-object definition but on the vicissitudes and defensive handling of instinctual drives. Such a transference replacement of one person by another is not a self-object distortion, but an object-object distortion, which serves to balance defensively fears and wishes. The transference is a creative distortion of reality to avoid and control feelings which might arouse anxiety. This distortion of the perceived reality gestalt is of a different order from the confusion of the reality of self and others, which comes from primary failure of assimilation and integration of introjects and projects, from failure of distinction between introjects and projects or from the accurate early learning of a narrow, peculiar, idiosyncratic reality which makes later, broader socialization difficult, if not impossible. Dora's wishes and fears pertaining to early love objects were transferred to Freud, Freud being used to displace the original love objects because of Dora's powerful emotional needs. Again assuming good self-object definition, this process was not a primary misperception or projective identification, but rather a secondary distortion of perception motivated by the anticipation, hope or wish for, and fear of, emotional gratification. As mentioned, Dora defined herself and was viewed by Freud, although neither she nor he used such terms, as having a clear self-object definition, distorted because of emotional conflict.

Although in retrospect, we can see that Dora did indeed have some impairment in the area of self-object definition and a need for affirmation, part of the analysis of her transference along instinctual lines would still have validity today with certain modifications. Originally, and to some extent today, self-object distortions were clarified in the therapy, and in life in general, in passing or implicitly. Today we are more explicit in the clarification and analysis of self-object distortions which are occurring in concert with instinctual transferences in therapy. Thus it is possible to comprehend, diagnose and treat more precisely and effectively a wider variety of psychopathology than was the case when the focus was so greatly on instincts and their vicissitudes. This binocular focus was expressed clearly by Erikson (1950) in his statement that the study of identity is as important in our time as the study of sexuality was in Freud's time. This by no means should be taken to mean, however, that the study of sexuality may be forgotten. The psychosexual stages—oral, anal, phallic-oedipal—and the instinctual vicissitudes of these stages will show themselves in powerful emotional terms in the transferences in marriages and in patient-therapist relationships.

WHAT IS NOT TRANSFERENCE

Although I have emphasized that the term "transference" should be used not to describe self-object distortion processes but only to describe emotional, sensual, gratification-seeking (per se), instinctual-drive vicissitudes in transactions, it does not follow, as mentioned earlier in discussing sensuality, that all sensuality or fear of it seen in therapy is transference. Although all transference processes have to do with issues of sensual gratification, not all searches for, or avoidance of, sensual gratification are transference processes. In instances of self-object distortion, sensual gratification or the absence or the avoidance of it can function in the service of achieving or limiting self-object definition. The need for sensual gratification operative in what have been termed "mirror" and "idealizing" transferences by Kohut (1971) represents an intense search for gratification not as a way of obtaining pleasure per se but as a way of achieving affirmation of a fragile sense of self through sensuality. As self-object definition develops, the need for constant and often indiscriminate sensual stimulation diminishes and/or is refined. In line with the thesis on transference presented in this paper, since the issue in so-called primitive or archaic transferences is primarily one of self-object development rather than of sensual gratification, even though sensuality is prominent, I believe the major part of this process should be called not an instinctual transference process but a self-object distortion process. The major work in the therapy of self-object distortions goes into assisting the patient in self-object development, a part of which involves establishing a working alliance along the lines described by Stone (1954), Dewald (1976), Greenson (1965), Greenson and Wexler (1969) and Zetzel (1956, 1970).

Although Kohut (1971) uses the term "transference" to describe self-object distortion processes in therapy, it is clear that he sees the sensuality here as I do, as being used in the service of transitionally acquiring missing parts of self: "The child does not acquire the needed internal structure, his psyche remains fixated on an archaic self-object, and the personality will throughout life be dependent on certain objects in what seems to be an intense form of object hunger. The intensity of the search for, and of the dependency on, these objects is due to the fact that they are striven for as substitutes for the missing segment of the psychic structure. They are not objects (in the psychological sense of the term) since they are not loved or admired for their attributes, and the actual features of their personalities and their actions are only dimly recognized. They are not longed for but are needed in order to replace the functions of a segment of the mental apparatus which had not been established in childhood" (pp. 45–46).

Nevertheless, in continuing this exposition he uses the term "transferencelike" to describe these processes: "One might say that the transferencelike condition which establishes itself in such analyses is indeed the reinstatement of an archaic condition. The analysand reactivates the need for an archaic, narcissistically experienced self-object which preceded the formation of psychic structure in a specific segment of the psychic apparatus" (pp. 46–47). He prefaces these comments, however, with the statement that "in the metapsychological sense of the word, the term transference may not be fully correct here" (p. 46), an acknowledgment that is congruent with the thesis presented in this paper—that the term "transference" should be used only to describe the vicissitudes of instinctual processes and that neither self-object distortion processes nor the sensuality connected with them should be considered as part of instinctual transference processes.

Parenthetically, it should be mentioned that although in persons with self-object impairment, sensuality is used excessively in the service of affirmation of self, sensuality serves also to affirm self in differentiated people as well, as emphasized by Binstock (1973) in his paper on the two forms of intimacy. Conflicts which block sensual gratification for pleasure per se can, through sensory deprivation, cause temporary deformities of self, which can be evident in therapy in conjunction with instinctual transference processes.

MATE SELECTION AND MARITAL TRANSFERENCES

Although the term "transference" was coined originally to describe a phenomenon occurring in the course of psychoanalysis, transferences are ubiquitous. The knowledge gained in analysis can be extrapolated to shed light on transferences in important relationships other than the analytic one. In particular, analytic experience over the years has helped us to learn about marriage dynamics.

Let us assume that a man and a woman meet. Each has a reasonable degree of self-object definition, yet each suffers from instinctual repression. Even if consciously seeking instinctual gratification, they will unconsciously, in the grip of unrecognized positive transferences, seek mates partly for reinforcement of repression. They may consciously rationalize their choice in such terms as "a decent man" or "a virtuous woman"; they may consciously marry someone manifestly sexual with the hope of receiving help in lifting or permission to lift repression; or they may be motivated in marriage by a wish to reform or rescue.

Although perhaps not visible early in marital relationships, as time goes on in the continuity of the marriage, negative transferences which were a hidden part of the original contract gradually become more manifest. Early in the marriage, the positive transferences which are operative blend with love or appear as love so that both partners are either passionately attracted to each other, attracted by a challenge, quietly contented and pleased by each other or at least not irritated by each other. There is a synergism or mutual adaptation of positive transferences for a while. In some marriages, as growth and change occur in one or both partners, positive and negative transferences are resolved and an ever-increasing capacity for genuine instinctual gratification of both partners occurs. Taking turns for times of introspection on the part of one and suspension of collusion on the part of the other are required for this to occur. A change in one spouse only, because of the development of a negative transference, a healthy awareness of sensual deprivation, a change in sense of self or an extramarital experience, may initiate a potentially creative turbulence and change in the, until then, homeostatic marital collusion of transferences. In creative marriages love and instinctual gratification grow ever deeper.

If a marriage gets stuck either in a collusion of negative transferences or in an unhappy combination of negative transferences plus healthy disinclinations to transfer or be transferred to positively or negatively, the marriage may continue unhappily on its course, a divorce or separation may occur or one spouse or the couple may seek treatment.

If one spouse comes for treatment alone or is "sent" for treatment, this "patient" spouse is often the one who is beginning to have emerging sexual and/or aggressive impulses. These impulses are causing either subjective symptoms or marital disharmony partly because of the instinctual repression in the transference of the "nonpatient" spouse, whose own guilt about expression is being projected and is impacting on the "patient." Other times the spouse coming or "sent" for treatment is the more repressed spouse, stirred up by the lifting of repression in a spouse who is breaking out of his or her own inhibitions and the marital collusion.

In transference, either positive or negative, there is always conflict and anxiety, with underlying fears that abandonment, loss of love, body damage or superego punishment will ensue if impulses are felt or expressed and gratified. In a positive transference, guilt and fear about hostile competitive impulses toward rivals or rival images are kept out of awareness, rationalized and temporarily partially overridden both by the urgency of the sexual impulses and the opposition to the superego offered by the love object. Guilt and fear associated with the need for sex and love from the love object, and the possibility that one might be rejected, feel frightened, angry and guilty, are also kept out of awareness, again temporarily assisted by the presence and availability of the love object. I am speaking here primarily of a heterosexual transference triangle, with fear and guilt toward the "father" or "mother," against whom he or she is competing, and guilt toward the "mother" or "father" one is both sexually attracted to and angry at. Similar mechanisms can be operative in a homosexual transference triangle.

It is unlikely that the positive transference will continue to exist for long, despite mutual sexual attraction, both because of the dynamic autoplastic interplay of internal id, ego and superego forces and because of the alloplastic interplay of repressive forces in the spouses. A wide variety of transactions can occur which reinforce repression in one or both spouses: Love and sensuality flowing from whichever spouse may be expressing it at the moment to the other can actually intensify the loved, but less sensual, spouse's guilt. The loved, more sensually repressed spouse then rejects the loving sensual spouse. The sensual spouse may then either experience a waning of love, attraction and desire or start to complain, gratifying the desired and loved spouse's need for punishment, intensifying guilt and repression.

The loving, sensually expressive spouse may feel guilty and complain in such a masochistic or condemning manner that the loved, sensually repressed spouse is not motivated to lift repression but may become further constricted by guilt and defend against guilt by counterattacking and gratifying the complaining spouse's need for punishment. The appealed-to or complained-against spouse may also naturally and realistically counterattack as a defense against what may have become definite abuse, or may realistically feel rejected, withdraw love and turn away. Love, lust and sensuality progressively diminish. One or the other spouse may seek affection elsewhere, which, as mentioned earlier, may in some instances break the downward spiral and start a healing battle against guilt and repression, or it may intensify guilt and resentment in one or both parties. As mentioned earlier, there may come a time when a marriage originally composed of a degree of mutual satisfaction and a collusion of reified positive transferences has shifted to a marriage composed of a mixture of negative transferences and realistic dissatisfaction. It is at this point that there is a separation or divorce; establishment of a chronic unsatisfactory homeostasis in the marriage with sado-masochism, apathy, somatic illness, affairs, sexual dysfunction, projection onto children or any of a variety of other psychopathologies as possible components; a serious struggle for self-healing and growth in the marriage; or the seeking of treatment by one or both spouses.

Two points should be borne in mind in considering this seemingly negative state of affairs which over time can develop in marriage. The first is that the emergence of negative transference is practically inevitable in marriage. The second point is that, just as a positive transference masks and is a defense against hostility, repression of which interferes with genuine and full expression of love, lust and sensuality, and hence is not such a good thing, a negative transference masks and defends against repressed love, lust and sexuality, and hence is not such a bad thing. The negative transference in the marriage contains an emergence of much of the hostility repressed in the positive transference. Thus, via the negative transference in therapy, it can be taken off the spouse and directed toward introjects of childhood competitors or frustrators. The hostility toward the spouse can be seen as a defense against having guilt and anxiety producing pleasure—i.e., it is easier to be angry at the spouse than face one's fear, grief, love, rage and guilt toward one's parents. A corollary of the positive value of the negative transference is that the expression of a degree of negative feelings toward the spouse, which is often greater than was ever expressed toward one's parents, indicates a greater degree of trust in or at least chance-taking with the spouse than was the case with the parents. Furthermore, the intensity of the anger toward the spouse can be seen not only as a measure of the anger toward parents and parent images (which, when focused and resolved, will free a great deal of libido for loving) but also as a measure of the desirability of the spouse, in that the spouse can represent a threat of happiness so great as to require such intense defensive measures.

The points about negative transference apply not only to marriage transferences but to transferences in therapy, the difference being that in marriage one has an available sensual love object upon resolution but in therapy an available sensual love object must still be found or, if present, will be more freely enjoyed when transferences are resolved.

THE THERAPIST AND THE THERAPY TRANSFERENCES

Just as it is important, in working with problems of self-object definition, for the therapist to have a clear sense of self, including a heterosexual reality sense and a family image, so in working with instinctual transferences it is important for therapists to be sensually and sexually uninhibited and have relationships outside the therapy situation which meet their needs to compete and to give and receive sexual pleasure. Therapists should not be vulnerable to desexualization by efforts to make them feel guilty or frightened about their heterosexuality, their assertive, or their competitive drives; nor should they be vulnerable to sexual seduction or be seductive. They should be able to handle whatever degree of anxiety they might experience if their own sexual and aggressive feelings are stirred up in the course of therapy, and they should use this anxiety creatively, without blocking emotional expression, exploiting it or being exploited by it. In short, therapists should have a family image and the well-developed triadic heterosexual sense of reality embodied therein, plus the capacity to handle the instinctual drives inherent in and pertinent to this gestalt as they are set in motion in the therapeutic experience. Just as the therapist should and can gain further clarity of his own self-object definition in helping patients clarify theirs, he should and can learn more about his own instinctual drives in helping patients with transference distortions. The responsibility for this lies primarily with the therapist (Saul, 1962). The therapist's situation here, even when clearly defined, is more difficult than when dealing with self-object processes, for in transference situations the therapist must remain relatively dispassionate in order to make credible transference interpretations and should not express feelings he or she may be having of sexual arousal, guilt, fear of rejection or hostility lest the patient's feelings be trapped with him or her and not be redirected to parent introjects, spouse or other people in the patient's social orbit. By contrast, in helping in areas of self-object definition, the therapist can feel more free to be expressive, since his or her efforts at clarification in these areas are not only self-expressive but therapeutic as well. In neither case should the therapist be too eager or too imposing, but the restraint required on his or her sexual and aggressive drives is greater when dealing with transference areas than with self-object areas. It is particularly important for the therapist to be able to interpret negative transferences, for it is when a spouse-therapist negative transference emerges (which is similar to a negative transference that has been operative in the marriage) that there is an opportunity for a major therapeutic gain. Through interpretation of such a spouse-therapist transference, not only is the therapist relieved of the pressures of the transference on him or her but, most importantly for his or her professional goal and for the couple's happiness, the similarly transferred-to spouse at this juncture is similarly relieved of forces which may have been impacting on him or her for some time. A way is opened for rechanneling emotions in the marriage and reworking feelings toward parents and parental images. In dealing with transference issues, therapists' instinctual drives must be sublimated into transference interpretations or into calm and patient study and reflection. By the act of eliciting, focusing and interpreting the negative transference, therapists expose themselves transiently to the impact of emotionally stimulating processes, which may motivate them to distort defensively their sense of reality, distort their perceptions of their patients and accept the patients' distortion of them. However, if therapists stay steady and interpret, and if their transference interpretations are accepted, their patients will give them the gift of freedom to use their feelings as they choose in their professional and personal lives, will no longer threaten to distort the therapists' triadic heterosexual reality sense, and will use the interpretations to deal with the past and move ahead in healthy sexual and aggressive ways in their marriages.

Transferences are usually more visible to the participants in the therapy situation than in marriage for several reasons. These are the therapist's relative objectivity and lack of collusion with, or gratification of, the originally unconscious but emerging transference wishes for sexual or aggressive pleasure or punishment; the neutrality and suspension of the need for instinctual gratification on the part of the therapist; and the mutual agreement of patient and therapist to examine the relationship processes. It is essential that the marital therapist understand the potentially positive forces in the combination of negative transferences and realistically based dissatisfactions which characterize the disharmonious marriage that comes to him or her for treatment. The couples do not see this, and therapists cannot help them unless they themselves do. The therapist must also not lose sight of whatever degree of genuine positive affection the spouses have for each other which, in concert with the positive transferences, originally drew them together, but which has become overshadowed and almost forgotten in the situation of anger, fear, guilt and mistrust that has evolved. As well as analyzing the negative transference to him or her, the therapist must help each spouse to delineate consciously the negative marital transferences and the realistically based complaints in the marriage, and help both spouses to see the wish for closeness and affection contained in each. When either spouse connects the guilt, anger, fear and grief contained in the negative spouse-therapist and marital transferences to parental introjects, sexuality emerges to cathect the other spouse. Increased flow of affection occurs also as the spouses see the desire for, and value of, the other, which is contained in the realistically based complaints. The release, which comes from resolution of the negative transference in the therapy and in the marriage, motivates the spouses to dissect their complaints and recognize the guilt and condemnation contained therein. The spouses come to see how guilt makes it difficult to ask clearly for gratification or to receive it if it is proferred, and how it also transforms potential requests into complaints and provocative behavior. They see how condemnation makes it difficult for a complained-against spouse to feel desired or valued, how it reinforces guilt and provokes defensive and realistic counterattacks.

As each spouse resolves his or her transferences, there is not only increased self-understanding and a change in self toward feeling and being more sensual, loving and lovable but also a simultaneous increased affection for, and understanding of, the other spouse as a nascently sensual, loving and lovable peer who is struggling with guilts and anxieties similar to one's own. There is an awareness of, and responsibility for, one's part in hurting one's spouse and oneself. Combined with expecting similar responsibility from one's spouse, there is a lessening of the tendency to take negative transferences personally. There is less vulnerability to the guilt and condemnation components of a spouse's complaint and an increased ability to hear the request contained in a complaint and to work toward a shared, responsible conversion of complaints into the pleasures of requests and gratifications.

A spillover gain accrues to the nonexploring spouse, who, at a given moment in observing and being part of an exploring spouse's resolutions, simultaneously experiences a better understanding of the resolving spouse. The "observing" spouse gains a degree of similar self-understanding and an increase in feeling and being sensual, loving and lovable in the process of listening, helping, participating and identifying. A combination of understanding, compassion, being trusted, the return of hope in seeing one's spouse work, plus the relief from the heavy burden of guilt-inducing condemnation, can release a wave of affectionate impulses, which can reinforce the resolving spouse's loving and lovable impulses. All of the foregoing processes described in one spouse or the other are alternately and sometimes almost simultaneously experienced by both spouses individually during therapy, and the spouses vicariously experience each other. Once this process starts, good things begin to happen quite rapidly. As mentioned earlier, the move that usually opens up this process is the intrusion of the therapist through interpretation of a negative transference and/or complaint toward him or her, which is similar to that which has been operating in the marriage. When good things reach a self-perpetuating level, the therapist turns away and at the same time is excluded by the couple.

In concluding this discussion of the therapist's handling of transferences, I would like to remind the reader of two major considerations. First, it is preferable that the transference therapist not have too much investment in the transferential field nor be too disturbed by defensively distorted perceptions of him or her by the patients. Secondly, although this paper artificially separates out transference distortions from self-object definition difficulties to facilitate understanding and identification of them as two distinct phenomena, I would like to emphasize that in every case both phenomena will be present. In fact, in reviewing a single therapy session one may find that he has been moving back and forth, dealing with both. Patients in the therapy communication system may recapitulate in a straight progression either the stages of psychosexual development or the stages in self-object definition, but they often do not, and a rigid theoretical expectation on the part of the therapist that this will occur over time, or that only one area or stage will be presenting itself for attention in any therapy, session or sequence of sessions, can ruin the therapy. People do compose themselves not exactly by the book but rather in their own unique way, and their reorganization can be equally unique and full of surprises.

CASE EXAMPLE

A clinical example of the therapy of a couple will illustrate the operation of some of the foregoing theoretical concepts and related technical considerations. The difficulties in this couple's marriage primarily involved instinctual transference problems. Although there were some self-object definition problems, I shall focus in this presentation on the marital transferences. Each mate was attractive, clear-thinking, talented and effective in life. The husband, who was sexually inexperienced, had married his wife because he had found her irresistible, and the wife, who was sexually experienced, had consciously seduced the husband in order to escape from a father who she feared might rape her. In the early marriage the husband soon felt trapped, that he had married before he had gone through his adolescence and, at that, had married someone who he felt was neurotic and dependent. They both remained attached to their own and each other's families in the early years of marriage and lived apart from one another for a time. Over the years they were unable to meet each other's needs, and they argued and complained excessively with each other about a variety of issues without coming to terms. They competed with each other as to how much time and money and attention each would devote to a career, how much prestige, money and pleasure would be obtained in the career, and how much each spouse respected and appreciated the other's career. They competed as to how money would be spent on clothing, housing, food, automobiles and recreation. They competed as to who was the better parent or who was the more expressive person. They used and were used by friends and families of origin to reinforce this competitive repulsion. As time went on, the husband, and less so the wife, sought intimate heterosexual companionship outside the marriage. They came into treatment as a couple, mutually motivated, after a period of stormy interaction, during which the wife had started to make frightened, outraged confrontations to the by-now-aloof husband about the pitiful state of their marriage and the husband had decided to give up his extensive outside sexual involvements.

A great deal of the work in the early therapy consisted of helping the wife, who was enraged at and demanding of the husband, to explore the homosexual trap she was in, which originated with her mother. She was unable to compete with her husband's mother or his extramarital women. On the husband's part, he was torn between feelings of attachment to his mother and a wish to escape from her influence. The wife was unable to let herself have her sexual feelings for her father without an accompanying fear that she would be given father by mother, and similarly, the husband was unable to let himself have his sexual feelings for his mother for fear he would be given mother by father. A difference existed between the two in that the wife was more aware of her sexual feelings toward her father than the husband was of his toward his mother. The wife had fled into peer sexual experience to escape the tensions she felt in her family, and the more repressed husband, who had handled his sexuality by intellectual and athletic accomplishments, was seduced into sexuality by his wife. Each spouse expected to be helped by the other to resolve the bonds with families of origin, but each was having trouble escaping or helping because of inhibitions which attached them to their own families. These inhibitions were acted out further and reinforced by the homosexual search for approval of the husband's mother by the wife and the wife's father by the husband. These processes meshed with the combined pressures of both families of origin to control the couple's sexual and procreative life. Both spouses had had a seeming oedipal victory in childhood that made them frightened of sexuality. "Winning" for the wife not only made her feel guilty but faced her with a fear of rape and domination by her father and a fear that both she and her mother might be killed by him. "Winning" for the husband made him feel not only guilty but meant to be trapped into a relationship with a seductive mother who would control and mold him into an intellectual accomplisher assigned to take care of a suffering, sick, unhappy woman who could not be gratified or gratify. The couple's marriage involved a transference by the wife to the husband of feelings she had about her father, and by the husband to the wife of feelings he had about his mother. After a brief initial override of repression, there was a rapid acting out of avoidance of sexuality and a seeking of approval and accomplishment on the wife's part, and the seeking of sexual expression outside the marriage and escape from control on the husband's part. The spouses were seeking emancipation from their families of origin, but were simultaneously complying with their early programming by transferring their struggle to the marriage, fighting with and repelling each other rather than attracting and enjoying each other. Although there was a degree of individual growth occurring in the spouses in this process, as far as the relationship was concerned they tended to drive each other back into the orbit of their families of origin and to throw each other away into the arms of other lovers. Instead of competing with their competition, they were competing with each other, and instead of cooperating with each other, they unwittingly were cooperating with their competition. It was clear in the early sessions that despite what they said to each other in anger, they saw each other as interesting, exciting, sexually desirable, admirable and attractive people. They were afraid of closeness, intimacy and sensuality with what they saw as forbidden, rejecting, guilt-inducing, controlling or menacing love objects.

Because of an initial, basically positive regard and respect for me on the part of both spouses, particularly the husband, it was possible for the couple to begin to explore, comprehend and change many of the patterns of interaction with their families of origin and in their marriage, as well as reorganize some of their psychic defensive processes. These gains involved, in particular, a lessening of guilt to mother and an increased ability to compete on the part of the wife. There was a developing willingness to learn from me and a recognition of some of her part in pushing her husband away to other women. Despite these seeming gains, however, her positive attitude began to shift to one of feeling that I was more fond of her husband than of her, that neither he nor I understood or cared for her but, in fact, were against her or wished her dead. Although she had bombarded her husband with an overkill of complaints to such a degree that he was hesitant and wary of expressing to her the feelings she was demanding he express, he was nevertheless more available to her than ever before. Certain aspects of their life situation had improved. He was responding to many of her requests, though not all, and was much more caring and honest. He was more real to her insofar as not giving in to irrational demands. Despite these partial improvements, her protests increased, she sought an outside love relationship and pressed for a separation or divorce at a point where I saw the chances for happiness as just around the corner. It was at this point that I was able to deal definitively with the wife's negative transference to me. I pointed out the many similarities in how she felt about me and how she felt about her husband. She saw both of us as authority figures, unfeeling and uncaring. I pointed out that she was probably unable to handle her positive feelings and had reversed them because of guilt and fear. In dealing with this, I pointed out, repeatedly and gently, all the positive evidences of warmth and care from me which she had previously at one time or another acknowledged, how she had expressed envy of my wife for having me and how she had wished her husband had more of my qualities. I said that she must be trying to deny her positive feelings, not only for me but for her husband. She wept at this point and agreed. A marked change occurred within a week in the marital relationship. She saw a vulnerability and a softness in her husband that she hadn't let herself see before, and she told him repeatedly how much she loved him. In the next session she brought in a nightmare, analysis of which revealed a theme of sex and violence with her father. She had split her sexual fantasies of her father into one of wanting to sexually gratify a poor, neglected disabled war veteran and one of being raped and killed by a violent soldier. All of the previously worked-on interactional and intrapsychic processes were reexamined from this now-open position, which had come from interpreting the negative transference to me, and it was possible for two phenomena to be seen convincingly. First, hostility and guilt toward her mother and memories of her father's temper had tilted the wife toward seeing men as "master sergeant-killer-rapists." Second, it was possible to see through a direct exploration of her masturbation fantasies that she had let herself have her sexual impulses in relation to safe, disabled men in masturbation over a period of intense sexual excitement in early marriage, during which time her husband, seen in the role of killer-rapist, was involved actively and secretly in sexual experiences with other women. She had made her husband into the sexually uncared-for father whom she could let herself enjoy and take care of only in masturbation and into the killer-rapist father she feared, repelled and gave away to other women.

The next problem to emerge was that the husband, although happy with the changes in his wife, was thrown into his own struggle, primarily with guilt about getting what he wanted, a struggle which he hadn't had to face or been given the opportunity to face as long as he was getting punished by his wife. He felt remorse about his past selfishness and cruelty toward his wife. He felt a fear of losing her. He struggled with questioning himself as to what a defensive selfishness was and what a healthy and deserved selfishness was. He needed strong reassurance from his wife that she did indeed love him, wanted to take care of him, that she saw him both as desirable and as deserving to be taken care of, that she was getting enough from him and that she saw him as a good father in whom she could entrust the care of a child. He was bewildered. His mother had never trusted his father to care for him and had been the dominant direction in guiding him in life and career choices. His mother had never really taken care of his father, and his father had always felt guilty toward his mother and encouraged the son to join him in catering to her. Not to care sufficiently for her could result in her death. The husband found himself struggling with feelings of guilt and grief about his mother, whom he was letting die in his imagery and whose recent actual death had freed him of any real burden of taking care of her. He now had a wife he could enjoy, but if this was possible, could he allow himself to enjoy her? He found himself worrying about his widower father, who both his wife and I reassured him was being pursued by many women. Although he had needed me to help him with his wife when we were both caring for a sick woman, now he was faced with the possibility of open competition with me, his father, her father and other men for her. Would he need permission to enjoy her, or could he claim her against fantasied or real competition? He had thoughts that maybe I didn't like him, and fleeting thoughts of jealousy that his wife might give me more than she would give him. Exploration of his feelings resulted in delineation and resolution of a negative transference to me, which was of much less intensity than that of the wife's.

It is common that the analysis of whichever spouse's negative transference is exposed second is easier and the transference less intense than the one exposed and analyzed first. I would speculate that there are three reasons for this. First is probably the gender of the therapist. If I had been a woman, it is quite possible the husband's negative transference to his wife could have been transferred to me and been analyzed first. Second is the nature of the couple's problem. If in this couple the man had had a great deal of distrust in men or a severe homosexual problem, and the wife a degree of respect in men and in me and my ability, the husband's negative transference to me might have emerged and been analyzed first. Third, as I have mentioned earlier, whatever resolutions occur in one spouse spill over and contribute to resolutions, sometimes unverbalized, in the other. This could apply to transferences as well. By the time the negative transference of the second spouse is dealt with, it is attenuated because of diminution in the marriage of negative transferences and because of the erosion of the negative transferences to the therapist. There is also an increase in therapist trust and motivation to analyze transferences that the second spouse experiences in seeing the spouse and therapist working on the first spouse's negative transference. In this process of observing and participating, the second spouse has all sorts of feelings around what he or she expects to happen or not happen (in contrast to what does happen or does not happen), many of which he or she may not verbalize. This process involves working on his or her transferences whether they are directly focused on or not.

A point should be made here relative to the manner of emergence and analysis of dyadic transferences in couple therapy with a single therapist compared to the resolution of marital and therapy transferences in couple therapy with a heterosexual co-therapy team. With the use of a heterosexual co-therapy team, resolution comes about through an analysis of triadic transferences to the co-therapy team "marriage." (Sonne and Lincoln, 1966).

A final point I would like to make about this case and similar cases is that with the analysis of the negative transferences there occurs a fairly rapid increase in the couple's sensual pleasure in each other, less intense involvement with the children and a joyousness of expression in other areas of fun and play. This is common in the analysis of instinctual transferences and is in contrast to what often happens with couples who are working more on self-object definition and who may have a drop-off from their previous sensuality for a time while improving and dealing formally and cognitively with self-object definition in themselves and their children before the sensuality returns in a new way in a new framework.

SUMMARY

In this chapter I have presented an argument for making a distinction between transference processes and self-object distortion processes in life, marriage and therapy. I have addressed myself to the confusion existing in the literature around the lack of clear definition of terms and have attempted to define what is and what is not transference. I have advanced the thesis that transference is primarily an affective process and that the term "transference" should be used only for those processes which involve the transfer of poststructural instinctual drive vicissitudes that pertain to the seeking of sensual gratification for pleasure per se, and not for sensual processes which are in the service of communication, learning, or self and self-object definition. The term "sensual" has been used frequently in this paper as an abstraction which is broader than "sexual" and which can be applied to self-object definition processes as well as to instinctual transference processes. A conceptualization of mate selection and marriage as involving the operation of an unconscious collusion of positive transferences and the shift from this situation over time to one of a marriage composed of a combination of negative transferences and healthy marital dissatisfaction has been outlined. The inevitability of the development of negative transferences in marriage and the positive connotations of this, plus the opportunity offered by the negative transferences, if successfully handled in therapy, have been emphasized. Movement occurs in therapy when a negative transference to the therapist which is similar to that which has been operative in the marriage can be analyzed. Personal qualities in the therapist and his or her having a reasonably gratifying sensual, sexual life are discussed, as well as the importance in therapy of being able to distinguish what are self-object processes and what are transference processes. A case has been presented of treatment of a husband and wife who were very competitive with and repelling of each other and who were struggling primarily with transference processes in their marriage.

REFERENCES

Abraham, K. Origins and growth of object-love. In *Selected papers on psychoanalysis*. (D. Bryan and A. Strachey, trans.). New York: Basic Books, 1954. (Originally published 1924.)

Abraham, K. Character-formation on the genital level of the libido. In *Selected papers on psychoanalysis*. (D. Bryan and A. Strachey, trans.). New York: Basic Books, 1954. (Originally published 1925.)

Abraham, K. *Selected papers on psychoanalysis*. (D. Bryan and A. Strachey, trans.). New York: Basic Books, 1954. (Originally published 1927.)

Binstock, W.A. On the two forms of intimacy. *J. Am. Psychoanaly. Assoc.*, 1973, *21*, 93–107.

Blum, H.P. The prototype of preoedipal reconstruction. *J. Am. Psychoanaly. Assoc.*, 1977, *25*, 757–785.

Dewald, P.A. Transference regression and real experience in the psychoanalytic process. *Psychoanaly. Quart.*, 1976, *45*, 213–230.

Erikson, E. *Childhood and society*. New York: W.W. Norton, 1950.

Frances, A., and Gale, L. The proprioceptive body image in self-object differentiation: A case of congenital indifference to pain and head banging. *Psychoanaly. Quart.*, 1975, *44*, 107–126.

Freedman, D.A. Congenital and perinatal sensory deprivation: Some studies in early development. *Am. J. Psychiat.*, 1971, *127*, 1539–1545.

Freedman, D.A. Congenital and perinatal sensory deprivation: Their effect on the capacity to experience affect. *Psychoanalyt. Quart.*, 1975, *44*, 62–80.

Freud, S. Studies in hysteria. *St. Ed., 2*, 1–305. London: Hogarth Press, 1955. (Originally published 1895.)

Freud, S. The interpretation of dreams. *St. Ed., 4* and *5*, 1–621. London: Hogarth Press, 1953. (Originally published 1900.)

Freud, S. Fragment of an analysis of a case of hysteria. *St. Ed., 7*, 7–122. London: Hogarth Press, 1953. (Originally published 1905.)

Freud, S. Character and anal eroticism. *St. Ed., 9*, 167–176. London: Hogarth Press, 1959. (Originally published 1908.)

Freud, S. From the history of an infantile neurosis. *St. Ed., 17*, 7–122. London: Hogarth Press, 1955. (Originally published 1918.)

Freud, S. Group psychology and the analysis of the ego. *St. Ed., 18*, 69–143. London: Hogarth Press, 1955. (Originally published 1921.)

Friedman, C.J., Sibinga, M.S., Steisel, I.M., and Sinnamon, H.M. Sensory restriction and isolation experiences in children with phenylketonuria. *J. Ab. Psychol.*, 1968, *73*, 294–303.

Greenson, R. The working alliance and the transference neurosis. *Psychoanalyt. Quart.*, 1965, *34*, 155–181.

Greenson, R., and Wexler, M. The non-transference relationship in the psychoanalytic situation. *Int. J. Psycho-Analy.*, 1969, *50*, 27–39.

Hebb, D.O. *The organization of behavior*. New York: Wiley, 1959.

Jones, E. A valedictory address. *Int. J. Psycho-Analy.*, 1946, *27*, 7–12.

Kernberg, O. *Object relations theory and clinical psychoanalysis.* New York: Jason Aronson, 1976.

Kestenberg, J.S. The role of movement patterns in development. I: Rhythms of movement. *Psychoanaly. Quart.*, 1965, *34*, 1–36.

Kestenberg, J.S. The role of movement patterns in development. II: Flow of tension and effort. *Psychoanaly. Quart.*, 1965b, *34*, 517–563.

Kestenberg, J.S. The role of movement patterns in development. III: The control of shape. *Psychoanaly. Quart.*, 1967, *36*, 356–409.

Klein, M. Notes on some schizoid mechanisms. In J. Riviere (Ed.), *Developments in psycho-analysis.* London: Hogarth Press, 1946.

Kohut, H. *The analysis of the self.* New York: International Universities Press, 1971.

Lilly, J.C. Mental effects of reduction of ordinary levels of physical stimuli on intact healthy persons. In *Psychiatric Research Report 5.* Washington: American Psychiatric Association, 1956.

Masterson, J.F. The borderline adult: Therapeutic alliance and transference. *Am. J. Psychiat.*, 1978, *135*, 437–441.

Nunberg, H. Transference and reality. *Int. J. Psycho-Analy.*, 1951, *32*, 1–9.

Prescott, J.W. Early somatosensory deprivation as an ontogenetic process in the abnormal development of the brain and behavior. In I.E. Goldsmith and Moor-Jankowski (Eds.), *Medical primatology.* New York: S. Karger, 1971.

Riesen, A.H. Brain and behavior: Effects of stimulus deprivation on the development and atrophy of the visual sensory system. *Am. J. Orthopsychiat.*, 1960, *30*, 23–36.

Robertson, J. *Young children in hospitals.* New York: Basic Books, 1962.

Rosenzweig, M.R., Krech, D., Bennett, E.L., and Diamond, M.E. Modifying brain chemistry and anatomy by enrichment or impoverishment of experience. In G. Newton and S. Levine (Eds.), *Early experience and behavior.* Springfield, Ill.: Charles C. Thomas, 1968.

Saul, J. The erotic transference. *Psychoanaly. Quart.*, 1962, *31*, 54–61.

Sibinga, M.S., and Friedman, C.J. Restraint and speech. *Pediatr.*, 1971, *48*, 116–122.

Sonne, J.C., Speck, R.V., and Jungreis, J. The absent-member maneuver as a resistance in family therapy of schizophrenia. *Fam. Proc.*, 1962, *1*, 44–62.

Sonne, J.C., and Lincoln, G. Heterosexual co-therapy team experiences during family therapy. *Fam. Proc.*, 1965, *4*, 177–197.

Sonne, J.C., and Lincoln, G. The importance of a heterosexual co-therapy relationship in the construction of a family image. In *Psychiatric Research Report 20.* Washington, D.C.: American Psychiatric Association, 1966.

Sonne, J.C. Entropic family communication in adolescence. *Int. J. Fam. Ther.*, 1979, *1*, 276–289.

Sonne, J.C., and Swirsky, D. Self-object considerations in marriage and marital therapy. In G.P. Sholevar (Ed.), *The handbook of marriage and marital therapy.* Jamaica, N.Y.: Spectrum Publications, 1981.

Spitz, R. Hospitalism: An inquiry into the genesis of psychiatric conditions in early childhood. *Psychoanaly. Study Child*, 1945, *1*, 53–74.

Spitz, R. Aggression: Its role in the establishment of object relations. In R.M. Loewenstein (Ed.), *Drives, affects, behavior.* New York: International Universities Press, 1953.

Spitz, R. *No and yes: On the genesis of human communication.* New York: International Universities Press, 1957.

Stone, L. The widening scope of indications for psychoanalysis. *J. Am. Psychoanaly. Assoc.*, 1954, *2*, 567–594.

Witkin, H.A., Lewis, H.B., Hertzman, M., Machover, K., Meissner, P., and Warner, S. *Personality through perception: An experimental and clinical study.* New York: Harper, 1954.

Zetzel, E.R. Current concepts of transference. *Int. J. Psycho-Analy.*, 1956, *37*, 369–376.

Zetzel, E.R. *The capacity for emotional growth.* New York: International Universities Press, 1970.

Zubek, J.P., and Welch, G. Electroencephalographic changes after prolonged sensory deprivation. *Science*, 1963, *139*, 1209–1210.

Zubek, J.P. (Ed.) *Sensory deprivation: Fifteen years of research.* New York: Appleton-Century-Crofts, 1969.

Zuckerman, M., Kalin, E.A., Price, L., and Zoob, I. Development of a sensation-seeking scale. *J. Consult. Psychol.*, 1964, *28*, 477–482.

Chapter 5

*Marriage Is a Family Affair: An Intergenerational Approach to Marital Therapy**

Geraldine M. Spark

With the increasing divorce rate, it is important to understand and find new and alternative therapeutic approaches to marital therapy. Instead of looking at the marital relationship as a closed system, it is necessary to study and treat it from an intergenerational point of view. This involves working on the interlocking between horizontal as well as the linear relationships in the nuclear family as well as both families of origin.

The marital relationship needs to be studied and treated from two vantages: first, as a horizontal peerlike relationship; and second, from a vertical-intergenerational point of view. The purpose of this paper is to emphasize and illustrate that clinically working on "unfinished business" between a parent and grandparents and even siblings can facilitate structural as well as symptomatic changes in the marital and family system.

*Reprinted from *Family Coordinator*, vol. 26, #2, 1977 with the permission of National Council on Family Relations.

To observe and treat the marital relationship as a unit totally independent of or isolated from families of origin would be to ignore the major significance and value of these interlocking relationships. It would also be treating the marital relationship as if it were a closed system. To concentrate only on the needs of each spouse would be to ignore the primary loyalty ties, indebtedness and obligations that exist with each one's family of origin. How these relationships are rebalanced to include those of the spouse and children within the nuclear family determines the degree of constructive functioning in these multiple and complex relationships. Marital therapy can provide an opportunity for such explorations.

MARITAL MYTHOLOGY

Myths that are passed on about the marital and parental relationships can lead to impossible expectations and failure. Marriages and families, both young and old, need an emotional support system which can facilitate responsible behavior among the spouses, parents and children, including both sets of grandparents. While an adoption of a communal family may temporarily provide such support for the young couple and family, the families of origin who are being rejected may be living in states of severe alienation, depression, depletion and despair. Even if these ties or bonds are seemingly ignored, guilt feelings may exist and, if not dealt with directly, may indirectly be channeled onto the mate or children.

To sustain closeness and intimacy and to balance it with separation and individuation throughout the various phases of marriage and family life are the paramount challenges.

In the past, when extended kin lived close by and were physically and emotionally available, there may have been conflict and competition, but generally alternate persons were available at times of need and crises. And of equal import, the very young could be a stimulus or resource to the older generation. Today, with the overemphasis on autonomy or "doing your own thing," when young or older families do depend on each other, they are considered weak or nonacceptable. We are living in a culture of denial. Supra-sex and violence are touted, as if steadiness, reliability, tenderness and romance are passé. Emotional and sexual intimacy in marriage is a longed-for goal, but for many it remains an unreachable ideal.

NUCLEAR-FAMILY FORMATION

Many couples believe that after taking the marital vows and from their growing bonds, they can and will establish a family similar to or better than their families or origin. They are set in a course of continuous integration of the old, the current and future goals. The marital choice is based on a physically and emotionally mutual attraction, trusting that the choice will lead to a gratifying and rewarding marital and family existence. The selection process often brings together partners who come from different backgrounds, but there is an expectancy that the difference may also help stimulate individual maturation and growth. For example, an individual who comes from a reserved, detached but stable background might seek a person who seems more spontaneous and open in his affectional areas. Or by contrast, both persons may have been raised in husband-fatherless or multiple-husband–father homes but hope and expect that their united efforts will correct such deprivations.

However, sometimes during the honeymoon or even shortly thereafter they discover that their idealization of the other turns into disappointment. And, too that the original families of origin reappear on the scene to make demands on one or both mates.

What has been given insufficient attention is that any separation, as reflected by a marriage, does restimulate the mourning process, reactivated from earlier losses. Leaving one's parents even for marriage can cause undue distress. Facing these feelings and concurrently changing one's behavior to shift the primary loyalty ties to the new spouse are demanding tasks. A rebalancing in each of these relationships—to the family of origin, to the spouse and to the new children that arrive—is a constantly challenging issue. With the help of a competent marital therapist, these struggles can be constructively undertaken.

Many couples and families that come for therapy are in a chronic, painful state of imbalance. Old obligations and indebtedness to the family of origin vie heavily with these new commitments.

The Marital Relationship

While marriage is essentially considered a twosome, the relationship must include and be rebalanced with those earlier relationships. In essence, then, marriage is a family affair in the sense that until and after the death of both sets of parents and siblings, they will continue to play a paramount part in the couple's adjustment to each other. Some marital and family therapists have argued whether families of origin are constructive or destructive forces. Sometimes it is one or both. But what is paramount is the quality of the relationships. The older parents are also moving into middle age or the aged phase, and these strong needs may temporarily be minimized or ignored. However, if they are not faced and dealt with, realistic and/or neurotic guilt feelings may accumulate and in the long run cost much in the marital and nuclear-family relationships.

Most young people, who are struggling with autonomy and interdependence, tend to postpone repayment of their original indebtedness. Severe symptoms and pathology can result without any awareness or insight into the process. The marital or family therapist who holds to an intergenerational accounting system often finds that he may be locked in a seemingly impossible impasse with these young patients. Some couples experience unbearable fears and anxieties about exploring these original interlocking relationships. They prefer coming to sessions with a full agenda of complaints about the spouse, and they cannot accept the intergenerational premises.

In many instances, then, they will sabotage the therapy, abruptly terminate or seek divorce as an ultimate solution. In some selected instances this is indeed a healthy decision. However, in too many situations the partner blames the emotional immaturity of the other instead of accepting therapy as a means of helping resolve the underlying conflicts and excess guilt feelings and of working towards rebalancing and repayment within his or her essential relationships.

More requests for therapy are being made by couples who are living with her, his and our children—and they are now experiencing even more difficulty with intimacy and sexuality than they had in their first marriage. But they have become aware that changing a mate is not the hoped-for solution. The loyalty ties are even more confused, and rebalancing and repayment are far more complicated than they might have been in the first or second marriage. These couples and families make the therapy process even more challenging. But those who can engage in treatment by accepting the interlocked, intergenerational dimensions can make more constructive gains in the long run than those who are not willing or able to work in this way.

TECHNIQUE AND TREATMENT

Just as the child's problems may be hidden behind the parent's request for marital therapy, so marital and intergenerational problems are often hidden behind a child's symptoms. In order to evaluate the pathological aspects, it is essential to study the marital, parental and grandparental relationships.

Couples who request therapy while stating that they have problems in communicating with each other generally show expertise in expressing negative criticism of each other. For some people verbal explosions can be devastating, even though there is no threat of violent verbal or physical abuse. But the more common, and by far the more powerful, weapon is the silent withdrawal for hours, days or weeks. Nothing ever gets settled or resolved. The couple may drift along for years communicating only on informational, factual levels. There is little capacity for emotional and sexual intimacy in such relationships.

In the initial phase, the complaints may concern money, housekeeping, work hours, vacations or children. More frequently, children are used for taking sides for or against the other spouse. Or children's needs are put ahead of those of our partners to a point where it is all family and no marriage. Or children are used as a reason for no sex: "They might overhear or walk into the bedroom." It is as if privacy was not an inviolable right for a married pair. Distance is maintained at all costs; the denial of gratification to the self is as great as to the other.

STRUCTURAL VERSUS SYMPTOMATIC CHANGE

Symptomatic relief may result in some areas if communication is improved, roles clarified and defined, tasks assigned and completed. But if we are concerned with structural change in a family system—that is, modification of destructive relationships from one generation to the next— intergenerational, marital and family therapy affords such an opportunity. In the more pathological situations, couples find themselves bound or caught in guilt-laden family relationships which not only cause suffering but are detrimental to change.

By taking a family history constructing a geneogram (see chart accompanying case illustration), which reveals the specific whereabouts of children, siblings, grandparents (including the illnesses or dates of death) and other important persons, one learns about the support system that may be available to the couple and family. The myths about little or no contact with families of origin or the in-law system begin to be penetrated. The behind-the-scenes powerful forces are brought out into the open and can begin to be dealt with. The loyalty ties, obligations and family accounting system begin to be revealed.

THEORETICAL DIMENSIONS

As Spark and Brody (1970) postulated, one could endlessly debate whether ties with maternal and paternal grandparents are sources of conflict and competition or resources of positive support and constructive influence on the nuclear family. Whether they fall into one or both categories, the reality is that these relationships do exist and are not peripheral ones that can be denied or minimized. Spark (1974) stated that as the focus of study and treatment moves from the individual to the family as a unit, the therapist must logically also include the extended and in-law family system.

Family-system theoreticians have long been aware of the nature of these interlocking physical, emotional and existential bonds among nuclear- and extended-family members, and their major treatment focus has been on the marital and/or parental relationships. Bowen (1966) focuses on a differentiation of self in the marital, parental and extended-family relationships to get out of the amorphous "we-ness" of the intense undifferentiated-family ego-mass. Ackerman, Lidz, Wynne and Jackson, pioneer family therapists, have also discussed generational issues in family systems. Boszormenyi-Nagy (1965) has consistently attempted to push his theoretical and clinical understanding beyond the known psychodynamics of the individual and the observable characteristics of his relationships with important others. Boszormenyi-Nagy and Spark (1973), in their current conceptualizations, introduce a dialectical perspective on family theory and therapy that revolves around the concepts of loyalty, justice and the balance of merits. In other words, two of the major and basic unifying tenets of intergenerational-family system theory are those of loyalty and obligation. These concepts include but go beyond the individual and his unmet dependency needs. For multiple reasons, some parents consciously try to give more both emotionally and materially to their children than they received from their own parents. They may do so at their own expense while, in addition, neglecting the grandparents. The underlying anger, resentment and guilt feelings toward their families of origin may remain untouched. Yet these experiences of exploitation and injustice may be important long-term motivational determinants.

In other words, whether the quality or quantity of the caring has been minimal or maximal, loyalty ties exist and indebtedness occurs. A family member may be caught in a denied or otherwise invisible loyalty bind and so may inevitably find himself in a guilt-laden position, which may interfere with his involvement and commitment in his marital and parental relationships.

By helping all family members face their invisible loyalties and obligations, a rebalancing of time, effort, interest or concrete services may begin to take place. The therapist may help dispel disappointment, anger or lack of trust, relieve guilt feelings and thus improve the functions of all family members. The scapegoated older person, marital partner or child may be relieved of these negative roles.

Many spouses often give the impression that there is little or no direct involvement with their families of origin or that repayment of emotional indebtedness is not expected of them. Such statements must be explored carefully and fully to determine the nature and extent of the involvements. Often it is the spouse or young children who make the most accurate comments regarding current relationships between the parents and their families of origin. The children carry the wishes and hope for reconnection and reconciliation. Since they are also less disappointed and guilt-ridden, it often will be the children who directly reveal the intensity of the current involvement with both sets of grandparents.

Family members who actively continue to appropriately balance their obligations as they pass through and into new phases of family life can then tolerate and support individual and family growth processes. For example, in the illustration that follows, as Mrs. P's relationship with her husband and her parents improved, her individual symptoms disappeared.

INTERGENERATIONAL-FAMILY THERAPY TECHNIQUES

In the course of marital and family treatment, when it has become evident to the marital pair that the relationships with one or both families of origin need exploration and improvement, the practice is to suggest that their parents become actively and directly a part of the treatment process whether physically present or not. The choice as to whether the older parents do or do not attend sessions is left up to the adult child and his parents. Bowen seems to bring this issue up much earlier with patients and family-therapy trainees. He "coaches" the person about their visits or "voyages" to their families of origin and other important extended-family members. (See also Anonymous, "Toward the Differentiation of a Self in One's Own Family," 1972.)

After working through much anxiety, fear and other resistances, some families eventually do bring grandparents into the sessions, while others even refuse to extend an invitation. It requires much discussion of purpose and aims before there is some relief of anxiety and fear about the grandparents attending sessions.

While the direct inclusion in sessions has provided in vivo learning for the family members as well as for the therapist, improvement has occurred even when the grandparents have refused to come. In some instances the grandparents live far away, yet changes in the relationships are reported verbally and are confirmed from the telephone exchanges, holiday visits and letters that are shared with the therapists.

The family therapist must help the spouse convey to his or her parents that the purpose is not to use either generation as a destructive target for each one's hurt, disappointed, angry feelings. Fears must be dispelled regarding verbal or physical loss of control as a result of underlying feelings of past injustices toward parents. The tentative *aims* are steadily clarified: hope for more adult-to-adult understanding and improved overall relationships. This can develop only as old feelings and accounts are faced and reworked. The parents must also rectify their own hopelessness about change ensuing between the generations. The more symbiotic the family, the more "certainty" may be expressed of "unchangeability" between the generations.

It should always be made clear that family members are free to arrive for any session in any combination of persons they may wish. There is no way of predicting who will have the courage for the explorations or at what point a grandparent or sibling will arrive. However, if the husband chooses to include his mother and father-in-law in a session, the therapist should emphasize that the focus will not be on the in-law relationship but that he will be placed in the observer's role. Some families are able to talk openly and freely in the presence of their in-laws, while others will be frozen. A parent may also decide not to include the children when the older parents attend the sessions. These choices and decisions should fundamentally be left with the person who is bringing in the older generation.

In an initial parent–older parent session, at first there is usually a polite but tense phase. The older parent must be helped by the family member and not by the therapist alone in openly stating the hope and purpose of the session. Invariably, there may be some degree of disappointment; bitter recriminations about past injustices and a seeming impasse may ensue. In other cases a defensive protectiveness blocks meaningful exchanges. The hope is to move out of the "blame syndrome" to a deeper level of reciprocal discussion between the generations.

The therapist may then encourage the older parents to share information about their lives. Frequently in the telling, painful affect is attached to the events, and this often is a very moving experience both for the parents and for their son or daughter.

This therapeutic intergenerational process enables a phase of reidentification to begin to take place between the parents and may replace the old, deprived or distorted aspects of their relationship. It does not develop as a result of mere confrontation of abreaction among generations. It can evolve only in a process that brings about a rebalancing of indebtedness and reciprocal repayment among the generations. Each family member in all three generations becomes aware of the complementary relational positions of being a parent and a child, as well as of changing phases and needs, both individually and family-wise. The inclusion of adult siblings from one's family of origin also facilitates the process of change.

CLINICAL ILLUSTRATION

In the situation to be presented, the couple came because they seemed concerned mostly over their children's reactions to their recent separation and reconciliation. In this situation the work with the extended family took place totally outside the sessions.

Mrs. P said that she and her husband were having violent physical battles so she left her husband, taking their three children upstate to stay with a maternal aunt. Mr. P came to claim his family, but because he was slightly intoxicated, Mrs. P's two brothers called in a local magistrate. A reconciliation was brought about after Mr. P agreed to go for marital therapy. Mrs. P said not only that Mr. P was intolerant and self-centered but that he was secretive about his work, his work hours and his income. Mr. P claimed his wife nagged him. She worried too much about his whereabouts and his drinking and did not trust him. They both agreed that the marital conflicts and tensions were increased after the birth of their youngest child, age seven, a son who had muscular dystrophy.

They readily described their difficulties on both sides of the family. After Mrs. P's mother died in 1968 at the age of 50 (heart condition), her father married a woman with young children. Mrs. P did not feel comfortable when visiting their home, but felt that her father seemed to prefer his stepchildren to his grandchildren. She could not discuss this with him, but was most hurt that her father showed little or no reaction to her son's illness or prognosis. Her guilt was excessive since she also felt her husband blamed her for the son's condition, and as a result, she could not accept comforting from her father or husband.

During this period, she was urged to write and visit her father more frequently, to make a special effort to discuss privately what she still needed or wanted from him. When she was able to be open and direct with her father, he was able to reassure her of his continued deep interest in both her son and her. This seemed to modify some of the anger that had been placed on Mr. P. Mr. P insisted that he had never blamed his wife for his son's defective health, which was in reality passed down through the maternal side.

There was an even more acute crisis in Mr. P's family. Several months prior to the separation, Mr. P's mother had a stroke and, after her hospitalization, had gone to live with a son and daughter-in-law, who insisted that she had to be moved from their home. Mr. P, as the second oldest son and his mother's favorite, felt that he had to come up with an alternative plan. He had always been the protector and later the provider of his mother and siblings when his alcoholic father had been abusive and irresponsible.

When Mr. P suggested bringing his mother into their home, Mrs. P became very upset. For the first time in their marriage and in a therapy session, she accused Mr. P of loving his mother more than he had ever cared for her. She felt his mother had always come first, and if she had ever needed any work to be done in their family home, he was immediately available. Last summer he had spent an entire week of his two weeks vacation doing this, and he had been upset when his wife and children expressed disappointment.

To the surprise of everyone, Mrs. P consented to taking her mother-in-law into her home. She stated that at first it was even repulsive to bathe, dress and feed her mother-in-law. During this phase Mr. P beamed with praise for his wife; came home promptly every evening and, for the first time, helped with many of the chores. His wife was overwhelmed by his expressed gratitude to his mother. There was a new kind of reconciliation between the two women.

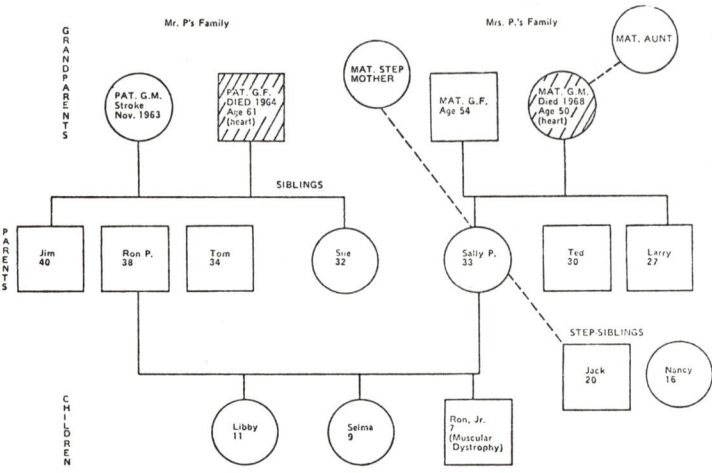

Figure 1.   Families of Origin.

After the mother-in-law died, Mrs. P said she had done for her only what she had done for her own mother before her death. Taking care of the paternal grandparent had brought Mr. and Mrs. P and the children much closer together. The mutual scapegoating, the accusations and guilt-producing comments that had characterized the early sessions no longer occurred. Mrs. P laughingly said that she was no longer an outsider as far as her husband and his siblings were concerned: "They were all openly grateful to her."

A major shift seemed to have taken place. Mr. and Mrs. P were less guilt-ridden, and they no longer used each other as a target for projecting their bad and negative feelings. Even when this was agreed on, neither seemed as vulnerable or insecure with the other. Even though Mrs. P was shy with anyone other than family, for the first time her husband invited her on a business-vacation trip, which they enjoyed immensely.

INTERLOCKING AND FAMILIAL DYNAMICS

From an individual and dyadic point of view, Mr. and Mrs. P can be seen as passively hostile, dependent, depressed, but collusively interlocked in who is to blame or who is responsible for giving more of themselves to their nuclear and extended family. However, from a familial perspective they are parentified children with their families of origin. In other words, each one had been the capable, responsible, available members who always felt that they had not received recognition for all that they had given or done.

In the marriage it might appear that they are vying for control of the other, but on another level the competition centers on who is the responsible one, who is irresponsible; who gives more and who gives less. Additionally, they are still struggling in the intergenerational sense with giving and receiving care: Mr. P assumes the physical and emotional care of his mother, who suffered a stroke; Mrs. P struggles with her father's seeming indifference, not only over her son's severe physical handicap, but essentially over recognition for herself. Even though she consciously states that she is glad her father is being taken care of by his second wife, she basically feels abandoned by him since the death of her mother.

We also get a clear picture of the sibling support system. When Mrs. P separated from her husband, a maternal aunt and two brothers effected a reconciliation based on Mr. P's promise to secure therapy. Mr. P feels obligated not only to take care of his mother but to relieve his siblings and an in-law of the care of a stroke patient. For the first time Mrs. P. feels accepted in the in-law system after the mother-in-law comes to live in her home.

In facing these conflicts and obligations as a parent, a spouse and part of a family of origin, each person is helped during the therapeutic process to rebalance his or her accounts. The ghosts from the past as well as the current problems are brought out in the three-generation perspective. This then provides a new and more constructive alternative behavior. When they first arrived for therapy, they were enmeshed in a mutually destructive scapegoating process, which made each one feel even more hurt and vulnerable. This process had escalated to such a degree prior to therapy that a separation had ensued and there was talk of divorce as a solution. These solutions were discarded, but the behavior helped to heal and strengthen the parental and grandparental relationships.

CONCLUSION

To treat a marital relationship as an entity separate from the parental and intergenerational dynamics can be as limited as treating an individual as if he were a closed system. By understanding and treating marriage within the full field of a two- or three-generation context, we are provided an opportunity not only for diminishing conflict and guilt but for rebalancing and thus improving all of the relationships.

REFERENCES

Anonymous. Toward the differentiation of a self in one's own family. In *Family interaction*, Framo, J. (Ed.). New York: Springer, 1972, pp. 111–166.

Boszormenyi-Nagy, I. A theory of relationships: Experience and transaction. In *Intensive family therapy*, I. Boszormenyi-Nagy and J. Framo (Eds.). New York: Harper and Row, 1965, pp. 33–86.

Boszormenyi-Nagy, I., and Spark, G. *Invisible loyalties: Reciprocity in intergenerational family therapy*. New York: Harper and Row, 1973.

Bowen, M. The Use of Family Theory in Clinical Practice, *Comp. Psychiat.* 1966, 7, 5, 345–374.

Spark, Geraldine. Grandparents and intergenerational family therapy, *Fam. Proc.* 1974, *13*, 225–238.

Spark, Geraldine, and Brody, Elaine. The aged are family members. In *Fam. Proc.*, 1970, *9*; 195–210.

Chapter 6

Bowen Theory and Therapy

Michael E. Kerr

Murray Bowen has usually presented his family-systems theory by organizing it around eight major concepts, namely triangles, scale of differentiation, nuclear-family emotional process, family-projection process, multigenerational-transmission process, sibling position, emotional cutoff and societal emotional process (Bowen, 1978). The goal of this chapter is not to again describe these concepts in detail, but to attempt to integrate them in a way that will, I hope, aid the reader's understanding of Bowen theory. A model of cardiovascular system dynamics in health and disease is introduced early in the chapter for the purpose of keeping the reader's focus on the fact that this is a *systems theory* and not a theory that can be integrated into an individual model. The chapter will be divided into a section on theory, a section on therapy and a conclusion.

BOWEN THEORY

Family Emotional System

The central formulation of Bowen theory is the existence of a family emotional system with illnesses or dysfunctions, such as schizophrenia, being viewed as symptoms of a disorder of this family emotional system.

The phrase "emotional system" introduces two concepts requiring some elaboration, namely systems and emotionality. Systems are comprised of forces that counterbalance one another through feedback mechanisms. The components of a system function interdependently, and so the activity of any part must be understood in the context of the function it serves in the total system. A family can be thought of as such a system, a family relationship system, in which the functioning of each member is related to the functioning of every other member. The concept of emotionality is introduced as the driving force that accounts for the activity of the family relationship system—in other words, that which is driving people to do what they do. This emotionality is considered a product of man's phylogeny.

This phylogenetic, or evolutionary, perspective of human emotional functioning is increasingly supported by research in a number of areas. One such area is MacLean's work on the triune brain (MacLean, 1978). MacLean has demonstrated that significant portions of man's brain are essentially identical to other animals' and that man's uniqueness rests in the elaborate development of a neocortex, or "thinking brain." According to MacLean, development of this neocortex does not negate the influence of the more primitive brain areas, namely the R-complex and limbic system, the areas man has in common with reptiles and lower mammals. MacLean hypothesizes that much of man's activity is influenced by these lower brain areas in much the same way that these areas influence the activity of other animals.

Another important research area has been sociobiology. The publication of Wilson's book *Sociobiology: The New Synthesis* has renewed attention to the similarities between human behavior and the behavior of animals (Wilson, 1975).

The concept of a family emotional system, then, describes the emotional chain reactions that occur among people in families, reactions that tie the emotional functioning of one family member integrally to another. Awareness of this family emotional system is critical for understanding the development and course of all types of symptoms in a family, whether they be physical illness, mental illness or social acting-out behavior.

Another important aspect of all systems, including the family system, is that they can exist in states of equilibrium or disequilibrium. Although systems are comprised of counterbalancing forces, these forces are not always in balance. When they are in balance, a state of equilibrium exists, and when they are out of balance, the system is in *disequilibrium*. When a family emotional system is in equilibrium, no new symptoms are appearing and any chronic symptoms are relatively stable. States of family disequilibrium are associated with the appearance of new symptoms and/or the deterioration of chronic symptoms, such as alcoholism or rheumatoid arthritis. Increasing anxiety is what drives a balanced family system toward imbalance or disequilibrium. As the system moves toward disequilibrium, automatic homeostatic or compensatory mechanisms come into play in an attempt to maintain equilibrium. At this point, introducing an analogy of the cardiovascular system might be helpful for illustrating the interrelationship of system equilibrium—disequilibrium, stress, compensatory mechanisms and symptoms.

Cardiovascular Systems and Homeostasis

The cardiovascular system consists of the heart (to pump blood), the arteries (to carry oxygen and nutrients to the tissues) and the veins (to carry metabolic products away from the tissues and return the blood to the heart). The counterbalancing forces of the system include blood pressure, vessel resistance to blood flow, volume of blood pumped per beat, heart rate and tissue requirements. All of these forces mutually influence one another through a series of feedback loops.

The cardiovascular system can be thrown out of balance by a number of things, one of which is heart failure. Heart failure means the heart cannot pump all the blood that is returned to it and tissue requirements are not met. Heart failure can be precipitated by many conditions, among which are high blood pressure and coronary artery disease. Heart failure is said to be *latent* when its presence is brought out only by significant stress, such as exercise. Latent heart failure, in other words, can be compensated for by homeostatic mechanisms as long as the stress on the system is not too great. Congestive failure, in contrast, is heart failure associated with chronic abnormal congestion of the circulation. Fluid has seeped out of the vessels and backed up into the lungs, liver and lower extremities.

When the cardiovascular system is thrown out of balance by something such as heart failure, reserve, homeostatic or compensatory mechanisms are called into action in an attempt to maintain balance or equilibrium. These are normal mechanisms designed to make sure the cardiovascular system meets tissue needs. One such compensatory mechanism is increased production of adrenalin and activation of the sympathetic nervous system. Both adrenalin and the sympathetic system stimulate contraction of the blood vessels, making their diameter smaller and increasing resistance to blood flow in certain less vital areas. This increased resistance helps maintain the blood pressure in spite of a weakened heart and also increases the force of the blood returning to the heart. The latter has the same effect as whipping a tired horse; in other words, the increased pressure of blood pouring back into the heart stimulates a stronger contraction. A second compensatory or reserve mechanism designed to maintain system equilibrium is increased retention of salt and water by the kidneys. This fluid retention increases the volume of blood in a relatively closed vascular space, thereby increasing pressure in the system and increasing stimulation of the weak heart. The third compensating mechanism is enlargement of the heart, with the heart then handling more blood, though pumping it less efficiently.

A healthy cardiovascular system, moderately impaired one and severely impaired system differ in the characteristic balance of forces in the system, use of compensatory mechanisms and amount of reserve or adaptability to stress. A healthy cardiovascular system can maintain balance or equilibrium under practically all levels of stress and will make only transient use of compensatory mechanisms. It has maximum reserve and experiences no acute or chronic symptoms. A moderately impaired system, on the other hand, can maintain equilibrium only under mild to moderate stress. It employs compensatory mechanisms chronically and, therefore, has less reserve. The moderately impaired system will develop symptoms when the stress increases above moderate levels, but the symptoms will disappear when the stress subsides. A severely impaired cardiovascular system can maintain equilibrium only under ideal low-stress conditions. It employs compensatory mechanisms chronically and excessively and has practically no reserve. The least additional stress can throw the system into irretrievable imbalance. This severely impaired system experiences chronic symptoms, symptoms that are complications of the compensatory mechanisms designed to maintain equilibrium. These mechanisms are helpful to the system up to a point, but when used excessively they become *the symptoms of the system problem* and can actually begin to drag the whole system down. Increased retention of salt and water, for example, although initially designed to increase pressure in the vascular space and stimulate the heart, can lead to fluid backing up into the lungs (producing difficulty breathing), into the liver (producing enlargement and damage), and into the legs (leading to numerous secondary complications). These parts of the body, in other words, are "sacrificed" to maintain equilibrium in the total system, but when they develop into serious symptoms, they come back to "haunt" the system and pull it down. Leaving the cardiovascular model, let us now turn the discussion of the counterbalancing forces in a family system.

Individuality and Togetherness Life Forces

Bowen conceptualizes two primary life forces that counterbalance each other in the family emotional system: a force toward *individuality*, or *differentiation*, and a force toward *togetherness*, or *fusion*. It is a disturbance in the balance of these forces that can precipitate physical, mental or acting-out symptoms in a family.

The togetherness, or fusion, force is rooted deep in man's biological makeup. Within the individual it is manifested in a strong need for a sense of connection with others, a sense of belonging. Within the relationship system, it is reflected in the forces that *act on people*, overriding their individuality and subjugating their functioning to the group. In essence, then, togetherness is a binding force, a force that makes the functioning of one person integrally tied to that of another. Emotional reactions, such as sensitivity to approval and criticism, a need to please others, feeling threatened by signs of rejection, concern with where one fits on the hierarchy, sympathetic reactions to the plight of others, a sense of responsibility *for* the well-being of others or the expectation that others are responsible for the well-being of self, are all components of the togetherness force. Even the development of belief systems can be totally or partially influenced by this togetherness force. Such beliefs are determined by the *emotional influencing* of the relationship system. This could mean blind compliance with the group's beliefs to retain approval and membership, *or* automatic rejection of the group's beliefs, as is the case with a rebel. Dogmatism is an example of emotionally influenced beliefs.

Activity of the togetherness force is most obvious when it is overriding in a relationship system. When this is the case, people have particular difficulty in permitting each other to be what they are and in not giving in to this kind of pressure. Projection, excessive blaming of self or others and scapegoating are prominent in such a system. There is significant intolerance for differences in thinking as the overriding togetherness force moves the system toward sameness. Decision making is highly emotionally reactive, aimed at relieving immediate anxiety without consideration of a long-term view.

When the togetherness force operates at an optimum level, it contributes to people enjoying each other, being attracted to each other, taking pleasure in closeness, affection and a sense of group belonging. In short, it contributes significantly to successful social organization.

The individuality, or differentiation, force is also rooted deep in man's biological makeup. Within the relationship system, it is reflected in the capacity for autonomous functioning, to be a separate self, counterbalancing the overriding of self by the togetherness force. Within the individual, it is manifested in an ability to keep intellectual and emotional functioning separate and also in an overall decrease in emotional reactivity. Most importantly, differentiation means an ability and willingness to stand alone and assume responsibility for one's own life. This ranges from not blaming others for your own anxiety to the courage to make decisions and stick by them.

The potential for the development of differentiation appears to be greatest in man, that potential being related to the evolutionary development of a massive neocortex, or "thinking," brain. "Its explosive growth [neocortex] in phylogeny is one of the most dramatic transformations known to comparative anatomy" (Herrick, 1933). There are, in a sense, many levels of differentiated activity, ranging from selfishness, a rather primitive form that can be observed in baboon troops as well as man, to the capacity to be a separate self while at the same time recognizing one's responsibility *to* others.

Differentiated beliefs, in contrast to togetherness-determined beliefs, are acquired through an intellectual process and are not dictated by emotionality within self or by emotional pressure from the relationship system. When stated, they are stated calmly and with an associated respect for the beliefs of others.

When at its optimum, the differentiation force makes a significant contribution to the cohesive, cooperative and altruistic qualities of social groups, successful social organization being a by-product of an optimum balance of the differentiation and togetherness life forces. There is probably no such thing as a totally differentiated act or totally togetherness-determined act. These two forces are mixed, much like two colors are mixed to produce a third color, and both forces permeate all aspects of human activity.

Variations in the Individuality-Togetherness Balance

While both the individuality and togetherness forces permeate all aspects of human activity, individuals, families and social groups differ in the *relative* influence or balance of these forces that are characteristic for them over time. One person's entire life, for example, may be characterized by an *average* high degree of differentiation-determined activity, while another's life course may reflect an *average* high degree of togetherness-determined activity. What constitutes equilibrium of these forces for one person or family may not be equilibrium for another person or family. This is analogous to the cardiovascular system in that the balance of forces in a healthy cardiovascular system is quite different than the balance in an impaired system, even though both systems may exist in equilibrium. These differing individuality and togetherness balances in families are a product of and are reflected in the life styles of family members and in the way they relate to one another. An example of how these differing individuality-togetherness balances are reflected in a family would be different sensitivity to fluctuations in closeness and distance in relationships. Families in which the balance of forces is strongly toward togetherness, also referred to as highly fused families, have a characteristic balance of a sense of distance and closeness that is comfortable for them. In one highly fused family this balance may be characterized by a lot of mandatory closeness and involvement in one anothers' lives, while in another equally fused family it may be characterized by a lot of distance. Better differentiated families, families in which the individuality-togetherness balance leans toward individuality, have similar closeness-distance balances in relationships, but disturbances in this balance stir less *emotional reactivity* than is the case with a highly fused family. Intense feelings of "too much closeness" or "too much distance" coupled with difficulty tolerating such feelings are more pronounced in highly fused or poorly differentiated families.

The reason for differences in the relative balance of individuality and togetherness forces in individuals, families and social groups can be understood by examining the evolution of family emotional process across many generations. A long chain of events that can eventually lead to rather marked differences in individuality-togetherness balance among individuals and families begins with the fact that within the same family the parents' relationships with their various children differ in the amount of togetherness- or fusion-determined activity that is characteristic of each relationship. Typically, if there are two children, one grows up more fused into the family emotional process than the other. The child who grows up more fused becomes "programmed" for equivalent degrees of fusion in all future relationships. Compared to the less-fused child or "free spirit," the more-fused one has a greater dependency on a sense of connectedness with others, greater intolerance for isolation *or* too much closeness, is more of an emotional reactor, has more fusion of his intellectual and emotional systems and is less capable of differentiated activity. This more-fused child *usually becomes more programmed in this direction than even his or her parents*.

Describing some of the differences in these two children as they progress through childhood and adolescence may be helpful in illustrating this concept. When the most-fused child and free-spirited one are small and the mother puts them outside to play, she worries more about the most-fused one. How will she keep him busy and entertained? She worries less about her free spirit, who has little difficulty setting his or her own direction, even at this early age. Mothers often say they react differently to their various children, but attribute this to the fact that their children are different. While differing reactions in the mother are *in part* related to differences in the children, *the process actually begins in the parents*, particularly in the mother, with the father supporting it. The differential reaction of the parents to the various children *leads* to emotional differences in the children. Within a short period of time, it does become a reenforcing process, with both parents and children being equal participants. The most-fused or most emotionally involved child (this being a relative difference between the children and not all-or-none) becomes exquisitely sensitive to the parents' reactions to him. If the mother leaves this one playing by himself, he quickly becomes bored and reinitiates involvement with her. She may become frustrated with this clinging and dependent child, seeing the problem as in the child and missing the role of her own emotional reactivity to the child as an influence on his or her behavior. The mother, for example, often feels responsible for keeping the child entertained and the child soon expects this of her.

When the children begin school, getting this most-involved child with the "right" teacher becomes all-important to the parents. In school, the less well differentiated child may become an emotionally driven overachiever or an emotionally reactive underachiever. He or she may be an unusually compliant child or an unusually rebellious one. In any event, this child is highly reactive to the harmony of the relationship systems in which he functions, and successful academic performance as well as control of behavior becomes integrally tied to the status of these relationships. The free-spirited child is less influenced by relationship harmony and disharmony. He or she is a more consistent performer and capable of structuring his or her own life. The school will often report that the most-fused child responds to a one-to-one relationship and a more structured atmosphere. This child may excel one year and droop the next, depending on the teacher's investment in him and on the classroom situation. Parents often put increasing effort into making sure their child is always in the right situation with a teacher who will take special interest in him, assuring good performance.

Much has been written about adolescence, but the experience of adolescence is not the same for the better differentiated and less well differentiated siblings. The poorly differentiated, more emotionally reactive child will often deal with his underlying dependence on the parents by making a "federal case" out of adolescence, asserting his or her "independence" by anti-parent, antiestablishment activities and joining the most "far-out" peer groups. This most-fused child will often cut off emotionally from his or her parents during adolescence with an intensity equivalent to his underlying dependence or fusion. He or she cuts off from the parents but replicates the fusion within his or her peer group and other relationships. The most-fused child may also react to adolescence by not getting involved with peers of outside activities, becoming a loner. Meanwhile, the better differentiated sibling is navigating through adolescence with less uproar. His or her relationship with the parents retains fairly open communication as he grows smoothly apart from them. The fused child "breaks away" from parents, while the less fused one "grows away." The peer groups of the less-fused child are more orderly, and there is less insistence on sameness within the group.

When these two children marry, they are attracted to mates of *equivalent* levels of differentiation or equivalent needs for fusion. In a couple, one mate may appear to be self-sufficient and independent, while the other may appear helpless and dependent, making one seem more differentiated than the other. This difference is more apparent than real, with the underlying basic differentiation of the mates being essentially the same. In any event, when each child does marry he fuses into the marital relationship to a degree equivalent to what had existed in his parental relationship. Since the most-fused child leaves home "programmed" more toward fusion or togetherness than even his or her parents were, then his marriage will be even more strongly fused than his parents' marriage. In contrast, the fusion in the less-involved child's marriage may be even *less* than the fusion of his parents' marriage. So two children from the same family establish marriages that differ in their relative balance of individuality and togetherness forces, one marriage balanced more toward togetherness than the previous generation and one balanced less toward togetherness than the previous generation or generation I. If there are several children in a family, typically one grows up less well differentiated than the parents, some much like the parents and another one more differentiated. Sometimes the differences between one generation and the next are fairly significant, but much of the time the changes are subtle.

The children of both of these marriages in generation II, then, will be subject to the same kind of emotional forces to which their parents were subjected. Generation III, the children of generation II, will then have its free spirits and most-involved children. Imagine, then, this process repeating over six, eight, ten generations, most-involved children marrying people like themselves, producing their most-involved child, who in turn marries someone like himself, etc. Another generational line of the family may be free spirits marrying other free spirits, who produce even freer spirits, etc. After this process repeats for many generations, the contrasts among the descendants become greater and greater. After, for example, eight generations descending from the original parents in generation I, there will be segments of the family significantly more fused than the original parents and segments significantly more differentiated. Equilibrium for one branch of the family will be tilted heavily toward togetherness, while equilibrium for another branch will lean more toward differentiation. There will also be segments of the family whose differentiation level is quite similar to the original ancestors. So the balance of individuality and togetherness in a family and in the people who make up that family is a product of many generations, not just one lifetime. This is important to keep in mind when thinking about helping families to "change."

Symptoms and System Balance

Given that individuals, families and social groups, based on the evolution of emotional process over many generations, differ in the relative balance of individuality and togetherness forces that is characteristic for them over time, what is its significance? While a system that is heavily balanced toward either togetherness or individuality can achieve equilibrium, *the more fused the family system, the more it behaves like an impaired cardiovascular system*. A highly fused family system is more vulnerable to shifting toward disequilibrium when under stress with associated symptoms and is more likely to have chronic symptoms present even when it is in equilibrium.

An explanation of the greater vulnerability to the development of acute and chronic symptoms of a strongly fused system should begin with a discussion of anxiety. The word "anxiety," as used here, is meant to convey something that runs very deep in the organism, affecting its internal systems. It is not simply equated with statements such as "I feel anxious," but would be better equated with states of anxiety that can be observed in groups of whales and other nonhuman animals. Clinical observations confirm that the more fused the family system, the more *chronic* anxiety it experiences. Explanations as to why this should be so are admittedly speculative, but a way to think about it is that the more strongly fused the system, the greater the people's need for one another in order to stabilize the functioning of self. In a strongly fused system, family members lean heavily on one another and pressure one another in many ways. This needing, leaning and pressuring generates anxiety. So the greater the fusion of the system, the more fusion-generated anxiety exists, and since the system is chronically fused, the product of many generations, the anxiety is chronic.

Now, as mentioned in the discussion of the cardiovascular system, stress or anxiety drives a system toward disequilibrium, or imbalance of the system's forces. In the case of a family, anxiety increases the activity of the togetherness force, creating an imbalance of the individuality and togetherness forces. When this occurs, again as is the case with the cardiovascular-system, compensatory or homeostatic mechanisms come into play to maintain equilibrium. Bowen has described four such mechanisms in a family system, which are the following: emotional distance, emotional conflict, fusion-exclusion (triangles) and pseudo-positions (dominant-adaptive). Each mechanism becomes more active as anxiety increases in the system in order to reduce that anxiety and maintain equilibrium.

The mechanism of *emotional distance* is perhaps the most obvious way of trying to cope with increased anxiety in a relationship. People close off from one another, either by physically removing themselves or through the use of internal mechanisms. The closing off can include the avoiding of emotional subjects in conversation, sexual turn-offs and a host of other things. While the need for others *remains* great, the sense of encroachment or "too much closeness" without this distance can make the distance an acceptable compromise. The distance can lower fusion-generated anxiety and maintain equilibrium, but a certain amount of capacity for closeness is sacrificed. Use of the word "compromise" is not intended to convey that this is an intellectual decision. It is, rather, an automatic emotional "decision."

The mechanism of *emotional conflict* allows intense relating and maintains distance at one and the same time. Typically, a marriage that employs this mechanism provides a type of equilibrium which, in spite of the relationship conflict, protects the individual functioning of each spouse, the anxiety being "bound" in the relationship and not within either spouse.

The use of the phrase *fusion-exclusion* to describe the third family compensatory mechanism as opposed to the word "triangle" is an attempt to keep focus on the emotional process that is the basis of triangles. This is a mechanism in which two people can stay in close contact with each other, avoiding fusion-generated anxiety, by either excluding a third person from their relationship or *focusing* their energies on a third person—for example, a child.

The final mechanism, pseudo-positions, is one in which people assume "pretend" postures in relationship to one another, for example, strong-weak, one-up and one-down, dominant-submissive, overresponsible-underresponsible, overadequate-inadequate polarities. Two strongly fused, insecure people can maintain harmonious closeness without significant anxiety by maintaining these "pretend" postures. One person *acts and feels* strong and secure while the other acts and feels weak and insecure. These positions have advantages to both parties and are fostered by both. The advantages rest in the reductions of the anxiety of too much closeness and maintenance of equilibrium in the system. The obvious disadvantage is that people go through life with an unrealistic appraisal of themselves. The word "pretend" is not intended to imply an intellectual process. This is, again, an emotional process that has some fascinating parallels in nonhuman animals. Dominant and submissive behaviors serve important roles in stabilizing social organizations of many animals.

Families, then, may use several or all of these homeostatic mechanisms to maintain equilibrium. *The more the family system is balanced toward togetherness, coupled with the associated chronic anxiety, the more these mechanisms are chronically in operation to preserve equilibrium.* All families use a certain amount of distance, experience some conflict, scapegoat, blame and pretend to be better or worse than they are, but the more-fused family does more of it. A highly fused system, chronically employing these mechanisms to retain equilibrium, has *minimal reserve* to cope with any additional stress. As in the case of the cardiovascular system, homeostatic mechanisms are designed to be helpful to the system as a whole, though they may be deleterious to some of its parts. But when these mechanisms are chronically in operation and excessively used, they eventually can become the symptoms of the system problem. The type of symptoms that develop, as with the cardiovascular system, are related to which homeostatic mechanisms are chronically in effect. Emotional distance, for example, driven to the extreme, results in alienation and isolation. Stabilizing distance, at the extreme, converts to destabilizing isolation. Emotional conflict can lead to fragmentation of the system or an inability to maintain the level of cooperation necessary for successful social organization. Fusion-exclusion, when, for example, the focus is on a child, can lead to symptoms in the child. Pseudo-posturing can, at its extremes, result in symptoms in either spouse. An overfunctioning, overadequate person can develop symptoms as well as an underfunctioning, underadequate person. The vulnerable spouse is the one making the most adjustments within self to preserve the harmony of the system. This adaptive one "absorbs" the problem of the system within him or herself.

To summarize symptom development, a well-differentiated family system, hypothetical only at this juncture in man's evolution, would behave like a healthy cardiovascular system. It would be highly adaptive to stress, experience minimal chronic anxiety, use homeostatic mechanisms transiently and have significant reserve. A moderately differentiated family system is analogous to the situation with latent heart failure. This system experiences moderate amounts of fusion-generated chronic anxiety, makes moderate chronic use of compensatory mechanisms, has moderate reserve, and symptoms will appear and disappear depending on the level of stress on the system. A poorly differentiated family system is analogous to congestive heart failure. Such a system experiences marked levels of chronic anxiety, makes chronic and excessive use of compensatory mechanisms, has little reserve or adaptability, and chronic symptoms are present, even when the system is in equilibrium. Any additional stress and increase in symptoms can destroy the system. A schizophrenic person, for example, can stabilize a family system up to a point, but eventually can drag the entire system down.

Anxiety and Life Events

Descriptions thus far have focused on the basic balance of individuality and togetherness forces that evolve over multiple generations in a family, a balance that is characteristic of an individual for a lifetime and of a family across generations. In addition to these basic long-term differences in individuality-togetherness balance among individuals and families, there are also more short-term shifts in this balance *within* the same family or person. These short-term shifts are triggered by events that increase or decrease the anxiety in that person or family system. In the nonhuman animal world, these anxiety-generating events can be a product of the relationship among animals of the same species or can be tied to the relationship between the species and its environment. In the study of homo sapiens, disturbances between man and nature as generators of anxiety are less well understood than distrubances between man and man, and for that reason the latter will be focused on here. This is not to imply that disturbances between man and nature are not equally important as generators of anxiety in human society; it is simply that less is known about this area.

Regardless of the basic balance of emotional forces in a system, *anxiety disturbs that balance by increasing the activity of the togetherness force.* With this increased activity of the togetherness force and resultant disequilibrium, the family's compensatory or homeostatic mechanisms also become more active. As mentioned previously, excessive use of these mechanisms can then lead to symptom development. When the anxiety decreases, equilibrium is restored, acute symptoms subside and chronic symptoms stabilize. The system, in other words, returns to its basic balance.

To make matters a bit confusing, addition of a person to a system can increase *or* decrease the anxiety in that system, and by the same token, removal of a person from a system can increase *or* decrease the anxiety. Simply a *change in functioning* of a person already in the system can have the same effects. It is not always easy to predict which way the anxiety will go when a person enters or leaves a system, but there are certain predictable events or phases when it does go one way or the other! Predictable events are events most families will experience in the course of their development. These predictable, potentially anxiety-generating periods include the following: a person leaving home, marriage, birth of the first child or subsequent child, children becoming less dependent on parents, children in the process of leaving home and retirement.

In looking at the first of these events, a person leaving home, some people function better when they leave, others worse, but it always has some effect and *the more fused the person to his or her family, the more pronounced this effect*. The anxiety that can occur during this period is not necessarily just in the person leaving or trying to leave home. For example, a nineteen-year old boy goes off to college and has an acute psychotic breakdown before the year is out. He drops out and returns home; family anxiety markedly increases. The next several years or more may be characterized by considerable instability in the parents' relationship with the son. The boy repeatedly fails at functioning independently, and the parents are in a state of near-panic in dealing with him. The opposite of this example is the person who can function effectively as long as he or she stays away from the emotional environment of his or her family. That person does "better" when he leaves home.

The second potentially anxiety-generating event is marriage. Problems surfacing in the year to two after a marriage are related usually to the anxiety generated by the fusion. Marriage, for some people, cuts off their sense of having an "escape" route. They feel trapped and anxiety escalates. Again, the more togetherness-oriented the people, the more likely this is to occur. On the other hand, a marital fusion can stabilize two unstable people, at least until the birth of the first child.

Pregnancy and childbirth, a third predictable event, can often lead to a striking buildup of anxiety in the system. Addition of a new person to a system can lead to a shift of emotional forces in the system that leaves one person in a compromised position and with serious symptoms. A certain amount of increased anxiety in the system with pregnancy and childbirth is not unusual. A reasonably well-differentiated system can adapt to this, and the system soon reequilibriates. At the other extreme, *a poorly differentiated system's ability to adapt can be exceeded by the birth of a child.* The resultant sustained imbalance in the system can contribute to the development of a serious symptom, like a cancer or a psychotic breakdown. On the other hand, when the anxiety dramatically decreases in a marital fusion following a pregnancy, this suggests the child will function as a mechanism to stabilize the marital fusion and portends future problems for the child.

Growing independence of children is a fourth development or phase that can foster shifts in the functioning of parents and changes in the system that can trigger anxiety. An example would be a mother who, as the kids get older, pulls up out of a functionally adaptive and dependent position and begins to set more of an individual direction. Her change in functioning can trigger reactions and counterreactions in the system.

When one or all the children leave home, a fifth predictable event, another imbalance in the system can occur.

Retirement-generated problems, the final phase, are frequently related to the anxiety of "too much togetherness." The disequilibrium can be transient or lead to serious symptoms.

There are also more unpredictable events, such as deaths of parents, divorces, illnesses, geographic moves, job instability, major changes in responsibility, etc., that can trigger an imbalance in the emotional system and influence symptom development. While the event may originate outside the family, usually the key factor is the family's ability to adapt to it. For example, five hundred families in a community may be subjected to the same disturbing events, but the better-differentiated families will adapt and have few or only transient symptoms. The more-fused families are more likely to develop serious protracted symptoms. It is important to keep in mind that one event is usually not enough to explain the development of a serious physical or mental symptom. It is, rather, usually a constellation of factors or events building up on a family over a period of time that is critical for symptom development. A well-differentiated family can sustain more such events without symptom development, but *any* family can get into difficulty if the stress is great enough and long enough.

Illness and Emotional Process

There are, then, three variables that are important to consider in understanding the onset and course of mental illness, physical illness and social acting-out behavior. The first variable is the basic individuality-togetherness balance of the person or family. As mentioned previously, the more fused the system, the more chronic anxiety is present, the more homeostatic mechanisms are chronically in use and the more likely even states of equilibrium will be associated with chronic symptoms. The second variable is the life event-generated level of anxiety that is over and above the chronic fusion-generated anxiety. The third variable in symptom development is the basic homeostatic mechanisms that are in use *where* a symptom appears, depending on which mechanism is most in use.

These three emotional variables are always in the background, influencing the onset and course of all illnesses or problems. The extremes of all illnesses can be thought of as *emotional equivalents.* Alcoholism, obesity, physical illness, mental illness and even criminal behavior, when at their extremes, all reflect significant lack of differentiation. Better-differentiated people and family systems can also experience these same problems, but they are likely to be in milder form. To a certain extent, the presence of one illness "protects" from the development of other illnesses. The "natural history" of any disease, then, is significantly related to the level of differentiation of the person and level of existent anxiety in the system.

The behavior of illnesses across generations in a family also appears to be tied to the level of differentiation. The theory would predict that if the same illness appeared in a family over successive generations, in the family lines evolving toward increasing fusion or togetherness, the illness would be expected to gradually appear earlier in life and be more severe. These more-fused segments of family would be more vulnerable to developing problems around life events that better-differentiated families can adapt to without symptoms. Any illness can cluster in a family, and when it does, there are, in fact, certain lines spanning four or five generations in which illnesses appear earlier in life with each successive generation and become more severe (Kerr, 1980).

The Extended Family

Thus far, the role of differentiation and the level of anxiety in the emotional field have been described as critical factors for understanding the development of physical, mental and social acting-out symptoms in a family.

Another major area meriting special emphasis and which affects the level of anxiety in the nuclear family and symptom development is the nuclear family's relationship to the extended family system. Bowen observed that the more a nuclear family maintains viable emotional contact with their extended family system, the healthier for the family. An important principle of therapy arose out of this observation that will be described later.

Every person grows up with a *degree* of fusion to their family system. When they leave home, this fusion or emotional attachment is really unresolved. People remain emotionally reactive to the interactions in their families and have views of various members of their extended family, ranging from overly idealized to overly critical. This emotional reactiveness to the family of origin is dealt with with distance or emotional cutoff. The person then fuses into his or her marriage and nuclear family, determined not to make the same mistakes he perceived his parents to have made. The greater the fusion that existed while growing up, the greater the tendency for emotional cutoff from the family of origin. The extreme of this would be leaving home and never going back. Most people, however, fall into the category of infrequent, brief, superficial visits home in which there is an effort to avoid emotional issues. There is also the other extreme of highly fused people who never leave their family of origin, geographically or emotionally.

It is a consistent clinical observation that the more isolated a nuclear family unit becomes from the families of origin, the more vulnerable it is to escalating buildups of anxiety. When the contact with extended family is more open, these buildups are less likely. One of the best examples of this is what happens to various segments of an extended family system after an important figure, such as a matriarch, dies. The incidence of the problems in the various segments of family often rises dramatically after such a death, as these segments become more isolated and experience more chronic anxiety. The matriarch, in other words, had been the stabilizing force for the system. Wolf has studied a similar process for the entire town of Roseto, Pennsylvania (Wolf, 1978). He observed that as the stability of the extended family and social network in the town deteriorated, there was a striking increase in the incidence of heart disease!

At the risk of implying one too many parallels, which is not intended, there is a fascinating example from the nonhuman animal world that may help convey the significance of cutoff from an extended network. Gorillas born in captivity frequently are injured, mutilated and even killed by their mothers (Rock, 1978). Gorilla mothers are gentle and affectionate in the wild, rearing their young in "families" protected by a dominant male and surrounded by other seemingly content mothers. The male plays with the babies and the mother spends hours feeding and cuddling them.

Ronald Nadler, a psychologist at the Yerkes Regional Primate Research Center, observed an infant born to a mother, Paki, alone in a maternity cage. She was a good mother for a little while, but after a week she got annoyed with the infant. She neglected the baby, would not answer its cries and began dragging it around the cage. Nadler initially thought this neglect and abuse stemmed from the fact the mother had been captured and taken from her own mother at an early age. This moderately abused infant eventually was removed from Paki, but the experience was a stimulus for Nadler to study the case histories of thirty first-time gorilla mothers at Yerkes. He found that only ten of them were able to care for their babies. The rest abused, killed or ignored their infants. Of the ten good mothers, *seven were in a group or with their male companions during and after childbirth*. Nadler developed a new hypothesis, that the mother's "loneliness" was the critical variable in the abuse. When the previously described mother, Paki, had her second baby, she started out the same way, annoyed by the clinging of the infant. But when another female gorilla was moved in with her, she calmed down and was able to raise the infant on her own! Nadler next developed a group of gorillas at Yerkes, settling on one male and three females living in a compound. In less than a year, all three gave birth, all first-time mothers, and all reared their infants completely without abuse. One particularly young, nervous mother is said to have been calmed by the "sympathetic cooling" of the other gorillas. Not only was the lack of abuse impressive, but three gorilla infant births occurring that quickly in captivity was highly unusual.

One final comment on extended networks is in reference to questions that often arise regarding the role of nonfamily networks as "support systems" for families. While neighborhood units or church groups, for example, are certainly important over the long term, the more critical support variable in the human family appears to be the extended family system. Cutting off emotionally from the past generation clearly increases the chances of transmitting one's own problems or "undifferentiation" to the next generation.

BOWEN THERAPY

Family Evaluation

The guiding assumption in evaluation of a family that seeks help because of the appearance of an acute symptom, such as a psychotic reaction, or because of deterioration of a chronic symptom, such as rheumatoid arthritis, is that *the symptoms are related to an anxiety-driven imbalance in the family emotional system*. This is the guiding assumption regardless of whether a single person, married couple or entire family seeks therapy. The goals of the evaluation, then, are to assess the factors contributing to this increased anxiety in the system, define the main homeostatic mechanisms in operation in the system and assess the basic level of differentiation of the people who present for therapy and of the family systems from which they come.

The first area of evaluation, assessment of the factors generating anxiety, has already been discussed to a certain extent in terms of life events and changes in functioning of people in a system. When evaluating these factors, it is important to keep in mind that the family usually sees the symptoms as generating the anxiety. While this is partly true, the family usually has limited awareness of the buildup of anxiety that *preceded and contributed to symptom development.* Family members' opinions about factors that contribute to the problems are important, but systematic data collection is perhaps even more important because families will often overestimate and focus on the importance of certain events and underestimate the significance of other events. People often fail to recognize the interconnectedness of events in their families, and the therapist can fall into the same trap if he is not reasonably systematic in his approach, disciplining himself to inquire about events and people the family may consider irrelevant.

The second area of evaluation, assessment of homeostatic mechanisms, is made primarily on the type of symptoms present. If marital conflict is a major problem, then it can be assumed that conflict is a major mechanism for dealing with the anxiety of too much fusion in the marriage. If one spouse is symptomatic, then it can be assumed the couple has functioned in pseudo-positions in relationship to each other; in other words, harmony in the relationship has been preserved at the expense of one compromising him or herself to the other, either as an overfunctioner or as an underfunctioner. When a child is symptomatic, the potential anxiety of the marital fusion has been projected onto an overinvolved child. Keep in mind that these mechanisms can be used in a family system without leading to overt symptoms. It is when the equilibrium is disturbed and the mechanisms are "overused" that symptoms appear. Usually more than one mechanism is employed by a family, and the more subtle levels of operation of these mechanisms are accurately assessed only with experience.

The third area of evaluation, assessment of the basic individuality-togetherness balance in a family system or individual, is the most difficult. In general, higher levels of differentiation are reflected in organized and stable lives of individuals over a lifetime and families over generations. Within the limits of available opportunities, better-differentiated people will advance educationally, be involved in more demanding occupations with considerable responsibility, experience better physical and mental health and have fairly stable marriages and children. No one piece of data is sufficient to evaluate differentiation; it is gleaned, rather, from a composite of data. In addition, assessment of just one person can be misleading. A father, for example, whose high level of functioning in the above-mentioned areas would appear to indicate good differentiation, but his alcoholic wife and schizophrenic son would correct that impression. Systems thinkers who have a reasonable understanding of differentiation still fall back, to a certain extent, on "intangibles" for assessing it; intangibles that appear to indicate an ability to separate intellectual and emotional functioning. Reliance on intangibles indicates the research still to be done in this area.

The actual data collection for a family evaluation is usually organized around three basic areas: history of the presenting problem, history of the nuclear family and history of each extended family.

When both spouses attend the initial sessions, with or without the children, the history of the presenting problem is obtained by soliciting the views of each member as to when the problems began, how they would define them, how they have evolved, what factors are contributing and what it takes to change them. A goal of these early sessions is getting the family *thinking* about the problems instead of just emotionally *reacting* to them, and this is accomplished through good questions. The husband of a depressed, dysfunctional wife, for example, has likely been putting pressure on her to pull up her functioning. Everything she says indicates to him she has a "sickness," for which she needs a cure. The therapist's questions should be aimed not at the wife's "sickness" but at the spouses' emotional vulnerabilities to each other. What specifically does the husband react to in his wife, how does he react internally and what action does he take based on that reaction? The same types of questions can then be asked of the wife. At this point, the spouses are *describing* the emotional process they live out instead of living it out *in the session*. These types of questions keep the focus on the family emotional process instead of on a preoccupation with the feeling states or symptoms of any one member. Remember that it is an assumption of systems theory that the internal states of an individual reflect the emotional process in the family, and it is this family process that receives primary focus in the evaluation.

Exact dates of when symptoms developed or changed are also important. These dates may later correlate with data obtained in other parts of the history and may suggest a relationship the family had been unaware of.

The history of the nuclear family begins with where and when the couple met, when they were engaged and the date of marriage. The husband may have been operating at loose ends with little life direction when he met his wife, but in the course of the marriage his functioning improved while the wife's declined. This gives an indication of the pattern of fusion in their relationship, with the husband being stabilized and the wife becoming the "inadequate" one. The extremes of length of courtship, very long or very short, are often indications of a less well-differentiated relationship. There is a beautiful parallel in nature, in which it has been observed that when considerable cooperation will be required of mates, they tend to have longer courtship periods (Barash, 1977).

Information about the early part of the marriage, again, can give indications of basic patterns of fusion. The marriage may have resulted in marked improvements in each spouse's functioning, an indication of fusion. The impact of the first pregnancy and childbirth can either disturb a balanced relationship or quiet a conflictual one. A serious disturbance in the marital equilibrium triggered by a childbirth may be the first *overt* indication of a degree of marital fusion. Geographic moves are important and, again, recording exact dates. Birthdates, education, occupation and health histories of each spouse are also recorded. Birthdates of children plus indications about their school performance, health history and social adjustment can give indications of which is the most emotionally fused child, even though overt symptoms may not be currently in evidence.

Nuclear-family emotional process is not static. It changes with additions and deletions from the system, moves, etc. One spouse may be the more adaptive one early in the marriage, but the pattern may later reverse. This part of the history is aimed at defining the evolution of the nuclear-family process as well as its current state.

Information about each spouse's extended family is collected next. Sibling position of the parents is a good place to begin. Bowen incorporated Toman's sibling profiles into his theory many years ago (Toman, 1969). It is a clinical fact that sibling position is an accurate predictor of certain aspects of a person's functioning. When an older brother of a sister, for example, marries a younger sister of a brother, it is likely that the husband will be the more dominant, decision-making person in the marriage. This kind of marriage can be a "perfect fit" under most conditions, with the husband content making the decisions and the wife content with him having that responsibility. Particularly under stress, however, such a marriage can reach a point where the overfunctioning of the husband can impair the functioning of the wife and vice versa. Marriage of an oldest daughter to a youngest son would tend to have the opposite profile and complications under stress. There are exceptions to Toman's profiles, depending particularly on the level of differentiation of the people. An oldest son, for example, who was quite fused into his family of origin may spend his life avoiding expectations and responsibility. There would be similar exceptions to all the other siblings profiles, but in general, knowing the sibling positions of the parents provides considerable information about what the basic characteristics of a marriage are likely to be.

In collecting extended family history, data on parents, siblings, aunts, uncles, cousins, grandparents, etc., should also include information about occupation, education, health history, geography, birth and death dates, causes of death and divorces. Comments like "Grandfather was an alcoholic" have to be heard as *opinions* and not facts. Such comments most often reflect the way the family emotional system *defines* the people in it and do not necessarily reflect an accurate picture of the person.

Once all of this information about the extended family has been collected, it can provide an assessment of three areas. The first is the basic level of differentiation of the overall family system. Better levels of differentiation are reflected in greater marital stability, good physical and mental health, occupational stability, educational achievement, etc.

The assessment of each family member over three or four generations provides a picture of what is average for the total system. Are you dealing with a relatively stable system or a relatively unstable one? Such information is, to a certain extent, predictive of the likely clinical course of the people who have come to you for help.

The second area that extended system data provides assessment about is where the undifferentiation of the system has most come to rest through the generations. Within his or her immediate family of origin, was this parent the most fused-in sibling or a free spirit? Was his immediate family of origin a relatively more stable or less stable segment of family than the rest of the extended system? Again, this has predictive value and implication for how therapy should proceed.

Extended-family data provides assessment of a third area and that is the degree to which recent events in the extended system may be triggering anxiety in the family seeking help. Recent deaths, divorces, moves, etc., in the extended system may not have been mentioned earlier in the history, but turn out to correlate precisely with symptom development in the nuclear family seeking therapy. An eight-year-old's school phobia, for example, may be found to have started two weeks after a cancer diagnosis of the paternal grandmother. This is not to imply that the eight-year-old is reacting to the cancer diagnosis, but that the diagnosis likely increased the anxiety in the system, with the child's parents becoming more anxious, reacting more anxiously to the child, and the child, in turn, being "infected" by parental anxiety.

A final but particularly important area to be assessed in this part of the history is the degree of emotional cutoff of each parent from their family of origin. The therapist's ability to assess cutoff grows with experience and the realization that statements like "I have a good relationship with my family" can mean many things. It is also important to assess the other "support" systems of the nuclear family as well—for example, how involved they may be in neighborhood, social, church and work-related systems.

THERAPY TECHNIQUES

Two principles guide the family psychotherapy based on Bowen theory: first, that reduction of anxiety in the system will automatically lead to reduction of whatever symptoms are present via restoration of system equilibrium; and second, that change in the basic individuality-togetherness balance in a family toward more individuality or differentiation will increase the adaptability of that system to stress and result in a *long-term* reduction of symptoms.

Reduction of anxiety in a person or family system is not a very well understood phenomenon. Anxiety-driven disequilibrium in a system can run its "natural" course without the intervention of a therapist in the same way that hurricanes, plagues of locusts and other natural phenomena gradually build up energy, peak and subside. Thinking of the family as a natural phenomenon about which our understanding is quite limited is useful in doing therapy. It is impossible for the therapist to really know what it takes to "fix" a family, but for that matter, it's not necessary that he know. The family knows. The therapist need only generate an atmosphere in which the family can find solutions. The system clearly has the ability to "heal" itself, but anxiety appears to interfere with that healing process. The calming influence of a relaxed therapist who can be closely involved with a family without fusing with it facilitates the reduction of family anxiety and mobilization of this "self-healing." This kind of change in a family, based on reduction of anxiety, can be accomplished short-term and is essentially symptom relief. It is functional improvement in the system, but the basic individuality-togetherness balance of that system has not changed.

Efforts to change the *basic* amount of differentiation in a system are, by necessity, long-term and are accomplished to different degrees by different people. For example, the more embedded people are in togetherness, where most of life energy is involved in trying to get from the other or protect self from the other, the more difficult it is to work toward differentiation. The intellectual and feeling systems of people in a strongly fused system are so merged that it is difficult for people to even be aware that separation of thinking and feeling is possible. This is not to imply that the theory does not "work" with poorly differentiated people, just that much, if not all of the "change" that can occur will be symptom relief. Basic change in the individuality-togetherness balance of a system grows out of the efforts of *individuals* in that system to improve their own functioning *in relationship to others*. If one person is successful at functioning on a more differentiated level, the entire system that person is in contact with will pull up its functioning in response to it. Differentiation is not accomplished by cutting off from a relationship, based on the assumption that the other person will never change. A basic tenet of systems thinking is that the functioning of an important other reflects the functioning of self and vice versa. Running away from the other is like trying to run away from yourself.

With the goals of therapy, then, being reduction of family anxiety and improvement in basic level of differentiation, the therapist's effectiveness can be evaluated based on his or her ability to accomplish these goals with a clinical family. Bowen has observed that for a therapist to be effective, "it's not what you do or say, but who you are that makes the difference." In other words, the level of differentiation of the therapist is the critical variable in the success of therapy. The family can go no further with their lives than the therapist has gone with his. So the training of family therapists based on Bowen theory emphasizes the trainee beginning what will be a lifetime effort toward improving his or her level of differentiation. The teaching of therapeutic technique is secondary.

If, then, the therapist's level of differentiation is the critical variable in therapeutic success, how does the therapist or potential therapist improve the degree to which differentiation influences his or her functioning? As usual, there is no simple answer to this question. Each person works at differentiation in his own way. Certainly successful efforts to function in a more differentiated way depend on several things. The first would be a person's ability to recognize his emotional reactivity and how that affects others. Secondly, efforts to improve differentiation also depend on awareness of the emotional process in the relationship systems in which he functions and how that process influences self. Finally, just awareness of emotional reactivity is obviously not enough. Differentiation also requires some ability to keep one's own emotional reactivity toned down to manageable levels and the *ability to keep intellectual functioning relatively free of emotional influence*. The gradual awareness of the degree to which emotion has influenced one's thinking and beliefs is perhaps, the most important dividend of a long-term effort toward differentiation. So much of every person's "thinking" about the world around them is a product of what they "bought" and "buy" from their relationship systems. Man's proneness to suggestibility and simple acceptance of what he hears and reads is notorious. This sorting out of the influence of emotion and the relationship system on one's own beliefs requires a tremendous amount of work and is something for which most people have limited motivation.

An effort toward differentiation begins in a person's important relationship systems, particularly the family relationship system. In the early days of training, Bowen encouraged therapists to get into family therapy themselves along with their spouse. In the early 1960's, he considered this the best available method of working toward differentiation of a self, namely in relationship to one's spouse. Around 1967, with the evolution of Bowen's thinking about the extended family, he began putting more emphasis on focusing primary attention on the family of origin as the method of choice for working toward differentiation (Bowen, 1978).

Development of this method grew out of the observation that most people have significant degrees of emotional cutoff from their original family and that the degree of cutoff is related to the degree of unresolved emotional attachment or fusion to the family of origin. The emotional cutoff from the past generations is accompanied by equivalent fusion into the present and future generations, namely spouse and children. With emphasis shifting off the nuclear-family emotional process and onto extended-family process, the assumption that is made is that what is observed and somewhat resolved in family of origin will permit the person making the effort to observe it and resolve it in his nuclear family.

The techniques for working toward differentiation in one's own family are as numerous as people making such an effort. What is effective for one person is not necessarily effective for another. What is absolutely essential is that a person is trying not to change his family, but to simply learn about the emotional process and how he fits into it. In general, such an effort requires more contact with the extended family than most people have. This means contact not just with parents and siblings, but with aunts, uncles, cousins, grandparents, etc. It means increasing one's knowledge about the multigenerational history of the family, going beyond genealogy to gain the kind of information that can lift into view the emotional process in a family across generations. Over the long term, a successful effort results in less emotional reactiveness to the family and more responsible involvement. The ability to maintain open relationships with various extended family members is increased. By "open relationships" is meant responsible communication—in other words, important subjects are not avoided and the privacy of certain communications is respected. The ability to think systems in relationship to one's family of origin is difficult. It is not simply an intellectual process. There are numerous emotional obstacles to be overcome within oneself. Sensitivities to disapproval, threats of rejection or withdrawal of love can undermine an effort to be a "self" in one's extended family. Changes in family emotional process occur slowly and are never fully resolved.

Family psychotherapy with a clinical population embodies the same principles as outlined above. Originally, Bowen focused on the marital relationship, including children in the sessions only on occasion. Experience has been that children living at home and financially dependent on parents are not capable of taking action toward more differentiation. The kids often have fascinating ideas and observations to contribute, but Bowen and those who have trained under him have made "change" in the family the responsibility of the parents. In the early days, the husband and wife were seen together regardless of whether the presenting problem was marital conflict, illness in a spouse or problems with a child. The goal of the therapy was to promote differentiation efforts in one spouse, then the other, through focus on their relationship. The implication was that differentiation in the parents would automatically lead to better differentiation in the children. Parents were, in effect, discouraged from trying to help their children do what they had been unable to do themselves, and focus was put back on the parents themselves to work out their own problems. The atmosphere of the therapy sessions was designed to increase the thinking about the emotional process and to decrease the reacting. The therapist's job was to maintain his own differentiation while relating to the family, not fusing in with it, taking sides, etc. The important thing was not the specific issues discussed in a session but the "background" emotional reactivity that underlay those issues. It is the emotional reactivity that interferes with the solution of a problem, and that is the focus of the therapist's questions.

Multiple-family therapy, established later in the 1960's, was a variant of work with individual couples. The therapist took turns working with each of three or four couples, all together in a session. The focus remained on the emotional process in each family and *not on group process*, so each couple had the opportunity to listen to and learn from the therapist's interaction with the other couples.

Recent years have witnessed increasing emphasis on family therapy with one family member, whether married or single. Spouses, for example, are often seen alternately about once a month. Several experiences have contributed to this change in emphasis in the therapy. First of all, the fact that many times when only one spouse was willing to come for therapy, significant changes occurred in the entire family system, including the other spouse, changes based on the differentiating efforts of just that one person. Second, increasing experience with conjoint family therapy began to highlight the sometimes "complications" of such an approach. For example, seeing two people together can do a beautiful job of equilibrating the togetherness and relieving symptoms, only to have serious symptoms emerge some years later in a spouse or one of the children. No differentiation has been achieved in seeing the couple together when, in fact, the family might have been capable of differentiation had the therapist approached them differently. Another complication of conjoint sessions is that sometimes one spouse, usually the compromised or "de-selfed" one, is unable to think clearly in the presence of the other. When these spouses are seen separately, it is often amazing the number of new ideas that emerge in their thinking. The third and perhaps most important experience that has influenced a change in therapy techniques toward focus on one family member has been development of the concept of differentiation of self in one's original family. Attempting to differentiate a self in one's family of origin is an individual project. The other spouse cannot help with it. The chances of the other spouse undermining the effort, even unwittingly, are far greater than his or her being helpful to it. Remember, the differentiation force is opposed by the togetherness force, and if one spouse is the least bit successful in trying to operate as more of a "self," the other spouse, 100 percent of the time, will oppose it. Differentiation, in its early stages, is a tenuous business. It behooves the therapist not to make it difficult for his people by designing therapy sessions that undermine their efforts.

Focus on the extended family and marked reduction in the frequency of sessions have clearly taken the therapy out of the consultation room. Most of the thinking and effort that determine the success of the therapy takes place in the person in the weeks between sessions, and the hour with the therapist is more a report about what the person has been doing than anything else. All of the techniques described—conjoint sessions, multiple-family therapy and focus on the extended family with one member—remain in active use. They have all of their advantages and disadvantages, but if differentiation of self is the goal, then individual sessions with a person motivated to focus on the extended family currently gets the highest success rating.

CONCLUSION

This concluding section will focus more specifically on marriage and marital problems. The reason so much time has been devoted to theory is to underline the importance of keeping a broad theoretical perspective when thinking about marriage, marital problems and marital therapy. Marital conflict is clearly only one of the many manifestations of the undifferentiation in a family. It is a mistake to think of marital tension or conflict as good or bad. It is simply one mechanism for dealing with undifferentiation, and the greater the anxiety, the more the mechanism is activated.

Much of the chapter has been devoted also to examples from the nonhuman animal world. Retaining a biological perspective on marriage seems indicated, particularly in an age when so much emphasis is placed on cultural determinants. Since man is not the only animal to attempt to bond for extended periods and cooperate in the raising of the young, the fact that man attempts it is determined, obviously, by more than just cultural influence. Culture and values are important, but biological determinants may ultimately prove to be a more influential variable. Although pair-bonding is not unique to man, the number of monogamous species in nature is relatively small. Among most mammals, including nearly all the rodents, the most abundant mamalian order, copulation itself provides the only adult sociality. The most persistent social bond is that between mother and young, which itself terminates at weaning. Males and females form distinct social bonds—monogamy in geese, songbirds, eagles, beaver, foxes and gibbons (Barash, 1977)—and although man is generally referred to as monogamous, Kleiman suggests that there are important ways in which he does not fit the criteria for a monogamous species (Kleiman, 1978).

The biological perspective has application in the daily practice of family therapy. When spouses seek help for marital difficulties, they are, to a great extent, anxious and issue-focused. The popular press frequently reports that issues such as sex, finances and the rearing of children are the important "causes" of marital disharmony and breakup. These issues are not causes. While any of these issues has the potential for generating anxiety in a marriage, it is precisely this anxiety or emotional reactivity that is the problem. Almost all couples can work out cooperative arrangements over money when each partner is calm, but when anxiety builds, each spouse fortifies self against the other lest he or she be the "loser" in the struggle. Other animals have been doing this for millions and millions of years. Sexual issues are much the same: spouses place each other in the same togetherness binds in this area ("If he is not interested in sex, then he is not interested in me and I am not a worthwhile person"). This is a common statement and is far more related to the togetherness balance in a relationship than to basic sexual drives. As one spouse gets more anxious about the frequency of sexual relations, he or she pressures the mate, who then reacts to the pressure with withdrawal, which increases the anxiety in the other spouse, etc. It is these *emotional chain reactions* that are the problem, and not the specific issues.

As described earlier, there are a number of ways anxiety can be absorbed or played out in a relationship system. Relationship harmony in a nuclear family, for example, can be preserved at the expense of one spouse who compromises his or her own functioning and desires to preserve that harmony. Marital harmony can also be preserved through distance and/or overfocusing by the parents on the well-being and functioning of a child. When significant marital disharmony does exist, it is an indication that much of the anxiety is being acted out in the marital relationship. When conflict exists, each spouse is usually feeling threatened and is on the defensive with the other lest the "self" be taken over or dictated to by the other. It is more the rule to have a mixture of these mechanisms in a nuclear family, with the anxiety being bound by one mechanism, making for less required activity of the other mechanisms. Marital conflict, for example, can keep the focus off the children and protect them from possible impairment.

The amount of anxiety to be "bound" in a system depends on several variables: namely, the chronic anxiety tied to the basic level of differentiation of the people; the acute and chronic fluctuations in anxiety related to changes in life situation; and finally, the anxiety related to emotional cutoff from the extended-family system and other support systems. All of these factors influence the degree of harmony and disharmony in a marriage.

In addition to consideration of factors influencing the amount of anxiety in a family system and the various mechanisms for dealing with that anxiety, there are variations in relationships that are not easily explained theoretically but are easily observed. One such variation is the different ways that the basic individuality-togetherness balance of a relationship can be disturbed. This point has particular reference to marital harmony and disharmony, and so will be discussed in some detail. As mentioned, Bowen theorizes that people differ in the degree to which individuality and togetherness influence their thinking and activity. Some people, in other words, are more differentiated than others. The theory posits that people of equivalent levels of differentiation are attracted to each other and marry. When they marry, the basic intensity of their togetherness needs determines the degree to which they fuse in the relationship. A basic individuality-togetherness balance is then established, and whatever disturbs that balance is reacted to with efforts to restore it. Interestingly, this fusion in a relationship may manifest itself in an intolerance for two people being alone together *or* in an intolerance for the intrusion of an outsider. This variation in what disturbs a fusion is one of those things that is more easily observed than explained. But as so often in nature, opposites are equivalent, and that certainly appears to be the case in this situation. When two people are intolerant of being alone together, yet are bound by their need for each other, they can feel tremendous encroachment and pressure. This is often the case when a marriage deteriorates in the first year or so or when it deteriorates when the kids leave home. Another equally fused couple, however, may be able to keep their relationship in balance provided there is no intrusion. With the addition of a third person, one mate becomes sensitive to the energy the other mate seems to be investing in that third person and the other mate feels caught in the middle. Protests ensue along with other efforts to shift the emotional forces in the system to make them more favorable for self. Addition of a child or bringing a parent to live in the home can often trigger such a chain of events.

A fascinating example of this two-person or three-person phenomenon occurred with the POWs in Vietnam. In the early years of the war, the prisoners were kept in small cells with anywhere from one to four people in a cell. When just one person was confined to a cell, it was usually lonely, but he found ways to adapt. When two were in a cell, there was usually a several-month "honeymoon" phase in which each prisoner relished the company. They got to know an awful lot about each other's experiences, knowledge, beliefs, etc. Then about three months out, the first signs of irritation would set in, which would progress to maximum emotional reactivity to each other. To cope with this intense reactivity in a confined space, the two prisoners would literally divide up the territory of the small cell and cease looking at each other, let alone speaking. Many of these twosomes could stabilize their situation with this kind of distance. But if a third person was added, it often proved to be an explosive situation. The inevitable outsider in the threesome would feel tremendous rejection, and the triangle was in a state of constant turmoil with efforts to alter the balance. When a similar situation has been created with mice, the outsider third mouse has tried to eat his way through a thick wall to find a mouse that would relate to him (Calhoun, 1978). In the POW situation, the addition of a fourth person would frequently produce a two-against-two stability with no outsiders. These same men, when placed in large compounds containing many prisoners, became the best of friends. Examples such as Vietnam POWs may seem far removed from the everyday practice of family therapy, but it is precisely this kind of buildup of anxiety and flow of emotional forces in a system that must be considered in evaluating and treating marital dysfunctions. The sense of confinement and no-exit feeling can be every bit as intense, whether it be produced by the emotional "constraints" of a marriage or the physical constraints of a small cell.

The principles of marital treatment were outlined earlier, namely reduction of anxiety and long-term efforts toward a better level of differentiation of self. The success of therapy, once a serious marital problem has surfaced, depends on a number of variables, but experience has suggested that the critical variable is the degree of emotional cutoff of each spouse from his or her extended family and the willingness of one or both spouses to work toward bridging that cutoff. Psychotherapy is a vague enough business that to make claims about anything can leave one on rather shaky ground, but this is one area—bridging the cutoff with past generations—that can contribute to rather remarkable changes in functioning and improvement in marital stability. It seems safe to say that people will make more progress on their marriage if they put primary emphasis on efforts toward resolving emotional attachments with past generations. The tedious, time-consuming process of sorting out the details of a marital fusion can be bypassed by the broader perspective gained with a multigenerational focus. It is extremely difficult to gain objectivity about people you live with when your focus is only on those relationships. The emotional matrix is always thick enough to make it difficult to see it clearly.

REFERENCES

Barash, D. *Sociobiology and behavior.* New York: Elsevier, 1977.

Bowen, M. *Family therapy in clinical practice.* New York: Jason Aronson, 1978.

Bowen, M., Toward the differentiation of self in one's family of origin. In M. Bowen, *Family therapy in clinical practice.* New York: Jason Aronson, 1978, pp. 529–547.

Calhoun, J.B. National Institute of Mental Health, Animal Center—personal communication, 1978.

Herrick, C. The functions of the olfactory parts of the cerebral cortex. *Proceed. Nat. Acad. Sci., 19,* 7–14, 1933.

Kerr, M. Emotional factors in physical illness: A multigenerational perspective. In R.R. Sagar (Ed.), *Georgetown family symposia: Volume IV (1977–1978),* Georgetown Univ., Washington, D.C., 1980.

Kleiman, D. Monogamy in mammals. In R.R. Sagar (Ed.), *Georgetown family symposia: Volume III (1975–1976),* Georgetown Univ., Washington, D.C., 1978.

MacLean, P. A Mind of three brains: Educating the triune brain. In *Education and the brain.*
   Chicago: Univ. of Chicago Press, pp. 308–342, 1978.
Rock, M. Gorilla mothers need some help from their friends. *Smithsonian, 9*; 58–63, 1978.
Toman, W. *Family constellation.* New York: Springer, 1969.
Wilson, E. *Sociobiology: The new synthesis.* Cambridge; Ma.: Belknap Press, 1975.
Wolf, S. Update on Roseto, Pennsylvania: Testing a prediction. Paper, American Psychoso-
   matic Society, March 31, 1978, Washington, D.C.

Chapter 7

Discussion of Psychodynamic Theories of Marital Therapy

Otto Pollak

The invitation to discuss the papers assembled in this volume was honorific, its acceptance burdensome and conflicted, and the carrying out of the task surprisingly enlightening and challenging. My contact with family therapy and family therapists goes back to 1949, when the Russell Sage Foundation made it possible for me to serve as consultant to the Child Guidance Bureau of the Jewish Board of Guardians in New York. At the time I came to know Nathan Ackerman and, a few years later, Alfred S. Friedman, and the Philadelphia group of family therapists who were instrumental in founding the Family Institute. In the course of years I have had occasion to meet Virginia Satir, John Bowen, Harold Lief and John Warkentin, to mention only a few, and to appreciate their contributions to the heroic age of family therapy. My contact with family therapists has persisted to this day and has made it possible for me to be part of the beginning and to remain part of the development of family therapy. This persistent contact has led me to form many friendships with family therapists and to become antagonistic toward some of them. Feelings of both types exist in me toward one or the other of the contributors. The nature of my comments will show whether I have learned—from family therapists—to control them and prevent them from spoiling my work.

As happens in the history of most scientific disciplines, the heroic age of the 1950's and 1960's was characterized by relatively simple and clearly stated messages. The primary message was that the family was a system and that improvement in one member of the system could produce the appearance of disturbance in another. In consequence, it was proposed and put into practice that, if possible, all members of the family unit should be seen in joint sessions. The much greater demand of such joint sessions on the perception and responses of the family therapist led to the establishment of co-therapist teams. Essentially, diagnostic thinking shifted from concern with the intrapsychic dynamics of one person to concern with the interactional dynamics and transactions in the family system. Furthermore, the proponents of family therapy in that period formulated theories of family dynamics which reflected largely their personalities, family histories or fit for a specific methodology of intervention: Ackerman's (1959) scapegoat theory, Bowen's undifferentiated-family ego mass (1959) and Jackson and Satir's (1961) double-bind and failure-in-communication theory come easily to mind.

The papers assembled in the volume here presented to the professional audiences of family therapists, psychiatrists, social workers and ministers show that we have come a long way from the simplistic optimism of the early period of the family-therapy movement. The first phenomenon that must strike the reader of these papers is the enormous complexity of the determinants of marital and other family relationships. I remember frequently how difficult it was for me to show that the practice of child-guidance work in the late 1940's was limited to seeing only the mother and child in treatment and that I had to search the literature for slips of the pen almost which revealed that this was so. Spark's paper on intergenerational therapy and Kerr's on Bowen's consideration of the extended family show how much we have increased our range of diagnostic perception and interventive methodology in thirty years. Although Ross Speck (1973) does not appear among the contributors, his pioneering in network therapy has to be mentioned in sketching this trend of "more and more" in the people and relationships considered of relevance in family therapy today. In this context it might be worth mentioning that James Bossard pointed out long ago that arithmetic increase of persons in a family led to an increase in the order of triangular numbers. According to this law, three persons in a family produce three interpersonal relationships, four persons six, five persons ten, and six persons fifteen relationships and so on (Bossard, 1948). The continuing extension of people and their relationships to be considered in family therapy has been paralleled by similar increases in the awareness of the variety of functions and dysfunctions that these relationships may assume. All case descriptions contained in this volume show the complexity of determinants in the working of a family system and the variety of results which they may produce. Sager's (1976) description of the Smith couple is the most instructive in this respect, although there is no case description in this volume that could not be used to demonstrate the same point.

Another important contribution of this volume is to show the main streams of theory building and new conceptualizations that can be traced in the work of family therapists over the last thirty years. It was strategically fortunate that Dr. G. Pirooz Sholevar, the editor, has given first place to the paper entitled "A Model of Marital Interaction," by Berman, Lief and Williams. Theory is always an attempt to cope with complexity, and it is regrettable that complexity also creates many theories. Berman, Lief and Williams have been courageous and successful in attempting to integrate the major theories in the field of family therapy by showing that they analyze the same phenomena from different points of view and that theories are essentially expressions of phenomenology. They discuss the same topic from different angles. Having different points of view, they are, of course, likely to identify determinants of the phenomenon that would escape perception in another perspective. The authors have been wise in avoiding "the trap" of endorsing one theory and objecting to another. Showing that they supplement one another was a meritorious undertaking. Claiming for their model not more than a "point of approach" which "can be used to form a multiple-intervention therapeutic approach or to allow the therapist using one preferred model to check her/himself against other points of view" shows modesty as well as sensitivity to the fact that therapists will have to find their fit among the many that may lead to similar results. It is truly acceptance of the principle of equifinality of systems theory. Actually, the model could and probably will also be put to another use. To therapists unsatisfied with their approach and methodology, it may offer alternatives to try with renewed therapeutic zest. It may give them deliverance from the loss of effectiveness due to routinization. It may help them to discover, test and enjoy their true fit in interventive methodology.

The volume also draws readers' attention to valuable conceptualization of recent vintage. Sager's (1976) concept of the marriage contract, introduced by him before, is well presented here. The same is true for the also previously presented concept of integenerational-family therapy by Spark. John Sonne's differentiation of self-object considerations and transference considerations constitutes a felicitous dichotomy connecting different developmental mishaps with different strategies of therapeutic intervention. This connection strengthens the case for differential diagnosis as a guide to differential intervention. It presupposes, however, or risks a strengthening of the probably erroneous belief that every therapist can do what a differential diagnosis suggests.

Another contribution of Sonne's is his description of the two different procedures that he follows in cases of self-object and transference consideration. This contribution is strengthened by Kerr's description of procedure, which derives from Bowen's principles and amounts to "being" rather than "proceeding." Sager's description of his intervention strategy in the Smith case with its self-questioning and lucid connection between his assessments of progress and planning of strategy completes this particular contribution of the volume.

A special tribute must also be paid to Kerr's references to animal behavior and his illustration of systems working and systems failure through his description of the cardiovascular system.

I have only three more reactions to the material presented in this volume. One is the impression of an apparent lack of understanding of what family therapy owes to psychoanalysis and what separates psychoanalysis from family therapy. The paper by Berman, Lief and Williams and the two papers by Sonne clearly show intellectual relatedness and indebtedness to Freud. They fail, however, to spell out the difference in goal setting. It is true that family therapists in the early times were psychiatrists who found psychoanalytic methodology ineffective in helping families, but they failed to see that this observation was due to a change in therapeutic goal setting.

It may be remembered that Freud (1966), in the first of his introductory lectures, described his initial contact with patients in a not exactly optimistic mood. He said that in contrast to the custom of physicians of his time, he warned his patients that treatment would be long and painful and that the outcome was uncertain. On another occasion he proposed that the result of a successful psychoanalysis was to help neurotics achieve what normal people accomplish for themselves without help (Freud, 1959). People who seek relief of family trouble and people who undertake to help them in obtaining such relief represent another mood and another type of goal setting. They are optimists and they want to help people to a better life. The application of Freudian methodology to the pursuit of goals which he never set for himself, of course, had to lead to disappointment. One should not conceal, however, the fact that practically all family therapists work with psychoanalytic concepts and should acknowledge the Freudian impact on their thinking in referencing their statements.

Another discomfort which I feel I have to express in this connection is the unfortunate terminology of referring to persons other than the patient as "objects." We are frequently informed about love objects, self-object connections and similar references to people as "objects." It is true that family therapists frequently meet patients who would like to treat their spouses and relatives as objects. However, this is their pathology, and it should not seduce professional people into at least linguistic acceptance of their patients' attitudes toward other people. There are no objects in family life. Every attempt to treat somebody as an object is likely to fail, and if it succeeds, it is severe pathology indeed. I would be happy to see therapists relate their patients linguistically to other "people" rather than to "objects." The term is dehumanizing and, as such, non-therapeutic.

I feel a similar discomfort about the use of the term "marriage contract" as a deliberate misnomer. Since Sager's work is concerned with contradictory expectations that two people have of their marriage, the term "marriage contract" will be disappointing to readers who trust the title of a publication to inform them about the content of the book. To a minor degree I also have a quarrel with the introduction of the term "accounting system" into the problem of conflicting loyalties. Dynamics are not easily quantified except perhaps with regard to the time which they consume.

These linguistic concerns should not be overrated, but they suggest that family therapists have a need to make themselves understood by the use of terms taken from other fields of human experience. It seems to me that the field has reached a stage of development where such strategic devices are not necessary and are potentially harmful. They may antagonize more people than they attract.

By way of conclusion, I should like to suggest that family therapists abandon the industrial model of productivity for the evaluation of their work. Helping people to a better family life is certainly praiseworthy as an undertaking, but it is beset by uncertainty of outcome. Actually, family therapy may even lead to deterioration. Jung (1972) has pointed out that releasing the unconscious is a dangerous undertaking, and, in cases of latent psychosis, may lead to mental disorder and possibly even to suicide. It is difficult to exclude the possibility that the entrance of therapists into the family system, one or the other occurrence in the process of their intervention or a specific change in interaction between two family members may have similar results. In human affairs the principle of indeterminacy is always at work. This is the risk of all medical intervention. It extends also to other interventions and it has two implications, one self-protective for the therapist and one philosophical and ego-enhancing for both therapist and patient. Therapists who tie their self-image to the number of successes or failures that they have experienced in practice run the risk either of having to become callous and cynical or of having to become depressed. Only recognition of the principle of uncertainty can secure their self-respect when faced with the disappointment of their therapeutic ambitions. As to the philosophical implications of this recognition, I should like to refer to a statement by Boszormenyi-Nagy (1965), who has pointed out that change is essentially a sign of health. May I offer an amendment? Change is always better than stagnation, even if it is change for the worse.

REFERENCES

Ackerman, N.W. *The psychodynamics of family life.* New York: Basic Books, 1958.

Bossard, J.H.S. *The Sociology of Child Development.* New York: Harper and Bros., 1948, p. 146.

Boszormenyi-Nagy, I. The concept of change in conjoint family therapy. In A. S. Friedman, I. Boszormenyi-Nagy, J. E. Jungreis, G. Lincoln, H. E. Mitchell, J. C. Sonne, R. V. Speck, G. Spivack, *Psychotherapy for the whole family*. New York: Springer, 1965, pp. 305–317.

Boszormenyi-Nagy, I., and Spark, G. *Invisible loyalties*. New York: Harper and Row, 1973.

Bowen, M. The family as the unit of study and treatment. *Am. J. Orthopsychiat.*, 1961, *31*, 40–60.

Bowen, M. A family concept of schizophrenia. In D.D. Jackson (Ed.), *Etiology of schizophrenia*. New York: Basic Books, 1960, pp. 346–372.

Freud, S. Analysis terminable and interminable. In J. Strachey (Ed.), *Collected papers, Vol. 5*. New York: Basic Books, 1959, p. 327.

Freud S. In J. Strachey (Ed. and trans), *The complete introductory lectures on psychoanalysis*. New York: W.W. Norton, 1966, p. 15.

Jackson, D.D., and Satir, V.M. Family diagnosis and family therapy. In N. Ackerman, F.L. Beatman and S.N. Sherman (Eds.), *Exploring the bases for family therapy*. New York: Family Service Association, 1961.

Jung, C.G. On the psychology of the unconscious. In *Two essays on analytical psychology* (R.F.C. Hull, trans.). Princeton, N.J.: Bollingen, 1972, p. 114.

Sager, J. *Marriage contracts and couple therapy*. New York: Brunner/Mazel, 1976.

Speck, V., and Attneave, C. *Family networks*. New York: Pantheon, 1973.

PART II

Theory and Technique in Marital Therapy

Existential Marital Therapy: A Synthesis* A Subsystem of Existential Family Therapy

Carl A. Whitaker
Alice Greenberg
Milton L. Greenberg

INTRODUCTION

Existential psychotherapy espouses three values—experience, reality and growth. It relies on the immediate experiencing of this very moment in all its fullness, the here and now. It emphasizes the impact of reality; the facts of life, which mold human experience. And it aims to help people grow, in contrast to helping people adapt.

One outstanding way to grow is through marriage. But this relationship is painful and demanding. In his *Devil's Dictionary*, Ambrose Bierce said that

---

*The content of this chapter derives primarily from Carl Whitaker's writings and teaching tapes, with additional original material of the three authors in close collaboration.

a marriage is a community consisting of a master, a mistress, and two slaves, making in all two. Verily. The tension in marriage is terrible. The only thing worse is being single.

But it is illusory to believe that a man and a woman are two separate people who come together to form a more perfect union. They are simply scapegoats sent out by their families to reproduce their kind. They are a fragment of each family system. In the same way, Existential Marital Therapy is just a subsystem of Existential Family Therapy.

Existential therapy's concern with growth is also a focus on change. In order to know what *can* be changed, it helps to recognize what can*not* be changed—that is, the context of the human condition. These facts of life are presented first. The foundation of this marital therapy is presented next, in the subsection "Assumptions About Human Growth and Marriage" and in the following section, "Existential Family Therapy." The chapter concludes with the two sections "Marital Theory" and "Marital Therapy."

The Facts of Life

The facts of life are the givens that confront each of us in our living. They are simply *there*. Some, like the psycho-biological facts, are universal and unchangeable. Others, like the psycho-social facts, vary for different groups of people or for different individuals. The facts of the life setting into which a person is born (particular year, country, family) are also immutable. With effort or "luck," a few facts of a person's current life circumstances may change.

This is not to make the job of people-changing seem hopeless. It can and does happen—with greater probability when we know what we're up against, including the huge odds that favor homeostasis. We have learned a great deal in our field about *feelings*. But we must also look at the *facts* involved in our living. It is a serious mistake to assume that we can straighten out the factual problems of life by intellectual decisions, behavior changes or feeling changes. The facts listed here are some of the most evident; they are not all-inclusive. They are meant to suggest some predicaments in which human beings find themselves.

The psycho-biological facts of life. The psycho-biological facts are so obvious that they are easy to overlook. We might remind ourselves that as the givens of life, these facts direct, limit and define the human condition for each of us. Of the many facts, five seem outstanding: (1) A body is born. (2) Every body is the same. Ninety-nine percent of a physical body is identical to every other body. Ninety percent or more of the bio-psycho-socio human being is just like every other human being. (3) A person is never as close to any other person as he/she is to his or her mother. (4) A person is a biological cripple: he can't reproduce himself. (5) A body dies. "I have eternal life" is a myth. Death is a constant haunt.

The psycho-social facts of life. The psycho-social facts are a set of givens on a different level. Some are cultural. Some are familial. Some are individual, as accidents of time, place or birth. But none is readily modifiable. And every fact is formidably real to each of us when we are confronted with it.

Five cultural facts of life seem especially basic to an understanding of existential psychotherapy: (1) A community is a supersystem. A family is a whole unit, but it is also one of the community's subsystems. A couple is a family's subsystem; and it is also a community's subsubsystem. (2) A person can belong only to his or her own generation. The generations are separated by time, experience and relationship (grandparents, parents and children), and the generation gap is a reality. (3) Each person has a yen to be a child again—to be silly, open and honest—and to use this regression in the service of his growth. (4) Each person has a yen to help, to fix it. Most people try to be psychotherapists. (5) Each person learns male and female roles very early. The roles are fixed, delimiting and hard to change.

Many social facts of life also determine profoundly the course of human development. The effects of poverty, hunger, unemployment and war are all devastating and often irreversible. Other predicaments can also have crucial impact. Cultural and educational starvation can deaden human vitality by way of a dull life or stimulus deprivation. Cultural pathology can constrict a person's or family's potential through a tradition of ethnic alcoholism, coldness or rage. Discrimination against a cultural minority can choke its members' initiative and creativity.

Finally, we recognize a whole set of influential family facts of life. Some of these family facts describe discrete events, clearly present or absent, with readily apparent tragic aspects. These include the facts of being orphaned, of desertion, divorce, suicide, murder, incest, adoption and physical disability. The first three, involving the loss of parents, undermine a child's ability to trust the source and reliability of his nurturance. In addition to their connection with loss and nurturance, the facts of suicide and murder force family members to confront their covert and overt violence. Incest, which also has violent undertones, is another major attack. One parent assaults while the other collaborates by withholding protection. Equally obvious, although not as dramatic, are the difficulties entailed in adoption and physical disability.

Other family facts have a more temporal, contingent character. Their impact depends on variables such as the particular time at which someone came into the family, the specific family situation at that point in its history or an implicit family commandment handed down through generations. They include the family facts of in-laws, mother's battle fatigue, and mother's symbiosis with an infant as a substitute for her husband. Other possibilities are situational or circumstantial: mother may fight with second daughter because she identifies that pregnancy with father's affair; increased wealth or fame may upset a family's life style. The multigenerational facts include a child's election to a scapegoat-Christ role as family savior; and the inheritance of a preset role from a family myth (e.g., "He's just like great-uncle Carter").

These sample human predicaments are sobering but necessary to consider. Awareness of them alerts us to their power to either handicap or help full human function. That people develop in spite of—or sometimes because of—the facts of life attests to a human resilience and drive for positive growth.

Assumptions About Human Growth and Marriage

The facts of life provide the framework within which humans develop. We make some basic assumptions about this human growth and relatedness.

1. Every human has a biological drive to unfold and to grow—to be the fullest self s/he* can be. This drive to grow may be forced underground in a person so that we cannot detect it, but we assume it is still present.

2. Personal growth occurs in phases, which are physically quite obvious in the child. In the adult the phases of growth are less predictable, less easily recognized and are likely to be set off by experiences which make the person very anxious.

Personal growth is intimately connected with affect—particularly with anxiety—and it is probably not possible to grow much without feeling anxious. We might well call the emotional as well as the physical phases "growing pains."

3. A person has major adjustment choices as to how he will deal with the stress of living: by emotional withdrawal, delinquency, physical illness or the development of neurotic and psychotic symptoms. During childhood the choice of expression or outlet is determined almost entirely by the family setting and climate. In adulthood the choice of symptoms under stress will be determined increasingly by friends, significant persons such as the pastor, and the psychotherapist.

4. Growth is irreversible. This is especially true of emotional growth.

5. People are good for each other to the degree that they are intimate. Such intimacy may or may not involve a sexual union or a sharing of

---

*The combined pronoun form s/he is used at the first appropriate place in a major topic. The male form (he, him) is used for the rest of that topic.

previously secret thoughts and feelings in words. Intimacy requires a physical presence with each other. It cannot be achieved by correspondence. A person who shows extreme affect hunger has usually had little or no intimacy in living with another.

6. Monogamous marriage is the best eventual arrangement to provide the opportunity for growing intimacy. The legal commitment provides maximum stability for the growth of the marital feeling relationship. While all marital partners feel/are shackled at times, in reality it is they who choose to make their marital ties into confining chains or supporting bonds.

7. The marital relationship is the dominant factor in determining the growth and feelings and behavior of all people in the home. The primacy of the marital relationship stems from the force of that power exerted by the marriage, which is greater than the sum of its two partners.

8. The emotional marriage has a natural growth history. It progresses through a series of nodal points, crises or impasses as the years go by. The more alive the partners, the more intense their interaction is likely to be at the points of crisis.

9. Marriage must become characteristically a sexual relationship, which increases with time as the couple becomes more intimate and less inhibited. Here "sexual" refers to sexual intercourse and much more. We also include the entire sense of the male and female relating their persons to each other, expressing their physical and emotional drive toward each other. The creativity of this relationship may be expressed by holding hands, which in itself may be a rich experience for marital partners who are sure of their desire for each other.

In this introductory section, the psycho-biological and psycho-social facts of life and assumptions about human growth and marriage have been presented. The facts and assumptions are closely connected with the existential values of the immediate experiencing of life, the impact of reality and the conditions of human growth and relatedness. All these elements contribute to an understanding of existential family psychotherapy.

EXISTENTIAL FAMILY PSYCHOTHERAPY

Existential Family Psychotherapy is the whole, of which Existential Marital Psychotherapy is a part. In the context of family therapy, marital therapy becomes clearer. An overview of Existential Family Therapy is presented in this section. This existential position is sometimes called nontheoretical. The term is used to warn against the dangers of theory, not to rule out the use of hypotheses. This view appears in the opening caveat on theory. Key concepts and basic premises are presented next, followed by main principles and processes. This section concludes with the major goals of treatment.

Included here are highlights of both theory and practice, which intermingle naturally. In later sections they are separated for convenience, but this does not reflect reality. The difficulty occurs because a linear form, writing, is used to describe circular, multilevel phenomena. Both living and therapy have a circular, feedback nature, as do theory and therapy with each other. For instance, does this statement describe theory or therapy? "Family treatment is a method which is applied to all referrals, not to a specific type." Obviously both. Separation between theory and therapy is arbitrary, although it can be useful.

Theory: Use with Caution

Dedication to theory in family therapy is a screen that will eventually conceal even the process of therapy. Theory is a left-brain abstraction of a two-brained operation. It has a chilling effect on intuition and creativity in general and on the therapy process in particular. If the therapist is dedicated to a theory, or even if he himself believes one theory of psychotherapy, he tends to make it into a theory for change, for growth, even for living. Although theories can be valuable in explaining processes and are important as a preliminary to work of any kind, a good blueprint does not guarantee a good house.

Experiential and Existential Psychotherapy

What can be used as a substitute for theory? Two precious human resources—the accumulated and organized residue of experience; plus the freedom to allow the relationship to happen, to be who you are with the minimum of anticipatory set and maximum responsiveness to authenticity and to your own growth impulses. These resources provide a wealth and a depth far beyond theory's grandest offering.

This process can help people to grow in any form of human relatedness, but it is especially valuable in psychotherapy. The experiential, existential form of therapy is related to the psychoanalytic pattern (Singer, 1965), but is concerned with what happens in the *fantasy life between* two people rather than in the *fantasy life within* a person or in the overt interpersonal life between two people. We assume that the unconscious-to-unconscious communications between doctor and patient are of a primitive character, once both are deeply involved in their efforts to grow. And the only personal response to primary process communication is primary process—that is, free association—by the therapist.

Two case examples will illustrate primary process communication.

Case example 1. When a therapist told her fifty-year-old male patient that she kept "seeing" a yarmulke (skull cap used in the synagogue) on his head, he readily shared the intense envy, fear and deprivation he had felt in his traumatic bar mitzvah some thirty-seven years earlier. The feelings were as alive and powerful in him as they had always been. He could now share and examine them from his adult perspective.

Case example 2. In another case where the therapist and patient were well into treatment and very close, and had reached an impasse, the patient said she felt a large black hole inside. "You have to go find your real father," the therapist said. "I know," replied the patient. "I've always known." "Why didn't you tell me before?" asked the genuinely surprised therapist. Only out of context might this interchange seem mystical. To the participants it was completely logical in the therapy's sequential flow.

Good therapy must include both the therapist's and the patient's physiological, psychosomatic, psychotic and endocrine reactions to a deeply personal interaction system. It also uses metaphors freely, as the case examples show. Appropriate metaphors further primary process communication and clarify issues, with singularly powerful and lasting impact.

The process of non-theoretical or non-technical family psychotherapy also includes a deliberate effort to increase anxiety. Anxiety is the motor that makes therapy move. The therapy team establishes a pattern of caringness, so the family dares to be more anxious instead of escaping into protective, defensive patterns. The therapist models with some member of the family an I-Thou relationship characterized by caring and flexibility, with the aim of pressuring the family into tolerating more anxiety. Much of this modeling is the freedom to share with the family the anxiety and the secret language that the therapist uses with himself or herself, including metaphorical allegories, free association and fantasies. For example, one family is forever stuck with the image of father as a wooden (cigar-store) Indian. Another family imagines itself boring a hole in great-uncle's head, and all climbing in to keep his brains warm.

Much more than facts or feelings, it is the experience of the interview that is important in inducing change. Insight is not enough to effect change; it is rather a by-product of change. Like discovering what one needed only after he got it, a person has to go past insight to see what it is. One young girl's experience provides an example of post-insight learning. She was compelled to ally herself with three delinquent brothers in another family, although she "knew" they couldn't be trusted. Shortly, she found that one of the brothers—which one she couldn't tell—had stolen her last ten dollars, leaving her with no carfare to get to work. Her gut-level rage and sense of betrayal gave her the experiential learning she needed; only then could she apply her insight.

When, without forethought, each person can share spontaneously his or her being, each can create for himself a series of immediate and fresh experiences which can encourage him to try for more exciting growth. Each uses his unconscious self on the way to becoming unself-conscious. First he lets himself experience the moment; he describes the process later, if at all.

While the therapeutic relationship is like other forms of human relatedness, it is also different. Its as-if character makes it an experiment, a pilot project. In addition to its primary process communication, therapy includes talking about life. This talking/thinking can free one to live more recklessly outside the therapy hour. Another freeing operation may occur when the therapist becomes the other "self" that stands off doing commentaries on the patient's ongoing living, so that he can abandon this function in favor of more living.

Experiential therapy aims toward maximal growth rather than symptom relief. Maximal growth includes such developments as increased integrity and greater freedom of choice. In contrast, theory tends to make symptom relief the objective of psychotherapy—whether through adaptation to culture, to family or to situational stress. A case fragment will illustrate a focus on growth rather than on symptom relief. In an initial family interview, a seventeen-year-old girl denied her anorexia and all problems associated with it. The therapists noted the danger of starvation, and asked if she wanted to live or die. The question surprised her. She chose life. The therapists then shared their concern that some family member might substitute another equally serious symptom if the girl were to abandon her anorexia. Daughter elected to explain the therapists' concern to her "un-understanding" parents. They denied this possibility. The topic was dropped. After two or three more interviews, daughter spontaneously abandoned her anorexia. No symptom substitution occurred in the family system.

Relieving the patient's symptom may destroy his effort to integrate the conflicting forces in his own life experience. The symptom may be an exquisite experience of regression in the service of the ego, and relieving the pain might well prevent the formation of a pearl. Patients mainly come into professional therapy out of hope. *Their symptoms indicate their hope for change. Otherwise they would stay hopeless and asymptomatic.*

Therapist and Family Needs

A therapist's own growth is a central aim of experiential therapy. We are here for the same reason that the families are here: we want to grow—to stretch our capacity to care and to expand our own personhood. If a therapist does therapy to extend herself or himself, both the patient and s/he get something out of it or it doesn't happen to either of them. When a therapist enjoys himself, the patients will grow. It helps to be looking for more and more of oneself in the other person, and for one's connections to the other.

Life is random, and openly meeting its randomness helps us grow. Adding any extra quantum, a random element, can give the whole process a twist. Then whatever comes of it will be unforeseen and unexpected. One can look for events that occur out of nowhere, that haven't been preplanned and that have never happened before. The therapist usually has to start the process, but shortly the book begins to write itself.

The more family members who are physically in the room, the easier the writing and the richer and more flowing the book. Whether a therapist sees one or twenty individuals together, all therapy should be family-oriented in his or her approach and thinking. *Family treatment is a method which is applied to all referrals, not to a specific type.* The difference is in kind, not in degree. Once one has worked with a family, he can never again see one or two people as completely separate entities who end with their own skins. And the more families he gets to know, the less he believes in people (as apart, instead of a part). He becomes more and more aware of all that is missing—other people, feelings, times, places, events—even in the simplest situation. These missing elements connect directly with what is happening right now in the office. It is much easier and more rewarding to invite all the ghosts to come in and help in the interview.

Help may come from unexpected sources. In one case, a loyal family maid provided a turning point in treatment. She gave information and loving comfort to the nineteen-year-old wildly suicidal son of a man who had left his family for the latest in a series of homosexual affairs. She recalled the son's confused panic when he was five and father had tried to capture mother's role and force son into a daughter's role by rolling up son's hair into rag curls. "I didn't think he shoulda done that," she said and shook her head. The son sobbed with the pain of the past and present confusion. The maid rocked and comforted him, a little boy again. "Now, Johnny, it's all right," she kept repeating. The maid was as deep into the family system as the mother and the scapegoat son—and as necessary in the treatment.

It is also important to have a co-therapist to work with. Just as the therapist increases the power on the family side by adding more people, he can increase the power on his side in the same way. One therapist can treat a couple, if necessary, but not a family. Here he or she desperately needs a co-therapist; any two-generation unit is too powerful for one therapist. The co-therapist need not be a trained therapist, but he or she must be someone the therapist can respect as a person.

The main advantages of co-therapy, besides that new entity, the dyadic system, are the teaming, the flexibility and the support—the sense of having someone on your side. The support of your co-therapist can enable you to be more open, honest and personal, which can help you push the patients into being more open, honest and personal. The co-therapy relationship is like a marriage, with the therapists modeling the roles of both parents. And just as in a healthy marriage, in a healthy co-therapy team the roles are reversible. Probably the only rule in co-therapy is that whoever moves does so for the twosome. If a therapist can't follow his co-therapist's lead at some point, it is better to oppose him or her directly and fight it out in the open. And in doing so, they again provide an important model for the patients—their children (Napier and Whitaker, 1972).

Separate Theaters of Operation: Therapist's and Patient's Life Spaces

Therapist's life space: the battle for structure. The therapist must be in charge of his or her professional living space—his office–operating room— the therapy itself. This process begins with the patient's initial phone call, and is most intense at the beginning of treatment. It includes the therapist's freedom to decide who shall be present, to schedule the time, to have consultants, to define how all will go about the process and to be, in essence, the rule-maker for the interview setting (Greenberg, 1978). This includes the process within the interview setting as well; a family member intruding between a therapist and another member should be firmly extruded.

The power politics of therapy are crucial. The therapeutic process is seriously impaired if the therapist lets himself or herself become one-down. No patient should trust a therapist who doesn't in a power sense belong to an older generation or who isn't secure and comfortable in his role as a parent-person. The therapist must be willing to confront patients, and he must have enough freedom to be spontaneous. He needs the kind of power that gives him the freedom to be creative. It helps to be clear that he is going to tell them how he sees it. But then he lets them know just as definitely that what they do about it is entirely up to them. All through the therapy he distinguishes between his power and responsibility and their lives. (This is similar to Bowen's distinction between his "I position" and the patients' rights to their life styles [Bowen, 1971].)

Patients' life space: the battle for initiative. Once the therapist defines his or her turf and integrity, he works to force the patients to define their turf. He demands that they live their lives and make their decisions. For example, when a patient asked if she should divorce her husband, the therapist replied, "Let's see now. I've been married for thirty-seven years. I think I'll keep my wife. Why don't you do what you want about your husband?" Once past the initial history, the direction should be up to the family. They have to live in their world in their style. First they have to be who they are before they can make any changes in their living pattern.

After the initial history, and a decision to enter therapy, a contract must be set up. The patients say, in essence, "I can't do it myself." The therapist says, "I can't do it to you or for you." Then he tries to establish the question of whether the family and the therapists can become a team, to mobilize the power of the joint system to help make changes. If this can't happen, there is no sense in going on. It is not psychotherapy; it is just game-playing and an imitation of therapy.

The whole money problem must also be settled early. Included in the contract is the explicit understanding that the family pays for the therapist's time, not for his affect. They have to earn his affection, interest and involvement; these are not under the therapist's control. What he can offer is where he is, who he is and what he has available.

The therapy contract may also include short- or long-term goals. These are highly individual and variable. As in learning to play the piano, some want to play rock; others, Bach. In addition, patient goals often emerge and change as patients change in treatment. It is easier to specify the general aims of the therapist.

Treatment Goals and Termination

Existential Family Psychotherapy has five main treatment goals: (1) Personal growth for all, therapists and patients alike, with a concomitant aim of becoming more of a person and less of a function. (2) Acceptance of generational boundaries and of membership in one's own generation. (3) Constructive use of affect, with these subgoals: to increase anxiety, to own and resolve one's anger, to recover the capacity to care and to meet and own one's creative craziness. (4) Increased intimacy, with these subgoals: to achieve real intimacy and cuddling; to discover that one can be symbiotically close without being bound, vulnerable or victimized; to increase unity and individuation; and to explore and experience the heights and depths of one's relationship. (5) Taking back one's own life fully, facing the terror and the unknown which makes living continue to be scary, exciting, terrible and fun.

The criteria for ending therapy also vary. Since people enter therapy when they are stuck, it can end whenever there is an end of the inertia in the patients' living process. Like a pendulum, it has to get moving. This could even happen in the first interview. Napier offers another answer to the question, How do you know when it's time to end therapy? He says, "When you've finished a meal, you're full."

MARITAL THEORY: DYNAMICS AND IMPASSES

The common developmental stages of marriage are examined in this section, with marital dynamics viewed from various perspectives. The first subsection, "Premarital Struggles," counterposes commonly held myths about marriage with the facts of the maturing needs of adolescents and young adults. The second subsection, "Marital Dynamics," examines several main processes in and characteristics of all marriages. The third subsection describes some major nodal crisis points which may help marriages to grow. The final subsection identifies the kinds of marriages more likely to be seen in psychotherapy.

Premarital Struggles: Myths About Marriage Versus the Facts of Life

A young person struggling toward growth, self-possession *and* intimacy is often tempted to embrace the *Myths About Marriage* in place of the facts of life. The first one is the *Myth of Unconditional Positive Regard.* No adult gives unconditional positive regard—not parent, spouse or therapist. One can get it only from a baby in the first nine months of life. Once s/he plays peek-a-boo, the love gets trickier. From then on, love is always a reciprocal trade agreement.

The agreement's terms and trades will be richer and more exciting, the further the individual has gone in his or her struggle for personhood before climbing on the marry-go-round. The problem for an adolescent is to become an adult in the framework of his own parents; to become an individual in a setting of teaming without being a prima donna. His high school project is to divorce his parents. If he can successfully separate from his family and still ultimately belong to it, then he can break the *Myth of the Delusion of Fusion.* This myth fantasizes that togetherness can be absolute, forever and unvarying. Coming out of a dependency on his family, he can either fight out his isolation or escape into premature fusion. If he can stand the isolation, he can grow from letting himself experience the feelings of just being: the beingness of non-doing. He can learn to be alone, without friends, without diversions and without dependence on others. He can learn to be with his dream self, with his infant self and with his body. He can learn Tillich's koan, "Being is becoming."

If he negotiates this demanding growth phase successfully, he is much more ready for the interpersonal dance, testing to see how well their parts complement each other: the fit of his silences with hers, of his head with hers, his genitals with hers, his silliness with hers, his hates with hers, his fears with hers. If their high school project is to divorce their parents, marriage then becomes their choice of a Ph.D. field. Here the complementary fit is his wholeness with her wholeness. It is a decision to enter into a lifetime of struggle.

If, instead, a young person flees from his forty days of wandering in search of himself in the desert, he is more prone to accept another popular *Myth: I'll Be Different After I'm Married.* This cliché fantasizes that marriage is a therapeutic experience leading to health. But marriage has no magic wand. Each person is already a lifetime member of a preexisting love-and-loyalty system: his and her families of origin. From early childhood each carries ingrained models for marriage, masculinity, femininity, motherhood, father-hood and all other family roles, as enacted in the drama of his particular family. These powerful models determine very much of the person's roles in his own life. It is amazing how little we live our lives. Jung said that you don't live life; it lives you.

Thus, each couple starts out as psycho-social remnant of two families. The mates are really two scapegoats, scouts sent out by their families to reproduce their kind. They are not two people deciding to get together; they are two families trying to get together. This happened at one wedding where, in unison, the bride's and groom's four parents gave their children to each other, despite the prior divorce and alienation from each other of one set of parents. Such an open acknowledgment of the two families' joint effort to come together can help the couple to establish a firmer "we."

The partners in a couple choose each other with exquisite accuracy; an exact unconscious-to-unconscious match. Each selects precisely a particular other who can best fulfill his or her emotional needs. Voltaire said that we each get exactly what we need, but the problem is we don't know what we need until after we've gotten it. Falling in love is transference: positive, negative and combined. The partners sense that the other is a carbon of a prototype—"She looks like my mother." The clues are hidden, but the partners hook themselves into this bilateral covert cue lock-in.

If they marry before each has successfully fought out his and her isolation, they simply assume that their courtship will lead to their identity completion and that their We-ness will solve their lack of personhood. This is trying to make believe that they can grow up overnight by marrying another sixteen-year-old and becoming thirty-two. There is no push to be a whole person in this arrangement. This marriage is a folie à deux. The couple buys the *Myth that You Are the Center of My World.* This reciprocal trade agreement is usually covert. ("I know I'm the center of my world,—but—it feels empty inside—so—let's 'play.'") 'I'll pretend you're the center of my world if you'll pretend I'm the center of your world.' This is a sham version of the childhood games of "You must be . . . (e.g., the mommy) and I must be . . . (e.g., the daddy)." It fosters a series of make-believes that move the partners further and further away from being honest with each other, while it aids their emotional suicide by absorption.

All intimate twosomes start out as friendships. Marriage itself begins as a fairly simple process having to do with the partners' yen to expand themselves and include somebody else, to be part of a whole that's greater than either one. Each individual is a subsystem, and their coupling creates a new, larger system, the marital relationship. It encompasses their current and past life experiences together, along with their fluctuating thoughts and feelings toward each other, their fantasies, memories, expectations, dreams, fears and everything else relating to each other. But as the relationship becomes more complex, they confront yet another *Myth: I Didn't Marry Your #$!&*# Family!* This fantasy stems from the transference phenomenon of the initial relationship. Each does become a part of, rather than apart from, his and her spouse's family. But the battle to remold the other, to 'make you like my family,' may go on long after the honeymoon. The struggle for whose family this is going to be modeled after often continues throughout the entire marriage.

The process of the struggle becomes clearer as we examine the marital dynamics.

Marital Dynamics

In every marriage there are two concurrent processes: the legal commitment and the feeling experience—the binding and the bonding. They are distinct from each other. The binding provides constraints and support; the bonding offers individual and marital growth.

The marriage's legal aspect is formalized by a ceremony. This ritual validates a legal/social partnership planned to have maximum stability. The object is to promote harmonious interaction based on fixed values, customs and habits to insure this stability. The partnership has to do with common property ownership, living on the same premises, joint checking accounts and sharing in all the realities and responsibilities of a business partnership, such as income-tax reports. The rules that apply in these business aspects of marriage are the same as those which apply in the business world at large, such as the rule of fairness between the contracting parties. But other than the gradual accumulation of real estate over the years, there is no provision for growth in this business aspect.

In contrast, the laws of society do not apply to the feeling experience of the marital process, and fairness is not an issue. John Warkentin said, "All's fair in love and war, and marriage is both" (Warkentin and Whitaker, 1967, p. 241). The feeling level is typically unstable and ever-changing, with peaks and valleys of love and hate. It is this constant flux which permits and encourages ongoing growth in the partners and in the marriage.

While the legal marriage emerges from the ceremony complete and full-grown, the emotional marriage is only in its infancy at that time. These two levels are connected: the legal marriage provides protection for the instability and stress of the emotional marriage. The heights and depths of marital joy and sorrow are made possible by the legal binding, so that they will not separate impulsively at times of mutual hatred. This firmness of the legal tie allows the marital partners to expect experiences of increasing intimacy and intensity in the course of their entire marriage.

Part of the precise partner-selection process lies in the apparent fact that the two partners' quantitative dynamics are equal, and probably identical. Both are equally powerful. Their aggression is equal. Their manipulativeness is equal. Their jealousy is equal. Their fragility is equal. Their dependency is equal. Their immaturity is equal. They are the same emotional age. Their quantum of emotional upset or pathology is equal. And their affect hunger is equal.

The feeling level of marital relatedness is constantly changing. The partners decide jointly, usually implicitly, how hot or cold they want their relationship to be at any particular moment, how much closeness or distance they need to satisfy their mutual affect hunger. And they set the emotional thermostat of their relationship accordingly. One partner functions as the heater and the other as the cooler. In this way, each one plays a part in maintaining their system's homeostatic balance within covert but well-defined upper and lower limits.

Thus the power of the marital relationship system controls its two individual members—the subsystems. This balance of power is very exact. To keep the balance, the system calls for the partners to behave in reciprocal, complementary patterns with each other. The dynamics are like a seesaw, with one partner more overt and the other more covert. She will act dominant, while he acts passive; she expressive, he withdrawn; she crazy, he sane; he loving, she hostile; he the chaser; she the chaste.

An observer hooked on seeing the partners as individuals will readily buy the *Dichoto-Myths* prevalent among therapists and other people: He is strong (inference: she is weak); he's responsible (she's irresponsible); she's honest (he's a con artist); he is good (she is bad); he is well (she is sick); she is growing (he is stagnating). But in a systems view of an established twosome, it is unimportant which partner expresses which specific behavior, since the behavioral roles are interchangeable. The central point is that whichever way the couple chooses to play it out, they have prearranged what role each one will play. Every act is bilateral, and both bear equal responsibility. Every interaction is the next in a long-term chain of interactions.

In healthy, unstable systems, as in competent ball teams, the members interchange roles according to what best fits each person and situation at the moment. In static, stable systems, people get stuck in fixed roles—one person to one function. The more fixed the role or function, the more one loses his personhood and *becomes* the function.

Throughout the marriage each partner strives for two seeming opposites: greater unity and greater individuation. They marry to be together, often to lose themselves in each other. And up to a point this teaming or solidarity can help each other to grow as an individual. Paradoxically, greater union and greater separateness do go hand-in-hand, so that the couple can continue growing closer *and* more unique as individuals throughout their marriage.

The partners can neither belong completely nor separate completely. Being part of a marriage and being a self have to be in balance with each other. More belonging and more individuating have to grow synchronously. The partners can be only as much married as they can be separate. They can be only as much separate as they can be married. The struggle for oneness and for separation is an endless dialectic (Singer, 1965). With the dialectic they can go on turning up their marital thermostat for the duration of their marriage.

How Marriages Grow: Nodal Crises

As the years go by, the emotional marriage progresses naturally through a series of nodal crisis points, or impasses. The more alive the partners, the more intense their interaction is likely to be at these points. The nodal points afford the best times, perhaps even the only times, when the partners can modify their relationship or reset their marriage's emotional thermostat.

The honeymoon is often a nodal point, even in this day and age. This may be especially true when a couple has not had premarital intercourse. It is surprising to see how long a shadow the experiences of the wedding night and honeymoon may cast in the marriage. The partners' anticipated culmination of sexual bliss may be thwarted by her early menstruation. Or he may be embarrassed to find himself impotent or otherwise sexually inadequate. The disappointment seems to raise an implicit omen of later disappointments to come and to suggest that other illusions will be shattered.

The first pregnancy and birth is a period of special stress. As the pregnancy progresses, even a young couple who wants their child wholeheartedly may feel threatened and upset by separate and different feelings. She has the normal fear of death as she prepares to give birth. He may have to cope with feelings of being a bystander or bit player in the tremendous drama about to occur, even when they plan for his inclusion and help during childbirth. (In one case, a prospective father who had long prepared for his part in the event was terrified and then furious at his last-minute exclusion and her Caesarean section.) Even though they may feel greater closeness in their joy that they can mutually produce new life, they also feel a sense of much greater responsibility and fear. After the birth, there is the intrusion of the third person. She may feel overburdened and have the "baby blues;" he may feel almost like a stranger. Although the couple often eagerly expects their first baby, as a means to deepen their love and encourage their marriage's growth, it does not reduce stress; it increases it. This is a time when the couple may question whether each was meant for the other and whether they really want to stay together forever.

The marital gap often widens as each partner has affairs; hers may be with the baby, his with the business (or vice versa). Within the family there are both the stresses and the joys of sexual triangles for the couple to cope with. Father may be able to be more loving with his little baby girl than he can be with his wife, and his wife is jealous. But these triangles can also give the partners greater emotional and role flexibility in their relationship. Any two can team up against the third, or one can mediate between the other two.

If the marriage survives the first baby, as many do, the second baby may pose an even more serious threat, as the couple again faces the difficulties of pregnancy and delivery. But this time they know more what lies ahead, and they may be much more disillusioned about their marriage being "heaven on earth." After the second baby, the wife may become desperately afraid of another pregnancy and the husband may become increasingly angry with her sexual unavailability, which he may diagnose as *her* problem of frigidity.

If the marital gap continues to widen, the partners may choose allies for their teams. There can be in-law wars and more choosing of sides. Everyone may gang up on mother and she may not be able to survive it without father's support. Or she may worry as father plays at castrating the boys so they will know they belong to the younger generation and are not yet adults. There are infinite possibilities for teaming and for triangles: two-generation, three-generation or the war of the sexes; some may be flexible and growth-inducing; others, rigidly fixed and deadly.

The Ten-Year Impasse Syndrome, give or take three years, is a characteristic time of stress. During the ten years, the couple has experienced turmoil, change and interaction. The partners have probably started whatever family they are likely to have. The transference feelings with which they initially married are largely exhausted, and they see themselves as having "fallen out of love." Each sees very clearly the character defects in the other. They often feel they made "the wrong choice." Disillusion leads to thoughts of dissolution. Each strongly suspects that neither is ever going to remold the other. They see that neither can win against the other, and they realize that each of them has somehow paralyzed the creativity and spontaneity in the other. They feel locked in. One or both may feel 'I can't change anything; all is lost.' Their marital growth has come to a grinding halt.

The ten-year syndrome may be resolved in one or more of several ways. Most constructively, there may be a "civil war," which results in the freeing of both "slaves." The partners may fight it out within the marriage and gradually regain their individuation. To achieve this they must pass through a "loss of face" and destruction of their fantasy constructs about each other. But instead they will find an increased acceptance of each other as real human persons. If they then feel very naked and defenseless with each other for a time, this is an added bonus to reward them for the struggle which they perpetrated. This process can make for the most magnificent and deepest experience they can have in the marriage.

In essence, it is only after a couple has "fallen out of love" that an adult, warm, loving, "I-Thou" relationship is possible for them. If they can find this deeper person-to-person love for each other, they may well achieve a higher level of marital integration and go on together from there. In our culture, the ten-year syndrome is usually the first opportunity for a couple to establish this kind of wholehearted marriage.

Unfortunately, there are other, less productive outcomes. The family squabbles may become more repetitive and pointless as the areas of mutual irritation and disappointment become symbolic and painful. The hostility underlying marital fights often stems from the partners' increasing frustration at the failure of their bilateral pseudo-therapy, where each has taken turns being therapist and patient to the other. In a marriage with this kind of continuing mutual pseudo-therapeutic character, the stop-growth point must come sooner or later. It may happen when one partner demands more than the other one wants to give—perhaps more supportive parenting—or when one wants more unity and the other more individuation. Or it can happen when both want more individuation but fear the reality of it. While marriage *is* therapeutic and people do help each other to grow during the early years, it may not merely resolve problems; it also often creates others.

The ten-year syndrome may also show itself in symptoms like psychosomatic illness, job maladjustment, social withdrawal or unfaithfulness in one or both partners. The affair may be merely affective, in the sense of admiration and dependent idealization inherent in falling in love with one's boss or with a talented colleague. However, it is often sexual as well.

This recalls another familiar *Marital Myth: If You're Going to Run Around with Somebody Else, Don't Tell Me.* There is probably nothing in a marriage which the other spouse doesn't know on some level. No secrets are possible; only implicit nonverbal plans. She says to him over breakfast, "Did you hear about Rocky Jones and his secretary?" "No," he answers, "but did you see what those swingers in Bayside are up to?" And they're off and running. Infidelity is always bilateral, preplanned (usually implicitly) by both, and both want it that way. They set it up so that each is having an affair at the same time. His may be with money and hers with school.

The affair is an effort to be growthful for each and for the marriage. It comes about when the partners agree that the temperature of the marriage is cooling. They decide implicitly that one of them is going out to gain some new kind of independence—to form a triangle by teaming up with someone else against the spouse. The third person is an amateur therapist. This activates the marital dyad through more intense fights, a warmer marriage bed, or both. The dyad takes on a new kind of spice.

The couple can also use the affair as a model, to demonstrate their marital goal. In effect, one partner points to the affair and says, "Look, this is what I'd like to have with you. *I'm* capable. How about you?"

Quaintly, the affair is never another new dyad. It's always a triangulation of the marital dyad. A person in a close dyadic relationship can't simply move to a different one. Instead, the partner replays his original mother-wife triangle: but now he makes his wife into his mother—the bad one; his new woman into his wife—the good one (for now); and he has a split transference, with all its complexities. With all the negative assigned to the wife and all the positive to the new woman, life seems magically beautiful. But while it's probably true that you can't go home again, it's also true that you can't get free of your home ties by this kind of triangulation. One woman in treatment described the problem in systems terms. "We hurt me. We hurt Dad, too. We made him lonesome. We made me steal the kids from Daddy, just like we stole Daddy from his mommy and daddy, and like we stole Mommy from her mommy and daddy."

Divorce. Another possible outcome of the ten-year syndrome is divorce. The couple, having "fallen out of love" and its bilateral transference broken up, may become locked in so tight to their mutual doctor-patient pattern that it looks like the partners have only two ways to be individuals: to break apart entirely or to actually destroy each other and maybe the family itself.

When divorce impends—and it usually does at some point(s) in every marriage—it involves a series of endless struggles, implied or explicit, with added threats. Many times what people really want, on the other side of their ambivalence, is help in reestablishing the balance of power. They need some sense that the hostility they feel ashamed of or guilty about is a pattern of the usual marriage. They need some sense of how identical their pathology is— that his pride is as bad as her pride, that her crying is no different from his pouting silence, that her rubber hammer is as lethal as his stiletto. If they can get the sense of these, and of the health and the love in their relationship, many times this is a major contribution to their changing the style of their fighting and making it more constructive.

But if they cannot make this change, the threats escalate until finally the hurt pride of one partner makes for a behavioral response that leads toward real divorce (Bateson, 1971). Up to this point, the major weapon has been only the threat of divorce. Now somebody in the relationship gets so desperate that they bring up the ultimate weapon—which is to change the rules. As in *Who's Afraid of Virginia Woolf?*, suddenly she feels the need not just to talk to the lawyer, to threaten her mate, but to move that one more behavioral step into insisting that the lawyer *do something*. And the lawyer, not understanding that she just wants support, may take her seriously.

If the final step is taken, the legal commitment, as symbolized by the divorce decree, is dissolved. Money, ownership of property, living arrangements and other realities connected with the business aspects of the marriage are divided in some final arrangement. Legally the separateness in these areas is complete. Just as the wedding ceremony symbolized the beginning of the legal business commitment, the divorce decree symbolizes its end.

But on the marriage's emotional level, the bonds are not so easily severed. When the couple in a well-established marriage tries to cut off their profound emotional investment in each other and in the marriage, they are trying to perform a Siamese twin operation which will leave each raw and bleeding for years, sometimes for life.

The couples' emotional investment may be likened to their money in the bank. Any marriage is like an irrevocable trust for the lifetime of the participants. The income from it may be withdrawn, but the principal always remains in the bank. One may be able to leave a first partner and subsequently deposit his feeling with another partner as they build a second marriage. But he cannot take his original feeling commitment away from the first partner and give that same feeling to a second partner. When a couple gets married emotionally, to whatever degree, the partners have irrevocably committed feeling to each other which they cannot then withdraw again and place elsewhere.

In many cases the first marriage is probably the best one a couple can achieve in their lifetime. The illusion that a person can start again is just that; it is like a delusional time machine. The second marriage doesn't make one nineteen again. It tends to be cooler and more distant. And the second partner is likely to be a close facsimile of the first.

The Empty-Nest Syndrome. If, on the other hand, the couple stays together, their next major stress period will develop at about the time their children, or particularly the last child, leaves home. The empty-nest syndrome may also coincide with the time when one or both partners retire from earning a livelihood. This period is always very frightening. It is tempting to give up, to feel that life is ended and to psychologically die. Actually, life at this time can be very warm, personal and rich.

The couple's choice between psychological death or life is real. The impact of the changes in their life is often greater than they could have expected, no matter how carefully they planned their retirement time and style. After the initial flush of release from routine, they may feel shelved in a way they didn't choose. Some find the long, unplanned hours lonely, and future prospects terrifying. Life is no longer structured by other peoples' needs and the demands of appointments. Each is free to do exactly what s/he wishes with all the hours of each day. No urgent pleas of "When can we eat, Ma?" No crucial board meetings. Each may feel that no one needs him or her anymore—he to do and provide, she to nurture. Life seems a series of losses, coming thicker and faster—of the comfortably familiar places and things, and of people. The neighborhood changes—always for the worse, it seems. The phone rings less often. Friends move away or die. Silence weighs. The very peace and quiet the couple may have craved in the busier years may now be oppressively endless.

The other side of this condition is that the partners can use this freedom to savor a new honeymoon. Responsible now only to themselves, they can linger over a drink or a sunset; they can more freely make love or a last-minute theater date. Each can live more spontaneously, for himself and herself, and together. And they can use their greater need for each other to develop their intimacy still further.

Some find excitement and challenge in the free time and the opportunities to pursue new activities—learning, art forms, travel, hobbies. They can enrich old friendships and make new ones. They can contribute time and energy to felt needs, giving of self in perhaps different ways from before.

They know they continue to have much to offer of their personhood to each other and to others—the richness of their lives and learning, the lifetime of experiences, shared jokes and predicaments—and an ongoing openness to new experience. They know that their children and grandchildren and other young people need not only their specific personhood, but need them in other roles. The young people need them as members of the front-line generation, both as models of vital living and as buffers between death and the next-younger generation. And they need them as time-binders, to link the past and the present to the future—to tell the stories of how it was in the family, to give the kids a richer, deeper sense of their roots and place in that particular family.

More than what they do, the ebb and flow of vital interests and energies the partners have available to invest in self and others will probably determine their choice of psychological life or death. If they actively pursued their I-ness and their We-ness in the earlier years, they will undoubtedly negotiate the transition through the empty-nest stage more easily. For the transition requires that they redefine their identities and roles, individually and as a couple. The task calls for each partner to recreate his and her life and their marriage. It is simply a continuation of their life task.

Kinds of Marriage

The material on marital theory which has been presented here indicates that marriages which seem different from one another may share common processes. These commonalities suggest that there are three major kinds of marriage systems. At any point in time, most well-established marriages will fall into one of these classes.

1. *Stable.* Any emotional fluctuations in a stable marriage stay well within the clearly defined upper and lower limits of the couple's emotional thermostat, so that its homeostatic system is always on an even keel. There are two types of stable systems: (a) *Stable and dead.* This kind of marriage is static and nongrowthful. The couple maintains a relationship frozen into either pseudo-mutual politeness or pseudo-mutual hostility. This stable marriage is like a stable person: dead. (b) *Stable and growthful.* Here the couple does allow emotional fluctuations. They can love or hate, be close or separate, sexual or aggressive in the marriage. But the growth stays within the thermostat's limits.

We rarely see a stable marriage in treatment. Either the partners are satisfied with it or they handle the unhappy or unstable times in private.

2. *Unstable and growthful.* Ideally, this kind of marriage can provide optimal conditions for continual individual and marital growth. The couple can tolerate emotional fluctuations within limits, and the partners can also set their emotional thermostat higher, so that they can increase the excitement in their entire marriage system as it goes on.

3. *Stalemated chaos.* This is the opposite of the stable and dead kind of marriage. Here the system lacks limits which are well-defined enough, and the partners are locked into interactions that are nongrowth-producing. This is like a car with its motor racing and its gears stuck.

Sometimes a marriage can change from being unstable and growthful to one of stalemated chaos. This is obviously one kind which needs marital therapy.

Besides highlighting common processes in marriages, the section on marital theory demonstrates that the most important dynamics and developments in marriage possess a basic sameness throughout the marital changes. This underlying continuity reappears in the discussions of premarital struggles, marital dynamics and nodal crisis points. It is also useful in developing treatment principles of Existential Marital Therapy, which follows.

MARITAL THERAPY: TECHNIQUES

A generation or two ago the unquestioned norm was for the partners to totally submerge their individuality in the twosome. Then, in the late 1960's, the pendulum swung drastically: each one demanded total individuality to "do his own thing." Now, some ten years later, we seem to be coming back to a more moderate position where couples are trying to have both unity and individuation in their marriages.

While styles and goals in marital relating are influenced by short-term societal trends, marriages possess an underlying continuity, as discussed in the previous section on marital theory. Existential Marital Psychotherapy builds on this continuity in developing its major concepts and tools for treating the marital partners and their relationship. These concepts and techniques are presented in this section. The areas include likely couples for therapy, marital and couple-therapist relations, the initial interview, the process, other techniques, therapeutic impasse and therapist impotence.

Marital Therapy for Whom?

When should a couple go to a psychotherapist? They should go when their increased union and their increased individuation have come to a grinding halt. Or at the first hint of one or both being lured into the amateur psychotherapy of a sexual affair. Or with any other split in the decision to work it out openly within the twosome of the marriage.

By the time they are desperate enough to seek professional psychotherapy, the couple will usually have a well-established system of relating to each other and to the marriage. Generally, there are three types of couples we see in treatment:

1. *Couples who are on the verge of divorce.* They try to find emotional freedom through legal divorce because their union is so tight that they can't individuate. It's as if the two partners in the intimate friendship are now caught in running a mom-and-pop store twenty-four hours a day, with no separate personhood of their own; everything happens in the store. They are victims of the twosome.

2. *Couples where one partner presents as the patient.* Here one has agreed to be the scapegoat, the symptom-carrier. It's his drinking or her infidelity or his prematurity or her frigidity or his asthma or her hypertension or his affair. Also by mutual agreement, the other partner compensates by being very solid, stable, conforming and helpful. This is a good example of the reciprocal seesaw pattern discussed in the section on marital dynamics, where one partner is overt and the other is covert. Couples presenting this pattern strongly tempt nonsystems therapists to believe the dichoto-myth that one partner is the angel and the other is the devil.

3. *Couples where the scapegoat presents in another generation.* It's his depressed mother or her alcoholic father or their son-the-car-stealer or their

daughter-the-dropout, etc. The scapegoat is in either the grandparents' or the children's generation. The couple appears perfectly "normal" aside from their great upset and concern over the scapegoat.

The truth is that, like the open-mouthed ceramic bird sitting atop the baking pie, the scapegoat is simply letting out the system's total steam. In these cases it is critical to see the scapegoat generation, too, for as many interviews as it takes to detumesce the scapegoat and inflame the marriage.

Styles of Marital Relating

Couples seeking treatment vary considerably in how they relate to each other and to their marriage. There are probably as many specific ways of marital relating as there are marriages. However, certain interactions are more typical in one marital style, while different interactions characterize other styles. The styles may overlap, but each appears often enough to warrant the labels below.

1. *Simple adoption.* In this type of marriage one partner agrees to be the child forever and the other agrees to be the parent forever. The marriage of Nora and her (father-) husband in Ibsen's *A Doll's House* is a good example.

2. *Bilateral adoption.* Here each of them plays child to the other's parent.

3. *Alcoholic.* This resembles the simple-adoption style, but is actually different in that it is not an adoption but a bilateral game. For instance, he plays the little brat and she plays the good little girl. If he's the alcoholic acting like a four-year-old still bottle-feeding, she's a pseudo-adult, a six-year-old doing a good job of taking care of little brother. But she is exhausted by her effort to be a nonperson, a function instead of a person. Her symptoms are those of battle fatigue, depression, a sense of hopelessness and a feeling that all is lost.

4. *Perverted.* This is an impersonal marriage, with no anger and no sex. It is all very cool. It is like a business where two colleagues just happen to share office space, or a friendship in which somewhat distant colleagues establish a good, long-range relationship.

5. *Lifetime affair.* The partners in this style skim life's surface, treat everything as equal fun and take nothing very seriously.

6. *Pseudo-marriage.* Here they sleep back-to-back, and each finds someone else with whom s/he can sleep.

7. *Bilateral pseudo-therapeutic.* This describes about 90 percent of American marriages. They start out with each trying to be therapist to the other's "child." Initially, this helpfulness is very valuable for their growth. But at about the time things are going well, it all starts to go sour. Each feels something has to change. Each increases the efforts to get help from and give help to the partner. The frustration increases as they get more locked in and

less satisfied. One or both want to break away, as though to leave home. At some point they have to stop trying to be helpful if they are going to be separate people and if the marriage is going to continue to grow.

Divorce is often the method chosen to get away from the "therapy impasse," with the conclusion that that one was a bad marriage, and the implicit hope that a new (amateur) therapist may solve it all. But couples usually can't individuate through divorce. (See previous discussion of dynamics in the affair and in divorce.) They simple remarry, repeat the pattern and develop another massive symbiosis. The way out is not *away*; it is *in, through, out* and *beyond*.

Couple and Therapist: How They Relate

Marital therapy is the process of the therapist trying to help the couple maintain the marital system while s/he is helping each partner to develop enough individuality so that neither feels enslaved. The object of marital therapy is to raise the marriage's emotional thermostat, not to interchange the heater and the cooler.

While a family is a biological unit of two, three or more generations, a marital couple is a social-psychological unit whose same-generation partners are transferred to each other. Thus, marital therapy is actually more like supervision within a couple's ongoing treatment of each other: the husband and wife carry on a one-to-one interview between them, and the therapist becomes a supervisor. The therapist is thus able to be a consultant to the relationship rather than the more symbolic person he is in one-to-one therapy. He can be much more directly confronting with them, and so, more useful to them.

Marital therapy has several advantages for a family therapist-in-training as well as for the couple. As a kind of half-function family therapy, it affords an ideal way to learn about whole-family therapy. Marital therapy also has similarities to treating a sibling adolescent group, that is, four or five siblings in the same family, without the parents being present. This offers an opportunity to establish peer solidarity as well as appropriate generational boundaries.

Another advantage of treating a couple is that there is an actual split transference to be examined and resolved. Early in therapy, when the partners relate to each other as children-siblings, each sees the therapist as his/her mother (all good), but also as his/her stepmother (all bad). This demands that each partner make the strange effort to handle this triangle, probably the most primitive triangle at the point of a beginning marriage. Later, as the couple can relate to each other as adult marital partners, each will see the therapist as his/her mother and mother-in-law. This is a split transference which they can resolve, since they no longer need to assign all the positive to one and all the negative to the other.

Throughout the treatment, the therapist forms and is part of a triangle with the couple. He is a mediator between the two, able to team up with the wife at one point, with the husband at another and with the marriage at still another. He also has considerable freedom to move in and out of the relationship, as well as sideways. The therapist's teaming must stay flexible, however. In general he is better off staying in the middle so that he can keep the third patient—the marriage—there, and treat it. If he gets stuck on one side of the husband-wife struggle, he simply gives them another problem and he will make it more difficult for them to resolve their struggle.

The Initial Interview

It is important to insist on seeing both partners together initially, and for however long it takes for all concerned to get the sense of the couple or family as patient—a crucial sense of the whole unit. This is especially true for a couple in the throes of the ten-year impasse syndrome, where it is most unwise for the therapist to undertake treatment of only one of the partners. Their temptation is so great to simply throw over the investment in living that they have made with each other that individual psychotherapy for either of them can easily be the final straw. We have observed that most individual psychotherapies of partners in the throes of the stay-or-leave struggle end in divorce. At the least, a therapist seeing one individual becomes that partner's soul-mate. This is even more so when both partners are seeing individual psychotherapists.

A therapist who sees only one partner to start with automatically becomes the mother-in-law to the other partner. To some extent he can compensate by seeing the other partner for his/her own interview(s) or by having a co-therapist see the partner, but these operations are expediencies. Seeing the couple together is preferable.

It is also most desirable to have a three-generation first interview, with both sets of the couple's parents and the couple's children present. It is very helpful to have the extended families in at the beginning of treatment; they have been in on the breakup one way or another, symbolically or in reality. And one can automatically assume that many ghosts are in the room with the couple: his and her parents, perhaps their grandparents, siblings of various generations, perhaps a housekeeper, a neighbor, a secretary—the list of possible ghosts is infinite.

The therapist can be freer if s/he goes in cold and does not preplan. The minimal information from the phone call is enough. It helps to start with the person farthest from the family's center—usually the father—and work into the center, where the mother and scapegoat are. With a full extended family present, the order could be father's father and then father's mother, followed by mother's father and mother's mother; then father, the other children, and finally mother and the scapegoat. Initial questions are usually quite system-oriented: "What's with your family?" or "Can you tell me about your family?"

The therapist should try to touch on all the crucial areas, so that the family knows they are important—suicide, homicide, death, divorce, incest, serious illness, family loyalty patterns, alliances of subgroups (e.g., all the males, mother-son versus father, younger siblings versus older sibs, middle child with parents). Many questions in this exploration, especially those about triangle dynamics, are best asked of others rather than of the principals. This can be done indirectly, as if it's the therapist's own fantasy: "Do you think Dad and Mother are going to get a divorce?" "Do you think Dad's playing around? No? Well, that's nice—How's school?" These loaded questions can be raised quite easily in an initial interview, where there is no therapeutic relationship. They cannot readily be asked later in treatment, when the relationship has begun to form but is still too tentative to support the weight.

Scapegoating dynamics as represented by symptoms should also be explored and identified. In addition to the more obvious forms, such as infidelity, scapegoating can include a family member's absence, physical illness, psychosis, temper tantrums, stealing, etc. When the symptoms are consistently manifested by one family member, s/he is the scapegoat—the decoy who only looks like "the patient." In truth, s/he is the ceramic pie bird, carrying the stress for the entire system.

It is assumed that at any particular point family dynamics are so thoroughly circular that there is no one person who is "doing anything" to the other—it's always a joint arrangement. The therapist must help all members to experience the reality that the system is responsible for whatever happens in the family, and that family life is based on the overall decisions of the unit. The therapeutic object is to distribute overt anxiety throughout the entire family, to equalize it, so that it becomes excitement and fun, and no longer the terror it is when the "designated patient" carries all of it alone. With the anxiety spread, everybody has a sense of his individual responsibility for changing himself as well as the whole family.

The therapist may take the number of interviews he needs to explore family patterns and to clarify the couple's roles and dynamics within the larger system. Then the therapist can tell the family or couple what he sees and what his experience of the interactions has been, can touch on the impasses in their current life and possibly in therapy, and state how he feels about both the couple's and his own strengths and what the therapeutic prospects seem to be.

Then, later, it is up to the couple to redecide whether or not to enter marital therapy. If they do return, they know they have chosen a person with a position, who is honest enough to say when he is bored, scared, angry, impotent or whatever. Only then can the partners and the therapist contract to try to mobilize the power of the joint system to make changes.

The Couple in Marital Therapy: The Process

Once the couple decides to enter therapy, the therapist has three patients in treatment: him, her and the marriage. All three need treatment first, simultaneously and concurrently throughout the therapy. As with the family anxiety, the couple must be helped to see that stress, pain and anxiety is in their whole system, not just in one partner. Each spouse must see how just like one another each is. that what each sees in the other is equally true for both. Each runs away when the tension gets high, or each blames the other or the other's parents, or they try to hide behind the parents' pathology. Each contributes to the intricate dance. Each must get the sense of the importance of the marriage.

To help them grasp the sense of the marriage as patient, they can be asked what would happen if each married somebody just like himself. If he married someone as cool as he, the marriage would be a deep-freeze forever. And if she married someone as revved-up as she, they would burn the place down. Then they can grasp the ways they coordinate and complement the relationship, and they can experience the relationship itself as patient. And then, when they can learn how to use "we" and "us" rather than "he" and "she," they can discuss themselves as a twosome. The story of the mother who said, "We hurt me. We hurt Dad, too . . ." illustrates this well. (This was mentioned in the discussion of the affair.)

At the same time that all are working on the marriage, the therapist is also helping the partners to decourt, that is, to disentangle, so as to recapture (or perhaps simply to capture) their individuation. To help the partners to resolve the locked-in impasse and to individuate, three basic steps and several additional specific techniques may be used:

1. The partners become peers in the same generation. This happens since each one looks on the therapist as his own (parent), and so on his spouse as a peer in the same generation; and, perhaps for the first time, as another adult. When one spouse attempts to be "helpful" to the other, the therapist can demand, "Cut it out! You failed as her therapist. Now let me do it. You can't

be her old man." (Or "his momma.") Once they can abandon the roles of child or parent to their spouse, they can both be kids to the therapist. They need to be helped to be children together, to have fun, play and be silly together.

2. The affect is increased. Another reason for stopping the couple's pseudo-therapeutic "helping" operation is the fact that such "helping" decreases the affect—especially the anxiety—that they have available for therapy. Since the couple and the therapist must be able to mobilize, channel and use as much constructive anxiety as possible for making changes, this spouse-"helping" is counterproductive.

3. The therapist focuses on the covert partner. He splits the now-increased available anxiety so that it is equal on both sides. The therapist does individual therapy with the symptom-free, non-scapegoat partner. He works with this covert spouse in the presence of the one who has the symptoms. He tries to help each find an individual self in the very presence of the coupling that they got so much from and that they are now scared of, fearing it will swallow them up. They need to work through this impasse and go beyond it to a new kind of union and a new freedom for individuation.

Decourting. A couple can try various methods to help the partners decourt. Most basically, each can go visit his family without his spouse. Each can thereby get from the real parents the parenting each has wanted from the marriage, and then return to be a spouse again when they have had enough. A weekend is usually more than enough.

With a couple who is massively involved, each can bring in his own friend who knows him individually, outside the context of the marriage. This will offer quite a different perspective of each one. Or if one partner is very angry, he can take another apartment as a temporary separation while still coming to therapy. If the couple is already separated or divorced and living with someone else of the same sex, those two can also come into therapy with the couple.

The therapist can always bring someone else into the therapy. If it turns out to be someone that one or both partners do not want, that person is probably valuable to have in; it means they have a strong negative relationship with the person. This can bring out intense negative feelings—envy, hatred, fear—which are powerful influences but which might otherwise be hidden or glossed over. (This is similar to the value placed on the "negative teacher" by the Eastern religions.) Usually after four or five decourting interviews, one accuses the other of courting again.

Other Techniques

Use with care. As with theory, the automatic or wholesale use of techniques may be dangerous to therapy's health—to its aliveness and growth. Techniques fade and wear out quickly. No matter how clever, any technique is dead and useless when it does not excite the therapist practicing it. There is apparent an increasing dependence on technique in today's methods. From behavior therapy to transactional analysis to transcendental meditation to est, "The 'expert' has an approach to his clients that is schematized and planned, and he essentially teaches it to them . . . [any] 'formula' approach can make a therapist emotionally dead if he becomes dependent on it.

"Technical expertise is not enough . . . [the therapist must] maintain an orientation around [his] own growth, and therapy will also become continually more exciting . . . one will continue to expand . . . Technique, plus personal involvement makes for continuing growth: not technical, not professional, but personal. There is no steady state. One must either grow or shrivel." (Napier and Whitaker, 1978, p. 190).

This is partially why books on techniques are often not helpful, because there is no personal involvement. A therapist can use very simple educational techniques, but only *after* s/he has a relationship with the people. For example, one can tell an elderly couple that if they want, they can just cuddle without active sex, where he worries about impotence and she fears upsetting him—but this simple reassurance can only help them once the couple and the therapist are connected with each other.

A therapist who dares to remain experiential and existential will continue to evolve, invent, adapt, modify and sometimes even rediscover his own creative techniques. He will, of course, develop a tried-and-true repertoire that can be counted on, but the choice, amount and timing of any technique will be flexible and on an as-needed basis. In all cases, the tool should fit the task.

Infinite resources. The most varied and productive "technique" available is the therapist's ability to call on an infinite number and variety of outside resources—both his and the patients'. In this way, s/he and the couple can play/work with life's random elements creatively. They can keep their affect high, and can maintain a sense of freshness throughout the therapy. (A rationale for this approach appears in the subsection on therapist and family needs.)

On the therapist's side, in addition to or as a substitute for a co-therapist, he can have a consultant in at the interview in which he shares his exploratory findings with the family or couple. While the co-therapist is a member of the therapy family, the consultant is a visitor. The consultant can be any respected colleague. Essentially the therapist tells the consultant what is going on with him and the patients, in front of the patients. A consultant can be brought in at any point where a therapist wants extra power and tension in the system. The therapist can have his or her spouse in on an interview. He can have another couple who is in therapy. Each change adds something valuable to the therapy.

The therapist can bring in the referral agent, too, either in the first interview or later, as needed. It helps initially to ask the referral person to function as an administrator, to be available over time to his referred people, to re-refer them, etc. He can ask for this "because they'll probably get mad at me and come back and complain to you, and if you'll encourage them to come on back and fight it out with me, that will be a big help."

The therapist also has unlimited outside resources available on the couple's side. He can bring in all or parts of the extended family to work with the couple for a period of time, as needed. A case example illustrates the value of bringing in the extended family. In an early interview with Nancy and Jim, a separated couple, and their parents, Nancy's mother said that before their marriage four years ago she had been concerned about the young couple's living next to Jim's aging parents, lest Jim's loyalty to his depressed mother interfere with the marriage. Nancy had now left Jim because she could not stand his "deadness." Both partners denied his mother's effect. But in an interview two months later, therapists, couple and Jim's sister and brother-in-law all felt the impact of mother's enormous power to silence Jim. He had planned to make clear to his mother how *his* worry about her depression served to keep him and his wife alienated from each other. But Jim clammed up and couldn't tell his mother anything. Mother showed herself to be a master playwright, and *her* family spoke only their scripted lines. But of course what was clearly exposed to all in the interview was exactly how she did this—messaging father to be completely deaf (in contrast to his lively involvement in the prior interview), tearfully protesting her total responsibility for the marital breakup, etc. Once they had experienced mother's power and her maneuvers, Jim and Nancy could start expanding their options.

In one way or another, bringing in members of the extended family always helps, and it never seems to hurt. When the therapist requests the visits, he can tell the couple this, and that "We need all the help we can get," and that it is not to make the others into patients, but to have them help the therapist. Members of the extended family can also be invited to drop in when they are visiting in the area.

An audio tape recorder is another valuable aid. It is useful to have the couple's parents make a tape about their family and/or their own life for the couple to hear. This is especially true if the parents are not available to come in to the interview. One can also use the tape recorder as a consultant, taping the interviews for the participants to hear later, when they can be observers of the interactions.

The whole area of therapist style in communicating has innumerable variations. What you say and when and how you say it are not the only important considerations. Equally so is to whom you say it—or do not say it. As we suggested, in touching on triangle dynamics in the initial interview a therapist can plant seeds by indirection and innuendo. He talks to one person through someone else. Rather than ask direct questions, it helps to infer from their preconscious or unconscious, and to leave the inference as questions in the therapist's mind, as his own fantasies. This can help the partners to expand their thinking. It is also useful not to repeat. You cannot say it again with your previous affect. That is what they want—to cut off the affect. So if you repeat, you have lost both—your affect and your effect. If they need to, they will have heard it on some level.

Keeping everyone's maximal affect available for interviews is a continuing prime objective. Anything major which interferes should be banned. Both sex and fights before interviews are in this category. Somatizing also seriously drains off anxiety. This should be discussed and the whole process interdicted. The therapist can tell them, "If you're going to work with me, you can't develop angina, asthma, hypertension or ulcers." Such interdiction often works.

The method of paradoxical intention and the use of the absurd can be a powerful therapeutic tool when used appropriately. As in an aikido encounter, the therapist goes with his opponent's force until the instant when he can use the force to lovingly disarm his opponent. He advocates the nongrowth side of a patient's ambivalence and augments its deviation. Essentially, it involves expanding on something significant to the point where it topples of its own ludicrous weight. The therapist takes an emotional pattern and extends it to where it becomes an absurd joint fantasy (Bateson, 1971; Hoffman, 1971).

For instance, when a woman threatens suicide, he can extend the possibility that maybe if she did kill herself her husband might marry that woman she had been thinking about for so long; or that maybe her husband would be so guilty that he would kill himself too, and then she would really have him fixed. But at any rate, suicide would be a great way to get back at a husband; it would be one of the ways of making him a murderer for life. Unless it backfired, as it did with a woman who jumped out of her third-story window when she learned that her husband had betrayed her. The brief news item concluded that she was "recovering in a hospital after landing on her husband, who was killed."

This method of extending to absurdity creates a strange kind of new fantasy that the patient cannot have for himself because the therapist is involved in it. His being part of the dream weakens it and changes it from a personal delusion-type fantasy to a social reality. This allows it to fade, because it has been shared.

But this move cannot be aggressive or cynical, nor can it be contrived. When it occurs in the therapy's organic flow, the therapist deeply feels the paradox: the life-and-death seriousness of the topic, the grim humor wrapped in a light touch, like the theater's two-faced mask of tragedy and comedy. It is a tongue-in-cheek game the therapist plays with the patient. If the therapist really feels it and it fits for them both, the patient cannot escape from either side of the double message—"I care for you and I'm laughing at you." And shortly he begins to laugh at himself (Keith and Whitaker, 1978).

The Therapeutic Impasse

At any point in treatment a therapeutic impasse can occur. An impasse is not so much a problem in technique as it is a disturbance of a human relationship. It is a stalemate or plateau in the process of achieving a therapeutic objective; a problem of decelerating progress and increasing emotional hesitancy. It is as though the therapeutic experience has lost its emotional voltage. Evidence of an impasse always includes loss of affect. The dynamics of a therapeutic impasse are essentially the same as those of the ten-year syndrome or of any other marital impasse the couple may experience.

It indicates that something is "wrong" between therapist and patient. The impasse is usually symbiotic, involving transference on both the therapist's and the patient's parts. They experience a deterioration in their relationship, with emotional withdrawal in its various forms—intellectual discussion, emphasis on symptomatology, interest in real life and its problems, or periods of futile silence.

The impasse may be around an issue of time, space, movement, sex, bilateral aggression or a previous therapist. The following case example illustrates an impasse around the issue of a previous therapist. Ann, a twice-divorced woman, had a strong positive transference to her previous therapist, Dr. C., even though ten years had elapsed since he had abruptly terminated treatment and disappeared. Her present therapist knew that her prior transference would strongly interfere with their ability to make progress in this therapy unless Ann could let go of her idealized Dr. C. The therapist dreamed that Ann drove him to a diner, where they unexpectedly met Dr. C. Ann ran to him. Dr. C. picked her up and, with her arms clinging tight around his neck, carried her back to the therapist's table. But she disappeared, leaving the therapist stranded. He awoke saying, "What a bitch!" His prediction was validated when she left therapy soon after. An unpaid bill can also be a very serious impasse problem. Regardless of its specific nature, it must be resolved before therapy can go on. Any of the techniques already mentioned can be tried, singly or in combination. A couple's children should come in especially when the partners are impassed or in crisis; the extended family might well come in, too. Again, this can increase the available affect and elicit more help and support.

The impasse may also be in the form of acting out. The behavior can be somatic, psychotic or criminal. As the therapist can ban illness, he can also interdict the other forms, insisting that the patient keep them out of the social structure. Going crazy and getting criminally caught are ways to try to avoid the anxiety of therapy. The patient may be told, "You must stay an outpatient to go on with me in therapy. If you go crazy outside, you can't be a patient of mine. You'll have to go to a state or private hospital, and then someone else will have to be responsible for you."

Therapist Impotence

Finally, sooner or later the therapist meets his own impotence. One of its bases is that he has been trained in linear causology, whereas the study of the family system shows clearly that this causology is circular. There is no single incidence or point of pathology in a family. And with the number of interactional balls to keep track of and juggle, it is easy to lose a few critical ones. In addition, the real power of the system can make the therapist impotent. Here the most he can do is to acknowledge directly the family's or couple's power, to confront his impotence and to admit failure, or its possibility, openly.

A therapist may choose to use what he believes to be an impotence ploy. He may withhold his power, to help the couple mobilize theirs—or he may feel that the resolution of this particular impasse is their responsibility, not his. He may also find another way of letting them know that he chooses not to use his power this time, perhaps by telling them, "That's not my department." However, if the impasse is not successfully resolved, the therapist may discover that what he put forth as an impotence ploy turned out to reflect his real impotence!

However, when s/he knows it is true therapeutic impotence, it can help to tell the couple something like, "I have gotten as far as I can go. I am afraid you are going to lose my affect, and if you do, then there is no more I can do about it than you can." When this happens—when the therapist cannot feel turned on and involved with his patients—this therapy cannot be helpful unless they can all resolve the impasse. It means that the combined power of the therapeutic team—the couple, therapist(s) and whoever else has been in on the journey—cannot overcome the system's resistance to change. The total system force for keeping the status quo is more powerful than that for significant change. There was a saying men used when they were still playing at seducing women: "We can't fight it; it's bigger than both of us."

Many factors may contribute to the therapist's impotence. The extended family may simply exert too great open or subtle pressure on the couple to conform to system expectations. Bowen says that when things start to change, the Queen may come out of the woodwork and make everything go back the way it was (1971). The therapist may or may not know the source and intensity of the power arrayed against his efforts. It may be a historical force going back two or more generations. For example, a wife may compulsively continue a string of affairs to act out the fantasies of her strait-laced grandmother—she accommodates dear old grandma by playing the whore side of the virgin-whore conflict.

The therapist may find the source of the opposing power later, either via additional factual information or by new insights. If the couple is still available—that is, alive—he can decrease the therapeutic impotence by adding the power of the new information into the therapeutic team. In the virgin-whore case, the therapist accidentally learned that wife and grandma had both had abortions at age sixteen—although wife had not known about grandma's abortion. Other striking parallels then emerged in the lives of the two women. After the therapist shared the new perspective with the couple, who had left treatment earlier, the wife went back to her grandma, told her that she loved her but that from here on grandma would have to tend to her own affairs. Grandma was totally "shocked" and "didn't understand" but did honor the wife's request to give her permission to cleave to her own husband. Shortly after, grandma found a lively male companion for herself.

But whatever the specific nature of the system power—hidden or known, past or current—the therapist can be certain that family loyalties are at work, and that the opposing power is surely connected with the kinds of formidable realities with which we began: the facts of life. The base may be psycho-biological, as was Jim's loyalty to his depressed mother (a person is never as close to anyone as to his mother). The base may be social (poverty and unemployment): a father jobless during the Depression swore he would give his son everything and worked single-mindedly to do so. The son had almost to kill himself on an exotic drug before father realized that the one thing he hadn't given the boy was—himself. Or the base may be familial, as in the following case example: A daughter was thirteen when her mother, loving another man, chose to die. Father, bitter at his dead wife and at all women, condemned daughter and favored her brother, four years younger. Daughter acquired from each of her parents a legacy of guilt and self-loathing, which in due time *her* two daughters acted out—each at age thirteen. It may be a husband still trying to maintain the myth of his parents' "perfect marriage." Or it may be a four-generational alliance of women who obey the unspoken family fiat of "us girls" and, like black widow spiders, kill their males after procreation.

With the right—or wrong—circumstances, any of these realities can overwhelm a therapeutic system. But the therapist's impotence may also be his or her ultimate therapeutic gift to the couple. Just as there are no perfect parents, so there are no perfect therapists, but there are therapists who have the capacity and willingness to share what they are and think and feel with their patients. This readiness of the therapist to present himself openly, to be profoundly known to his patients, is contagious, for it encourages them to be more open and honest. What can happen then is that together couple and therapist can de-mythologize and de-pedestalize the therapist—along with *their* parents, each other and the marriage.

They can joyously shout, "The Emperor has no clothes!" And then add, "And neither do we!" If therapy ends with the couple seeing their therapist's impotence, it gives them one valuable way to repossess completely and take full responsibility for their own lives. And that, after all, is the ultimate treatment goal: "To take back one's own life fully, facing the terror and the unknown, which makes living continue to be scary, exciting, terrible and fun."

REFERENCES

Bateson, G. The cybernetics of "self": A theory of alcoholism. *Psychiat.*, 1971, *34*, 1–18.

Bowen, M. Toward the differentiation of a self in one's own family. In J. Framo (Ed.), *Family interaction*. New York: Springer, 1971.

Greenberg, A. Through the looking glass—psychotherapy ground rules in family and marital therapy. *Interaction*, 1978, *1*, 3, 20–29.

Hoffman, L. Deviation-amplifying processes in natural groups. In J. Haley (Ed.), *Changing families*. New York: Grune and Stratton, 1971.

Keith, D.V., and Whitaker, C.A. Struggling with the impotence impasse: Absurdity and acting-in. *J. Marr. & Fam. Couns.*, 1978, *4*, 1, 69–77.

Malone, T.P., Whitaker, C.A., Warkentin, J., and Felder, R.E. Rational and non-rational psychotherapy. *Am. J. Psychother.*, 1961, *15*, 212–220.

Napier, A.Y., and Whitaker, C.A. A conversation about co-therapy. In A. Ferber, M. Mendelsohn, and A.Y. Napier (Eds.), *The book of family therapy*. New York: Science House, 1972.

Napier, A.Y., with Whitaker, C.A. *The family crucible*. New York: Harper and Row, 1978.

Singer, E. *Key concepts in psychotherapy*. New York: Random House, 1965.

Warkentin, J., Felder, R.E., Malone, T.P., and Whitaker, C.A. The usefulness of craziness. *Med. Times*, 1961, *IX*, 86.

Warkentin, J., and Whitaker, C.A. Serial impasses in marriage. In I.M. Cohen (Ed.), *Family structure, dynamics and therapy*. Psychiatric Research Reports, American Psychiatric Association, Report 20, 1966.

Warkentin, J., and Whitaker, C.A. The secret agenda of the therapist doing couples therapy. In G.H. Zuk and I. Boszormenyi-Nagy (Eds.), *Family therapy and disturbed families*. Palo Alto, Ca.: Science and Behavior Books, 1967.

Whitaker, C.A. Psychotherapy with couples. *Am. J. Psychother.*, 1958, *12*, 18–23.

Whitaker, C.A. Acting out in family psychotherapy. In L.E. Abt and S. Weisman (Eds.), *Acting out: Theoretical and clinical aspects*. New York: Grune and Stratton, 1965.

Whitaker, C.A. The growing edge. In J. Haley and L. Hoffman (Eds.), *Techniques of family therapy*. New York: Basic Books, 1967.

Whitaker, C.A. *Making marriage work* (10 Cassette Audiotapes). Chicago: Instructional Dynamics, 1970.

Whitaker, C.A. *What's new in husband-wife counseling* (30 Cassette Audiotapes). Chicago: Instructional Dynamics, 1970.

Whitaker, C.A. The chemistry of the extended family—an implosion can bring 'em back alive. *Voices*, 1972/73, *8*, 4, 42–44.

Whitaker, C.A. My philosophy of psychotherapy. *J. Contemp. Psychother.*, 1973, *6*, 1, 49–52.

Whitaker, C.A. Psychotherapy of the absurd: With a special emphasis on the psychotherapy of aggression. *Fam. Proc.*, 1975, *14*, 1, 4–19.

Whitaker, C.A. The hindrance of theory in clinical work. In P.J. Guerin (Ed.), *Family therapy*. New York: Gardner Press, 1976.

Whitaker, C.A. A family is a four-dimensional relationship. In P.J. Guerin (Ed.), *Family therapy*. New York: Gardner Press, 1976.

Whitaker, C.A. Family therapy and reparenting myself. *Voices*, 1976/77, *12*, 4, 66–67.

Whitaker, C.A. Process techniques of family therapy. *Interaction*, 1977, *1*, 1, 4–19.

Whitaker, C.A. Symbolic sex in family therapy. In G.P. Sholevar (Ed.), *Changing sexual values and the family*. Springfield, Ill.: Charles C. Thomas, 1977.

Whitaker, C.A., and Miller, M.H. A reevaluation of psychiatric help when divorce impends. In J. Haley (Ed.), *Changing families*. New York: Grune and Stratton, 1971.

Whitaker, C.A., Warkentin, J., and Johnson, N. The psychotherapeutic impasse. *Am. J. Orthopsychiat.*, 1950, *20*, 641–647.

Chapter 9

Behavioral Approaches to the Treatment of Marital Discord

Norman Epstein
Ann Marie Williams

The behavioral orientation to analysis and treatment of marital problems represents not a uniform approach, but rather a number of approaches grounded in a common set of general premises regarding interspousal behavior. In this chapter, the term "behavioral approach" will be used to describe three major subcategories of concepts (operant, repondent and cognitive), each of which has different implications for problem definition, therapeutic goals and treatment procedures within a general behavioral orientation. The more global term "behavioral orientation" will be used to refer to basic assumptions and characteristics of a body of behavioral principles applied to interpersonal interactions, distinguishing these assumptions and principles from those of other major theoretical orientations (e.g., psychodynamic).

There is a common misconception that behavioral marital therapy is a narrowly defined "technology," but in fact therapists with a behavioral orientation vary widely in the procedures they employ. Each of the operant, respondent and cognitive approaches includes a variety of procedures, and any individual practicing therapist is likely to use different combinations of these, hopefully based on client needs as much as on therapist preference. This chapter is intended to illustrate the breadth of behavioral marital therapy (BMT). It cannot serve as a "how-to" manual, but it should provide the reader with a sense of what this expanding field has to offer.

A historical perspective suggests that the major approaches described in the earliest publications on behavioral marital therapy have since received uneven attention, but that recently there has been renewed interest in those approaches that were relatively neglected. As a result, BMT is becoming more broadly based and more integrated. In this chapter we will trace the development of the major behavioral approaches to marital treatment and will describe the wide range of specific intervention procedures available to clinicians. In addition, we will describe what presently seem to be major trends for the future of behavioral interventions with couples.

BEHAVIORAL APPROACHES TO MARITAL TREATMENT: A HISTORICAL PERSPECTIVE

The behavioral orientation traditionally has focused on how an individual person's positive and problematic behaviors are influenced by his/her interactions with the environment. The functioning of the individual is thought to be due to past and present learning experiences through direct influence of the environment. The improvement of dysfunction calls for unlearning/relearning processes involving respondent, operant and cognitive responses.

In a classical conditioning (respondent) paradigm, emotional and behavioral responses, such as phobic avoidance of environmental stimuli, are learned through an associative process and can be treated with deconditioning procedures (such as systematic desensitization) designed to break associative patterns.

In an operant model, the frequency of a behavior can be increased or decreased by its consequences. When a behavior *increases* in frequency after it has been followed by a consequence, the consequence is labeled a positive reinforcer. For example, if one spouse's talk about physical complaints increases after the other spouse has paid attention to such complaints, the talking was positively reinforced by attention. On the other hand, when a behavior *increases* after it has led to termination of an aversive condition, the consequence (termination of the aversive stimulus) is a negative reinforcer. Thus, a behavior that increases after it has stopped another person's nagging has been negatively reinforced. In contrast to the two forms of reinforcement, which increase rates of behaviors, punishment has occurred when a behavior *decreases* when followed by a particular consequence (inferred to be aversive). In this model, which will be described in greater detail later in the chapter, deficits and excesses in social behaviors can be modified by systematically varying the pattern of consequences for the specific behaviors.

The general cognitive-behavioral model suggests that except for a simple reflex response, such as jerking one's hand away from a hot stove, a person responds to his/her subjective perceptions of environmental stimuli rather than to their objective characteristics. Thus, one person may perceive an animal as dangerous and flee while another person may perceive the same animal as cuddly and pet it. The recent increase in behaviorists' interest in cognitive variables (appraisals, attitudes, beliefs) represents a departure from Skinner's "radical behaviorism" that eschewed events that were not directly observable.

At a general level, in contrast to psychodynamic therapeutic approaches that focus on modifying underlying internal processes such as conflicts and motives, behavioral approaches are intended to change problematic behaviors (including cognitions) by creating specific environmental conditions for new learning.

Although behaviorists traditionally have focused on the individual as the target for treatment, they consistently have recognized that a major portion of a person's environment is interpersonal. Other people regularly serve as stimuli that elicit an individual's emotional and behavioral responses (e.g., when the sight of a feared person makes one tense). Similarly, other people have control over the major reinforcers (e.g., attention, approval) that shape one's behavior.

A gambler responding to a slot machine that provides quarters as a consequence for the particular behavior of arm-pulling is involved in a one-way pattern of influence: the machine shapes the person's behavior, but the person's responses do not change the preprogrammed "behavior" of the slot machine. In contrast, a person interacting with another person who provides reinforcers for particular responses is likely to influence the other person's behavior in return. The other person's behavior *also* can be elicited and reinforced by social stimuli. Thus, the basic behavioral tenet that an individual's behavior varies as a function of his/her environment can be extended easily to a conceptualization of an interpersonal system of mutual influence. As writers such as Weiss (1978) have noted, behavioral theory applied to interpersonal interactions has much in common with general systems-theory approaches to relationships. Although an extended discussion of parallels between behavioral theory and systems-theory views of marriages and families is beyond the scope of the present chapter, the reader may find treatment of these issues in Weiss (1978) and in this volume's chapter by Berman, Lief and Williams.

DEVELOPMENT OF BEHAVIORAL MARITAL THERAPY

Of the three major behavioral approaches, the operant model has been much more influential in the development of behaviora: marital therapy than either the respondent or the cognitive model (O'Leary and Turkewitz, 1978). The respondent model has been applied regularly in sex therapy but minimally in treating other areas of marital dysfunction. The idea of applying the general cognitive model to the treatment of relationship problems has achieved significant popularity only recently. Even within the popular operant perspective, different treatment formats exist, but histori- cally these formats have received uneven attention. At present, it appears that behaviorally oriented marital therapists are using a wide variety of procedures based on all three major approaches, and that the field is moving toward greater diversity, incorporating a variety of old and new concepts. In this chapter we intend to illustrate the diversity of behavioral marital therapy as currently practiced.

The earliest papers describing behavioral approaches to marital problems tended to focus on changing an individual spouse's dysfunction. Goldia- mond (1965) taught self-control procedures to individuals in order to reduce particular behaviors that were disrupting their marriages. Within the behavioral orientation, a person exercises "self-control" by identifying environmental conditions that control the occurrence of his/her positive and negative behaviors, and then by manipulating those conditions to maximize the positives while minimizing the negatives. For example, Goldiamond reduced a jealous husband's yelling at his wife by instructing him to spend time with her in settings (e.g., restaurants) where quiet, civilized talk was expected. With a couple who reported a very low frequency of sexual contact due to the husband's busy schedule, sexual frequency was increased when the husband scheduled appointments with his wife and when the spouses' highly valued appointments with beautician and barber were made contingent on the sexual encounters.

Goldstein (Goldstein, 1971; Goldstein and Francis, 1969) noted the importance of mutual influence patterns between spouses, integrating Skinner's (1953, 1957) ideas of behavior control through reinforcement with social exchange concepts of theorists such as Goffman (1959) and Thibaut and Kelley (1959). While Skinner tended to focus on behavior control of single organisms, the social psychologists suggested that *mutual* exchanges of positive reinforcers produce satisfaction for both partners in a relation- ship. Marital satisfaction is thought to be directly related to spouses' abilities to maximize individual rewards and minimize individual costs in their ongoing interactions.

Although he subscribed to the view that spouses influenced each other in a system of mutual behavior control, Goldstein worked with a population of wives whose husbands would not take part in marital therapy. He trained the wives to apply reinforcement systematically to change their spouses' distressing behaviors. Unknown to their husbands, each wife identified a specific distressing behavior of her spouse, recorded its daily frequency with a small hand-held counter and instituted reinforcement contingencies designed to reduce the target behavior. Goldstein (1971) clearly stated that in order to change a husband's behavior, the therapist must change the wife's behavior toward her spouse. Thus, although the behavior of one partner still was defined as the problem and the focus of treatment, the interdependence of spouse behaviors was recognized. One implication of the effectiveness of Goldstein's interventions may be that the wives' pretreatment behaviors had been as problematic as those of their husbands in that they had maintained the husbands' distressing behaviors. Theoretically, one could apply this operant format in conjoint treatment, with both spouses trained to reinforce systematically their partner's preferred behaviors.

Stuart (1969) also viewed the marital dyad in terms of mutual behavior control, based on the concept of reciprocity in "behavior exchange." In Stuart's view, each spouse gives the other positive reinforcers with the expectation that the partner will reciprocate. Increases in one's output of positive reinforcers are expected to yield similar increases in positives provided by one's partner. In contrast, members of disordered marriages give their partners few positives since they expect few positives from the partner and are attempting to minimize their own costs in the exchange. Stuart's (1969) operant solution to such problems was conjoint marital treatment in which spouses identified specific positive responses they would like to receive from each other (e.g., more conversation time, more sex) and exchanged these positives through a "token reinforcement system." Stuart identified the *relationship* as the "client" and sought equal, simultaneous change in both spouses.

Although Goldstein and Francis (1969) and Stuart (1969) published their initial reports in the same year, and both of their approaches were grounded in operant behavioral concepts, they emphasized different formats for mutual behavior control. In spite of the conceptual overlap between the two operant approaches, they had different implications for treatment. Stuart's model emphasized agreement for mutual exchanges in which each partner's provision of positives is linked in some way with the other's exchange pattern. Subsequently, practitioners have developed a number of behavioral contracting formats to facilitate such exchanges (see discussion of behavioral contracting below). Goldstein's model focused on how each member of a couple can increase or decrease a partner's specific behaviors by changing the interpersonal environment he/she provides for the partner. Goldstein's data indicated that wives' overuse of aversive control tactics (e.g., nagging) could be supplanted by new skills in using positive behavior-change procedures. Wives were taught to reinforce desired behaviors selectively (e.g., with affection), to provide environmental stimuli likely to increase their husbands' awareness of desired responses (e.g., posting a graph of a husband's daily response frequency) and to reinforce desirable behaviors that compete with the occurrence of an undesirable behavior (e.g., reinforcing a husband for making household repairs, since his problematic drinking tended not to occur while he was working).

Publications describing behavioral approaches to marital therapy over the past decade (e.g., Jacobson, 1979; Jacobson and Martin, 1976; Weiss, Hops and Patterson, 1973) indicate that efforts to apply operant behavioral principles to marital problems primarily have followed the format initiated by Stuart (1969), and that Goldstein's approach to teaching couples systematic reinforcement skills has received considerably less attention. In fact, the term "behavioral marital therapy" (BMT) has been equated with behavioral exchange or contracting procedures in some publications (e.g., Gurman and Knudson, 1978). Although other procedures, such as training in decision making and communication skills, have been used in behavioral treatment packages, the "bottom line" has tended to be the formulation of behavior-exchange contracts. Only recently has attention shifted to other parameters of the interpersonal behavior system. This trend seems to be due at least in part to a growing body of evidence that formal exchange contracts may not be necessary and that training in other interpersonal skills can produce positive changes in disturbed marriages (Jacobson, 1978a; O'Leary and Turkewitz, 1978; Weiss, 1978). Encouraging preliminary data, such as those reported for Goldstein's (1971) approach, suggest that procedures other than contracting warrant further evaluation.

Applications of classical conditioning principles to the treatment of individuals' marital problems began with Wolpe's (1958) work on the desensitization of dysfunctional emotional responses, particularly the treatment of anxiety that inhibited sexual performance. Masters and Johnson's (1970) widely used procedures for treating sexual dysfunctions similarly facilitate desensitization of partners' performance anxieties.

Lazarus (1968) noted that a person may develop a variety of conditioned emotional responses to his/her spouse and described the use of systematic desensitization to reduce a wife's severe emotional responses to thoughts of her formerly alcoholic husband's drunken behavior. Such an approach may make it easier for a person to tolerate a partner's presence, but it is unlikely to be sufficient treatment in itself because it does not modify problematic mutual interactions. However, the fact that classical conditioning (respondent) procedures other than sex therapy have received attention from only a few writers (e.g., Knox, 1971) is unfortunate. The lack of attention to this approach in the absence of research evaluating its efficacy seems premature.

Cognitive behavior therapy has experienced considerable growth in recent years. The major influences in this trend toward examining cognitive mediators of emotional and behavioral responses to stimuli have been Ellis' (1962) rational-emotive therapy, Beck's (1976) work on cognitive styles and Meichenbaum's (1977) work on self-instruction. An increasing body of literature indicates that therapeutic strategies based on cognitive behavioral principles have considerable promise (Meichenbaum, 1977), but cognitive behavioral procedures have not been applied in any systematic way with couples. The proposal that marital dissatisfaction and maladjustment may stem from irrational expectations of marriage that spouses bring to the relationship (Ellis and Harper, 1975) has received little attention from researchers and other writers who discuss marital therapy (O'Leary and Turkewitz, 1978). Eisenberg and Zingle (1975) found that clinic couples scored higher than nonclinic couples on the Zingle (1965) Irrational Ideas Inventory (III), but that III scores were not correlated significantly with scores on the Locke-Wallace Marital Adjustment Scale (Locke and Wallace, 1959). Epstein, Finnegan and Bythell (1979) found that observers who had scored high on Jones's (1968) Irrational Beliefs Test (IBT) were more likely to interpret disagreement in videotaped couples as indicative of marital maladjustment than were observers who had scored low. Ratings of agreeing couples did not vary significantly with observers' IBT scores. The research in this area can be considered preliminary only, and the potential for applying cognitive principles to marital problems is unknown at present. Later in this chapter we will discuss possible directions for cognitive behavior therapy with couples.

The focus in the behavioral marital therapy literature on the exchange model may be due in part to its conceptual elegance, but also to the fact that of the approaches described above, it is the approach that best reflects an orientation toward conjoint intervention at the level of dyadic *interaction*. Goldiamond (1965) intervened at the level of individual self-control, and although Goldstein's (1971) model could be applied conjointly, he reported work only with the wives. Classical conditioning and cognitive behavioral procedures traditionally have been applied to individual dysfunctions as well. Since the predominant orientation in contemporary marital therapy involves a focus on the relationship as the unit for assessment and treatment, it is not surprising that more individually oriented approaches would be less popular among theorists and researchers. However, the conjoint sex therapy work of Masters and Johnson (1970) and others illustrates how desensitization of dysfunctional emotional responses can be a dyadic issue. Similarly, Sager's (1976) work on expectations that partners bring to their marriages illustrates how cognitions of two individuals may interact and reinforce one another. Thus, it appears that a variety of behavioral approaches may be applicable to marital problems. Certainly no conclusions pro or con can be made until extensive research evaluating the less popular approaches has been conducted.

Although the literature dwells on the exchange model, in fact many behavior therapists employ a wide variety of procedures based on other approaches to marital dysfunction. In practice, these procedures are more diverse, more flexible and less mechanistic than much of the basic literature suggests. Also, the practice of behavioral contracting has evolved toward less formality (O'Leary and Turkewitz, 1978; Weiss, 1978). Currently, behavioral marital therapy is developing the capacity to meet the needs of distressed couples with a wide variety of marital problems. The remainder of this chapter will describe the range of behavioral procedures available to the clinician, with suggestions regarding the most appropriate uses for each. Specific procedures are outlined in as much detail as possible, given space limitations, and the reader is referred to other sources for additional information.

BEHAVIORAL PROCEDURES FOR MARITAL THERAPY

What does a behavior therapist *do* with the couples he or she sees for marital therapy? Does *every* therapist use a behavior-exchange contract? Do you need videotape equipment and three student assistants to use a behavioral approach? In this section, we will try to answer these questions and, at the same time, to dispel some popular misconceptions about behavioral marital therapy (BMT). While much has been written about the *outcome* of BMT (e.g., Gurman and Kniskern, 1978a; Jacobson, 1978a; Williams and Miller, this volume), there have been relatively few descriptions of the *process* of BMT (e.g., Jacobson, 1977c; Knox, 1971; Liberman, Wheeler and Sanders, 1976), with the exception of articles describing a particular treatment program in a research-oriented setting (e.g., O'Leary and Turkewitz, 1978; Stuart, 1976; Weiss, Hops and Patterson, 1973). We will, therefore, describe the general application of behavioral principles in dyadic counseling.

Although the modular format has been emphasized in the BMT *research* literature (Jacobson, 1979), it is not necessarily used in *practice*. In the sections that follow, we will present the range of available behavioral procedures in the order they are often used in therapy. Except for the practical considerations of logical order (e.g., pinpointing a deficit in problem-solving skills before training in those skills), there are no rigid rules as to the order in which the procedures are to be used. Furthermore, not all of these procedures are appropriate for every couple or client. The *if* and *when* of the various behavioral procedures is left for the clinician to decide based on the ongoing evaluation of the couple's pattern of functioning and current level of distress. The various procedures which will be discussed below are (1) preparations for behavior change, (2) pinpointing and discrimination training, (3) operant behavior change procedures (e.g., schedules of reinforcement and punishment), (4) increasing positive interactions (e.g., recreation and leisure time), (5) stimulus control, (6) classical conditioning and desensitization, (7) building communication skills, (8) building skills in assertion and problem-solving and (9) contingency contracting.

PREPARATIONS FOR BEHAVIOR CHANGE

An area of utmost importance in behavioral marital therapy (BMT), as in other treatment approaches, is the preparation of the clients for the behavior-change process. These necessary preliminary steps have often been overlooked or understated in reports of BMT research. However, they are most certainly included in clinical practice, to a greater or lesser extent, according to the style of the individual therapist.

Presenting complaints and ventilation. If often requires considerable skill and patience for the therapist to "take a history" from an angry or vindictive couple who have come to the first session prepared with a list of grievances against each other. A detailed description of the "thirty years' war" must be discouraged because otherwise attention and tacit approval are thus given to counterproductive behavior. On the other hand, if the therapist completely ignores the presenting complaints of a conflicted couple, he/she is unlikely to be perceived as an understanding person whose attention has positive value. Since the effectiveness of behavioral interventions often depends in part on social reinforcement provided by the therapist, it is important that the therapist become a salient dispenser of positives. Some empathic listening to each client's complaints is likely to increase the therapist's reinforcing value.

Thus, the task of the therapist is to maintain a delicate balance between listening too much and listening too little. As soon as the complaints have made one complete cycle (this usually occurs in the first fifteen to twenty minutes), the therapist may tactfully mention that the clients are beginning to repeat themselves. By using focused questions and selective attention, the therapist can gather the necessary biographical and relationship information without eliciting useless diatribes. Client comments of the "He never . . ." and "She always . . ." variety can be gently but firmly rephrased (see "Discrimination Training and Pinpointing" below).

Presenting complaints can be diagnostically useful for differentiating clients who want help to improve their relationships from those who want "permission" to separate or divorce. It would be inappropriate to apply relationship-enhancing treatments with clients who seek therapy only to be able to say to themselves, their in-laws, relatives and attorney, "See how hard I tried." These clients may be more likely to benefit from therapy focused on individual decision making. Similarly, clients who "bring" their spouses to therapy with a "repair request" for the therapist to "make him (or her) change" or "make him (or her) love me" will need some orientation to systems concepts before they will be willing to change *their* half of the marital interaction. Weiss (1976) formulated a typology of presenting complaints and noted that referrals for individual therapy or divorce counseling may be necessary in some cases.

Building the therapist-client relationship. Behavioral marital therapy (BMT) is far from impersonal or mechanistic. A study by Mickelson and Stevic (1971) showed that there were differential effects according to whether behavioral therapists were facilitative or nonfacilitative. Facilitative therapists were high in their offerings of nonpossessive warmth, genuineness and accurate empathy (Truax and Carkhuff, 1967). The facilitative therapist emerged as a more potent reinforcer because of the reinforcing value of the therapist-client relationship. It was postulated also that a facilitative therapist is better able to discern when to stimulate the clients to try new behaviors and when to be empathic and supportive.

In addition to the potency of the therapist as a reinforcer, the potency of the therapist as model and as an authority figure is important to the therapist-client relationship. Presumably, a facilitative therapist is more effective as a model and more persuasive as an educator than is a therapist who is perceived as distant, hypercritical and insensitive. Thus, there are both theoretical and empirical grounds for maintaining that behavioral marital therapists should develop rapport with clients as an essential element of the therapeutic process.

O'Leary and Turkewitz (1978) have conceptualized the therapeutic relationship as composed of four stages: (1) the courtship stage, involving assessment of client functioning and dysfunctioning and, concurrently, rapport-building; (2) the engagement stage, involving the development of the therapeutic contract; (3) the marriage stage, involving the actual treatment program; and (4) the disengagement stage, in which the clients are weaned from the active participation of the therapist in their marital interaction. These authors have suggested that rapport can be "enhanced by focusing on specific behaviors that can be changed, and by showing a serious concern for the spouses' feelings toward one another" (p. 257). They also suggest that rapport can be facilitated during the initial interview by careful listening with minimal interruption. Accurate, nonjudgmental paraphrasing of both clients' statements is recommended in order to model "active listening" and gradually to decrease any anxiety associated with entering therapy. O'Leary and Turkewitz (1978) suggest that as a means of strengthening the couple's belief in the therapist's ability to help them solve their marital problems, occasional reference can be made to previous successful cases.

Finally, O'Leary and Turkewitz suggest that the limited use of self-disclosure of personal, nonintimate details of the therapist's own experiences as a married person (e.g., ways of structuring one's day so that regular communication is guaranteed) may help clients who lack adequate role models of satisfying dyadic interaction. The models thus created should be realistic rather than idealistic, since unrealistic or idealistic models would tend only to frustrate the clients by presenting behaviors impossible for them to emulate.

Liberman, Wheeler and Sanders (1976) have offered several concrete suggestions for building a successful therapist-client relationship. They suggest (p. 386) that the therapist try the following:

1. Give careful directions for finding the office on the first visit
2. Remove a desk between therapist and client
3. Ask permission before addressing the patient by his or her first name
4. Apologize when late for an appointment
5. Show the patient where the bathroom is and indicate that it is all right to use it at any time
6. Not look at one's watch while the patient is talking
7. Let the session last a little longer than the exact time when the patient has made good use of the time, and
8. Acknowledge the patient's birthday and anniversary.

These behaviors by the therapist will be seen as thoughtful, considerate and understanding. Moreover, the therapist can convey the belief that each person (even one's spouse) is "special" and should not be taken for granted.

Other facilitative therapist variables (e.g., stimulating interaction, gathering data and giving support in the early sessions rather than labeling unconscious motivations) have been surveyed from the marital and family literature by Gurman and Kniskern (1978, p. 11–13). These variables have been reviewed in detail elsewhere in this book (see chapter by Williams and Miller).

Structuring client expectations. When a distressed couple begins marital therapy, they often bring the expectation that the therapist will do the "work" for them. It is assumed that this work will involve only one hour each week, for an indefinite period of time, limited to the therapist's office. These expectations are consistent with the medical model in which the doctor diagnoses and treats the patients in his office. The medical patient is responsible only for keeping appointments, taking medicine and paying bills. A more appropriate analogy for behavioral marital therapy would be taking piano lessons. Restructuring the couple's expectations includes replacing the image of the medical model with a more suitable set of expectations. For example, in the case of piano lessons, the teacher initially takes a more active role. The students are responsible for attending the lessons *and* for practicing several times each week. Once the basic material is mastered, the teacher can give pointers on ways to improve "style," but the final performance will express the personalities of the students rather than that of the teacher. It is obvious that each student's level of achievement is determined by the amount of work that is done *between lessons*. Gradually, as the students progress, less input is needed from the teacher. This model emphasizes collaboration between therapist/educator and client/student.

Furthermore, the education analogy also holds that interpersonal skills must be practiced if they are to be maintained. Developing a healthy, satisfying marital relationship is a continuous process. Without practice, the skills fade. Many couples entering marital therapy find this reality depressing. Often it is encouraging to tell them that the same interpersonal skills will be valuable in parent/child and employee/employer relationships as well.

The behavioral orientation assumes that faulty behaviors have been learned and can be replaced with more functional behaviors. It also assumes that attributions should be made to a person's *behavior* ("He did a hostile thing") rather than to his or her *character* ("He is a hostile person"). Characterological attributions have been found to be counterproductive because they *describe* without *explaining* or *predicting* and they negate the hope of meaningful improvement. Behavioral attributions, on the other hand, encourage the couple to look at a pattern of faulty behaviors as a problem to be solved through cooperative efforts by both spouses. The transformation of characterological attributions ("She's a lousy housekeeper, just like her mother") into behavioral attributions ("She does not dust or vacuum the living room as often as my mother did") is a necessary preliminary step to making behavior changes. This point should be emphasized to clients as soon as possible.

As part of structuring the couple's expectations, Goldstein (personal communication, 1973) has suggested that the couple consider therapy an "experiment in new ways of behaving." Since the therapeutic interventions are designed for the idiosyncratic needs of each couple, the first procedures suggested may not be entirely successful. Through the use of continuous assessment (e.g., using rating scales, charting, counting specific behaviors), the program can be modified to maximize desired outcomes. This behavioral orientation is a departure from the traditional stance, which assumes that "the therapist knows best." Because of its roots in experimental psychology, the BMT orientation emphasizes the need for an open-minded, flexible attitude: "The *data* will tell us what works." Readers familiar with the BMT research literature may feel that the behavioral orientation has been narrow or inflexible because of the attention paid to modular programs in which all clients seem to be "processed" through a set series of training experiences. In practice, however, the behavior therapist needs to model for the couple the open-minded, flexible *attitudes* which are an essential part of problem-solving skills. The *procedures* for problem-solving skills are then presented in later therapy sessions.

Structuring therapist-client interaction. Behavioral marital therapy tends to be both structured and time-limited. During the initial orientation sessions, the therapist outlines the general format: the fixed or most probable number of sessions, length of each session, spacing of sessions, whether the program will include maintenance and follow-up visits, the nature of the homework assignments and any contingencies that will be applied to the therapeutic contract—e.g., that therapy will continue only if both partners agree to discontinue any extramarital affairs (Liberman, Wheeler and Sanders, 1976).

The basic information that must be given to the couple follows the format *who, what, when, where,* and *why.* For some behavior therapists, these expectations for the couple are stated formally. For other behavior therapists, these expectations are implied or stated indirectly over the course of the therapy:

WHO Changes are made *by the couple*; the therapist will act as a teacher, consultant, and coach.

WHAT He/she will try *new ways of acting* with the partner which are not historically tied to the couple's chronic pattern of arguments or aversive control.

WHEN This will be done *at least daily*, preferably several times a day (e.g., acknowledging behaviors which are pleasing).

WHERE It will be practiced at home, while shopping, *everywhere* the couple goes together, not just in the therapist's office.

WHY First, the ways in which the couple have been interacting in the past obviously have *not been successful*, and second, these new ways of interacting have been successful with other couples with similar problems.

Some behavior therapists may ask a couple to read a book (e.g., *Families* by Patterson, 1971, or *A Couple's Guide to Communication* by Gottman et al., 1976) which describes these expectations as part of a behavioral orientation. No matter how these expectations are presented to the clients, they represent a repetitive theme in BMT programs.

DISCRIMINATION TRAINING AND PINPOINTING OF BEHAVIORAL OBJECTIVES

Couples who seek marital therapy frequently present global complaints and do not have a clear sense of what changes in their relationship would relieve their distress. Even when a complaint centers on a specifiable event (e.g., "He/she has a drinking problem," "He/she had an affair"), clients often have difficulty identifying what their partners might do differently in order to improve the relationship. Most often, the client is upset about a *pattern* of interaction with the spouse rather than a single event. For example, the client who complains about a spouse's drinking is responding to a pattern in which the actual drinking behavior is only part, and issues such as neglect of the client's various needs are quite important. In addition, the client usually is unaware of what *he* or *she* might do to modify the relationship. As noted by Weiss (1978), clients often are not aware of the complex cause-effect relationships in their interactions with spouses. The behavioral marital therapist assumes that marital dissatisfaction is a function of specific interchanges between spouses and that these behavioral events must be modified to maximize satisfaction. Since research has tended to support the idea that spouses' subjective marital satisfaction is related to concrete events (Weiss, 1978), having clients learn to discriminate positive from negative relationship behaviors is a crucial component of therapy.

Rather than attributing marital problems to personality characteristics (e.g., "He's inconsiderate"), which provides little direction for treatment, a client needs to specify which of the partner's behaviors are pleasing and which are displeasing. Identification of positives is quite important, since it provides directions for behavior change, i.e., pleasing behaviors can be increased. Also, it is easier to reinforce a spouse for doing more of something than for doing less of something. Couples who seek therapy quite often are preoccupied with the negatives in their relationship and overlook the strengths with which they might rebuild it.

Behavioral marital therapists commonly ask their clients to keep daily records of specific "pleases" and "displeases" that their partners direct toward them. These events must be concrete and observable (e.g., "He kissed me when he got home from work"). In order to facilitate this record-keeping, therapists often give clients extensive checklists of possible pleasing and displeasing behaviors (Liberman et al., 1976; Weiss, Hops and Patterson, 1973) that can be categorized as either "instrumental" (action taken to achieve a goal, such as preparing a meal) or "affectional" (overt expressions of love and caring). Weiss et al. (1973) stress that the pleasing or displeasing quality of each behavior is defined by the spouse who receives it, not by the giver, therapist or other outsider.

Ratios of "pleases" to "displeases" have been shown to be higher for nondistressed (nonclinic) couples than for distressed (clinic) couples (Weiss, 1978), and increase following behavioral marital therapy (e.g., Jacobson, 1977a). Liberman, Wheeler, and Sanders (1976) ask spouses to share their lists and to discuss their desires for increases in "pleases." This procedure draws their attention to relationship strengths and helps each spouse discriminate specific things he/she can do to satisfy the other. Each spouse's behavior-change task becomes much more manageable than attempting to modify global traits. Behaviors specified in this manner then can serve as targets in behavior-exchange contracts (see discussion below).

A more informal approach that the present authors sometimes find useful, especially in initial sessions when one is attempting to orient clients toward a behavioral view of relationships, is to ask the spouse who makes a global complaint the question, "What specific things that I, as an outside observer, could see would your partner need to do more of or less of in order for you to be happier with the relationship?" Clients commonly need coaching in specifying behavioral examples.

As Weiss (1978) notes, another purpose of behavioral pinpointing is to increase clients' awareness of cause-effect patterns in their relationships. An important goal is to identify not only the "pleases" and "displeases" produced by one's partner but to discover what situational conditions (including one's own behavior) contribute to the frequencies of those behaviors. Clients can be coached in conducting a "functional analysis" (Kanfer and Saslow, 1969) of the problematic behaviors in their relationships, identifying antecedent and reinforcing events that control their occurrence. For example, it would be important for spouse A to recognize that spouse B withdraws more after spouse A has been nagging. It is especially important for spouses to understand the circular causality in their interactions, in which each person's behavior serves as both a consequence and an antecedent for the other's behavior. Such data are crucial for setting up mutual positive control programs, such as that described by Goldstein (1971).

The therapist should provide detailed feedback regarding the couple's interaction *sequences*. This necessitates careful observation of live interactions in the office, supplemented by client reports of interactions they have had at home. Since clients often have difficulty reporting past incidents with the degree of accuracy necessary for a behavioral functional analysis, teaching them to monitor their interactions in the office is an important step in discrimination training. Each spouse's behaviors must be viewed in the context of the partner's behaviors that preceded and followed it. Initially, videotape playback of the couple's interactions is likely to be helpful in facilitating clients' awareness of how each spouse's responses influence the other's responses. The therapist's task is to guide clients into a participant-observer role and to increase their understanding of how both spouses contribute to problematic *and* positive behavior patterns. Once clients become aware of specific ways in which their behaviors are interdependent, the therapist can introduce suggestions regarding contributions *each* spouse can make toward modifying dysfunctional interaction patterns. This orientation often has a benefit of reducing mutual blaming.

A recent study by De Torres (1979) indicated that spouses in distressed and nondistressed marriages were equally coercive with each other when discussing a high-conflict topic, but that distressed couples used more coercion than nondistressed couples when discussing low-conflict topics. Ryder (1968) found that distressed spouses had more positive interactions with strangers than with their partners. These studies suggest that negative behaviors of distressed spouses more likely represent situation-specific responses to their partners rather than consistent traits, and that these individuals are failing to discriminate one interaction situation from another. When the condition of holding a discussion has greater control over their behavior than the topic of discussion, the couple needs training in discriminating different ways of interacting, based on variation in the situation.

Another important area for discrimination training is the identification of discrepancies in the perceptions the two spouses have of the time they spend together. Williams (1978; in press) has demonstrated that spouses may judge the quality of a particular time period spent together differently and may not be aware of the discrepancy. Using a "time line" assessment procedure, in which each spouse independently charts the hours spent with the partner each day (in quarter-hour segments) and rates the quality of each segment on a five-point scale (++ = very pleasant to -- = very unpleasant), Williams found frequent instances in which one spouse rated the time positively and the other rated it as neutral or negative. In order for a couple to be able to restructure their interactions to maximize mutual satisfaction, they need to become aware of differences in their experiences of interactions and to discriminate specific events that produce satisfying and dissatisfying experiences for each of them. Having spouses compare their "time line" ratings is a useful way of drawing their attention to such issues. Once spouses are aware that they had different perceptions of an interaction, the therapist can guide them in exploring what behaviors of their partner made the interaction positive, neutral or negative for them, and what specific behaviors might be increased in order to make future interactions more positive.

Stuart and Stuart's (1972) Marital Precounseling Inventory (MPI) also is useful for focusing clients' (and therapists') attention on specific aspects of a couple's interaction that are satisfying and on those that are dissatisfying. Clients complete items that emphasize identification of desired behaviors and specification of their current frequencies as well as set goals for *preferred* frequencies. The MPI's focus on positive behaviors that can be increased shifts clients' attention from negatives to the potential for constructive change.

In summary, behavioral approaches to marital therapy focus on changing concrete events in order to maximize interactions that both spouses find subjectively satisfying. A prerequisite for the various procedures, which will be described in the remainder of this chapter, is a clear and thorough assessment of the interaction events that each partner experiences as positive and negative. Training clients to discriminate events in their behavioral system and to pinpoint objectives for behavioral change not only serves this assessment function but is likely to begin the change process by giving each spouse behavioral guidelines.

OPERANT PRINCIPLES AND BEHAVIOR-CHANGE PROCEDURES

In the operant model, emphasis is placed on the probability that a certain behavior will occur. When we say that the frequency or rate of occurrence can be increased or decreased by manipulating the consequences, we mean *in all probability* but not with certainty. As we shall see, behavior-change procedures with couples may look deceptively simple but are difficult to apply because of the lack of a clear cause-effect relationship. For the sake of clarity, we will assume great complexity in human behavior but will use simplified definitions and examples to explain basic principles.

As mentioned in the introduction, consequences which tend to *increase* the probability of occurrence of a behavior they have followed are *positive reinforcers*. On the other hand, consequences that involve avoidance or escape from aversive conditions (e.g., escaping heat by turning on an air-conditioner in mid-August) also will increase the probability of engaging in that behavior in the future. The relief from the heat and humidity could be considered a *negative reinforcer* because the adverse environmental conditions have been *subtracted*. As even this simple example demonstrates, positive and negative reinforcement may occur simultaneously; that is, the act of turning off the heat (aversive stimulus) requires turning on the coolness and dryness (pleasant stimulus) at the same time. Whether escaping the heat or seeking the coolness, the instrumental response is rewarded and becomes highly probable in the future.

Punishment has the reverse effect. It involves consequences which tend to *decrease* the probability that the behavior they follow will occur in the future. If a wife puts a new dress in mothballs after her husband tells her that "it looks faded," he has, in effect, punished her for buying a dress with muted colors. A major reason why punishment is avoided as a behavior-change procedure in BMT is that its consequences can be quite unpredictable. It may suppress an undesirable behavior temporarily, at least when the punisher is present, but it provides the punished person no guidelines for positive behavior change. In the present example, even the husband's simple comment that "it looks faded" can have at least three separate sequelae. First, the wife may not wear the dress again. Second, she may buy brighter colored dresses in the future. Third, she may resent her husband's derogatory remark about her choice of clothes and may criticize him in return. Without knowing the *history* of the marital relationship, it would be impossible to predict which responses are likely to occur. A common occurrence in marriages is that the spouse forgets what was being punished

and remembers *only* that a punishment was received. A secondary consequence is that the punished spouse avoids the punisher in order to decrease
the probability of receiving future attacks. The wife may avoid asking her
husband's opinion when she buys another dress.

A second kind of punishment is the *withholding* of desirable behaviors or
consequences after an unwanted behavior by the spouse. If a husband
returns from a business meeting smelling of cigar smoke, his wife may
adamantly refuse to kiss and embrace him until he brushes his teeth, uses a
mouthwash and changes his clothes. Again, her withholding physical
affection may have multiple effects on the husband's behavior. First, he may
refuse cigars when they are offered at meetings. Second, he may instead
brush his teeth, etc., before he approaches his wife for a kiss. And third, he
may *avoid her* for being "picky" about something he feels he has a perfect
right to do. Again, without knowing the history of the marital relationship,
it would be impossible to predict his response.

The behavior therapist may suggest that the wife greet her husband with a
kiss on the cheek and then embrace him more warmly as soon as he has met
her reasonable request (presented in a non-offensive manner). The emphasis
is on positive consequences rather than on aversive control.

These four types of contingencies for behavior—positive reinforcement,
negative reinforcement, punishment and withholding desired behaviors—
have been described more fully elsewhere in this book (see the chapter by
Berman, Lief and Williams). Precise definitions of the operant terms are
available in Reynolds (1968). Explanations and examples are available in
Gambrill (1977) and Whaley and Malott (1971).

In dyadic interactions, these four types of behavior contingencies can
form at least two major social reinforcement patterns—*reciprocity* and
coercion. Reciprocity involves the mutual exchange of positive reinforcers in
a way which the partners see as equitable over time (Patterson and Hops,
1972; Weiss et al., 1973). Whether the reciprocity model involves a one-for-
one exchange or a "bank account" arrangement (Gottman et al., 1976), in
which spouses give each other positives at high rates without regard for how
the partner is behaving at a particular time, has yet to be empirically
determined. Nevertheless, predominantly positive exchanges are characteristic of couples who are more satisfied with their marital relationships
(Jacobson, 1979; Weiss, 1978). Behavior therapists, therefore, seek to
increase the number of interspousal interactions which are perceived by the
couple as mutually reinforcing and satisfying.

The second social reinforcement pattern emphasized by behavioral marital therapists, *coercion*, involves the use of aversive control to force desired
responses from one's partner. Using "arm-twisting" to effect an immediate
goal causes long-term strain in the relationship, despite any short-term
achievement of the goal. Thus, a husband may coerce his wife into accepting

his sexual advances and the wife may comply, but the marital bond may be weakened rather than strengthened as a result. The wife is rewarded for her *compliance* because, temporarily, her husband will "leave her alone" sexually. Since her compliance stops his aversive demands, it is rewarded by *negative reinforcement*. The husband is directly rewarded for his demands by getting the sexual gratification he wants (*positive reinforcement*). However, because of the coercion used, the exchange engenders resentment instead of satisfaction. Escalating exchanges of aversive control between spouses are common and counterproductive (Raush et al., 1974).

Building positive behaviors. How are new behavior patterns *initiated*? How are the more satisfying interaction patterns to be *maintained*? The behavior therapist follows two different procedures, depending on the preexisting rate of the preferred behaviors. First, if the target behavior (for example, greeting the spouse pleasantly when the spouse enters the house or returns from another room) *never* occurs, the therapist will model the appropriate response and will have the partner "prompt" it (for example, "Hello, dear"). After the target response has occurred once, the partner needs to acknowledge and reward its occurrence on a *continuous reinforcement schedule* until the new behavior is established. It is imperative that the acknowledgment be given *immediately*, not at the next therapy session. Also, the acknowledgment needs to be positive and genuine from the perspective of the recipient. If the verbal message is positive but the nonverbal presentation is sarcastic, the nonverbal behavior will speak louder than the words and the efforts at trying a new response will have been punished. On the other hand, if the desired response is successfully established, a second procedure—*intermittent* reinforcement—is used to maintain it. In intermittent reinforcement, the rewarding consequence occurs after a certain number of responses have occurred (e.g., every fourth greeting) or after a certain length of time has passed (e.g., after three or four hours, the next greeting will *immediately* be acknowledged and thanked). Intermittent reinforcement may be on a fixed (regular) schedule or may be random. Spacing the reinforcements in this way helps to keep the acknowledgments from becoming stale and losing their value as rewards. Also, a person who receives continuous reinforcement is likely to stop responding sooner when reinforcement stops than someone who receives intermittent (less predictable) reinforcement. Random reinforcement, such as that used with slot machines, tends to produce a strong response tendency.

It is imperative that an acknowledgment or other reinforcement be given immediately so that unwanted or unrelated behaviors will not be rewarded and increased *accidentally*. If the grateful spouse waits thirty minutes, until the partner is leaving the room, and *then* reinforces the greeting, the act of leaving might be increased instead of the act of greeting.

Another important requirement for social reinforcement between spouses is that an acknowledgment be clear so that the partner knows which behaviors are desired and which are extraneous. Sometimes "superstitious" behaviors are rewarded which are not necessary to the interaction pattern. These accidentally reinforced behaviors are continued as part of a ritual because they have been reinforced along with other behaviors which *are* essential. The therapist's task is to help the clients decide which behaviors are necessary and which are optional. On an individual level, athletes often develop superstitious behaviors (e.g., wearing a particular pair of socks) if they have been reinforced (win a game) while engaging in that behavior.

Similarly, some couples feel they must go through a ritual before they can engage successfully in sexual intercourse. They may start with sexual suggestions at breakfast, a phone call in the afternoon, a candlelight dinner, a shower together and then a massage with mood music *before* they can engage in sexual behavior. While therapists may prescribe this chain of behaviors to add romance to a dull or cursory pattern of sexual encounters, it is not recommended that this pattern be followed rigidly every time. A chain of behaviors this long and complicated would discourage the couple if they have only one hour to spend alone together after their children are in bed. If the pattern has been set up with superstitious behaviors, rewarded by several enjoyable intercourse occasions, one or the other spouse may feel that he or she will not be able to respond sexually (receive reinforcement) if one of the steps is omitted. They may postpone the final initiating gestures until they have all of the preliminary steps in proper sequence. The therapist can help the couple break this chain so that less formal, more spontaneous encounters can be added to their "special occasions."

What if the new behavior does not occur in the exact from that is desired? It may be necessary for the therapist to *shape* clients' behaviors gradually until they more closely resemble the criterion behavior. If a newlywed husband wants his bride to bake desserts like his mother used to make, and if she agrees to try, then it may be necessary for her to learn to beat egg whites first before she tackles a lemon meringue pie with a flaky crust. The husband needs to encourage her as she makes closer approximations to the desired goal. If he *withholds* reinforcement when she tries her best at her current level of culinary competence, he may find that she refuses to try anything more difficult than jello. Although this example may be somewhat trite, it illustrates the important behavioral principle of selective reinforcement for successive approximations to the desired end-product.

The acquisition of skills, such as driving a car, is a relatively simple example of shaping behavior. The establishment and maintenance of new social interaction patterns are much more complex and difficult. They are different from basic skill acquisition, since most of the component skills are already in use in nonmarital social interactions (Ryder, 1968); i.e., distressed spouses often exhibit positive social skills with strangers but not with their partners. Frequently, faulty marital behaviors must be removed or un-learned at the same time that more functional behaviors are practiced or increased. The chronically dysfunctional behaviors are decreased through the process of *extinction*, in which they are purposely ignored and not rewarded. As the newer, more functional behaviors are reinforced and increase in frequency, they compete with the previous behaviors and, hope-fully, displace them in the client's repertoire. As the dysfunctional behaviors are extinguished and fade from the current behavior patterns, the therapist needs to be watchful regarding three potential problems. First, the couple's interaction must be *monitored* closely to ensure that the reinforcers maintain their positive value. Second, *consistency* is needed both in rewarding the competing behavior (continuous reinforcement at the start) and in ignoring or extinguishing the aversive behavior. Third, both therapist and clients need *patience*. When an undesirable behavior has been maintained by an intermittent reinforcement schedule, interruption of this schedule during extinction may not produce a quick decrease in the behavior, since a person who has received intermittent reinforcement is accustomed to responding without reinforcement for some time. Change will be slower if the reinforce-ment has been highly intermittent and unpredictable. Therefore, expecting relatively rapid change in long-standing interaction patterns is unrealistic unless the intermittent reinforcement is abruptly stopped. Even so, the client will test the old schedule several times to be certain that it is still obsolete. Couples need to be warned that the negative behaviors may reoccur several times before they disappear. Unless warned in advance, they may interpret the periodic reappearance of the aversive behavior as an exacerbation or acceleration rather than as a normal part of the extinction pattern.

Cost/benefit analysis. In behavioral marital therapy, the social-exchange theory first described by Thibaut and Kelley (1959) has been applied to a cost/benefit analysis of husband-wife interaction. The therapist must con-sider the cost/benefit ratio of each negative behavior for each partner before initiating a specific behavior-change procedure. Each partner, theoretically, has something to gain and something to lose in any interaction. The goal for each individual is obviously to increase the former while decreasing the latter. Moreover, if the cost/benefit ratio within the marital relationship is not "profitable," the individual may seek an alternative source of reinforce-ment (according to his or her comparison level for alternative sources of reinforcement) outside of the marriage.

The task of the therapist is to present the proposed behavior change as beneficial enough to compensate the clients for the time, energy and emotional cost of unlearning the old behaviors and relearning the new. Part of this therapeutic task involves overcoming the client's behavioral inertia and relinquishing the comfort of the status quo (Goldstein, 1976, p. 195). Recent research by Williams (1978; in press) suggests that the costs and benefits of the marital relationship include not only the behaviors and events that *do* occur but also those that are expected but that *do not* occur. It was suggested that these *omissions* (e.g., compliments expected, prompted, but not received) are as important to the cost/benefit formula as are the *commissions* (e.g., attention, affection, approval, etc.) that are given at other times. Thus, in the behavioral analysis of marital interaction, the cost/benefit ratio is also influenced by the spouses' expectations for the relationship. When a spouse expects a positive response (e.g., "I'll fix his favorite dessert. He'll like that"), and when the expected compliment is received ("You always make the best red raspberry pie"), the value of the expected response is a single positive. However, if the compliment was not prompted or is not routinely given, it comes as a doubly valued "unexpected pleasure." Similarly, when an insult or critical remark is expected ("She always bugs me about my driving. It doesn't bother me anymore"), the impact seems less negative than it was the first time the critical remark occurred in the history of the relationship. In contrast, when a spouse prompts and expects a positive response, receiving an insult or critical remark can be perceived as devastating ("When I brought home sixty dollars worth of groceries, she only commented on the hamburger I forgot"). The substitution of a negative consequence for a positive one seems to have double negative impact. The task of the therapist is to change the husband-wife interaction so that positive responses are justly rewarded and not ignored (extinguished) or punished. The negative impact of constructive criticism then can be counterbalanced in the cost/benefit ratio by the positives received.

One interaction pattern which couples often misunderstand deserves special comment. When the impact *intended* is not congruent with the impact *received* (Gottman et al., 1976), the "giver" may demand that the "receiver" express his or her gratitude after the giving behavior has been ignored or rejected. The "ungrateful" spouse, feeling unjustly accused, may respond with anger or hostility ("Why should I thank you for doing something I didn't want in the first place? Nobody asked you to do it for me"). The task of the therapist is threefold.

First, he or she needs to help the clients understand that the value of a given behavior is decided by the receiver. A positive reinforcement is judged by its consequences, which are in part determined by the person, place and time of its occurrence. These circumstances may shift and change as a person's levels of deprivation and satiation change. Moreover, the attributions of the receiver must also be considered. A dozen red roses may have a positive impact on the wife if they are received *before* the husband sees the therapist but may have little positive impact *after* the therapy session if the wife attributes them to the therapist's suggestions and not to her husband.

Second, the receiver needs to learn how to give corrective feedback as to which behaviors or situations are currently potent reinforcers and which have lost their reinforcing value. Without explicit feedback, the giver will have to deduce the loss of potency or change in interest by trial and error. As can be seen by the example already given, these reinforcement "errors" can be costly to the marital relationship.

Third, the receiver can learn to acknowledge the positive intentions of the giver ("It's the thought that counts") as a prelude to giving the constructive corrective feedback. In the case of intent/impact incongruity, the good intentions need to be rewarded even though the actual behaviors emitted need to be shaped to be more appropriate for the recipient. Otherwise, the act of giving itself will be extinguished, since the benefits of giving will be outweighed by the costs (or risks) of being rejected or ignored. Again, these three therapeutic tasks are important if the therapist is to increase reciprocal reinforcement, decrease aversive control and facilitate the behavior changes necessary so that the benefits of the relationship more than balance the costs.

Schedules of reinforcement. As noted earlier, the schedules with which reinforcements are given will affect the strength and maintenance of learned responses. We are surprised by the scarcity of discussion about reinforcement schedules in the BMT literature and feel that this topic has not been given the attention that it deserves. It has certainly proven to be an important aspect of behavior therapy in other areas (for example, in the management of chronic pain) and is a relatively unexplored area in BMT which could have great influence on the field in the future.

There are four types of schedules. Two types involve *how often* a response is reinforced, and two involve *how many* responses must occur before a reinforcement is given. The first two types are *interval* schedules, which include either *fixed* or *variable* lengths of time. The second two types are *ratio* schedules, which include either *fixed* or *variable* numbers of required responses on which the reinforcements depend or are contingent.

The first type of schedule, the *fixed-interval* schedule, is familiar to the reader as the period one must wait before receiving a weekly, biweekly or monthly paycheck. Many couples fall into a fixed interval schedule in their marriages because of convenience or expediency. For example, they may eat dinner at a restaurant on Sundays ("Mother's day off") as a reward for the meals she has prepared the previous week. Efforts at aversive control may also follow a fixed interval schedule, as in the case of the Monday/Thursday trash-collection schedule. A nagging wife may increase the rate of her requests to her husband to empty the trash compactor as the Monday morning and Thursday morning deadlines approach. After each trash pickup, there is a pause (post-reinforcement) for a couple of days, followed by a gradual increase in the frequency or intensity of the "don't forget to take out the trash" reminders.

When a therapist is analyzing marital-interaction patterns, two characteristics of fixed-interval schedules can be important clinically. At the end of the interval, the person who has been doubling and tripling his or her efforts to meet the deadline will take a post-reinforcement pause. This pause has been referred to as "the pause that refreshes" and as "the pause that depresses." While the person is resting before starting to work on the next deadline, the activity level may be very low. Others may perceive this lack of activity as "lethargic," "depressed" and "lazy." However, the lethargy, depression and laziness disappear as the rate of responding gradually accelerates in the next fixed interval. This may be important information for the guilt-ridden client who wants to learn to work at a steadier pace. A change to a variable-interval schedule (described below) will alleviate extremes of activity levels.

Another problem generated by the fixed-interval schedule is that a nonworking spouse may feel neglected while the partner responds at an extremely high rate just before the end of the interval. It may be helpful to remind the neglected spouse that a vacation (post-reinforcement pause) is soon to follow. If the nonworking spouse interrupts the hard-working spouse, the frustration before the goal is reached will likely result in overt hostility. In cases when the pattern is less blatant, it may help the couple to monitor how the level of stress and irritability cycles with the response schedule.

The second type of schedule, the *variable interval*, is similar to the fixed-interval schedule in that it is also time-dependent. However, the intervals between reinforcement or punishment are variable. The individual who is responding under this schedule is unlikely to exhibit discrete bursts of activity, since he or she cannot predict when the next deadline will occur.

Variable-interval schedules can be imposed on a couple by the outside world. The families of physicians, firemen and clergymen are familiar with the pattern of having one spouse "on call" on a twenty-four-hour basis. Often the tension which is produced by this type of unpredictable schedule changes the behavior of the entire family unit. The person "on call" is usually tense and unable to relax fully, depending on how fast and to what extent he or she is expected to "get in gear." A surgical resident, who will be required to reach a high pitch of life-saving activity in the shortest possible time, may be tense for the entire period that he or she is assigned to the emergency room. The partners must work harder in the marriage to develop "quality time together," since the time for recreation, meals, child care, problem-solving and decision making may vary from five minutes to five days. Both partners must be efficient in prompting each other for reinforcement and in giving rewards. Since reinforcement is available from the spouse only during limited periods, the individual must respond during this limited "window" of time in order to capitalize on the opportunity to receive reinforcement (Whaley and Malott, 1971). This schedule may be difficult to adjust to, since many reinforcements lose their potency rapidly once the behavior is emitted.

For example, it may be too late to thank the working spouse for giving the baby a bath when the spouse returns after a twenty-four-hour shift and the baby already needs another bath.

If this type of schedule is detrimental to the marital relationship, the therapist can problem-solve with the couple to see if the *variable*-interval schedule can be modified into a *fixed*-interval schedule. Physicians usually accomplish this by setting up group practice, in which the "call" schedule is shared. Any member of the group is on call only every fourth night and every fourth weekend. Both the work load and the tensions are lessened during the nonworking periods.

Within the marital relationship, one spouse may provide reinforcement for the other on a variable-interval schedule. For example, a spouse may pay attention to the partner's behavior on some occasions but not at other times, based on the former's moods and preoccupations. Thus, a wife may notice and reinforce her husband's efforts at helping with housework on days when she is not preoccupied with other concerns, and the time intervals between reinforcements may vary considerably. The husband receives reinforcement if he helps around the house on a day when his wife is likely to pay attention. This type of schedule can be problematic when reinforcements are too few to maintain a spouse's positive behavior or when the recipient of reinforcement resents a low frequency of reinforcement. Such a problem may be alleviated by increasing the awareness on the part of the reinforcing spouse that the partner is performing the desired behavior and that reinforcements should be dispensed more regularly. The partner who receives the reinforcements can facilitate this process considerably by acknowledging the reinforcement when it occurs.

The third type of schedule, *fixed ratio*, involves reinforcement after a fixed number of tasks have been completed, regardless of how long the tasks take. When a door-to-door salesperson must sell $500 worth of merchandise in order to get a $50 bonus, how soon he or she gets paid is determined by his or her diligence and efficiency in selling the product. Watching the clock is irrelevant, since reinforcement is independent of the time elapsed. First, a post-reinforcement pause is likely to occur before the next batch of work (ratio) is begun. The length of this pause is related to the quantity of responses required before reinforcement is given, i.e., the size of the ratio (Whaley and Malott, 1971). Second, the response rate is more consistent than on the fixed-interval schedule in that it does not gradually build up over the interval. On the contrary, once the individual makes the first response, he or she works as rapidly as possible until the requirement is completed; then the pause is taken. Fixed-ratio schedules of reinforcement are not common in couples' interactions, because it is rare for one spouse to set an *unchanging* quota of any response for the other to fulfill.

The fourth type of schedule, the *variable ratio* (VR), was seen in the slot-machine example above. Once the first response has been rewarded, the person continues to work consistently and rapidly *without* a post-reinforcement pause. Because the schedule of payoffs is variable and unpredictable, two responses in a row could be rewarded, or six could occur without rewards. Many gamblers attribute frequent rewards as evidence that "Lady Luck is with me," whereas a period without rewards is referred to as "a string of bad luck." Gambling casinos arrange the VR schedules to maximize the probability of gambling behavior while minimizing the probability of payoffs.

Most reinforcement schedules in nature and in our social relationships are *variable ratio*. We speak of being industrious, but a hard-working person on a VR schedule knows that the more you work, the more you succeed. A schedule in which the reinforcements occur *on the average* after a few responses may be considered a *rich* schedule. A spouse who is thanked after an *average* of three chores (i.e., making the bed, washing the dishes and walking the dog) may continue to do these same things at a consistent rate. On the other hand, a spouse who is thanked only once out of fifty times on the average may be on too *lean* a schedule to maintain the behavior. When the reinforcements are spaced too far apart on the average, the target behaviors gradually begin to decrease.

Extinction. Extinction is a "schedule" in which *no* reinforcements are provided for a person's responses. This schedule is used to eliminate a person's undesirable behavior, usually in combination with a schedule of positive reinforcement for an alternative (competing) prosocial response. When a person is attempting to extinguish a partner's particular response, he or she must be highly consistent in withholding reinforcement. Otherwise, intermittent reinforcement will produce a reinforcement schedule (e.g., variable ratio) that in fact may *strengthen* the partner's undesirable response. Spouses may unwittingly maintain each other's negative behaviors by providing intermittent reinforcement rather than extinction.

INCREASING POSITIVE INTERACTION THROUGH RECREATIONAL TIME

Behavior therapists are very much concerned that distressed couples no longer enjoy spending time together. It is not enough that therapists decrease the couples' heated arguments and icy silences, since the lack of negative marital interaction does not strengthen the marital bond enough to compete successfully with warmth and companionship available outside the marriage. In an effort to strengthen the marital bond (Weiss, 1978; Williams, 1978), the therapist seeks to improve the *quality* of leisure (and nonleisure) time spent with spouse and moderate the *quantity* of time together.

It was suggested by Williams (1978) that some couples need a period of time *alone* together each week before they can begin to interact with each other on an intimate (nonsexual) basis. She found that distressed spouses spent less time with each other than did nondistressed spouses, yet they spent an adequate amount of time together doing the chores necessary to maintain the *household*. What appears to have been lacking for the distressed couples was adequate good-quality time for maintaining the *marital relationship*. For couples with children, this relationship time is generally referred to as "leisure" or "recreational," since it occurs *outside* the home environment, where responsibilities for home and family compete with the focus on the dyadic interaction.

In situations where the couple disagrees on *what* activity to engage in, the therapist can suggest several options. For example, if the husband prefers a trip to the art museum and the wife prefers to take their child to a baseball game, they could do the latter on Saturday and the former on Sunday. Alternatively, they could spend Saturday afternoon in separate activities and then go out alone together for a quiet dinner. The leisure activities which occur daily or weekly offer more opportunity for flexible arrangements than do annual or semiannual vacation trips. Knox (1971) has outlined some suggestions for handling major disagreements on how to spend the family vacation. Desensitization can be used for vacation activities that attract one spouse but terrify the other (e.g., a burro ride into the Grand Canyon). Knox suggested modeling to help the hesitant spouse develop more favorable attitudes toward a specific activity or location (e.g., talking with friends who have made the trip and have returned safely). Selective verbal and behavioral reinforcement (e.g., praise, hugs) can be given for planning and positive verbalizations about the trip. Finally, the Premack principle could be used by making more attractive activities (e.g., nightclub shows) contingent on the spouse's participation in the less attractive activities desired by the rest of the family.

Liberman, Wheeler and Sanders (1976, p. 388) give their group-therapy couples the following guidelines for the beneficial distribution of their leisure time:

1. Each person needs his or her own individual recreation, alone or with his/her own separate friends.

2. Each couple needs to do things they enjoy as a dyad.

3. Every couple needs to have some recreational time with other couples, preferably *happily* married ones. (*Authors' note:* Happily married couples can serve as positive role models.)

4. Each couple has, as part of a well-rounded pattern, recreation with the children, such as family outings or celebrations.

As a couple matures together, their interests and activities are bound to change. These changes need to be discussed and new joint activities initiated. The communication skills needed for negotiating which activities to pursue individually and which to pursue as a dyad (or family unit) will be discussed in this chapter's section on building communication skills.

STIMULUS CHANGE AND STIMULUS CONTROL PROCEDURES

The behavioral principle involved in stimulus control is that if a response is reinforced a number of times in the presence of a particular stimulus, that stimulus comes to "control" the given response. If a couple enjoys holding hands during several movies while they are dating, the theater may become a *discriminative stimulus* (S_D) for hand-holding. The frequency of hand-holding is high in the presence of the stimulus (the theater) and lower in its absence. The stimulus does not *elicit* the response but *sets the occasion* on which the hand-holding has previously been reinforced. The stimulus is said to "control" the response because the probability of the response (hand-holding) can be *increased* by presenting the stimulus (going to the movie) or decreased by withholding the stimulus (not go to the movie) (see Reynolds, 1968). Thus, the discriminative stimulus is an informational cue to a person that a particular response is likely to produce a particular consequence.

A discriminative stimulus can also signal when a response is more likely to be punished. If a husband has yelled at his wife several times for bothering him when he is reading the paper, the newspaper can signal an occasion on which she will probably be punished for speaking to him. Conversely, the absence of a newspaper on his lap or the newspaper lying on the table (where he leaves it when he's finished) can signal an opportunity to start a conversation, which will probably be rewarded. The wife's behavior of initiating conversations may be under stimulus control of seeing her husband with or without the newspaper.

A therapist can use these behavioral principles to facilitate the occurrence of positive interactions or eliminate conditions which make arguments or attacks more likely. A closely related behavioral principle is that a novel environment (new stimuli) can speed up the change from an old behavior pattern to a new one. By changing the environment, discriminative stimuli for problematic responses can be eliminated and new discriminative stimuli for positive responses can be added.

Historically, stimulus change and control were the first behavioral principles to be applied to marital problems. Goldiamond (1965) instructed a chronically jealous husband to rearrange the use of the rooms and the furniture in them so that the couple's home would appear different and unfamiliar. The husband was not allowed to yell in the house, and his prolonged sulking was relegated to a "sulking stool" in the garage. The unprovoked yelling and sulking were thus disassociated with the wife and their home and were instead associated with the stool in the garage. Moreover, since he was alone in the garage, his sulking could not be accidentally reinforced by attention from the wife. In addition, since the bedroom had become a discriminative stimulus for *both* bickering and love-making (and the former interfered with the latter), its stimulus qualities were changed. The couple was instructed to turn on a yellow night light whenever they were in the mood to make love. In this way the environmental discriminative stimuli for bickering were changed and a new stimulus just for love-making was created.

Goldiamond (1965) described the rationale for these procedures as follows (p. 856):

> One of the most rapid ways to change behavior is by altering the conditions under which it usually occurs. This is called *stimulus change* or the effects of novel stimuli. If the novel stimuli are then combined with new behavioral contingencies designed to produce different behavior, these contingencies are apt to generate the new behavior much more rapidly than they would in the presence of the old stimuli.

A stimulus that signals when reinforcement probably is *not* available rather than when a reinforcement or punishment *is* available is called an S-delta. For example, a wife has repeatedly been ignored when her husband is reading (rather than being yelled at for interrupting). If he does *not* answer her first attempts at a conversation, she gives up (discriminated extinction) until he puts the paper down (S_D to try again). She has learned that he will ignore her attempts at conversation until he has finished the paper (Whaley and Malott, 1971).

If a therapist were asked to change this interaction pattern, there would be several behavior-change procedures from which to choose. One method would be to change subscriptions from an evening paper to a morning paper, which the husband could read at work or at lunch. Coming home from work could then be associated with a pleasant family activity (e.g., taking a walk before dinner) rather than with an activity that produces resentment in the wife or frustration in the husband. Another method would be to have the husband read the paper aloud to the wife (or vice versa) while dinner is being prepared. The newspaper could then become an S_D for pleasant interaction instead of an S_D for yelling-when-reading-is-interrupted or an S_D for the wife being ignored. This change could be reinforced by having the wife listen attentively. Third, a behavior-exchange contract could be set up which allowed the husband thirty minutes of uninterrupted reading time in exchange for thirty minutes of active listening and problem-solving with the wife. Exchange contracts and contingency management will be discussed below.

The type of stimulus change and stimulus control procedures described by Goldiamond (1965) have not been reported extensively in the more recent BMT literature. However, several variations of the stimulus control theme have been described and warrant our attention here.

Goldstein (1976) used a form of stimulus control with severely distressed couples when he had them post a behavior chart on their refrigerators. He used this highly visible recording device to remind both husband and wife to acknowledge positive behaviors emitted by their spouse. The chart set the occasion for the behaving spouse to be reinforced by the recording spouse. Furthermore, it also set the occasion for the recording spouse to be rewarded by the therapist for recording the data.

In another procedure, Goldstein (1976) used a kitchen timer to mark off thirty-minute intervals for rating marital interaction. During the timed intervals, pleasant interaction was likely to be reinforced with a "plus" rating while unpleasant interaction was likely to be punished with a "minus" rating.

Another type of stimulus control comes in the form of instructions from the therapist. Some behavior therapists have instructed couples to set up "executive time" (Liberman, Wheeler and Sanders, 1976), "administrative sessions" (Weiss et al., 1973) and "Family Meetings" (Gottman et al., 1976). During these structured, preplanned periods (e.g., two to three in the afternoon, Sundays), the couple is instructed to practice problem-solving, decision making or some other communication skill.

Some form of stimulus control can be introduced by the therapist. However, many marital behaviors are under stimulus control from our culture, from society and from our childhood experiences. An authority figure—"mother," "boss," "policeman"—can embody dozens of rules simply through their presence ("Don't drop crumbs in the living room." "Don't waste time at the water cooler." "Don't park by a fire hydrant"). Their presence signals an increased probability that certain behaviors will be punished or rewarded under certain circumstances (see Weiss, 1978, p. 194).

Williams (1978) suggested that extraordinarily happy spouses and severely distressed spouses may become S_Ds because their *presence* reliably signals an opportunity for rewards in the former case and punishment or aversive control in the latter case. It was suggested that this stimulus control property is not contingent on the occurrence of any particular *behavior* by the spouse. Some partners in severely disturbed relationships may avoid interacting with their spouses because they feel they will be attacked *on sight*, regardless of their being on "good behavior." At the other end of the spectrum, we speak of honeymooners enjoying each other's company regardless of the specific behaviors emitted ("Love is blind"), because the history of the relationship predicts the opportunity for mutual reinforcement.

The application of these behavior principles in marital therapy is three-fold: first, to identify when faulty behaviors are under stimulus control (e.g., when the wife sees the newspaper and begins to feel rejected); second, to *clarify* and strengthen stimuli which are supposed to signal the opportunity for satisfying interactions (e.g., when the wife's nightgown is supposed to signal a receptive mood for sex, but the husband tends to miss the signal [Liberman, Levine, Wheeler, Sanders and Wallace, 1976]); and third, to *modify* stimulus conditions so that signals for aversive interactions become signals for enjoyable intimate interactions (e.g., when the spouse's car pulls in driveway, the homecoming includes a cold drink and a warm kiss rather than a reenactment of the woes of the day).

In summary, marital partners learn that when they act in a certain way under certain conditions (discriminative stimuli), there are known probabilities that a positive (or negative) consequence will occur. The therapist works to *increase* the probability of positive consequences while working to *decrease* the probability of negative consequences. The stimulus can be a person, place, object, gesture or verbalization. What matters is the meaning (cueing function) that has gradually become attached to it.

Jacobson (1978d) has proposed that the effectiveness of the most popular BMT strategy to date, contingency contracting, is less determined by the terms of the contract itself than by the stimuli (self-statements) generated by the contract negotiation process. If the negotiation process includes mutual cooperation and efforts at constructive problem-solving, the probability that behavior change will occur is enhanced. On the other hand, if the negotiation process is characterized by nonproductive debate, criticism and recriminations, the probability that the desired behavior change will occur is diminished. Theoretically, in the former case, self-statements are generated which reinforce cooperative behaviors ("I'm a good person, I'm not holding a grudge"). In the latter case, the self-statements generated are presumed to be detrimental to the marital relationship ("Why should I compromise with that creep?! Who wants to live with someone who acts like that, anyway?"). If Jacobson's hypothesis proves to be correct, the emphasis in treatment may shift from contingency contracting (to be discussed below) to the stimulus conditions generated by the negotiation process. As we shall see, this would be a major change in the practice of behavioral marital therapy.

CLASSICAL CONDITIONING BEHAVIOR-CHANGE PROCEDURES

Classical conditioning (respondent) principles have been used to explain how an emotional or behavioral response can come to be elicited by an environmental stimulus that initially did not elicit that response; for example, how a person can learn to feel anxiety when in the presence of a sexual partner. Conditioning occurs when the initially neutral stimulus (one that did not elicit the emotional response) is paired temporally with unconditioned stimuli (events that already elicit the response). Thus, while the sexual partner's presence initially produces no anxiety, if his/her presence is paired with events that *do* elicit anxiety (e.g., failure to perform adequately in sex), then the mere presence of the partner can elicit anxiety in the future. The strength of the conditioning increases in proportion to the number of pairings and to the strength of the unconditioned event, in this case the strength of the anxiety response to sexual failure (Gambrill, 1977). Respondent learning commonly is thought to account for the acquisition of a variety of pleasant and unpleasant emotional responses to particular stimuli. Conditioned responses can generalize to stimuli that bear some similarity to the stimuli present in the original conditioning situation; e.g., the above individual may have anxiety responses in the presence of *other* sexual partners.

Bandura (1969) notes the important role of human cognitive processes (e.g., the ability to anticipate and imagine an event) in facilitating respondent conditioning. For example, if a person imagines poor sexual performance *and* negative responses such as ridicule and rejection from the partner, these thoughts are likely to elicit a strong negative emotional response on the former's part. This emotional response is then paired with the presence of the partner (in vivo or in the person's imagination), and through classical conditioning the partner becomes a stimulus that elicits negative emotions, such an anxiety. The fact that people can imagine worse consequences than would occur in reality suggests that an important aspect of assessment and treatment of negative emotional responses involves understanding what the client is *thinking* about himself/herself and the partner's reactions.

Whether or not there is direct evidence that unwanted emotional responses were classically conditioned, one approach to eliminating them is extinction. In this procedure, the person is exposed repeatedly to the (assumed initially neutral) emotion-eliciting stimulus without pairing it with the unconditioned stimuli. In the above example, the anxious individual would be instructed to spend gradually increasing amounts of time with the sexual partner under conditions requiring no performance. As these experiences are repeated, the associative link begins to weaken and the person can be in the presence of the partner without experiencing anxiety. Next, the sexual intimacy or performance demands of the situation can be increased enough to elicit mild anxiety, and a new series of extinction trials can be run. This procedure, which is common in the treatment of sexual dysfunctions such as psychogenic impotence, can be conducted in a series of steps until the person no longer experiences the emotional response to the partner or other environmental stimulus (cf. Kaplan, 1974). Extinction of negative emotional responses necessitates overcoming clients' attempts to avoid the stimuli that elicit unpleasant feelings.

With severe emotional responses that may be difficult to eliminate with extinction procedures, Wolpe's (1958) systematic desensitization paradigm can be used for "counterconditioning." Systematic desensitization is based on the idea of classically conditioning a new, positive response to the stimulus that presently elicits the undesirable response, such that the new response will compete with and replace the old response. In the treatment of anxiety, clients often are taught reliable procedures for relaxing in the presence of the anxiety-eliciting stimulus. Goldfried and Davison (1976) present a clear introduction to relaxation training procedures. Other constructive responses incompatible with anxiety, such as assertiveness, also can be used in counterconditioning (Wolpe, 1958).

Desensitization is conducted either by having the client imagine stimuli that elicit the undesirable emotional response or (preferably) by actually exposing the client to those stimuli. A spouse with a problematic emotional response can be trained in deep muscle relaxation and then desensitized to imagined aversive interactions with the partner. The therapist helps the client identify a hierarchy of emotion-eliciting situations, varying from those that are fairly neutral to those that produce strong negative emotion. Beginning with the lowest-level situations, the client *imagines* interacting with the partner and uses relaxation techniques whenever he/she experiences the negative emotion. When able to imagine the particular scene with no appreciable discomfort, the client moves to the next highest level in the hierarchy of problematic situations and repeats the desensitization process. In order to maximize generalization of desensitization to actual marital interactions, the client then could be instructed to repeat the entire hierarchy in vivo, with the partner.

As noted earlier, Lazarus (1968) and Knox (1971) have applied desensitization procedures to reduce one spouse's dysfunctional emotional responses to the other's behavior, especially when the mere presence of the partner elicits an emotional response strong enough to interfere with communication or therapeutic efforts. Since cases in which the only dysfunction is one spouse's unrealistic emotional response to the other's prosocial behavior are likely to be rare, desensitization most often will serve as a *preliminary* intervention that allows the couple to work together on other problems. Nevertheless, since strong emotional responses such as anger and anxiety can impede therapeutic work, it behooves the marital therapist to be competent in applying procedures to reduce such responses. Useful sources for the interested reader include Lazarus (1971), Wolpe (1973) and Goldfried and Davison (1976).

An additional approach to conditioned emotional responses, which integrates concepts of classical conditioning and concepts about human cognitive processes, involves changing the qualities of an eliciting stimulus by giving it a new cognitive meaning. A person's subjective appraisal of a stimulus, rather than the objective qualities of the stimulus, often elicits respondent emotional reactions (Gambrill, 1977). As noted earlier, phobic responses often are mediated by imagined aversive events rather than actual events, and an individual may fear an object (e.g., snakes) even though he/she has never had a traumatic experience in the presence of the object. Similarly, a person may develop an emotional response (e.g., anxiety, anger) to a marital partner's particular behavior based on *imagined* aversive consequences associated with the behavior. Thus, one spouse may experience anxiety when the other disagrees with any of his/her opinions, based on an imagined association between disagreement and rejection by the partner. If a therapist can break the client's disagreement-equals-rejection association by relabeling moderate disagreement as a *positive* event that can add interest or "spice" to a relationship, the anxiety-eliciting capacity of imagined rejection may be detached from the disagreement situation. In general, assessment and treatment of emotional responses to a spouse or other stimuli must take into account the sophisticated human capacity for imagining associations among events.

BUILDING COMMUNICATION SKILLS

Perhaps the most common complaint presented by couples who seek marital therapy is some variation of the theme "We can't communicate," and some form of training in communication skills is included in most behavioral treatment programs for couples (e.g., Jacobson, 1977a; Liberman, Wheeler and Sanders, 1976; Weiss, Hops and Patterson, 1973). However, due to the emphasis that has been placed on behavior-exchange procedures, descriptions of behavioral marital therapy commonly have not detailed the varieties of communication training programs in use. In order to provide a more comprehensive survey of behavioral procedures for couples, the present chapter includes a relatively extended discussion of these programs.

While the various behavioral programs may focus on somewhat different aspects of communicative exchanges between spouses, they share some basic assumptions. First, as emphasized by Watzlawick, Beavin and Jackson (1967), all interpersonal behavior has message value, and couples who say that they cannot communicate most likely mean that they do not like the messages they are receiving or that the messages they send are misinterpreted. Second, communication is considered to be a set of skills. It is assumed that when individuals have failed to learn communication skills or have learned dysfunctional skills (those producing interpersonal problems), an educational approach can be used to teach effective ways of interacting.

The general behavioral orientation to marriage proposes that in a cost/benefit analysis, dissatisfied spouses do not receive sufficient positive reinforcers from their partners to counterbalance costs in the relationship. In order for two individuals to function effectively as a unit that maximizes rewards and minimizes costs to each member (the reciprocity model), they need to exchange information in a manner that is both clear and constructive.

Distressed couples commonly report that their needs are not being met in their relationships, and they frequently perceive that their partners are letting them down. Unhappy spouses have tried in a variety of ways, particularly through the use of aversive control such as nagging, to elicit more rewarding behavior from their partners, but their behavior-change tactics tend to be ineffective. While coercive control, such as threats, may produce some compliance by a partner, in the long run the partner is likely to reciprocate with coerciveness or withdraw. When spouses become involved in a frustrating spiral of mutual aversive control and/or withdrawal, they are likely to develop the impression that their partners do not *care* to be more positive. Over time, each person's desire to give the partner positives does decrease, and by the time such a couple reaches a sufficient level of distress to seek therapy, they may expect few positives from each other and in fact have few positive exchanges.

From a communication viewpoint, positive exchanges may fail to occur because (1) a spouse does not clearly send the partner information about the positives he/she would like to receive, (2) a spouse does not perceive information about his/her partner's needs accurately, (3) information about desired positives is sent and received accurately, but the sender uses aversive means of requesting positives (e.g., demands) and thus decreases the receiver's tendency to comply, (4) a spouse intends to give a partner positives, but does not do so in a clear enough manner for the partner to perceive the positives, (5) a spouse intends to give a partner positives, but what he/she gives is *not* a reinforcer for the partner, (6) a spouse fails to perceive the positives given by his/her partner, (7) a spouse perceives the positives given by his/her partner but fails to acknowledge them, thus extinguishing the partner's positive responses or (8) partners are unable to engage in problem-solving communication that would produce positive outcomes for each of them (e.g., reducing external stress on the relationship due to financial problems or pressure from in-laws). In order to produce more positive exchanges, each member of a couple must develop skills in both sending and receiving unambiguous, direct messages. It is important to note that when a person intends to send a partner negatives rather than positives and the partner perceives this accurately, the problem is not one of unclear communication (Weiss, 1978).

The process of clarifying messages and increasing their positive quality begins during discrimination training and pinpointing of targets for behavior change. As noted earlier, the therapist guides each client toward operationalizing *global* complaints and preferences into *specific* behaviors he/she would like the partner to decrease or increase (especially the latter). The therapist must be attentive to his/her own tendency to accept general descriptive terms (e.g., "He ignores me") and needs to emphasize the potential for miscommunication when one person assumes understanding of another's global messages. When a spouse fails to provide positives for a partner because he/she does not know what specific positives the partner desires, pinpointing can be a valuable remedy. Given that no other major relationship problems exist, couples who have mutual good will may need little more than discrimination/pinpointing training to shift their interaction patterns in a positive direction. When the level of good will is lower, other behavioral procedures may be needed to overcome spouses' unwillingness to give their partners positives (see Goldstein, 1976).

Gottman, Notarius, Gonso and Markman (1976) differentiate between the message a person *intends* to communicate and the actual *impact* the message has on the recipient. In good communication, intent equals impact, and Gottman et al. emphasize the responsibilities both speaker and listener have to ensure that messages are communicated accurately. As described above, one way of clarifying messages is for the speaker to describe specific behaviors for the partner to increase or decrease. Likewise, the listener is responsible for identifying miscommunication by giving the speaker feedback about the message's impact. Of course, the speaker must ask for and acknowledge the feedback as well. Unfortunately, distressed couples often carry on a conversation without feedback, which often leads to misunderstanding and fighting. It is not unusual for a poorly communicating couple to fight over a perceived disagreement when in fact they agree!

Mutual feedback between spouses is unlikely to occur when each person is invested in proving the superiority of his/her viewpoint and repeatedly restates that position rather than listening to the partner's message and describing its impact. Gottman et al. (1976) refer to this problematic pattern as the "Summarizing Self Syndrome" and suggest that both partners feel a lack of respect and understanding from each other as a result of these frustrating interactions. Spouses often engage in "mind-reading," responding to assumptions about the other's thoughts and feelings without checking the validity of those assumptions. Even when one spouse is aware that the other has a specific complaint, the response tends to be "cross-complaining," summarizing one's own complaints rather than trying to understand the other's point of view. Gottman et al. describe the "Summarizing Self Syndrome" as a pattern of negative exchange that at its worst becomes a highly dissatisfying sequence of escalating quarrels and periods of withdrawal. A couple can reach a "standoff," in which each spouse refuses to move from a position that he/she sees as "right." Gottman et al.'s procedures for ending a "standoff" focus on increasing spouses' understanding of each other's perspective and their acknowledgment that each other's position has validity. Since some of the major positives that members of a couple can exchange involve approval and validation (affectional "pleases"), increasing the frequencies of such messages is quite important.

Gottman et al. propose a set of communication skills that can decrease the "Summarizing Self Syndrome" and produce more positive exchanges. First, couples can increase their awareness of this destructive pattern through therapist feedback (perhaps facilitated by playback of the couple's video-taped interactions) and can learn to stop such exchanges as soon as they notice them developing. Next, each spouse is to ask the other for feedback regarding the impacts of messages he/she has sent and to provide brief but specific feedback when the partner requests it in return. Discrepancies between intents and impacts are to be noted and discussed in order to clarify misunderstandings. In order for each spouse to understand the other's subjective experiences, careful listening to both the content and feelings communicated when a partner states a position *or* provides feedback is considered necessary. Giving one's partner the positives of understanding and validation involves both paraphrasing the messages one has received regarding the partner's thoughts and feelings *and* communicating that those thoughts and feelings are reasonable. Thus, even in the face of disagreement, it is important for each spouse to let the other know that he/she accepts the possibility of different points of view, each with some merit. These concepts of paraphrasing/summarizing and validation are quite similar to Rogers' (1957) concepts of empathy and unconditional positive regard. Validation overlaps with unconditional positive regard in that a partner is valued and respected whether or not what he/she says and does conforms to the listener's own preferences.

Gottman et al.'s approach to communication also places responsibility on the speaker to make clear, direct, but nonattacking statements of thoughts and feelings. Consistent with Raush, Barry, Hertel and Swain's (1974) work that described the advantages of such communication over patterns of avoidance and attack in resolving marital conflicts, Gottman et al. train couples in a skill they label "constructive leveling." In contrast to forms of "destructive leveling," in which one spouse attacks the other with complaints and insults, constructive leveling involves making statements in the form "When you do X in situation Y, I feel Z." The speaker is obligated to be specific about the action (X), situation (Y) and feeling (Z). It is recognized that at times it may be appropriate for couples to avoid conflict or to fight. However, in the long run constructive leveling (or for Raush et al., "constructive engagement") is expected to facilitate the exchange of infor-mation necessary for partners to resolve conflicts and to avoid escalation of mutual attack. Gottman et al. note that leveling involves assertiveness, and they have clients explore "catastrophic expectations" (e.g., "My spouse will not love me anymore") that inhibit assertive expression. Since some clients may have difficulty discriminating their emotional states, Gottman et al. provide a "feeling chart" with lists of positive and negative affects from which they can pick labels for their emotions. Clients also are instructed to pay attention to bodily indications of their emotional states. Procedures for dealing with clients who are not accustomed to self-disclosure are not specified in this program.

O'Leary and Turkewitz (1978) also stress the importance of increasing feeling expression on the part of clients who tend to self-disclose minimally, noting that this is more often true of males than females. Clinically distressed wives commonly complain of emotional distance from their partners. O'Leary and Turkewitz describe how the husbands' negative feelings frequently are communicated nonverbally (e.g., through sulking), such that their partners have difficulty responding. It is important in these cases for the therapist to give the client feedback on his/her nonverbal cues of emotional response. "Feeling talk" also can be shaped by asking the client to describe feelings he/she has about some nonthreatening topic unrelated to the marriage. Modeling of appropriate self-disclosure by therapists can be used to encourage and guide clients. O'Leary and Turkewitz also suggest that the therapist can respond to a nondisclosing spouse's statements with empathic reflections at a level low enough for the client to acknowledge the feeling; for example, speaking of "annoyance" rather than anger. As the client becomes more comfortable "owning" feelings, the therapist can gradually increase the level of the empathically reflected emotion. A spouse who has requested greater feeling expression from such a reticent partner also may need to become comfortable with increases in the partner's self-disclosure, since he/she may not be prepared to hear expressions of negative feelings in addition to the positive ones.

O'Leary and Turkewitz set ground rules for the expression of negative feelings. Feelings regarding conditions that a spouse cannot change (e.g., family members) are not encouraged, since these issues cannot be resolved. Also, an important distinction is made between a description of negative feelings, such as "I am angry because you did not respond to what I said," and punishing remarks such as "You are selfish and you disgust me." The former statement conveys useful information and is less likely to elicit defensiveness and counterattacks from the partner. As is the case with other communication training programs, O'Leary and Turkewitz teach couples the above skills by means of a variety of social learning procedures, such as therapist modeling, instructions, behavior rehearsal, and shaping through selective reinforcement.

Increasing mutual empathy. Training couples to exchange positives through empathic listening is a central goal of Guerney's (1977) "Relationship Enhancement" approach to communication. As in Gottman et al.'s approach, both speaker and listener bear responsibility for accurate communication of each person's thoughts, feelings and needs. In a group setting, couples are taught expressive skills and listening skills. Guerney's educational, as opposed to therapeutic, model also is intended to change clients' *attitudes*—e.g., increasing acceptance of one's own feelings and those of others; recognizing that each person's views are subjective and should not be reason for blame. Mutual empathy is expected to facilitate resolution of marital conflicts by clarifying needs, preferences and feelings and by increasing communication of respect.

The methods used to teach Relationship Enhancement skills are based on social learning principles (Bandura, 1969) and are highly structured and detailed. They include modeling of good communication skills by group leaders, didactic presentations and instructional aids such as videotaped examples of communication patterns, maximizing of successes through "graded expectations" (leaders begin with low expectations for client performance and gradually increase them as clients gain skill), selective reinforcement of successes and in vivo practice of communication skills with "homework" assignments. In order to minimize disruption of learning by emotion-laden material, group members are instructed to practice their new skills initially with nonthreatening topics (not involving the partner), first in same-sex pairs and then with their spouses. As their skills develop, partners move to discussing positive aspects of their marital relationships and eventually to low-level and high-level conflict topics.

The Relationship Enhancement program is intended to strengthen affectional bonds, but it also may lead to divorce if spouses learn that their needs are incompatible. Guerney (1977) stresses that improving communication skills serves a primary preventive function since couples can apply these skills to future relationship problems they may face. Mutual empathy not only creates a supportive, caring atmosphere but also facilitates the accurate (and nondefensive) exchange of information regarding relevant thoughts and feelings in a conflict situation, which then is expected to improve a couple's problem-solving ability.

The basic format of the Relationship Enhancement program is to have two partners in an intimate relationship take turns operating in an expressive mode of communication or an empathic mode. One person explains his/her thoughts and feelings, and the other person communicates understanding and acceptance; when accurate communication has been achieved, the two people switch modes. Participants also learn skills for switching between these modes smoothly and for teaching others the communication skills. Guerney presents behavioral criteria for performance in each of the communication modes.

The expresser is expected to follow six guidelines:

1. *Reports of perceptions and judgments should be acknowledged to be subjective.* Rather than dogmatically stating something as true, the speaker can use qualifiers such as "I believe . . . " or "It seems to me. . . ." This guideline is intended to decrease the listener's defensiveness and increase understanding of subjectivity in personal experiences.

2. *Specific feelings (in contrast to ideas) associated with an issue should be expressed directly.* The basic format of such statements would be "I feel [some emotion] because [some perception or belief]." A statement in this form acknowledges the subjectivity of the expresser's experience *and* informs the listener of the impact that experience has on the expresser's emotional state.

3. *The expresser should include an acknowledgment of the positive side to the issue.* An example of a message that includes the positive reference is "I enjoy working together with you on projects to improve the house, and I know you share my interest in having an attractive home, so I have felt disappointed and irritated that you seem to leave me all the work lately." Focusing on the positive is intended to reduce the listener's defensiveness and provide some goals for change. It also is likely to change the expresser's perspective in favor of constructive suggestions rather than blame.

4. *Descriptions of thoughts, feelings and perceptions of events should be specific.* Observable events that have elicited particular feelings should be detailed. This process involves discrimination and pinpointing of behaviors in terms of their topography, time, place, frequency, etc. An example of a specific message is "I like it when you kiss me and talk with me when you get home from work."

5. *The interpersonal message, or what specific constructive action the expresser would like from the listener, should be stated explicitly.* The positive consequences that could follow from the listener's compliance (e.g., making the expresser happy) can be stated. Statements of specific positive solutions can give the listener both motivation and direction for changing behavior. Factors that may inhibit clients from making requests (e.g., the belief that it is selfish to make requests; fears of rejection) should be explored.

6. *A message concerning the expresser's feelings or personal request also should convey empathy for the listener's position.* The expresser is to assume that the other person's behavior is based on his/her *own* personally valid perceptions and feelings. Empathic statements are expected to elicit reciprocal cooperation rather than defensiveness. An example of an empathic preface for a request would be "I know that you are tired when you come home from a day's work, but. . . ." Guerney stresses that empathic statements should only be used when the expresser is sure that he/she under-

stands the listener's position, based on previous concrete information (no "mind-reading") and that empathic acceptance is expressed both verbally and nonverbally.

The goal of *empathic listening* by clients is the same as that for empathic therapists (Truax and Carkhuff, 1967): achieving and communicating to one's partner an accurate understanding of the partner's subjective state. The empathic responder is to engage in reflective listening and should *not* (1) ask questions to guide the expresser's discussion, (2) present his/her own opinions and perceptions, (3) make interpretations, (4) make suggestions or (5) make judgments about what the partner says.

Guerney's (1977) communication training program is one of the most comprehensively presented programs in the literature to date. Studies applying the Relationship Enhancement program to marital and parent-adolescent relationships have indicated some positive treatment outcomes. However, subjects in the reported studies tended to be highly educated, of high socioeconomic status and not identified as clinically distressed. Further evaluation of the program with clinical populations and subjects from various social strata is needed. Also, as Jacobson (1978a) and Weiss (1978) have noted, overreliance on self-report measures that are susceptible to halo effects and other distortions limits the conclusiveness of existing outcome studies on Relationship Enhancement. Additional studies that include more behavioral measures and follow-up assessments are needed.

Liberman, Wheeler and Sanders (1976) consider communication training to be the most important element in their behaviorally oriented group treatment for couples. They also employ procedures based on social learning principles, including therapist modeling, coaching, prompting, behavior rehearsal and feedback from therapists and group members. As in Guerney's program, results of weekly homework assignments for practicing communication skills are processed in the next group session, and therapists provide corrective and positive feedback as appropriate. Training deals with both verbal content and nonverbal parameters (e.g., voice volume, facial expression) of communication. Specific areas of communication addressed include (1) giving compliments, (2) acknowledging and reinforcing "pleases" received from one's partner, (3) making assertive, non-demanding requests, (4) communicating negative feelings in a nonattacking manner and (5) communicating openly about sexual desires and preferences. In the area of sexual communication, male-female co-therapist teams deal with clients' inhibitions about telling a partner what is physically pleasing by modeling mutual hand massage with verbal feedback and coaching couples in doing the same.

Liberman et al. also instruct couples to conduct regularly scheduled five-to-fifteen-minute "executive sessions" in which they practice expressing feelings to each other in a setting with minimal distractions. Spouses take turns expressing and listening reflectively, in a manner quite similar to that in Guerney's model.

Communication as operant behavior. Thomas (1977) focuses on verbal communication as operant behavior that is controlled by its consequences, and he examines marital interaction as an interplay of two individuals' complex response repertoires. Each spouse's verbalizations can influence the occurrence of the other's verbal behavior by reinforcing or punishing it. In addition, each spouse provides verbal discriminative stimuli (e.g., instructions, demands), signaling that the other spouse is likely to be reinforced for producing certain responses. For example, the statement "I am feeling romantic" may serve as a cue for the partner that sexual advances would be reinforced. Furthermore, a spouse's verbalizations can elicit classically conditioned positive and negative emotional responses from the other. Thus, the statement "I am feeling romantic" may elicit positive sexual arousal if it has been associated with arousing sexual activity in the past. The complexity of marital communication is clear when one considers that each spouse's verbal responses can serve all these functions simultaneously, and that nonverbal behaviors constitute another set of stimuli that may be consistent or inconsistent with verbal messages.

Content of a verbal response does not necessarily reflect its function; e.g., the therapist must observe increases and decreases in a spouse's behavior to determine whether the partner's verbal responses were reinforcing or punishing stimuli. For example, when a husband finishes a meal that his wife has prepared specially and says to his wife, "That was better than what my mother used to make," one should not necessarily conclude that his wife will find the response rewarding and cook more special meals in the future. It is possible that due to past unpleasant conversations in which the husband compared his wife unfavorably to his mother, his present comment will be aversive (punishing) for her and will decrease the probability of her preparing special meals in the future.

Thomas' (1977) analysis of potential sources of difficulty in marital verbal interaction includes a wide range of interpersonal, intrapersonal and other environmental factors. Consistent with the general behavioral orientation, he focuses on current influences that may be modified directly rather than on historical issues (although the client's learning history is relevant). Since each of the following sources of communication difficulty has different treatment implications, a careful assessment is needed:

1. *Repertoire deficits.* Deficits in communication skills based on prior individual learning histories may exist in any area (e.g., knowledge of how to make a direct verbal request or how to acknowledge understanding of what another person says). Treatment generally involves training in the particular communication skills by means of social learning procedures, such as

therapist modeling, instruction, coaching, behavior rehearsal and feedback. An example of such treatment is assertiveness training (see the chapter by Epstein, in this volume).

2. *Referent conditions.* These are life conditions, such as job or financial pressures, that affect marital communication by producing stress, with its accompanying disruptions of emotional and thought processes. The locus of a referent condition may be outside the couple (e.g., pressures from relatives) or within the couple (e.g., a partner's abuse of alcohol). These conditions often need to be modified before possible communication repertoire deficits are treated.

3. *Setting events.* These are internal states of the individual (e.g., sex deprivation, anger, fatigue) that affect responses to stimuli related to verbal communication. For example, spouses may be more likely to argue when they are tired. When setting events are not temporary and cannot be remedied easily, as by getting a good night's sleep, treating them formally may be prerequisite to any communication training.

4. *Structural deficits.* This issue involves the absence of environmental stimuli likely to facilitate good communication. Many couples could communicate more often and more effectively if they set up conditions of time and place free of distractions. Attempts to communicate about relationship issues during the family dinner time or while watching television are likely to fail because these stimulus conditions produce many competing behaviors. Treatment involves restructuring the communication environment, usually including the scheduling of discussion time in a relatively nondistracting setting.

5. *Partner interaction.* As in Goldstein's (1971) operant model, each marital partner may elicit or maintain the other's problematic response deficits and excesses through positive and negative reinforcement, punishment, stimulus control (discriminative stimuli that cue the other's responses) and stimuli that elicit emotional responses, such as anger. For example, one spouse may positively reinforce the other's excessive use of coercive messages by paying attention to those verbalizations but ignoring more positive messages. A spouse's *deficit* of positive talk may be maintained because the partner fails to reinforce such talk, punishes it or fails to cue it with questions. Given the pattern of mutual influence in a relationship, *conjoint* treatment using the behavioral procedures described in this chapter may be advantageous. Gurman and Kniskern (1978) concluded from their review of outcome research on marital and family therapy that conjoint treatment is more effective in reducing problematic interaction than is individual treatment for marital dysfunction.

Thomas' (1977) program for modifying problematic communication patterns focuses on deficits and surfeits that can be operationalized and measured in terms of criteria such as frequency or duration. He identifies five dimensions of verbal behavior in which these deficits and surfeits may exist: (1) *representation* of events and objects, which may be inaccurate (e.g., due to overgeneralization and lack of specificity); (2) *content*, which may involve problems with thematic continuity (e.g., avoiding particular content; shifting topics excessively) or handling of content (e.g., excessive blaming; too little positive talk); (3) *information given*, which may be excessive, insufficient, redundant or ambiguous; (4) *conversational guidance*, in which a spouse may influence the other's talking in a destructive way (e.g., by excessive interruption) and (5) *vocal properties*, which may involve problems with rate, amount, latency, volume, tone and fluency. It should be noted that these problem categories have been derived *intuitively* rather than on the basis of empirical evidence that they produce less satisfying marital interactions.

Thomas' approach to assessment includes the identification of each spouse's problematic verbalizations from actual communication samples. A couple is instructed to discuss topics relevant to their relationship (e.g., strengths and problems of the marriage), and potentially problematic responses can be rated according to a Verbal Problem Checklist. Other information regarding communication problems, strengths and mitigating factors (such as setting events and referent conditions) is obtained from clinical interviews. After any primary mitigating factors have been treated, the therapist selects verbal response categories to be modified. Thomas reports that an average of three to four problematic behaviors usually are identified for each spouse. Selection of target behaviors for intervention is left to the therapist's judgment. Once the couple agrees to comply with the therapist's recommendations for behavior change, specific modification procedures are implemented. Thomas does not explain how he deals with ambivalent or resistant clients except to note that work may be terminated if "further discussion" does not increase cooperation.

Interventions that combine procedures for accelerating positive responses *and* procedures for decelerating negative responses are preferable, since changing one type of behavior will not necessarily influence the other (Thomas, 1977; Weiss, 1978). Modifying complementary behaviors of the two partners simultaneously (e.g., when one talks too much and the other talks too little) also may maximize change in dyadic interaction.

Thomas' major intervention methods include (1) *corrective feedback and instruction*, in which the therapist describes (and often illustrates with playback of the couple's taped interaction) the partners' verbal strengths and target problems at intake, then explains how the couple should behave differently; (2) *provision of oral or written "rules" for marital interaction*, designed to minimize negative mitigating factors and to maximize open exchange of information (e.g., "Do not fault your spouse"; "Stay on one topic until each has had a say"; "Be specific"); (3) *interactional cueing* (stimulus control), by which partners can be taught to start or stop each other's verbal behaviors with particular responses such as "How did you like my suggestion?" and "Let's not discuss that issue now"; (4) *practice*, involving role playing and in vivo rehearsal of positive verbal skills; (5) *feedback*, by therapist comment and tape replay, regarding performance of the new skills; (6) setting up operant *response contingencies*, such as selective reinforcement, in which each partner modifies the other's verbalizations, and (7) *behavior exchange systems* (to be described later in this chapter).

The procedures used in Thomas' (1977) approach to assessing and modifying problematic verbal interactions can be taxing and expensive in terms of time and money, so they may be less convenient for the average clinician than for the clinical researcher who has laboratory resources and assistants. However, identification of specific verbal strengths and problems, assessment and treatment of mitigating factors such as referent conditions, and systematic modification of dysfunctional communication patterns are important goals for any marital therapist (see Jacobson, 1978a).

Differentiating communication goals. Once couples have the opportunity to talk in a favorable environment, they also need to clarify what *kind* of communication is to transpire. For example, if one partner intends to ventilate feelings and the other wants to problem-solve, neither person's goal is likely to be achieved. Weiss, Hops and Patterson (1973) note the confusion that can arise when partners are communicating in different modes, and suggest that couples set aside "Administrative Time" restricted to problem-solving activity. Some manner of compartmentalizing communication functions is likely to reduce clients' confusion and frustration. In addition to planning special times for particular modes of communication, it is helpful for each spouse to preface interactions with a statement of what his/her communication goals are, e.g., "I need to let off some steam." If spouses discover that they have different expectations or goals, they have the option of delaying one of the goals or taking turns.

Nonverbal behavior and consistency of communication channels. The communication training programs described above tend to focus on parameters of verbal content and paralinguistic behavior (voice qualities such as tone, speech rate) that increase or decrease the accurate transmission of information and maximize partners' exchanges of positives. Nonverbal communication ("body language") clearly is acknowledged to be important (e.g., O'Leary and Turkewitz, 1978), but most references to work with nonverbals are brief and sketchy. Given the strong influence of nonverbal behavior on the impact of messages (Gottman, Markman and Notarius, 1977; Mehrabian, 1972), and the fact that nonverbal behaviors (e.g., facial expression; body posture) can communicate messages that are inconsistent with verbal content, it is important that communication programs address these issues. Therapists need to increase each spouse's awareness of how he/she sends messages nonverbally and how these messages impact upon the partner. When a client is conscious of his or her nonverbals, discrepancies between intent and impact (Gottman et al., 1976) need to be identified. On the other hand, many nonverbal behaviors, such as facial expressions and postures, occur without the actor's awareness, and the impact these have on the partner needs to be clarified for both parties. Inconsistencies among verbal, paralinguistic and nonverbal channels should be noted, since they are likely to produce confusion, frustration and conflict. Although verbal feedback from therapists can be helpful, videotape playback can provide more complete, detailed information. A client can actually see how he/she smiled while saying "I am angry," and the partner can describe the impact of the inconsistent messages. While videotape feedback can be inappropriate and even detrimental with some clients (Alkire and Brunse, 1974), it has considerable therapeutic utility (c.f. Berger, 1978). Clinicians who have access to video equipment are likely to find it a valuable aid in communication work.

Summary. Although the various communication training procedures we have reviewed have somewhat different foci, they have some common goals: first, increasing positive exchanges and decreasing negative exchanges in order to maximize spouses' satisfaction with their interactions; and second, increasing clarity in the transmission of information. Direct communication can be used to facilitate mutual understanding through the exchange of information regarding each partner's needs, preferences, thoughts and feelings. Couples also can communicate mutual empathy and acceptance. Positive exchanges of accurate information also are necessary for constructive problem-solving. The skills necessary for effective communication can be taught, and a variety of social learning procedures, such as therapist modeling, use of taped models, specific instructions, coaching, behavior rehearsal and performance feedback are available. Direct communication may not be wise or appropriate in all situations, but in the long run it is likely to produce greater satisfaction of both partners' needs than either avoidance or attack. The next section of this chapter describes some special applications of communication training in marital therapy.

BUILDING SKILLS IN ASSERTION AND PROBLEM-SOLVING

A couple's ability to make changes in their relationship requires more than clear communication and empathy. Each partner must be able to make and refuse requests for behavior change constructively, contribute to effective problem-solving and negotiate when the two parties have different goals or desires. In addition to the expressive and listening skills described in the previous section, other specific skills are useful for facilitating these functions.

Assertion training. Training clients in the direct but noncoercive expression of thoughts, feelings and preferences has become a popular intervention for individuals with a variety of presenting problems (e.g., anxiety, social inhibition). The goals of assertion training are also quite consistent with those of behavioral marital therapy (decreasing coercive control; increasing clear, direct communication), and assertive skills are being taught with increasing frequency to spouses with marital problems. Assertion training is intended to substitute direct noncoercive communication for aggressive (coercive) and avoidant or passive communication. It includes the development of skills for making assertive requests, which are likely to elicit more compliance and less anger than aggressive requests (Hollandsworth and Cooley, 1978). Assertiveness also involves the ability to refuse requests in a nonhostile manner that is less likely than aggression to alienate the requester. A detailed description of theoretical and practical issues in assertion training for couples is presented in this volume's chapter by Epstein.

Problem-solving. Any couple is faced with a variety of problems, ranging from the relatively trivial (e.g., what movie to see) to core relationship issues (e.g., distribution of power) that require resolution in terms of reaching some agreement. Decisions must be made and strategies for coping with problems must be selected. As Jacobson (1977b) has noted, negative exchanges between spouses are likely to interfere with problem-solving activity and preclude agreement. In distressed relationships, coercive attempts to solve problems often are unsuccessful and lead to despair. The result is a backlog of unresolved issues which further exacerbate marital tensions. As noted earlier, Jacobson (1978d) also suggests that agreements reached under unpleasant circumstances are less likely to be carried out than those reached in a cooperative atmosphere of good will. Thus, effective problem-solving requires (a) a positive interpersonal environment, characterized by exchanges of rewarding rather than punishing responses, and (b) specific problem-solving skills.

Positive interaction between spouses is more likely to occur if certain communication guidelines are followed. Although communication of feelings, both positive and negative, is to be encouraged in *other* contexts, neutrality provides the best context for problem-solving, which should remain a basically cognitive process (Jacobson, 1977b). In order to minimize negative feelings, each partner should define problems in as positive or neutral a manner as possible. Use of negative remarks and trait labels (e.g., "You are inconsiderate") only serves to elicit defensiveness, anger and counterattack from the other person. Inferring that one's partner has negative motives presents an unreasonable problem and is likely to elicit unproductive self-justification. It is important for the therapist to stress the difference between intentions and actions, noting that only the latter are realistic targets for change. If one spouse's behavior bothers the other, no matter what the other's intention was, a request for change in the behavior is legitimate. On the other hand, requesting simultaneous changes in behavior *and* attitudes is unrealistic and unwarranted. A partner can control behaviors but cannot necessarily change attitudes at will. A common trap is to ask one's partner to change a behavior and to *like* doing so as well. Therapists often need to stress that a spouse who agrees to change a behavior is exhibiting some good will, and that attitudes often change in time as people become accustomed to new ways of relating to each other. The discrimination and pinpointing skills described earlier in this chapter are likely to help clients formulate concrete descriptions of problems (e.g., "You don't call when you are going to be home late"). Prefacing criticisms with expressions of appreciation (stating the positive side of an issue first) also is likely to minimize the listener's defensive reactions, as is empathic paraphrasing of a partner's complaints.

Positive exchanges are also more likely to occur when there is an expectation on the part of both spouses that solutions will involve mutual, rather than unilateral, change. Even when the presenting problem clearly involves one spouse more than the other, the partner should be involved actively in helping the other change. When change becomes a collaborative effort, problem-solving can occur in a positive atmosphere where each spouse reinforces the other. Jacobson (1977b) illustrates this point with a case in which a wife's chronic tendency to leave her clothes on the floor changed when her husband agreed to walk hand-in-hand with her, picking up the clothes. Similarly, the wife's desire for her husband to spend more time with their daughter was actualized when the wife planned activities for the husband and daughter. The husband had been unaware of appropriate ways of interacting with the child.

Other communication difficulties that should be avoided during problem-solving sessions include: excesses and deficits in talking; overgeneralization; content shifts; excesses in agreement, disagreement, giving opinions and giving information; references to past transgressions; cross-complaints; negative nonverbal behaviors; and other behaviors that are likely to escalate and distract spouses from their task (Jacobson, 1977b; O'Leary and Turkewitz, 1978; Thomas, 1977; Weiss, 1978). The findings that distressed spouses exhibited more problem-solving behaviors with strangers than with their partners (Vincent, Weiss and Birchler, 1975) and could produce more problem-solving behaviors when instructed to "fake good" (Vincent, 1976) suggest that useful skills often are inhibited or disrupted by partners' negative responses *to each other* (Weiss, 1978). Clearly, couples who communicate in negative and ineffective ways will have considerable difficulty carrying out the problem-solving procedures described below. Therefore, interventions for increasing positive interaction and constructive communication can be considered prerequisites for training in problem-solving.

The process of problem-solving and decision making. A problem situation is one for which no agreed-upon solution immediately exists. Problems can be due to factors outside the relationship (e.g., job pressures), between the partners (e.g., conflict over child-rearing), or within an individual (e.g., alcohol abuse). Marital problem-solving involves issues and solutions that affect both partners to some extent and are based on the partners' preferences rather than on established facts (Thomas, 1977).

Problem-solving focuses on producing particular outcomes or products (Weiss, 1978). It is a set of behaviors that should not be confused with the basic communication skills described earlier. The first major step in problem-solving is identification of a particular situation for which there is no agree-upon solution, and specific definition of the problem's components (Jacobson, 1977b; Thomas, 1977). Thus, if a couple becomes aware that they are having difficulty maintaining discipline with their children and that they seem to be taking different approaches to discipline, they might identify the following problem components, among others: (1) lack of clear standards for the children's behaviors, (2) inconsistent discipline methods between the parents, (3) lack of clarity regarding *who* is responsible for disciplining the children and (4) conflict when the parents communicate about discipline issues in the presence of the children. D'Zurilla and Goldfried (1971) suggest that relationships among components be examined, and that the components judged as most important be given priority for problem-solving. As in other behavioral approaches, descriptions of problem components should be in terms of specific, observable events (e.g., "Should a child who disobeys be lectured, deprived of privileges, spanked, etc.?") rather than abstract concepts. Descriptions of relevant behaviors are appropriate, but blaming and guessing about etiology are not (Jacobson, 1977b; O'Leary and Turkewitz, 1978).

Harrell and Guerney (1976) have couples select relationship issues that clearly involve both spouses and that both spouses would like to see changed. Having identified "our" problem, each member of the couple is instructed to describe his/her own behavioral contribution to it. Therapists reduce defensiveness and aversive exchanges further by encouraging spouses to use empathic listening and reflection in all stages of their problem-solving program.

Once the problem's components have been described and given priorities, information relevant to the important components should be collected (Thomas, 1977). If in the above example the issue of how two parents can communicate about discipline in their children's presence was rated most important, relevant information might include: (1) how the children respond (e.g., are they less obedient?) when the parents disagree openly, (2) how each parent feels when they disagree openly and (3) what nonverbal cues the parents have available for signaling each other at these times. It is important for the therapist to keep the couple focused on the identified problem, since sidetracking to another problem detracts from resolution of either problem (Jacobson, 1977b).

The next major step in problem-solving is the generation of alternative solutions. Couples should be encouraged to "brainstorm" possible solutions without regard to their quality (Jacobson, 1977b; Thomas, 1977). This process encourages flexibility in problem-solving and is likely to generate some solutions that are acceptable to *both* partners (Harrell and Guerney, 1976). Solutions should be stated in objective behavioral terms and preferably should involve increases in low-rate behaviors, when possible, rather than decreases in high-rate behaviors (Jacobson and Martin, 1976).

Next, each potential solution should be evaluated for its assets and liabilities, its potential for solving the problem and its feasibility (Jacobson, 1977b; Thomas, 1977). Costs to be assessed would include personal sacrifices and discomfort each spouse would suffer.

When a solution has been selected, the specific actions to be made by each spouse should be specified, or as Thomas (1977) states (p. 116), "Who will do what, when, and how." Behavior changes required of each partner are more likely to be achieved if shaped in graduated steps rather than expected in all-or-none fashion (Jacobson, 1977b). For example, a solution that involves a spouse keeping the house clean might represent an overwhelming change for him/her. However, an *initial* solution might involve only one or two cleaning tasks (e.g., picking up things from the floor; washing the dishes after meals), with additional tasks added as the spouse masters the initial ones. Criteria for compliance with these agreements should be specific and observable so that success can be judged objectively. Harrell and Guerney (1976) suggest that each spouse should agree to emit a behavior that both of them have judged a helpful solution. The behaviors selected for this "exchange" should be similar in terms of costs and benefits. Harrell and Guerney note that such an agreement to work on a *mutual* problem differs from behavioral exchanges in contracting programs (e.g., Stuart, 1969; Weiss, Hops and Patterson, 1973). Harrell and Guerney's approach is intended to increase couples' awareness of how both partners do contribute to the existence of a problem and can contribute to its solution. The details of the various versions of behavior-exchange/contracting programs will be discussed later in this chapter.

As each spouse proceeds with the agreed-upon actions, ongoing assessment is an important source of feedback regarding adequacy of performance. If goal behaviors have been specified properly, it should be possible for both spouses to observe and record them in terms of frequency, duration, rate, etc. A spouse whose problem-solving behavior has not met the criteria can then modify it accordingly. Similarly, the adequacy of the problem *solution* should be evaluated in terms of objective criteria. In the example regarding parental discipline, outcome could be evaluated in terms of latency and frequency with which the children comply with specific parental requests. When there is evidence that spouses are performing as intended but that the planned solution is not having the expected effect on the problem, the couple may need to select a new solution from their list or reevaluate the components of the problem.

Thus, problem-solving is a sequence of specific skills that rely on effective communication, cognitive flexibility, discipline and an atmosphere of cooperation. On the whole, the messages sent during problem-solving should be instrumental and task-oriented rather than affective. Therapists can teach couples these skills by means of social learning procedures, such as modeling, instructions, behavior rehearsal, coaching, feedback and stimulus control (Jacobson, 1977c; O'Leary and Turkewitz, 1978; Thomas, 1977).

Behavioral feedback should occur at two major points: (1) before treatment, when the couple provides a sample of their problem-solving skills and the therapist gives feedback (often aided by videotape playback) about the strengths and problems in their performance, and (2) regularly during training, as corrective feedback and reinforcement for successes. This feedback should be specific and should clarify any relevant stimulus-response links; e.g., "John, when you make negative criticisms, Mary tends to respond with criticism in return, but when you make positive suggestions, Mary tends to ask for more information regarding changes she could make." Feedback can be evaluative when the therapist is letting the client know whether or not he/she is exhibiting constructive problem-solving behavior (Jacobson, 1977c). *Immediate* feedback is used to prevent long chains of ineffective and anger-inducing interactions, especially in the early stages of training. As couples become experienced and competent with problem-solving skills, the therapist can give more *delayed* feedback. Above all, the emphasis should be on positive rather than negative feedback.

Most complex human learned responses are acquired by observing competent models (Bandura, 1969). Consequently, therapists should provide examples of problem-solving skills that clients may imitate. It is useful to expose clients to videotapes of couples exhibiting examples of good skills. Also, co-therapist pairs can demonstrate skills for their clients (Epstein, DeGiovanni and Jayne-Lazarus, 1978; Epstein, Jayne-Lazarus and DeGiovanni, 1979; Weiss, Hops and Patterson, 1973). Therapists also model constructive skills by giving clients specific feedback in reasonable doses rather than by using global statements and making attributions regarding personality traits (Jacobson, 1977c).

Instructions and coaching commonly are used to guide clients in practicing new skills. Often, the therapist describes how each spouse should behave and then provides a model for them to imitate. As spouses try to imitate the modeled behaviors, the therapist coaches them, giving suggestions for improving particular aspects of their performances. Jacobson (1977c) notes that in order to insure that clients are actually learning problem-solving principles rather then merely imitating the model, the therapist should ask them to describe constructive aspects of the model's behavior *and* discrepancies between the model's behavior and their own.

Behavior rehearsal is crucial for couples to master problem-solving skills that they can apply to future problems. Although the therapist guides the learning process, clients will be able to solve problems on their own if the therapist provides no actual solutions (Jacobson, 1977c). Mastery of skills requires repeated live practice with instructions, modeling, coaching and feedback. As noted earlier with respect to communication training, couples should begin practice with neutral, nonthreatening problems and move to significant relationship issues only when their competence with the problem-solving steps is quite high. Rehearsal can involve role-plays with topics the couple identifies as common issues *and* "re-plays" of instances in which a problem-solving attempt did not progress smoothly at home (O'Leary and Turkewitz, 1978). The major goal of behavior rehearsal is to shape skills that the couple can apply in the future without a therapist.

Stimulus control is used when a couple has difficulty engaging in good problem-solving behavior due to their problem-solving environment. A common difficulty noted earlier is that many couples try to solve problems at times and in circumstances that are not conducive to such behavior. Since problem-solving behavior is complex and requires concentrated thought, couples should set aside "administrative time" (Weiss, Hops, and Patterson, 1973) when there are likely to be no distractions. Further stimulus control can be attained when couples give themselves problem-solving instructions; e.g., by announcing to each other that they are going to sit down and work out a solution to a problem.

In the next section on behavior exchange and contingency contracting, we will discuss the use of an exchange contract as a form of stimulus control to cue each partner as to *what* they have agreed to change, *when* and *how*.

BEHAVIOR EXCHANGE AND CONTINGENCY CONTRACTING

The last behavioral marital therapy procedure to be discussed is the negotiation and execution of a behavior-exchange contract between husband and wife. This BMT procedure has been saved for last because in clinical practice it tends to *follow* rather than precede the behavior change procedures we have described above. As the areas of BMT which have predominated in the literature, behavior-exchange and contingency contracting have themselves undergone the most change over the last decade. There has been a trend away from a legalistic concern with the details of the contract and its enforcement and a shift toward the problem-solving and communication skills needed to negotiate the marital agreement.

The behavioral contract, based on the principle of reciprocity in social exchange—i.e., quid pro quo—assumes that both parties have resources potentially rewarding to the other party. Furthermore, early reports on the use of contracts in marital therapy assumed that both parties were willing and able to bargain for mutual exchange of these resources (see Rappaport and Harrell, 1972; Stuart, 1969). It was assumed further that complying with the articles of the contract is the necessary means to a desirable therapeutic end, since "each person can gain only by holding to the contractual obligations" (Weiss et al., 1973, p. 328).

The early enthusiasm among behavior therapists for the use of this technique is exemplified by Knox (1971, p. 321): "Exchange contracts are one of the most effective and efficient procedures of the behavioral marriage counselor. By specifying what behaviors are to occur, when, with what consequences, marital happiness becomes a realistic possibility." The "increasing popularity of contracting and negotiation training" (Weiss, Birchler and Vincent, 1974) was, in part, demonstrated by the relatively large number of behavioral marital therapy articles on the use of the procedure that had been published (Azrin et al., 1973; Eisler and Hersen, 1973; Friedman, 1972; Hickok and Komechak, 1974; Knox, 1971, 1973; Patterson and Hops, 1972; Rappaport and Harrell, 1972; Stuart, 1969; Weiss, Hops and Patterson, 1973). Although these studies each included four to ten separate procedures (modeling, charting, role-playing, selective reinforcement, etc.), Weiss et al. (1973, p. 311) stressed that "contracting and negotiating skills are the main vehicles for bringing about these behavioral changes between the spouses."

Earlier articles describing some of the first behavior-exchange contracts emphasized the formality, therapeutic control and specific contractual agreements. Later articles emphasized the transient nature of contracts as temporary aids in the demonstration of constructive interaction and mutual social exchange between conflicted partners. The therapeutic focus shifted from how to write an air-tight contract to how to reciprocate and reward the positive changes made by one's spouse. The contract by Patterson and Hops (1972, Appendix A, Part II) illustrates the earlier emphasis on exactness and formality:

> That the Defendant, Bill, does throw newspapers about
> the floor when finished reading.
> That the Defendant, Betty, does leave dinner dishes
> overnight without reason.

> Therefore, the Defendant, Bill, violating the above shall
> mop the floor and/or wash the windows for not less than
> three (3) days.
> Also, the Defendant, Betty, violating the above, shall
> wash the Volkswagen and clean interior.

The technical intricacies and limitations of the quid pro quo contract have been discussed in detail by Weiss, Birchler and Vincent (1974) and Tsoi-Hoshmand (1975) and need not be explored further here. However, an important feature of the early exchange contracts, which was not explicitly mentioned in those articles, should be emphasized. Many of the contracts in the early BMT literature were predominantly *coercive* in that as much or more attention was paid to the penalty clauses and negative consequences for noncompliance (e.g., Azrin et al., 1973; Patterson and Hops, 1972) as was paid to the rewards inherent in cooperation and compliance. If the *medium* (a coercive contract) is the *message* (noncompliance is expected and will be punished), the mutual exchange of positive behaviors may be impeded rather than facilitated. Any coercive interaction between husband and wife tends to generate resentment.

A statement made by Thibaut and Kelley (1959, p. 105) regarding coercive demands in social exchange is particularly relevant to this discussion of contracts: "If B is controlled solely by augmentation (say he is offered rewards for compliance), he will monitor himself . . . In contrast, when reduction (decreased rewards or increased costs) is threatened for noncompliance, A must keep B's compliance under surveillance." Thus, contingency contracts which specify only the rewards for compliance eliminate the need for negative spouse-monitoring (that is, scanning for failures and omissions).

Weiss et al. (1974) argue for the use of a *good-faith* contract in which the contingencies for compliance are parallel rather than interlocking. Instead of the "*If* wife does A, *then* husband does B" (and vice versa) format, the good-faith contract uses the format "Wife agrees to do A regardless of husband's behavior *and* husband agrees to do B regardless of wife's behavior." Rewards for compliance are dispensed by the therapist or by oneself, and exclude behavior changes contracted for by the spouse. This format solves the problem of *neither* partner wanting to be the first to change an undesirable behavior. Since the good-faith (parallel) contract is structured so that each partner's rewards and penalties are independently determined (i.e., by self or by therapist), it is a useful procedure with distressed couples whose willingness to change has been limited by their mutual distrust.

Weiss (1975, p. 17) offered several clinical pointers for guiding a couple to write the initial parallel contract: (1) focus on behaviors which can be accelerated, (2) begin with low-cost behavior changes and (3) make use of non–spouse determined rewards.

Knox (1973), moreover, recommended that therapeutic contracts be developed in two stages so that the introduction of contingency management was less abrupt. In the first stage, *individual* contracts would be negotiated between the therapist and each spouse. These behavior-change agreements were parallel and noninteractive. While the other partner may benefit from increased positive behaviors (e.g., more compliments to the wife), only the therapist monitors and mediates the negative consequences for noncompliance. Furthermore, the therapist's time and fees can be made contingent on completion of individual contracts. Compliance is rewarded with a five-dollar fee reduction; noncompliance results in a five-dollar fee increase. When the target behaviors are being emitted at the appropriate rate, then *husband-wife* contracts can be negotiated. The role of the therapist would be phased out gradually.

In order to estimate the impact of this technique, Knox asked ten couples seen in private therapy if they had continued to use either individual or husband-wife contracts in the six to twelve months since therapy termination. All ten couples said no. Based on the feedback received on follow-up questionnaire, Knox (1973, p. 24) concluded:

1. Behavior contracts in marriage counseling are helpful for some couples in improving marital interaction.
2. Marriage problems are rarely solved by marriage counseling; rather, the frequency of their occurrence is reduced.
3. Although behavior contracts may be helpful in increasing happiness, they are not necessary for the maintenance of that happiness.

What *is* the role of contingency contracting in BMT? Weiss (1975, p. 22) described the role of contracting as "a vehicle for stimulus control over their exchange of gratification." Thus, as mentioned in our discussion of stimulus control, the contract serves a cueing function to make the occurrence of the desired behaviors more probable. Liberman, Wheeler and Sanders (1976, p. 392) described the contract as "a temporary aid in structuring positive exchange and fairness as well as an opportunity to practice communication and problem-solving skills."

Is contingency contracting the sine qua non of BMT? Is contracting necessary or appropriate for every distressed couple? The obvious answer to these questions is no. In answer to both questions, Liberman (1975) presented four case studies of marital and family therapy in which an explicit contract was not employed. He used shaping, modeling, role playing, behavioral rehearsal and instructions (but not contracting) to alter the maladaptive reinforcement contingencies of the clients. With increasing clinical experience using contracts, behavior therapists began to realize that formal contracts were *not necessary* in some cases and *not* appropriate in others. The beginning of the trend away from reliance on the exchange contract as the principal tool of marital therapy can be seen in Knox's (1973,

p. 23) article: "Some clients also reported that 'contracts are silly and too immature.' The counselor asks, 'What is the alternative?' When clients suggest an alternative treatment strategy and agree to collect data, the contract issue is dropped. Some spouses do not need behavior contracts to initiate positive behavior."

The characteristics of behavioral marital therapy described by Jacobson and Weiss (1978, p. 161) perhaps best explain the trend away from the original legalistic exchange contract which had become widely popular: "In our view BMT is a flexible, versatile, and often effective model for helping couples. It is also an approach that is fluid, open to disconfirmation, and subservient to empirical verification." The fact is that several review articles on BMT (see the chapter by Williams and Miller, in this book) called for studies of the "active ingredients" of behavioral programs. Systematic research was (and is) needed to determine *which* therapy modules are necessary for *which* problems of *which* couples.

In their extensive review of BMT, Jacobson and Martin (1976) suggested that if quid pro quo and good-faith contracts were found to be equally effective, then the quid pro quo would be the contract of choice because it is easier and less time-consuming to use in therapy. In a subsequent study of mildly to moderately distressed couples, Jacobson (1978b) tentatively concluded that the two types of contracts were interchangeable. He noted, however, that the good-faith contract may still be preferable for *severely* disturbed couples, as had been suggested previously by Weiss, Birchler and Vincent (1974).

Ewart (1978a, b) compared the effects of quid pro quo and good-faith contracts in *severely* distressed couples. These couples were somewhat older than most research participants had been (husbands averaged forty years of age; wives averaged thirty-eight years of age). Ewart added a third comparison group in which the individual partners set goals without arranging any contingent consequences. He concluded (1978b, p. 5): "Merely pinpointing a behavioral goal was as effective as arranging quid pro quo enforcement arrangements or programming performance-contingent rewards." Again, quid pro quo and good-faith contracts were equivalent. However, noncontingent goal setting was found to be no less effective than formal procedures designed to *insure* performance of the behavior-change agreements. Further empirical investigation is needed to replicate this finding and to determine the implications for BMT. Since the field is "subservient to empirical verification" (Jacobson and Weiss, 1978), the direction of clinical practice will be, presumably, to follow the data as the implications of goal setting are explored.

Are contingency contracts needed at all in behavioral therapy with distressed couples? Clinical experiences reported by Liberman, Levine,

Wheeler, Sanders and Wallace (1976) suggested that communication skills training is a necessary prerequisite to writing a formal behavior-exchange contract. Liberman et al. (p. 32) were not enthusiastic about contracting as a panacea for marital distress: "Contingency contracting is worth just about the paper it's printed on without the family members having adequate interpersonal communication skills." They used contracting selectively with clients who had adequately mastered skills such as negotiation and assertive communication.

Jacobson (1978c, d) has also questioned the effectiveness of contingency contracting as a treatment strategy. In a recent study (1978b), Jacobson had found that the two forms of contracting had equivalent effects, and he suggested (p. 39) "the possibility that contingency contracting itself was an extraneous procedure, and that problem-solving training served as the primary active ingredient in both conditions." It is interesting to note that the consumer reactions in the Liberman, Levine, Wheeler, Sanders and Wallace (1976) study pointed to the role playing of communication skill as the most helpful behavioral procedure.

The above opinions and unsubstantiated observations were challenged by Ewart (1978a, b), who evaluated his data from somewhat older couples by means of visual inspection and time-series analyses. By having different couples begin contracting at different times and by having each individual contract at successive intervals for different behavior changes, Ewart was able to separate the effects of contracting from those produced by communication skills and problem-solving training. He reported that 93 percent of the behavioral marital contracts had produced a significant change, over and above improvements due to the communication and problem-solving training.

The trend toward informal contingency contracting is clear in O'Leary and Turkewitz's (1978) use of "marital agreements." Spouses identify specific behaviors they would like each other to increase, and make a written agreement regarding the behaviors to be changed. Rather than setting up formal contingencies (rewards and punishments) for each spouse's compliance, O'Leary and Turkewitz focus on "intrinsic positive consequences" (e.g., increased cooperation) each spouse will receive.

As we mentioned earlier, behavioral goal setting was posed as one of the essential active ingredients sought by behavioral therapists and researchers. If this proves to be the case, then *contingency contracting*, which was argued to be "cumbersome, time-consuming, and arduous" at best and "potentially self-defeating" at worst (Jacobson, 1978d, p. 33), may be obsolete in favor of *pinpointing of specific behavioral goals, problem-solving training and behavioral rehearsal* of effective communication. The answer to the question "Are contingency contracts necessary?" must await more definitive research.

TRENDS FOR THE FUTURE OF BEHAVIORAL APPROACHES TO MARITAL THERAPY

In our reading of behavioral marital therapy literature, we have noted a trend toward deemphasis of contingency contracting. Behaviorally oriented therapists seem to be taking a more thoughtful look at other procedures within the operant, respondent and cognitive-behavioral approaches. Consequently, the well-versed clinician has a broad repertoire of skills to apply to marital problems. Procedures such as discrimination training, stimulus control and communication training can be used singly or in combination, depending on clients' needs.

In addition to this trend toward a more differentiated behavioral marital therapy, there seems to be increasing interest in two other areas: applications of cognitive-behavior therapy to marital problems and a focus on marital therapy for particular types of problems or clients. We will first consider cognitive-behavior therapy.

Cognitive-behavior therapy with couples. Increasingly, behavior therapists have taken into account the role of thought processes as mediators of a person's emotional and behavioral responses to environmental stimuli. The basic cognitive model postulates that a person responds to perceptions and appraisals of an event rather than to the objective characteristics of the event. For example, an individual's stress response varies directly with the level of danger he/she perceives in the situation (c.f. Lazarus, 1966).

Although therapeutic procedures designed to modify problematic cognitions have been applied to a wide range of clinical problems, including social anxiety, depression, phobias and childhood hyperactivity (Beck, 1976; Meichenbaum, 1977), cognitive-behavioral principles rarely have been applied to marital problems (O'Leary and Turkewitz, 1978). However, it is clear that spouses continuously serve as stimuli for each other, and their responses to these stimuli are likely to be influenced by cognitive mediators. Marital therapists are beginning to acknowledge the importance of perceptions, thoughts, beliefs, etc., and we expect that the focus on cognitions will become significant in the coming years.

Ellis (1962; Ellis and Harper, 1975) has presented the most detailed cognitive-behavioral analysis of marital dysfunction to date. His "rational-emotive therapy" (RET) is based on the assumption that disturbed emotions and behaviors occur when a person holds irrational, unrealistic beliefs about himself/herself and the world. The irrational beliefs Ellis has identified, which are learned through socialization into Western culture, tend to be negative, self-deprecating and unrealistically demanding (e.g., "It is awful if I do not have everyone's love and approval," "It is terrible if I do not perform perfectly all the time"). They base a person's self-worth on extreme standards and the opinions of other people, and in fact they often involve imagined negative consequences (e.g., rejection by a significant person) much more severe than any consequences the person has actually experienced. Rational-emotive therapy is intended to convince the client that his/her disturbed emotions and behavior (e.g., anxiety, procrastination over a job) are due to irrational thinking, and to substitute more realistic thinking for the problematic beliefs. More positive beliefs would include, "It is nice to have other people's love and approval, but I am a worthwhile person even without that," and "I enjoy performing well, but it is human to make mistakes."

Irrational beliefs are not necessarily fully conscious but, as firmly established attitudes, often occur "automatically," involuntarily and with minimal awareness (Beck, 1976; Meichenbaum, 1977). They generally occur instantaneously and often involve imagined visual pictures rather than covert verbal statements. For example, a person who fears snakes may imagine being bitten and suffering a painful death. The therapist encourages the client to pay attention to thoughts and images that occur in conjunction with the disturbing emotions and behaviors. This procedure of keeping a "diary" of associations between cognitions and problem responses is consistent with the behavioral orientation toward functional analysis. The therapist also encourages the client to adopt the view that faulty cognitions mediate problematic responses to events. Meichenbaum (1977) stresses that it is less important that the client actually engaged in an irrational self-dialogue before therapy than it is that he/she be willing to believe that problematic responses can be maintained *and modified* by cognitions. Meichenbaum also suggests that nonclinical subjects may hold the same irrational beliefs as clinical populations but may be better at "compartmentalizing" them and using positive coping, such as humor.

The therapist instills the cognitive viewpoint by means of some combination of encouraging, goading, challenging, educating, providing information, conducting rational analyses of the client's responses, etc. (Meichenbaum, 1977). Ellis' forceful manner of challenging a client's irrational beliefs need not be adopted by all therapists who choose to take a cognitive-behavioral approach. Some research studies evaluating RET have suggested its effectiveness (Ellis and Grieger, 1977), but definitive data supporting the efficacy of RET still are lacking (Mahoney, 1974; Meichenbaum, 1977).

According to Ellis (Ellis and Harper, 1975), marital dysfunction is due to one or both spouses' cognitively-mediated neurotic responses. Unrealistic expectations of oneself and the marriage lead to anger, disappointment, anxiety and other negative emotions, as well as counterproductive behaviors such as nagging and blaming. The therapist points out how these expectations produce only negative interpersonal consequences; e.g., the wife's blaming does not make her husband make fewer mistakes and in fact makes him more defensive. It is noted that it is irrational for either spouse to believe that the husband *should* be blamed for mistakes, and stressed that human beings *do* make mistakes. Since blaming one's partner for past mistakes is counterproductive, both spouses' attention could be applied more productively to efforts aimed at improving performance in the present and future (Ellis and Harper, 1975). In general, RET is intended to convince spouses that it is not their partners who make them upset but rather their own ways of thinking about their partners' behaviors. This is not an interactive view of marital dysfunction but an extension of Ellis' approach to individual psychological disturbance. However, it is likely that spouses "fuel" and reinforce each other's irrational expectations, since Ellis sees these as shared by most members of society. Also, it may be to one spouse's advantage to reinforce the other's irrational thinking if this produces compliance with the former's wishes. For example, suggesting to one's partner that he/she *should* feel guilty for making mistakes may increase the likelihood that the partner will try hard to avoid similar mistakes. However, since such a strategy provides the partner with no constructive suggestions for behavior change, it is more likely to result in rumination and defensiveness than a positive outcome.

Eisenberg and Zingle (1975) found that spouses' scores on Zingle's (1965) "Irrational Ideas Inventory," which was designed to measure the irrational assumptions postulated by Ellis, were not correlated with their scores on Locke and Wallace's (1959) measure of marital adjustment. However, this finding might be due to the nature of the two scales. On the one hand, a general adjustment measure may not assess marital processes that are influenced by irrational thinking. On the other hand, the III may not assess particular versions of irrational beliefs that are relevant to marital interaction. For example, the III does not assess beliefs such as the following: "If people love each other they sense each other's thoughts and feelings without having to ask" (Lederer and Jackson, 1968); "If I express my feelings, I will hurt our relationship beyond repair" (Gottman et al., 1976); "Planned positive interactions between spouses are unromantic and insincere" (Gambrill, 1977); and "If spouses disagree, they have a poor relationship" (Epstein, Finnegan and Bythell, 1979). Future research in this area would be aided if measures of *irrational relationship beliefs* were developed.

In terms of clinical assessment, it behooves the therapist to spend more interview time probing for possible irrational beliefs that each spouse may hold and exploring how each partner's negative responses to the other's behavior may be due to unrealistic expectations. This goal is consistent with Sager's (1976) view that marital dissatisfaction occurs when spouses' idiosyncratic expectations of marriage are not met by their actual patterns of interaction. Each spouse brings to the marriage a set of expectations, both conscious and beyond awareness, regarding benefits he/she will derive and obligations he/she will have in return. Some of these expectations will be realistic and constructive, but others may be neurotic or conflictual. Since many of these "needs" are not expressed directly, spouses often are not aware of the partner's expectations. Thus, each partner has an individual "contract" involving assumptions that each spouse will give and receive certain relationship commodities, and he/she may behave as if the couple had agreed to these terms overtly. When the *actual* pattern of exchange does not fulfill significant aspects of a partner's individual contract, he/she is likely to respond with negative feelings (e.g., disappointment, anger, depression) and behaviors (e.g., withdrawal, attack). A central goal of Sager's approach to marital therapy is to make each spouse aware of the expectations he/she has brought to the relationship and how these mesh with the partner's expectations and actual marital interactions. Changes might be made in either individual or interactional "contracts."

Meanings attributed to behavior. Discrepancies between the intents and impacts of messages often are due to idiosyncratic meanings that one spouse attributes to the other's behavior. Weiss (1978) notes that spouses frequently go beyond the concrete qualities of their partners' behaviors to make inferences about the partner's motives and intentions. A partner's failure to complete a household task may be interpreted as a sign that he/she does not care about the marriage. Gottman et al. (1976) suggest that when problem-solving efforts seem to go in circles with no clear resolution of issues, one or both spouses will likely have a "hidden agenda" or unexpressed issue that is not being addressed. For example, spouses who fight over seemingly trivial household tasks and who try to agree on a plan for sharing responsibilities may have difficulty solving the problem if one or both interprets the issue as one of power, in which there must be a winner. In order for the couple to proceed with constructive problem-solving, the meanings attributed to behaviors and the relevant "hidden agendas" need to be made explicit. Gottman et al. have identified three major categories of hidden agenda: (1) *positiveness*, including issues of emotional investment, such as caring, trust, love and attraction; (2) *responsiveness* or interest; and (3) *status*, including issues of influence and importance of each spouse's needs. Since these hidden agendas involve needs and expectations for a relationship, their clear disclosure can lead to further problem-solving and negotiation aimed at maximizing their fulfillment. The communication skills described earlier will be important tools for resolving these issues.

Self-instruction. Meichenbaum's (1977) "self-instructional" aproach to cognitive-behavior therapy offers some interesting possibilities for conjoint marital therapy. The goal of self-instructional training is to teach clients how to use cognitions intentionally to mediate their own behaviors and emotional responses. For example, Meichenbaum and others (e.g., Bornstein and Quevillon, 1976; Spivack and Shure, 1974) have taught impulsive children, who generally do not analyze their experiences before acting, to think about task demands and solutions before responding. The children are trained to emit self-verbalizations, first overtly and then covertly, that guide their behavior; e.g., "What am I supposed to do? I am supposed to copy these words. Okay, first I'll copy the letter A, and now the letter N . . ." Clients also are taught to evaluate their own performance, instruct themselves to make corrections as needed and reinforce themselves as appropriate (e.g., "Good job"). Research findings regarding the application of self-instructional training to reduce "hyperactive" children's impulsive behavior, to increase socially withdrawn children's interactive skills, to increase college students' creativity, and to decrease schizophrenics' task-irrelevant behaviors have been quite encouraging (Meichenbaum, 1977).

Since couples who are attempting to communicate clearly and solve problems frequently are distracted by task-irrelevant thoughts and emotions (e.g., memories and anger about past injustices by the partner), self-instructional training might be used to increase their focus on constructive behavior, such as empathic listening. When spouses tend to respond rather impulsively toward each other, increasing their ability to regulate their own behavior would seem to be a valuable goal.

Self-instructional training might be used to interrupt destructive spouse interactions in the following manner. First, spouses would be trained to notice both intrapersonal and interpersonal cues that destructive interactions were occurring. Intrapersonal cues would include feelings of anger, frustration, anxiety and confusion; behaviors such as rapid talking, interrupting one's partner and raising one's voice; and distracting thoughts such as concerns about winning an argument. Interpersonal cues include negative and task-irrelevant behaviors on the part of a partner. Both spouses would be given considerable behavioral feedback, especially by videotape playback, and would be coached in identifying these "red flags." Next, they would be instructed to use these cues as discriminative stimuli for engaging in constructive self-instruction. Each client should verbalize (1) the demands of the present task (e.g., "I am supposed to communicate clearly by telling my partner what I think and feel, and by listening empathically to my partner in return"); (2) instructions to speak slowly, to stay calm and to listen carefully; (3) ongoing self-corrective statements (e.g., "You interrupted your partner; now slow down and listen to him/her"); and (4) self-rewarding statements. The therapist should give clients specific instructions for generating self-verbalizations, model overt self-verbalization, coach clients as they rehearse overtly and shape the client's skills with both corrective and reinforcing feedback. Once a client has become proficient at overt self-instruction, he/she can rehearse *covert* verbalization. As in the development of other skills, couples initially should practice self-instruction while discussing topics that are not emotion-laden, and should only proceed to more significant relationship issues when their skills are highly developed.

Since applications of cognitive-behavior therapy with couples have not been evaluated empirically, clinicians should approach them with caution. Data from studies testing the effects of cognitive-behavioral therapies with individuals have been promising, but controlled outcome studies with couples are lacking at this time. The present authors hope to encourage the inclusion of cognitive variables in marital therapy research.

Problem-Oriented Behavioral Marital Therapy

Gurman and Kniskern's (1978) review of the behavioral and nonbehavioral marital therapy outcome literature indicated that many of the nonbehavioral studies were problem-oriented (e.g., for the treatment of alcoholism, drug abuse, gambling and family violence). On the other hand, while there have been some common themes in the problems treated with BMT (e.g., the wife is disinterested in sex and wants more verbal communication with her career-oriented husband, who devalues conversation), behavioral treatment programs generally have not been tailored to specific undesirable behaviors. Behaviorally oriented sex therapy (e.g., LoPiccolo and Lobitz, 1973) is a notable exception, and the application of social skills training and behavioral contracting with alcoholics and their spouses (Miller, 1976) is increasing. However, in spite of the emphasis placed on assessment for treatment in the behavioral orientation (Hersen, 1976), matching of particular behavioral interventions with particular types of marital problems remains fairly unsystematic. In the future it may be advantageous for behavioral marital therapists and researchers to identify optimal treatment programs for homogeneous target problems, especially those of significant social concern (e.g., wife abuse).

SUMMARY

We have maintained that behavioral analysis and treatment of marital problems represent not a uniform approach but rather a collage of approaches to dysfunctional dyadic behavior. We have described the array of behavioral procedures currently available and argued that the behavioral marital therapy *research* literature may not accurately represent the clinical practice of BMT. A historical perspective has suggested that the major approaches described in the earliest publications on BMT have since received uneven attention. Some of the relatively neglected approaches (e.g., stimulus control) recently have attracted renewed interest.

In order to describe the range of interventions a behavior therapist can use with a distressed couple, we have presented nine behavior-change procedures in some detail. Although behavior-exchange contracts have been widely used and publicized, obviously not every behavior therapist uses this procedure. When contracts *are* used, it is often in the context of a more broad-based treatment program.

We wish to stress that behavioral marital therapy is neither simplistic nor mechanistic. It requires knowledge of operant, respondent and cognitive behavioral principles, as well as a careful approach to ongoing assessment. Perhaps the most important requirement for the therapist is an open-minded, flexible approach in which one is prepared to discard favorite procedures that have not produced desired results in favor of alternative procedures. Given a commitment on the part of behavioral marital therapists to identify treatments that work best for particular clients and problems, the behavioral orientation should continue to evolve as a creative solution to the problems of distressed couples.

REFERENCES

Alkire, A.A., and Brunse, A.J. Impact and possible casualty from videotape feedback in marital therapy. *J. Consult. & Clin. Psychol.*, 1974, *42*, 203–210.

Azrin, N.H., Naster, B.J., and Jones, R. Reciprocity counseling: A rapid learning-based procedure for marital counseling. *Behav. Res. & Ther.*, 1973, *11*, 365–382.

Bandura, A. *Principles of behavior modification.* New York: Holt, Rinehart and Winston, 1969.

Beck, A. *Cognitive therapy and emotional disorders.* New York: International Universities Press, 1976.

Berger, M.M. *Videotape techniques in psychiatric training and treatment* (rev. ed.). New York: Brunner/Mazel, 1978.

Berman, E., Lief, H.I., and Williams, A.M. A model of marital interaction. In G.P. Sholevar (Ed.), *The textbook of marriage and marital therapy.* New York: Spectrum Publications, 1981.

Bornstein, P., and Quevillon, R. The effects of a self-instructional package on overactive preschool boys. *J. Appl. Behav. Analy.*, 1976, *9*, 179–188.

De Torres, C.D. Marriage, power, and conflict. Paper, Eastern Psychological Association, Philadelphia, April 1979.

D'Zurilla, T.J., and Goldfried, M.R. Problem solving and behavior modification. *J. Abnor. Psychol.*, 1971, *78*, 107–126.

Eisenberg, J.M., and Zingle, H.W. Marital adjustment and irrational ideas. *J. Marr. & Fam. Couns.*, 1975, *1*, 81–91.

Eisler, R.M., and Hersen, M. Behavioral techniques in family-oriented crisis intervention. *Arch. Gen. Psychiat.*, 1973, *28*, 111–115.

Ellis, A. *Reason and emotion in psychotherapy.* New York: Lyle Stuart, 1962.

Ellis, A., and Grieger, R. *Handbook of rational-emotive therapy.* New York: Springer, 1977.

Ellis, A., and Harper, R.A. *A new guide to rational living.* Englewood Cliffs, N.J.: Prentice-Hall, 1975.

Epstein, N. Assertiveness training in marital treatment. In G.P. Sholevar (Ed.). *The textbook of marriage and marital therapy.* New York: Spectrum Publications, 1981.

Epstein, N., DeGiovanni, I.S., and Jayne-Lazarus, C. Assertion training for couples. *J. Behav. Ther. & Exper. Psychiat.*, 1978, *9*, 149–155.

Epstein, N., Finnegan, D., and Bythell, D. Irrational beliefs and perceptions of marital conflict. *J. Consult. & Clin. Psychol.*, 1979, *47*, 608–610.

Epstein, N., Jayne-Lazarus, C., and DeGiovanni, I.S. Cotrainers as models of relationships: Effects on the outcome of couples therapy. *J. Marit. & Fam. Ther.*, 1979, *5*, 53–60.

Ewart, C.K. Behavior contracts in couple therapy: An experimental evaluation of quid pro quo and good faith models. Paper, American Psychological Association, Toronto, 1978a.

Ewart, C.K. Behavioral marriage therapy with older couples: Effects of training measured by the Marital Adjustment Scale. Paper, Association for Advancement of Behavior Therapy, Chicago, 1978b.

Friedman, P.M. Personalistic family and marital therapy. In A. Lazarus (Ed.), *Clinical behavior therapy*. New York: Brunner/Mazel, 1972.

Gambrill, E.D. *Behavior modification: Handbook of assessment, intervention, and evaluation*. San Francisco: Jossey-Bass, 1977.

Goffman, E. *Presentation of self in everyday life*. New York: Doubleday, 1959.

Goldfried, M.R., and Davison, G.C. *Clinical behavior therapy*. New York: Holt, Rinehart and Winston, 1976.

Goldiamond, I. Self-control procedures in personal behavior problems. *Psychologic. Rep.*, 1965, *17*, 851–868.

Goldstein, M.K. Behavior rate change in marriages: Training wives to modify husbands' behavior. Ph.D. diss., Cornell Univ., 1971.

Goldstein, M.K. Increasing positive behaviors in married couples. In J.D. Krumboltz and C.E. Thoreson (Eds.), *Counseling methods*. New York: Holt, Rinehart and Winston, 1976.

Goldstein, M.K., and Francis, B. Behavior modification of husbands by wives. Paper, National Council on Family Relations, Washington, D.C., October 1969.

Gottman, J., Markman, H., and Notarius, C. The topography of marital conflict: A sequential analysis of verbal and nonverbal behavior. *J. Marr. & Fam.*, 1977, *39*, 461–477.

Gottman, J., Notarius, C., Gonso, J., and Markman, H. *A couple's guide to communication*. Champaign, Ill.: Research Press, 1976.

Guerney, B.G., Jr. *Relationship enhancement*. San Francisco: Jossey-Bass, 1977.

Gurman, A.S., and Kniskern, D.P. Research in marital and family therapy: Progress, perspective and prospect. In S.L. Garfield and A.E. Bergin (Eds.), *Handbook of psychotherapy and behavior change* (rev. ed.). New York: Wiley, 1978.

Gurman, A.S., and Knudson, R.M. Behavioral marriage therapy. I. A psychodynamic-systems analysis and critique. *Fam. Proc.*, 1978, *17*, 121–138.

Harrell, J., and Guerney, B.G., Jr. Training married couples in conflict negotiation skills. In D.H.L. Olson (Ed.), *Treating relationships*. Lake Mills, Iowa: Graphic, 1976.

Hersen, M. Historical perspectives in behavioral assessment. In M. Hersen and A.S. Bellack (Eds.), *Behavioral assessment: A practical handbook*. New York: Pergamon, 1976.

Hickok, J.E., and Komechak, M.G. Behavior modification in marital conflict: A case report. *Fam. Proc.*, 1974, *13*, 111–119.

Hollandsworth, J.G., Jr., and Cooley, M.L. Provoking anger and gaining compliance with assertive versus aggressive responses. *Behav. Ther.*, 1978, *9*, 640–646.

Jacobson, N.S. Problem-solving and contingency contracting in the treatment of marital discord. *J. Consult. & Clin. Psychol.*, 1977a, *45*, 92–100.

Jacobson, N.S. Training couples to solve their marital problems: A behavioral approach to relationship discord. I: Problem-solving skills. *Int. J. Fam. Couns.*, 1977b, *4*, 22–31.

Jacobson, N.S. Training couples to solve their marital problems: A behavioral approach to relationship discord. II. *Int. J. Fam. Couns.*, 1977c, *5*, 20–28.

Jacobson, N.S. A review of the research on the effectiveness of marital therapy. In T.J. Paolino and B.S. McCrady (Eds.), *Marriage and marital therapy: Psychoanalytic, behavioral, and systems theory perspectives.* New York: Brunner/Mazel, 1978a.

Jacobson, N.S. Specific and nonspecific factors in the effectiveness of a behavioral approach to the treatment of marital discord. *J. Consult. & Clin. Psychol.*, 1978b, *46*, 442–452.

Jacobson, N.S. Contingency contracting with couples: Redundancy and caution. *Behav. Ther.*, 1978c, *9*, 679.

Jacobson, N.S. A stimulus control model of change in behavioral couples' therapy: Implications for contingency contracting. *J. Marr. & Fam. Couns.*, 1978d, *4*, 29–35.

Jacobson, N.S. Behavioral treatments for marital discord: A critical appraisal. In M. Hersen, R.M. Eisler and P.M. Miller (Eds.), *Progress in behavior modification.* New York: Academic Press, 1979.

Jacobson, N.S., and Martin, B. Behavioral marriage therapy: Current status. *Psychologic. Bull.*, 1976, *83*, 540–556.

Jacobson, N.S., and Weiss, R.L. III. Critique: The contents of Gurman et al. may be hazardous to our health. *Fam. Proc.*, 1978, *17*, 149–164.

Jones, R.G. A factored measure of Ellis' irrational belief system, with personality and maladjustment correlates. Unpub. Ph.D. diss., Texas Tech. Coll., 1968.

Kanfer, F.H., and Saslow, G. Behavioral diagnosis. In C.M. Franks (Ed.), *Behavior therapy: Appraisal and status.* New York: McGraw-Hill, 1969.

Kaplan, H.S. *The new sex therapy: Active treatment of sexual dysfunctions.* New York: Brunner/Mazel, 1974.

Knox, D. *Marriage happiness: A behavioral approach to counseling.* Champaign, Ill.: Research Press, 1971.

Knox, D. Behavior contracts in marriage counseling. *J. Fam. Couns.*, 1973, *1*, 22–28.

Lazarus, A.A. Behavior therapy and marriage counseling. *J. Am. Soc. Psychosom. Dent. & Med.*, 1968, *15*, 49–56.

Lazarus, A.A. *Behavior therapy and beyond.* New York: McGraw-Hill, 1971.

Lazarus, R. *Psychological stress and the coping process.* New York. McGraw-Hill, 1966.

Lederer, W.J., and Jackson, D.D. *The mirages of marriage.* New York: W.W. Norton, 1968.

Liberman, R. Behavioral principles in family and couple therapy. In A.S. Gurman and D.G. Rice (Eds.), *Couples in conflict: New directions in marital therapy.* New York: Jason Aronson, 1975.

Liberman, R.P., Levine, J., Wheeler, E., Sanders, N., and Wallace, C.J. Marital therapy in groups: A comparative evaluation of behavioral and interactional formats. *Acta Psychiatr. Scand.*, 1976, supple. *266*, 3–34.

Liberman, R.P., Wheeler, E., and Sanders, N. Behavioral therapy for marital disharmony: An educational approach. *J. Marr. & Fam. Couns.*, 1976, *2*, 383–395.

Locke, H.J., and Wallace, K.M. Short marital adjustment and prediction tests: Their reliability and validity. *Marr. & Fam. Living*, 1959, *21*, 251–255.

LoPiccolo, J., and Lobitz, W.C. Behavior therapy of sexual dysfunction. In L.A. Hamerlynck, L.C. Handy and E.J. Mash (Eds.), *Behavior change: Methodology, concepts and practice.* Champaign, Ill.: Research Press, 1973.

Mahoney, M. *Cognition and behavior modification.* Cambridge, Ma.: Ballinger, 1974.

Masters, W.H., and Johnson, V.E. *Human sexual inadequacy.* Boston: Little, Brown, 1970.

Mehrabian, A. *Nonverbal communication.* Chicago: Aldine/Atherton, 1972.

Meichenbaum, D. *Cognitive-behavior modification: An integrative approach.* New York: Plenum, 1977.

Mickelson, D.J., and Stevic, R.R. Differential effects of facilitative and nonfacilitative behavioral counselors. *J. Couns. Psychol.*, 1971, *18*, 314–319.

Miller, P.M. *Behavioral treatment of alcoholism.* New York: Pergamon, 1976.

O'Leary, K.D., and Turkewitz, H. Marital therapy from a behavioral perspective. In T.J.

Paolino and B.S. McCrady (Eds.), *Marriage and marital therapy: Psychoanalytic, behavioral, and systems theory perspectives.* New York: Brunner/Mazel, 1978.

Patterson, G.R. *Families: Applications of social learning to family life.* Champaign, Ill.: Research Press, 1971.

Patterson, G.R., and Hops, H. Coercion: A game for two: Intervention techniques for marital conflict. In R. Ulrich and P. Montjoy (Eds.), *The experimental analyses of social behavior.* New York: Appleton-Century-Crofts, 1972.

Rappaport, A.F., and Harrell, J. A behavioral-exchange model for marital counseling. *Fam. Coord.*, 1972, *21*, 203–213.

Raush, H.L., Barry, W.A., Hertel, R.K., and Swain, M.A. *Communication, conflict and marriage.* San Francisco: Jossey-Bass, 1974.

Reynolds, G.S. *A primer of operant conditioning.* Glenview, Ill.: Scott, Foresman, 1968.

Rogers, C.R. The necessary and sufficient conditions of therapeutic personality change. *J. Consult. Psychol.*, 1957, *22*, 95–103.

Ryder, R.G. Husband-wife dyads versus married strangers. *Fam. Proc.*, 1968, *7*, 233–238.

Sager, C.J. *Marriage contracts and couple therapy: Hidden forces in intimate relationships.* New York: Brunner/Mazel, 1976.

Skinner, B.F. *Science and human behavior.* New York: Macmillan, 1953.

Skinner, B.F. *Verbal behavior.* New York: Appleton-Century-Crofts, 1957.

Spivack, G., and Shure, M. *Social adjustment of young children: A cognitive approach to solving real-life problems.* San Francisco: Jossey-Bass, 1974.

Stuart, R.B. Operant-interpersonal treatment for marital discord. *J. Consult. & Clin. Psychol.*, 1969, *33*, 675–682.

Stuart, R.B. An operant interpersonal program for couples. In D.H.L. Olson (Ed.), *Treating relationships.* Lake Mills, Iowa: Graphic, 1976.

Stuart, R.B., and Stuart, F. *Marital Pre-counseling Inventory.* Champaign, Ill.: Research Press, 1972.

Thibaut, J.W., and Kelley, H.H. *The social psychology of groups.* New York: Wiley, 1959.

Thomas, E.J. *Marital communication and decision making: Analysis, assessment, and change.* New York: Free Press, 1977.

Truax, C.B., and Carkhuff, R.R. *Toward effective counseling and psychotherapy: Training and practice.* Chicago: Aldine, 1967.

Tsoi-Hoshmand, L. The limits of *quid pro quo* in couple therapy. *Fam. Coord.*, 1975, *24*, 51–54.

Vincent, J.P. The susceptibility of marital observation data to faking. Paper, Western Psychological Association, Los Angeles, April 1976.

Vincent, J.P., Weiss, R.L., and Birchler, G.R. A behavioral analysis of problem-solving in distressed and nondistressed married and stranger dyads. *Behav. Ther.*, 1975, *6*, 475–487.

Watzlawick, P., Beavin, J.H., and Jackson, D.D. *Pragmatics of human communication—A study of interactional patterns, pathologies, and paradoxes.* New York: W.W. Norton, 1967.

Weiss, R.L. Contracts, cognition, and change: A behavioral approach to marriage therapy. *Counseling Psychologist*, 1975, *5*, 15–26.

Weiss, R.L. Strategies for couples' therapy. Workshop, Association for the Advancement of Behavior Therapy, New York, December 1976.

Weiss, R.L. The conceptualization of marriage from a behavioral perspective. In T.J. Paolino and B.S. McCrady (Eds.), *Marriage and marital therapy: Psychoanalytic, behavioral, and systems theory perspectives.* New York: Brunner/Mazel, 1978.

Weiss, R.L., Birchler, G.R., and Vincent, J.P. Contractual models for negotiation training in marital dyads. *J. Marr. & Fam.*, 1974, *36*, 321–330.

Weiss, R.L., Hops, H., and Patterson, G.R. A framework for conceptualizing marital conflicts, a technology for altering it, some data for evaluating it. In L.A. Hamerlynck, L.C. Handy, and E.J. Mash (Eds.), *Behavior change: Methodology, concepts and practice.* Champaign, Ill.: Research Press, 1973.

Whaley, D.L., and Malott, R.W. *Elementary principles of behavior.* New York: Appleton-Century-Crofts, 1971.

Williams, A.M. The quantity and quality of marital interaction related to marital satisfaction: A behavioral analysis (Ph.D. diss., Univ. of Florida, 1977). *Diss. Abstr. Int.*, 1978, *38*, 7. (Univ. Microfilms 77–29, 296).

Williams, A.M. The quantity and quality of marital interaction related to marital satisfaction: A behavioral analysis. *J. Appl. Beh. Analy.*, 1979, *12*, 665–678.

Williams, A.M., and Miller, W.R. Evaluation and research on marital therapy. In G.P. Sholevar (Ed.), *The textbook of marriage and marital therapy.* New York: Spectrum Publications, 1981.

Wolpe, J. *Psychotherapy by reciprocal inhibition.* Stanford, Ca.: Stanford Univ. Press, 1958.

Wolpe, J. *The practice of behavior therapy* (2nd ed.). New York: Pergamon, 1973.

Zingle, H.W. A rational therapy approach to counseling underachievers. Unpublished Ph.D. diss. Univ. of Alberta, 1965.

Chapter 10

Assertiveness Training in Marital Treatment

Norman Epstein

The recent trend toward short-term, structured treatment for marital discord is particularly evident in the application of assertion training to couples' dysfunctional relationships. Although assertion training initially was developed as a behavioral approach for reducing anxiety and inhibition of individuals (Salter, 1949; Wolpe, 1958), increasingly it has been used to treat a variety of interpersonal skill problems. While Wolpe's early description of assertion training stressed the need to increase inhibited clients' overt expressiveness, theoreticians and practicing clinicians have refined the definition of unassertiveness to include inappropriate expressiveness, such as coercive aggression (Alberti and Emmons, 1974; DeGiovanni and Epstein, 1978; Hollandsworth, 1977). The central goal of training is to substitute clear, direct expression of an individual's thoughts and feelings for inhibited and/or aggressive behaviors that have undesirable social consequences. It is assumed that training in assertive social skills will maximize the degree to which a person's needs will be fulfilled in interpersonal relationships without coercing and alienating significant others. Such skills would seem especially valuable in intimate relationships such as marriage.

Application of assertion training to the treatment of couples is consistent with the goals of both marital communication training and behavioral marital therapy. Modification of problematic communication has become a common component of marital treatment, based on the assumption that clear communication is a prerequisite to need fulfillment and problem-solving in intimate relationships. Empirical studies (e.g., Murphy and Mendelson, 1973; Navran, 1967) tend to support the idea that clear communication and marital satisfaction are associated, although the corre-lational nature of the data limits one's ability to conclude that clear communication produces marital satisfaction, that marital satisfaction produces clear communication or that some third factor produces both. In ongoing relationships, it is likely that poor communication and marital dissatisfaction reinforce each other in a spiraling of dysfunction. Raush, Barry, Hertel and Swain (1974) describe two major forms of problematic marital communication likely to interfere with conflict resolution: active escalation of conflict through attack (e.g., disparagement) and withdrawal from conflict through passivity or active avoidance. The close parallel between these dysfunctional forms of communication and the unassertive modes of aggression and inhibition suggests that assertion training may be an appropriate treatment for communication problems. Assertive skills allow spouses to send and receive information necessary for mutual need fulfillment. Whether assertive communication also is *sufficient* for marital satisfaction is an issue to be addressed later in this discussion.

A basic tenet of behavioral marital therapy, supported by empirical research (Gambrill, 1977; Jacobson and Martin, 1976; Weiss, Hops and Patterson, 1973), is that dysfunctional marriages are likely to be character-ized by spouses' disproportionate use of aversive means of controlling each other. A partner's compliance with one's wishes is gained through coercion (punishment and threats of punishment), but at the cost of having the partner retaliate or avoid contact. A central goal of behavioral treatment packages, such as that developed by Weiss and his associates, is to reduce spouses' use of aversive (aggressive) control and increase their exchange of positive reinforcement, using skill training in communication, contracting and negotiation. Jacobson (1978, p. 30) suggests that negotiation is more likely to produce positive change in marital interactions if agreements are reached in a pleasant context than in a context of aversive exchanges: "Positive problem-solving sessions serve as discriminitive stimuli for initial desirable changes, whereas negative problem-solving sessions render suc-cessful change unlikely." Jacobson notes the importance of increasing "positive relationship behavior" before behavioral negotiation sessions are attempted. It seems reasonable to expect that assertion training procedures designed to decrease aversive control in marital interaction will help create a positive context for negotiation. Assertion training for passive or avoidant spouses also is likely to reduce frustration in marital interaction and create a pleasant problem-solving atmosphere. Thus, there are substantial theoretical reasons for applying assertion training to marriages characterized by problematic aggression and inhibition.

Although assertion trainers commonly cite benefits of assertive communication between intimates, and few would argue with the idea that training both members of a couple will maximize impact on the marital system, only recently has the marital system been a focus of treatment. Assertion training for inhibited and aggressive clients has been used primarily with individuals and groups of individuals, focusing on *general* assertive skills for a variety of situations (e.g., refusing unreasonable requests from friends; protecting one's rights with a coercive salesperson). It is important to note that this focus on the individual has not reflected any argument with a systems view of marital treatment. Instead, the focus on individual assertiveness seems to have stemmed from assertion training's origin as a treatment for individual anxiety and the philosophical emphasis on individual rights prevalent in the 1970's (e.g., in the development of the women's movement). Unfortunately, a common stereotype portrays assertion trainers as teaching individuals to satisfy their own needs regardless of the impact on others. On the contrary, while assertion training is designed to enhance individual self-actualization, its means is self-definition with minimal coercion of others. It is recognized that aggressive insistence on achieving one's goals may be the most adaptive response in some situations (e.g., in protecting one's rights from a consistently coercive person); however, over the long run mutually satisfying interactions with others are thought to be characterized by clear but noncoercive communication. Thus, the social consequences of the individual's assertive and unassertive behavior are important considerations, particularly when training is applied to dysfunctional marriages. The interpersonal system, in which members of a relationship mutually influence each other's assertive and unassertive behavior, increasingly has become the focus of treatment. While modification of one spouse's behavior may shift the equilibrium of the marital behavioral system somewhat, theory and research (Gurman and Kniskern, 1978) suggest that treatment of both spouses will produce more extensive change.

The clinician who believes that assertion training for both members of a couple is desirable still must decide whether treatment is to be conjoint or concurrent (each spouse receiving individual training, with potential responses of the partner considered). Factors bearing on this issue are discussed below.

CONJOINT VERSUS INDIVIDUAL ASSERTION TRAINING FOR COUPLES

As a social skill, assertion tends to be situation-specific, such that a person who is quite assertive with co-workers may be unassertive with a mate

(Gambrill, 1977; Rich and Schroeder, 1976). Individual or group training that produces desired changes in the treatment room may not generalize to relationships with significant others, where the costs of alienating recipients of assertiveness are greater. In many instances, unassertive behavior (inhibited or aggressive) may have been an individual's most adaptive response to a living situation that reinforces such behavior and/or punishes assertive behavior. An individual's new assertiveness may be undermined by a mate who is not prepared for changes in the marital system. For example, if a person who is inhibited in marital interactions (and is dissatisfied with the marriage) has a spouse who is insecure and who responds to perceived threats with aggression, assertion training for the former's inhibition may be unsuccessful unless the latter's ability to receive assertiveness from his/her partner is treated simultaneously (Alberti and Emmons, 1976). If individual spouses are trained with "confederates" or other clients who are strangers, it may not be possible to anticipate responses of their actual partners. Conjoint assertion training allows a couple to practice sending and receiving assertive messages in vivo, and to deal with significant issues in their relationship. The relevant idiosyncratic social environment of each marital system is changed when the clinician identifies the spouses' patterns of mutual control and has them practice responses likely to elicit and reinforce assertive behavior.

Of course, the issue of whether conjoint assertion training is in fact superior to individual assertion training for modifying dysfunctional marital interactions remains an empirical question. To date, even the majority of treatment outcome studies directly evaluating the effects of assertion training on couples rather than on the individual's nonmarital assertiveness (Eisler, Miller, Hersen and Alford, 1974; Lehman-Olson, 1976; Muchowski and Valle, 1977) have provided treatment for only one spouse. Two studies (Epstein and Jackson, 1978; Epstein, DeGiovanni and Jayne-Lazarus, 1978) evaluated conjoint assertion training, but no studies reported in the literature have compared effects of individual and conjoint assertion training for marital problems. Preferences for conjoint training have been based on theoretical rationales, clinical judgments and research results indicating limited generalization of assertive skills from one type of interpersonal situation to another. All these may be compelling reasons for conducting conjoint assertion training, but it is important to note the need for research directly addressing the issue.

ASSESSMENT ISSUES IN ASSERTION TRAINING

The development of specific treatments, such as assertion training, for marital discord calls for equally specific assessment procedures in order to provide clients with appropriate treatment. For example, while both assertive and aggressive behavior are expressive and likely to produce *some* compliance from other people, aggression is more likely to produce retaliatory aggression and noncompliance (Hollandsworth and Cooley, 1978). Failure to distinguish clearly between these two forms of expressiveness may lead a clinician to forgo assertion training for inappropriately aggressive clients. Since most existing questionnaire and behavioral measures of assertiveness have not been designed to differentiate assertion from aggression (DeGiovanni and Epstein, 1978), the practicing clinician is faced with making personal assessments of candidates for assertion training. The following definitions, based on current research and theoretical literature, may be helpful in distinguishing forms of assertive and unassertive behavior. The division of aggression into direct and passive forms is based on descriptions of passive aggression in the clinical literature as a qualitatively distinct form of behavior that is particularly resistant to treatment (Bach and Wyden, 1968; Lazarus, 1971). These definitions, presented by Epstein and DeGiovanni (1978), differentiate assertion, aggression, passive aggression and submission in terms of two dimensions: degree of coerciveness and degree of direct versus indirect expression. This two-dimensional model of assertive and unassertive behavior is presented in Figure 1. Assertion is direct and noncoercive, aggression is direct and coercive, passive aggression is indirect and coercive, and submission is indirect and noncoercive.

More detailed definitions of the four behavior modes are as follows:

Assertion: Expressing one's opinion, feeling or preference in a direct manner, without attempting to force compliance through aversive control, such as punishment and threat of punishment. One may express assertively both positive feelings, such as affection, and negative feelings, such as anger.

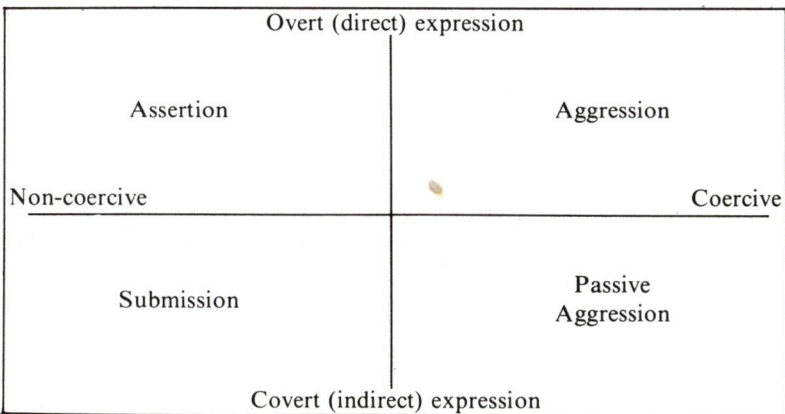

Figure 1. A two-dimensional model of assertive and unassertive behavior.

Assertion does not guarantee that others will comply, but at minimum it is a means of self-definition that can bolster self-esteem.

Aggression: Expressing one's opinion, feeling or preference in a manner that includes the explicit use of coercive power to force another's compliance (i.e., removing his/her behavioral options). Coercion includes the expression of punishment and threats. Overt punishment includes disparagement, name-calling, aversive physical stimulation and direct statements of social ostracism. Overt threats include warnings of future punishment.

Submission (avoidance): Failing to state clearly and directly one's opinion, feeling or preference, and *submitting* automatically to another's preference, power or authority. Submission includes no direct or indirect attempts to make the other person comply.

Passive aggression: Failing to state clearly and directly one's opinion, feeling or preference, while indirectly attempting to coerce the other person to comply. Indirect coercion includes indirect infliction of punishment and threat, particularly by means of attempts to oppose or manipulate others. Examples of indirect coercion are withdrawal of affection, pouting, passive obstruction, insinuation of disparagement and covert social ostracism through the cutting off of communication.

These definitions differ somewhat from conceptualizations that emphasize personal rights (e.g., Alberti and Emmons, 1974). Heimberg, Montgomery, Madsen, and Heimberg (1977) note that defining assertion as "exercising one's rights without denying others' rights" necessitates arbitrary value judgments. Since most of the "assertive rights" noted in the literature emphasize freedom from coercion, definitions based on dimensions of coercion (punishment and threats of punishment) and expressiveness provide a relatively value-free system for classifying assertive and unassertive behaviors.

Accurate assessment of assertive and unassertive behaviors must take into account verbal content, paralinguistic factors (e.g., voice tone and volume) and nonverbal behaviors (e.g., posture). Paralinguistic and nonverbal behaviors commonly cited as distinguishing assertion from submission include duration of eye contact, duration of speech, loudness of speech, degree of affect in speech (expressive versus flat), use of body gestures for emphasis, speech fluency, facial expressiveness and congruence between verbal and nonverbal behavior (Alberti and Emmons, 1974; Eisler, Miller and Hersen, 1973; Galassi, Hollandsworth, Radecki, Gay, Howe and Evans, 1976; Lange and Jakubowski, 1976). Lange and Jakubowski suggest that assertive nonverbals strengthen and emphasize verbal content, while passive nonverbals (e.g., hand wringing, low voice volume) communicate anxiety, weakness, pleading or self-effacement. People who are afraid of offending others use such behavior to soften their messages. On the other hand, aggressive nonverbals (e.g., staring, pointing a finger) convey an attempt to dominate the other person. Hollandsworth (1977) describes how nonverbal aggression fits the basic definition of aggression as coercive behavior that punishes or threatens to punish another person. Unfortunately, empirical support for nonverbal and paralinguistic indices of assertiveness and unassertiveness has been inconsistent (DeGiovanni and Epstein, 1978), and further research differentiating these cues is needed. However, the fact that spouses can provide immediate feedback about specific components of their partners' behavior that they perceive as assertive, aggressive, submissive or passive aggressive can be quite useful in assessing the role of nonverbal communication in a dysfunctional marriage.

Assessment for assertion training with couples necessitates an evaluation of the behavioral system; i.e., each spouse's own range of assertive and unassertive behavior *plus* responses of the partner that control each spouse's behavior. It also is important to assess whether each individual's unassertiveness (aggression, passive aggression or submission) is specific to interactions with his/her spouse or an example of a more general response style that might call for more intensive individual treatment. While assertiveness and unassertiveness tend to be situation-specific, relatively general personality factors (e.g., severe inhibition and depression) may override an individual's specific responses to a spouse. A clinical decision to supplement conjoint assertion training with individual therapy may be made when the conjoint treatment is impeded by individual psychopathology.

One also must assess whether an individual's unassertiveness reflects a skill acquisition problem (i.e., faulty learning of assertive skills) or a choice not to be assertive based on beliefs that assertion is dangerous, socially unacceptable or otherwise inappropriate. Inhibited individuals often mistake assertion to be negatively valued aggression (Ludwig and Lazarus, 1972). This confusion may be particularly problematic for women, whose traditional social roles have emphasized subordination and have included negative sanctions for assertiveness (Butler, 1976; Phelps and Austin, 1975). Although assertion may elicit unfavorable responses from some people in some situations, an individual may have unrealistic expectations of negative reactions that inhibit his/her expressiveness. Thus, assessment in marital treatment includes an evaluation of the individual's expectations of disapproval and rejection by the spouse. A number of writers have stressed that socialization into Western culture includes teaching children an unassertive belief system emphasizing self-sacrifice and denial of personal feelings (Alberti and Emmons, 1974; Lange and Jakubowski, 1976; Smith 1975). These writers present lists of "assertive rights" (e.g., the right to change one's mind; the right to have personal needs and feelings) and routinely teach an "assertive philosophy" to inhibited clients. On the other hand, Ellis (1976; Ellis and Harper, 1975) describes how irrational beliefs (e.g., that one *must* get one's way; that one cannot tolerate frustration) may lead a person to respond to a frustrating spouse with anger and aggression rather than inhibition. Ellis suggests that when one substitutes wishes and preferences for absolutistic demands (i.e., assertively stating one's preferences rather than aggressively demanding one's way), strong anger toward one's spouse will be replaced by only moderate displeasure or annoyance. Rational-emotive therapy (RET), which is based on the assumption that emotional responses, such as anger, stem primarily from an individual's interpretation of external events rather than from the events themselves, focuses on changing the individual's absolutistic belief system of "musts" and "shoulds." Severe marital distress is conceptualized as a failure of spouses to perceive unfair treatment by their partners as inconvenient and frustrating rather than as a catastrophe. Disturbed spouses tend to believe that their partners *must* always be accepting, loving and fair. Lange and Jakubowski (1976) employ RET procedures in assertiveness training by determining the irrational beliefs underlying a client's unassertiveness, by challenging those beliefs and by substituting more rational ideas (e.g., "It is unpleasant that my spouse is treating me this way, but it is not *terrible* and I can stand it"). Problematic beliefs involved in spouses' unassertiveness may include Ellis' list of ten common irrational beliefs (Ellis and Harper, 1975), but irrational expectations specific to marriage may be particularly relevant to interventions with couples. Common examples of the latter are "If my spouse and I argue, we must not love each other," "A mate should satisfy all one's needs" and "A loving mate knows what his/her partner feels and needs without having to be told." Assessment of the particular beliefs associated with each spouse's unassertiveness toward his/her partner provides a more complete view of the marital system than one would achieve by assessing only the range and frequency of assertive and unassertive responses per se. The roles of beliefs and expectations as mediators of assertive and unassertive behavior also suggest that training in assertive expressiveness may be necessary but not sufficient for change in the marital system. Spouses who cling to irrational beliefs regarding themselves, their partners and the institution of marriage are unlikely to develop assertive skills or accept assertiveness from their mates.

COMPONENTS OF ASSERTION TRAINING

Although there is no standard approach to assertion training, most programs include a number of basic components. These procedures are not specific to assertion training but are basic behavioral approaches to skill training. Treatment is designed to increase assertive responses *and* decrease unassertiveness. Since unassertive behavior frequently has been adaptive within the individual's social environment, merely teaching assertive skills does not guarantee that instrumental unassertiveness will decrease. Thus, clients need to learn what *not* to do as well as what to do. As noted earlier, conjoint treatment allows one to create a new social environment that will elicit and reinforce assertive rather than unassertive behavior. The behavioral training procedures of modeling (often with instructions), overt and covert rehearsal, feedback and coaching are most commonly used to achieve these goals. Cognitive therapies such as RET frequently are used to supplement skill training.

Modeling. Presenting examples of competent assertive behavior for clients to imitate is a common training procedure based on behavioral research indicating that observation can be an efficient mode of learning. Modeling may teach clients with skill deficits new ways of responding, may demonstrate under what conditions it is socially advantageous to be assertive and may "legitimize" assertive behavior for clients who *choose* not to be assertive due to unassertive beliefs. Models may be presented by trainers themselves, by skilled "confederates" or by means of taped examples. Samples of unassertive and assertive responses to the same interpersonal situation may be contrasted, and narrative commentary may focus clients' attention on important aspects of the modeled behavior. Co-trainer teams may model the sending and receiving of assertive messages for client couples. Modeling may be accompanied by specific instructions describing verbal and nonverbal components of assertive and unassertive behavior, e.g., "Make eye contact when expressing your opinion." The principle of modeling suggests that assertion trainers need to be proficient at the skills they intend to teach, i.e., they must practice what they preach. The relationship between co-trainers may require special attention.

Rehearsal. Repeated practice of assertive behavior is central to training programs and takes a variety of forms. In covert rehearsal, the client is asked to imagine an interpersonal situation and his/her typical response to it. After exposure to appropriate modeling and/or instruction, the client imagines successful assertion. This procedure may be particularly appropriate for inhibited clients and may develop into a systematic desensitization program for highly anxious individuals.

Advantages suggested for overt over covert response practice include engagement of disinterested clients, generalization of learned responses and more effective training of nonverbal assertiveness (Rich and Schroeder, 1976). Clearly, trainers are better able to shape clients' behavior when continuous observation of overt responses is possible. A combination of overt and covert rehearsal may be used in order to take advantage of each procedure's strengths.

Overt rehearsal may involve the client's attempts to imitate an assertive model, the practice of specific assertive skills with sets of exercises or role-play sessions with confederates and significant others. Exercises that break down assertive behavior into its verbal, nonverbal, and paralinguistic components may be particularly helpful for clients whose difficulties primarily involve basic skill deficits rather than an unassertive belief system. Epstein, DeGiovanni and Jayne-Lazarus (1978) had spouses focus on communication with nonverbals (e.g., facial expressions), practice expression of the same verbal content with different voice tones, repeat "I" statements and send direct messages to their partners by completing sentence stems such as "When I am angry, I . . ." Lange and Jakubowski's (1976) exercises for group assertion training (e.g., giving and receiving compliments; asking open-ended questions) also can be used with couples.

Content of role-plays may be situations contrived by the clinician (either predetermined as problematic for most couples or individually designed for each couple based on an assessment of their particular difficulties) or material selected by spouses. Role-plays with the clinician or a trained confederate may be useful when significant others, such as a spouse, are not available for training or when a client's anxiety over interacting with an intimate initially would minimize success.

During role-play sessions, each client is instructed to rehearse changes in specific components of assertive behavior. Eisler, Miller, Hersen and Alford (1974) identified assertive deficits of passive male patients (e.g., long response latency; low voice volume) from videotapes of the patients' interactions with their wives, and then asked the patients to role-play appropriate changes in these behaviors with a female surrogate. In Epstein, DeGiovanni and Jayne-Lazarus' (1978) treatment program, spouses selected their own role-play topics and rehearsed changes in unassertive behaviors identified during the set of exercises described above. As clients become more skilled, they may need fewer specific orienting instructions for role-plays.

Behavioral changes shaped during role-plays may be more likely to generalize to real-life marital interactions when the role-play conditions are similar to actual conditions (Eisler, Miller, Hersen and Alford, 1974). Consequently, the clinician may reduce the "as-if" quality of practice sessions by treating couples conjointly and having them negotiate emotionally significant issues from their own relationships. Although the artificiality of rehearsals cannot be eliminated entirely as long as the clinician is monitoring the clients, a reasonable degree of realism can be achieved in the office or research laboratory for practice purposes.

An important consideration in the rehearsal of assertive skills is that the training program should maximize clients' opportunities for success, particularly in early sessions. Since anxiety and defensiveness commonly contribute to unassertive behavior, conditions that minimize these responses during training sessions will facilitate substitution of assertion for aggression, passive aggression and passivity. Clients will be less likely to rely on familiar problematic modes of responding if they have early interpersonal successes with assertive behavior. Trainers and clients can rank assertion situations in a hierarchy in terms of likelihood of success as well as of their anxiety-eliciting potential. Consistent success (i.e., competent production of assertive responses and favorable feedback from recipients of assertion) at lower levels of the hierarchy should precede attempts at assertion in more difficult situations. Trainers frequently will need to encourage the spouse who receives assertive communication to reinforce the partner's new behavior. Defensive responses by the recipient spouse become additional targets for treatment, requiring an assessment of how this individual may irrationally interpret his/her partner's assertiveness and what benefits s/he stands to lose if the partner becomes more assertive.

Feedback and coaching. Rehearsal procedures generally are accompanied by extensive feedback to the client regarding the success of his/her efforts to behave assertively and coaching in performance of more effective responses. Although response rehearsal alone may be sufficient to produce increased assertion in well-functioning individuals, such as college students, more guidance is necessary with patient populations (Heimberg et al., 1977). Feedback focuses the client's attention on specific verbal, nonverbal and paralinguistic components of assertive behavior that s/he can control, rather than on global impressions. The trainer notes even small improvements and emphasizes successes rather than failures. The central goal of feedback is for the client to achieve successive approximations of the desired assertive behaviors, with sufficient reinforcement to motivate continued efforts. Feedback helps the client learn to discriminate effective from ineffective behavior and increases the probability of successful attempts in the future.

Feedback procedures in assertion training have taken several forms. The client may provide self-feedback by comparing self-monitored responses against a model or verbal instructions. Placing the responsibility solely on the client for detecting failures and planning constructive change may be unreasonable with all but the most competent of clients. A partial compromise is audiotape or videotape playback of the client's behavior, in which the client is responsible for detecting and correcting discrepancies between his/her behavior and the model. Feedback becomes coaching when the trainer takes responsibility for detecting the client's errors and suggesting changes (Rich and Schroeder, 1976). The option also exists of having the client and trainer collaborate in generating feedback from tapes. *Guiding* the client in accurately assessing his/her own behavior may enhance self-perceived competence. Rich and Schroeder note that no research has compared the effectiveness of the various forms of feedback.

In conjoint assertion training for couples, each spouse may provide feedback for the other. An advantage of this procedure is that clients develop their own ability to discriminate constructive from problematic behaviors by observing both their partners and the feedback provided by trainers. Premature use of spouses as trainers for each other may undercut progress if the feedback is critical and defensive rather than supportive.

Cognitive restructuring. All assertion training programs involve an attempt to change clients' beliefs about assertive and unassertive behavior. Rich and Schroeder (1976) note that trainers typically preface exercises with speeches extolling the virtues of assertiveness and describing how assertive behavior can be substituted for problematic unassertive behavior. In addition, some trainers provide lists of "assertive rights." A major goal of these "pep talks" is to counteract client beliefs that assertive expression is socially undesirable.

Some trainers use cognitive therapies as a major component of their treatment programs. For example, Ludwig and Lazarus (1972) bring clients' irrational cognitions (e.g., perfectionism; unrealistic approval needs) to their attention, stress their negative ramifications for the clients' lives and note how these beliefs are untenable. Clients are coached in new "self-talk," involving conscious subvocalization of constructive statements, such as "I will get a better response from most people if I sincerely express my views rather than simulate agreement." Lehman-Olson (1976) used rational-emotive therapy to modify anger-eliciting irrational beliefs of aggressive female clients. Lange and Jakubowski (1976) make the important point that trainers should be supportive rather than critical in challenging clients' irrational beliefs (i.e., traditional therapeutic characteristics such as empathy still are quite important). Long-standing irrational beliefs have been functional for the client and may be central to his/her view of the world. Many people will not perceive or acknowledge that their behavior is mediated by these beliefs, particularly if the trainer is highly disapproving. Clients are more likely to modify irrational beliefs when trainers illustrate their negative consequences (emotional upset; ineffective interactions with other people) in an informative and minimally judgmental manner. Comparisons with positive consequences already achieved when the client has engaged in constructive thinking can be helpful in underlining his/her potential for effective thought and action. Emphasis on the emotional and behavioral benefits of positive cognitions will help motivate clients to challenge their old beliefs. During conjoint marital treatment sessions, spouses should be encouraged to report their emotional responses to their partners' behavior *and* their cognitive appraisals of that behavior. The realization that a partner's behavior can have alternate (and nonthreatening) meaning can be a quite enlightening and reassuring experience for a distressed client.

Assertion training programs for couples, as well as for individuals and groups, typically include each of the above components to some degree. After a rationale for assertiveness is presented and clients' particular deficits are assessed, a series of behavioral procedures is instituted to shape appropriate responses. Competent models of assertiveness are presented, with instructions to focus clients' attention on components of effective and ineffective behavior. Clients practice a graded progression of behavioral changes through covert and overt rehearsal. Specific goals for each treatment session are based on assessment of each client's deficits and strengths. Continuous feedback and coaching aid in shaping their behaviors toward matching the criteria represented by effective models. Assessment and treatment of problematic beliefs and attitudes throughout training are used to facilitate behavioral change. As clients become adept at assertive communication during training sessions, they are encouraged to practice their skills outside the office. These "homework" assignments for natural settings continue to focus clients' attention on components of assertiveness rather than on global goals.

Conjoint assertion training for couples is guided by systems theory concepts common to other treatments of relationships. Trainers pay considerable attention to each spouse's habitual responses and beliefs, but always in the context of relationship dynamics. An individual's behavior with his/her spouse is not assumed to be characteristic of a general interpersonal style. Modification of problematic behavior requires intervention with the spouses' system of mutual control. Thus, assertion training for couples represents an integration of individually oriented behavior change principles and the expanding field of conjoint marital treatment.

LIMITATIONS OF ASSERTION TRAINING FOR COUPLES

By definition, assertion training is a focused program of skill development. Although it is applicable to a variety of problems in interpersonal functioning, any temptation to view it as a panacea for relationship difficulties should be tempered by the fact that the goals of training are circumscribed. When assertion training is successful, spouses send and receive information more openly about their feelings, thoughts, values and needs. However, clear communication may be a necessary but not sufficient condition for marital satisfaction and adjustment. Even when cognitive therapy reduces the threats spouses perceive in their partners' messages, it is quite possible that members of a couple will communicate clearly that they do not share basic life values, goals and needs. Such a clear exposition often is lacking during courtship or has been impeded by adult developmental changes in each spouse's needs. Some couples' communication difficulties may be defensive strategies for avoiding open conflict. Thus, assertion training may pave the way for negotiation training and conflict resolution, but it also may uncover irreconcilable differences and facilitate relationship dissolution. Of course, the latter outcome need not be assessed as a therapeutic failure if treatment has improved each individual's relationship skills and potential for maximizing fulfillment of significant personal needs, if not in the present relationship, then elsewhere.

The short-term (e.g., Lehman-Olson used four weekly two-hour sessions; Epstein and Jackson used five two-hour sessions over three weeks), structured format of assertion training makes it a convenient adjunct to a more comprehensive marital treatment program that includes conflict-resolution training and work with other dynamics of the interpersonal and intrapsychic systems. Assertion training may be sufficient treatment for couples whose difficulties primarily involve faulty communication or rigid interaction patterns. The breadth of assertion training's impact on marital systems has yet to be assessed.

Since assertion training involves a considerable amount of confrontation through behavioral feedback, a caution regarding its use with clients having low self-esteem and tolerance for confrontation is warranted. The negative outcomes (e.g., suicide) that may result from inappropriate confrontation of clients has been illustrated in studies such as that by Alkire and Brunse (1974). As noted earlier, assertion training can be effective with individuals exhibiting at least moderate psychopathology, but these clients are likely to need more highly structured training than less dysfunctional clients.

At present, the body of existing research on assertion training, particularly with couples, is insufficient to conclude that training is better than alternate treatments, although it clearly is more effective than no treatment or placebo interventions (Heimberg et al., 1977). Research on assertion training for couples is in an early stage, especially with respect to the identification of the components that are effective and those that may be inert. Preliminary studies (e.g., Eisler, Miller, Hersen and Alford, 1974; Epstein, DeGiovanni and Jayne-Lazarus, 1978) suggest that assertion training can change marital interactions in desired directions. Important tasks now facing clinicians and researchers include development of procedures for selecting couples whose dysfunctions are most responsive to assertion training and the demonstration that training is more effective than other available treatments.

REFERENCES

Alberti, R.E., and Emmons, M.L. *Your perfect right* (2nd ed.). San Luis Obispo. Ca.: Impact, 1974.

Alberti, R.E., and Emmons, M.L. Assertion training in marital counseling. *J. Marr. & Fam. Couns.* 1976, *2*, 49–54.

Alkire, A.A., and Brunse, A.J. Impact and possible casualty from videotape feedback in marital therapy. *J. Consult. & Clin. Psychol.* 1974, *42*, 203–210.

Bach, G.R., and Wyden, P. *The intimate enemy.* New York: Avon, 1968.

Butler, P. *Self-assertion for women: A guide to becoming androgynous.* San Francisco: Canfield Press, 1976.

DeGiovanni, I.S., and Epstein, N. Unbinding assertion and aggression in research and clinical practice. *Beh. Mod.,* 1978, *2,* 173–192.

Eisler, R.M., Miller, P.M., and Hersen, M. Components of assertive behavior. *J. Clin. Psychol.,* 1973, *29,* 295–299.

Eisler, R.M., Miller, P.M., Hersen, M., and Alford, H. Effects of assertive training on marital interaction. *Arch. Gen. Psychiat.,* 1974, *30,* 643–649.

Ellis, A. Techniques of handling anger in marriage. *J. Marr. & Fam. Couns.,* 1976, *2,* 305–315.

Ellis, A., and Harper, R.A. *A new guide to rational living.* Englewood Cliffs, N.J.: Prentice-Hall, 1975.

Epstein, N., and DeGiovanni, I.S. Distinguishing among assertion, aggression, submission and passive aggression: A two-dimensional model. Unpublished ms., State Univ. of New York at Buffalo, 1978.

Epstein, N., DeGiovanni, I.S., and Jayne-Lazarus, C. Assertion training for couples. *J. Beh. Ther. & Exper. Psychiatr.,* 1978, *9,* 146–156.

Epstein, N., and Jackson, E. An outcome study of short-term communication training with married couples. *J. Consult. & Clin. Psychol.,* 1978, *46,* 207–212.

Galassi, J.P., Hollandsworth, J.G., Jr., Radecki, J.C., Gay, M.L., Howe, M.R., and Evans, C.L. Behavioral performance in the validation of an assertiveness scale. *Behav. Ther.,* 1976, *7,* 447–452.

Gambrill, E.D. *Behavior modification: Handbook of assessment, intervention, and evaluation.* San Francisco: Jossey-Bass, 1977.

Gurman, A.S., and Kniskern, D.P. Research on marital and family therapy: Progress, perspective and prospect. In S.L. Garfield and A.E. Bergin (Eds.), *Handbook of psychotherapy and behavior change: An empirical analysis* (2nd ed.). New York: Wiley, 1978.

Heimberg, R.G., Montgomery, D., Madsen, C.H., Jr., and Heimberg, J.S. Assertion training: A review of the literature. *Behav. Ther.,* 1977, *8,* 953–971.

Hollandsworth, J.G., Jr. Differentiating assertion and aggression: Some behavioral guidelines. *Behav. Ther.,* 1977, *8,* 347–352.

Hollandsworth, J.G., and Cooley, M.L. Provoking anger and gaining compliance with assertive versus aggressive responses. *Behav. Ther.,* 1978, *9,* 640–646.

Jacobson, N.S. A stimulus control model of change in behavioral couples' therapy: Implications for contingency contracting. *J. Marr. & Fam. Couns.,* 1978, *4,* 29–35.

Jacobson, N.S., and Martin, B. Behavioral marriage therapy: Current status. *Psychologic. Bull.,* 1976, *83,* 540–556.

Lange, A.J., and Jakubowski, P. *Responsible assertive behavior: Cognitive/behavioral procedures for trainers.* Champaign, Ill.: Research Press, 1976.

Lazarus, A.A. *Behavior therapy and beyond.* New York: McGraw-Hill, 1971.

Lehman-Olson, D. Assertiveness training: Theoretical and clinical implications. In D.H.L. Olson (Ed.), *Treating relationships.* Lake Mills, Iowa: Graphic, 1976.

Ludwig, L.D., and Lazarus, A.A. A cognitive and behavioral approach to the treatment of social inhibition. *Psychother.: Theory, Res. & Prac.,* 1972, *9,* 204–206.

Muchowski, P.M., and Valle, S.K. Effects of assertive training on trainees and their spouses. *J. Marr. & Fam. Couns.,* 1977, *3,* 57–62.

Murphy, D.C., and Mendelson, L.A. Communication and adjustment in marriage: Investigating the relationship. *Fam. Proc.,* 1973, *12,* 317–326.

Navran, L. Communication and adjustment in marriage. *Fam. Proc.,* 1967, *6,* 173–184.

Phelps, S., and Austin, N. *The assertive woman.* San Luis Obispo. Ca.: Impact, 1975.

Raush, H.L., Barry, W.A., Hertel, R.K., and Swain, M.A. *Communication, conflict and marriage.* San Francisco: Jossey-Bass, 1974.

Rich, A.R., and Schroeder, H.E. Research issues in assertiveness training. *Psychologic. Bull.*, 1976, *83*, 1081–1096.

Salter, A. *Conditioned reflex therapy.* New York: Capricorn, 1949.

Smith, M.J. *When I say no, I feel guilty.* New York: Dial Press, 1975.

Weiss, R.L., Hops, H., and Patterson, G.R. A framework for conceptualizing marital conflict: A technology for altering it, some data for evaluating it. In L.A. Hamerlynck, L.C. Handy and E.J. Mash (Eds.), *Behavior change: Methodology, concepts and practice.* Champaign, Ill.: Research Press, 1973.

Wolpe, J. *Psychotherapy by reciprocal inhibition.* Stanford, Ca.: Stanford Univ. Press, 1958.

Chapter 11

Marital Therapy From a Structural/Strategic Viewpoint*

M. Duncan Stanton

The view of marriage and marital therapy from a systems theory perspective has been comprehensively presented by Steinglass (1978), with further explication by Feldman (1979), Gurman (1979), Sluzki (1978) and others. These authors compare and contrast the various theoretical and operational ramifications of systems approaches within a marital context, and the reader is referred to them for an overview. The present chapter is an attempt to describe a particular approach to marital treatment drawn from two of the systems or communication "camps" defined by Madanes and Haley (1977). These are the structural and strategic approaches. As background, some basic principles and practices of structural and strategic therapy will first be presented. These will be followed by case material demonstrating the

*Appreciation is extended to the following for helpful comments on an earlier version of this chapter: Ellen Berman, M.D., Sandra Coleman, Ph.D., H. Charles Fishman, M.D., Lynn Hoffman, A.C.S.W., Jay Lappin, M.S.W., Braulio Montalvo, M.A., Monica McGoldrick, A.C.S.W., John Rosenberg, Ed.D., Thomas Todd, Ph.D., and Ann Williams, Ph.D.

contrapuntal use of these two approaches and, finally, by a discussion of the context and expansion of the marital treatment.

Before we deal with them separately, it seems appropriate to note some of the common threads between structural and strategic therapy. As a rule, both schools subscribe to the following ideas or methods of treatment:

View of the Couple or Family

1. People are seen as interacting within a context—both affecting it and being affected by it.
2. The family life cycle and developmental stage are important both in diagnosis and in defining therapy strategy.
3. Symptoms are both system-maintained and system maintaining.
4. The couple or family can change, allowing new behaviors to emerge, if the overall context is changed. Further, in order for individual change to occur, the interpersonal system itself must change. This would permit different aspects of such family members' (potential) "character" to come to the fore.

Therapy and the Therapist

1. Treatment is viewed pragmatically, with an eye toward what "works."
2. Emphasis is on the present rather than the past.
3. Repetitive behavioral sequences are to be changed.
4. While structural therapists may not be as symptom-focused as strategic therapists, both are much more symptom-oriented than psychodynamic therapists.
5. Process is emphasized much more than content. This includes interventions which are nonverbal and noncognitive—in a sense, "doing away with words." Such interventions derive from viewing the system from a "meta" level and recognizing that verbalizations per se by therapist or family are often not necessary for change.
6. The therapist should be active.
7. Diagnosis is obtained through intervention.
8. Therapeutic contracts are negotiated with clients revolving around the problem and the goals of change.
9. Interpretation is usually employed to "relabel" rather than to produce "insight."
10. Behavioral tasks are assigned.
11. Considerable effort may go into "joining" the couple positively and reducing apparent "guilt" or defensiveness. This is more than simply

"establishing rapport," as it is often done selectively and in regard to what the therapist deems is necessary for system change.

12. Therapy cannot usually progress from the initial dysfunctional stage to a "cure" stage without one or more intermediate stages which, on the surface, may appear dysfunctional also. For instance, a therapist may have to take sides with a spouse (thereby "unbalancing" the couple in an opposite way from which it entered treatment) in order to restabilize at a point of parity.

13. Therapy tends to be brief and often does not exceed six months.

It may be apparent that some of the above points are shared by other, more active marital therapies also, such as the behavioral and "communications-training" approaches. However, many of them are distinctive of structural and strategic therapy.

STRUCTURAL THERAPY

The literature on structural therapy has been covered in at least two reviews (Aponte and Van Deusen, 1981; Stanton, 1980), and the principles and techniques appear in two books (Minuchin, 1974; Minuchin, Rosman and Baker, 1978). However, although Minuchin (1974) presents an interview with a "normal" couple, and Heard (1978) describes a case in which marital treatment evolved from a presenting problem with a child, Gurman (1979) notes that there has been very little writing on structural approaches to treatment of the marital subsystem "in isolation"; most of the publications to date on this approach have not provided much in the way of guidelines to marital treatment. Gurman also suggests this is probably due to the historical development of structural therapy as primarily two-generational in its clinical emphasis. It might appear at first glance that the structural approach is faced with the dilemma of not being able to apply one of its hallmarks—i.e. its emphasis on the boundary between generations—when the problem is presented as existing within one generation, that of the spouse system. However, this notion can be misleading, as structurally oriented clinicians commonly do treat couples, whether the initial problem concerns an offspring or not.

Basic Aspects of Structural Therapy

In this therapy the focus is less on theory of change than on theory of family (Stanton, 1980). The model is not particularly complex, theoretically. The most primary concept is that of *proximity and distance*, whether between individuals, such as two spouses, or groups of individuals (subsystems) within a family. One way of defining such proximity/distance is through the concept of *boundaries*, which are the rules that define "who participates and how" in the family (Minuchin, 1974, p. 53). Proximity/distance might be determined by examining a couple's respective "turfs," such as where one member has primary influence (e.g., concerning budgets, children) compared to the other member. The boundaries can also denote coalitions, such as when one or all children are united with one parent against the other or where one or more of the spouses' parents are involved in coalition(s) against the other spouse.

A central concept in structural therapy is the continuum of *enmeshment-disengagement*. These are the extremes of proximity/distance or boundary functioning within families or within family subsystems (with most families or subsystems falling between the two poles). The enmeshed family or family subsystem is overly tight, and members are allowed little or no autonomy. If the integrity or "closeness" of the system is threatened, the enmeshed couple often responds rapidly and defensively. Further, behavior change or reaction to stress in one spouse greatly affects the other and may reverberate throughout the system. The heightened sense of belonging in enmeshed systems or subsystems comes at the cost of individual independence (Minuchin, 1974).

In disengaged couples and families, members may function autonomously, but there is little loyalty and a distorted sense of independence. They cannot request support when needed and lack a capacity for interdependence. In such families, members tend to operate within their own, separate little domains relative to the spouse or rest of the family. Stresses in one member do not readily affect the others (Minuchin, 1974). In general, then, the thrust of structural therapy is toward differentiating enmeshed members and increasing the involvement of couples who are disengaged.

Structural Techniques

It is important to note that a structural aspect of treatment applies to therapies and therapists of all persuasions, as follows: *any therapeutic intervention made by any therapist necessarily includes a structural component.* For example, by choosing to talk to or interact with one member of a couple or the other, or with both spouses together, the therapist makes a structural decision, whether or not he is aware of it. Not to do so would mean that the therapist interacts at random with the participants, and while some therapists may seem to behave randomly at times, it is perhaps fairest to give them credit for doing so intentionally. Nonetheless, by focusing his attention on, or making a statement about, a given member (or subsystem) at a particular point, he is, by nature of the power and status vested in him as a therapist, elevating that person and separating him from the other(s). He shares his power by his attention, so that, as Haley (1976) states, "a comment by the therapist is not merely a comment but also a coalition with one spouse in relation to the other or with the unit against a larger group" (p. 160). The therapist cannot (and probably should not) avoid doing this in most marital treatment contexts, so the important point is whether he does it with some plan in mind and remains consistent with his plan. In other words, does his (structural) intervention lead him toward change that is consonant with his goals?

Ignoring the above notion can be disasterous to treatment. In marital therapy it commonly crops up when a therapist is contacted by one spouse about his/her own problems or about problems with the other spouse. If the therapist ignores the structural context which includes both spouses (and any others who may be involved with the problem), he may get trapped into becoming overly empathic with the complainant spouse. He may mistakenly accept the complaints at face value without making contact with the other, absent member so as to (a) hear that other person's "side," (b) observe the interaction and (c) determine the balances between the two members. He thus establishes a coalition with the complainant—a kind of "side-taking"— which he might not otherwise have done if he had first seen the couple together. This error in procedure or strategy may partly underlie the conclusion, drawn by Gurman and Kniskern (1978) from the marital therapy outcome literature, that individual therapy for marital problems is significantly less effective than conjoint or conjoint-group marital approaches.

Treatment goals. Minuchin (1974) defines the goal of structural therapy as inducing a "more adequate family organization" of the sort which will maximize growth potential in each of its members. The thrust of the therapy is toward "restructuring" the system, such as establishing or loosening boundaries, as appropriate, for a given couple. Consequently, there is less emphasis (compared with behavioral and strategic approaches) on directly correcting the "problem" or symptom, per se. Instead, problems are seen to result from a rigid, dysfunctional structure, and their functionality or usefulness will disappear with system transformation. With an enmeshed couple which demonstrates overinvolvement in each other's duties, daily affairs, individual friendships, etc., boundaries must be established. A disengaged couple would dictate the opposite approach, often requiring more proximity, mutual activities and appropriate nurturance. Again, the idea is to alter and derigidify the structure, thus promoting a context which allows more complexity to emerge. Symptom elimination, then, becomes a "spinoff" of structural change.

Diagnosis. In structural therapy the tendency is often to move in fast to break up dysfunctional patterns. The diagnostic process involves joining and knowing a couple or family—accepting and learning its style in a sort of blending experience. The therapist accommodates and adapts, thus gaining a subjective knowledge of the transactional patterns. From there he can probe for flexibility and change, with an eye toward transforming the system. He may (temporarily) join one spouse in order to strengthen that person (e.g., getting a browbeaten woman to speak up to her husband by asserting that "your wife has some important things to say"). Reactions to such restructuring help to give the therapist a more complete picture. Throughout he is trying to stay both within and without the system. He accommodates but retains enough independence both to resist the couple's pull and to challenge it at various points. His diagnosis will less likely be a single term than a sentence which implies a direction for treatment, e.g., "the husband's sloppiness provides a vehicle for disengagement; it furnishes the wife with a job and keeps her busy, while allowing the husband to spend an excessive amount of time in his work activities." Such diagnoses are rarely static, but are revised as the couple responds to interventions and systemic changes.

Interventions. Structural therapists think to a great extent in visual, spacial terms. Conceptualizing a treatment plan usually involves a sort of map, with symbols for diffuse, clear and rigid boundaries, affiliations, overinvolvement, conflict, coalitions and detouring. While a given map depicts only a momentary status of a system, it can help the therapist to diagnose and also define what interventions are to be made. A typical sequence of maps would show at least three stages: present status, status expected after first structural intervention and final status for the treatment or for a particular session. A therapist may enter a session with such a schema in mind.

The therapist's plan is gauged against his knowledge of what is "normal" for a couple or family at a given stage in its development. For example, his interventional format would probably differ for a newly married couple compared with an "empty-nest" marriage or a recently retired marital pair. His aim is to help the couple establish a developmentally appropriate structure, with due consideration, of course, for their socioeconomic, cultural, ethnic and religious context.

More emphasis is placed on process than content in structural therapy. Patterns such as "who speaks to whom," and how often, are important to identify, despite the content of the message. These patterns give clues as to proximity and distance. Using them, the therapist can then apply various nonverbal techniques, with the particular intent of *establishing boundaries.* Such techniques could include separating a couple by chair placement, seating oneself between an intrusive spouse and another family dyad, asking a spouse to watch from an observation room, etc. Boundaries can also be made more permeable by getting disengaged members or subsystems to relate differently. The therapist might ask a member to "see if you can get your husband to talk to you." If it doesn't work, the therapist could press again with, "The way you are going about it isn't working. Can you try a different way, a way so that he might be able to hear you better?" The point here is that the content of the dyadic communication is less important than the process whereby disengaged entities are reengaged, consequently altering the structure of the couple or family at that point.

A crucial aspect of structural therapy is that the desired interactional change must take place *within the actual session*, rather than depending (alone) on its occurrence when the participants return home. In other words, the therapist consciously tries to revise relationships during the session, while the couple is sitting in the room (Hoffman, 1976). In the same vein, the therapist might, for instance, want to make a marital battle "live" again by reenacting it rather than talking about it. These features of interpersonal "enactment" and "reenactment" distinguish structural therapy from most other marital therapies, such as the behavioral and strategic types.

Structural therapists for the most part deal with those members of a family who live within a household or have regular contact with the immediate family. Rarely, for instance, are spouses' parents brought to treatment if they live some distance away or are not in touch. The general idea is to involve in treatment those interpersonal systems which have regular or daily impact on the problem. This might even include an employer if the problem centers around the work situation of one of the spouses.

Some other aspects of the interventional process are the following:

1. Most structural therapists, particularly Minuchin, will refuse to let a spouse talk *about* the other spouse in a session. They do not like people to speak for or about others in a way that squelches individuality.

2. Minuchin (1974) notes that people will change for three reasons. First, their perception of reality has been challenged. Second, alternative possibilities are presented which make sense to them. Third, once alternative transactional patterns have been tried out, new relationships appear which themselves become self-reinforcing.

3. It should be understood that the structural therapist is not trying to wrench spouses apart and make each stand emotionally naked and alone. The whole idea of restructuring is to shift supports around, recognizing that people will not move to the unknown in a situation of danger. The healing potential of the relationship is assumed, and supports are provided to facilitate movement (Minuchin, 1974).

4. The usual preference in this approach is to bring a couple to a level of

"health" or "complexity" and then stand ready to be called in the future, if necessary. Such a model is seen to combine the advantages of short- and long-term therapy.

STRATEGIC THERAPY

Haley (1973) has defined strategic therapy as that in which the clinician initiates what happens during treatment and designs a particular approach for each problem. Strategic therapists take responsibility for directly influencing people. They want to at least temporarily enhance their influence over the interpersonal system at hand in order to bring about beneficial change. In fact, they are not as concerned about family theory as they are with the theory and means for inducing change.

A number of people and groups are considered representative of this school, such as Milton Erickson, Jay Haley, the Mental Research Institute (MRI) group (including Don Jackson, John Weakland, Paul Watzlawick, Richard Fisch, Arthur Bodin and Carlos Sluzki), Gerald Zuk, the Center for Family Study group in Milan, (including Mara Palazzoli-Selvini, Luigi Boscolo, Gianfranco Cecchin and Giuliana Prata), Lynn Hoffman, Richard Rabkin, Peggy Papp and others. Gregory Bateson should be most accurately deemed the theoretical "father" of strategic therapy, while most of the clinical techniques derive from the original work of Erickson. These therapists do not operate in exactly the same way. Rather than devote inordinate space to their individual contributions, styles and differences, the approach here will be more superficial—presenting the principles and practices which apply to most of them. The reader interested in greater detail is referred to their various published works or to several synopses which have emerged in the literature (Madanes and Haley, 1977; Stanton, 1980, 1981a; Steinglass, 1978).

Basic Aspects of Strategic Therapy

Strategic therapists see symptoms as the resultants or concomitants of misguided attempts at changing an existing difficulty (Watzlawick, Weakland and Fisch, 1974). However, such symptoms usually succeed only in making things worse—as, for example, in the case of the depressed person whose spouse frantically tries and tries to cheer him up, making him only more and more depressed. Thus the attempt to alleviate the problem actually exacerbates it. Further, individual problems are considered manifestations of disturbances in the marriage or family. A symptom is regarded as a communicative act, with message qualities, which serves as a sort of contract between two or more members and has a function within the interpersonal network. It is a label for a *sequence of behaviors* within a social organization (Haley, 1976). A symptom usually appears when a person is "in an impossible situation and is trying to break out of it" (Haley, 1973, p. 44). He is locked into a sequence or pattern with his significant other(s) and cannot see a way to alter it through nonsymptomatic means. The symptom is thus a homeostatic mechanism regulating marital or family transactions (Jackson, 1957, 1965).

From the above, the marital pair can be viewed, then, as an interpersonal system which is in many ways analogous to other cybernetic systems (Hoffman, 1971). It is of the nonlinear type (e.g., the relationship between A and B is cyclic rather than A causing B), with complex interlocking feedback mechanisms and patterns of behavior that repeat themselves in sequence. If one observes a given couple long enough, such sequences can be observed and particular phases within a sequence can even be predicted before they occur.

Haley (1973) and Erickson, endorsed by Weakland, Fisch, Watzlawick and Bodin (1974), have stressed the importance of the family developmental process as a framework for explaining symptomatology. In fact, these therapists were among the first to focus on the relevance of this process to human dysfunction and treatment. Within such a framework, dysfunctional couples can be seen to develop problems because they are not able to adjust to transitions which occur within the family life cycle. They become "stuck" at a particular point. As examples, Haley (1973) cites the difficulty that families of schizophrenic young people have in allowing them to leave home, while Stanton et al. (1978) note this and a related pattern revolving around inability of parents to allow an offspring to maintain a viable marriage in families of drug addicts. The "problem," then, is not the "identified" patient but rather the crisis stage the couple has entered. It thus might make more sense to talk of couples in relation to where they are developmentally than to try to define a marital typology or symptomatology (Haley, 1971).

Strategic Techniques

A basic tenet of strategic therapy is that therapeutic change comes about through the "interactional processes set off when a therapist intervenes actively and directively in particular ways" in a family or marital system (Haley, 1971, p. 7). The therapist works to substitute new behavior patterns or sequences for the vicious, positive feedback circles already existing (Weakland et al., 1974). In other words, his goal is to change the dysfunctional *sequence* of behaviors shown by the marital couple appearing for treatment.

Strategic therapists are very wary of getting caught in overt power struggles. Thus they will employ skill and maneuvering to get covert control, but do so in the service of the situation as defined by the couple. They tend to "go with" resistance offered by clients and avoid power struggles whenever possible—especially in initial sessions. They find it wisest to travel a path of least resistance, accepting what the marital partners offer, since that is what they are ready to work on, and then may use implicit or indirect ways of turning the couple's investment to positive use (Weakland et al., 1974). Further, the problem to be changed must be put in solvable form. It should be something that can be objectively agreed upon—e.g., counted, observed or measured—so that one can assess if it has actually been influenced.

Just as dynamic therapy is largely based upon interpretations, the main therapeutic tools of strategic therapy are tasks and directives. *This emphasis on directives is the cornerstone of the strategic approach.* Much of the discussion that takes place early in a session is aimed at providing information necessary for the therapist to arrive at a directive or task. Subsequent interaction might then center either on how to carry the directive out or on actually performing the task in the session. Haley (1976) notes that the best task is "one that uses the presenting problem to make a structural change" in the couple or family; for instance, by prescribing to a couple who compete over the running of a family business (while at the same time agreeing that the husband should be in charge) that the wife "see to it" that her husband arrives at the business well before she does so that he can get it running properly at the start of each day (Erickson, in Haley, 1973). In such a case the wife's cooperation is obtained toward her "slacking off" in her involvement with the husband's duties, thus giving him greater license while also permitting her more time to complete activities which she desires to do at home in the morning. Tasks such as this are usually designed to be carried out between sessions as a means of using time more fully and generalizing what transpires in the session to the outside world.

Like behavioral therapists, and unlike most structural therapists, strategic therapists tend to be quite symptom-focused. They assume that elimination or reduction of the symptom results from system change, but their therapeutic operations include considerable symptom monitoring. They differ from behavioral therapists in being much more indirect and in placing a great deal more emphasis on chains or sequences of behavior rather than on reinforcement per se.

Their emphasis on the therapist's responsibility for change also differentiates strategic therapists from most other marital therapists. Of course they want to enlist the couple's cooperation in the treatment process, but they do not view treatment as requiring the kind of "joint collaborative effort" subscribed to by some others. Again, the preferred practice is to enter (or at least emerge initially from) treatment with a plan designed for the particular problem at hand.

Paradoxical intervention. Perhaps more than any of their other techniques, strategic therapists have been identified with the use of paradoxical interventions. Such techniques have been described by a number of writers (Erickson, in Haley, 1967, 1973; Frankl, 1960; Haley, 1963, 1976; L'Abate and Weeks, 1978; Watzlawick, Beavin and Jackson, 1967; Watzlawick et al., 1974; Weakland et al., 1974) and recently reviewed by Soper and L'Abate (1977). Watzlawick et al. (1967) define paradox as a "contradiction that follows correct deduction from consistent premises" (p. 188). In a therapeutic context, Hare-Mustin (1976) has described paradoxical interventions as "those which appear absurd because they exhibit an apparently contradictory nature, such as requiring clients to do what in fact they have been doing, rather than requiring that they change, which is what everyone else is demanding." The use of paradoxical intervention is partly based on the assumption that there is great resistance to change within a couple (or family) and that a therapist entering their context is put under considerable pressure to adopt their ways of interacting and communicating. Succumbing to this pull will render the therapist ineffective. In addition, the couple resists the therapist's efforts to make them change. If, however, the therapist tells them to do what they are already doing, they are in a bind. If they follow his instructions and continue the prescribed behavior, they are doing his bidding and, therefore, giving him undue power; he gains control by making the symptom occur at his direction. If they resist the paradoxical instruction, and therefore the therapist, they are moving toward "improvement" (and in the long run also doing his bidding). The confusion which occurs as to how to resist leads to new patterns and perceptions and thus to change—or at the very least it can help to achieve a certain amount of detachment from the disturbing behavior (Hare-Mustin, 1976). In this way a directive which appears on the surface to be in opposition to the goals being sought actually serves to move toward them. It is often couched to the couple in terms of "getting control" of the symptom—e.g., "If you can turn this symptom on when you try, you will be able to control it instead of it controlling you." The paradoxical directive can be given to both spouses, the whole family, or to certain members.

If a client improves too rapidly following a directive, or the therapist has other reasons to expect symptom recurrence, he might prescribe a relapse. This could also be justified as a means for the client's "maintaining control," but Erickson often introduces a nostalgic flavor to such a directive. He might say to the client, "I want you to go back and feel as badly as you did when you first came in with the problem, because I want you to see if there is anything from that time that you wish to recover and salvage" (Erickson, in

Haley, 1973, p. 31). Such moves take into account the benefits that usually accrue from symptoms and also serve to anticipate that improvement may increase apprehension about change; this danger is thus met paradoxically through "redefining any relapse that might occur as a step forward rather than backward" (Weakland et al., 1974, p. 160).

Haley (1976) has outlined eight stages in undertaking a paradoxical intervention: (1) there is a client-therapist relationship, defined as one to bring about change, (2) there is a clearly defined problem, (3) there is a clearly defined goal(s), (4) the therapist offers a plan, usually with rationale, (5) the therapist gracefully disqualifies the current authority on the problem, e.g., spouse or a parent, (6) a paradoxical directive is given, (7) the response is observed and the therapist continues to encourage the (usual) behavior— no "rebellious improvement" is allowed, (8) the therapist avoids taking credit for any beneficial change that occurs, such as symptom elimination, and may even display puzzlement over the improvement. Haley (1963) has stated that the basic rule is "to encourage the symptom in such a way that the patient cannot continue to utilize it" (p. 55). Sometimes this can be done by making the cure more troublesome than the symptom itself, such as by prescribing an increase in the frequency or intensity with which the symptom is to occur.

Recently, several attempts have been made to provide alternative explanations of the ways in which paradox works. Andolfi, Menghi, Nicoló and Saccu (1980) describe a sequential approach (summarized in Stanton, 1981b) based on the balance between the family and therapist as to the extent to which they display either homeostatic or "transformational" (ability to change) tendencies. In short, the therapist, by advocating more homeostatic behavior than the family (e.g., denying the IP's "craziness," warning against "moving too fast," etc.), secures a position of greater power and control as the family moves toward transformation in its efforts to unseat him; they have to change in order to resist him.

Stanton (1981a, 1981b) has proposed a mechanism of "compression" to explain paradox. Dysfunctional nuclear families are seen as vacillating, in cyclic form, between an overly close "undifferentiated" or "fusion" state, through a disintegrating or expansive state directed outward, to another fusion state with the family of origin. Upon imploding toward a point of near-fusion, a counterreaction occurs outward, away from fusion among spouses and toward fusion with the families of origin. This repetitive expansion and contraction are manifested by the behavioral sequences observed in couples and are especially obvious in marriages which are severely dysfunctional. The paradoxical intervention, by compressing the spouses toward fusion, accelerates the process and causes an explosive counterreaction. However, the therapist blocks the usual path of the reaction, diverting it in a new direction—one which requires different responses and an expanded repertoire. In this way a pattern is broken and transformation has occurred. Stanton proposes that such a model can be applied not only to paradox and positive interpretation but also to other therapeutic devices, such as "flooding," crisis induction, certain aspects of "provocative" therapy (Farrelly and Brandsma, 1974), etc.

Positive interpretation. The tendency of people who practice this treatment is to ascribe positive motives to clients. This is primarily because blaming, criticism and negative terms tend to mobilize resistance, as spouses muster their energies to disown the pejorative label. Such negative or depressive maneuvers can render the therapist impotent. Consequently, the therapist might, for example, relabel "hostile" behavior as "concerned interest" (Weakland et al., 1974) or perhaps as a desire to "get the best care possible" for the identified patient. This approach has a paradoxical flavor, as the couple finds that its efforts to fight are redefined (Haley, 1963). It is also a form of reframing (Soper and L'Abate, 1977). Another facet of this tack is that simply defining problems as interactional or marital stumbling blocks serves to have them viewed as *shared* rather than loading the blame entirely on one member—this is a "we're all in this together" phenomenon (Weakland, 1976).

Certain strategic groups have taken positive interpretation beyond the application of a simple nonblaming stance or the avoidance of pejoratives alone, however. They have adopted the position that all symptoms are highly adaptive for the couple or family, in a sense holding that "everything that everybody does is for good reason and is understandable." This notion developed somewhat independently within several quarters. Erickson and Haley, of course, had been glancing this way for some time in their emphasis on nonblaming, as had the MRI group, Minuchin, L'Abate (1975) and others. Ivan Boszormenyi-Nagy and Geraldine Spark (1973), nonstrategic therapists who eschew "techniques," have used positive interpretation indirectly for a number of years by noting to clients that their symptoms are adaptive for the family group across generations; members are thus, in a sense, fulfilling a script and are absolved of blame. Stanton and associates, although unaware at the time of the emphasis on such an approach by strategic therapists, found in working with (tremendously defensive) addict families that for treatment to proceed, they needed to attribute noble motivations to even the most "destructive" behaviors shown by these families (cf., Stanton, 1977). They have termed this technique *ascribing noble intention* (Stanton and Todd, 1979; Stanton, Todd et al., 1981). While influenced by Boszormenyi-Nagy, their approach differs from his in that they took this tack intentionally, with full cognizance of the effect desired.

A group which has been particularly creative in applying what they term *positive connotation* has been that of Palazzoli-Selvini and associates in Milan. "Positive connotation" is one of their trademarks. They use it to gain access to the family system, generally preferring to positively address the homeostatic tendency of the family system rather than its individual members. For instance, they might praise a wife for being symptomatic and sacrificing herself so that her husband would not be at the bottom of the totem pole after losing his job. Or they might express appreciation to a husband for keeping tight rein on the family purse strings so his wife does not have to suffer the fear of going outside to go shopping. Palazzoli-Selvini et al. (1974) note that through positive connotation, "We implicitly declare ourselves as allies of the family's striving for homeostasis, and we do this at the moment that the family feels it is most threatened. By thus strengthening the homeostatic tendency, we gain influence over the ability to change that is inherent in every living system" (p. 441). In other words, total acceptance of the marital or family system by the therapists enables them to be accepted in the family game—a necessary step toward changing the game through paradox (Palazzoli-Selvini et al., 1978).

Among other things, what positive interpretation seems to do is to address, in a respectful way, the resistance and ambivalence which the couple feels toward change. The therapist recognizes and acknowledges the functional and desirable aspects of the symptom. Thomas Todd* notes that clients who have previously engaged in other forms of therapy often feel that the therapist who uses this approach is the first person they have met who really "understands" them and (what they perceive as) the magnitude of their struggle.

THE INTERPLAY BETWEEN STRUCTURAL AND STRATEGIC APPROACHES

Within the systems or communication approach presented here it is possible to apply either a structural or a strategic approach separately, or to use the two both conjointly and contrapuntally.

General Rule 1

The first general rule being proposed is to *initially deal with a couple through a primarily structural approach*—joining, accommodating, testing boundaries, restructuring, unbalancing, increasing intensity, etc. An example is given below.

Case A. A couple presented with the wife complaining of being "unhappy" and both spouses agreeing that "something seemed wrong" in their relation-

---

*Thomas C. Todd, personal communication, January 1979.

ship, but they were not sure what it was. Further exploration revealed that the husband kept extremely close tabs on the wife's activities, especially in the financial area. She had to justify every penny that she spent during the week, providing him with a rationale and accounting of expenditures so that he could be assured that nothing was wasted. She, of course, contributed by assuming a dependent stance and asking him often whether she should purchase this or that and how much she should pay, such as for a loaf of bread; some of these requests for guidance even *he* found trivial and excessive. Upon learning these facts, I commenced with coaxing, complimenting and pressuring the wife in order to get her to express her dissatisfaction with this arrangement. Eventually she was able to tell her husband that his requirements made her feel "like a child" and that she thought her judgment was good enough not to spend money on anything that was not necessary for the family. Following this outburst, which was not typical of her style and which took the husband aback, I turned to him. I praised him for his frugality and his close attention to matters which too many husbands tend to neglect. I told him, however, that I thought he was overworked, and that if things did not change, he might have to take a second job because his marriage would eventually land on the rocks and he would have support and perhaps alimony payments to make. This scared him and he asked what else was he supposed to do. I asked him how much "insurance" would he be willing to pay per week to possibly avoid such a turn of events. After thinking a minute, he estimated that "maybe twenty dollars" came to mind, although it was hard for him to gauge such a proposition accurately. I then asked if he felt fairly sure about paying ten dollars per week, and he did. I then asked him if he would agree to have his wife act as the insurance company—to pay her the money—and that I would explain further if he could go along with this. Since he was relieved at the prospect of only paying ten rather than twenty dollars, the second amount did not seem like much and he consented. He was then requested to take ten dollars from his wallet and give it to his wife as the "initial payment." He also agreed to make the second payment one week hence. I then turned to the wife and said I would like her to do two things. First, she should take the money and during the week spend it on anything she wanted for herself, preferably something totally frivolous or useless—the more wasteful the purchase, the better. In fact, she could even burn the money or tear it up if she wanted—"that would be super," I said. She was not to ask her husband's counsel in what to do with the money. Laughing slightly, she agreed to do this.

The second task I asked of her was that at least once during the week she should buy a small item without approaching her husband about it beforehand. I asked him what item this should be, and he suggested any grocery items less than a dollar or two were probably not worth being brought to his attention. I also asked him if he wanted to be told about this purchase on the day it happened, to wait until our next session or some other time. He said that being informed the day after the purchase was fine.

When they returned the next week the wife reported difficulty at first in deciding what to do with the ten dollars. She said she had thought about spending it on one of the kids, but eventually bought a phonograph record and a couple of posters that she had seen in a store several weeks before. The husband was pleased because during the week she had told him of at least three items (rather than just one) that she had not pestered him about. He was also relieved because her demeanor had changed and she "seemed a little happier—I even heard her humming on Tuesday." A more positive mood was reflected in both of them, so I did not assign new tasks but left them with a warning that the next week might be tougher than the past one had been.

In subsequent sessions such issues were dealt with as establishing a more equitable distribution of funds between the two people (according to their separate responsibilities), giving the husband a "rest" so that he did not have to do "all the work and worrying," etc.; these will not be covered here. Rather, this material is given to demonstrate the use of several principles common to structural therapy. While the nature of the directive, the warning to the couple about future difficulties, and several other facets of the treatment are also typical of strategic therapy, most of the work rests on a structural model. The intrusion (enmeshment) of the two partners into each others' space should be apparent, as certain of the boundaries were diffuse. The (ostensible) complementarity between them (the husband seemingly in a hierarchically greater, "one-up" and controlling position) also comes through. The therapy was aimed at (a) the therapist joining both members at various points, (b) elevating the wife (unbalancing) by having her confront her husband in the session (increasing intensity) and thus enacting the conflict, (c) devising and enacting tasks that drew firmer boundaries between them (wife having her own ten dollars, husband not being pestered by wife with unimportant financial matters) and (d) altering the previous sequence by pulling the husband out of the pattern of monitoring every penny and by preventing the wife, at least once, from soliciting her husband's opinion about what he saw as small and irritating matters. Couching the ten-dollar task in terms of buying something "frivolous" or "useless" is a different kind of unbalancing perhaps better termed *relative contrast* (Stanton, 1981b). It was done to alter her pattern of being overly dutiful by granting permission to go much farther in her frivolity than was her usual tendency: if she was given license to do something completely untoward, maybe she could actually do something just a little bit foolish, thereby gaining a modicum of freedom and independence. While there are elements in this example which correspond to techniques used by behavioral, cognitive and other kinds of therapists, it is important to note that the interventions were oriented less toward solving the problem than toward changing the structure and balance within the relationship.

General Rule 2

The second general rule is to *switch to a predominantly strategic approach when "structural" techniques either are not succeeding or are unlikely to succeed.* This might include the heavy use of positive interpretation, the introduction of paradoxical instructions and the use of distancing (discussed below). There are at least three situations which might dictate such a switch: (1) some sort of impasse is reached by the therapist in which resistance is so great that movement cannot easily be obtained with conventional structural techniques; (2) the therapist has prior knowledge about a case which leads him to believe that structural techniques, at least initially, will not succeed; (3) the therapist feels adrift and has lost his understanding of what is transpiring with the couple. These three situations will be dealt with separately below, with primary attention given to the first of them.

1. *Switching from a structural to a strategic approach.* In this kind of situation the therapist works within a structural framework and finds that "resistance" mounts progressively in the family or simply that no change is occurring. Of course this could be due to an inappropriate application of structural techniques or a misdiagnosis of the structural changes needed, but we will assume that the structural work has been competent up to this point. There are certain kinds of couples in which the somewhat confrontational structural approach only leads to escalation in defensiveness by the partners. The therapist finds himself beset by two people working overtime to bring him around to their respective points of view. A good example has been provided by Wellisch, Gay and McEntee (1970) in their work with couples in which one or both members were drug-addicted; the two clients competed constantly in attempting to triangulate the therapist against the other partner, thwarting therapist interventions at every turn. Another example is the "warring" couple, with the partners engaging in an ongoing battle involving matters both large and small. Any attempt by the therapist to suggest change (or certainly to attribute error) to a spouse or to the couple is met by massive counterattack; the therapist's confrontation, no matter how gentle, mobilizes all the couple's energy to resist him, thus minimizing the possibility that efforts can be rechanneled in the direction of positive change. A third situation where a switching of approach may be indicated is with couples in which an extremely strong homeostatic tendency is noted. The therapist makes structural interventions which seem accurate, but nothing happens—there is no "second-order" change (Watzlawick et al., 1974). Tasks are never followed or are distorted to disadvantage. The resistance is often covert and the therapist starts to sense defeat. This kind of pattern is not atypical in couples with a schizophrenic member or an addict, or in which one or both spouses display what historically has been termed a "personality disturbance." Often such couples are entwined with other

systems, commonly those of their parents, and therapeutic leverage is slight or nonexistent.

Encountering problems such as the above requires a change in tactics. When bumping up against these kinds of resistances, it may be helpful for the therapist to switch immediately to a (strategic) technique of profuse positive interpretation. He should take the tack that everything the couple does is wonderful, is based on noble intentions and probably should not be changed. He notes the benefits which the symptom provides for the spouses. He may then direct that they continue to do things as they have in the past, because change would result in the loss of some very helpful and functional attributes (much in the therapeutic manner of Andolfi et al., 1980, and Palazzoli-Selvini et al., 1978). Another related device is to use "compression" (Stanton, 1980b, 1980c) and push the couple toward each other. The case below gives an example of such a tactical change.

Case B. This couple had been seen for twelve sessions one year earlier; that treatment will be only briefly covered here. During the first therapy experience, in which they had been arguing frequently, two major themes had prevailed. One was a cultural and racial difference—he being raised in a black ghetto and she coming from a large Midwestern Jewish family. Work on this area revolved around (a) the husband learning new behavior in terms of an ability to be "gentle" with her—a style which he respected but which was dystonic with his early upbringing and experience, and (b) the wife becoming more inured to what she considered his aggressively provocative and confrontative style, which was different from what she had been used to. The second issue concerned child bearing. During their marriage she had had an abortion and one or two miscarriages. She complained of still feeling hurt because he had not supported her (with empathy and soft words) during the trauma of the last miscarriage. Since both of them were encroaching on each other's space in other areas and held unrealistic expectations for each other's contribution to the relationship, a major intervention was to reframe any future pregnancy so that it be treated as if she were to "go it alone." This "boundary" permitted her to expect less of her husband at such a time. Paradoxically, it also allowed him to help her as best he could, without resenting what he thought were unfair expectations of him related to her previously expressed "needs."

As noted, the couple called again for therapy one year later. The husband asked me for a single marital consultation session. The wife was now five or six months pregnant and, with apparently good medical supervision, seemed like she would complete a successful pregnancy. The husband complained that his wife was cutting him out of the pregnancy. She had done much reading on the topic, and when they were with friends or at a social gathering, he would start to discuss the pregnancy and she would cut in on him, spouting a lot of technical and medical information about pregnancies, babies, etc. I responded—as a way of testing them—that having a baby was a big step in their lives and maybe they were not ready for it, maybe this was not a good time. The way in which they protested and opposed me on this point indicated that perhaps they were indeed ready. Overall, my hypothesis was that while the husband had a profession and a certified area of expertise, the wife had not been working for several years and had not had an area in which she felt particular competence. The pregnancy and the baby had resolved this problem for her, except that she had overcompensated, becoming so expert and dominant on the topic that she was excluding her husband from satisfying the normal curiosity and activity of an expectant father; it was not so much that either of them expected him to do more for her, but rather that he wanted more information about the baby and the combination of his wife and the baby. An overly rigid boundary had formed between them around a developmentally normal process. I thus began by confirming in a number of ways the wife's expertise in the area of pregnancy and babies—stating that her husband could never equal her knowledge of such matters, that she had ways of knowing physically more about pregnancy (feeling the baby kick and turn, experiencing hormonal changes, etc.) then any man ever could, etc. The idea here was to unequivocally establish her superiority in this domain in hopes that if she knew she could be secure in her expertise she might be able to share the baby a little more with her husband—the boundary could be made more permeable. I made and embellished these and related points to both spouses until I was satisfied that they agreed with me (in this case, on what was obvious). Then I asked if she would allow him to feel the baby. She consented and I had him explore the baby through her abdomen, instructing him to ask whatever questions came to mind and instructing her to answer each question.

The affective tone was warm while they went through the above exercise, and after five or ten minutes I decided to try to cap it off by getting something for the wife. She had mentioned earlier that she would like to see more spontaneous affection from her husband, so I thought of extending the present tone to one more exercise. The husband did not seem adverse to showing affection, so I supported him by noting that he was probably "chomping at the bit" to be affectionate to his wife but simply had not had enough experience in doing this. He agreed that perhaps this was so. The task—to be done in the session—was for her to stand up and pretend to perform some task she might commonly be doing alone during a normal day; in this case it was standing by the sink washing dishes. I then took the husband outside the room and asked if he would go in to his wife and be affectionate to her in some new way while she played at doing the dishes. I told him to take only twenty or thirty seconds to do this and to call me in when he had finished. (My self-exclusion was in deference to his privacy and to a sense that it would be easier for this man to perform if I was absent. The short time period for the task was to prevent them from getting too close for too long, perhaps resulting in a negative rebound.) He summoned me after about half a minute, and when I entered they were giggling together. The warm tone had been maintained, at least for the moment, and the wife seemed pleased with the result.

At this point I started to move toward terminating the session. After a minute or two, however, they started to get into a mild argument. I had been concerned that they might rebound soon and had hoped to avoid it. I tried a bit of moderating to see if it was a minor issue amenable to quick resolution. They continued to pick at each other, as if to tell me that "the affection was nice, but we need this (fighting) too." Thus I changed strategy. I emphasized (paradoxically) that their fighting was much too important to be abandoned and that I was not advocating this: "I would never want to take that from you." I reframed their battles as a source of excitement which, like carnival rides or TV mystery shows, could be frightening and upsetting but still fun to experience. I instructed them to have at least one good fight a week—more if need be—to keep the "juices flowing." They were somewhat confused by this tack, but after a moment they seemed a bit relieved. They left the office in good spirits. No problems and less fighting were noted in our agreed-upon telephone follow-up one month later.

I consider this session a fairly clear example of the sequential use of what are commonly viewed as structural and strategic techniques. In most of the session emphasis was on the structural, with considerable joining, renegotiation of a boundary, establishment and maintenance of marital parity and, particularly important, enactment of the exercise within the session. At the end, when a homeostatic swing back began to occur, this was dealt with strategically—I became more homeostatic than the couple, concomitantly disengaging myself and uniting them against me. In order to resist me they had to fight a little less. This final, paradoxical move was introduced to (a) firm up earlier gains, (b) extricate myself from the fray and (c) set in motion a different sequence which included more "affectionate" elements and fewer antagonistic behaviors.

2. *Determining strategy from prior knowledge.* This is the second situation in which a switch in tactics may be indicated. Based on what is learned before ever seeing a given case, the therapist may decide to lean toward more strategic techniques. The most common example might be when one has pretherapy information that a family has a severely dysfunctional member, often one diagnosed as schizophrenic. Such couples or families have apparently not been as responsive to conventional structural therapy techniques (or for that matter to most other psychotherapies) as they have been to strategic modes. In such situations, the model applied by Andolfi et al. (1980) might be fitting. As described briefly before, these therapists tend to work paradoxically from the start with such cases. They constantly take a

position which is more homeostatic than that of the couple, at least in the early phases of treatment. Interestingly, as a couple progresses and its members start to behave more as separate people than as a system which only reacts massively and in concert, Andolfi et al. tend to move toward a more structural approach. It almost seems as if such severely disturbed families need to experience a strategic intervention first before they become individuated enough to respond to structural techniques.

A somewhat similar approach is used by Berenson (described in Stanton, 1981b) in dealing with alcoholic couples. Whereas he initially shies away from paradoxical instructions, from the outset of treatment he commonly employs directives. It is a planned approach, seen as progressing through identifiable stages, in which much reframing (but not "interpretation") is used. Berenson places much emphasis on being able to establish space between the partners, particularly in the early phase of therapy. He also works toward building more extensive external support systems for both spouses. Later on, in the second major phase, he moves to a variety of other techniques which are also consistent with a structural view.

3. *Confusion and loss of "understanding" by the therapist.* There come times in therapy when the therapist becomes befuddled, unsure of what is occurring with the couple and unclear as to where to go with treatment. At such times, Sluzki (1978) offers the following principle: "If you find yourself not understanding what is going on with the couple, *then* cease paying attention to content, and observe verbal patterns, sequences, gestures and postures, and/or observe your own emotions, attitudes or postures" (p. 389). He notes that such occurrences usually indicate that the therapist is being pulled by a fascination for content and has probably been "sucked in" by the marital system: he has allowed himself to be inducted by the couple and has lost control of his own behavior. He needs to get some distance. At this point, then, it behooves him to change his behavior. Sluzki notes that simply acknowledging his confusion—stating "I don't understand"—is one way of differentiating from the system. There are other ways, also, which have a more strategic flavor to them.

It is sometimes hard for a therapist to resist getting drawn into a couple's quarrels. He can easily slide toward working hard with them in an effort to "patch things up," serving as a kind of matchmaker or trying to pour oil on troubled waters. Too often this is a trap, as was seen in Case B (above). At such points the therapist may want to disengage almost entirely, leaving the couple, in a sense, alone—almost abandoning them momentarily, or at least bowing out of the battle. Carl Whitaker is particularly good at this. When he senses that a couple or family is both strongly resisting change and trying to leave him with the responsibility, he might counter with a calm withdrawing statement, such as "I can see . . . you've got a problem." When they agree and then ask what to do about it, such a therapist might say, "It's a tough one." If they pursue further, asking (or telling) him to help, he might respond with "I don't know what you should do" or "It beats me." This tactic is similar to one used by Palazzoli-Selvini et al. (1978), of declaring "total impotence" in a case. Such a retreat, in addition to differentiating the therapist, can have at least two effects. First, it shifts the responsibility for change back onto the couple; the intent is to bring them, in effect, to the conclusion, "Gee, if the therapist can't do anything about this, or is not competent to help, maybe we'll have to do it ourselves." Related to this, a second effect may be to unite the couple, possibly against the therapist, but nonetheless placing them in a position where they are no longer diverting their energies toward triangulating a third person; they must turn to each other and perhaps try to find a common ground for cooperation, problem-solving and change.

Stemming from the above, a third option might be not only to disengage but to "flip-flop" into praising the couples' behavior. The therapist draws upon his creative energy to come up with a noble rationale (positive interpretation) for their problem, much as was described earlier in Case B. The couple is left not only with a disengaged therapist but with an indirect and paradoxical message to keep on doing what they have been doing. When faced with such a dilemma, their capacity to change toward a different or more beneficial pattern is increased, even if they only do it out of recalcitrance.

EXPANDING THE THERAPEUTIC SYSTEM

A key contribution made by structural, strategic and some other family approaches has been to insist that marital therapy encompass not only the marital dyad but also the *context* within which it functions. The basic principle here is to address the interpersonal systems which may be affecting the marriage, in a sense to broaden one's scope. Thus it is desirable both from a diagnostic and an intervention standpoint to determine the *systems of import* which impinge upon the marriage. This is in contrast to the tendency prevalent in traditional marital counseling to confine treatment to the marital system in isolation, ignoring other important and often primary influences, such as extended family, children and spouses' parents. This difference in philosophy has a historical basis, since traditional marital counseling developed from treating adults, while the structural and strategic modes evolved more in relation to problems in children and unmarried young people. However, recent years have seen these two traditions moving closer together.

In line with treating the marriage within its context, Haley (1976) has emphasized the practice of viewing the marital system as a triad in which a couple's struggles "spill over" and a third entity (child, parent, sibling, lover, job, etc.) is drawn into the interaction, often as a means for detouring the conflict. Marriages rarely involve only two people and the therapist may need to incorporate other members, if for no other reason than to observe their effect on the marital interaction. Indeed, such others may actually serve to undercut the gains made in marital sessions, thereby reducing the therapist's effectiveness. Sluzki (1978) puts it thusly: "On occasion the couple may not be the critical unit of analysis, as it may not include all the protagonists of the interpersonal drama. It is not an infrequent observation that, when treatment of a couple fails to show progress, a qualitative leap takes place when the couples' offspring—or her mother, or his sister, or any other relative—is included in the session. The effect is often the unveiling of issues that were up-to-then mystified, showing other sides of conflicts or triggering confrontations that appeared dormant until then" (p. 391). In addition, expansion of what Minuchin (1974) calls the "therapeutic system," as appropriate, is in line with the notion of effecting total system (rather than individual) change—considered a necessary condition of durable change. Of course, the sheer increase in numbers which occurs with the addition of these other family members is itself no guarantee of success, since change is more contingent on the therapist's interventions than on simple system inclusiveness. The remainder of this chapter will deal with the inclusion of two particular subsystems in the marital therapy, those of the offspring and of the parents.

Involving Children

At first glance it might not make much sense to involve a couples' children in their marital treatment. It would seem to be an excessive and unnecessary complication—out of line with "where it's at." Of course, with treatment centered around a child as the presenting problem, the therapy inextricably either involves working indirectly with the marital problem or, in some cases (e.g. Heard, 1978), evolves toward couple therapy. Here, however, we are concerned with treatment which revolves around the marital relationship, at least at the outset.

There are at least two situations in which offspring should be brought into marital therapy, although both are in a sense different sides of the same coin when viewed from a systems perspective. The first is when either or both parents break ranks and rope one or more of their children into the fray. Sometimes the therapist has served as a conflict-detourer between the partners, and as he extricates himself or moves toward termination, the couple triangulates someone else. As Haley (1976) posits, "One can note that the therapist replaces the child with the couple and thus stabilizes the dyad.

Then the problem becomes one of how the therapist can exit without the couple unstabilizing and without bringing in the child" (p. 154). Whether or not the child was an integral part of the original presenting (marital) problem, he is now, and this turn of events indicates that true structural or system change has not taken place. The therapist's work is thus cut out for him.

The second situation that prompts including offspring in therapy is when they have been directly involved in the problem from the start—i.e. their importance is apparent and cannot be discounted—and the system of import is one encompassing both parents and children. In this situation, strides made in sessions with the spouses can be neutralized upon return home. Such events are particularly likely when older children are living with their parents. The intergenerational coalitions which existed prior to treatment, while perhaps weakened, are still there. The offspring, not being involved in changes which take place in the therapist's office, do not feel party to what has happened. They thus can put considerable pressure on the parents to maintain homeostasis by amplifying their own actions, causing the parents greater difficulty, exaggerating their sidetaking, etc. Faced with this problem, the therapist is well advised to enlarge his scope and either (a) include the offspring or (b) work intensively with the parents toward anticipating their kids' next actions, planning what to do about them and in general determining how to regain control of their household. Whatever road he chooses, however, the therapist will have to think in terms of hierarchy and general family structure, directing his efforts toward family restructuring (e.g., breaking up coalitions) and changing the family's repetitive, predictable sequences.

Involving Parents

Including parents of a marital couple in treatment has been perhaps practiced less by structural therapists than by certain strategic therapists, such as Erickson and Haley, who have spent more of their professional time dealing with problems in adult populations. Structural therapists may have been hampered by their preference for dealing with members of a system who are living in the same household. It should be emphasized, however, that this is an operational shortcoming rather than a theoretical one, since structural theory, as defined by Minuchin (1974), would in no way preclude this option. In fact, recent years have seen an increasing interest by structural therapists in the inclusion of spouses' parents in treatment (e.g., Stanton and Todd, 1979).

The most common situation dictating parental involvement in the therapy is when there is enmeshment between one or both spouses and their respective families of origin. Typically this emerges in patterns of everyday life. For instance, parents may foist money or large gifts on the spouses, serving to limit their autonomy as individuals and as a couple. Or the parents become involved in issues pertaining to the grandchildren, offering intrusive and unwanted child-rearing instructions or making it clear that they want to handle all the baby-sitting duties, perhaps becoming "indispensible" in this role. Sometimes the couple enters conflict over responsibilities to parents versus other social activities, such as when one spouse refuses to go anywhere but to the parents' home on Friday nights. Of course, such patterns are not unidirectional, since they would not occur without collusion on the part of one or both spouse(s); they are systemic, nonlinear phenomena involving all members within both generations. Nonetheless, when issues of enmeshment with the family of origin arise, the therapist is usually well advised to at least temporarily include parents in the treatment process.

Permission to marry. One always has to ask, when confronted with a marital problem, what was its genesis and what is maintaining it. In contrast, perhaps, with most of the present thinking in the structural and strategic camps, and certainly in contrast with traditional marital counseling, it is my experience that roughly *80 percent of marriages that fail do so because one or both spouses have not had permission to succeed in the marriage.* Usually this lack of permission extends from parents. While there may be other justifications for marital difficulty—such as might arise with racial, ethnic or religious differences—I would posit that such espoused differences pale in relation to parental disapproval per se. (A similar point has been made by Boszormenyi-Nagy and Spark, 1973.) Such disapproval can loom like a malevolent specter over a marriage. It may occur because one of the partners is instrumental in keeping his or her parents' marriage together, because a parent is undergoing bereavement and is giving the message that "I need you more than your spouse" to the partner, or for other reasons frequently tied into critical points in the family and parental life cycle. The disapproval is a way of not letting go of the son or daughter—they exert a pull on him/her— often because they feel their own needs are greater. It can be conveyed in subtle ways, such as brushing the spouse off over the phone, criticizing the spouse, or even siding with the spouse against the offspring with statements such as "I don't blame you for getting mad at [our daughter]; she doesn't deserve good treatment." This is an insidious message which can serve to undercut the stability of the offspring's marriage; while ostensibly joining with the son or daughter-in-law, the parent-in-law is also giving the message both that the marriage has good reason not to work and that it should not work. Another way of withholding permission for the marriage is to say nothing negative but to (usually unconsciously) allow a cataclysmic event to occur. In one case known to the author, a father expressed "approval" of the marriage, gave his daughter away at her wedding and then suffered a heart attack the next day.

Sometimes the spouse whose marriage is not approved can be "freed up" through incidental means. For instance, I have seen marriages flourish after the death of one of the spouses' parents. In other cases, a spouse or couple may "buy" a degree of freedom through the transfer of a newborn or other child to the parent(s) to raise. The marital partner thus substitutes another person for himself in his parents' relationship. If this alternative is acceptable, the child becomes a member of the key triad and the spouse is released to his partner and family of procreation (Boszormenyi-Nagy and Spark, 1973; Stanton et al., 1978).

Death-bed instructions. Another phenomenon related to the permission-to-marry dilemma which occasionally occurs (and which is rarely acknowledged by structural and strategic therapists, except perhaps Erickson) is the "death-bed instruction." The partner is given a directive by a dying parent (or other significant person, such as a spouse) not to marry or to watch over the remaining parent until that parent dies. Such instructions can be extremely powerful. The surviving offspring or spouse is put in an untenable conflict between opposing loyalties. A common option under these conditions may be for the constrained spouse not to leave the marital partner but to have a tentative, at best marginally successful, marriage, thereby partially fulfilling the requirements of both opposing forces.

Death-bed instructions are frequently (and often inappropriately) viewed as noble in present-day society. The mass media reflect this. An example comes from the television program *Quincy*, which deals with the adventures of a medical examiner who is also a bachelor. In one episode, pressure is put on Quincy by his girlfriend to get married. Quincy cares for the woman, so he buys her a ring and sets a date for the wedding. Then he starts to reminisce about his former wife, who died from a tumor while they were married. During their marriage his wife wanted children, but Quincy was opposed to this because he was so devoted to his career that he did not want to dilute his energies and affections. When his wife became hospitalized and was dying, Quincy felt great guilt, first, because he did not agree to her request for children—lamenting to a friend that "I've denied her her immortality"—and, second, because in his overcommitment to his profession he had neglected their marriage. He also felt bad because in his neglect he had not spotted various early symptoms and other changes in her behavior which were diagnostic of her condition. Just before she died the couple had a moment alone. Quincy's wife took the opportunity to tell him, in what came across as a half-kidding but mostly serious injunction, not to, in effect, "do this to some other woman." The ostensible intent of her message was to save some poor woman the troubles she herself had faced by letting Quincy know that he could not maintain a viable marriage. The *effect* of the message, in its denial that Quincy might one day be able to marry successfully, was to practically insure that he would never remarry, i.e. that no other woman would ever get him. It hamstrung him in his future relationships, and Quincy, after completing his reminiscence, called off the relationship with his present-day fiancée. This example, then, demonstrates the popular tendency to attend to the content of such instructions and ignore their results or consequences. In this (fictional) case the results were unfortunate for the survivor, Quincy, and it is doubtful whether either the producers or most viewers picked up the discrepancy.*

Typical Syndromes. The refusal of parental permission for an offspring's marriage can occur in many different kinds of cases and situations. However, there are at least three clinical conditions where it seems to be particularly pervasive and potent—where the requirements and overinvolvement of parents are especially common. While the patterns are often similar among them, three such (usually severely dysfunctional) conditions are presented below.

Psychosis. Haley (1976) has stated that "an individual is more disturbed in direct proportion to the number of malfunctioning hierarchies in which he is embedded" (p. 117). While it is not common for a psychotic (adult) spouse to be overly bound by both his parents and grandparents, it is my experience that such overinvolvement with parents alone is quite usual. Families in schizophrenic transaction typically show clinging by parents to offspring and vice versa, even in cases where the offspring has taken the individuating step of getting married (Haley, 1980).

Alcoholism. While some male alcoholics become "cut off" from their families of origin in the sense that Bowen (1978) uses the term, it is also my experience that many (perhaps the majority) of them, even if married and with children, are in close contact with their parents, especially mother. Frequently the wife of such a man may complain about a pattern in which her husband comes home drunk late at night on weeknights—so that she does not see him—and then on weekends goes over to his mother's house to perform chores or repairs, so that she does not see him again. As discussed below, the drinking can serve a function of keeping distance from the spouse and thereby staying loyal to the parent(s). In one case, the husband was no longer drinking but would change his behavior when his mother telephoned him. The pattern was common and became predictable, as follows: The mother would call and her son (the husband) would answer or come to the

---

*The similarity between this case and one presented by Watzlawick et al. (1967, pp. 252–253) is striking. The point in the present chapter is not that such death-bed instructions are immutable, but that, as in the Watzlawick et al. case, they must be dealt with if they are relevant to the problem.

phone. As soon as he began talking to her he assumed a demeanor of intoxication, slurring his speech, mumbling, hiccuping, etc. Soon the mother would ask to speak to his wife. When the wife got on the phone, the mother would berate her for not taking proper care of her son. Meanwhile the husband, sober as a judge, would go about his business. This is a nice example of how a triangulated person was able to resolve the opposing loyalties between parent and spouse.

Drug addiction. A pattern somewhat similar, although generally more intense, than that above has been observed in our work with married drug addicts (Stanton et al., 1978). We noted how events in the marital system of these people, while symptom-maintaining in themselves, were also being modulated by the addicts' relation to the parental system. To quote:

> If the addict has not "checked in" at the home recently or the parents have some other reason to fear they are "losing" him, a crisis may occur in their home—often a fight between them—and he will be alerted to it. At this point, he is liable to start a fight with his wife—a move which serves two purposes. It shows the parents that they have not lost him to marital bliss, and it gives him an excuse to return home to help, since he has "no place else to go." He will usually succeed in diverting attention from the problem in the parental home and once again function to reduce conflicts between adults.
>
> At other times the precipitating event(s) will be less obvious and he and his wife will fall into a cycle of periodic altercations. Their temporal regularity may seem almost servo-controlled. [In this case, "servo-controlled" refers to an automatic return to a prior behavioral state, once a certain limit (i.e., the end of a time period) is reached.] These appear to be maintenance cycles. They may not result in his moving out, but instead he will show up with some regularity at his parents' home to complain about connubial problems. He seems to be saying, "I just dropped by to let you know that things aren't going well and you haven't lost me." (In one case, every time the addict's mother called, he would tell her he had just had a fight with his wife, even if this was not true— a rather ingenious way of keeping both systems simultaneously intact and pacified.) Marital battles thus become a functional part of the integenerational homeostatic system, possessing both adaptive and sacrificial qualities . . . In other words, issues between spouses, while real, cannot be viewed apart from the relationship between the addict and his parents—the two subsystems are often highly interdependent. [Stanton et al., 1978, p. 141]

In the early phases of the above work, we started by working with the marital couple in some cases. This made sense, since more time was generally spent in the marital context and it did appear to contribute to the symptom. It was also easier because the addicts much more readily acknowledged a marital problem than difficulties with their parents. They tended to pronounce their independence from parents, saying they had outgrown the family or the family had given up on them. However, as our work progressed and we began to make interventions, we found that this approach did not go far enough. Couples treatment appeared to stress the marriage so that the addict would leave his spouse and return home to his parent(s). It sometimes seemed as if he was just waiting for an excuse to rebound back to them. It became evident that we could not deal with the spouse system alone and ignore the parental system if treatment was to succeed. Again, parental permission was quite tentative for the addict to have a viable marriage. There was a certain pull for him to return and a conveyed message of "Well, if you have trouble with your wife you can always come back and stay with us." Like the Quincy example, this might have a noble, "caring" ring to it, but covertly it was an instruction not to be too content with his spouse. A truly successful marriage would signify that his parents had "lost" him. His unavailability would then make them more available to each other and increase the probability that their marital conflicts came to the fore.

Treatment strategy. The practice of including spouses' parents in treatment has been emphasized by Boszormenyi-Nagy and Spark (1973) and, especially, by Framo (1976) and Headley (1977). These clinicians routinely move in this direction in their work. However, the techniques and rationale that they employ differ in some ways from those being proposed here, since they consider themselves neither structurally nor strategically oriented. In dealing with a therapeutic system composed both of the marital couple and one or more parents, it is possible to apply the general two-step procedure described earlier: start with a more structural approach, and if that is not feasible or working, switch to a more strategic operation.

When working with spouses and their parents, it is preferable to have the parents actually present in the session rather than try to deal with them through the couple. Working "blind" requires that the therapist be able to estimate from talking only with the couple what the situation is and what effect his interventions will have on the parents; as Haley (1976) notes, the average therapist does not usually have this skill, and if he can avoid working at such a handicap, he should. This is particularly true when taking a structural approach, as so much depends on changing relationships, restructuring, etc., within the actual session. Although roundabout methods may be employed, such as use of the telephone, it is harder to draw boundaries, to separate generations and to apply other structural techniques without the parents being in attendance so that they can (a) experience the interventions themselves, (b) be dealt with directly, (c) be given a chance to respond and (d) provide the therapist with the opportunity to observe systemic feedback and intervene accordingly in the "here and now."

When for economic, logistical, medical or geographic reasons it is not possible for parents to attend sessions, it may not be possible to apply conventional structural techniques. This is not to say that the clinician stops *thinking* structurally, but that he may have to shift his modus operandi somewhat. Some strategic therapists, notably Erickson, Haley and the MRI group, can work "long distance" quite handily when they have to. This is partly because they have found that effective intervention can be made through any member of the system (Weakland, 1976). As a brief example, in a (nonmarital) case in which Haley was called in as consultant, a girl in her early twenties was being treated for trichotillomania. She had persisted in pulling hair from her head and, especially, from her eyelids and eyebrows. Haley was asked if he had any ideas as to treatment strategy. He suggested the therapist direct the girl that every time she pulled her hair out she was to put it in an envelope and mail it to her mother. The girl was not pleased with this suggestion. However, she followed the instruction for a brief period and then, rather than continue, stopped her hair pulling. The case was terminated soon after.*

SUMMARY

In this chapter a rationale has been presented for the use of both structural and strategic techniques in treating couples. The general rule proposed is to start with a structural approach and move to more strategically anchored interventions when the structural methods do not succeed or are unlikely to succeed; this is done while recognizing that such strategic moves are inescapably based on a structural framework. Emphasis is also given to including the systems of import in the treatment, a notion which contrasts with traditional marital counseling. As appropriate, this could mean children, parents, siblings, coworkers or other persons or groups of persons important to the problem. The point is underscored that many marriages fail because one or both partners have not had parental permission to succeed in the marriage.

REFERENCES

Aponte, H.J., and Van Deusen, J.M. Structural family therapy. In A.L. Gurman and D.P. Kniskern (Eds.), *Handbook of family therapy.* New York: Brunner/Mazel, 1981.

Andolfi, M., Menghi, P., Nicolò, A.M., and Saccu, C. Interaction in rigid systems: A model of intervention in families with a schizophrenic member. In M. Andolfi and I. Zwerling (Eds.), *Dimensions of family therapy.* New York: Guilford Press, 1980.

Boszormenyi-Nagy, I., and Spark, G. *Invisible loyalties.* New York: Harper and Row, 1973.

Bowen, M. *Family therapy in clinical practice.* New York: Jason Aronson, 1978.

---

*Jay Haley, personal communication, October, 1979.

Farrelly, F., and Brandsma, J. *Provocative therapy.* Fort Collins, Co.: Shields, 1974.

Feldman, L.B. Marital conflict and marital intimacy: An integrative psychodynamic-behavioral-systemic model. *Fam. Proc.*, 1979, *18*, 69–78.

Framo, J.L. Family of origin as a therapeutic resource for adults in marital and family therapy: You can and should go home again. *Fam. Proc*, 1976, *15*, 193–210.

Frankl, V. Paradoxical intention. *Am. J. Psychother.*, 1960, *14*, 520–535.

Gurman, A.S., and Kniskern, D.P. Research on marital and family therapy: Progress, perspective and prospect. In S.L. Garfield and A.E. Bergin (Eds.), *Handbook of psychotherapy and behavior change: An empirical analysis* (2nd ed.). New York: Wiley, 1978.

Gurman, A.S. Dimensions of marital therapy: A comparative analysis. *J. Marit. & Fam. Ther.*, 1979, *5*, 5–16.

Haley, J. *Strategies of psychotherapy.* New York: Grune and Stratton, 1963.

Haley, J. (Ed.) *Advanced techniques of hypnosis and therapy: Selected papers of Milton H. Erickson.* New York: Grune and Stratton, 1967.

Haley, J. A review of the family therapy field. In J. Haley (Ed.), *Changing families.* New York: Grune and Stratton, 1971.

Haley, J. *Uncommon therapy.* New York: W.W. Norton, 1973.

Haley, J. *Problem solving therapy.* San Francisco: Jossey-Bass, 1976.

Haley, J. *Leaving home: Therapy with disturbed young people.* New York: McGraw-Hill, 1980.

Hare-Mustin, R. Paradoxical tasks in family therapy: Who can resist? *Psychother.: Theory, res. & prac.*, 1976, *13*, 128–130.

Headley, L. *Adults and their parents in family therapy.* New York: Plenum Press, 1977.

Heard, D.B. Keith: A case study of structural family therapy. *Fam. Proc.*, 1978, *17*, 338–356.

Hoffman, L. Deviation-amplifying processes in normal groups. In J. Haley (Ed.), *Changing families.* New York: Grune and Stratton, 1971.

Hoffman, L. Breaking the homeostatic cycle. In P. Guerin (Ed.), *Family therapy: Theory and practice.* New York: Gardner Press, 1976.

Jackson, D.D. The question of family homeostasis. *Psychiatr. Quart. Supple.*, 1957, *31*, 79–90.

Jackson, D.D. The study of the family. *Fam. Proc.*, 1965, *4*, 1–20.

L'Abate, L. A positive approach to marital and family intervention. In L. R. Wolberg and M.L. Aronson (Eds.), *Group therapy: 1975.* New York: Stratton Intercontinental Medical Book Company, 1975.

L'Abate, L., and Weeks, G. A bibliography of paradoxical methods in psychotherapy of family systems. *Fam. Proc.*, 1978, *17*, 95–98.

Madanes, C., and Haley, J. Dimensions of family therapy. *J. Nerv. & Ment. Dis.*, 1977, *165*, 88–98.

Minuchin, S. *Families and family therapy.* Cambridge, Ma.: Harvard Univ. Press, 1974.

Minuchin, S., Rosman, B., and Baker, L. *Psychosomatic families: Anorexia nervosa in context.* Cambridge, Ma.: Harvard Univ. Press, 1978.

Palazzoli-Selvini, M., Boscolo, L., Cecchin, G.F., and Prata, G. The treatment of children through brief therapy of their parents. *Fam. Proc.*, 1974, *13*, 429–442.

Palazzoli-Selvini, M., Boscolo, L., Cecchin, G., and Prata, G. *Paradox and counter-paradox: A new model in the therapy of the family in schizophrenic transaction.* New York: Jason Aronson, 1978.

Sluzki, C.E. Marital therapy from a systems theory perspective. In T.J. Paolino and B.S. McCrady (Eds.), *Marriage and marital therapy: Psychoanalytic, behavioral and systems theory perspectives.* New York: Brunner/Mazel, 1978.

Soper, P.H., and L'Abate, L. Paradox as a therapeutic technique: A review. *Int. J. Fam. Couns.*, 1977, *5*, 10–21.

Stanton, M.D. The addict as savior: Heroin, death and the family. *Fam. Proc.*, 1977, *16*, 191–197.

Stanton, M.D. Family therapy: Systems approaches. In G.P. Sholevar, R.M. Benson and B.J. Blinder (Eds.), *Emotional disorders in children and adolescents: Medical and psychological approaches to treatment.* Jamaica, N.Y.: S.P. Medical and Scientific Books, 1980.

Stanton, M.D. Fusion, compression, expansion and the workings of paradox: A theory of systemic/therapeutic change. Paper in prep., 1981a.

Stanton, M.D. Strategic approaches to family therapy. In A.S. Gurman and D.P. Kniskern (Eds.), *Handbook of family therapy.* New York: Brunner/Mazel, 1981b.

Stanton, M.D., and Todd, T.C. Structural family therapy with drug addicts. In E. Kaufman and P. Kaufmann (Eds.), *The family therapy of drug and alcohol abuse.* New York: Gardner Press, 1979.

Stanton, M.D., Todd, T.C., Heard, D.B., Kirschner, S., Kleiman, J.I., Mowatt, D.T., Riley, P., Scott, S.M., and VanDeusen, J.M. Heroin addiction as a family phenomenon: A new conceptual model. *Am. J. Drug & Alcohol Abuse,* 1978, *5,* 125–150.

Stanton, M.D., Todd, T.C., and Associates. *The family therapy of drug addiction.* New York: Guilford Press, 1981.

Steinglass, P. The conceptualization of marriage from a systems theory perspective. In T.J. Paolino and B.S. McCrady (Eds.), *Marriage and marital therapy: Psychoanalytic, behavioral and systems theory perspectives.* New York: Brunner/Mazel, 1978.

Watzlawick, P., Beavin, J.H., and Jackson, D.D. *Pragmatics of human communication.* New York: W.W. Norton, 1967.

Watzlawick, P., Weakland, J., and Fisch, R. *Change: Principles of problem formation and problem resolution.* New York: W.W. Norton, 1974.

Weakland, J.H. Communication theory and clinical change. In P.J. Guerin (Ed.), *Family therapy: Theory and practice.* New York: Gardner Press, 1976.

Weakland, J., Fisch, R., Watzlawick, P., and Bodin, A.M. Brief therapy: Focused problem resolution. *Fam. Proc.,* 1974, *13,* 141–168.

Wellisch, D.K., Gay, G.R., and McEntee, R. The easy rider syndrome: A pattern of hetero- and homosexual relationships in a heroin addict population. *Fam. Proc.,* 1970, *9,* 425–430.

Chapter 12

Transactional Analysis in Marital Therapy

Betty Magran

The last ten years have seen a proliferation of theories and therapeutic techniques that explain and deal with marital dysfunction. According to what aspect of the problem they emphasize, these theories fall into three main schools: the intrapsychic, the behavioral and the systems-transactional. Each one's focus is significantly different from one another.

Transactional analysis offers a new, integrated approach to the understanding and treatment of marital conflicts. Its method bridges the gap, the "either-or" state of this field, by combining the three main schools into a coherent theory of personality and a specific treatment modality. In this way transactional analysis allows for a structured eclecticism on the part of the therapist. Thus, it prevents a dogmatic or rigid alliance to one theory emphasizing one aspect of the problem to the exclusion of others that are equally significant. Like a happy and harmonious marriage, it works.

Transactional analysis was created by Eric Berne, a psychoanalyst who questioned established dogma and was flexible in its application. He adopted and adapted to his work what seemed to be useful in other forms of psychotherapy. As a psychoanalyst, he was fully aware of the intrapsychic, unconscious determinants of human behavior. Berne was also a social scientist, and as such he was particularly interested in observing the transactions between people with the purpose of understanding how these contributed to determine the quality and future of their relationship. In addition, he noted that people seemed to have individual patterns of behavior that elicited consistent responses from others. These in turn seemed to reinforce and energize the original behavior, regardless of the pleasure or pain involved. Berne thus began the process of integrating the study of unconscious motivation, interpersonal transactions and repetitive behavioral patterns.

How does transactional analysis work, particularly in the treatment of marital dysfunction? I will not attempt to describe the entire theory. The interested reader is referred to the transactional analysis books listed in the references. I will, however, review some of its basic concepts when these are used in this chapter. For the purpose of clarity I will illustrate the method by using the case material of the actual treatment of a couple, Mary and Jim Tate.

THE THERAPEUTIC CONTRACT

Transactional analysis is a contractual form of therapy. Negotiating a therapeutic contract is the beginning and most crucial part of treatment. It clarifies unrealistic expectations, sets the tone and mode of treatment and, most importantly, defines the treatment goals. The therapeutic contract needs to be agreed to by both the Adult ego state of the patient and the Adult ego state of the therapist.

What is an *ego state*? The personality is comprised of three functional parts, called ego states. According to Berne, an ego state is "a system of feelings accompanied by a related set of behavior patterns" (Berne, 1961; p. 17). The segregation and analysis of ego states is called *structural analysis*.

Briefly, the Parent (P) ego state is that part of the personality that has directly taken or incorporated attitudes, beliefs and behaviors from one's parents and/or authority figures. It is expressed in prejudicial, critical and nurturing behaviors (Critical Parent, or CP, and Nurturing Parent, or NP). It is often an arbitrary basis for decisions. The Parent ego state also has an important survival value: storing traditions and cultural standards.

The Adult ego state (A) focuses on reality. Much like a computer, it gathers information and processes data in a dispassionate and unbiased way to estimate probabilities and make decisions. Its main function is reality testing.

The Child (C) ego state contains all the impulses, feelings, spontaneity and creativity that characterize the chronological child. Often in response to environmental stimuli perceived as parental, the individual reacts in an adapted fashion (Adapted Child or AC) or a rebellious manner (Rebellious Child, or RC).

Each ego state has concomitant behavioral manifestations, verbal and non-verbal, that allow it to be easily identified by oneself or others. This is in itself important, particularly in the treatment of dysfunctional couples, since the awareness of which ego state one is cathecting at the time is the first step toward actual behavior control and change.

Problems arise when the individual uses an ego state, consistently and rigidly, that is inappropriate to the situation and without Adult control, as for instance, a young wife who panics and reacts with helplessness and despair (C) when she has to make a decision (A) in the absence of her husband.

We need to go back now to the first stage of marital treatment, the therapeutic contract, and describe it further. "A contract must be clear, concise, and direct. It involves (1) a decision to do something about a specific problem, (2) a statement of a clear goal to be worked toward in language simple enough for the inner Child to understand, and (3) the possibility of the goal being fulfilled" (James and Jongeward, 1971, p. 242).

Contracting in marital therapy is a more complex transaction, particularly because the therapeutic contract is negotiated among three people. The astute therapist will pay special attention to this part of treatment in order to avoid future difficulties. What he/she will find at times is that although both spouses declare that they are seeking treatment in order to help their failing marriage (A$\rightleftharpoons$A), one of them may have already made an unconscious decision to leave the other and is intending, again without awareness, to use the therapy to play a psychological game of Look How Hard I've Tried, in this way assuaging feelings of guilt (Berne, 1964). In a closely related variation of this game, the guilty spouse has decided consciously to break up the marriage and seeks "treatment" in order to leave the other on the therapist's lap, so to speak, to pick up the pieces.

Another situation, often detectable in the first session, also has an ulterior motive. Although both husband and wife state that they come to therapy to improve their relationship, one of the spouses, consciously or unconsciously, is there to try to prove the other "crazy" (wrong, guilty, inadequate, in need of hospitalization, etc.). This is Courtroom, a psychological game often used by clients in the family or marital-therapy sessions. The more inexperienced the therapist, the more the couple will tend to use the session as a perpetual game of Courtroom, in which nothing is resolved and where the therapist is used as a sometimes unwilling, often helpless judge. In this game the spouses will usually take turns at playing the roles of plaintiff and defendant (Berne, 1964).

This was the initial tone of the first session with Mary and Jim Tate. This couple was, at the time, in their early thirties. Both were college graduates.

They has been married seven years and had a one-and-one-half-year-old daughter when they first sought marital therapy. They were not getting along, they fought and argued often and, in general, were not happy together. They had considered separating several times.

Mary and Jim have had individual psychotherapy. This had been successful in helping Jim with a severe case of colitis that had plagued him on and off since his college years. Unemployed for the last two years, Jim spent his time dabbling in the arts.

Mary had a long history of personality problems. She had difficulties relating to people in an even, mature fashion. At times she was abrupt, critical and intolerant, while at other times she was impulsive and explosive, or loving and friendly. However, she was able to maintain a well-paying job because she could do it on her own terms and it did not require dealing with people. Mary's previous therapy helped her through some crises, but it also reinforced her poor self-esteem and her secret suspicions of being "crazy." Mary fluctuated between dealing with people from her Parent ego state (mostly Critical Parent) and being in her Child—impulsive, unreasonable, explosive, loving. Jim, on the other hand, had his Child ego state cathected a great deal of the time and dealt with most situations and people from his Child. Charming and ineffectual, he was passive but dreamed dreams of glory. Because he was "waiting for Santa Claus" to fulfill his fantasies, he made no efforts himself. Periodically he used his Parent to take care of Mary when she had one of her temper tantrums.

The first session was used ostensibly to negotiate a therapeutic contract. The process of this intervention allowed for the opportunity to arrive at a tentative clinical diagnosis of each individual and at a preliminary understanding of the nature of their marital relationship.

Mary and Jim agreed that they both wanted to improve their marriage and change specific aspects of it, particularly the fighting and arguing. Their initial game of Courtroom was easily broken by a simple rule: to use the second person (you) in their communications, instead of the third (she, he). This game also alerted the therapist as to the manner in which they dealt with their problems, namely shrugging their individual responsibility for their troubles and blaming the other.

With the help of the therapist, the Tates became aware of some of these patterns in the here-and-now of the first treatment session. They were encouraged to observe themselves more realistically. This new understanding led them to agree on their overall therapeutic contract: for each to assume responsibility for the nature and outcome of their transactions with each other. To take the first steps toward achieving this goal, both needed to learn to cathect their Adult ego state. Tasks (behavioral contracts) were used for this purpose.

The person's understanding and his ability to control his/her transactions with others have important implications. Aware of his modes of dealing with others and of the responses that these most likely will elicit, the individual can assume responsibility for the type of interaction that will develop and the outcome most likely to occur as its consequence. Understanding allows for choices. Analysis of the transactions with others allows for social control.

Psychological games are a clear example of these repetitive patterns of interaction and of the problems that they can cause in a relationship. Berne defined *game* as "an ongoing series of complementary ulterior transactions progressing to a well-defined, predictable outcome. Descriptively it is a recurring set of transactions, often repetitious, superficially plausible, with a concealed motivation" (Berne, 1964, p. 48).

Games are learned, unconscious maneuvers, repetitious in nature, that have a social, acceptable component and an ulterior, concealed aspect. Games always start with a discount of the self and/or the other person, and they have a psychological payoff at the end: bad feelings for one or all the players. They serve some important needs in people: games help structure time and they confirm and further the individual's feelings about himself and others. Games prevent honest, intimate and open relationships.

People play a small number of favorite games in varying intensities, according to how casual or close that relationship may be.

First-degree games are socially acceptable and do not have major consequences, but do have some excitement or mild upsets.

Second-degree games lead to stronger, more unpleasant reactions or payoffs.

Third-degree games may involve tissue damage. They usually have catastrophic outcomes, often ending in the hospital, jail, courtroom or morgue.

Intuitively, game players seek others who will play complementary games. This is one of the unconscious contracts in the marriage.

Mary and Jim had an armamentarium of games at their disposal. Each knew how to start them and what moves were needed to keep their games going. They had no choice, since they were unaware of their individual roles in the unfolding of their stereotyped patterns of interaction and of the motivations underlying their behavior. In this sense they were victims.

A way in which Mary and Jim avoided looking at their own roles in their marital conflicts and assuming responsibility for themselves was through playing If It Weren't for You (Berne, 1964). This is a marital game that is played often by women who, in order to avoid looking at their phobic, inhibited nature, tend to blame their domineering husband for their own lack of success (lack of social life, fun, education, glamorous career, etc.). In this case, the Tates took turns at blaming. Mary made Jim responsible for her poor and inconsistent parenting of their daughter ("If you would have a job, I would not need to work and I would be a better mother"). On the other hand, Jim blamed Mary for being too domineering and unstable, thus causing him too much upset and anxiety to be able to hold a job.

A crucial issue with both Mary and Jim was their fear of closeness. Partially determined by parental messages and injunctions, and possibly in part by their own early childhood conclusions that to be close to their needy mothers meant to be overpowered and destroyed, this fear shaped their marriage. Their fights had the definite patterns, moves and payoffs of Uproar, a game designed to avoid intimacy. When one of them sensed that they were getting too close, Jim or Mary managed to start a fight. This would establish an emotional and physical distance between them and would allow them to move to a more "comfortable" level of relating, reinstating in this way the original terms of their unconscious marital contract.

Games need to be uncovered and exposed in the therapy sessions for changes to occur, if closeness between the spouses is a goal. The results are often dramatic.

The objection might be raised that helping people change their maladaptive behavior patterns does not necessarily change their unconscious need to act in that particular way. Knowing the consequences of relating (talking, acting, etc.) in a certain manner may not be enough to offset the need that motivates it. This objection is valid. In problems that are less deep-rooted or less threatening to the psychological survival of the individual, a mere change in the stroking pattern between the spouses is sufficient to modify their interaction to a more gratifying behavior pattern.

A stroke is a unit of recognition, a form of stimulation. Strokes can be physical, verbal or nonverbal. They can be positive or negative, conditional or unconditional. Strokes are necessary for survival. This recognition hunger is an inherent psychological need of human beings. Children are programmed to behave in specific ways by the manipulation of strokes. This is the process by which we learn to get and elicit particular types of strokes—the kind that was most often used to help us adapt to our parents' demands and expectations during the formative years. One of the most important functions of marriage is that through it the spouses are insured a steady diet of the strokes they are used to and need (being praised, criticized, discounted, etc.). At times this stroking pattern creates difficulties in the relationship, and as was mentioned above, helping the couple change the patterns may result in substantial changes in the relationship itself.

However, in those cases where the conflict has greater significance, there is a need for deeper insight and for the resolution of the original conflict that causes the problematic behavior in the present. It is at this point that transactional analysis switches to the analysis of the unconscious intrapsychic issues underlying the maladaptive behavior: script analysis. A psychological script is a blueprint for life, an unconscious life plan. Like the script of a theatrical play, it has a theme, plot, stages, roles, drama and an outcome. It is developed and arrived at piece by piece over the first few years of life, although there are occasional corrections, additions and subtractions later on. Dynamic rather than static, it has a direction and a movement that is unique.

A child is born with certain genetic and individual characteristics. Berne used to say that we are all born princes and princesses and that life and our experiences in it transform us into frogs. He also added that the role of therapy is to reverse this and change us back to being princes and princesses. How does the "frogging" process take place? Parents transmit to their children, from birth on, a multitude of attitudes and messages, verbal and nonverbal, that begin to shape the child's view of himself and the world. In addition, the individual's early experiences also contribute to the establishment of that person's *existential or life position*. The existential position influences how the individual thinks, acts, feels and relates to others. There are four basic life positions:

1. I'm O.K., You're O.K.
2. I'm O.K., You're Not O.K.
3. I'm Not O.K., You're O.K.
4. I'm Not O.K., You're Not O.K.

The existential position arrived at early in life shapes the personality and is at the basis of each person's script and of the psychological games that are played to further and confirm one's script. They also determine the type of psychopathology the individual may develop.

Parental attitudes and messages are reinforced by parents through stroking certain behaviors in the child while ignoring or discounting others. Thus the individual learns, early in life, that to survive (get along, please, be loved, be accepted) in his family he has to be and behave in the way prescribed by his parents, based on their own personality and needs (Steiner, 1974).

Early survival conclusions become childhood decisions that are incorporated in the script and determine its course and outcome. The implication is that the individual's basic life course is, in a sense, decided on in the first few years of life. Success or failure, happiness or loneliness in adult life can be traced back and be better understood in the context of the person's life script.

I often describe to my clients some of the personality and cognitive characteristics of the two- to four-year-old child: concrete thinking, no sense of time, illogical, unable to postpone gratification, poor impulse control, poor frustration tolerance, dependent, vulnerable, etc. They are confronted with the idea that they may now be governed by someone like that, and that some of their conflicts stem from it. Understanding and insight facilitate redecision, the next step before change occurs.

Because of its unique nature, the marital relationship is the perfect stage upon which are acted out old parental messages, injunctions and attributions, feelings about oneself and others, and early childhood conclusions about one's life and destiny.

Jim and Mary Tate are a good example of how individual scripts complement and support each other in a marriage. Jim was the younger of two sons. His parents had a precarious but lasting marriage that resembled the Tate's. His father was quiet and fairly passive, while his mother had a long history of what appeared to be a manic-depressive psychotic condition. Their messages to him had to do with being adaptive, taking care of mother when she was emotionally upset and not succeeding like father. His childhood conclusions and decisions appeared to be that in order to be loved and accepted by his parents, he needed to be good and passive, to suppress anger, to not succeed and to take care of mother when she went "crazy." He became a pleasant, sickly underachiever. In this way, he learned to get strokes from them, positive as well as negative. He learned also that to get to be taken care of, he had to be completely helpless. Like his mother, being sick—colitis—insured him the nurturing he did not get otherwise.

Unconsciously he married a woman who would help him further his script and carry out his childhood decisions about his life and relationships.

Mary was the older in a family of two daughters. Her role in the family was twofold: she was the buffer between her parents and she provided the excitement for them. Being the "parentified" child, she took emotional care of her parents, while her temper tantrums and volatile personality offered a constant source of attention and concern for them. In the first role she was domineering and critical. In the second, she was unpredictable and irrational. Her parents' emotional divorce was masked by her behavior, as it was unconsciously prescribed by them through nonverbal messages ("Take care of us," "Be crazy," "Be good") and injunctions ("Don't be close").

Their marriage allowed Jim and Mary to continue their individual scripts and confirm them. Mary still had to be either in her parent role or in her explosive childlike role. Jim's passivity and his earlier psychosomatic condition provided the justification for both. She either persecuted Jim or felt victimized by him, while at other times she was his rescuer (Karpman, 1968).

On the other hand, Jim was following his own life plan, aided actively by Mary's. He was unsuccessful in most areas of life despite his high potential, and he married a woman who would need and accept it. He was still following his parental messages ("Be passive," "Be nice") and injunctions ("Don't succeed," "Don't be close"). The psychological games that Jim and

Mary played served to perpetuate and further their scripts by providing the strokes that they sought, maintaining their life positions and confirming parental messages and injunctions. Furthermore, their games established a distance and lack of intimacy between them that was prescribed by their scripts.

In marital therapy these issues were dealt with as they came up in the sessions as the result of their interaction. Both became aware of the complementarity of their behavior in maintaining their relationship at a frustrating, unhappy level. They realized what their individual roles were and how they used patterns and games to keep their relationship as it was. With the help of therapy, they were able to look into options and choices made by them as adults of how they wanted their lives to be and what they needed to do to change those aspects of it that they did not like. They learned to ask for what they wanted from each other in direct ways. They learned to talk to each other and to have fun together.

They changed.

The mechanism often used to implement those changes is contracting over specific issues between the spouses and with the therapist.

As I have described elsewhere, following the initial commitment, contracting is negotiated over specific issues. Specific contracting is used on many levels. On one level the therapist uses negotiations over contracting issues to restructure the couple's mode of interaction, with the aim of helping them experience in the here-and-now a more satisfying way of relating to each other, much as in the structural approach to family therapy (Minuchin, 1974). Each of the spouses has the opportunity to express his or her wants and learn to listen and respond to his partner's needs.

On the content level, each marital member is asked to express clearly and concretely those changes that his/her partner could make that would allow for the growth of trust and the development of more positive feelings between them. The couple learns to account and be accountable for each other's needs.

On another level, the therapist implicitly and explicitly grants permission and support for changes of old established patterns. This acceptance and support form the foundation that allows the client to change. It should be noted that the content is not the most important aspect of the contract. Its value resides in negotiating, which offers the opportunity to (1) expose the dysfunctional interactional patterns so that they can be reworked, (2) help the couple learn communication skills, (3) help the individual ask for what he/she needs, (4) help the couple develop trust in each other and (5) receive permission to change through the therapist's support.

Contracting in this model appears to be similar to the one elaborated by Sager in that it is a tool that provides a structure for couples to respond to each other's needs in a "quid pro quo" fashion (Sager, 1976). Contracting helps the couple examine the underlying assumptions in the marriage, explicit and implicit, and furnishes the therapist with an information-gathering mechanism. The difference between contracting as used by Sager and this approach resides in how this tool is used.

Contracting over specific issues is a vehicle used by the therapist to bring to the surface, in the here-and-now of the therapy session, the basic conflicts that disturb the marriage. Once exposed, these conflicts are dealt with in terms of the psychological games they represent and the payoff that these offer for the individual. In turn, their games are looked at and understood from the larger context of their scripts and their early childhood conclusions and decisions. This new awareness not only brings a new understanding of each other in terms of the past but allows for options and ultimately leads to redecisions.

Fulfillment of specific contracts is positively reinforced by the therapist and again viewed in the light of new options and decisions regarding the couple's marriage. Lack of fulfillment of the contract offers the opportunity to look at the ways in which the individual's Child is sabotaging his/her Adult decision to change and the reasons why. It is a warning signal that there is a need to rework the problem at hand.

Changing the stroking pattern in the couple is an essential part of treatment because it helps to implement their decision to change. This is done not only at a behavioral level; the need to give and get negative strokes or to discount positive behavior is dealt with at every step of treatment from the larger perspective of each spouse's background, his or her relationships in the family of origin and their individual scripts (Fisher and Magran, 1978).

The *marital contracts* are also examined, understood and demystified. They are discussed in terms of (a) the formal, verbalized Adult contract agreed on by the couple ($A \rightleftharpoons A$); (b) the relationship or psychological contract that is not verbalized and may resemble a tacit symbiotic agreement, which is usually a preconscious commitment to take care of or be taken care of ($P \rightleftharpoons C$, $C \rightleftharpoons P$); and (c) the script or unconscious contract ($C \rightleftharpoons C$) (Berne, 1961).

These were the tools used with the Tates in the slow process of helping them change. When last contacted, two years later, those changes had been sustained. John had been successfully employed for one-and-one-half years and had recently been promoted. Their marriage was solid, not "perfect," but rewarding to both. They were parents of a six-month-old baby boy and were doing reasonably well in handling their family. They were not fighting as they used to. Most important, they were in control of their lives.

Mary summed it all up when she stated, "And I love my life now."

CONCLUSIONS

Transactional analysis, originally designed to be used as a therapeutic approach in groups, has proven to be an extremely effective tool when applied to marital therapy.

Transactional analysis succeeds because it considers and deals with aspects of the personality that other techniques may tend to exclude: the behavioral, the interpersonal and the intrapsychic. Accounting for all three modalities by means of a coherent therapeutic technique insures that intentional or nonintentional biases on the part of the therapist will be minimized.

In a sense it offers the therapist the opportunity of being eclectic in an organized, systematic way.

Transactional analysis's effectiveness also derives from its goal: not merely to help people resolve their conflicts but to give them a tool that is experienced and learned and that they can use and resort to when needed. The process of the acquisition of these tools *is* the therapy.

Combining the rational with the emotional, the cognitive with the affective, transactional analysis deals with the here-and-now while it emphasizes the individual's past and the intergenerational components of human behavior. Marital problems viewed from this frame of reference are understood in the larger context of each individual's unconscious script, interlocked with that of the spouse and reinforced by it. Resolution of conflicts is achieved through insight into the original childhood conclusions and decisions that underlie them, through redecision and by changing the stroking pattern between the spouses.

REFERENCES

Berne, E. *Transactional analysis in psychotherapy.* New York: Grove Press, 1961.

Berne, E. *Games people play.* New York: Grove Press, 1964, pp. 92–109.

Fisher, S., and Magran, B. *Behavioral contracting to create a therapeutic event in marital therapy.* Unpub. Paper, 1978.

James, M., and Jongeward D. *Born to win.* Reading, Ma.: Addison-Wesley, 1971, p. 242.

Karpman, S. *Script drama analysis.* Transactional Analysis Bull., 1963, 7, *26* 39–43.

Minuchin, S. *Families and family therapy.* Cambridge, Ma.: Harvard Univ. Press, 1974.

Sager, C. *Marriage contracts and couple therapy.* New York: Brunner/Mazel, 1976.

Steiner, C. *Scripts people live.* New York: Grove Press, 1974, pp. 55–75.

Chapter 13

Couples Group Therapy: Rationale, Dynamics and Process

Florence Kaslow
E. James Lieberman

The literature on treating couples conjointly in group therapy was relatively sparse until the past decade. Since then, articles have begun to appear with greater frequency as leading practitioners of couples group therapy have begun to write about their work (Kadis and Markowitz, 1972; Framo, 1973; Alger, 1976; Liberman et al., 1976; Neiberg, 1976; and Jacobson, 1977). Despite the growing number of published articles, this method is probably more frequently utilized than the literature would suggest, but less than is warranted by patient need. In a society recently experiencing a million divorces per year, there is not enough high-quality therapy time available to deal with the majority of couples experiencing serious marital dissension. Couples group therapy often offers an effective, comparatively inexpensive form of psychotherapy.

Traditional psychoanalytic therapy does not usually include spouses of patients. Many analysts scrupulously avoid meeting the spouse of a patient, and debates about the wisdom of seeing couples together still echo (Gottlieb and Pattison, 1966). More surprising, even in classical marriage counseling, conjoint therapy has not always been the rule (Mace, 1974). In recent years, conjoint therapy with husband and wife has become more common and is relatively standard practice in sex therapy. The latter is also being practiced in couples' groups (Baker and Nagata, 1978). Some group therapists separate partners into different groups, believing each needs his/her own space to work out problems and that this is preferable to having the spouse present so that fuller disclosure can take place.

Historically and contemporaneously, then, couples experiencing marital discord and seeking professional help might be seen in individual therapy by the same or different therapists; conjointly by one therapist or a co-therapy pair; or in group therapy, in separate groups or the same group by one or a pair of therapists. The modalities may be combined for one or both members of the dyad, so that a wide range of possibilities exists.

Conjoint work with one husband and wife dyad has limitations as well as advantages not found in individual or group therapy. The benefits of conjoint couple treatment cluster in the area of receiving total attention from the therapist and learning more effective communication and mediation skills. Some intrapsychic explorations may be undertaken and roots of the difficulties which emanate from past family relationships explored.

The therapist may impart certain ideas and model certain skills but, after a few sessions, too often tends to become a mediator or referee. Once the therapist's philosophy and style have been demonstrated, the intense concentration on that pair may begin to be more of a liability than a benefit. Some couples focus the whole week's interaction into that hour. They may lose spontaneity in their relationship and may depend on the therapist to structure tasks for them. This is appropriate in some sex therapy, but less so for other relational distress. Along with Cohen (1977), we believe that some relationships may shrivel rather than bloom under the spotlight of regular conjoint sessions over a prolonged period. Too much stress may fall on continually "working" to improve the marriage; this can become laborious and may inadvertently divest it of all fun and playfulness.

In individual therapy the work with one spouse may be deeper because that person believes he/she can risk more alone and become more vulnerable with the therapist than would be possible in the presence of another. There may be facts or feelings which cannot constructively be shared with the spouse, and other feelings, transference or real, directed toward the therapist which might not emerge with the spouse present. In couples group, depth may be reached by vicarious use of, or identification with, the dilemmas and frustrations expressed by others. Paul's use of videotapes, with which patients can identify to stimulate growth in marital therapy, seems to follow this principle (Paul, 1975).

Following several sessions of conjoint therapy with husband and wife, and occasional subsequent conjoint sessions, one author (E.J.L.) believes a combination of individual and group psychotherapy works best. He has also found family therapy to be useful as an adjunctive modality when issues which involve children surface. However, many issues of concern to married couples cannot be discussed as constructively with children present; they are of import to the parent subsystem and the generational boundary should not be transgressed. Such areas include marital sexual issues, certain parenting disputes, favoring or disparaging a child, and certain financial matters.

The other author (F.K.) uses an initial conjoint interview to determine what is likely to constitute the treatment of choice. If couples group therapy is selected, that is the only modality utilized and all issues and feelings are dealt with in the one context. Requests for separate sessions are seen as a way of diluting one of the salient values of the group experience. The intensity of sharing and relating in an interpersonal situation lacks the total, undivided attention the patient receives in a therapeutic one-to-one encounter. Such requests may also be interpreted, where pertinent, as stemming from the patient reexperiencing sibling rivalry in the group and seeking the separate session in order to form a special, stronger alliance with the therapist, thereby finally becoming the favorite child and/or obtaining enough nurturance.

Two major schools of thought about theory and technique of therapy seem to undergird, and have been adapted for, couples group therapy. The first is psychodynamic and is reflected in the work of the clinician—authors we have chosen to summarize and amplify here. This theoretical orientation is also a major element in our own practices, although we are eclectic and draw on transactional, holistic and humanistic-existential ideas and techniques. The major second force in treatment is predicated on learning theory and behavioral therapy, and much couples group therapy is practiced within this framework. Because of space limitations, this will not be described herein, but interested readers are referred to articles by Liberman, Wheeler and Sanders (1976), Jacobson (1977) and Paolini and McCrady's book (1978) for a comprehensive view of this approach.

We see the marriage encounter and marriage-enrichment approaches (Mace and Mace, 1977; L'Abate, 1977) as emanating from a nontherapeutic base, and therefore as outside of the scope of a chapter focused on treatment. However, it is important to note that thousands of couples who are unsatisfied in their marriages have been attracted by these programs and report finding the experience beneficial. The widespread appeal of such a group phenomenon causes us to ponder the reasons for the resistance or antipathy people have to seeking couples group therapy. The implication of illness implicit in the word "therapy" may constitute a stumbling block. The prolonged nature of most treatment and the anticipated cost, which far exceeds that incurred in a marriage-encounter weekend, may serve as other deterrents. To have the promise beckon of truly encountering one's spouse or of enriching one's most significant relationship rather quickly is no doubt a more appealing prospect than to contemplate facing one's deep-seated anger, deprivation, narcissistic wounds and egocentrism.

INTERVENTION PHILOSOPHY AND STRATEGY

We identify three rather distinct approaches to couples group therapy, which emanate from a psychodynamic framework. They also share in common the utilization of a combination of techniques drawn from group, marital and family therapy, a systems understanding of the interaction of the marital pair and a preference for a heterosexual co-therapy pair of equals as the co-leaders. This latter stipulation is a requirement in the first approach discussed below, that promulgated by Kadis and Markowitz (1972), and so will be summarized in the context of their material.

Short-Term, Closed-End Analytic Treatment of Married Couples in a Group

The model evolved by Kadis and Markowitz (1972, p. 463) flowed from an appreciation of the "effects in the here-and-now of the spouses' residual characterological problems originating in early familial experiences." In most instances, compulsive strife between mates can be broken if either can be made aware of the similarity between his* perception of his relationship to and expectations of the other and his perception of a significant parental figure. It can then be brought to awareness that these old problems are being replayed in the present marital situation. Much marital distress is diminished when the spouses realize that they are projecting intrapsychic difficulties and needs unmet in their family of origin in the past onto the current partner. Thus, in a group composed of five couples, each members' intrapsychic mechanisms are explored, and the male-female co-therapy team is used as a screen upon which to project the earlier unresolved conflicts and unfulfilled longings.

The theme of separation and union is perceived as a major one. Most of the participants selected for inclusion in the group have been inadequately weaned, are incompletely individuated and lack autonomy. They often marry someone similar and demand excessive nurturance. During the courtship, each has promised the other tremendous love and caring and,

---

*"His" is used in the generic sense with no political-sexist connotations intended.

overtly or covertly, has required the same in return. After the wedding, neither is able to provide such tremendous and continuous sustenance; increasingly, each feels deprived on the receiving end and frustrated that no matter how much they give, it is perceived as insufficient. The fury over once again experiencing unmet needs and unkept promises motivates them to seek therapy. The unconscious fantasy of omnipotence, total gratification and emotional fusion is brought into the group context.

The co-therapists function partially as parent surrogates and recreate in the group a substitute family. This allows for the shifting of total responsibility for need satisfaction from the mate, thereby reducing some of the pressure on the spouse by permitting the separation problems to surface. Some of the deficit needs are attended to by others in the group and by the leaders. The implications become clear, that is, (1) that it is not possible for any one person to constantly be with us or to fulfill all of our needs; (2) that it is legitimate and healthy to have friends, activities and interests that one shares with one's mate but also that that may be important to only one partner and need not be sacrificed or forced upon the other, since total immersion in each other is no longer a goal (such expansion of the family and friend support system and of areas of interest is encouraged, thus fostering individuation and providing space for each to be his own person); (3) that we cannot project responsibility for our behavior and our satisfaction onto anyone else, not even our spouse, but rather each individual is ultimately responsible for his/her own thoughts, feelings and actions; and (4) that neither parent is or was all good or all bad, but that both had some good and bad qualities. This latter emphasis, which is heightened by the fluidity of roles played by the co-therapists, who avoid being trapped into a competitive relationship or being split by rivalrous group members, promotes in the members a synthesis of the parent image, thus allaying the tendency toward ego-splitting regarding the parents, ultimately the therapists, spouse and, most importantly, the self.

The co-therapists not only model a healthy substitute parent couple who communicate clearly and candidly with each other and with group members, but they also subtly serve as a new kind of role model for their patients in parenting their own children. They build in necessary limits through contracting for session length and fee (for example, by explicitly establishing that this is brief treatment, to last for ten sessions, and that no one may take a vacation or plan other activities in conflict with therapy sessions). The value of fulfilling a commitment or promise made to self and others is thereby underscored. Such structure confronts the neurotic superego's magical expectation of unlimited time and gratification and harnesses the energy and intention of group members to settle in quickly to utilize the time available for problem resolution. It also provides many with a sense of the positive and comforting aspects of setting limits and adhering to these so that *termination of the therapeutic relationship when originally specified is an important dynamic* in helping each patient to complete, finally and successfully, a separation process and to feel full approval from the therapist-parent for moving away.

The rationale for this approach to short-term couples group therapy is that it helps patients shift from a primarily pleasure-principle orientation of anticipating total gratification to a reality-principle orientation, which accepts rational limitations. It also enables patients to finish the incomplete process of individuation from their family of origin, thereby disengaging from overly dependent ties, and to handle the attendant separation anxiety and blame for deprivation which has been erroneously projected from parents onto spouse. When led by a competent, confident male-female co-therapy team, "sex-syntonic identifications are . . . easily evoked" (p. 480) and alliances with others of the same sex take place during group meetings. When the therapists are free of anxiety about relating to and caring about members of the opposite sex, everyone present has greater freedom to achieve a sex-syntonic self-concept.

In such couples groups, transferences can be responded to and handled directly. There is little likelihood that either therapist will assume the role of sexual savior. Transferential acting-out is confronted with appropriate affect and a direct interpretation. Given the group context, interactions, identification and mirroring phenomena are "less transferentially distorted, since there are constantly parents and children simultaneously present" (p. 481). The attempts at splitting and the transferences are sharply etched and become responsive to corrective feedback; the patients find the exposure to and experiencing of the complimentary and balanced co-therapy parental interaction quite curative. The planned feedback session a month after termination is usually filled with reports that the gains made during treatment have been solidified and with some analysis of the regressive pulls being experienced.

The first author has used a modification of the above approach with twelve different patient groups during the past five years, and concurs with Kadis and Markowitz as to the benefits of such groups. Note that ten is not a magic number. If therapists work better on a twelve or fifteen week schedule, they should tailor initial contract to their own rhythm. What is crucial is that the originally agreed-upon time schedule not be modified. This method is particularly suitable with outpatients who are neurotic and immature. It falters if a member is severely borderline or psychotic. It is highly suitable to upper and upper-middle-class intelligent and articulate patients. It is adaptable for lower-class inner-city populations who are unwilling to enter treatment without knowing how long it will take but who can make a commitment for ten to twelve weeks and who can afford therapy more easily when the cost is split with four other couples.

Marital Therapy in an Open-Ended Couples Group

By contrast to the closed-ended, short-term group with much interaction between members described above, the Framo model is an open-ended one involving three couples (Framo, 1973). Instead of fostering spontaneous communication, support and cross-confrontation among couples, Framo allocates twenty-five minutes to each of the three couples in sequence for the ninety-minute session. He helps them focus on the secret agendas that went into their mate selection, residual unresolved conflicts with their families of origin, the discrepancy between the conscious and unconscious demands placed on the marriage and the current marital turmoil.

Framo indicates that he originally formed a couples' group to allow himself more freedom to effect change and to avoid being placed in a judge or referee role. Groups held promise of preventing feeling bored and thwarted by repetition and lack of progress. After seeing hundreds of couples in groups, Framo attests that this is a "powerful form of treatment in its own right" (p. 89), a conclusion shared by others who utilize this method, yet one not adequately documented through psychotherapy outcome research (DeWitt, 1978).

Through becoming involved in group, couples come to recognize that their problems are not unique; some marriages improve when the partners realize how frequent difficulties like theirs are. Ventilation in frank discussions with other couples is an uncommon occurence in our society; couples group therapy provides novel opportunity for sharing of troubles, getting varied inputs regarding oneself in interpersonal dealings, and reworking of relationships. A great deal of mirroring and identification occur through seeing how other spouses act, react, and think. It is sometimes easier to work out an issue after hearing another couple who have successfully resolved it than by attempting to do it alone without any road maps. Patients often tend to listen to and be more willing to accept critical feedback from other patients than from their own spouse or the therapist. They also derive support from one another in their struggle toward happier and healthier functioning and gain an expanded view of how to consider alternative solutions and behaviors.

Framo lets his patients know that in order of priority, their first obligation is to themselves, the second to their spouses and only third to the group. Although he utilizes group process, it is deemphasized in that he does not focus on "relationships and distortions between individuals across couples" (p. 90). While one couple is being worked with, the other four patients are instructed to attend carefully and, at the end of the allocated time, to give their reactions to what they have observed.

Framo uses similarity of age and stage of life cycle as the major criterion in forming a new group. He does not find that differences in social class or educational attainment impede therapeutic gains; rather, such differences can mean varying perspectives are brought to bear on problems under consideration, and can enrich the options formulated. He gives a few simple ground rules to his patients in the initial session. Framo places a premium on candor and on members being free to reveal their thoughts and feelings, but states that no physical violence will be permitted. Spouses are free to discuss sessions afterward with each other but not to discuss the other couples with nongroup members. All criticisms of one another are to be voiced in a constructive fashion. We concur with the importance of these basic rules and believe they do help to fashion a safe, trusting environment.

Once the group is underway, a couple may terminate whenever they choose to—either because they have completed what they wanted to accomplish or because they no longer care to continue. Another couple is added so that the size of the group is maintained. If one partner must be absent, the other is still permitted to attend so that continuity is maintained and the spouse's individual identity is fostered.

The kinds of games married couples play repetitively are soon obvious in group, as are the ways they sabotage each other's growth. The group helps them recognize their patterns, why they play such seemingly unrewarding games, and to explore better ways of interacting.

If one partner wants to continue the marriage and the other partner longs to dissolve it, the issue is confronted head on and trial separation may be proposed. During this phase, treatment continues so that they can gain some experiential knowledge of how it feels to be apart, what it might take to get back together or whether a divorce should be contemplated.

Helping the partners achieve their separate identities, a major thrust for Framo, as for Kadis and Markowitz and the current authors, paradoxically also creates a favorable climate to and the freedom for increased intimacy between them. It flows from feeling whole and therefore being clear as to one's own boundaries, for their closeness becomes less threatening and more exciting.

Framo does not discourage couples from having contact outside the group. Rather, some of the more isolated pairs become friendly. Relationships established in the group sometimes prove to be quite lasting. In his experience, and in ours, patients have not acted out sexually across couples in the group. We have observed that such acting-out occurs only when the therapist, overtly or covertly, gives permission for patients to have affairs with one another or is sexually provocative with the participants.

I (F.K.) have found, as has Framo (1972, p. 96), that the unfinished business of the past with one's parents must be dealt with before the marriage can flourish fully, so I may hold a session with a patient and his/her family of origin separate from the group sessions *if* the issues cannot be adequately worked through without such a multigenerational session.

This supplements the ongoing therapy process, often serving to clarify the underlying dynamics and to release previously bound energy as the necessary healing takes place within the locus of the real family system. Conflicted relationships are worked through in what are often lengthy, tearful, deeply moving and rewarding sessions.

Couples Group Psychotherapy

In the approach favored by therapist-author Lieberman, four couples meet weekly for ninety minutes for a minimum of a year. The group process is unstructured; the content of each session flows from the needs and offerings of the participants and the leader. Members are regarded as individuals who relate as such to each other. In contrast to Framo's procedure, there is no attempt to structure couple interaction; on the contrary, members are encouraged to relate independent of spouse rather than to focus on marital interaction. Group membership, not spousal identity, provides the pivotal leverage.

Of course, members are present as couple subgroups. Each dyad interacts intimately during the intervals between group sessions. A few guidelines help to prevent subversion of this special factor. Partners may not intimidate one another by threatening to bring something up in group or by retaliating at home for something said in group.

Unlike other group therapy but similar to family therapy, here each spouse is accountable for possible harm to an enduring relationship. To help resolve these dilemmas, the therapist is available for individual or separate couple sessions. Group patients may be in individual therapy, preferably with the therapist who conducts the group. This is a radical departure from the standard practice of seeing group patients only as a unit in order not to set up special alliances or arouse rivalry for extra attention and favoritism. The therapist must be able to keep confidences, not revealing to the group (or spouse), deliberately or accidentally, material heard in individual session. For some therapists, keeping clear what is and what is not confidential can pose a serious problem.

Some therapists abhor secrets, but improved communication can—indeed must—be achieved with regard for the capacity of all concerned to deal with revelations. We do not believe that couples or family therapy calls for free expression of any and all feelings which may arise. Only individual psychotherapy or psychoanalysis provides that kind of freedom.

All other relationships require a mixture of honesty and discretion, or in Thoreau's classic phrase, "tact with truth." When others beside the therapist are present, the patient is responsible for the content and style of his/her communication—though not for the underlying feelings. No group, couple or family can exist if members utter every strong feeling whenever it arises, regardless of its potential harmful impact on others. Some capacity for selection and restraint is required. This selectivity is not the same as censorship of powerful or disquieting feelings. However, one should strive to express anxiety, sadness, love, anger and joy in ways which enhance relationships.

A therapist cannot simply encourage patients to lay everything out in the open when some revelations may result in permanent damage to a relationship. The consulting room provides shelter against threats and recriminations, but it cannot absolve one of responsibility for what is said. Becoming able to accept such responsibility is a manifestation of increasing emotional health. Therapists must learn—and teach—the difference between information which may hurt but must be revealed and that which would surely hurt and need *not* be expressed. These limitations require ego development of a nonrepressive kind, which is consonant with therapeutic endeavor and essential for a capacity to experience and express emotions. "Free" and impulsive expression may block more meaningful emotional experience, especially if the former lacks personal ego investment. We are not responsible for the feelings we have, but we are for the way we act on them; therapy tries to stimulate a wider range of feelings and behaviors, but the latter are not free of accountability.

In couples work, we find massive clouds of silence veiling important marital concerns. Often dramatic changes occur as group sessions dispel the clouds after years of collusive masking. In group, both men and women hear other husbands talk about matters that men rarely discuss. They also hear other wives tell about problems which can now be aired and responded to— in ways which were not possible earlier—because of the new perspective and improved self-concept. Individuals find support for enriched and more meaningful emotional communication, and the therapist can share responsibility with other participant-observers. Group members respond to each other; the therapist ceases to be the referee or sole authority. Presuming a strong group and an egalitarian leader, sexist bias is unlikely with four group members of the opposite sex present to provide balance.

For full benefit of this mode of group therapy to be derived, considerable time is required, a year of weekly meetings. A commitment is requested, therefore, but no one is required to stay in the group if it fails to meet important needs. A basically sound marriage is necessary for people to be able to participate in this kind of couples group therapy. "In group, good marriages get better; bad ones get worse in a hurry" (Cohen, 1977). Other members do not want to be helpless witnesses to the deterioration of a marriage, or to be constant referees. Patients embroiled in aggravated conflict will be unable to contribute much to fellow group members. The orientation is toward exploration of relationships among the *individuals* present. The group is not a place for a litany of complaints or recitation of "the week that was" in a marriage.

The group is open-ended; most couples remain for one to two years. As in the second model, new couples are introduced as old ones leave. This provides for an ongoing group-therapy situation in which couples with more experience or with greater need become senior, and may move from a position of passivity or poor insight to activity and therapeutic strength, thus consolidating gains while contributing support and guidance to newer members.

Implicit in the *commitment* to marriage is sexual exclusivity. This extends to excluding the presence of a third party "waiting in the wings," although it is not always possible to eliminate such diversions. Nevertheless, if this is an issue, it should be discussed thoroughly between the patient involved in an affair and the therapist, in private individual sessions. An affair must be ended, whether or not the spouse knows about it, if the marriage is to improve. If a revelation is important, the therapist is not the one to make it. Even if he recommends telling something, the responsibility for the decision still resides with the person who would have to make and live with the disclosure. In either case, telling or not telling, the therapist cannot promise that therapy will be successful. All one can do is guide and offer to help; there are times when one can be sure therapy will *not* work unless certain things are done, and the requirement to bring to closure and sometimes to disclose an affair is made in this spirit.

Selectivity helps create a coherent group. Some diversity is desirable. The second author finds that stage-of-life differences among couples ranging from grandparents to relative newlyweds can be beneficial; this is in contrast to Framo's position that people should be of similar age and phase of life cycle. Cultural, racial and religious heterogeneity is invigorating, and subtle similarities in values and life style are often more remarkable than the more obvious sociocultural differences. Yet with couples of widely divergent educational background, a common idiom must exist. It may be as unreasonable for professorial types to try to communicate at a high school level as the reverse, but the less well educated can keep the rest of us—therapists, especially—alert and challenged. Of course, to be effective the therapist must be able to engage with a broad spectrum of people, and in some cases, he may be an excellent model for reaching diverse group members. We have found considerable scope for creativity in combining people who we think can benefit from one another and can stay together for intense psychotherapeutic work.

Members of the group are informed that matters discussed in the group are to be kept confidential. Last names of couples are not revealed. Social contacts outside of the group are discouraged; in this I (J.L.) differ from Alger (1977), Neiberg (1976) and Framo (1973). If contacts occur by chance or by design, they are subject to scrutiny by the whole group. These interactions are hazardous because some relationships may gel more than others; individuals or couples "left out" may not be able to talk about their feelings of being excluded. Also, comments may be passed between couples outside group which become secrets and can never be dealt with in therapy. This impedes the group process and often causes a reenactment of earlier bitter in-group/out-group experiences.

Since the therapist cannot use his time in other pursuits if a member is absent, everyone pays for all sessions. The ongoing charge means absences are dealt with as a group issue, not in monetary terms. If one spouse has to miss a session, the other should come anyway. There are occasions when a sole spouse may tell something to the group that might not be revealed in the presence of his/her partner. Remarkably, the group tacitly respects the privacy of that communication, although the members are not bound to keep it secret; they accept the information as appropriate, supporting the risk-taker and often helping the one present to find a good way to communicate the matter to his/her spouse. In this process, group members identify with the therapist, who supports risk-taking and respects and protects privacy of certain substantive revelations while striving to improve communication of feelings.

A member is not entitled to information from a session which he missed. A spouse may relate the essence of a session at home so that the absent one will not be completely left out, but such summarizing can never be complete and may be quite biased. One might avoid this problem by taping the session for the missing member; however, this may reduce the spontaneity of the participants and lacks the immediacy of context.

The "principle of spousal independence" holds also for exodus from some therapists' treatment groups (J.L.). If one leaves, the other may remain. This procedure removes the power of one spouse to terminate the other's participation. Thus, in Lieberman's groups, but not in Framo's, Kadis and Markowitz's, or Kaslow's, it is possible to have group with one or more unaccompanied spouses. The others believe couples group is for couples only, except for a rare absence of a spouse, and that the dyadic interaction can be focal only when both are present. Out of consideration for the group, a member should not leave without warning; but if one does, the group must deal with the occurrence.

When there is only one therapist and he/she needs to be absent, group may be rescheduled. If all members want to meet without the therapist, this can be a useful experiment; taping may be justified in that event. If more than three of eight members expect to be absent, it may be well to cancel the session. However, if four members are eager for a meeting, the therapist's discretion should be used.

The problem of cancellation rarely occurs when a co-therapy model, much preferred by Kaslow, is utilized. As a matter of fact, if one of the co-therapy pair cannot attend, group members are likely to try splitting the therapy couple in much the same way they did earlier regarding their own parents— the one present, and therefore available to them, is good; the one absent is neglectful and rejecting, and therefore bad. It provides a fine in vivo opportunity for patients to relive the implications of the splitting mechanism and for the therapist to indicate: (1) that absence is not equal to abandon- ment, (2) that he has no need to be the favorite therapist (parent), as the relationship is collaborative and not competitive, and (3) that the group (family) does not need both therapists (parents) all of the time to survive and function well. If the other therapist misses a session some weeks later and the patients indicate, as they usually do, how poorly the meeting went when the first one was absent and how glad they are he/she is here tonight, the dynamics of playing one therapist off against the other again must be explored and exploded.

The emphasis in our groups on relationships permits each person to view and be viewed by his/her spouse in a relatively objective but supportive atmosphere. Interaction across couples is cultivated. This takes pressure off each marriage, widens the perspective and allows one to feel empathetically toward one's spouse with the help of a benign third person, who may or may not be the therapist. Spouses are discouraged from continually bringing up marital issues as such. "My husband won't talk about his feelings" must be converted to a statement about how the wife herself feels and what she does about it or could possibly do to change something about herself. It is simple to be an expert on the other person's problems while denying one's own; yet each must be helped to recognize and modify his/her contribution to the marital contention. In principle, each member requests feedback and interpretation; however, often such comment is best delivered by those more objective and less enmeshed than the spouse.

One of the remarkable dynamics seen is the contribution of each spouse to the pathology which he/she ostensibly wishes to change in the other. Napier (1978, pp. 5–12) describes such an interaction in his discussion of the rejection-intrusion pattern; and Rubenstein and Timmens (1978), pp. 13–24) describe the precarious seesaw quality in the depressive dyad. Group members are usually quick to see that the complainer often helps maintain the "undesired" behavior in the spouse (Rabinowitz, 1974). It is necessary to find unexpressed needs of the complaining spouse which have no obvious link to the specific grievance. For example, a wife complains that she has to persuade her husband to come to the group against his will, and that he reluctantly promised her that he would give it a try. As the husband becomes involved in the group, however, the wife becomes increasingly distressed, apparently because the husband is now in the group for his own reasons. She has lost a measure of control. This is the critical issue, not her husband's resistance to therapy.

CONCLUSION

Three different models and modes of couples group therapy have been depicted as illustrative of current approaches subsumed under this umbrella heading. We have tried to highlight the essence of each and believe some notable differences as well as some common themes emerge clearly from the mélange. The theoretical framework is an integrative one incorporating analytic, humanistic-existential and behavioral approaches. It becomes clear that there is no single entity called couples group therapy. There are choices available to therapists, clients and agencies, depending on personal and professional predilection, patient diagnosis and preference, time available, setting, cost and staff competence. Each of the major modes presented has value, and every therapist should explore more than one mode in order to know personally the advantages and limitations of several approaches and which is most compatible with his/her style, rhythm and patient population.

A second major theme which emerges is that the essential issue which surfaces in all couples groups is that of individuation and intimacy, separation and togetherness—and in what proportion each of these aspects of health and wholeness is desirable. For too much separateness produces alienation and isolation, and too much togetherness reflects or comes from a loss of self and too much fusion. In couples therapy, strides are made toward achieving the vital balance and toward facilitating a marital bond that is dynamic and ethical.

Of the three approaches described, Framo's approach gives the therapist most control and keeps the process oriented to couple communication. Although he states that the individual is a principal emphasis, we think an important expression of individuality is hindered by the deemphasis on cross-couple interactions. Problems similar to those encountered in conjoint marital sessions may arise—the tendency to overscrutinize the relationship and to encourage replay of redundant and collusive arguments. At least the presence of other commentators prevents the therapist from falling into the role of referee.

Not only is separation from the family of origin a goal in all psychodynamically oriented couples group therapy, but so, too, is the strengthening of each individual's personal identity within the couple. *Capacity for intimacy without fusion* depends upon mature individuation. Couples groups foster this uniquely by helping a person work it through in the presence of his/her own spouse, who thereby also gains some awareness of the dilemma and process and is therefore less likely to sabotage the effort.

In the Kadis and Markowitz, Kaslow, and Lieberman models, healthy intimacy is developed both within and across couple boundaries. A solid marriage requires the recognition by each spouse that attraction toward, and being attractive to, others is desirable as long as it does not jeopardize basic trust. Sensitivity and leadership skill are required of the therapist, who must balance between a stultifying assumption of rigid couple boundaries and a casual disregard for boundaries when structure and commitment are needed.

As clinicians who sometimes utilize couples group therapy as the treatment of choice, we posit that the rewards and benefits to patients and therapist alike outweigh the difficulties encountered.

Couples group therapy does not belong exclusively under the rubric of family therapy, group therapy or marital therapy. It builds upon and draws from all three, in some ways achieving a new, potent and more meaningful synthesis.

REFERENCES

Alger, I. Multiple couple therapy. In P.J. Guerin (Ed.), *Family therapy: Theroy and practice.* New York: Gardner, 1976.

Baker, L.D., and Nagata, F.S. A group approach to the treatment of heterosexual couples with sexual dissatisfactions. *J. Sex Ed. & Ther.*, 1978, *4*, (1), 15–18.

Cohen, H. Family counsel. Interview broadcast Feb. 22, 1977, WAMU-FM, American Univ., Washington, D.C.

DeWitt, K.N. The effectiveness of family therapy: A review of outcome research. *Arch. Gen. Psychiat.*, 1978, *35*, 549–651.

Framo, J.L. Marriage therapy in a couples group. In D. Bloch (Ed.), *Techniques of family psychotherapy: A primer.* New York: Grune and Stratton, 1973.

Gottlieb, A., and Pattison, E.M. Married couples group psychotherapy. *Arch. Gen. Psychiat.*, 1966, *14*, 143–152.

Jacobson, N.S. Problem solving and contingency contracting in the treatment of marital discord. *J. Consult. & Clin. Psychol.*, 1977, *45*, (1), 92–100.

Kadis, A., and Markowitz, M. Short term analytic treatment of married couples in a group by a therapist couple. In C. Sager and H.S. Kaplan (Eds.), *Progress in group and family therapy*, New York: Brunner/Mazel, 1972.

L'Abate, L. *Enrichment: Structured interventions with couples, families and groups.* Washington, D.C.: Univ. Press of America, 1977.

Liberman, R.P., Wheeler, E., and Sanders, N. Behavioral therapy for marital disharmony: An educational approach. *J. Marr. & Fam. Couns.*, Oct. 1976, *2*, 4, 385–395.

Mace, D. Marital and sexual counseling: The state of the art. In D.W. Abse, E.M. Nash and L.M.R.. Louden (Eds.), *Marital and sexual counseling in medical practice.* New York: Harper and Row, 1974, 1–14.

Mace, D., and Mace V. *How to have a happy marriage.* Nashville, Tenn.: Abingdon Press, 1977.

Napier, A.Y. The rejection-intrusion pattern: A central family dynamic. *J. Marr. & Fam. Couns.*, 1978, *4*, 1, 5–12.

Neiberg, A. The group psychotherapy of married couples. In H. Grunebaum and J. Crist (Eds.), *Contemporary marriage.* Boston: Little, Brown, 1976, 401–410.

Paolini, T.J., and McCrady, B.S. *Marriage and marital therapy.* New York: Brunner/Mazel, 1978.

Paul, N.L., and Paul, B.B. *A Marital Puzzle.* New York: W.W. Norton, 1975.

Rabinowitz, S. Marital conflicts and group psychotherapy. In S.W. Abse, E.M. Nash and L.M.R. Louden (Eds.), *Marital and sexual counseling in medical practice.* New York: Harper and Row, 1974, 174–183.

Rubenstein, D., and Timmens, J.F. Depressive dyadic and triadic relationships. *J. Marr. & Fam. Couns.*, 1978, *4*, 1, 13–24.

Chapter 14

Couples Communication and Marital Enhancement: A Didactic Approach

Mirta T. Mulhare

THE BACKGROUND

Culture is a shared system of symbols, a learned system of expectations, of meanings. This symbolic system is based on language, both verbal and nonverbal. It is the binding thread of all interpersonal relations.

Couples, families, groups of all sorts, form their own microcultures and evolve their own special system of expectations, of symbols, of meanings. Because each individual is also a culture unto himself, each member of a couples' system brings to the relationship his/her own set of symbols and expectations. They must both learn from and teach each other new meanings. The acquisition of new meanings continues throughout one's lifetime. We keep on learning how, when, what and to whom to communicate.

It is this basic aspect of communication, which is acquired, not innate, that has resulted in a variety of couples and family treatment modalities. Programs of studies emerging from the growing emphasis on learning theory, client-centered approaches (Rodgers, 1951) and the impact of systems theory on contemporary relational therapy (Von Bertalanffy, 1968) now exist.

Those who wish to explore further the influence of systems on relational therapy are directed to the chapter by Stanton in this volume. Undoubtedly, the work of Haley and Minuchin and other contemporary thinkers has had a salutary impact on the emergence of didactic modalities emphasizing communication.

Many approaches for couples and marital treatment have been developed based on educational, marital-enhancement and preventive models. Contractual arrangements, negotiation techniques and conflict resolution combining instructional modalities with systems analysis are now in use.

Olson's (1976, pp. 4–5) overview of trends in treating relationships identifies four major conceptual and programmatic directions being followed today:

1. Emphasis on increasing specific skills rather than global treatment
2. Increasing use of educational and preventive models
3. Greater reliance on groups versus individual approaches
4. Shorter-term contracts rather than open-ended treatment.

These trends are illustrated in the programs selected for review here. This brief review also provides a basis on which to design other couples communication workshops and marital-enhancement programs, utilizing the guidelines given in the last part of this paper.

All of the programs reviewed have in common:

1. A stress on the couples building on their own resources prior to building additional ones (Mace and Mace, 1973, 1974).
2. Couples progress viewed as a breakthrough in communication (Mace and Mace, in Olson, 1976; Miller, 1971; Karlsson, 1951).

Good communication has been shown to be highly correlated with good marital adjustment (Rappaport, 1976). In *The Mirages of Marriage* (Lederer and Jackson, 1968), communication as the key to a successful relationship was already stressed. Marital adjustment, however, is difficult to define. Locke and Williamson (1958) have called it a tendency for couples to provide means to avoid or resolve conflict, which is the desired result for all treatments (Bateson and Jackson, 1968; Navran, 1967; Watzlawick et al., 1967; Williams and Womble, 1966).

All techniques possible for treating an individual couple can and have been used in group approaches emphasizing communication: role-playing, role reversal, psychodrama, sculpting and others.

Whatever the technique used, the main difference with individual couples treatment is the emphasis on a carefully structured plan, with clearly defined goals and rules and procedures for reaching these goals.

THE PROGRAMS

One of the most notable examples of a carefully structured program is the Minnesota Couples Communication Program (MCCP). It was developed and first used with premarital couples in 1968 at the University of Minnesota.

The originators of the program summarized their goals as follows: "First, increase each partner's awareness of self and his contribution to interaction within significant relationships; second, increase each partner's skill in effectively expressing his own self-information—that is, making this self-awareness available to one's partner; and third, enhance each partner's sense of choice within the relationship for maintaining changing ways of relating in a mutually satisfying manner" (Miller, Nunnaly, and Wackman, in Olson, 1976, p. 38). These goals are basic to any program of this sort and relevant to any form of relational treatment. Results of their first research project are encouraging. The program seems to be beneficial at any point in the couple's life cycle. By 1976, approximately twelve hundred couples had gone through this training. Since the initial experiment, a classroom setting has developed. The group context has been a significant learning environment. Each couple has multiple models immediately available to them to watch and question—most necessary for the premarital couples, who are usually isolated from each other.

All programs reviewed underlined the acquisition of skills through learning procedures and of principles for effective communication within a group setting. Interaction among participating couples in communication and enhancement programs was generally promoted—except for "Catholic Marriage Encounters." This program was initiated in New Jersey in 1967. Originally, it was imported from Spain (Bosco, 1972). Catholic Marriage Encounters is a private affair between the couple, who is part of a participating team of married couples led by a priest. No modeling or learning from other couples takes place.

Other marital-enrichment programs have been emerging. A survey of them was conducted by Otto in 1975. One of the oldest and best known is ACME (Association for Couples for Marriage Enrichment). It conducts a variety of programs and utilizes the retreat approach. The effectiveness of the retreat as a learning medium for couples seeking a better relationship was studied in 1974 by Swicegood. The conclusion was that follow-ups were needed after intense retreats. A one-time program on a weekend or otherwise does not appear to provide, according to Swicegood's study, the depth of learning and understanding needed by the couple to give long-range relief.

Conflict resolution, negotiation skills and other approaches built on the open expression of discomfort and dissatisfaction have developed (Harrell and Guerney, 1976). Play fighting or expressing constructive aggression as a good basis for building a good relationship has been explored as early as 1968 (Bach and Wyden, 1968).

One of the main problems in all these programs is the measurement of their effectiveness. Having accurate instruments to measure before and after training becomes a necessity for evaluation. Bienvenue (1970) conducted a pilot study of 172 couples, which revealed significant contrasts in patterns and degrees of communication among them. He used as a measuring instrument a "communications inventory," which attempted to differentiate between good and poor communication, the handling of anger and differences, tone of voice, understanding, good listening habits and self-disclosure.

Bienvenue states that "happy" couples report an absence of irritating tone. Effective control and direction of communication processes were associated with "satisfying" marriages. There have been other attempts at producing measuring instruments (Rotter, 1967; Farber, 1957). Measuring program effectiveness is still difficult. Long-term follow-ups of couples who have undergone training are probably better indicators of effectiveness of training.

Another approach which should be mentioned here is the use of programmed instruction to improve communication. Programmed texts based on learning principles had been used as early as 1964 (Bugelski). Hickman and Baldwin (1971) also worked with thirty couples from "Conciliation Court," referred there because of marital problems, and used programmed text training with them versus a control group receiving no treatment and another group which had marital counseling emphasizing marital communication. According to Hickman and Baldwin, the group receiving programmed texts changed positively on the variables in semantic differential scores pre- and post-test. The text used was *Improving Communication in Marriage*, a publication of the Human Development Institute, 1967.

STRUCTURING A DIDACTIC COUPLES GROUP

Basic Guidelines

More and more couples are asking for shorter-term, less costly preventive and group approaches to better relationships. Should an experienced couples therapist wish to begin a didactic group, the following should prove helpful:

1. Preferably, have a co-leader of the opposite sex, and make sure you are both in complete agreement as to the nature and style of the program.

2. Limit your first group to no less than five and no more than seven couples *who are not in therapy at the time.* The obvious disadvantage of a couple being in therapy and also participating in a group program is the possible dilution of the effect of both experiences. Maintaining a small number will allow the development of a good communication flow and better control for the therapist leaders.

3. Do not include any couples you or your co-leader have seen in therapy before. It could alienate the other couples and jeopardize the program.

4. Set a specific number and length of sessions, and stick to it. The model that will be given was set for eleven sessions of ninety minutes each, with a few minutes break in between two sessions of approximately forty minutes each, and one review session four weeks after the last session.

5. Set other rules as well, governing such things as tardiness, attendance, smoking or not smoking, and other group behavior.

6. Goals must be clearly specified and the program must be given an identifiable title related to the goals to be accomplished. For example, the model that will be provided here could be called "Role and Contract Clarification: A Workshop for Couples," "Redefining the Marital Contract" or any other title that would clearly indicate what will be done. Do not promise too much in setting the goals or the title of the workshop. Have realistic goals which can be attained in a first workshop; think of more advanced goals possibly emerging as you reach the first ones and leave them for a future program.

7. Include all of the above in a program manual to be duplicated and distributed to participants to show applicants what the structure and function of the program are all about. As you are writing the manual, think of other questions that would be commonly asked:

   a. What can be expected from participating?
   b. Will there be homework assignments?
   c. What about confidentiality?
   d. What about contacting the leaders after the group meets on personal matters?

Many of these rules are personal choices of the leaders, hence not elaborated upon here. Common sense and experience in therapy can dictate what is best. For example, the matter of being contacted by participants for personal issues outside the group setting is controversial. One approach is to limit contact to questions about the course and around the discussion of personal matters, counseling or treatment on the telephone. Some therapists might feel differently about these contacts and could set different rules. The important guideline is that there be consistency and equal treatment for all.

Selecting an Area

By working on a specific aspect of interaction, good communication skills can be learned well, since "communication may be viewed as *how* people exchange feelings and meanings as they try to understand one another and come to see problems and differences from the other person's point of view" (Bienvenue, 1970, pp. 26–27)

A couples group can provide an excellent means for exploring how communication is or is not taking place and for focusing on communication as the basic process of marital interaction.

Role definition and contract clarification is a topic that could provide a workable structure, one that couples can easily relate to and also one that can provide realistic, attainable goals. In the course manual, a general focus for this program could be described as "clarification of role definition, task allocations, and agreements on basic issues concerning money, children, relatives, relationships, leisure activities and attitudes."

The ultimate objective could be explained as "emerging with a new couples contract that specifies roles and tasks for each partner and a series of agreements as to life style and living conditions."

In terms of communication skills to be learned, the following should be listed: "Listening, constructive verbalization of disagreement, use of substitutions, exchanges and compromises [Harrell and Guerney, 1976], learning to take care of one's feelings without insult or injury to the other person [Hobart and Klausner, 1959] and incorporating another's point of view into new agreements without ego losses for either side."

The main eleven sessions should be divided in such a manner as to limit the discussion of each area into manageable time sections.

The first session can be devoted to a general discussion of male and female roles and task allocations. Couples are left with the directive of returning with a listing of tasks that each one has been doing and reviewing them with an eye on changes and more equitable distribution—if such is needed.

Armed with these lists in the following session, the leaders launch a discussion around the agreements and disagreements brought by the couples.

From the very first session, the leaders must promote the learning of the communication skills which were listed above. As the group begins to identify problems in communication, each should be encouraged to point out to the other, "You were not listening" or "Is there a substitution possible to change this deadlock?" "Could you rephrase that without hurting John's feelings and still express your own concerns?"

Deadlocks are always possible, but the group should endeavor to help one another overcome and change deadlocks into agreements through the use of substitutions, exchanges and compromises.

Value systems will enter deeply into all the topics covered. People's ethnic backgrounds, religious and ethical systems will come into play constantly. As these differences become obvious, the leaders should point to the need to learn from each other, tolerate and compromise.

Homework varies for each couple. It is built around problems in the redefinition of roles, allocation of tasks and marital contract clauses. Couples that leave a session deadlocked must try to bring new answers and compromises to the next session. By the ninth session, each couple will have drafted its own written contract, divided by the areas covered.

By the final session, couples should sign their contract with the understanding that it will be in effect for a trial period of four weeks, after which the group will meet for a contract-review session, in which each couple will share their experiences with the new contract.

The program described provides a flexible format to enable the leader to apply creatively his/her own experience. Needless to say, anyone with severe pathology cannot be included in this program; nor can couples on the verge of divorce or couples whose excessive battling would totally prevent an effort at establishing better communication. Not unlike the other programs reviewed, this is a program for couples with relatively manageable relational problems who are not so embittered as to be ready for termination or in need of intensive therapy, individual or relational. "Marital adjustment is an adaptation between husband and wife to the point where there is companionship, agreement on basic values, affectional intimacy, accommodation, euphoria, and certain other unidentified factors. Studies should be made to discover the unidentified factors in marital adjustment and to validate these by comparing sub-scores with independent criteria" (Locke and Williamson, 1958, p. 569)

Until these studies are conducted, helping couples to draft agreements that are workable while learning communication skills can be a productive endeavor. Measuring effectiveness is difficult, but follow-ups can help to know how well the couple is applying the learned skills and adhering to agreed attitudes and behavior.

In summary, what most couples need is an opportunity to learn communication skills through better listening, constructive expression of feelings and compromise. The topic selected as a point of departure should offer the opportunity for learning basic communication skills and also help couples to emerge with a clearer agreement for a more satisfactory relationship.

REFERENCES

Bach, G.R., and Wyden, P. *The intimate enemy*. New York: William Morrow, 1968.

Bateson, G. and Jackson, D.D. Some varieties of pathogenic organization. In D.M. Rioch and E.A. Weinstein (Eds.), *Disorders of Communication*, Baltimore: Williams and Wilkins, 1968.

Bienvenue, M.J. Measurement of marital communication, *Fam. Coordinator*, Jan. 1970, *19*, 26–31.

Bosco, A. *Marriage Encounter: The rediscovery of love*. St. Meinrad, Indiana: Abbey Press, 1972.

Bugelski, B.R. *The psychology of learning applied to teaching*. New York: Bobbs-Merrill, 1964.

Farber, B. An index of marital integration. *Sociometry*, 1957, *20*, 117–134.

Harrell, J., and Guerney, B.G., Jr. Training married couples in conflict negotiation skills. In Olson, H.L., *Treating relationships*, Graphic, 1976.

Hickman, M.E., and Baldwin, B.A. Use of programmed instruction to improve communication in marriage. *Fam. Coord.* 1971, 121–125.

Hobart, C.W., and Klausner, W.J. Some social interactional correlates of marital role disagreement, and marital adjustment, *Marr. & fam. living*, August 1959, 256–263.

Human Development Institute. *Improving communication in marriage* (3rd ed.). Atlanta: HDI, 1967.

Karlsson, G. *Adaptability and communication in marriage: A Swedish prediction study of marital satisfaction*, Uppsala, Swed: Almquist and Wiksells, Boktrycheri Aktiebolag, 1951.

Lederer, W., and Jackson, D. *Mirages of marriage*. New York: W.W. Norton, 1968.

Locke, H.J., and Williamson, R.C. Marital adjustment: A factor analysis study, *Am. Sociologic. Rev.* 1958, *28*, 562–569.

Mace, D., and Mace, V. Marriage enrichment retreats: Story of a Quaker project, Friends General Conference, 1973.

Mace, D., and Mace, V. We can have better marriages—If we really want them, Nashville, Tenn. 1974.

Mace, D., and Mace, V. Marriage enrichment—A preventative group approach for couples. In Olson, H.L., *Treating relationships*, Graphic Publishing Co., Inc., 1976, 321–336.

Miller, S. *The effects of communication training in small groups upon self-disclosure and openness in engaged couples' systems of interaction: A field experiment*, Unpublished Ph.D. Thesis, University of Minnesota, 1971.

Miller, S., Nunnally, E.W., and Wackman, D., Minnesota couples communication program premarital and marital groups. In H.L. Olson, *Treating relationships*, Graphic, 1976.

Navran, L. Communication and adjustment in marriage, *Fam. Proc.*, 1967, *6*, 173–184.

Olson, D.H.L. (Ed.). *Treating relationships*, Iowa: Graphic, 1976.

Otto, H. Marriage and family enrichment program in North America—Report and analysis, *Fam. Coord.*, 1975, *24*, 137–142.

Rappaport, A.F. Conjugal relationship enhancement program. In D.H.L. Olson (Ed.). *Treating relationships*. Graphic, 1976.

Rodgers, C. *Client-centered therapy*. Boston: Houghton-Mifflin, 1951.

Rotter, J.A. A new scale for the measurement of interpersonal trust, *J. Personality*, 1967, *35*, 651–655.

Swicegood, M.L. An evaluative study of one approach to marriage enrichment, Unpub. Ph.D. Diss., Univ. of North Carolina at Greensboro, 1974.

Bertalanffy, L. von, *General systems theory*. New York: George Braziller, 1968.

Watzlawick, P., Beavin, J.H., and Jackson, D.D. *Pragmatics of human communication*. New York: W.W. Norton, 1967.

Williams, D.D., and Womble, D.L. Interpersonal communication in marriage, *J. Home Econ.*, 1966, *58*, 35–39.

PART III

Special Issues and Techniques

Chapter 15

Evaluation and Research on Marital Therapy

Ann Marie Williams
William R. Miller

INTRODUCTION

Often a body of literature takes on a personality of its own as it comes to reflect the values and concerns of its contributors. Even reviewers, through the standards they set and the criteria they offer, tend to shape the direction of future research efforts. This review of the reviews will analyze the marital-therapy-outcome literature as an organic whole, as a "client" with a history to be understood and a prognosis to be predicted. By analyzing the "behavior" of this body of literature, looking at what has been done and what has been omitted, we will try to see what steps are needed to make it healthier and more productive in the future.

This overview of marital therapy outcome research is not meant to duplicate the recent exhaustive reviews contributed by Gurman and Kniskern (1978b) and Jacobson (1978b, 1979). Rather, in order to "take the history" of the outcome literature, we will summarize the strengths and growing pains of our literary "client" as reported in the reviews published in the decade since 1969. This history will be followed by a discussion of the methodological problems which have made our growing up difficult. Finally, the implications of our history and current status will be discussed with some specific suggestions for improving our prognosis.

This chapter is limited to reviews of couple counseling outcome studies. For reviews of the effectiveness of marital enrichment programs, the reader is referred to Gurman and Kniskern (1977) and Hof, Miller and Green (1980). The sex therapy literature has been reviewed by Jacobson (1978b) and Marks (1976), and reviews of the evaluation of family therapy are available in Dewitt (1978) and in Gurman and Kniskern (1978b).

THE HISTORY OF OUTCOME STUDIES

Since the late 1960's, there has been a growth spurt in the literature on the effectiveness of marital therapy techniques and treatment programs. When Emily Mudd surveyed the field in 1957, there were no outcome studies to be found. When David Olson did the decade review in 1969, he surveyed over two hundred articles but found fewer than twenty studies which could be considered marital therapy research. He reported that seven of these twenty studies amounted to therapy case follow-ups. Four other studies had analyzed the advantages and disadvantages of various therapy formats, namely conjoint (Beck, 1966; Dicks, 1967; and Fitzgerald, 1969) and group versus individual-couples therapy (Burton and Kaplan, 1968). Only one completed study included a control group (Ely, 1970). Lastly, one study systematically analyzed the effects of training wives in behavior change methods (Goldstein and Francis, 1969). The remainder of the twenty outcome studies reviewed by Olson dealt with the characteristics of the clients and the marital therapists as well as the methodological difficulties in doing research in marital therapy. In summary, Olson found only thirteen completed studies which evaluated the effectiveness of marital therapy. He concluded that "more methodological research is needed in this field before adequate research methods can be developed" (p. 41). Due to the lack of many of the fundamentals of scientific research, Olson (1970, p. 530) further concluded, "Little is actually known about the process or effectiveness of the clinical approaches now in use." However, he was optimistic about future research efforts.

Alan Gurman, as a Ph.D. candidate, published his first review of the outcome literature in 1971. After reviewing twenty-six articles describing marital therapy done in a group format, he concluded that the three studies which did include systematic evaluations (Maizlish and Hurley, 1963; Targow and Zweber, 1969) lacked the methodological sophistication needed to substantiate their reported results. Relying on self-reports of positive attitude changes, the criteria for improvement were indirect (unobservable), were subject to rater bias and contamination and lacked any kind of control or comparison groups. Gurman (1971) recommended that future outcome studies include:

1. Comparative study of various group marital therapy methods (psychoanalytic, client-centered, behavioral, etc.)
2. Comparative study of group and other marital therapies—e.g., conjoint, concurrent, collaborative
3. "Comparative study of the effects . . . through multiple evaluation (i.e., patients, therapists, and independent judges). The measurement of response generalization must include evaluation of the effects of treatment on other significant figures in a couple's lives, especially, a couple's children" (p. 186)
4. Investigation of primary therapist characteristics . . . (e.g., warmth, empathy, regard, position on the A-B scale)
5. "Investigation of the effects of group composition on therapeutic effectiveness (e.g., age of participants, length of marriage, SES level, symptomatology)" (pp. 184–186).

After describing the debate between psychoanalytic goals for individual personality change and relationship goals for marital interaction, Gurman concluded: "Intra-individual change by itself is not a meaningful index of an improved marital relationship—it is meaningful only when it constitutes an active ingredient of more effective behavior between marital partners." Gurman was neither optimistic nor pessimistic; he frankly stated the urgent need for better empirical research.

In his second review, Gurman (1973a) analyzed the marital therapy literature through August 1972. His content analysis of a 415-item marital therapy bibliography revealed a trend toward "growing interest in empirical and methodological issues." By searching four previous bibliographies and the current *Psychological Abstracts*, Gurman found forty-three outcome studies, thirty of which had been written *since* 1967. In view of the rapid recent growth of the field, he was optimistic that it "suggested that the marital clinician of the next several years will become increasingly eclectic, pragmatic, and, hopefully, effective [p. 53]."

In a paper given in October 1972, David Olson presented the first review and critique of behavior therapy research with couples and families. His paper has not been published to date and thus has not been widely available for review. However, it appears to have influenced subsequent reviews (Gurman, 1973a; Gurman and Kniskern, 1978a, 1978b, 1978c) because of its use of a systems analysis approach to the evaluation of both the methodological and theoretical limitations of behavioral research.

Olson's critique of behavior therapy strongly recommended the analysis of marital and family problems on five system levels: (1) intrapersonal (individual), (2) interpersonal, (3) quasi-interactional (during structured task in a controlled setting), (4) interactional (self and relationship to others), (5) transactional (marital or family group as total system). He also suggested that therapy assessment include measurement of generalization of change to nontarget behaviors and to nontarget relationships (e.g., parent-child interaction). Furthermore, Olson noted that behavior therapists have used self-reports of behaviors to assess both therapy *process* and *outcome*, although "surprisingly little research has been done to assess the reliability and validity of this data." Finally, he exhorted behavior therapists to focus in the future on *how to improve* behavior therapy rather than on the *need to prove* it. Presumably, the "need to prove" statement was in reference to the debate current at that time in individual psychotherapy regarding symptom substitution.

In this third review, Gurman (1973b) analyzed the marital therapy outcome literature from 1950 through October 1972. Of the forty-three studies previously mentioned, seventeen were omitted because they predated 1950, did not include explicit statements of the outcome assessment procedures used, or did not involve the treatment of three or more couples. The remaining twenty-six studies were examined microscopically to determine whether or not the "growing trend toward experimentation and empiricism" was as promising as it seemed at first glance. Some of the strengths of these twenty-six studies were the following: (1) The clients ranged in age from early twenties through mid-fifties; (2) the therapists represented a wide range of disciplines; (3) they introduced interaction testing, in which both spouses' behavior was observed in a structured setting (Goodrich and Boomer, 1963; Olson and Ryder, 1970; Olson and Strauss, 1972; Strodtbeck, 1951); (4) they introduced also the use of multidimensional assessment rather than just global ratings in about half of the studies; (5) the length of treatment in the twenty-six studies seemed to be "quite representative of the duration of most therapy practiced in outpatient clinics"; (6) the overall improvement rate was 66 percent across the variety of treatment types and therapist orientations; and (7) they introduced the repeated single-case design by clinician-researchers. To summarize the positive aspects of the growth trend, Gurman observed that "it is clear that there are potent change-inducing elements active in the marital therapies." However, as will be seen in the discussion of the shortcomings, in 1973 we had almost no idea what the active change-inducing elements were.

The methodological weaknesses of the outcome literature were made evident by Gurman's (1973b) intensive analysis: (1) Since most of the therapists were also the researchers and authors, the reports ran the risk of lacking "investigative objectivity"; (2) although eight of the outcome studies *did* include a nontreatment control group, eighteen of the studies *did not*; (3) while eleven studies used ratings of individual changes and another eleven studies used ratings of couple changes, only four studies assessed *both* individual and dyadic effects of treatment; (4) while thirteen studies used ratings from more than one perspective (patient and/or therapist and/or independent judge and/or behavioral records), thirteen of the studies *did not* use multidimensional assessments, which Gurman felt were "generally acknowledged as requisite" for psychotherapy outcome research, based on the standards outlined by Bergin and Strupp (1972) and Strupp and Bergin (1969); (5) although the studies that *did* include follow-up evaluations reported slight increases in improvement after therapy termination (Fitzgerald, 1969; Goldstein, 1971; Linden, Goodwin and Resnik, 1968; Stuart, 1969; Targow and Zweber, 1969), twenty-one outcome studies lacked adequate follow-up; (6) while nine specific criteria were used among the studies (e.g., sexual satisfaction, communication skill or specific change in problem behavior), "the most commonly used outcome criterion has been a global rating of change, which has many serious shortcomings"; (7) few of the twenty-six outcome studies indicated either the number of treatment dropouts or what became of them; (8) no satisfactory baseline for spontaneous improvement of untreated marital problems has been determined; (9) only three of the twenty-six studies included documentation of deterioration among a few (2 percent) of their marital-therapy clients; (10) because relevant patient characteristics were not routinely reported (e.g., age, SES level, diagnosis, previous therapy), information was not available to answer the question, "Effective treatment *for whom*?"; and (11) we didn't know exactly *what* worked or *why*—that is, "clinically relevant assessments of the specifics of the change process" were lacking.

Gurman (1973b) rated these outcome studies for "Adequacy of Design," using the following six criteria:

1. Random assignment of patients to treatments/therapists
2. Follow-up of patients
3. Inclusion of pre/post-measurement of outcome
4. Research predictions stated in advance
5. Appropriate statistical analysis
6. Authors are not also the therapists in the study (footnote, p. 155).

The ratings were assigned "grades," as follows:

Level 1. 0–2 criteria met = poor
Level 2. 3 criteria met = fair
Level 3. 4 or 5 criteria met = good
Level 4. 6 criteria met = very good

Overall, the research design grades were bimodal, in that ten studies were rated "poor," while eleven studies were rated "very good," with the five remaining studies either "fair" or "good." Gurman did not comment on the qualitative improvement in these outcome studies over the history of the literature. This trend can be seen clearly in Figure 1, in which the grade-point average for each year is graphed against the year of publication. As can be seen in the ratios of quality points to number of studies, there was a decrease in the number of outcome studies written after 1969, but an increase in adequacy of research design. We suspect this qualitative increase is in part due to the development of individual psychotherapy research, described by Bergin (1971), Bergin and Strupp (1970) and Strupp and Bergin (1969). We will see in our later discussion of the more recent reviews whether this decrease is a trend in the literature or an artifact of the number of articles available at the time the review was written.

Finally, Gurman ended on a positive note by observing that marital-therapy research "had nòt yet become ensnared in narrow, theoretical dogma" so that the field was free to grow and develop according to what worked best rather than try to follow "pre-established notions."

In the same year, Weiss, Hops and Patterson (1973) published their review

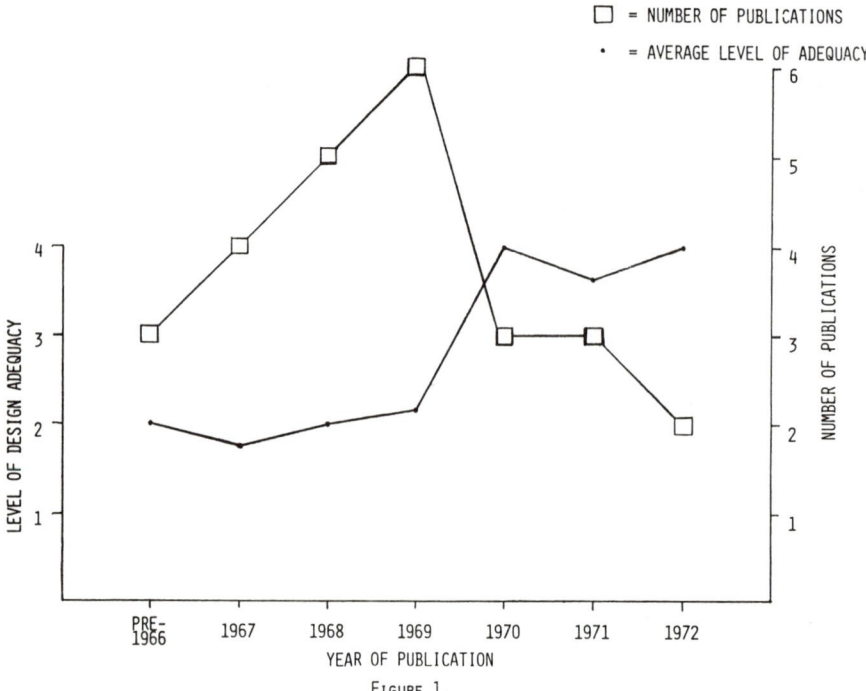

FIGURE 1.

*BASED ON DATA FROM GURMAN (1973 B).

of behavioral marital therapy. Although their review did not include nonbehavioral studies, it is important for our consideration because it was the first lengthy description of the Marriage Research Project at the Oregon Research Institute and University of Oregon. The project directors, Gerald Patterson and Robert L. Weiss, worked with four doctoral students, who produced dissertations and theses which were valuable additions to the marital research literature: Birchler (1973), Reid (1967), Vincent (1973) and Wills (1971). During the same period, Hops, Wills, Patterson and Weiss (1971) formulated the Marital Interaction Coding System (MICS). The Weiss et al. (1973) report presented six newly developed techniques for assessment of dyadic interaction:

1. The Willingness to Change (W-C) scale, which is a self-report survey of specific activities and behaviors each spouse would like his or her partner to change
2. The Marital Activities Inventory: Together, Alone, Others (MAITAO) survey, which asks the frequency of occurrence of eighty-five common recreational, self-enhancing, affectional and utilitarian activities during the previous month
3. The Pleasurable-Displeasurable (Ps and Ds) count, which is a quasi-observational self-report procedure for daily coding of spouse behaviors recorded at home
4. A structured interview, during which the interviewer rates both verbal and nonverbal exchanges between spouses as positive or negative
5. Samples of ongoing problem-solving behaviors, which are coded using the MICS
6. Home observation of family interaction, in which specific behaviors (e.g., talk, whine, yell) and specific consequences (e.g., attend, ignore) are coded.

The Oregon group presented a comprehensive behavioral treatment program, which included communication skills training, discrimination and pinpointing of problem behaviors, negotiation skills training and exchange contracting. A group of five couples participated in the first study, which showed somewhat significant improvement on both observational and self-report measures of marital interaction. In the second study, a slightly older group of couples participated in the therapy program for a longer period of time (fifty-six to ninety-one days on a weekly basis, rather than ten to sixty days on a weekly basis). The results of the second study showed significant improvement on counts of Pleasurable and Displeasurable behaviors at post-treatment testing. At the three- to six-month follow-up, the Locke-Wallace (1959) scores showed maintenance of their significant improvement ($p < .01$), as did the Willingness to Change survey ($p < .05$). The inventory of activities, MAITAO, did not show a group mean change, even though seven of the ten participants reported an increase in percent time spent with spouse. Although the outcomes for both studies were positive, the purpose of the chapter was more than just data presentation. It was to describe "the continual interplay between case study and technique building," which involved "moving from case study to technique development, then to replicated case studies with the new techniques [pp. 337–38]," rather than to simply state "what we did worked." By modeling the *process* of applied clinical research—from conceptualization through intervention to evaluation—this detailed report made an important developmental step in the growth of marital therapy outcome literature.

The review of the behavioral literature done by Greer and D'Zurilla (1975) covered the period from 1968 to 1974. They found thirteen completed studies which can best be characterized as *demonstration* studies. The first three were individual case studies which demonstrated the use of negotiation and exchange contracts (Hickok and Komechak, 1974; Rappaport and Harrell, 1972; and Wieman, Shoulders and Farr, 1974). The next five articles were reports on the use of a mechanical apparatus to evaluate and, in some cases, modify the verbal or nonverbal communication of distressed couples (Eisler, Hersen and Agras, 1973a, b; Carter and Thomas, 1973a, b; Thomas, Carter and Gambrill, 1971). In addition to the work of the Oregon research group already described (Weiss et al., 1973), Greer and D'Zurilla (1975) summarized three studies which demonstrated their behavioral intervention on a single experimental treatment group without either control or comparison groups (Goldstein, 1971; Goldstein and Francis, 1969; and Stuart, 1969). The last completed study in the review was Azrin, Naster and Jones (1973), which had a modular treatment package with negotiating and contracting skills similar to the program developed by Weiss, Hops and Patterson. In comparing the Oregon marital-therapy program with the Azrin et al. package, Greer and D'Zurilla (1975, p. 311) added their commentary on the relative practicality of the two programs:

> At this point a marriage counselor reading this paper may . . . be wondering how he is supposed to translate the MICS into a viable assessment device when he has no videotape equipment, not to mention research assistants for coding (even if he had time to train them); when he does not have the staff to conduct home observation visits; and when he rarely has clients cooperative enough to spend their time and money completing assessment instruments or daily reports of P's and D's.

The Azrin et al. program, on the other hand, required only a daily pencil-and-paper rating of nine specific marital problems and of overall marital happiness. The reviewers also commented favorably on the use of a placebo-control condition ("catharsis counseling") during six one-hour sessions prior to the introduction of the reciprocity procedures. Although this own-control procedure was seen as a "decided methodological improvement," Greer and D'Zurilla (p. 313) were cautious about the implications of the results:

> Designs which include matched no-treatment groups and placebo control groups are still needed before a definite cause-effect relationship can be concluded.

The tone of their comments on the behavioral outcome literature was neither complacent nor overly critical and demanding. On the contrary, the *implied* message was acknowledgment and encouragement: "What you've done so far is good. Now try more difficult research designs."

Dorothy Fahs Beck (1975), the director of research for the Family Service Association of America (FSAA), reviewed the outcome literature from the perspective of a service provider. Her review summarized six different types of research projects: (1) the 1970 FSAA census of 1,919 agency cases involving marital problems; (2) eight published studies (with a minimum of ten cases each) reporting global outcomes without control-group comparisons; (3) eight studies, originally doctoral dissertations, reporting the results when individual, joint or group marital counseling was utilized as one approach; (4) twelve controlled-outcome studies using only structured communication training; (5) nine controlled-outcome studies using behavioral techniques; and (6) three controlled-outcome studies, originally doctoral dissertations, which analyzed marital-enrichment groups.

The FSAA report reviewed by Beck is an important addition to the marital-therapy-outcome literature. For each of the 985 marital cases in the nationwide study, both the counselor and client independently rated changes in marital and family functioning. The outcome criteria included global ratings of improvement in the clients' total problem situation and in sub-areas, as well as a composite change score from the average of the change scores reported in four major areas. Counselors and clients independently rated multiple indicators of change in the client's presenting problems, the client's approach to problem-solving, changes in family relationships and changes in individual family members. Follow-up data were received from 585 clients; overall improvement was seen in 66 percent of these cases. Specific marital problems were reported as improved by counselors in 55 percent of the cases and by clients in 60 percent of the cases. Only 5 percent of the follow-up group were reported *worse* by the counselors and only 8 percent by the clients themselves. It is important to note that although clients with alcoholism and mental illness problems were omitted from the data analysis, these Family Service clients were not the well-educated, middle-class young couples from university settings usually seen in outcome studies.

In her review, Beck came to the following conclusions about the outcome literature: (1) excluding studies reporting only global outcomes, twenty-three of the thirty-two studies showed gains significantly above control-group levels; (2) the short-run changes in the absence of treatment (no-treatment control) were consistently small, of mixed direction and, with rare exceptions, not statistically significant; (3) significant improvement was the prevailing finding regardless of the type of measure used; (4) all except a few of the studies with control groups were done as doctoral dissertations; (5) despite the relatively high quality of research design, only a small proportion of the studies were published; (6) the details of the findings appear to favor the newer modalities that utilize more structure and simultaneously involve both husband and wife in direct communication exchanges; (7) marital therapy was more successful in the FSAA study than with general social casework studies because of the heterogeneous nature and multiple problems of the general clients who are studied. Regarding the future of behavioral marital therapy, Beck predicted that "the deficits in behavior therapy (as described by Olson, 1972) will undoubtedly be moderated as both research in the area and the method itself mature and are integrated into the eclectic approach typical both of family agencies and marital counseling in general."

In Gurman's fourth review of the marital therapy literature (1975), he briefly reviewed and updated the outcome data he had reported in 1973. He then discussed treatment, patient and therapist variables and their impact on the clinical practice of marital therapy. Although this review was published in *Couples in Conflict* (Gurman and Rice, editors) in 1975, the data "update" (see Gurman, 1975, Table 1) did not include Weiss, Hops and Patterson (1973), Azrin, Naster and Jones (1973) and Beck and Jones (1973), since the chapter was apparently written for presentation in June 1973. Although the numbers of couples treated would have been markedly increased by these additions, Gurman's earlier conclusion would have remained valid: "Differential marital therapies have not yet been adequately demonstrated to produce significant differential treatment outcomes."

Regarding therapist variables related to treatment effectiveness, Gurman found that both of the studies that investigated therapist impact (Freeman et al., 1969; Griffin, 1967) found experienced therapists had better outcomes than did inexperienced therapists. Two other studies (Gurman, 1973c; Rice, Fey and Kepecs, 1972) found that co-therapists were more successful in their therapeutic efforts if they were more similar in their amount of clinical experience. Other than in a training setting, there appeared to be no persuasive evidence that two therapists are better than one.

Client characteristics which affect therapy outcome had been only minimally explored. Demographic variables, such as age and length of marriage, were not predictive. It was found, however, that having both spouses involved in treatment improved the probability of a successful treatment outcome. Spouses who were able to develop more empathy, warmth and genuineness were also likely to benefit from marital therapy.

Regarding treatment variables, Gurman noted that the data, to date, were all on relatively short-term courses of therapy (i.e., about four months of treatment). Since there was *no* evidence to show that longer, costlier courses of therapy were more effective, clinicians were invited to "prove" that the increased time and expense were warranted.

Based on the then-available data (five studies), Gurman estimated that *at least* 5 percent of couples undergoing marital therapy suffered deterioration of their relationship due to the treatment. This rate was felt to be comparable to the estimated deterioration rates in individual psychotherapy.

Finally, with a note of optimism, Gurman (p. 425) admonished clinicians "to avoid getting stuck in a unidimensional theoretical or technical rut" because marital therapy is "a field in which genuinely creative and clinically useful innovations are being evolved with increasing frequency."

Jacobson and Martin (1976) did a comprehensive review of the behavioral therapy (BMT) literature, which appeared as a *Psychological Bulletin* article. At the time the article was written, there were seven research reports—all primarily uncontrolled case studies without comparisons to other treatment techniques (Azrin et al., 1973; Goldstein, 1971; Goldstein and Francis, 1969; Hickok and Komechak, 1974; Stuart, 1969; Weiss et al., 1973; Patterson, Hops and Weiss, 1972). Jacobson and Martin (1976) concluded that existing evidence for the effectiveness of BMT was "suggestive rather than experimentally demonstrated." After reviewing each of the behavioral reports and describing the methodological weaknesses of each one, Jacobson and Martin made several specific suggestions for future research. First, they called for controlled studies with either between-groups design (e.g., waiting list versus treatment group) or within-subject design (e.g., Jacobson, 1978a), in which baseline data are taken during a no-treatment period, an intervention is introduced and its impact recorded, it is removed and the impact of its absence recorded, then the intervention is reintroduced (see Sidman, 1960).

Second, Jacobson and Martin emphasized the need for control of nonspecific treatment variables, such as client expectancies for improvement, demand characteristics of the therapist-client relationship and social-desirability response bias on global measures of adjustment and satisfaction. In a subsequent study Jacobson (1978a) dealt with these nonspecific variables.

Third, these reviewers also recommended a finer grain analysis of some of the specific treatment variables (e.g., contracting, roleplaying, modeling, individual couples versus couples-group format, etc.). In a more recent study, Ewart (1978a, b) conducted the comparison study of quid pro quo and good-faith contracts, which had been described in the Jacobson and Martin (1976) review.

Fourth, it was noted that assessment of couple interaction in the home needs further development. The reliance on direct observation by nonfamily observers sent to the home may be unwise because of the reactivity involved in obtrusive measures. In a recent pilot study, Williams (1978) offers one example of a less reactive home-assessment procedure for investigating couple interaction.

Fifth, the authors recommended an idiographic approach tailored to the needs of each individual couple instead of standardized treatment procedures "applied without a thorough analysis of each individual case."

Sixth, the exchange of assessment instruments and intervention techniques was suggested in order to facilitate the comparison of results from various programs and settings.

Finally, consideration should be given to the needs of other intimate dyads, heterosexual and homosexual, premarital and postmarital. They gave a clear reminder of social reality: "Married couples are not the only category of adult dyadic relationships in need of assistance."

In addition to this advice to researchers, Jacobson and Martin advised clinicians that *any set of clinical procedures currently advocated should be viewed skeptically and used cautiously.* They were hopeful that future investigations of the application of social learning principles to marital therapy would end the long-standing problem in the outcome literature of "no empirical support" for a particular therapeutic approach.

In an article published in October 1976, Olson and Sprenkle presented an overview of the growth and development in both marriage and family counseling. This article appeared concurrently with Olson's book, *Treating Relationships* (1976), which contained many of the recent works referred to in their analysis of "emerging trends in treating relationships." Using a phrase that has been repeated throughout the early marital therapy outcome literature, Olson and Sprenkle (1976, p. 317) described the field as developing with "a great amount of vigor but without a sufficient amount of rigor." They also used the analogy of young "fraternal twins" to describe the parallel but separate development of marital and family therapy. At that time, the twin disciplines were perceived as showing encouraging signs of maturity.

Citing several examples, including the change of the American Association of Marriage Counselors (AAMC) into the American Association of Marriage *and Family* Counselors (AAMFC) in 1970, Olson and Sprenkle concluded that the structural and functional distinctions between marriage counseling and family therapy were fading. They noted the emergence of alternative life styles and variant family forms (e.g., communes and group marriages), and the need to choose the treatment unit (e.g., dyads versus single parents) on practical rather than on ideological grounds. With the expansion of technical knowledge and of the professional literature, the need for specialization within the marriage and family therapy fields had become apparent. Olson and Sprenkle pointed to the development of several subspecialty areas, including sex therapy and divorce counseling.

Three theoretical approaches were seen as influential in recently developed treatment programs. First, social learning theory was an integral part of both behavioral marital therapy (Stuart, 1969; Weiss, Hops and Patterson, 1973) and the new sex counseling programs (e.g., Masters and Johnson, 1970). Second, systems theory was seen as the dominant theoretical framework in family therapy. Olson and Sprenkle also traced the influence of systems theory on the development of communication principles. One product of the integration of systems theory with communications approach was the Minnesota Couples Communication Program (Miller, Nunnally and Wackman, 1976). Third, Rogerian client-centered techniques were used in the development of the Conjugal Relationship Enhancement Program (Guerney, 1977). The reviewers saw these three programs as the first major efforts to integrate theory with practice.

Olson and Sprenkle (1976) noted a trend away from the traditional model of treating one couple at a time for unspecified individual and relationship problems. They welcomed the use of educational and preventive models (Mace and Mace, 1976) to teach specific skills (e.g., assertiveness and communication skills), particularly in a group format (e.g., Lehman-Olson, 1976; Leichter, 1973). They observed also that therapists were beginning to use structured, short-term therapist-client contracts rather than unstructured, open-ended treatment agreements common in the past.

Regarding trends in the outcome literature, Olson and Sprenkle (1976) heralded the "intensified emphasis on research and evaluation of both the process and outcome of treatment." They elaborated (pp. 324–25) the following points as identifiable recent trends:

1. *Clearer and more researchable questions are being asked* (e.g., Does behavioral role reversal increase the frequency of the client's assertive statements?).

2. *There is an increase in systematic studies of treatment programs* (e.g., Miller, Nunnally and Wackman, 1976).

3. *Greater rigor in evaluation research is being practiced* (that is, more clearly focused multidimensional studies, with independent raters, using a multi-method approach, and rigorous experimental designs with matched control groups).

4. *Increased use of multi-method approaches involving both self-report and observational methods* (e.g., Weiss, Hops and Patterson, 1972).

5. There is more attention to change in both the treatment outcome and the treatment process (e.g., daily recording of specific behaviors).

Olson and Sprenkle saw two critical issues on the horizon for marriage and family counseling, which they felt would "determine the shape and scope of the field in the coming decade." First, the interface between *the family* and other economic, political, educational and social-cultural institutions or systems (e.g., Figley, Sprenkle and Denton, 1976). Their strong preference for the general systems theory perspective was evident in their statement (p. 325) that "Such interchange . . . is mandatory for the survival of systems."

Second, professional competence and accountability were seen as pivotal issues in establishing the credibility of marriage and family counseling within the mental health field. Regarding research, they emphasized the need for sophisticated programmatic research by professionals with a lifelong commitment to marital and family therapy. Regarding counseling, they stressed the need for quality control through the licensure or certification of marriage and family practitioners.

As part of our continuing analysis of the "personality" of the marital therapy literature, we note that their preferences (e.g., systems theory) influenced their perception of the current status and future development of the field. Their writing also suggested an awareness of political practicalities in their consideration of marriage and family counseling as a single profession. Obviously, if marriage and family counseling were united in their quest for licensure and certification as health-service providers, the probability of success of the joint efforts would be greatly increased. It is interesting to note the evolution of this concept throughout the article. In the beginning, marriage and family counseling were described as fraternal twins "developing along parallel but surprisingly separate lines." By the end of the article, the twins were described as *one* energetic, awkward adolescent showing encouraging signs of maturity. The further integration of research, theory and practice was seen as a healthy trend in future growth. Taking on the adult responsibilities of *credibility* and *accountability* is a complex and difficult task which Olson and Sprenkle (1976) saw as imperative but not impossible.

Gurman's fifth review, and his first co-authored with Kniskern (1978a), was an in-depth analysis of evidence of deterioration then available in the outcome literature (as of June 1976). Their analysis included both marital and family reports. Our summary will, however, focus only on the marital therapy literature.

Among the more than two-hundred outcome studies reviewed, there were thirty-six non-behavioral and five behavioral studies which reported at least gross improvement/unimprovement rates due to marital therapy. Of thirty-six nonbehavioral reports, only two (Alkire and Brunse, 1974; Most, 1964) included a control group. Without sufficient experimental controls, it cannot be determined whether the reported deterioration was *caused* by the intervention or by extraneous factors which occurred *during* the therapy. In addition to the use of a control group, another (and perhaps better) way to demonstrate a cause/effect relationship between treatment and outcome is the use of an ABA design with multiple baseline measurement. At the time that the Gurman and Kniskern (1978a) review was written, this had not yet been done.

Based on the forty-one studies they analyzed, individual marital therapy rated least effective compared with other marital therapy formats. Individual therapy for marital problems yielded improvement in only 48 percent of its clients and had twice the rate of relationship deterioration reported when both partners were treated simultaneously (11.6 percent versus 5.6 percent), whether therapy was conjoint, concurrent or collaborative.

The reviewers extrapolated (pp. 11–13) from both the marital and family literatures in order to describe the *therapist* variables that are suspected of contributing to deterioration. The following "styles" were noted as increasing the chances of negative therapeutic effects:

1. The therapist does relatively little structuring and guiding of early treatment sessions.

2. The therapist uses frontal confrontations of highly affective material very early in therapy.

3. Unconscious motivations are labeled early in therapy instead of stimulating interaction, gathering data or giving support.

4. The therapist does not actively intervene to moderate interpersonal feedback from others when a member of a group has very low ego strength (e.g., during group marital therapy).

5. Inappropriate remarks by a therapist which accept or promote sex-role stereotypes without comment (e.g., implicit acceptance of wife abuse as masculine behavior).

The evidence regarding *patient* variables related to deterioration was not impressive. If premature termination is included as one form of deterioration, then only one study which dealt with continuance/discontinuance (Hollis, 1968) was found in the marital therapy outcome literature. Four family therapy studies were reviewed which suggested that severity and chronicity of family and individual problems were not related to premature termination or deterioration. None of the articles found by Gurman and Kniskern (1978a) dealt directly with *patient* variables predicting early termination in marital therapy. *Why* some couples terminate soon after intake and *which* couples are at higher risk of either individual or relationship deterioration due to the "therapeutic" interventions have not yet been systematically examined in the outcome literature.

In this same review, Gurman and Kniskern proposed an assessment scheme for evaluating relative degrees of deterioration within an intra- and interpersonal hierarchy. In the priority hierarchy, there are seven units or levels of assessment, ranging from the individual (the identified patient may be the child, parent or spouse) to the total family system, including all combinations of individual functioning versus relationship functioning among the dyads and triads formed by the family members. Since improvement at one level can disrupt the balance at other levels and result in symptomatic behavior in other family members or relationships, the authors concluded (p. 15) that "in marital-family therapy, deterioration is not necessarily the opposite of improvement." In order to determine whether "worsening" is the result of necessary imbalances in a dysfunctional system versus unnecessary deterioration in an individual or relationship, Gurman and Kniskern suggested continuation in therapy: "Had therapy been of longer duration, some of these couples and families might have 'worked through' this intermediate stage to an improved level of functioning." Whether more therapy would indeed help in some cases seems to be an empirical question.

As part of our analysis of the "personality" of the outcome literature, we note that this deterioration article and the review chapter which follows (Gurman and Kniskern, 1978a, b) echoed the perspective previously presented by Olson and Sprenkle (1976). By including both marital and family studies in the same review, the message was implied that the *marital* therapy literature should be coupled with the *family* therapy literature. Often observations were made and conclusions were drawn from both sources interchangeably. References were made to "marital-family therapy," as if the two disciplines, with their diverse histories, were now wedded and had decided to use a hyphenated last name. This style of review—in which both literatures are analyzed simultaneously, yet without loss of their separate identities—may reflect Gurman and Kniskern's preference for a systems-theory approach to the evaluation of treatment impact. This systems theory perspective, which combines both literatures and calls for the assessment of a "matrix of change," has not yet been adopted by subsequent reviewers.

Finally, Gurman and Kniskern were not disheartened by the therapy-induced deterioration that had been reported. Borrowing from the individual psychotherapy literature, they argued that the capacity to harm inadvertently is evidence of the potency of the therapy process. Thus, whether therapeutic tools are used constructively or destructively, they are nonetheless powerful. Moreover, through careful analysis of our failures we may hope to increase the number of our successes.

Gurman's sixth review, and his second review co-authored by Kniskern (Gurman and Kniskern, 1978b), is a landmark achievement in the outcome literature. They collected more than 200 published and unpublished outcome studies, approximately 120 of which were evaluations of marital therapy. We will consider some of the ways in which a reviewer's perspective can influence the trends he or she perceives in the literature, and will then take a second look at some of their conclusions.

The structure of the chapter itself is interesting. Marital and family therapy were described, compared and contrasted concurrently. Although the two fields were described as having two parallel histories and as developing from two different theoretical frameworks, in their introduction, the authors referred to "marital-family therapy" as a single entity on twelve occasions. From their perspective: "Recently the histories of marital-family therapy in theory and in practice have converged." Later, they clearly stated their biases regarding the relationship between the two areas: "Marital therapy, when conducted with a couple who have children, is not a unique treatment format, but represents one subtype of family therapy." They were concerned that their semi-independent format, necessitated by the current labeling practices in the field (i.e., marital therapy *and* family therapy, not marital-family therapy), would imply a different conceptual position.

The opinion of the reader as to whether marital therapy requires a *unique treatment format* may depend on the type of clients most often seen and the nature of their presenting problems. Therapists who work in a child-guidance or family-service setting may deal primarily with problems involving *mother-father* and parent-child roles. On the the other hand, therapists who work in an adult outpatient setting may deal primarily with clients seeking help with *husband-wife* and *male-female* roles (e.g., extramarital affairs, sexual dysfunctions, financial problems, dual career ambitions and age-thirty crises). These latter therapists may respect the position held by Gurman and Kniskern while not sharing it. In any case, what is important for the purposes of this chapter is the impact their perspective had on the outcome literature, as seen in their discussion of marital and family therapy as a single discipline.

A second observation about the structure of the Gurman and Kniskern chapter is that behavioral and nonbehavioral techniques and outcomes were reviewed separately. The rationale given was that "the large body of empirical work recently emerging from that (social learning) orientation is sufficiently conceptually integrated to be deserving of independent examination." While segregating behavioral research in a separate section does facilitate conceptualization of the ways in which social learning theories have been studied and applied, it may also deter the integration of behavioral theories and practices with other major therapeutic approaches (cf. "A Model of Marital Interaction" in this book).

A third observation on the structure of this major review chapter is that studies lacking either control or comparison groups were listed on separate tables and were *not* rated for "Adequacy of Design." Specifically, the thirty-six uncontrolled nonbehavioral studies reporting essentially only gross improvement rates and the eight behavioral studies of single-treatment groups were summarized separately from the other research. This suggests that Gurman and Kniskern have a strong preference for the use of control and comparison groups in outcome research. We share their desire for high standards in research methodology. However, if these criteria are accepted without qualification, we are concerned about the impact these value judgments may have on both the design of future research and the editorial standards for publication of outcome studies. Therefore, two comments are warranted. First, the standards and criteria set by Gurman and Kniskern are *not* meant to be inflexible. Later in their chapter, considerable praise is given to the researchers at the Philadelphia Child Guidance Clinic for their *un*controlled investigations of life-threatening disorders. The reviewers noted that the criteria used for measurement of change were highly objective (e.g., weight gain, blood sugar levels, respiratory function tests), which thus have the advantage of being relatively free of rater bias and subjective interpretation. Moreover, they suggest that an untreated control group is not necessarily required in the case of a disorder in which the prognosis for untreated or routinely treated cases is known to be poor. While a waiting list or no-treatment group is recommended in analog or naturalistic studies with mild or moderately distressed couples and clients, it is not advocated in life-threatening situations or with severely disturbed clients (O'Leary and Borkovec, 1978). This issue will be discussed more fully in the section on methodological problems, which follows.

Our second comment is that the fourteen criteria published in Gurman and Kniskern (1978b) were written with the traditional between-groups design in mind, so that points were given for random assignment to groups and for equivalence of concurrent treatments across groups. Obviously, other criteria regarding appropriateness of treatment reversals in the ABA design would need to be substituted for evaluating a within-subjects design. Concurrent treatment would need to be either consistently present or consistently absent (preferably the latter), across both baseline and treatment conditions in the within-subject design.

Furthermore, we would hope that an additional set of criteria would also be used in determining priority for publication. These criteria would give "points" for degree of relationship distress or individual disturbance (e.g., wife abuse or child abuse), originality of the assessment or intervention techniques (e.g., anger-control module used before problem-solving or contract negotiation) and applicability of the assessment or intervention technique for clinical practice. It would be unfortunate if narrow or rigid publication standards discouraged creative variability.

Because of the large number of studies reviewed and because of the potential impact of the design-quality ratings, the Gurman and Kniskern

(1978b) chapter is expected to influence greatly the future development of the marital outcome literature. As described previously, Gurman's (1973b) review proposed four levels of adequacy, based on the degree of fulfillment of six research design criteria. In the 1978 review, one of the original six criteria was dropped ("research predictions stated in advance") and the following new criteria were added (1978b, pp. 820–21):

1. No contamination of major independent variables (5 points)
2. Treatments equally valued, control of therapist bias (1 point)
3. Treatment carried out as described or expected; clear evidence (1 point), presumptive evidence ($\frac{1}{2}$ point)
4. Use of multiple change indices (1 point)
5. Use of multiple assessment viewpoints (e.g., clients, therapist, independent rater, objective records) (1 point)
6. Measurement of change generalization beyond "identified patient" (e.g., spouse, children) (1 point)
7. Evidence that concurrent treatment, if any, is same across groups (1 point), mention of presence of concurrent treatment without control of equivalence across groups ($\frac{1}{2}$ point)
8. Comparison groups have equal treatment length (1 point)
9. Outcome assessment includes both possibility of improvement and deterioration (1 point)

The original criteria, "random assignment to groups," "pre-post measurement of change" and "appropriate statistical analysis," were each assigned 5 quality points. Studies meeting 0 to 10 criteria were rated "poor"; $10\frac{1}{2}$ to 15 criteria were rated "fair"; $15\frac{1}{2}$ to 20 criteria were rated "good"; and $20\frac{1}{2}$ to 26 were rated "very good."

These criteria are obviously more rigorous than the implicit ones used by Olson in the 1970 decade review or the six proposed by Gurman in the 1973a review. The evolution of these criteria can, perhaps, best be seen in the way they have been applied to an outcome study which has been rated at three points in time. The study by Goldstein and Francis (1969) was among several studies singled out by Olson as "exemplary" and "one of the most carefully designed and executed marital therapy studies to date." In 1973 Gurman rated the same study as Level 4 or "very good." When Gurman rated it again with the new criteria added, the Goldstein and Francis study received only a "fair" rating. The history of the outcome literature is such that as our research methodology becomes more sophisticated, our breakthroughs are soon taken for granted and still later seem almost primitive.

In presenting the conclusions drawn by Gurman and Kniskern in their extensive review, we will not repeat the conclusions reported previously in this chapter.

Regarding the growth of the nonbehavioral outcome literature, Gurman and Kniskern noted "a recent quantum increase in research sophistication in the field" (including both marital and family therapy). In order to better assess the trend in marital therapy research, separate from family research, we plotted the number of controlled and/or comparison group studies and the number of single-group uncontrolled studies by the year of publication. Behavioral and nonbehavioral studies are presented together. As seen in Figure 2, there were twelve controlled/comparison studies as compared with fifteen uncontrolled/single-group studies during the period 1967–1971. This ratio of twelve to fifteen changed to a ratio of thirty-eight to sixteen during the period from 1972 to 1976. Thus, the number of uncontrolled/single-group studies remained roughly the same, while the number of controlled/comparison studies *more than tripled.* In order to assess the trend in level of design adequacy over the decade, we graphed the average level of adequacy for each year and the total number of publications per year. These ratings are calculated from Tables 4, 6, 8 and 9 in Gurman and Kniskern (1978b), which did *not* include ratings of the thirty-six nonbehavioral marital studies reporting global improvement rates or ratings of the eight behavioral marital studies of a single, uncontrolled group. It should be remembered that in comparison with Figure 1, *the four levels here are based on fourteen criteria rather than on only six.*

As seen in Figure 3, between 1967 and 1971 there were twelve controlled or comparison group studies which averaged 2.63 quality points. Between 1972 and 1976, there were thirty-six controlled/comparison studies which

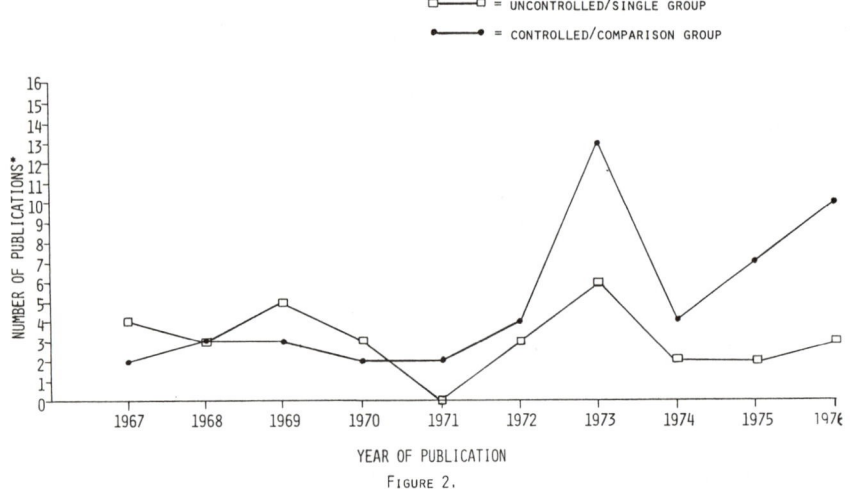

FIGURE 2.

*BASED ON DATA FROM GURMAN AND KNISKERN (1978 B) TABLES 1, 4, 6, 8, & 9.

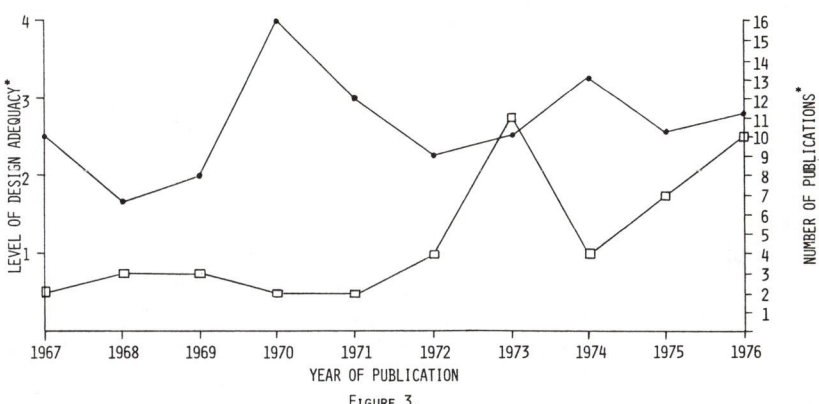

□ = NUMBER OF PUBLICATIONS

• = AVERAGE LEVEL OF ADEQUACY

FIGURE 3.

*BASED ON GURMAN AND KNISKERN (1978 B) TABLES 4, 6, 8, AND 9.

averaged 2.68 quality points. The retrospective application of the research design criteria to this subset of outcome studies suggests *no change* in quality while the quantity was *tripled.* In summary, the "quantum increase," according to Gurman and Kniskern's rating system, is actually a threefold increase in amount, *without* a quantum increase in sophistication. It is possible, however, that many recent studies have scored more points within a level (e.g., 20 points rather than 16) and have still been rated "good" rather than being rated "very good."

Looking at the behavioral and nonbehavioral studies separately may not warrant the "no difference" implied but not stated in the Gurman and Kniskern analysis. Based on their rating system, the thirty-one nonbehavioral studies averaged 2.4 quality points. During the first five-year period, they averaged 2.6 points but dropped to 2.33 points during the second five-year period. In contrast, the seventeen behavioral studies averaged 3.0 quality points overall. During the first five-year period, there were only two eligible outcome studies, each of which earned a Level 2 rating. The remaining fifteen studies were published since 1972 and averaged 3.13 quality points, which is equivalent to a "good" (Level 3) rating.

While these calculations can be used to study objectively the historical trends in the outcome literature, they do *not* reflect the subjective criteria suggested above, which could be used to gauge the *utility* of these outcome studies for the improvement of marital-therapy effectiveness. Several of the observations made by Gurman and Kniskern relate to this issue. They suggested that evidence of the power of Behavioral Marital Therapy (BMT) was limited by several types of research which have been emphasized and other types which had not as yet been systematically explored.

They pointed to the too frequent use of demonstrations of therapy techniques with mildly distressed nonclinical volunteers. In twelve of the twenty-seven BMT studies, the participants were not as distressed as the couples who incur the expense and stigma of "seeing a marriage counselor." In comparison with the Locke-Wallace average adjustment score of 71 for distressed therapy couples, these studies, on quick inspection, averaged in the middle 80s and low 90s. Although eight BMT studies did evaluate moderately to severely distressed couples, including a total of 328 cases, Gurman and Kniskern pointed out that only Jacobson (1977c) and Tsoi-Hoshmand (1976) have done *controlled* BMT studies.

Another limitation of the BMT studies noted by Gurman and Kniskern (1978b) was the insufficient number of group-design studies (N = 7) and the use of a very small number of therapists and patients (average patient sample = 8.8 couples per group). They also noted an "essential lack of replication" of the Oregon work by researchers outside that center, although they did describe the "near-replication" done by Jacobson (1977c and 1978a). However, Gurman and Kniskern's comment that BMT suffered from infrequent follow-up may not have been warranted, since seven of the fifteen naturalistic BMT studies included follow-up ranging from one month to five years.

On the other hand, Gurman and Kniskern pointed to a potential problem in BMT studies which does seem to warrant serious consideration by future researchers, namely the use of outcome measures which were susceptible to the demand characteristics of the therapy situation. These daily assessment procedures, especially the tracking of pleasurable and displeasurable behaviors, were used to *stimulate* behavior changes as well as to *document* the impact of other intervention techniques. It would seem advisable to measure the actual reactivity of these procedures by using a placebo or waiting-list control group. It is noted that the BMT studies have supplemented the use of daily behavioral recording by also using a traditional self-report questionnaire (i.e., the Locke-Wallace Marital Adjustment Test). According to Gurman and Kniskern (1978b), in Tables 8 and 9, twelve of the twenty-seven BMT studies have included marital adjustment data among their outcome criteria. While this instrument measures only global, retrospective data and is weakened by sex-role stereotypes (see Laws, 1971), it does facilitate comparison across studies of both baseline level of marital distress and pre-post changes due to therapy. In comparison with the nonbehavioral outcome studies, marital adjustment tests were used in only three of the thirty-five comparative or controlled nonbehavioral reports, which precluded comparison of results on marital adjustment across studies.

An additional limitation of the BMT studies that Gurman and Kniskern

(1978b) reviewed was the lack of therapist ratings of treatment effectiveness. They suggested the value of the clinician's perspective *in addition to* self- and spouse-ratings and objective records.

Beyond the methodological issues of research-design adequacy and limitations of published studies, did the behavioral and nonbehavioral marital-therapy work? Looking at the thirty-six nonbehavioral studies reporting gross ratings of outcome, nonbehavioral marital therapy *excluding* individual treatment produced improvement in 65 percent of the clients evaluated (N = 1,122 cases). Of the fifteen nonbehavioral marital therapy outcome studies, which included a no-treatment control group, ten studies showed the treatment program to be superior to a lack of treatment.

The effectiveness of BMT is more difficult to interpret, in part because behavioral researchers have used multiple-outcome criteria. When several criteria are favorable to BMT, but one or two others show no change or are favorable to an alternative treatment, reporting "overall improvement" becomes a subjective task. Does improvement require a plurality, a majority or the totality of the three to eight assessment procedures used? Gurman and Kniskern (1978b) concluded that among the eight controlled analog (non-clinical) BMT studies, only Fisher (1974) and Roberts (1975) *clearly* demonstrated the superiority of BMT over a no-treatment control group. The five naturalistic (clinical) studies comparing BMT with alternative treatments showed that four of the five favored BMT (Crowe, 1978; Liberman, Levine, Wheeler, Sanders and Wallace, 1976; Margolin, 1976; McLean, 1973). These four studies included a total of 98 couples. Based on Table 9 in Gurman and Kniskern (1978b), we calculated that roughly 205 of the 267 (about 77 percent) couples treated in *uncontrolled* single-group BMT studies were improved at therapy termination. This 77 percent of 267 couples would be more impressive compared with the 65 percent of 1,122 couples reported in the *uncontrolled* nonbehavioral studies *if* the number of couples in the behavioral studies had been larger and more representative of the general population of distressed marital therapy clients.

Continuing with our analysis of the "personality" of the outcome literature, we note that there was an unevenness in the way in which Gurman and Kniskern presented their conclusions regarding the relative merits and shortcomings of nonbehavioral and behavioral therapy. They tended to be more demanding of the behavioral researchers than of the nonbehavioral researchers since the behavioral treatments were believed to "not . . . offer more than a very conservative suggestion of efficacy," while the nonbehavioral treatments were believed to "offer reasonable evidence of the salience of nonbehavioral marital and family therapies." The behavioral outcome studies had shown a higher rate of improvement in uncontrolled studies (77 percent versus 65 percent), had a larger number of follow-up studies (seven of fifteen versus three of thirty-two) and had a higher level of research-design adequacy (3.0 versus 2.4, using the set of fourteen criteria). Our purpose is *not* to argue for the superiority of either behavioral or nonbehavioral methods, but rather to point to interpretations made by reviewers which may be influenced by their values and preferences.

As the following quote will illustrate, Gurman and Kniskern (1978b) seemed to want to deflate what they *perceive* as a group of overzealous behavioral researchers: "*Behavioral marital and family therapies, while offering testable models and relatively precise intervention packages, currently offer insufficient research support to justify the training of neophyte therapists in this framework alone* . . Nonbehavioral therapies, of course, also lack a sufficient evidential base to support 'single-system' training."

The same conclusion could be written in a more balanced fashion as follows: Neither behavioral nor nonbehavioral marital and family therapies currently offer sufficient research support to justify the training of neophyte therapists in either framework alone.

This apparent effort to lessen the enthusiasm of behavioral researchers and therapists was continued in a series of four articles published in *Family Process* in June 1978. The lead article by Gurman and Knudson presented an analysis and critique of BMT from a psychodynamic systems theory perspective. It is beyond the scope of this chapter to comment on the *theoretical* issues presented and debated by Gurman and Knudson and refuted by Jacobson and Weiss (1978) in the third article in the series. However, Gurman and Knudson (1978, p. 134) did make one observation of empirical importance, albeit in a derogatory tone: "It is unfortunate that, in a zealous effort to expand the technological base and powers of couples therapy, behavior therapists have not emphasized the importance, in the therapist's behavior, of those very same interpersonal skills the therapist teaches to his clients."

While the therapist-client relationship *has* been considered in the practice of behavioral marital therapy (e.g., role modeling and shaping through selective reinforcement), this relationship has not yet been formally studied in BMT research in the same way that a therapist's nonpossessive warmth, genuineness and accurate empathy have been emphasized in research on individual psychotherapy (Truax and Carkhuff, 1967).

The companion article by Gurman and Kniskern (1978c) was an empirical review of BMT in "the broader context of outcome research on nonbehavioral marital therapy." Summarizing briefly the Gurman and Kniskern (1978b) chapter previously discussed, the authors presented evidence of the efficacy of nonbehavioral therapy. In eleven well-designed nonbehavioral studies (average level of design adequacy = 3.54 out of 4.0), there were fifteen treatment comparisons. In ten comparisons, the treatments were *superior* to a no-treatment control condition; in four comparisons they were *equal* to the lack of treatment; and one atypical treatment was inferior to the no-treatment condition. Gurman and Kniskern were defending nonbehavioral therapy from some comments made by Nathan Azrin as a discussant in a symposium in December 1975. Although Azrin's remarks were not available for our review, they were taken to represent an our-evidence-is-more-convincing-than-theirs position. We do not know what data, if any, Azrin used to support his comments. Since we have not seen any we-are-better-than-they-are statements in the published BMT literature to date, this unpublished remark was perhaps the source of Gurman and Kniskern's concern that nonbehavioral marital therapy is under attack from advocates of behavioral couples therapy.

The Gurman and Kniskern review (1978c) in *Family Process* (their third review written together and Gurman's seventh review as senior author) updated the BMT reviews previously published by Greer and D'Zurilla (1975) and Jacobson and Martin (1976). In addition to the BMT articles analyzed in their previous paper (1978b), they analyzed Follingstad, Haynes and Sullivan (1976), Jacobson (1978a), Mayadas and Duehn (1977) and Turkewitz and O'Leary (1976).

After adding these four studies, Gurman and Kniskern concluded (p. 140): "There does not yet exist even one controlled comparative study of behavioral couples therapy with real clients involved in severely disturbed relationships." This statement needs to be qualified in that they excluded studies using a placebo, attention or nonspecific control condition (Crowe, 1978; Jacobson, 1978a; O'Leary and Turkewitz, (1978a). Only no-treatment and waiting-list control conditions were credited as "controlled." Moreover, the controlled comparative studies by Crowe (1978), O'Leary and Turkewitz (1978a), and Wieman (1973) were excluded because the patients were mildly to moderately distressed rather than *severely* disturbed. Both the Crowe (1978) and O'Leary and Turkewitz (1978a) studies involved patients felt to be representative of the general clinical population. Thus, the statement by Gurman and Kniskern regarding severely disturbed clients apparently refers to patients *more* distressed than the general clinic cases referred by general practice M.D.'s or clients seeking help at local mental health clinics.

Furthermore, the Jacobson (1978a) study, which compared two behavioral treatments with a nonspecific attention-placebo condition *and* a waiting-list no-treatment condition, was also disqualified. Although the participants were shown to have had severely disturbed relationships, they were not considered "real patients" because they sought help through answering an advertisement for a research program rather than identifying themselves as therapy patients. This article (Jacobson, 1978a) was further questioned (Gurman and Kniskern, 1978c, p. 142) because of the particular multi-level assessment procedures used: "The immediate clinical relevance of this study is questionable, however, in that all the behavioral change measures (MICS) were based upon couples' problem-solving behavior while dealing with *hypothetical* marital problems (from an inventory) and actual but *minor* problems in their own relationship."

It should be noted that in addition to these behavioral-change measures (namely, the Hops et al. [1971] MICS and Olson and Ryder [1970] IMC vignettes), Jacobson used two rating scales (namely the Locke-Wallace [1959] Marital Adjustment Scale and the Stuart and Stuart [1972] Marital Happiness Scale). These four outcome criteria would seem to compare favorably with the "gross improvement rates" reported in the thirty-six nonbehavioral studies cited by Gurman and Kniskern as "far more positive and less equivocal [p. 140]." The eleven well-designed nonbehavioral controlled studies praised by Gurman and Kniskern used patient reports of "self-concept," "self-esteem," "communication," "self-exploration," etc., as indicative of improvement as well as objective records of reconciliation or divorce. We feel that this discrepancy regarding which criteria are accepted and which are questioned suggests an implicit double standard for nonbehavioral and behavioral outcome studies.

As suggested previously, having multi-trait, multi-level outcome criteria may be disadvantageous for behavioral studies since the results are often not uniformly favorable for either the behavioral or the comparison treatment. It should be noted that the thirty-one *behavioral* studies (analog/nonclinical *and* naturalistic/clinical) reviewed by Gurman and Kniskern (1978b, 1978c) had an average of 4.03 outcome criteria, which was almost twice the number of criteria (i.e., 2.28 per study) used in the thirty-two *nonbehavioral* controlled or comparative studies in the Gurman and Kniskern (1978b) review. To the extent that different assessment procedures are aimed at different levels of individual and relationship functioning, it might be predicted that the greater the number of outcome criteria, the lower the probability that *uniformly* positive or negative results will be found. Thus, when the results of complex criteria are simplified for the purposes of literature reviews, the results might be interpreted as ambiguous or conflicting rather than as indicative of having more impact on one or two levels of functioning than on other levels.

In his 1972 review recommending a systems analysis approach to evaluating marital therapy outcomes, Olson described his study with forty-eight couples, which showed that none of the assessment variables (namely assertiveness, effective power, mutual support, creativity and activity level) correlated with the others across methods (namely, the MMPI, the SIMFAM game, a marital satisfaction test and therapists' ratings). Olson found this "not surprising." This difference in outcome criteria between the behavioral and nonbehavioral studies is noted here because a superficial look at the results summarized by Gurman and Kniskern (1978b, 1978c) might lead to the conclusion that the nonbehavioral studies *were* able to clearly demonstrate their effectiveness, but many behavioral studies *were not*. While some behavioral studies had positive results which were easy to interpret (e.g., Knox, 1973; Stuart, 1976; Jacobson, 1977c), other behavioral studies had more complex results which were more difficult to interpret (e.g., Liberman et al., 1976; Margolin, 1976). The literature is faced with the task of defining "improvement." Is improvement on one or two criteria equivalent to improvement on five out of eight criteria?

Finally, in their review in *Family Process*, Gurman and Kniskern (1978c, p. 142) concluded that their reanalysis of the BMT literature found "little additional evidence of either the superiority of behavioral treatments to other strategies or even its consistent superiority to no-treatment." This conclusion was challenged by Jacobson and Weiss (1978) in their reply in the same series of articles.

Although Jacobson and Weiss agreed that BMT at that time remained unproved with *severely* distressed couples, they also noted that the same can be said of *nonbehavioral* marital therapy. However, for less distressed couples, they asserted (p. 157) that "BMT is successful for a substantial majority of mildly to moderately distressed couples." Jacobson and Weiss argued (p. 161) with the conclusion drawn by Gurman and Kniskern (1978c) on the grounds that their review was at least partially inaccurate: "In their analysis of the empirical literature, Gurman et al. form erroneous conclusions based largely on faulty scholarship. The most blatant example involves citing research with which they are unfamiliar."

In their reply, Gurman, Knudson and Kniskern (1978) admitted that one clinical study (Becking, 1972) was incorrectly listed as an analog study. Also, they agreed that the Cotton study (1976) was incorrectly classified as a no-treatment control study when it has actually used an attention-placebo condition. However, Gurman et al. continued to disagree with Jacobson and Weiss as to the correct classification of Epstein and Jackson (1978) and concluded that there were *six* controlled analog BMT studies (rather than five or seven). This list of six studies (Becking, 1972; Epstein and Jackson, 1978; Fisher, 1974; Harrell and Guerney, 1976; Roberts, 1975; and Wieman, 1973) *again* incorrectly included the Becking (1972) study as an analog/non-clinical study rather than as a naturalistic/clinical study.

We are confused by what seems to be a typographical error in Table 2 in the Gurman and Kniskern (1978c) article. The table is labeled twice (pp. 143–44) as "uncontrolled comparative studies," yet it included the Jacobson (1978a) study with both a waiting-list control group (N = 6 couples) and a nonspecific-condition control group (N = 7 couples). The Tsoi-Hoshmand (1976) and Turkewitz and O'Leary (1976) studies were also incorrectly listed under the "uncontrolled" heading. These three *controlled* studies should have been listed as such under a separate heading.

To dispute the comment by Gurman et al. suggesting little evidence that BMT had shown "consistent superiority to no-treatment," Jacobson and

Weiss (p. 157) emphasized that BMT had been effective in every controlled clinical study in the Gurman and Kniskern (1978c) review: "Disregarding the study that Gurman *et al.* identify correctly as methodologically deficient (Tsoi-Hoshmand, 1976), three controlled studies remain that attest unanimously to the effectiveness of the behavioral approach (Jacobson, 1977, 1978; O'Leary and Turkewitz, 1978)."

Jacobson and Weiss (1978) not only found fault with the Gurman and Kniskern (1978c) review of BMT but also disputed their summary of the *nonbehavioral* marital therapy. Referring to Gurman and Kniskern (1978c), Jacobson and Weiss wrote (p. 159): "Thus, the authors have combined unspecified approaches, approaches categorized by their theoretical framework, approaches categorized by their structure (e.g., conjoint vs. concurrent), and approaches categorized according to the client population treated; they have then compared the cumulative results from this group to the research on behavior therapy."

Perhaps the best indication of the lack of identity among the nonbehavioral marital-therapy studies is the fact that they have been categorized by a characteristic they lack (i.e., *not* being behavioral) rather than by an easily recognizable characteristic they share.

Although Jacobson and Weiss agreed that BMT had not yet been demonstrated to be *more* effective than nonbehavioral marital therapy, they questioned whether *any* single nonbehavioral approach had been shown to be effective. Conjugal relationship enhancement had only two outcome investigations (Collins, 1972; Wieman, 1973), and both these were dissertations which used a nonclinical/analog design. In order to be considered a "theoretical approach," as contrasted with a "pilot study," a series of investigations must be done in which the therapeutic interventions are conceptualized clearly and verbalized adequately so that they can be replicated. Moreover, as a treatment program is developed, the treatment components which are the "active ingredients" necessary for effectiveness must be identified. Jacobson and Weiss felt that this kind of systematic examination of a single marital-therapy model or approach was essentially absent from the nonbehavioral marital-therapy literature. Thus, they concluded that BMT is "the only approach that is demonstrably effective [p. 159]."

In their defense of BMT, Jacobson and Weiss may have overstated their case. Despite the lack of theoretical and methodological cohesiveness, the sixty-eight nonbehavioral marital studies reviewed by Gurman and Kniskern (1978b) certainly exist as an entity. As we described previously regarding the relatively good design quality of the thirty-two controlled and comparison studies, the evidence of effectiveness is adequate. The problem is a lack of specificity as to *what was done, what worked* and *why.*

To some extent the precedent for a cohesive theoretical model has been set in nonbehavioral *family* therapy. The "structural family therapy" approach (Minuchin, 1974; Minuchin, Baker, Rosman, Liebman, Milman and Todd, 1975; Rosman, Minuchin, Liebman and Baker, 1976; Stanton and Todd, 1976; and Stanton, 1978) is an example of a nonbehavioral approach which is "clearly delineated, highly teachable." However, as Gurman and Kniskern (1978b) also noted, "The effective treatment components in the structural therapy for these disorders [anorexia, asthma, diabetes and heroin addiction] have not been identified." Again, we have the problem of not knowing which treatment components are the necessary active ingredients in the therapy approach.

Our next series of papers for consideration were published in a recent book edited by Paolino and McCrady (1978). We will look briefly at three of the chapters (i.e., Weiss, 1978; O'Leary and Turkewitz, 1978a; Gurman, 1978) and then take a closer look at the fourth (Jacobson, 1978b). These particular chapters were chosen because of their concern with the systematic evaluation of marital-therapy process and outcome. The first three chapters will be discussed in the order in which they appeared in the book.

In the first chapter, Weiss (1978) focused on the behavioral conceptualization of *marriage* as opposed to the behavioral model of *marital therapy* (cf. O'Leary and Turkewitz, 1978a). In the course of his excellent review of research investigating *how marriage works* (including both sociological and psychological data), Weiss reviewed selected therapy studies relevant to our analysis. For example, in his reviews of Margolin's (1976) dissertation research, Weiss explained what the study contributed to our understanding of helpful or supportive spouse responses as well as the benefits gained in therapy from adding a cognitive attribution procedure to a behavioral model. This perspective—"What did this study teach us about how to make marital therapy more effective?"—is quite different from the perspective presented in Gurman and Kniskern (1978c), in which the Margolin study was mentioned as an *uncontrolled* study of couples with *severely* disturbed relationships. The outcome criteria and results are presented (Gurman and Kniskern, 1978c, Table 2), but are not interpreted or explained. A similar difference in perspective was noted for other outcome studies as well (i.e., Follingstad, Haynes, and Sullivan, 1976; Follingstad, Sullivan, Ierace, Ferrara, and Haynes, 1976; Harrell and Guerney, 1976; Wieman, 1973). At the risk of oversimplifying the differences in perspective, it could be said that Gurman and Kniskern focused on the question *Did* the marital therapy work? while Weiss's conceptual review focused on the question *How* did the marital therapy work and *why*? It seems to us that both perspectives are valuable and necessary for the development of the field.

The second chapter of interest from Paolino and McCrady (1978) was a sample of the behavioral marital therapy model by O'Leary and Turkewitz. Their chapter also summarized the development of BMT from operant, classical and cognitive therapy origins. Their chapter took a narrower perspective than Weiss's overview of marital interaction in that it focused on the assessment, treatment procedures and outcome data of the Stony Brook marital-therapy program. The treatment model based on behavioral principles was presented in a step-by-step manner which should facilitate both its modeling by interested clinicians *and* its replication by interested researchers.

It is important to note that both Weiss (1978) and O'Leary and Turkewitz (1978a) emphasized (1) that there is no one behavioral approach, but rather a group of different therapy models sharing the same behavioral orientation; (2) that the current emphasis in BMT incorporates many forms of cognitive therapy; and (3) that formal marriage agreements or behavior contracts are no longer the cornerstone of BMT (O'Leary and Turkewitz, 1978a, p. 276). For a discussion of this last issue, see the Epstein and Williams chapter in this book.

The third chapter of interest in Paolino and McCrady (1978) was Gurman's (1978) conceptual overview of psychoanalytic systems theory and of behavioral approaches to marital therapy. In this integrative chapter, Gurman included a section on the current status of marital therapy research (p. 548), summarized from chapters we have already discussed (Gurman and Kniskern, 1978a, 1978b, 1978c). Although Gurman repeated his conclusion that "no single approach has won all the prizes in the Alice in Wonderland race for superiority," he conceded (p. 552) that BMT had changed from his earlier conception of it: "Behavior therapists, having established that they have a legitimate place in the therapeutic sun, have, in general, toned down their earlier claims of superior efficacy, and, indeed, have recently even begun to incorporate methods that would have been considered heretic, if not blasphemous, a decade ago."

Gurman suggested two directions for future research which warrant our consideration. First, that empirical study was needed of "what marital therapists of different persuasions actually do with couples." And second, that marital therapists as a group need to use some common indexes to assess change.

Finally, Gurman's evaluation of the current status of our "client" was reminiscent of conclusions drawn in previous reviews. The key phrases were "cautious optimism" and "not a finished product yet." Regarding contemporary marital therapies, the analogy used to describe this developmental phase was an adolescent period in which the therapies have been "struggling to establish their own boundaries," have been "very caught up in their own identities," but have "matured rather well of late." While Gurman's optimism was *cautious*, it was optimism nonetheless.

The fourth chapter of interest from the Paolino and McCrady book in Jacobson's (1978a) review of the research on the effectiveness of three therapy approaches, although *not* the same three approaches (psychoanalysis, systems theory and behavior therapy) featured in the rest of the text. Instead, he reviewed the outcome literature on (1) communication skills training, (2) behavioral marital therapy and (3) problem-oriented therapies, focusing on two specific clinical problems, namely alcoholism and sexual dysfunctions.

Jacobson (1978a) was unable to review outcome research which systematically analyzed the effectiveness of the psychoanalytic and systems theory approaches to marital therapy because he found *no such literature*. It was suggested that systems theory has been a *family* therapy approach applied primarily to child-related problems rather than a *marital* therapy approach applied to husband-wife problems. The scarcity of psychoanalytic research, on the other hand, was felt to be related to a lack of interest or to a lack of research training among the analysts.

From the perspective of behavior exchange theory and social psychology (Thibaut and Kelley, 1959; Homans, 1950), we might also suggest the importance of the lack of psychoanalytic role models to demonstrate methods of conducting controlled and comparative outcome studies. Furthermore, the cost/benefit analysis for systematic investigations of psychoanalytic marital therapy suggests that there may be few payoffs and considerable response cost to a psychoanalyst for acquiring and applying the principles and practices of scientific research.

In his section on communication skills training, Jacobson (1978a) reviewed three major models or programs: (1) training based on Carkhuff's model, with three studies; (2) Conjugal Relationship Enhancement (CRE), with four studies; and (3) Minnesota Couples' Communication Program (MCCP), with two studies. There were six other studies which used "eclectic" or miscellaneous communication training procedures. Based on these fifteen communication studies, Jacobson concluded (p. 412): "There seems to be some cause for cautious optimism that structured, systematic communication training, particularly communication training of the CRE variety, can be an effective treatment for mildly distressed couples."

In his review of behavioral marital therapy (BMT), Jacobson (1978a) summarized two analog studies (Roberts, 1975; Margolin, 1976) and six controlled studies (Harrell and Guerney, 1976; Jacobson, 1977a, 1977b, 1978b; Tsoi-Hoshmand, 1976; Turkewitz, 1977). Based on these studies, Jacobson challenged the assumption that contingency contracting is a necessary ingredient of BMT. Two studies, Jacobson (1977b) and Turkewitz (1977), reported positive outcomes *without* written contracts. The hypothesized active ingredients of the treatment package in Jacobson's three recent studies were thought to be training in communication, problem-solving and contingency management skills (without explicit contract writing).

Jacobson (1978b) summarized the results of the six controlled studies by

saying that all of the studies except Turkewitz (1977) found BMT significantly more effective than the control conditions. The results of the five
comparative BMT studies were equivocal so that BMT's superiority in the
comparative studies was "open to question" [p. 424].

Several of the outcome studies in the literature involved neither communication training nor BMT, but rather focused on the *format* of the marital
therapy. These variables involved how therapy was done rather than the
theoretical approach or conceptual model used. Among these miscellaneous
format variables were group versus conjoint versus concurrent sessions; the
use of programmed instruction; time-limited, brief treatment versus open-
ended, extended treatment; need for male-female co-therapy teams; and
importance of therapist's experience. Jacobson (1978a) felt that no conclusions were warranted from the available literature.

After reviewing seven studies of marital therapy with alcoholics and their
spouses, Jacobson (1978a) concluded tentatively that "there is some evidence
that treating alcoholism as a marital problem can facilitate the diminution of
alcohol consumption [p. 433]." He hastened to add that measuring the level
of alcohol consumption was difficult in these clients, and all of the studies
were "plagued by methodological limitations."

Jacobson's review of the sex therapy literature is beyond the scope of this
chapter.

In his suggestions for future research, Jacobson focused on the therapy
format and procedural parameters as variables which had been overlooked.
Three suggestions were made:

> *First*, component analyses of both conjugal and behavioral exchange
> approaches must be conducted in order to determine which aspects of these
> treatment packages are contributing most to their effectiveness.
> *Second*, group treatment versus individual conjoint treatment must be
> evaluated more thoroughly.
> *Third*, the merit of involving a co-therapist must be investigated (p. 440).

In our analysis of the "personality" of the literature as it has been shaped
by the biases of each reviewer, we note that Jacobson was explicit regarding
his own perspective and his preferences for the future development of the
field. The key words were "behavioral," "rigorous methodology," "scientific
inquiry" and "experimental analysis." It is primarily the last phrase, *experimental analysis*, which distinguishes Jacobson's research and his reviews
from the others' we have analyzed. He has been working to improve the
quality of marital-therapy research from the level of a preliminary *study* to
the level of a systematic *experiment*. In an experiment, the investigator
varies only one factor at a time for the purposes of testing an hypothesis
(e.g., the hypothesis that problem-solving alone is effective in improving

marital interaction). The controlled application of the empirical method requires that variables not specific to the experimental condition be held constant so that they cannot affect the target behavior and confound the results of the treatment (Jacobson and Baucom, 1977).

While some of the studies on couple counseling previously reviewed did include some of the basic methodological requirements of experimental design (e.g., random assignment to groups, follow-up data, detailed description of treatment procedures to be used, and control groups), Jacobson (1977a, 1977b) added the use of single-case, within-subject design and multiple baseline analyses. As mentioned previously, in a within-subject design, each couple serves as its own control, so that matching subjects is obviated. Baseline data are taken during a no-treatment period, then an intervention is introduced and its impact recorded, then the intervention is removed so that the impact of its absence can be recorded, and then the intervention can be reintroduced. As Jacobson (1978a) noted (p. 407), a causal relationship between treatment and outcome cannot be established by simply measuring pre-test to post-test changes: "In order for within-subjects designs to be internally valid, it must be demonstrated that the changes which occurred in the treatment group were due to the treatment itself; this can only be accomplished through the use of reversal designs, multiple baselines, or another similar procedure (cf. Hersen and Barlow, 1976)."

Jacobson's two studies (1977a, 1977b) clearly demonstrated his preference for experimental research designs. When Jacobson said, "Marital therapy is slowly moving toward a firmer foundation in scientific inquiry [p. 441]," he was obviously referring to his own recent studies (both published and in press). If he continues to lead the way in the use of experimental research designs, rather than just *observing* or *predicting* future trends, he will have the advantage of *shaping* them.

Our last paper for consideration is a recent review of BMT by Jacobson (1979). In his overview of the past decade, Jacobson has observed three trends: *first*, that BMT has been presented in a modular format with a preprogrammed sequence of interventions; *second*, although there has been a proliferation of sophisticated assessment devices, BMT researchers have become increasingly aware of the complexities inherent in measuring the behavior of intimate dyads, so that they are reserving judgment pending the emergence of definitive data; and *third*, although a conceptual model has recently been introduced (Weiss, 1978), a "comprehensive, empirically validated behavioral model of relationship distress remains a hope for the future."

In this paper, Jacobson interwove theory, measurement and treatment. Since our focus is marital *therapy* outcome studies, we will try to unravel that thread from the other two. However, we heartily agree with Jacobson's proposition that the development of one area—say, measurement—affects and is affected by the development in the remaining two—that is, both theory and treatment.

In his discussion of therapy outcome research, Jacobson (1979) reiterated the conclusion made in the earlier review (Jacobson, 1978b). He suggested that "contingency contracting itself was an extraneous procedure, and that problem-solving training served as the primary active ingredient" [p. 39]. Problem-solving training was also seen as "a prime candidate as the change-inducing ingredient of greatest power" [p. 39].

Although the inclusion of *cognitive* techniques in behavioral marital therapy programs has caused concern among some behavior therapists, the "cognitive restructuring" described by Jacobson (1979) seems easily acceptable (p. 48). The cognitive restructuring involved instructing the couple to attribute their relationship problems to deficient communication skills (i.e., *behavioral* deficits) rather than to faulty personality traits in the partners (i.e., *characterological* deficits).

Jacobson made the suggestion that future research should be longitudinal, sequential and experimental. Moreover, he noted an excessive preoccupation with *verbal* communication out of proportion to the small part of a couple's time spent in verbal communication. Jacobson speculated that our focus would be different if we spent more time studying working class couples (p. 55).

Finally, Jacobson continued the same biases discussed in the previous paper. His summation statement was that "optimism is warranted." However, his optimism was not without the warning that "whether or not the promise suggested by this research is fulfilled depends upon an enduring commitment to the scientific study of behavior change."

As we will see in the next section, there are methodological problems which will test our "commitment" in the coming decade.

METHODOLOGICAL ISSUES IN MARITAL THERAPY RESEARCH

As we have seen, virtually every review of research in marital therapy has included at least some reference to the need for more methodological rigor in studies of the outcome of marital therapy. In fact, Gurman (1973b) and Gurman and Kniskern (1978b) have provided us with a system for grading the methodological design adequacy of marital therapy studies.

Two recent articles are particularly useful for those planning to conduct or evaluate marital therapy research. O'Leary and Turkewitz (1978b) present a concise discussion of the common methodological errors in marital therapy research and suggest procedures by which researchers may avoid these errors. The second article discusses the problems in using placebo and no-treatment groups in psychotherapy research (O'Leary and Borkovec, 1978).

O'Leary and Borkovec (1978) suggest that both placebo and no-treatment controls raise ethical concerns in that the control subjects are placed at risk by the experimental procedures. In addition to the risks that may result from deception of subjects, risks to the placebo or no-treatment control subjects are seen as stemming from "(a) lack of potentially active intervention, (b) treatment deterrent, and (c) frustration as a consequence of minimal improvement [p. 825]." O'Leary and Borkovec suggest several alternative research methods, which are intended to control for nonspecific treatment effects while minimizing the potential risks to the subjects. As O'Leary and Borkovec noted, the alternative research strategies have some problems of their own. Nevertheless, the research designs that they have described are interesting and should be considered by those doing marital-therapy research.

In spite of the urgings of reviewers of the marital therapy research literature, the evidence presented in Figure 3 suggests that the methodological quality of the studies has not improved substantially between 1967 and 1976. We can suggest four reasons for the slow rate of growth in the methodological sophistication in marital therapy research. First, the fact that so much of the research in the field has been conducted as part of doctoral dissertations indicates that a major part of marital therapy research has been done by beginning investigators who lack extensive research experience, have very limited or no funding, and have relatively tight time constraints. The supervision of doctoral students' research by more senior investigators may decrease to some extent the chances that the research design of the inexperienced researcher will contain methodological flaws. The fact remains, however, that marital therapy research is expensive in terms of both time and money. It is unlikely that doctoral students would be able to afford the inclusion of such factors as large numbers of couples per treatment condition, the participation of a number of different therapists and provisions for long-term follow-up.

The second factor which is a likely contributor to the methodological inadequacy of much of the marital therapy outcome research is the apparent lack of interest and involvement in the field of marital therapy on the part of academic clinical psychology departments. These departments are the training grounds for many, if not most, of the researchers in the fields of psychotherapy and behavior change. Yet, as a recent survey has shown (Prochaska and Prochaska, 1978), only 7 percent of the psychology departments in this country provide any specific training in the field of marital therapy.

Another factor affecting the quality of marital therapy research is the difficulty of assessing and quantifying the outcome of marital therapy. The number of outcome measures for marital therapy with documented reliability and validity is limited. In addition, the researcher faces the problem that the unit of assessment—the dyad—may not exist after treatment, i.e., some couples get separated or divorced. Most clinicians would agree that the dissolution of the relationship is a positive outcome in some cases and a negative outcome in others. Yet the typical measures of outcome in marital therapy research—e.g., measures of marital adjustment or communication skills in the dyad—probably will not distinguish between the positive and negative cases in which separation or divorce has occurred.

The fourth and probably most important influence on the frequent presence of methodological weaknesses in marital therapy research is the practical difficulty inherent in conducting such research. As we already mentioned, it is costly and difficult to obtain large numbers of couples and a number of different therapists. The use of measures of behavioral interaction often require rather expensive videotape equipment and necessitate the addition of carefully trained independent raters to the research team. Those who attempt to conduct research in clinical settings frequently encounter resistance from the non-research clinical staff, who may resent what they view as an intrusion upon their usual ways of doing things. Locating and obtaining the cooperation of subjects at follow-up is always difficult in psychotherapy research. In marital therapy research, however, this difficulty is increased in degree because some of the research couples may have separated or divorced. These are but a few of the practical difficulties in conducting marital therapy research that may lead researchers to compromise some of the principles of research design in order to be able to complete the research within a reasonable time and with a limited budget.

PRESCRIPTIONS

Based on the above explanation for some of the inadequacies in the marital therapy outcome literature, we would like to suggest some "prescriptions" to help overcome these methodological difficulties and promote the optimal development of the field:

First, referral should be made to the O'Leary and Turkewitz (1978b) paper in order to avoid the more common methodological errors in marital treatment research (e.g., inadequate description of therapists' backgrounds, levels of expertise, previous experience and theoretical persuasions).

Second, in the case of marital therapy research with severely distressed clients or couples with disturbed relationships, if a waiting list control or a placebo condition would place the control subjects at serious risk of deterioration, then an alternative method for control of nonspecific treatment effects might be used—for example, the "best alternative method" or a neutral expectancy control condition (see O'Leary and Borkovec, 1978).

Third, marital therapy skills and methods for systematic treatment evaluation should be included in clinical psychology and in applied behavior-analysis training programs.

Fourth, more active participation of experienced researchers in the design of doctoral dissertation research on marital therapy is needed in order to promote better quality research designs.

Fifth, doctoral students should be supported and encouraged in their struggle to prepare their dissertation research for publication in a professional journal. Many of the better quality studies done by graduate students remain *unpublished* and are thus unavailable to practicing clinicians and all but the most diligent reviewers.

Sixth, reliable assessment procedures which can measure dyadic functioning in areas other than specific communication skills (e.g., *Inventory of Marital Conflict,* by Olson and Ryder, 1970) or behavior exchange patterns (e.g., *Marital Interaction Coding System,* by Hops et al., 1971) need to be developed. In particular, assessment procedures are needed which can be used by clinician researchers without extraordinary expenditures of time and money for equipment and personnel.

Seventh, standards for research methodology *should be high* (e.g., Gurman's fourteen design adequacy criteria), but should not be so narrow or inflexible that the standards become obstacles to the development of meaningful innovations in marital therapy or outcome evaluation. Flexibility does not connote lack of careful planning. Rigorous standards should likewise not result in rigor mortis of the field.

And finally, *eighth,* we should encourage active collaboration between experienced researchers and skilled clinicians so as to decrease the response cost to both groups of doing well-designed investigations of marital therapy process and outcome.

PROGNOSIS

As we have seen, the consensus of the reviewers is that there is cause for both optimism and concern. The current level of attainment in marital therapy outcome research is *not* adequate. However, the rate of growth and development of the field is healthy and shows good potential. We should note that our conclusions may well be influenced by our own biases in favor of a positive outlook. However, we hope that our analysis of the research literature has been objective enough so that the reader has by now drawn his or her own conclusions.

Our analysis of the "personality" of the research literature suggests that our "client" is entering a phase of normal, albeit turbulent, adolescent growth (Olson and Sprenkle, 1976; Gurman, 1978). For some of us, this period will be a trial of our patience. For others of us, however, it will be an interesting challenge to watch and enjoy.

REFERENCES

Azrin, N.H., Naster, B.J., and Jones, R. Reciprocity counseling: A rapid learning-based procedure for marital counseling. *Behav. Res. & Ther.*, 1973, *11*, 365–382.

Alkire, A.A., and Brunse, A.J. Impact and possible casualty from videotape feedback in marital therapy. *J. Consult. & Clin. Psychol.*, 1974, *42*, 203–210.

Beck, D.F. Research findings on the outcomes of marital counseling. *Soc. Casework*, 1975, *56*, 153–181.

Beck, D.F. Marital conflict: Its course and treatment as seen by caseworkers. *Soc. Casework*, 1966, *47*, 211–221.

Beck, D.F., and Jones, M.A. *Progress on family problems: A nationwide study of clients' and counselors' views on family agency services.* New York: Family Service Association of America, 1973.

Becking, E.P. Pretraining effects on maladaptive marital behavior within a behavior modification approach. (Ph.D. diss., California School of Professional Psychology, San Francisco, 1972). *Diss. Abstr. Int.*, 1973, *33*, 5007 B.

Bergin, A.E. The evaluation of therapeutic outcomes. In A.E. Bergin and S.L. Garfield (Eds.), *Handbook of psychotherapy and behavior change.* New York: Wiley, 1971.

Bergin, A.E., and Strupp, H.H. New directions in psychotherapy research. *J. Abnor. Psychol.*, 1970, *76*, 13–26.

Bergin, A.E., and Strupp, H.H. *Changing frontiers in the science of psychotherapy*, Chicago: Aldine, 1972.

Birchler, G.R. Differential patterns of instrumental affiliative behavior as a function of degree of marital distress and level of intimacy. (Ph.D. diss., Univ. of Oregon, 1972). *Diss. Abstr. Int.*, 1973, No. 73–7865.

Burton, G., and Kaplan, H.M. Group counseling in conflicted marriages where alcoholism is present: Clients' evaluation of effectiveness. *J. Marr. & Fam.*, 1968, *30*, 74–79.

Carter, R.D., and Thomas, E.J. Modification of problematic marital communication using corrective feedback and instruction. *Behav. Ther.*, 1973a, *4*, 100–109.

Carter, R.D., and Thomas, E.J. A case application of a signaling system (SAM) to the assessment and modification of selected problems of marital communication. *Behav. Ther.*, 1973b, *4*, 629–645.

Collins, J.D. The effects of the conjugal relationship modification method on marital communication and adjustment. (Ph.D. diss., Penn. State Univ., 1971). *Diss. Abstr. Int.*, 1972, 6674–B.

Cotton, M.C. A systems approach to marital training evaluation. Unpubl. Ph.D. diss., Texas Tech. Univ., 1976.

Crowe, M.J. Conjoint marital therapy: A controlled outcome study. *Psychologic. Med.*, 1978, *8*, 623–636.

DeWitt, K.N. The effectiveness of family therapy. *Arch. Gen. Psych.*, 1978, *35*, 549–561.

Dicks, H.V. *Marital tensions.* New York: Basic Books, 1967.

Eisler, R.M., Hersen, M., and Agras, W.S. Videotape: A method for the controlled observation of nonverbal interpersonal behavior. *Behav. Ther*, 1973a, *4*, 420–425.

Eisler, R.M., Hersen, M., and Agras, W.S. Effects of videotape and instructional feedback on nonverbal marital interaction: An analog study. *Behav. Ther.*, 1973b, *4*, 551–558.

Ely, A. L. *Efficacy of training in conjugal therapy.* Unpub. Ph.D. thesis: Rutgers Univ., 1970.

Epstein, N., and Jackson, E. An outcome study of short-term communication training with married couples. *J. Consult. & Clin. Psychol.*, 1978, *46*(2), 207–212.

Ewart, C.K. Behavior contracts in couple therapy: An experimental evaluation of quid pro quo and good faith models. Paper, American Psychological Association, Toronto, 1978a.

Ewart, C.K. Behavioral marriage therapy with older couples effects of training measured by the Marital Adjustment Scale. Paper, Association for Advancement of Behavior Therapy, Chicago, 1978b.

Figley, C.F., Sprenkle, D.H., and Denton, G.W. Training marriage and family counselors in an industrial setting. *J. Marr. & Fam. Couns.*, 1976, *2*, 167–175.

Fisher, R.E. The effect of two group counseling methods on perceptual congruence in married pairs. (Ph.D. diss., Univ. of Hawaii, 1973). *Diss. Abstr. Int.*, 1974, *35*, 885-A.

Fitzgerald, R.V. Conjoint marital psychotherapy: An outcome and follow-up study. *Fam. Proc.*, 1969, *8*, 260–271.

Follingstad, D.R., Haynes, S.N., and Sullivan, J. Assessment of the components of a behavioral marital intervention program. Paper, Assoc. for Advancement of Beh. Therapy, New York, December 1976.

Follingstad, D.R., Sullivan, J., Ierace, C., Ferrara, J., and Haynes, S.N. Behavioral assessment of marital interaction. Paper, Association for Advancement of Behavior Therapy, New York, December 1976.

Freeman, S.J.J., Leavens, E.J., and McCulloch, D.J. Factors associated with success or failure in marital counseling. *Fam. Coord.*, 1969, *18*, 125–128.

Goldstein, M.K. Behavior rate change in marriage: Training wives to modify husbands' behavior. (Ph.D. diss., Cornell Univ., 1971). *Diss. Abstr. Int.*, 1971, *32*, 559B.

Goldstein, M.K., and Francis, B. Behavior modification of husbands by wives. Paper, National Council on Family Relations, Washington, D.C., October 1969.

Goodrich, D.W., and Boomer, D.S. Experimental assessment of modes of conflict resolution. *Fam. Proc.*, 1963, *2*, 15–24.

Greer, S.E., and D'Zurilla, T.J. Behavioral approaches to marital discord and conflict. *J. Marr. & Fam. Couns.*, 1975, *1*(4), 299–315.

Griffin, R.W. Change in perception of marital relationship as related to marriage counseling. (Ph.D. diss., Florida State Univ., 1967). *Diss. Abstr. Int.*, 1967, *27*, 3956A.

Guerney, B.G. *Relationship enhancement.* San Francisco: Jossey-Bass, 1977.

Gurman, A.S. Group marital therapy: Clinical and empirical implications for outcome research. *Int. J. Group Psychother.*, 1971, *21*, 174–189.

Gurman, A.S. Marital therapy: Emerging trends in research and practice. *Fam. Proc.*, 1973a, *12*, 45–54.

Gurman, A.S. The effects and effectiveness of marital therapy: A review of outcome research. *Fam. Proc.*, 1973b, *12*, 145–170.

Gurman, A.S. Therapist, patient and treatment factors influencing the outcome of marital therapy. Unpub. ms., Univ. of Wisconsin Med. School, 1973c.

Gurman, A.S. Some therapeutic implications of marital therapy research. In A.S. Gurman and D.G. Rice (Eds.), *Couples in conflict.* New York: Jason Aronson, 1975.

Gurman, A.S. Contemporary marital therapies: A critique and comparative analysis of psychoanalytic, behavioral and systems theory appoaches. In T.J. Paolino and B.S. McCrady (Eds.), *Marriage and marital therapy: Psychoanalytic, behavioral, and systems theory perspectives.* New York: Brunner/Mazel, 1978.

Gurman, A.S., and Kniskern, D.P. Enriching research on marital enrichment programs. *J. Marr. & Fam. Couns.*, 1977, *3*, (2), 3–11.

Gurman, A.S., and Kniskern, D.P. Deterioration in marital and family therapy: Empirical, clinical, and conceptual issues. *Fam. Proc.*, 1978a, *17*, 3–20.

Gurman, A.S., and Kniskern, D.P. Research on marital and family therapy: Progress, perspective, and prospect. In S.L. Garfield and A.E. Bergin (Eds.), *Handbook of psychotherapy and behavior change: An empirical analysis* (2nd ed.). New York: Wiley, 1978b, 817–901.

Gurman, A.S., and Kniskern, D.P. Behavioral marriage therapy. II. Empirical perspective. *Fam. Proc.*, 1978c, *17*(2), 139–148.

Gurman, A.S., and Knudson, R.M. Behavioral marriage therapy: A psychodynamic-systems analysis and critique. *Fam. Proc.*, 1978, *17*, 121–138.

Gurman, A.S., Knudson, R.M., and Kniskern, D.P. IV. Reply: Take two aspirin and call us in the morning. *Fam. Proc.*, 1978, *17*(2), 165–180.

Gurman, A.S., and Rice, D.G. *Couples in conflict.* New York: Jason Aronson, 1975.

Harrell, J., and Guerney, B. Training married couples in conflict negotiation skills. In D.H.L. Olson (Ed.), *Treating relationships.* Lake Mills, Iowa: Graphic, 1976.

Hersen, M., and Barlow, D.H. *Single case experimental designs.* London: Pergamon, 1976.

Hickok, J.E., and Komechak, M.G. Behavior modification in marital conflict: A case report. *Fam. Proc.*, 1974, *13*, 111–119.

Hof, L., Miller, W.R., and Green, S. *Marriage enrichment: Philosophy, process, and program.* Bowie, Md.: Charles Press, 1980.

Hollis, F. A profile of early interviews in marital counseling. *Soc. Casework*, 1968a, *49*, 35–43.

Homans, G.C. *The human group.* New York: Harcourt Brace, 1950.

Hops, H., Wills, T.A., Patterson, G.R., and Weiss, R.L. Marital interaction coding system. Unpub. ms., Univ. of Oregon, 1971.

Jacobson, N.S. Training couples to solve their marital problems: A behavioral approach to relationship discord. Part I: Problem-solving skills. *Inter. J. Fam. Couns.*, 1977a, *4*, 22–31.

Jacobson, N.S. Training couples to solve their marital problems: A behavioral approach to relationship discord. Part II: Intervention strategies. *Inter. J. Fam. Couns.*, 1977b, *5*, 20–28.

Jacobson, N.S. Problem-solving and contingency contracting in the treatment of marital discord. *J. Consult. & Clin. Psychol.*, 1977c, *45*, 92–100.

Jacobson, N.S. Specific and nonspecific factors in the effectiveness of a behavioral approach to the treatment of marital discord. *J. Consult. & Clin. Psychol.*, 1978a, *46*, 442–452.

Jacobson, N.S. A review of the research on the effectiveness of marital therapy. In T.J. Paolino and B.S. McCrady (Eds.), *Marriage and the treatment of marital disorders from psychoanalytic, behavioral, and systems theory perspectives.* New York: Brunner/Mazel, 1978b.

Jacobson, N.S. Behavioral treatments for marital discord: A critical appraisal. In M. Hersen, R.M. Eisler, and P.M. Miller (Eds.), *Progress in behavior modification.* New York: Academic Press, 1979.

Jacobson, N.S. Increasing positive behavior in severely distressed marital relationships: The effects of problem-solving training. *Behav. Ther.*, 1979, *10*(3), 311–326.

Jacobson, N.S., and Baucom, D.H. Design and assessment of nonspecific control groups in behavior modification research. *Behav. Ther.*, 1977, *8*, 709–719.

Jacobson, N.S., and Martin, B. Behavioral marriage therapy: Current status. *Psychologic Bull.*, 1976, *83*, 540–566.

Jacobson, N.S., and Weiss, R.L. III. Critique: The contents of Gurman et al. may be hazardous to our health. *Fam. Proc.*, 1978, *17*(2), 149–164.

Knox, D. Behavior contracts in marriage counseling. *J. Fam. Couns.*, 1973, *1*, 22–28.

Laws, J.L. A feminist review of marital adjustment literature: The rape of the Locke. *J. Marr. & Fam.*, 1971, *33*, 483–516.

Lehman-Olson, D. Assertiveness training: Theoretical and clinical implications. In D. Olson (Ed.), *Treating relationships*, Lake Mills, Iowa: Graphic, 1976.

Leichter, E. Treatment of married couples groups. *Fam. Coord.*, 1973, *22*, 31–42.

Liberman, R.P., Levine, J., Wheeler, E., Sanders, N., and Wallace, C.J. Marital therapy in groups: A comparative evaluation of behavioral and interactional formats. *Acta Psychiatr. Scand.*, 1976, suppl. *266*, 3–34.

Linden, M.E., Goodwin, H.M., and Resnik, H. Group psychotherapy of couples in marriage counseling. *Int. J. Group Psychother.*, 1968, *18*, 313–324.

Locke, H.J., and Wallace, K.M. Short marital adjustment and prediction tests: Their reliability and validity. *Marr. & Fam. Living*, 1959, *21*, 251–255.

Mace, D., and Mace, V. Marriage enrichment—A preventive group approach for couples. In D.H.L. Olson (Ed.), *Treating relationships*. Lake Mills, Iowa: Graphic, 1976.

Maizlish, I.L., and Hurley, J.R. Attitude changes of husbands and wives in time-limited group psychotherapy. *Psychiatr. Quart. Suppl.*, 1963, *37*, 230–249.

Margolin, G. A comparison of marital intervention: Behavioral, behavioral-cognitive and nondirective. Paper, Western Psychological Association, Los Angeles, April 1976.

Marks, I.M. Management of sexual disorders. In H. Leitenberg (Ed.), *Handbook of behavior modification and behavior therapy*. Englewood Cliffs, N.J.: 1976, 255–300.

Masters, W.H., and Johnson, V.E. *Human sexual inadequacy*. Boston: Little, Brown, 1970.

Mayadas, N.S., and Duehn, W.D. Stimulus-Modeling (SM) videotape for marital counseling: Method and application. *J. Marr. & Fam. Couns.*, 1977, *3*, 35–42.

McLean, P.D., Ogston, K., and Grauer, L. A behavioral approach to the treatment of depression. *J. Behav. Ther. Exp. Psychiatr.*, 1973, *4*, 323–330.

Miller, S., Nunnally, E.W., and Wackman, D.B. Minnesota Couples Program (MCCP): Premarital and marital groups. In D.H.L. Olson (Ed.), *Treating relationships*. Lake Mills, Iowa: Graphic, 1976.

Minuchin, S. *Families and family therapy*. Cambridge, Ma.: Harvard Univ. Press, 1974.

Minuchin, S., Baker, L., Rosman, B., Liebman, R., Milman, L., and Todd, T. A conceptual model of psychosomatic illness in children. *Arch. Gen. Psychiatr.*, 1975, *32*, 1031–1038.

Most, E. Measuring change in marital satisfaction. *Soc. Work*, 1964, *9*, 64–70.

O'Leary, K.D., and Borkovec, T.D. Conceptual, methodological, and ethical problems of placebo groups in psychotherapy research. *Am. Psychologist*, September 1978, 821–830.

O'Leary, K.D., and Turkewitz, H. Marital therapy from a behavioral perspective. In T.J. Paolino and B.S. McCrady (Eds.), *Marriage and marital therapy: Psychoanalytic, behavioral, and systems theory perspective*. New York: Brunner/Mazel, 1978a.

O'Leary, K.D., and Turkewitz, H. Methodological errors in marital and child treatment research. *J. Consult. & Clin. Psychol.*, 1978b, *46*, 747–758.

Olson, D.H. Marital and family therapy: Integrative review and critique. *J. Marr. & Fam.*, 1970, *32*, 501–538.

Olson, D.H. Review and critique of behavior modification research with couples and families: Or, are frequency counts all that count? Paper, AABT, New York, October 1972.

Olson, D.H.L. *Treating relationships*. Lake Mills, Iowa: Graphic, 1976.

Olson, D.H., and Ryder, R.G. Inventory of marital conflicts (IMC): An experimental interaction procedure. *J. Marr. & Fam.*, 1970, *32*, 443–448.

Olson, D.H.L., and Sprenkle, D.H. Emerging trends in treating relationships. *J. Marr. Fam. Couns.*, 1976, *2*(4), 317–329.

Olson, D.H., and Strauss, M.A. A diagnostic tool for marital and family therapy: The SIMFAM technique. *Fam. Coord.*, 1972, *21*, 251–258.

Paolino, T.J., and McCrady, B.S. *Marriage and marital therapy: Psychoanalytic, behavioral and systems theory perspectives*. New York: Brunner/Mazel, 1978.

Patterson, G.R., Hops, H., and Weiss, R.L. A social learning approach to reducing rates of marital conflict. Paper, AABT, New York, October 1972.

Prochaska, J., and Prochaska, J. Twentieth-century trends in marriage and marital therapy. In T.J. Paolino and B.S. McCrady (Eds.), *Marriage and marital therapy: Psychoanalytic, behavioral, and systems theory perspectives*. New York: Brunner/Mazel, 1978.

Rappaport, A.F., and Harrell, J. A behavioral exchange model for marital counseling. *Fam. Coord.*, 1972, *22*, 203–212.

Reid, J. Reciprocity and family interaction. Unpub. Ph.D. diss., Univ. of Oregon, 1967.

Rice, D.G., Fey, W.F., and Kepecs, J.G. Therapist experience and 'style' as factors in co-therapy. *Fam. Proc.*, 1972, *11*, 1–12.

Roberts, P.V. The effects on marital satisfaction of brief training in behavioral exchange negotiation mediated by differentially experienced trainers. (Ph.D. diss., Fuller Theological Seminary, 1974). *Diss. Abstr. Int.*, 1975, *36*, 457B.

Rosman, B., Minuchin, S., Liebman, R., and Baker, L. Impact and outcome of family therapy in anorexia nervosa. Ms. submitted for publication, 1976.

Sidman, M. *Tactics of scientific research: Evaluating experimental data in psychology.* New York: Basic Books, 1960.

Stanton, M.D. Some outcome results and aspects of structural family therapy with drug addicts. In D. Smith, S. Anderson, M. Buxton, T. Chung, N. Gottlieb, and W. Harvey (Eds.), *A multicultural view of drug abuse: The selected proceedings of the National Drug Abuse Conference—1977.* Cambridge, Ma.: G.K. Hall/Schenkman, 1978.

Stanton, M.D., and Todd, T.C. Structural family therapy with heroin addicts: Some outcome data. Paper, Society for Psychotherapy Research meeting, San Diego, June 1976.

Strodtbeck, F.L. Husband-wife interaction over revealed differences. *Am. Sociologic. Rev.*, 1951, *16*, 468–473.

Strupp, H.H., and Bergin, A.E. Some empirical and conceptual bases for coordinated research in psychotherapy. *Int. J. Psychiatr.*, 1969, *7*, 18–90.

Stuart, R.B. Operant-interpersonal treatment for marital discord. *J. Consult. & Clin. Psychol.*, 1969, *33*, 675–682.

Stuart, R.B. An operant interpersonal program for couples. In D.H.L. Olson (Ed.), *Treating relationships.* Lake Mills, Iowa: Graphic, 1976.

Stuart, R.B., and Stuart, F. *Marital pre-counseling inventory.* Champaign, Ill.: Research Press, 1972.

Targow, J.G., and Zweber, R.V. Participants' reactions to treatment in a married couples' group. *Int. J. Group Psychother.*, 1969, *19*, 221–225.

Thibaut, J.W., and Kelley, H.H. *The social psychology of groups.* New York: Wiley, 1959.

Thomas, E.J., Carter, R.D., and Gambrill, E.D. Some possibilities of behavioral modification of marital problems using SAM (signal System for the Assessment and Modification of behavior). In R.D. Rubin, H. Fensterheim, A.A. Lazarus, and C.M. Franks (Eds.), *Advances in behavior therapy.* New York: Academic Press, 1971.

Truax, C.B., and Carkhuff, R.R. *Toward effective counseling and psychotherapy: Training and practice.* Chicago: Aldine, 1967.

Tsoi-Hoshmand, L. Marital therapy: An integrative behavioral-learning model. *J. Marr. & Fam. Couns.*, 1976, *2*, 179–191.

Turkewitz, H. A comparative study of behavioral marital therapy and communication therapy. Unpub. Ph.D. diss., SUNY at Stony Brook, 1977.

Turkewitz, H., and O'Leary, K.D. Communication and behavioral marital therapy: An outcome study. Paper, AABT, New York, December 1976.

Vincent, J.P. The relationship of sex, level of intimacy and of marital distress to problem-solving behavior and exchange of social reinforcement. (Ph.D. diss., Univ. of Oregon, 1972.) *Diss. Abstr. Int.*, 1973, No. 73–13, 778.

Weiss, R.L. The conceptualization of marriage and marriage disorders from a behavioral perspective. In T.J. Paolino and B.S. McCrady (Eds.), *Marriage and marital therapy: Psychoanalytic, behavioral, and systems theory perspectives.* New York: Brunner/Mazel, 1978.

Weiss, R.L., Hops, H., and Patterson, G.R. A framework for conceptualizing marital conflict, a technology for altering it, some data for evaluating it. In L.A. Hamerlynck, L.C. Handy and E.J. Mash (Eds.), *Behavior change: Methodology, concepts, and practice.* Champaign, Ill.: Research Press, 1973.

Wieman, R.L. Conjugal relationship modification and reciprocal reinforcement: A comparison of treatments for marital discord. Unpub. Ph.D. diss., Penn. State Univ., 1973.

Wieman, R.L., Shoulders, D.I., and Farr, J.H. Reciprocal reinforcement in marital therapy. *J. Behav. Ther. & Exper. Psychiatr.*, 1974, *5*, 291–295.

Williams, A.M. The quantity and quality of marital interaction related to marital satisfaction: A behavioral analysis. (Ph.D. diss., Univ. of Florida, 1977.) *Diss. Abstr. Int.*, 1978, *38* (7).

Williams, A.M. A behavioral analysis of the quantity and quality of marital interaction related to marital satisfaction. *J. Appl. Behav. Analy.*, 1979, *12*(4), Winter issue.

Wills, T.A. Measuring pleasurable and displeasurable events in marital relationships. Unpublished Masters Thesis, Univ. of Oregon, 1971.

Wills, T.A., Weiss, R.L., and Patterson, G.R. A behavioral analysis of the determinants of marital satisfaction. *J. Consult. & Clin. Psychol.*, 1974, *42*, 802–811.

Chapter 16

Overview of Sex Therapy

Stephen B. Levine

Most human beings can expect to have some sexual difficulties during their lifetimes. Of course, the specific problems, their causes and duration will vary widely—but few individuals will escape. Cross-sectional studies of diverse cultural groups have consistently shown a high prevalence of variously defined sexual difficulties (Frank, Anderson and Rubenstein, 1978; Levine and Yost, 1976a; Martin, 1977; Golden et al., 1977). Although these studies have not yet fully captured the subjective aspects of sexual functioning, they point to its troubled state. Should more sophisticated epidemiologic data ever become available, they are likely to demonstrate that it is statistically normal for sexual life to be problematic.

This dour prediction, obviously a clinical bias, is consistent with the opinions derived from both psychoanalytic theory and practice and the recent more direct behavioral approaches to sexual complaints—i.e., sex therapy. From the clinical perspective, the major characteristic of sexual life is the ease with which it can be disturbed.

CATEGORIES OF SEXUAL DISTURBANCES

The disturbances of human sexual life fall into four major categories: gender-identity disorders; perversions; homosexuality; dysfunctions. Although these disturbances are conceptually and subjectively quite different, some individuals have difficulties in more than one category. These four categories will be briefly reviewed in order to clarify the problems treated with sex therapy.

Core gender-identity disorders. Individuals with disturbances of their self perceptions as masculine or feminine are unable to live comfortably as members of their biologic sex. Men with these problems live, secretly dress or fantasize themselves as women. Women may live as men, as highly masculinized women, or fantasize themselves as men. Core gender-identity disorders are variously labeled transsexualism, transvestism or gender dysphoria syndromes. Though rare, they are more common among men and are the most basic and severe of all sexual problems.

Perversions. Sexual behaviors which involve masochism, sadism, voyeurism, exhibitionism, pedophilia and rape have traditionally been classified as perversions or paraphilias. Most of these widely censured sexual patterns are forms of eroticized aggression which involve a victim rather than a partner. They are infrequent among men and very rare among women. The inordinate excitement and pleasure associated with these sexual behaviors may explain why they are rarely brought to psychiatric attention unless a powerful external force is exerted—e.g., court, convincing threat of divorce.

Homosexuality. The persistent sexual attraction to a member of the same sex has traditionally been viewed as a disorder of sexuality. In 1973, however, the American Psychiatric Association decided that only those who were unable to accept their homoerotic preferences were diagnosable as having a disorder. Homosexuals per se were no longer to be considered mentally ill. Regardless of its classification, the process of accepting one's homosexuality can be quite painful. As many as 10 percent of both sexes may have homoerotic preferences.

Dysfunctions. The dysfunctions are the various inabilities to experience sexual arousal to orgasm with a partner in a smooth, well-integrated manner. Almost anyone may develop dysfunctional symptoms at some time. Dysfunctions are highly influenced by life changes. They are subclassified according to four separate component capacities of sexual functioning: desire, arousal, orgasm, emotional satisfaction. Although an isolated disturbance of a single component can exist, one disturbance often leads to other component problems—e.g., an emotionally dissatisfied man may soon lose his capacity to be aroused; a woman with orgasmic problems may soon develop desire problems.

Table 1 is a list of recognized dysfunctional symptoms and their common terminology. These are the simple, irreducible units of sexual problems— i.e., the chief complaints, the apparent reasons for seeking help. There are three reasons for the table's seeming complexity. It includes both rare

Table 1
Classification of Sexual Dysfunctions by Component Symptoms

Component	Sex	Symptoms	Common Terminology
Desire (Libido)	Male and female	Absent desire Infrequent desire Excessive desire	None
Arousal	Male	Inability to obtain erection Inability to maintain erection }	Impotence or erectile dysfunction
	Female	Inability to become aroused Inability to stay aroused }	Frigidity or excitement phase dysfunction
Orgasm	Male	Rapid, uncontrolled ejaculation Ejaculation too difficult to achieve Inability to ejaculate with partner Inability to ejaculate in the vagina }	Premature ejaculation Retarded ejaculation Ejaculatory failure or ejaculatory incompetence
		Ejaculation without orgasm Orgasm without ejaculation Orgasm with no apparent ejaculation (semen in bladder)	Pleasureless orgasm Dry orgasm Retrograde ejaculation
	Female	Orgasm too rapid Orgasm too difficult to achieve Inability to achieve orgasm with partner } Inability to achieve orgasm during intercourse Pleasureless orgasm	Orgasmic phase dysfunction Coital anorgasmia Pleasureless orgasm

Table 1 (continued)
Classification of Sexual Dysfunctions by Component Symptoms

Component	Sex	Symptoms	Common Terminology
Satisfaction	Male and female	Little or no emotional satisfaction	None
Other Problems	Male	Penile anesthesia during coitus	None
		Penile pain during coitus or with erection	Male dyspareunia
	Female	Vaginal anesthesia during coitus	None
		Vaginal or pelvic pain during coitus	Dyspareunia
		Intolerance of intromission	Vaginismus

complaints and more common clinical varieties. There is as yet no common terminology for similar component symptoms which occur in both sexes. Some dysfunctional symptoms are sex-limited—e.g., vaginismus, the involuntary contraction of the perivaginal musculature, which makes intercourse painful or impossible; retrograde ejaculation, orgasm accompanied by ejaculation into the bladder. By emphasizing the variety of specific component dysfunctions, the table enables an appreciation of the psychophysiologic integration of aproblematic sexual functioning.

Sex therapists are invariably called upon to treat individuals with gender-identity problems, perversions or homosexuality—some of whom are also dysfunctional. The term "sex therapy," however, usually refers to treatment strategies aimed at dysfunctional symptoms. In this chapter, the category "dysfunctions" will be used in reference to symptoms developed by apparent heterosexuals without obvious gender-identity problems or perversions.

CLINICAL REALITIES

The literature on sexual dysfunctions, like that of any field of patient care, does not always fully reflect clinical realities. Dealing with patients requires the establishment of a special relationship and the exercize of good clinical judgment—intangible factors rarely mentioned in the literature. Instead, the literature concentrates on techniques or theories of therapy. Lag times of three or more years between the collection of data and their appearance in a journal are inherent in the publication process (Ingelfinger, 1977). If authors should come to some other conclusion in the interim—as a result of subsequent data or clinical maturation—the new view rarely appears in print. Positive findings tend to be overrepresented in the literature because authors are disinclined to report negative ones. Those reporting positive results are usually academicians whose careers are based on their innovations. Their total immersion in their subject and extra enthusiasm may provide their patients with subtle bonuses not available to the patients of other clinicians. Moreover, their specially selected patients may not be comparable to the range of patients encountered in other clinical settings.

In addition, editorial review results in publication of articles which present succinctly expressed ideas—i.e., one dominant theme per article. In the clinical setting, the same idea has to compete with many other ideas, viewpoints and "facts." Clinicians who are new to sex therapy may feel their own work is inadequate because their patients have not responded with the ease, completeness and permanence of those described in the literature. Their difficult cases, however, should not necessarily be considered indications of their incompetence.

The clinician dealing with sexual dysfunctions is involved in four routine pursuits, which are not well described in the current literature: the identification of organic causes; separation of psychological factors that are intrapsychic from those that are interpersonal; the attempt to get the patient(s) to become as sexually normal as possible; stabilization of therapeutic gains.

Dysfunctional symptoms may be the result of direct physical factors. The development or maintenance of any symptom may be at least partly due to an organic factor. Organic factors which directly contribute include (a) physical disease—e.g., renal failure, diabetes; (b) drugs—e.g., reserpine, methadone; (c) surgery—e.g., prostatectomy, vulvectomy; (d) aging—e.g., idiopathic loss of vigor. Neither the basic neurophysiology of sexual response nor the effect of organic factors on it is well understood. In fact, some symptoms now thought to be psychologic in origin may ultimately be attributed to an organic factor.* Organic factors, however, may also indirectly contribute to dysfunction by incuding psychologic and social changes—e.g., mastectomy, response to knowledge of one's own or partner's cancer (Jamison, Wellisch and Pasnau, 1978; Wellisch, Jamison, Pasnau, 1978). Most of the literature on the effectiveness of sex therapy presumes—sometimes without justification—the absence of organic factors.

The literature is preoccupied with methods of therapy. However, careful differential diagnosis must precede therapy. The mere existence of some symptoms is of value in separating organic from psychologic cause—e.g., retrograde ejaculation suggests an organic cause; most premature ejaculation suggests a psychologic cause. Symptoms become more meaningful for differential diagnostic purposes, however, when they are temporally related to the life cycle. Symptoms which have always been present during partner sexual behavior are referred to as primary dysfunctions. Symptoms which appear after an established period of better sexual functioning are classified as secondary.† Secondary dysfunctions are prime suspects for organic contributants. Primary *psychological* dysfunctions are usually related to a developmental failure to achieve comfort with sexuality. The basic therapeutic task, therefore, is to facilitate growth. Secondary *psychological* dysfunctions are more likely to involve an important interpersonal problem. The therapeutic task will often, therefore, involve altering a marital equilibrium. Careful differential diagnosis is very important. Organic and psychologic problems require different forms of interventions—as do primary and

---

*Peyronie's disease has been suggested as a cause of some cases of "psychogenic" impotence (Karacan, 1978).

†The adjective "situational" is often applied to secondary psychological dysfunctions that are present only with a particular partner. The most frequently described situational dysfunction,

secondary psychologic problems. For example, the husband's presence throughout therapy for secondary psychologic excitement-phase dysfunction may quickly reveal the source of the symptom as the wife's anger at him and enable its resolution. In primary excitement-phase dysfunction, his presence throughout may prevent the wife from dealing effectively with her guilty childhood fears of sexuality.

Subjectively, there really is something called "sexual normality." Sexual normality is not captured by the epidemiologists' attempts to measure performance—e.g., erectile or ograsmic attainment. In a clinical setting, limiting the evaluation of normality to performance criteria results in defensiveness, anxiety and altered marital balances. The concept of normality becomes clearer when discussed in subjective terms. During therapy, dysfunctional couples or individuals know when they become normal. They feel normal when they are relaxed, willing to make love and able to concentrate on sensations. It is interesting that when these subjective requisites of sexual normality are fulfilled, most psychologic dysfunctions disappear. (The psychologic sequences that mediate most dysfunctions are unwillingness to make love, inability to relax and the inability to concentrate on sensation (Levine, 1976b).

Normality can also be said to exist when both partners are aproblematic in the four components of sexual functioning: desire, arousal, orgasm, emotional satisfaction. Resolution of only one component of the problem may result in improvement—but not normality. For the individual couple, it is the subjective, not the statistical, aspects of normality that are important.

The sexual relationship of a couple is a product of complex, highly interdependent psychodynamic forces. Masters and Johnson's often-quoted statement to dysfunctional couples beginning treatment somewhat exaggerates this basic concept: "Sexual dysfunction is a marital unit problem—not a husband's or a wife's problem" (Masters and Johnson, 1970). An individual is always dysfunctional with a partner—but not necessarily the same one at all times. There are, in fact, many dysfunctional single and divorced individuals. The partner's attitude and behavior not only influence the quality of sexual life, but can account for the presence or absence of dysfunction. For example, a premature ejaculator may be helped to develop ejaculatory control. If his partner is uncomfortable with his new sexual capacity, however, his rapid, uncontrolled ejaculation may soon return. The positive results of any therapy with individual partners do not necessarily have a positive effect on the couple's sexual adjustment.

---

situational anorgasmia, illustrates the imprecision of commonly used terminologies. The term "anorgasmia"—failure to achieve orgasm—does not distinguish between arousal and orgasmic component problems.

THE CHANGING THERAPEUTIC ATMOSPHERE

Prior to 1970, psychoanalytic theory and practice dominated the therapeutic approach to sexual problems. (Behavior therapists were becoming interested in sexual dysfunction at this time, but their work was not well known.) Cautious conservative attitudes toward sexual symptoms were shared by psychoanalysts and the large numbers of professionals they influenced. The outcome data presented in *Human Sexual Inadequacy* (Masters and Johnson, 1970) challenged these attitudes and suggested a radically different therapeutic approach. The rapid acceptance of the new form of therapy by both the lay and the professional public testifies to the failure of the psychoanalytic tradition to deal with the widespread presence of sexual problems.

Psychoanalytic theory is a slowly evolving collection of ideas that attempts to integrate the forces that influence psychological life. It attempts to relate sexual and other symptoms to the patient's past psychological development and current mental state. Psychoanalytic discussions of sexual symptoms may include all of the following factors: constitutional predispositions; parent-child relationships over time; psychosocial development (biologically programmed ontogeny through oral, anal, phallic, oedipal and genital stages); sociocultural and biological alterations. The general nature of psychoanalytic theory makes it equally as impossible to convince the skeptic as to disenchant the believer. Even most of its opponents accept its basic tenets: there are important unconscious influences on all mental functioning; no psychological event occurs entirely by chance (Brenner, 1955). There are various schools of psychoanalytic thought, but all psychoanalysts recognize the critical importance of the complex internal psychological life.

The typical therapies for sexual problems that have evolved from psychoanalytic tradition are dyadic. Their aim is to achieve more complete understanding of the individual's mental life. The sexual problem is seen as a manifestation of an underlying, usually unconscious, internal conflict. The therapeutic goal is not to just relieve the symptom, but to resolve its infrastructure—the underlying conflict. Insight, understanding, mastery, and pyschological growth are highly valued therapeutic goals. Other means of symptom removal are regarded simply as "transference cures" or "suggestion," likely to be followed by symptom substitution. The rate at which psychoanalysis and psychoanalytic psychotherapy proceed is largely controlled by the patient's inner life. After the evaluation phase, a married patient with a sexual problem is usually seen alone. Interpersonal problems tend to be viewed as the acting out of the patient's internal conflicts.

Psychoanalytic notions are often intellectually rich and clinically useful. The analytic therapies have, however, left a number of significant deficiencies in regard to the dysfunctions. There have never been convincing data to support the great conviction about the efficacy of psychoanalytic therapies— especially psychoanalysis. Actually, the capacity of such therapies to cure sexual problems (efficacy) has not been seriously questioned; their effectiveness (i.e., number of cures per one hundred cases), however, has been.

Psychoanalytic thought has paid relatively little attention to the various forms of dysfunctions. Most male problems were loosely referred to as "impotence," all female problems as "frigidity." No advances in the understanding of the dysfunctions were made since the initial great discoveries about sexual life made by Freud and the early analysts.

Psychoanalytic therapies were expensive and apparently best suited to psychologically minded, relatively young people—thus excluding a large percentage of the population with a high prevalence of sexual problems. The emphasis on past developmental problems, unconscious factors and long-term therapy frightened away many prospective patients who "didn't believe in psychiatry." Besides sympathy and an offer of a separate therapy, nothing was provided for the spouse of a dysfunctional person.

Masters and Johnson's initial work suggested a number of exciting possibilities for dealing with the dysfunctions. Both partners are included in the treatment. The concerns of each partner have to be considered without placing blame for the dysfunction. The symptoms belong to the marital unit, not the symptom-bearer.

The psychologic mechanisms of dysfunction could be largely related to current, rather than past, influences—e.g., performance anxiety; spectatoring; anger at the dysfunctional spouse. A new emphasis was placed on social forces rather than intrapsychic causes—e.g., cultural expectations which prevent the normal development of female sexual expression; religious orthodoxy.

Key psychoanalytic teachings about female sexuality were in error. The traditional male interpretation of normal female sexual response had to be carefully avoided. The ingrained notion that the "clitoral orgasm" was immature, pathological and inferior to the normal "vaginal orgasm" was proven to be a myth (Masters and Johnson, 1966). This enabled therapists to convince women they should not consider themselves "neurotic" on the basis of their means of orgasmic attainment.

Male and female co-therapy teams were uniquely suited to fostering communication and mutual understanding between spouses. They were also more effective in dealing with the high frequency of serious interpersonal problems. Correction of misinformation and the imparting of knowledge were facilitated by co-therapists.

Perhaps Masters and Johnson's most important innovation, however, was the collection of data on the results of their therapeutic efforts. They claimed to have achieved stable improvements and eradication of various dysfunctions with large numbers of patients in two weeks of daily therapy. Comparable results with individual psychotherapy were thought to require months or years of treatment.

THE NEW SEX THERAPIES

These new principles were quickly adopted and modified by others. In spite of the many subsequent innovations, most sex therapies with couples still consist of Masters and Johnson's basic format: thorough evaluation of psychological and organic factors; use of sensate focus exercizes; sex education; improved communications; attempts to help with apparent personal and interpersonal conflicts.

There have been three major modifications of these principles:

1. Application in a hometown ambulatory setting. The couples are seen less frequently—e.g., weekly for twelve weeks, rather than daily for two. This forces the couple to integrate their therapy into their normal life pattern. Masters and Johnson deliberately attempted to create an atmosphere for couples that was free from mundane interfering problems.

2. Co-therapy teams have often been replaced by individual male or female therapists. This modification evolved due to the double cost of two therapists, difficulty in coordinating the schedules of two professionals with other commitments and the basic problem of finding two professionals who worked well together. Co-therapy is still used in some clinics by therapists who believe it is a more effective approach. Often an experienced therapist works with a beginner for training purposes. There are no definitive data on the effectiveness of co-therapists (Roman and Meltzer, 1977).

3. Addition of various psychological theories. Many of Masters and Johnson's ideas are intuitively understood by dysfunctional individuals. There is no consistent, unifying psychological theme in either their therapeutic innovations or their explanations for dysfunction, however. Their contributions cannot be completely subsumed under any existing psychological theory—e.g., psychoanalytic, learning, social-psychological, gestalt. The impact of this "deficiency" is lessened, however, by the realization that no theory is powerful enough to explain most behavior.

Sex therapy involves all professionals in activities which cannot be easily classified. Although there are now psychodynamic sex therapists (Kaplan, 1974) and behaviorist sex therapists (Lazarus, 1977), sex therapy is quite eclectic. Regardless of the therapist's theoretical bias, the initial approaches to a given dysfunction are remarkably similar. There are great differences, however, in the conceptualization of therapy and the alternative approaches employed when a dysfunction is not quickly reversed. For example, a psychologically impotent man who does not respond to sensate focus may be treated with either individual talking psychotherapy or assertiveness training.

THERAPEUTIC TACTICS

There are two basic ingredients to any sex therapy: sensate focus exercizes and some form of psychotherapy. Sex therapy for couples is often erroneously equated with only the first element.

Sensate focus is an elegantly simple method based on the principle that sex is the totality of a couple's physical sharing, rather than just intercourse. The therapist(s) briefly directs the couple's sexual behavior, usually beginning by instructing them to touch and kiss each other everywhere except the breasts and genitals. This first instruction, by freeing the couple from performance worries, encourages relaxation and the drift into sensation awareness. It provides the opportunity to explore and talk about giving and receiving pleasure. The ideal end result is sexual excitement. When mastery of these tasks is achieved, the breasts and genitals are added to the areas of pleasuring. Major emphasis continues on learning about and providing for partner desires and on giving and receiving pleasure, rather than on performance. Breast and genital pleasuring usually generates a high degree of arousal; orgasm may follow through extravaginal means. The third major instruction, after good sexual functioning in noncoital modes is achieved, is to include intercourse.

When sensate focus progresses smoothly, the results are hard for everyone—patients, therapist and professional peers—to believe. A couple with a long history of dysfunction may, in the course of a few days or weeks, find sexual experience to be an easy, richly pleasurable recreation. The dysfunctional physiology is reversed. The couple grows together, having shared a very intimate process of learning about one another.

The ideal state, often present early in sensate focus, frequently does not last. The progress of sensate focus is blocked by other feeling states. Attention to these affects, and not to the technique of sensate focus itself, comprises the psychotherapy component of sex therapy. Good sexual functioning usually cannot be achieved if the intensity, source and meaning of these feelings are not appreciated. The presence of interfering feelings or attitudes is signaled by the couple's inability to carry out the sensate focus instructions or become emotionally involved in the sexual behavior. The major challenge for the sex therapist is essentially a psychotherapeutic one: working with persons to overcome their resistance to emotional participation in the tasks of sensate focus.

The sources of resistance vary from person to person and are not always completely definable. They do, however, frequently derive from couples' nonsexual relationships, their sense of gender-appropriate sexual behavior and their individual capacities to tolerate emotional and physical intimacy.

The actual course of a couple's sex therapy is determined by the specific dysfunctions present. Arousal problems lead to an emphasis on early sensate focus. Orgasmic problems require concentration on genital pleasuring techniques. Vaginismus is typically treated by vaginal dilation and relaxation exercises. Desire problems, the most recalcitrant of dysfunctions, are increasingly being dealt with by traditional psychiatric explorations, rather than sensate focus.

The following is a typical set of instructions given by a sex therapist to a couple with uncomplicated premature ejaculation—i.e., no other component problems. The psychic distress caused by these instructions would be dealt with during the office sessions with the therapist. The entire sequence may take two to three months of weekly sessions.

1. First sensate focus instruction: kiss and touch everywhere but genitals.

2. Second sensate focus instruction: add breast and genital stimulation. Don't worry about having an orgasm. It doesn't matter if or when it occurs.

3. Third sensate focus instruction: focus on extravaginal penile stimulation.
   a. Allow partner to stimulate genitals manually.
   b. Male concentrates *only* on sensation.
   c. Male tells partner to stop when he feels he is building up to orgasm.
   d. Rest for two minutes and return to genital stimulation three times.
   e. On the fourth approach, allow orgasm to occur.
   f. Whenever orgasm occurs, experience all the contractions; do not apologize; savor the pleasure.

4. Fourth sensate focus instruction: quiet vagina exercises (begun after man can "endlessly" tolerate extravaginal stimulation).
   a. Male supine; female inserts penis; no thrusting; concentrate on sensations of containment. When man can remain in vagina for a minute,
   b. female may slowly thrust. She stops when he is nearing orgasm. On fourth approach to orgasm she should not stop. He should have orgasm and savor it without apology.
   c. Male begins to thrust, stopping when he feels increasing arousal.
   d. Side-to-side and man-on-top positions used if desired.

EXTENSIONS OF SEX THERAPY

Therapists are constantly trying to assist people who do not qualify for the sex therapy described above—e.g., unmarried couples; single or divorced individuals without partners; homosexual couples; physically handicapped patients; those who are unwilling to regard themselves as patients or clients. Their sex therapies often consist of combinations of group therapy, films, bibliotherapy, surrogate partners, relaxation techniques, assertiveness training, marathon weekends and factual discussions. Most of these methods include some attention to affects, attitudes and relationships—elements of psychotherapy.

In a very short time many different activities and techniques have been classified under the rubric "sex therapy." Behavior therapists have been especially active and interested in treating dysfunctional symptoms. Sex therapy is clearly still evolving. Its unchecked growth has generated a number of concerns—e.g., how to distinguish between legitimate sex therapy and quackery; minimum training standards for sex therapists; evidence that sex therapy works. Solutions to such basic problems might be facilitated by a period of assessment, scrutiny and conservatism.

EFFECTIVENESS OF SEX THERAPY

A number of diverse influences maintain the growth of sex therapy. There is a strong belief that Masters and Johnson have already demonstrated its effectiveness and superiority over other approaches. Kaplan's work has made it palatable to dynamically oriented professionals by combining psychodynamic understanding with a direct approach to sexual symptoms (Kaplan, 1974). It is relatively easy to obtain a positive response early in therapy with many patients. There is no precedent for scientific rigor in evaluating the effectiveness of other psychotherapies prior to their widespread use. There is a growing public demand for assistance with sexual concerns.

The optimism expressed in reviews of sex therapy is not entirely based on the objective analysis of outcome data (Wright et al., 1977; Kinder and Blakeny, 1977). There are relatively few studies dealing with specific dysfunctions. Many reports treat the dysfunctions as a group—disregarding the significant differences between primary and secondary or excitement-phase and orgasmic-phase problems. Also, little attention has been paid to problems of desire, which are often hidden by arousal difficulties (Kaplan, 1977). Techniques used in group settings are not really comparable to those applied in individual or couple therapy. Most importantly, however, there are no standard evaluative methods or parameters (Kuriansky and Sharp, 1977).

An evaluation of any therapy should begin with a thorough description of the degree and frequency of the pretreatment problems. The immediate and long-term effects on these problems should be presented separately, using a standard, clinically meaningful approach. It is important to make certain that the patient subjectively experiences the improvement shown on the objective measures used. The degree of initial short-term recovery and the relapse frequency must be evaluated for the target symptom being studied. The effects of therapy on the other component problems, however, must also be evaluated.

Table 2 illustrates the complexity found in groups which are homogeneous for any specific dysfunction. It lists the component profiles of five hypothetical forty-eight-year-old married men with secondary psychological impotence. Case 1 has uncomplicated impotence. His previous sexual life was aproblematic and he still experiences sexual desire. Case 2 was dysfunctional prior to being impotent. His uncontrolled rapid ejaculation will also have to be reversed before he will feel sexually normal. Case 3 suffers from an acute loss of libido, probably because of a mild depression. In addition to restoring potency, the therapist will have to help resolve the emotional problems in his devitalized, mutually unsatisfactory marriage. Case 4 has never found sex very satisfying—perhaps because of his lifelong low libido and poor ejaculatory control. His impotence is the consequence of long-standing personality or constitutional problems. Case 5's impotence is also due to desire problems. His problem is only ten years old, however, and is not constitutional.

The information in Table 2 leads to the question, should sex therapy be judged according to its capacity to restore erectile functioning or its capacity to resolve all major component problems? There is no easy answer. The following case illustrates the effective restoration of erectile functioning without resolution of component problems.

A brooding, bitter, chronically depressed thirty-nine-year-old man and his hopeful wife sought sex therapy to prevent the ultimate dissolution of their relationship. She could no longer tolerate his sexual disinterest and complete impotence. He was concluding a five-year psychoanalysis and claimed to have no understanding of his sexual incapacity [sic!]. Prior to marriage he had functioned normally with other partners. Emotional attachment caused him to lose sexual interest in one relationship. His libido did not return until he recovered from a near-fatal sucide attempt that had been precipitated by her terminating the relationship. He was regularly desirous of and potent with his wife premaritally until their relationship became serious. They had intercourse about ten times in their ten-year marriage. The last time was two years ago after he discovered she was having an affair. He had anxiety attacks if she tried to initiate sex.

They were afraid to separate. Their relationship was tender and affectionate. They both felt he would probably suicide if she left. Extramarital

Table 2
Secondary Psychological Impotence in Married Men

Component Problem	Case 1	Case 2	Case 3	Case 4	Case 5
Desire	Stable	Stable	Acute absence	Always low	Low × 10 yrs.
Arousal	Impotent	Impotent	Impotent	Impotent	Impotent
Orgasm	Normal	Lifelong premature ejaculation	Normal	? Normal	Normal
Previous Emotional Satisfaction	Normal	Normal	Little when potent in recent years	Eh!	Normal when potent

liaisons had intensified her conflicts by showing her what she had been missing. She loved her husband dearly, in spite of his hyperintellectual, obsessive, controlling style.

Because the man was terrified by the prospect of touching in the nude, therapy began with breathing exercises. Throughout the treatment his behavior was either anxious, bored, neutral or mechanical. He enjoyed giving pleasure more than receiving it. Even when he was firmly erected, he denied pleasure and lacked motivation to penetrate. He was eventually able to maintain erection for intercourse until she was orgasmic, but then felt his "duty was over" and was unable to ejaculate. He recalled his previous postorgasmic depressions and joked about the dangers of unrecognized long-term effects of "harmless" activities. After months of cheerful optimism, she concluded he was incapable of emotional involvement and lost all pleasure in having intercourse with him.

In a letter written six months after termination of therapy, she reported that they had made love three months ago and both had orgasms. It was brief, but great. A combination of her threat to leave him and his knowledge of her recent affair had enabled the intercourse. Since, there had been only stated intentions to make love. Their nonsexual relationship was very good and there were no plans for separation. "I fear I shall grow unused and desiccated."

In her follow-up letter one year after therapy terminated she reported that three months ago she had been feeling desperate about the absence of sex. They agreed to make love each weekend at a specific time, after having a few drinks. Sex occurred at least twice a month. The quality was much improved and both were orgasmic. He admitted to a great anticipatory fear, which probably accounted for his taking so long to erect. "I know he is enjoying it a lot more now." She hoped someday sex would be good enough for her not to need a lover.

In this case, is it fair to say sex therapy was ineffective? It succeeded where psychoanalysis had failed. Erectile functioning was restored; eventually he overcame his inability to ejaculate. Clearly it is not completely honest to say this man was cured. Here is the dilemma. If the criterion of effectiveness is too narrow—e.g., simply erectile function—sex therapy will be erroneously rated as highly effective. If the criterion is too broad—e.g., capacity to make patients subjectively normal—the power of sex therapy will be unappreciated.

The ideal solution is to evaluate sex therapy for target symptoms subclassified according to associated component problems. Thus, in secondary psychological erectile dysfunction, the uncomplicated cases would be separated from those with antecedent premature ejaculation or absent libido. While this method makes it harder for clinicians to collect large numbers of cases for review, it is more likely to provide a useful measure of the effectiveness of sex therapy for this problem.

These problems are further complicated by the fact that the wives of married impotent men may have their own component problems. If sex therapy is going to result in a stable long-term improvement, the wives' problems may also have to be resolved. Such evaluation expectations are clinically reasonable, but make evaluation enormously complicated. Methods of assessment which oversimplify the clinical realities have usually been used. These range from simply classifying each patient as cured, improved or not improved to the use of various pre- and post-therapy rating scales.*

The remainder of this section will focus on the quality of the evidence documenting the effectiveness of sex therapy. One male and one female dysfunction are used as examples of the prevailing views on the subject. The conclusions would not be measurably strengthened by reviewing the data for each dysfunction.

SECONDARY PSYCHOLOGICAL IMPOTENCE

In 1969, Cooper presented data on sixty-seven married men evaluated at a psychiatry clinic for "potency" disorders (Cooper, 1969). These disorders included acute onset impotence, insidious onset impotence, inability to ejaculate and premature ejaculation. This pre-Masters and Johnson sex therapy was described as "practical, superficial, aimed at the symptom rather than the underlying cause." It consisted of deep muscle relaxation, optimal sexual stimulation, sex education and psychotherapy. Forty-nine patients completed the minimum treatment requirements of twenty fortnightly sessions. Cooper described his results as poor: seven recovered, twelve improved. Although Cooper stated that acute onset impotence had the best prognosis, he provided no data on the response of each specific problem to therapy. This is a significant methodologic limitation. Cooper's clinical impressions about prognostic factors seem reasonable, especially since there were no stringent selection criteria. Factors associated with a good outcome included short duration of problem, heterosexuality, desire for coitus, mutual marital happiness and love, cooperative spouse and absence of personality disorder.

Masters and Johnson's data dealt with 213 cases of secondary impotence (Masters and Johnson, 1970). Their sample was highly selected and not strictly comparable to unscreened patients in psychiatric clinics. Criteria for

---

*Eastern Association for Sex Therapy (EAST) has recently compiled a *Handbook of Measures in Human Sexuality* to assess the results of sex therapy.

success were never specified, probably because no information on success rates was given. They reported a 26.2 percent failure rate at the end of two weeks of treatment; only ten men relapsed during the five-year follow-up. Their five-year overall failure rate was 30.9 percent. Follow-up was apparently conducted with phone conversations, episodic interviews and letters.

In 1976, Ansari added a sobering dimension to outcome studies of clinic patients—control groups. He compared a modified Masters and Johnson treatment format with two others: chemotherapy and supportive psychotherapy (Ansari, 1976). There were no significant differences in outcomes! In the modified Masters and Johnson group, 67 percent had either recovered or improved after therapy; 33 percent were in the same categories at eight months. Ansari stressed important clinical differences among the sample of 65, many of whom had histories of lifelong low libido. He found prognosis was related to the subjects' clinical features, not the form of therapy. Those whose impotence was caused by a specific psychological or physical trauma had a better prognosis than those with an insidious decline in potency or lifelong low libido. His data, however, probably contain some cases of primary impotence.

Levine and Agle (1978) reported detailed results on sixteen couples presenting with chronic secondary impotence (mean duration, 8.8 years). Table 3 lists their component problems. Sex therapy was immediately effective with fourteen men in restoring fully turgid erections. The accomplishment of at least one lasting penetration followed shortly. There was, however, a high relapse rate during therapy. Relapses were also frequent between the four follow-up interviews, conducted at three-month intervals. Most couples were better at the end of one year than when they came to therapy, but not free of component problems. Problems of desire were especially recalcitrant to treatment. Unresolved female dysfunctions undermined some of the male accomplishments during the follow-up period.

Depending upon the definition used, success rates could vary from 6 percent (restoration of the couple to normality for one year) to 69 percent (improved erectile function one year after treatment, regardless of interim relapses). The authors were more impressed with the diagnostic utility of sex therapy in quickly revealing a couple's interpersonal and intrapsychic dynamics than with its lasting curative powers.

This small study lacked a control group. It did, however, include well-defined admissions criteria, an unbiased non-therapist evaluator, pre-post objective measures and regular follow-ups with standardized questions. While everyone had sensate focus exercises, there were wide differences among the psychotherapeutic interventions used with each couple. Thus the therapies could be considered identical only in a limited sense. The fact that a large percentage of Levine and Agle's patients subsequently sought

Table 3
Sexual Problems Associated with Impotence†

Case	Male			Female			
	Rapid Ejac.	Other Ejac. Disturbances	Desire Problem	PEPD*	SEPD*	POPD*	Desire Problem
1							
2							
3	X	X					
4							X
5							
6			X		X		
7			X				
8	X					X	X
9							

Table 3 (continued)
Sexual Problems Associated with Impotence†

	Male			Female		
10	X	X			X	
11	X			X		
12		X				X
13		X	X			X
14	X			X		X
15						
16						

Male sexual problems, including impotence = 27
Female sexual problems = 11

*PEPD = Primary Excitement Phase Dysfunction
 SEPD = Secondary Excitement Phase Dysfunction
 POPD = Primary Orgasmic Phase Dysfunction

†From Levine, S.B., Agle, D. The effectiveness of sex therapy for chronic secondary psychological impotence. *J. Sex. & Marit. Ther.*, 1978, *4*, 235–258.

additional therapy was consistent with Levay and Kagle's (1977) earlier report about the treatment needs following sex therapy.

PRIMARY ORGASMIC PHASE DYSFUNCTION

According to the previous definitions, "primary orgasmic phase dysfunction" refers to a woman's lifelong inability to experience orgasm with a partner by any means in a smooth, well-integrated fashion. For practical purposes, the diagnosis also applies to a woman who has an orgasm only on rare occasions. Women who can achieve orgasm only after Herculean stimulation (e.g., one hour with a vibrator) or who must dissociate during orgasm (e.g., "I feel outside myself, like it isn't happening to me!") are diagnosed as dysfunctional according to this definition. Because the definition refers only to sexual response with a partner, these women should be conceptually separated into two groups: those who can achieve orgasm by self-stimulation and those who have never tried masturbation or are incapable of a masturbatory orgasm. Dysfunctional patients who can masturbate to orgasm are quite common; the literature on this subject, however, is largely restricted to those who cannot. The latter group has been variously labeled "primary anorgasmic," "primary inorgasmic," "primary nonorgasmic," "primary orgasmic dysfunction" and "preorgasmic."

Masters and Johnson had an immediate treatment failure rate of 16.8 percent in treating 193 women for primary orgasmic dysfunctions; their five-year failure rate was 17.6 percent (Masters and Johnson, 1970). Since means of orgasmic attainment were never specified, their data probably apply to orgasms achieved with a partner by any means: manual, oral, coital. There are also no data on the frequency, ease or integration of orgasmic attainment. Nonetheless, 82.4 percent of 193 women is an impressive success rate.

In 1972, LoPiccolo and Lobitz introduced an innovative approach for the woman with primary orgasmic-phase dysfunction—a nine-step masturbation program used during couple sex therapy (LoPiccolo and Lobitz, 1972). The first six steps were to be accomplished alone: (1). visual exploration of the genitals and use of pubococcygeal exercizes; (2). tactile stimulation of the genitals; (3). localization of the pleasurable areas; (4). deliberate stimulation of these areas to induce pleasure; (5). attempt to masturbate "until something happens." (Therapists suggest use of fantasy and erotica.) (6). If 1 through 5 have been unsuccessful, the woman is asked to use a vibrator and pornographic materials to achieve orgasm. (7). Masturbation with husband watching. (8). Husband "does for his wife what she did for herself." (9). Intercourse with simultaneous stimulation of the clitoris. LoPiccolo and Lobitz's criterion for success was orgasm through self-stimulation. At the end of treatment all eight women were successful. At six-month follow-up, six were orgasmic during coitus, four without simultaneous clitoral stimulation. Three years later this same program was used with another six women, all of whom became orgasmic during coitus at least 25 percent of the time (McGovern, Stewart and LoPiccolo, 1975).

Barbach introduced group treatment for "preorgasmic women" with or without partners (1974). The groups consisted of six clients and two female co-therapists who met twice weekly for five weeks. The clients were educated about female sexual functioning, given reading assignments and assigned one hour of "homeplay" a day. They saw and discussed a movie of a woman masturbating. Women were encouraged to be assertive in this feminist therapy. LoPiccolo and Lobitz's nine-step masturbation program was slightly modified. The criterion of success in this study was masturbatory orgasm by any means—e.g., hand, vibrator, running water. Of eighty-three women, 91.6 percent achieved success by the end of therapy. Of the seventeen follow-ups, eleven were orgasmic with partners by some means at least 50 percent of the time eight months after therapy (Wallace and Barbach, 1974).

Munjack et al. (1976a) utilized a wait-list control group in studying twenty-two "happily married" women who had been unable to achieve orgasm with their partners for at least a year. The sample was divided into two subgroups: those who had never experienced orgasm (primary) and those who had had at least one orgasm (secondary). The husbands were present only at some of the twenty sessions. The major criterion of success was orgasmic attainment in at least 50 percent of partner sexual activities. Treatment was shown to be more effective than no treatment. Twenty-two percent of the primary and 40 percent of the secondary group were successful at the end of treatment. Average duration of follow-up was nine months. None of the primary, and 60 percent of the secondary, group were successful at follow-up.

The definitions of success used in research studies are not necessarily consistent with clinical realities (Munjack and Kanno, 1976b). Most women with primary orgasmic phase dysfunctions complain they cannot achieve orgasm with a partner. They usually add "during intercourse." Beginning dysfunctional women on a masturbation program is probably common practice now. The realistic therapeutic goals with these women are (1). enabling masturbatory orgasm in a smooth, well-integrated manner; (2). enabling orgasm with partner in similar manner, not necessarily during coitus; (3). enabling the maintenance of these gains. Based on research with Barbach's "successfully" treated clients, Payn has recently described the frequent failure to comfortably integrate their orgasmic capacities into partner sexual behavior (Payn, 1978). Payn's work supports the clinically obvious—i.e., there is more to helping sexually dysfunctional women than motivating them to masturbate to orgasm. Success is a matter of comfortable integration. Partner sexuality is more complex than solitary sexuality. Both are at least dependent upon intrapsychic and interpersonal dimensions. Improved sexual functioning involves more than behavior; it is a matter of personality.

CONCLUDING REMARKS

The appearance of sex therapy has been associated with a number of positive changes in the mental health professions: new clinical services—often to individuals who previously would not have sought help; graduate and postgraduate educational programs in sexuality; public discussion of many sexual issues; stimulation of research. A prominent critic has claimed that sex therapy dehumanizes sex by removing it from its natural context (Shaines, 1978). Similar comments have been made by dissatisfied patients. It is possible to dehumanize sex by oversimplifying its emotional components. However, such criticism is more useful as a caveat than as a blanket indictment of the aims and quality of all clinical work done in the entire field. Sex therapy is just another activity that enables professionals to provide service while studying behavior. There are three major clinical dangers of sex therapy: its naïve application to unskillfully selected patients; the assumption that any specific dysfunction can best be treated by a specific sex therapy; therapists who violate the ethical guidelines for dealing with patients.

This chapter has emphasized the fact that sex therapy will probably not restore most individuals to subjective sexual health. This does not mean it is of little or no value! To keep the issue of effectiveness of sex therapy in its proper perspective, it is necessary to consider the documented effectiveness of every form of therapy—e.g., individual, marital, group, family.

Sexual functioning may be improved through frank, calm, direct discussion of sexual behavior combined with some specific technique—e.g., sensate focus, assertiveness training. The sad fact remains, however, that many individuals with "treatable" sexual problems remain dysfunctional after therapy.

EPILOGUE

I once described a fifty-nine-year-old previously potent church deacon to a large class of second-year medical students. During sex therapy, this man experienced impotence, inability to ejaculate, penile anesthesia, retrograde ejaculation, pleasureless orgasm, normal sexual functioning and, finally, an attack of chest pain. His wife had been institutionalized two years before for Alzheimer's disease. He had previously cared for her at home for six years against everyone's advice. He became progressively more isolated and depressed and prayed for his own death—until he met the woman he called his "angel." They waited eight months before attempting intercourse. In spite of firm erections while necking in the living room, he was anxiously impotent and self-disparaging in the bedroom. He reported nightmares about someone murdering his wife. His guilt about wishing his wife dead and having an "extramarital" affair were obvious to his partner—and the medical students. His progression through most of the dysfunctions was a dramatic illustration of the power of his internal conflicts. Shortly after finally having a series of good sexual experiences with his "angel," he was admitted to the cardiac intensive-care unit. His ailment was eventually diagnosed as psychosomatic pain.

One student raised his hand and commented that this man's sexual problems were just part of a larger existential dilemma. I hope that student became a sex therapist!

ACKNOWLEDGMENT

The author wishes to thank Mrs. Barbara Juknialis of the Department of Psychiatry, Case Western Reserve University, for her editorial assistance.

REFERENCES

Ansari, J.M.A. Impotence: Prognosis in a controlled study. *Br. J. Psychiatr.*, 1976, *128*, 194–198.

Barbach, L.G. Group treatment of preorgasmic women. *J. Sex & Marit. Ther.*, 1974, *1*, 139–145.

Brenner, C. *An elementary textbook of psychoanalysis.* New York: International Universities Press, 1955.

Cooper, A.J. Disorders of sexual potency in the male: A clinical and statistical study of some factors related to short-term prognosis. *Br. J. Psychiat.*, 1969, *115*, 709–719.

Frank, E., Anderson, C., and Rubenstein, D. Frequency of sexual dysfunction in "normal" couples. *N. Eng. J. Med.*, 1978, *299*, 111–115.

Golden, J.S., Golden, M., Price, S., and Heinrich, A. The sexual problems of family planning clinic patients as viewed by the patients and the staff. *Fam. Plan. Perspect.*, 1977, *9*, 25–29.

Ingelfinger, F.J. Shattuck lecture: the general medical journal: For readers or repositories? *N. Eng. J. Med.*, 1977, *296*, 1258–1264.

Jamison, K.R., Wellisch, D.K., and Pasnau, R.O. Psychosocial aspects of mastectomy. 1. The woman's perspective. *Am. J. Psychiatr.*, 1978, *135*, 432–436.

Kaplan, H.S. *The new sex therapy.* New York: Brunner/Mazel, 1974.

Kaplan, H.S. Hypoactive sexual desire. *J. Sex & Marit. Ther.*, 1977, *3*, 3–9.

Karacan, I. Advances in the diagnosis of erectile impotence. *Med. Asp. Human Sexual.*, 1978, *12*, 85–97.

Kinder, B.N., and Blakeny, P. The treatment of sexual dysfunction: A review of outcome studies. *J. Clin. Psychol.*, 1977, *33*, 523–530.

Kuriansky, J., and Sharp, L. Guidelines for evaluating sex therapy. *J. Sex & Marit. Ther.*, 1977, *2*, 303–308.

Lazarus, A. The behavioral approach to treatment. In J. Money and H. Musaph (Eds.), *Handbook of sexology.* Amsterdam: Excerpta Medica, 1977.

Levay, A.N., and Kagle, A. A study of treatment needs following sex therapy. *Am. J. Psychiatr.*, 1977, *134*, 970–973.

Levine, S.B., and Yost, Jr., M.A. Frequency of sexual dysfunction in a general gynecological clinic: An epidemiological approach. *Arch. Sex. Behav.*, 1976a, *5*, 229–238.

Levine, S.B. Marital sexual dysfunction: Introductory concepts. *Ann. Inter. Med.*, 1976b, *84*, 448–453.

Levine, S.B., and Agle, D. The effectiveness of sex therapy for chronic secondary psychological impotence. *J. Sex & Marital Ther.*, 1978, *4*, 235–258.

LoPiccolo, J., and Lobitz, W.C. The role of masturbation in the treatment of orgasmic dysfunction. *Arch. Sex. Behav.*, 1972, *2*, 163–171.

McGovern, K.B., Stewart, R.C., and LoPiccolo, J. Secondary orgasmic dysfunction: 1. Analysis and strategies for treatment. *Arch. Sex. Behav.*, 1975, *4*, 265–275.

Martin, C. Sexual activity in the aging male. In J. Money and H. Musaph (Eds.), *Handbook of sexology.* Amsterdam: Excerpta Medica, 1977, 813–824.

Masters, W.H., and Johnson, V.E. *Human sexual response.* Boston: Little, Brown, 1966.

Masters, W.H., and Johnson, V.E. *Human sexual inadequacy.* Boston: Little, Brown, 1970.

Munjack, D., Cristol, A., Goldstein, A., Phillips, D., Goldberg, A., Whipple, K., Staples, F., and Kanno, P. Behavioural treatment of orgasmic dysfunction: A controlled study. *Br. J. of Psychiatr.*, 1976a, *129*, 497–502.

Munjack, D., and Kanno, P. An overview of outcome on frigidity: Treatment effects and effectiveness. *Compr. Psychiatr.*, 1976b, *17*, 401–413.

Payn, N.M. Beyond orgasm: A study of the effect on couple systems of group treatment for preorgasmic women. Eastern Association of Sex Therapy, New York, March 1978.

Roman, M., and Meltzer, B. Co-therapy: A review of the literature (with special reference to therapeutic outcome). *J. Sex & Marit. Ther.*, 1977, *3*, 63–77.

Shaines, N. Sexual ethics in America. *Psychiatr. Opin.*, 1978, *15*, 13–14.

Wallace, D.H., and Barbach, L.G. Preorgasmic group treatment. *J. Sex & Marit. Ther.*, 1974, *1*, 146–154.

Wellisch, D.K., Jamison, K.R., and Pasnau, R.O. Psychosocial aspects of mastectomy. II. The man's perspective *Am. J. Psychiat.*, 1978, *135*, 543–546.

Wright, J., Perreault, R., and Mathieu, M. The treatment of sexual dysfunction. *Arch. Gen. Psychiat.*, 1977, *34*, 881–890.

Chapter 17

Blue Collar-White Collar: Sexual Myths and Realities

Ilda V. Ficher
Sandra B. Coleman

INTRODUCTION

Since sexual problems are inextricably related to the emotional conflicts of everyday life, it is apparent that a "satisfactory sex life," despite idiosyncratic differences in meaning, makes an important contribution to the maintenance of a secure marital relationship. Although the sexual revolution has had considerable impact on all social classes, its effects appear to be mediated by varying socioeconomic and cultural factors. Kinsey's (1948, 1953) findings that social status effects the marital couple's sexual values and influences the quality of their sexual behavior are still supported by contemporary research (Rubin, 1976).

A stable marriage facilitates a considerable amount of personal growth for both husband and wife; its success is reflected by the extent to which interpersonal relationships are enhanced and sexual fulfillment achieved. But traditional attitudes toward marriage and sexuality have undergone profound modification in recent years, and attitudinal changes of this magnitude are not easy for either men or women.

There seems little doubt that sexual attitudes are changing most rapidly among middle-class couples. Although the road is not without mishaps, most researchers report that husband and wives of the middle class, better educated and perhaps exposed to more sexual freedom, appear more comfortable with today's rapidly changing attitudes. In clinical practice, however, we find that these attitudinal changes pose particular difficulty for the poor and culturally disadvantaged.

The purposes of this chapter are (1) to give an overview of the current literature on interclass differences and similarities with regard to sexual attitudes; (2) to describe some of the social behavior that is a function of class differences in sexual knowledge; (3) to examine class-related sexuals myths; and (4) to provide case studies that demonstrate class-relevant strategies for treating sexual dysfunction in women.

THEORETICAL ISSUES

Sexual Attitudes and Social Class

Cross-cultural studies from the United States and elsewhere indicate that there are substantial differences in sexual attitudes among diverse socioeconomic classes. In general, as one moves from higher to lower social status, the proportion of men and women expressing strong interest and enjoyment in sex declines. When specific sexual matters, such as foreplay, positional variations, coital nudity, frequency of intercourse and sexual experimentation, are examined, middle-class couples consistently report more gratification in sexual relations than do members of the lower class.

Rubin (1976) discusses the effects of the sexual revolution on the lives of a large number of blue-collar working-class Americans. From her interviews with working-class couples and a matched group of professional middle-class couples, Dr. Rubin notes that *all* couples reported some problem in sexual adjustment. She describes the extremely complex task that both men and women face when they attempt to incorporate ever-changing sexual mores into a conservative traditional value system. Many areas of sexual expression are more sensitive than ever before, possibly due to the gap between today's social expectations and previous standards of morality. Although it appears that couples are more open in expressing sexual needs and desires, many men still differentiate between "the girls they marry and the girls they use." Rubin views this conflict as partly related to the working-class man's struggle to gain control over his daily job-related activities. As a consequence of the insecurity that often surrounds employment, relationships with women become highly significant measures of male self-esteem.

Often this leads to performance anxiety, impotence, premature ejaculation, the withholding of sex and many other emotional problems.

In this context female sexuality becomes troublesome. Among the lower classes, the woman's conflict is relatively easy to understand, due to the double standard of sexual behavior that is still operant. "Nice girls" do not do certain things, no matter what the newly liberated sex experts say. Rubin notes that the wife's innocence in sexual matters is valued among working-class people, the I-taught-her-everything-she-knows claim being a recurrent motif in her interviews. Thus the "blue-collar woman" has been socialized to conceal her sexual awareness, causing her considerable difficulty in adjusting to the demands of today's seemingly uninhibited sexual climate. The traditional inequality of the double-standard mentality—the attitude that men can enjoy sex within or outside of marriage, whereas women cannot, or that men are expected to have premarital experience, whereas women are not—seems more ingrained in men and women of the lower socioeconomic class and is one of the factors most resistant to change. Thus, too much knowledge of sexual technique or too ready a response might be interpreted by the young lower-class husband as evidence of his wife's questionable background.

In examining the sexuality of the American black ghetto, Brown (1968) points to the maternal role as a prime factor in the structure of the family. He traces this back to the time of slavery, when mother-child relationships were often the only source of stability in the family. Black women in the ghetto are often "protected" from sex in order to become good mothers and child raisers. They are taught from childhood that "sex is dirty and evil; it's something you just don't talk about, even when you do it." This protective attitude provides power and freedom for the male, who is not so protected, and helps to distinguish between the girls that marry and the ones who remain unattached and promiscuous.

Staples (1972a) states that there is a higher incidence of sexual activity at an earlier age among lower-class blacks in the United States. This is not the result of a higher sex drive but derives from the absence of both parents from the home and the lack of supervision of preteen and teenage youngsters. On the average, black lower-class females have their first sexual experience two years earlier than white middle-class females. He reports that this phenomenon is more closely related to social class than race. Vincent (1961) found that unwed mothers from various cultural and socioeconomic groups expressed markedly different attitudes regarding their pregnancies. For example, both black and white unwed lower-class mothers reported that their pregnancies were products of casual relationships, whereas middle- and upper-class women, regardless of race, viewed their pregnancies as "love related." Although the difference is not great, more black than white lower-class unwed mothers became pregnant in casual relationships. Lower-class women often perceived their behavior as necessary to please the male and as a ploy to acquire a husband.

Sexual Myths and Social Class

Sexual attitudes are not the only source of conflict for men and women of the lower socioeconomic classes. They are also burdened by the inaccurate sexual stereotypes projected onto them by therapists and others of the middle and professional classes. (Wyatt, Strayer and Lobitz, 1978) For example, for years the lower classes have been considered far more sexually active than other groups; they are often thought to have far more premarital experience and sexual knowledge than middle-class people of the same age. Research indicates, however, that the reverse is true; when young men and women of the lower classes are questioned carefully, it appears that they are quite conservative in matters such as premarital sex and nudity. They report that both sex relations and orgasms are experienced less frequently than by comparable members of higher socioeconomic groups (Rainwater, 1960; Hunt, 1974).

In another study, Staples (1972b) adds to the issue of the stereotypical view of the lower class the additional burden of the minority groups within this class. He states that myths such as that "black women are the most sensual of all females" or the commonly held fantasy of "the uncontrolled animal sexuality of the blacks" may be due to the repression which white society has experienced. These myths serve only to confuse and complicate the issue of sexual behavior in the lower socioeconomic population.

SEXUAL KNOWLEDGE AND INTERCLASS SOCIAL BEHAVIOR

In European and Latin American cross-cultural studies, the same gulf in sexual knowledge and behavior appears between lower and middle socio-economic classes. Sociologist Lee Rainwater has long been interested in lower-class marital sexuality. In one of his studies (Rainwater, 1975), he focused on four cultures of poverty in Puerto Rican, Mexican, North American and British lower classes. Among the groups studied, he noted that sexual instruction was almost never given to daughters. Modesty and prudishness were the female tradition, and since these were highly valued, most women of these classes report that they were totally unprepared for sexual relations in marriage. Although marriage is the only way they can escape the increasing demands of parental homes, women of these impover-ished cultures expect little in the way of sexual fulfillment or gratification from their husbands. Not surprisingly, in several different studies of marriage among the lower classes, women report little or no positive feelings about sexual relations.

These responses and their associated marital dysfunction must be seen as an extension of the traditional separation and isolation of men and women of the working classes. In their working life and in recreational activities, men of these classes tend to congregate with other men, usually outside of the home and family unit. Women, on the other hand, generally remain at home and relate mostly to other women, often family members.

Conjugal role relationships appear to function quite differently among better-educated middle- and upper-middle-class couples. These men and women participate in jointly organized activities both within the home and outside of it. The "togetherness" of joint activities seems to be valued in middle-class families, while lower- and working-class couples emphasize the separation of their interests and activities.

Rainwater (1975) suggests that the closed and relatively exclusive social networks of the lower classes greatly complicate individual adjustment to today's changing sexual morality. Again, when husband and wife roles are well defined and sharply segregated, each spouse tends to interact almost exclusively with same-sex family members and peers rather than with each other. Thus, while men and women of the middle classes may experience improved sexual relations as a result of their socialization, the same opportunities usually do not exist for members of lower socioeconomic groups.

Some research indicates that the traditional separation of the sexes continues with undiminished force in some societies today. Quijada (1977), after interviewing a thousand men and women, indicated that the basic precepts of male superiority, or "machismo," are presently as strong as ever in Mexican society. He also points out that although the feminist movement has achieved some victories, it has changed few attitudes. According to this study, the reasons for machismo are complex, stemming largely from the male's reaction to what historically has been a matriarchal society. Quijada asked in his study, "Isn't it possible that behind the gross and grotesque caricature of male domination there should be a real female domination? The man who shouts his masculinity is often guided and controlled by a woman. His shout is only that reaffirmation of something he has lost."

According to Quijada's study, female domination comes only through the figure of the mother, who is seen as a saintly person uncontaminated by eroticism. The mother naturally becomes the model for a wife, who must be a virgin, have a respectable reputation and a need to sacrifice. But since the wife can never match the mother's perfection in the eyes of most Mexican men, she can be punished through ill treatment and unfaithfulness. This infidelity is seen in their strong need to conquer women because of feelings of insecurity and inadequacy about their own masculinity.

In describing the Puerto Rican lower-class culture, Lewis (1965) diverts some of his focus to the nature of their sexual encounters. He describes clearly a population that is not as informed about sexual matters as their middle-class counterparts. As in the lower-class black family, the mother is a central character in the family composition, and the male often distinguishes between wife and lover. The male-oriented sexuality of this population puts sex into the realm of power, and often there is a power struggle in the marriage.

TREATMENT ISSUES

The cultural variances in the sexual expectations of men and women of the lower socioeconomic classes have broad implications for those treating them for sexual dysfunction. When working-class couples require marital counseling, some specific therapeutic problems emerge.

For example, it was found (Settlage, 1975) that problems of "self-esteem, body image and sex-role stereotyping are greater than in middle-class populations." With regard to sexual behavior generally, these couples have insufficient information, negative experiences, inadequate sexual communi-cation and individual self-concept deficiencies. In addition, motivation is often low, particularly when the partner is resistant to treatment. Frequently there is denial that a sexual problem exists, especially among black and Hispanic males.

Finally, the therapist's reluctance to treat people from an unfamiliar ethnic group may pose significant obstacles. This is often due to the therapist's lack of experience in relating to sexual norms that are dissimilar to his/her own. Also, there is a commonly held misconception that blacks and Hispanics are sexually hyperactive and do not require intervention.

An investigation (Calneck, 1970) of the interpersonal transactions be-tween the black patient and the black therapist showed that although the black professional was expected to treat the lower-class minority patient more effectively than his/her white colleagues, this was not the case. It was also found that the therapeutic relationship can be seriously affected by "traditional American racial" factors. For example, if the therapist was formerly a lower-class minority member, he/she may now want to reject previously held lower-class values because of having "made it" to the middle class. This indoctrination into the middle class presents a serious hindrance to the black patient/black therapist relationship.

Koegler and Williamson (1973) speak of the treatment of lower-class Spanish-speaking patients. They note that this population is quite different from the middle class, and that they are much in need of heightened attention from the professional community. Koegler and Williamson point out that "until recently the mental health professional thought psychotherapy was not effective for patients from lower socioeconomic levels." They indicate that there is the need for a new kind of therapist, one who has flexibility in treating multi-ethnic groups and varying socioeconomic classes.

Kranz (1973) proposes a schema for achieving meaningful interactions with minority group patients. He suggests the need for "greater ease and openness in dealing with relevant racial material." Also, the therapist needs to be more sensitive and less defensive when dealing with racial issues with a patient. Finally, he proposes the need for a greater ability to listen to the minority-group patient rather than setting one's self up as an authority. Kranz calls for expanded training for professionals, including cross-cultural educational programs, sensitivity training and increased exposure to minority group patients.

Unfortunately there is a dearth of literature on the relationship between professional therapists and lower-class clients. The few studies that do exist indicate that there are a number of misconceptions regarding the sexual activity of this population; that this group is in great need of accurate sexual information; that there is both a high need for treatment and a great deal of resistance by patient and therapist. Finally, there is a need for significant change in the training of the professional if he/she is to work effectively with multi-ethnic, lower-class patients.

Clinical Considerations

Our experiences in working with different cultures and multi-level socioeconomic groups provide an extensive base of information regarding the varied range of sexual dysfunctions and the most effective class-relevant strategies for treating them. From this clinical exposure we have developed a framework of considerations which every therapist should consider as he/she initiates contact with the client(s). Before developing a strategy for treating any presenting dysfunction, the therapist must understand fully the sociocultural context within which the treatment methodology must fit. Most importantly, the following represent some of the major issues which require therapeutic attention:

Sociocultural norms. Sexual behavior is a function of an amalgam of customs which derive from a society's institutions, e.g., religion or politics. These sociocultural norms influence one's moral attitudes toward sexuality, thus regulating the degree to which people accept various sexual activities, such as homosexuality or oral sex. Also within the broader society there are varying socioeconomic substructures that have class-relevant attitudes and values.

Gender-linked role expectations. All societies have gender-linked expectations of the roles that males and females "should" assume. These expectations provide a foundation for the interpretation of sex-linked behavior. Thus, a therapist must be familiar with gender-linked expectations of the roles and associated behaviors that emerge from the clients' particular class and culture.

Sex-linked traits. Although there may be a general attitude that certain characteristics are universally linked to either males or females, sociocultural conditions may be more responsible for the development of certain traits than previously believed possible. Therapists must therefore be aware of their clients' background and any idiosyncratic sex-linked cultural characteristics that may take precedence over biological traits.

Culturally imposed restrictions. Along with the various norms which apply to sexual behavior in general, there are societal restrictions on specific types of sexual activities at certain times. These usually vary according to the degree to which a culture sanctions sexual intercourse during menstruation, pregnancy, lactation, etc. Also, positions during intercourse are culturally and socioeconomically influenced and often legally controlled. For example, in the United States the male superior, or missionary, position (male on top) was the only acceptable position until recently. Now the U.S. imposes no legal restrictions on intercourse positions, but this may not be representative of other societies. Even when it is within a couple's *legal* rights, religious doctrine may be antithetical. It is the therapist's obligation to become aware of the prevailing cultural influences of a client's behaviors.

Language expectations. It is especially important that a therapist be sensitive to the language norms that influence his/her clients. Since almost all contemporary therapy depends on a verbal process, language is the major vehicle for determining the effectiveness of one's interventions. If the therapist's language is either offensive or misunderstood, the treatment strategies cannot be successful. Although the use of street language or slang expressions may be appropriate and even desirable for a young American "hippie" couple, it could be an affront to others to the extent that it might preclude working with them. It is clearly the therapist's responsibility to learn and to apply the most culturally appropriate language to the treatment situation.

These are a few of the major considerations which the therapist must understand in order to treat effectively those from multi-level socioeconomic groups and different cultural backgrounds. The therapist must know the myths, beliefs and customs that influence his/her clients' behavior, for without this understanding he/she may develop therapeutic strategies that conflict directly with the clients' personal attitudes and values regarding sex. Further, this becomes even more significant when working with multi-ethnic couples whose own mixed backgrounds may present a significant amount of cultural discord.

There are additional factors to be taken into account in specific situations, and each therapist should investigate and delineate those variables, which are likely to influence the process and eventual outcome of therapy. Overall, the sensitive therapist will be able to enhance his/her treatment interactions when the *clients' point of reference*—their sociocultural overlapping systems—are used as the context within which the therapeutic model is developed.

CONCLUSIONS

This chapter has examined some of the class-related attitudes and values regarding contemporary sexual issues. Despite the liberal views that characterize the media and seem to dominate our lives, the effects of the sexual revolution on minority groups and lower classes are less profound. Overall, the double standard still pervades a large segment of our population, compelling men to tenaciously hold on to traditions that secure their male prowess, while female innocence is protected and glorified vis à vis the maternal role. Although sexual activity is initiated much earlier among lower-class women, they still are less apt to experience orgasm and sexual fulfillment. In contrast, middle- and upper-middle-class women embrace a more open sexual morality, enjoy more varied sexual activity and expect their sexual relationships to provide optimal satisfaction.

Unfortunately the literature reflects a lack of new data on sexual patterns among varied populations. The information presented here represents the body of existing knowledge. We have attempted to discuss some of the clinical considerations and approaches that can be adapted to the special needs of different populations.

One of the major problems in resolving sexual dysfunctions is that minorities and lower-class populations are reluctant to seek treatment. To encourage their involvement in sex-therapy programs, the following procedures are suggested: (1) Special attention must be paid to the cultural background and sexual attitudes of both patient and therapist; (2) the identified patient should be afforded flexibility in treatment and should not be confronted with rigid requirements for couple therapy when this is contrary to tradition (especially among Hispanics); (3) alternative treatments should be presented when marital therapy is contraindicated, e.g., group or individual therapy; (4) the therapist must have an understanding of ethnic and class-relevant norms and must incorporate them into all aspects of treatment when needed; (5) the therapist must be flexible about hours, length of sessions, immediate contact with patients and his/her availability to them.

Very few treatment outcome studies with crosscultural populations and varied socioeconomic classes have been done, yet there is an important need for such research. Until such controlled, systematic studies are undertaken, we are left to speculate and stumble in our theoretical and clinical attempts to help the blue-collar and white-collar folk with their many sexual dilemmas.

REFERENCES

Brown, T.E. Sex education and the life in the Negro ghetto. *Pastoral Psychol.*, 1968, *19*, 45–54.

Calnek, M. Racial factors in the countertransference: The black therapist and the black client. *Am. J. Orthopsychiatr.*, 1970, *40*, 39–46.

Ficher, I. The influence of changing roles on the sexual relationship in marriage. In G.P. Sholevar (Ed.), *Changing sexual values and the family*. Springfield, Ill.: Charles Thomas, 1976.

Ficher, I. Sex and the marriage relationship. In W.W. Oaks, G.A. Melchiode and I. Ficher (Eds.), *Sex and the life cycle*. New York: Grune and Stratton, 1976.

Hunt, M. *Sexual behavior in the 1970's*. New York: Playboy Press, 1974.

Kaplan, H.S. *The new sex therapy*. New York: Brunner/Mazel, 1974.

Kinsey, A.C., Pomeroy, W.B., and Martin, C. *Sexual behavior in the human male*. Philadelphia: Saunders, 1948.

Kinsey, A.C., Pomeroy, W.B., Martin, C.B., and Gebhard, P.H. *Sexual behavior in the human female*. Philadelphia: Saunders, 1953.

Koegler, R.R., and Williamson, E.R. A group approach to helping emotionally disturbed Spanish-speaking patients. *Hosp. & Commun. Psychiatr.*, 1973, *24*, 334–336.

Kranz, P.L. Toward achieving more meaningful encounters with minority-group clients. *Hosp. & Commun. Psychiatr.*, 1973, *24*, 343–345.

Lewis, O. *La vida*. New York: Random House, 1965.

Masters, W.H., and Johnson, V.E. *Human sexual response*. Boston: Little, Brown, 1970.

Quijada, O.A. Sexual behavior in Mexico. In Mexico: Machismo thrives in a matriarchy. *N.Y. Times*, September 19, 1977, p. 40.

Rainwater, L. *And the poor get children: Sex, contraception and family planning in the working class*. Chicago: Quadrangle, 1960.

Rainwater, L. Some aspects of lower-class sexual behavior. *J. Soc. Iss.*, 1966, *22*, 96–108.

Rainwater, L. *Behind ghetto walls*. Chicago: Aldine, 1970.

Rainwater, L. Marital sexuality in four cultures of poverty. In W.C. Sze (Ed.), *Human life cycle*. New York: Jason Aronson, 1975, 481–496.

Rubin, L.B. *Worlds of pain*. New York: Basic Books, 1976.

Settlage, D.S.F. Heterosexual dysfunction: Evaluation of treatment procedures. *Arch. Sex. Behav.*, 1975, *4*, 367–387.

Staples, R. Research on black sexuality: Its implications for family life, sex education and public policy. *Fam. Coord.*, April 1972a, 183–188.

Staples, R. The sexuality of black women. *Sex. Behav.*, 1972b, *2*, 4–15.

Sze, W.C. *Human life cycle*. New York: Jason Aronson, 1975.

Vincent, C.E. *Unmarried mothers*. Ill.: Free Press of Glencoe, 1961, 83–84.

Wyatt, G.E., Strayer, R.G., and Lobitz, W.C. Issues in the treatment of sexually dysfunctioning couples of Afro-American descent. In J. LoPiccolo and L. LoPiccolo (Eds.), *Handbook of sex therapy*. New York: Plenum Press, 1978.

Chapter 18

The Legal Factors Facing a Family in Custody Proceedings and Separation

Arnold H. Winicov

As indicated in the main text on the subject in *Pennsylvania Family Law*, the question of custody of the children is one of the main issues facing a family after separation or divorce.

The Family Court is usually the instrument through which this is decided when there is no agreement between the parties. As can be expected, it is an advocacy procedure with each side represented by counsel. The court operates in fragmented situations. A petition for support is heard by one judge and a custody petition may be heard by another judge. There is no systematic procedure encompassing the entire family situation. There is no rule that the parties—the husband, wife or children—must have an attorney. Usually both the husband and wife have counsel and the children involved do not have any legal representation. Thus, the court must decide on what is best for the children. In the event the adverse parents come to an agreement (to satisfy their own needs), the courts may not even be part of how the parents decide on custody, support or visitation rights for the children. Even when the judges are a part of the decision-making process, in most cases they are not trained to deal with the emotional problems of the marriage and its demise, which have been foisted upon the children and the spouses.

To illustrate the division within the courts on the treatment afforded children, in one case the court awarded custody of the children to a parent who intended to reside permanently in Scotland. In another case the court permitted a child to remain in the United States with its father rather than live with its mother in India. The same kind of conflict can occur where support is the issue between the couple. In practically identical cases the court can award different amounts for support. The courts in question are lower courts in the state of Pennsylvania and, in effect, are a realm all their own. The decisions of these courts are reviewed upon appeal to a court of appeals. In Pennsylvania, that is the Superior Court. The Superior Court will not reverse the decisions of the lower court (known as the Court of Common Pleas) unless the lower court has abused its discretion, made an error of law or decided facts on the basis of insufficient evidence or improper conclusions.

In order to understand the role of the courts in custody matters, one must first see how they come to have jurisdiction. Custody proceedings are initiated by the party or parties out of possession of the child. The action is known as a writ of habeas corpus (the act of February 18, 1785), which in effect means, "produce the body." The writ will be heard by the Common Pleas Court only if it has jurisdiction. The elements necessary for the court to have jurisdiction are as follows: the child in question must be actually present in the state; the child or the parent that has the child must be domiciled within the state; both parents (if adversaries) are subject to the jurisdiction of the state of Pennsylvania, i.e., present in the state or domiciled in the state. "Domicile" means that the state is the intended permanent residence of the party in question. The date the writ of habeas corpus is issued is the date deciding the question of jurisdiction.

The child takes the domicile of both parents or, if they are separated, the one with whom he or she lives. Even if a child is illegally in the custody of one of the parents, unless that parent is subject to the jurisdiction of the state of Pennsylvania or the child is so subject, the courts in this state have no jurisdiction in a custody matter.

It is important to note that a decree awarding custody of a child in one state need not be enforced in another state. The reason for this is that all awards are temporary and may be changed or modified in the best interests of the child. Such awards are temporary even with the state of Pennsylvania itself. Many times a husband and wife may enter into a written separation agreement which will provide for the custody of a child. The court will not be involved at all unless one of the parties or some interested third party files a writ of habeas corpus in order to break the agreement. The agreement in question will yield to any court award of custody. This is because the court's award is in the best interests of the child. Naturally, if there is no conflict between the spouses on the issue of custody and if no one challenges the agreement as to whether it is in the best interests of the child, the agreement will stand.

The court's actions regarding children in custody cases is dependent to a large degree on the act of the Pennsylvania legislature known as the Juvenile Act. Its purposes are to preserve the unity of the family whenever possible and to provide for the care, protection and wholesome mental and physical development of the children coming within its provisions. A child under the act is an individual under eighteen years of age. The provisions of the act refer to children that are deprived. "Deprived child" means one that is without adequate education required by law. He is also deprived if he does not have support of his physical, mental or emotional health or morals or has been placed for care or adoption in violation of the law. Any child that has been abandoned by his parents, guardian or legal custodian or is habitually and without justification truant from school is also considered deprived.

If the court, after a hearing, determines that a child is deprived, the court may (1) permit the child to remain with his parents or guardian subject to the conditions and supervision of the court; (2) transfer custody to anyone in or out of the state qualified in the court's opinion to care for the child, or even an agency or private organization; (3) transfer custody of the child to the juvenile court of another state. If the child is mentally ill or retarded, then the provisions of the Mental Health Act are determinative.

There is also a Child Protective Services law to discover and correct abuses of children. It defines an abused child as one that is under eighteen years of age and has evidence of serious physical or mental injury not explained. This includes sexual abuse or physical neglect.

The basis of all awards of custody are in the "best interests of the child." The court making that decision is usually a lower court, which acts as a fact-finder and decision-maker. There is no jury involved. The judge serves that function. The lower court decision is appealable to the Superior Court here in the state of Pennsylvania. This is the first higher court granting the right of appeal or judicial review. The Superior Court may review the entire record of what happened in the lower court and affirm or reverse the decision of the lower court. It also may send the case back to the court below to take additional testimony if it feels the record is incomplete. The Superior Court has the widest possible scope of reviewing the lower court's decision. It is not bound by the deductions and inferences the lower court has made. Nor must the Superior Court accept the findings of fact that the lower court has made unless the findings are based on competent evidence. The lower court is the sole determiner as to the credibility of all witnesses that appear before it. Of course, the Superior Court has a right to review all legal issues in the case and determine whether the lower court ruled correctly or not. The Superior Court has seven justices sitting, and a majority vote by those justices present decides the matter.

Thus, if the lower court, on the basis of competent evidence which it deems credible and with no errors of law, makes a decision to award a child to one spouse or another or to a third party, there is not much reason for the reviewing court to reverse that decision. Only if the lower court has abused its discretion or made an error in the law will the Superior Court reverse.

The Supreme Court is the final stop in the reviewing line. However, it will not hear an appeal from the Superior Court unless it agrees to accept it for review. An appeal to the Supreme Court is a matter not of right but of permission. Usually the Supreme Court will not accept a case unless the question of law involved is unique, there is some question as to what the law is or they want to change the law. Thus, the Superior Court decisions in these matters stand as final in most cases.

The award of custody of a child is determined by "the best interests of the child." In past years a mother was presumed to have superior rights to custody of children under fourteen years of age, assuming both parents were fit. This was known as the tender-years doctrine. Of course, the closer the child was to age fourteen, the more the court would or should consider the preference of the child. So, in cases of twelve- and thirteen-year-old children, the preference of the child could outweigh the tender-years doctrine and the court could accept the child's preference. The tender-years doctrine could also be rebutted by showing that the best interests of the child would be with the father of the child or some third party. This is a matter of proof by the party wanting custody.

Another basis for the rebuttal of the tender-years doctrine would be if the child in question was already with the father and the fitness of either parent was not in dispute. In these cases the courts are loath to change the environment of the child. This is especially the case if other siblings are also with the father.

What does the court mean when they refer to "the best interests of the child"? They are referring to four needs, in the following order: (1) physical welfare, (2) intellectual welfare, (3) spiritual welfare and (4) emotional welfare.

By "physical welfare" the court does not mean that the party with the most money will be awarded custody. It does mean, however, that if one party has insufficient wealth to maintain the reasonable physical welfare of the child, the court "could" award custody to another.

The courts, when referring to the "spiritual welfare" of a child, mean that the disruption of religious and educational development should not take place by awarding custody of the child to one party rather than to another.

Certainly a party that could not provide a continuation of education or religious training would not be looked upon favorably by the court.

If one of the spouses, whether already having custody or wishing it, shows a lack of interest or has so shown it by not visiting the child, not caring for the child in the home or by any action that creates an unfavorable moral climate for the raising of the child, the court is not likely to award custody.

The courts also look to the emotional stability of the parties contending for custody. Unfortunately, most of the discussion by the courts concerning the welfare of the child is about good health and lack of physical abuse. There are too few cases decided that have even discussed the emotional needs of the child. Unfortunately, too, the court has little personal knowledge or understanding in most cases of which factors would militate against a good emotional environment and which would be beneficial.

Keep in mind that anyone with a legal or family tie to the child, even temporary foster parents, may file for custody of a child. Included are grandparents, welfare agencies, sisters, etc. All of the foregoing statements as to the best interests of the child are operative no matter who moves for custody. Thus, in the proper case, grandparents may successfully be awarded custody of a grandchild living with its mother. Or an agency may be able to remove a child from a parental home and place him or her with foster parents.

It is a new development in the law that questions of race, as well as the question of whether the illegitimate father is entitled to custody or not, are nonapplicable in custody proceedings.

It is now possible, under the "right" circumstances, for a black father or mother to obtain custody of their child, which may be of a different hue. Such was never the case in the past. The Supreme Court of the United States has just decided that an illegitimate child may inherit from its natural father. As yet, the rights of the illegitimate father as to his ability to aquire custody are in doubt, but it appears likely that he will soon stand equal with the legitimate father in custody matters.

In most cases a parent will be able to successfully retain or obtain custody of his or her child against a nonparent. This is the case assuming the parent in question is fit and the best interests of the child are so indicated. Naturally, if the parent has not or cannot provide essential parental care in the opinion of the court, this may be a different case. The fact that a mother may be working full time, for example, is no bar to her fitness per se. The court prefers to avoid having the children testify in open court. Usually, if the child is testifying, it is out of parental hearing. Counsel for the parents may or may not be present, according to the discretion of the judge. In these custody hearings, only oral testimony under oath and subject to cross-examination is permitted. No reports or transcripts, whether under affidavit or not, will be allowed. The judge should and will hear testimony from all interested parties. Even disinterested objective parties may be heard if any are available.

It should be remembered that in order to obtain child custody, one need not prove a parent unfit but merely show that the best interests of the child lie with the party seeking custody. Unfortunately, the court system historically has seemed to favor showing one or the other parent unfit. Obviously, anger, rancor, anxiety, are hovering over the proceedings.

The fact that one parent is not married is also in itself insufficient to deny custody. A case in point is one in which a white mother had a black lover. The two were living together. The court indicated that the mother was fit and provided good care for the child, and she retained custody.

Although in the past morality of the mother or the father was the concern of the court, there is a definite change in emphasis today. There are still some lower courts that disapprove of so-called immorality and that remove the child from a parent who in their opinion is immoral, but almost uniformly, the Superior Court, in reviewing the case, will overrule if the child's best interest seems to lie with that parent.

As part of the custody proceeding, the court must grant visitation rights to the parent who lost the custody battle. It must be reasonable, based upon the relationship in existence and the abilities of the parent to adequately provide for the child while in his or her custody. The mere fact that a parent waited several years to request visitation rights is no basis in itself for denying it. On the other hand, a child cannot be forced to visit a parent if he or she is over eighteen years of age. This is so even if the child (adult) is being supported by the father by court order or voluntarily. Minor children (under eighteen) can be required to visit a parent, even against their wishes. Where the visit to the parent is considered by the court to be detrimental to the child, there can be a denial of visitation temporarily. The court cannot make an order permanently denying visitation.

Many times, if a woman or man has been deserted by his or her spouse, the question comes up, perhaps after a divorce and a remarriage, of adoption by the new spouse of the children born of the previous marriage. This action of adoption is covered by statute.

In the event there is consent on the part of one of the parents, it is possible to begin an action for voluntary relinquishment of parental rights. This proceeding is also necessary for unwed mothers who wish to give their illegitimate children up for adoption. It is also possible for married parents to give up their rights to their children voluntarily, if there is an agency or adoptive parents that will take custody of them. The alternative to voluntary relinquishment is involuntary termination of parental rights, which the court also has jurisdiction over and may order.

The proper court is the Common Pleas Court where the petitioner or adoptee resides or in the county where the agency having custody has an office. It is also possible, with the permission of the court in the county where the adoptee formerly resided, the bring the action there.

The natural parents may petition to relinquish all parental rights if they, the parents, are over eighteen years old; otherwise, only the parents of the relinquisher or guardian may give consent with the minor parent. Any agency with custody shall join in consenting to accept custody of the child from the relinquishing parent or parents until adoption of the child.

The child must have been at the agency and in its custody for five days or in custody of an adult other than the parent for five days, not including the parties intending to adopt. The court will always order a hearing both for voluntary relinquishment and for involuntary termination as well as for any adoption.

Involuntary termination is approved by the court when for a six-month period the natural parent has by conduct evidenced a settled purpose of relinquishing parental claim, has failed to perform parental duties or has repeatedly been abusive to or neglectful of the child, causing the child to be without essential parental care, control or subsistence necessary for the physical or mental well-being of the child (and when these conditions cannot or will not be remedied by the parent). Under the law the parent is the presumptive, not the natural, parent of the child. The law will not allow anyone to bastardize a child born from a woman with a husband. So the natural father, if he is not the husband of the mother, has no rights to the child in most cases.

The law has been, up to now, that where the mother has no husband, the natural father of an illegitimate child has no rights in preventing the adoption of his child. There is no need, nor has there been a need, for any involuntary termination petition in that case by the natural father. This situation is now in a state of uncertainty because the United States Supreme Court and the Pennsylvania Supreme Court could change this in their present sessions. In fact the United States Supreme Court has just handed down a decision allowing an illegitimate child to inherit from its natural father, leaving open, therefore, the rights of the natural father.

Either parent may file for the involuntary termination of the other's parental rights. So, too, may an agency or individual with custody, if there is shown an intention to adopt. The courts in the past have been rather restrictive in the qualifications necessary for adopting parents, such as requiring the same religion or race as the natural parents, but there is constant change on this.

The cases indicate that even unwed minor parents cannot have their parental rights terminated unless they do so voluntarily or unless the best interests of the child so demand. The court will be very careful in the case of any voluntary relinquishment by a minor or unwed parent to see if the decision is intelligent, deliberate and uncoerced. The law with regard to natural fathers in these cases is still unclear, and in Pennsylvania it will be determined by the Equal Rights Amendment to the state constitution.

REFERENCES

The Adoption Act of Pennsylvania, 1970.
Child Protective Services Law of Pennsylvania, 1975.
The Civil Procedure Support Law of Pennsylvania, 1978.
The Law of Marriage and Divorce in Pennsylvania. Athens, Pa.: Riverside Press, 1957.
The Marriage Law of Pennsylvania, 1953.
Pennsylvania Family Law. Philadelphia: Momjian and Perlberger, Bisel and Co., 1978.
Pennsylvania Habeas Corpus Act, 1785.
Pennsylvania Juvenile Act of 1972.
Pennsylvania Mental Health Act of 1976, as amended.
Pennsylvania Mental Health Procedures Act of 1976.
Revised Uniform Reciprocal Enforcement of Support Act, 1968.
Uniform Child Custody Jurisdiction Act, adopted 1971.

Chapter 19

The Emotional Impact of Family Disruption on Children

G. Pirooz Sholevar

INTRODUCTION

The significant increase in family dissolution by divorce and separation and its impact on child development have posed major challenges to the child mental-health profession for the 1980's. The problem is formidable in numbers alone. There are currently twelve million children under the age of eighteen in this country whose parents are divorced. Around one million children a year are affected by the dissolution of their families. It is estimated that 45 percent of all children born in this country in any given year will live with only one of their parents sometime before they are eighteen (Francke et al., 1980). The emotional impact on children of family disruption is significant and tends to vary according to a variety of factors, including the phase of family disruption and the developmental stage of the child. In addition to the emotional impact, the financial burden on the family is also significant, due to the costs of litigation and of maintaining two households. A recent Census Bureau report found that only 25 percent of divorced, separated or single mothers received child support.

Legal issues and custody battles can create a traumatic situation for everyone involved, and children involved in disputed custody battles suffer more than most children in disrupted families. They can be swayed by appeals from either parent into shifting allegiances. Recently, many families have attempted to turn to joint custody as a way of avoiding the no-win situation of custody battle.

The principle of the "best interest of the child" has become a guiding force in the establishment of custody and adoption of children through the intensive work of Goldstein, Freud and Solnit (1973). This is to counter lawyers' tendency to fight for the wishes of their clients regardless of the best interest of the children involved. To protect the optimal development of the child, some states are either referring such cases to conciliation courts, where the families can work out a compromise with an impartial third party, or appointing a guardian to represent the child. In contested custody cases in Wisconsin, the court is required by law to appoint an attorney for the child. The lawyer interviews people who have daily or regular contacts with the child and the family for guidance as to which living arrangement is best for the child.

Another serious threat to the developmental process in the child is kidnapping by parents. Each year, 25,000 children are "snatched" or hidden by one parent from the other. Children's Rights, Incorporated (CRI), a Washington-based clearinghouse for information on parental kindapping, estimates that if snatched children are not found within six months, they probably will not be found for years. Parents on the run move frequently and often do not enroll the children in school for fear of being traced (Francke et al., 1980).

In order to reduce the chances of child snatching by the parents, attempts are being made to make kidnapping one's own children a federal offense. While thirty-nine states have enacted the Uniform Child Custody Jurisdiction Act, the remaining eleven are potential havens for parental kidnappers. The parental kidnapping prevention act, once passed, would honor and enforce custody and visitation decrees of other states and make it a federal misdemeanor to restrain or conceal a child in violation of a custody or visitation decree (Francke et al., 1980).

The parental attempts at socialization and dating following divorce can lead to temporary neglect of the children. Divorced men and women feel compelled to join the social world to reestablish their sense of attractiveness. Parental dating often heightens the fear of the children that a new partner will replace the departed parent. Although the parental sexual activity may compete with the parenting function of the divorced parent, the absence of parental social and sexual involvement can also be damaging to the child. A child's concept of heterosexual life and family image may be interfered with by living with a single parent who has a limited social life.

All children of divorce are subjected to immediate crisis created by the divorce situation. The long-term effect of family disruption on the developmental process of the children is not known completely. Wallerstein and Kelly (1973, 1976, 1977) have found that five years after the separation, a third of the children they studied seemed to be resilient; an equal number were coping and muddling through; and the rest were troubled noticeably, looking back at their life before the divorce with intense longing.

THE IMPACT OF FAMILY DISRUPTION ON THE DEVELOPMENT OF CHILDREN

Divorce may be the single largest cause of depression in children. Additionally, it is implicated frequently as a contributing factor in antisocial and other disturbances of children and adolescents. The impact of family disruption on the developmental process of children varies according to a variety of factors, including the phase of family disruption, the developmental stage of the child, the emotional and social status of the custodial and noncustodial parent, the relationship of parents with each other and the nature of their relationships with their extended families and secondary social support system.

PHASES OF FAMILY DISRUPTION

Family disruption should be studied as a process with several specific phases rather than as a distinct event. Each phase of the marital disruption impacts on the developmental process in children, although the nature and the character of the impact may vary from one phase to another. The phases of marital disruption can be divided into:

1. The phase of conflict preceding the actual separation
2. The phase of separation
3. The phase of legal and relational conflicts over issues of child custody, support, division of property, etc.
4. The phase of resolution or stabilization of conflict, such as legal and physical separation, legal and emotional divorce, establishment of custody and visitation arrangement, etc.

The children may be affected significantly by the conflictual phase preceding the separation. At times, young children may be the first ones who sense the dissolution of marriage before the parents have recognized its inevitability. They may react strongly to the crises and stresses of this phase by exhibiting behavioral and physical symptoms or a lowered functioning in their everyday activities. In the phase of *separation*, a variety of behavioral reactions, such as anger, sadness, disruptive behavior in school, problems with peers or social withdrawal, may be noticed. The exact nature of the child's reaction will be further discussed later in this chapter. The loss of one parent in the phase of separation is common and frequently results in some form of mourning or grief reaction in the child. In the *phase of legal and relational conflict* between the parents, the children are invariably brought into the parental conflict. More intense and protracted conflict between the parents imposes a heavier toll on the children. When, for a variety of reasons, the phase of conflict between the parents is mild or short-lived, the children's adjustment to the crisis situation is enhanced. It is particularly helpful if the parents can keep the child's interest as a separate point of view in mind while they continue their own marital conflicts. Cramer (1975), in discussing three of forty-five subjects studied longitudinally with "optimal development," discussed the fact that one child was of divorce and one of a depressed mother in a conflicted marriage. He hypothesized that these children developed optimally because of the spoken and unspoken parental alliance regarding the child.

The *phase of resolution or stabilization* of conflict will give the child the opportunity for integration of the disordered element in his family life. One should keep in mind that legal divorces are seldom followed by an emotional divorce between warring parents. The parental fights continue due to "incomplete emotional divorce," which can actually heighten the child's involvement in the parental conflict with deleterious impact on his or her development. The parental grievances against the other parent are generally delegated to the child in a subtle fashion. He becomes the vehicle to carry the parental accusation back and forth—a function which will impair his development and adjustment in the present and in the future. In fact, it is a major task of mental-health professionals to intervene when the child is caught in loyalty conflicts between two divorced parents who have not completed their marital battles or their mourning over the loss of the spouse.

The Developmental Stages of the Child

The impact of marital disruption on the child varies according to the child's developmental stage at the time of the dissolution (Derdeyn, 1976). *Very young children* of less than one year of age may encounter significant parental deprivation prior to the separation phase, as the parents are preoccupied significantly with their own conflicts, which leave little time and energy for the infant. Following the separation phase, the custodial parent may be depressed significantly, which will further deprive the infant of parental stimulation and affection. In severe cases the infant may be afflicted by "failure to thrive." The presence of older and more demanding siblings may result in further deprivation of the infant by the parent. Interference with adequate object relationship and the development of basic trust has been described in such young children at the time of marital disruption (Kelly and Wallerstein, 1976; Cline and Westman, 1971).

In the *toddler age* group, the major tasks in the achievement of separation-individuation and autonomy may be disturbed significantly. The departure of the noncustodial parent is a major factor, which is further complicated by the decrease in the availability of the custodial parent, who may have to obtain a new job, return to school or be depressed and emotionally unavailable to the child. The introduction of strange and new people to assist with care of the child can further complicate the situation. The stresses of this developmental phase, such as a confrontation over toilet training, negativism and autonomy between the toddler and the parent, can result in heightened conflict due to limited tolerance and understanding of the custodial parent.

The child in the *phallic-oedipal stage* may encounter significant difficulties in the resolution of the oedipal phase, especially if the departing parent is the same sex as the child. In the preseparation phase, the child's omnipotent and aggressive fantasies heighten his fears of harm to self or his parents. In the separation phase, the child may feel his fantasies have been actualized, resulting in excessive feelings of guilt.

Wallerstein and Kelly (1976) have described the reaction of *latency-age children* to marital disruption in two groups of younger latency-age children (seven to eight years of age) and older latency-age children (nine to ten years of age). The younger children were more vulnerable to the effects of parental divorce, and they experienced more difficulties in dealing with the trauma. The responses included sadness, grief, fear, feeling of deprivation, fantasies of reconciliation, feelings of guilt, feelings of loss for the departed parent, anger and anxiety in relation to the custodial parent. Older latency-age children were not as immobilized by the parental divorce. They attempted to master their feelings of anger, fear, phobia, loneliness and loyalty conflicts. Some exhibited somatic symptoms and showed a lowering in their performance in school.

Adolescents were severely affected by parental divorce (Sorosky, 1977). They experienced fear of abandonment, of rejection and of loss of love. Many showed fear and apprehension in regard to their own future marriages and exhibited difficulty in resolving their own sense of identity. There was a heightening of conflict over sexuality and aggression. The adolescents showed particular difficulties when the parents resumed dating and sexual activities following divorce.

The vulnerability of children to parental divorce has been described in detail by Wallerstein and Kelly (1973, 1976, 1977). They concluded that even after the brief interventions and one year following divorce, 44 percent of preschoolers, 26 percent of early latency and 24 percent of older latency-age children experienced some deterioration of behavior. This vulnerability was attributed to the developmental and cognitive immaturity of the child and the continued conflict between the parents. When one of the parents was suffering from mental illness, the impact of the divorce on the children was heightened significantly.

The Role of Parents and the Extended Family in Family Disruption

Longfellow (1979) has described many aspects of divorce that impact on the child. In addition to the age of the child, the presence of mental illness in one of the parents exposes the child to a double jeopardy in his development. Other factors, including disputed custody and visitation, the continuation of conflict between parents and incomplete emotional divorce, can prolong the crisis and distort the development of the child. For example, the anger toward the departed spouse can be generalized and extended to the children of the same sex as the spouse. In a family where men were feared and demeaned for generations, the departure of the husband resulted in intensification of such feelings, which were quickly extended to the two young boys in the family. The boys reacted to the perceived hostility by becoming withdrawn and exhibiting regressive behavior.

The relationship with families of origin can be a source of emotional, ego and social support or additional stress on the divorced parents. The extended-family members can be helpful if they recognize the pain of the divorced couple and attempt to be supportive without being infantilizing or encouraging of the regressive tendencies. However, the old conflicts within the extended-family group are revived frequently by the divorce of their children. At such times, the grandparents can become accusatory, feel guilt-ridden or be infantilizing. The mother of a divorced woman who was caught in an ungratifying marriage for many years continued to attack her daughter mercilessly as her own long-standing wishes to break up her own marriage were revived by the action of her daughter. Furthermore, having considered herself an unloving and inadequate mother for her daughter, she accused her daughter of being selfish, uncaring for her children and wishing to live like a "hippie" and a "whore."

The presence of one or more *siblings* can interfere with or facilitate the adjustment to the crisis of family disruption. The presence of older and demanding siblings may result in relative environmental deprivation for infants and very young children. On the other hand, older siblings can act as substitute parents and facilitate the postseparation adjustment of their younger siblings. A large sibship group can enhance the reality-testing for the children and reduce their feelings of guilt and responsibility for the parental breakup. Only children generally have a strong tendency to feel guilt-prone and may feel excessively responsible for the divorce of their parents, particularly if the marital disruption has occurred around the oedipal phase when the children have many related fantasies about their parents.

The future marriages of children of divorce have been described as problematic due to their lack of a firm family image, poor self-concept and disturbed gender identity. The children of divorce tend to have a higher incidence of divorce in their own marriages due to their own unsatisfactory earlier experiences. Even when their marriages are intact, their ability to satisfy themselves and their marital partner and to function as an adequate parent may be interfered with due to the deficiencies in their development and upbringing. However, it should be noted that some children of divorce form very stable marriages as a way of compensating for the painful experiences they were subjected to as children.

INTERVENTION

Intervention on behalf of young children at the time of marital dirsuption should take into account the immediate crisis situation, as well as the possible future difficulties in adjustment and development of the youngsters, and also the complexities of the divorce situation itself with its emotional, legal and economical components. In addition to the acute crisis situation, it should address the long-term deficiencies in divorcing families where the long-standing marital conflicts, mental illness in parents or other factors have significantly distorted the development of the child.

The reason for divorce should be openly and frankly discussed with the children. Gardner (1980) suggests that the children be told the real reasons for the divorce. Just telling the child that "we don't love each other anymore" is insufficient. The child should be told the real reasons, such as "Your father drinks too much" or "I have met someone else I care about more." But no matter what deficiencies are presented to the child, it is essential that the other parent's assets be acknowledged as well.

Although divorce is an upsetting time for everyone involved, it is equally disturbing, perhaps worse, for children to live in an embattled household. Divorce is actually beneficial for the children raised in very conflicted and unhappy families.

Recently, the principle of serving the "best interest of the child" has been emphasized significantly through the work of Goldstein, Freud and Solnit (1973). They have emphasized the need of children for a stable relationship to enhance their development and provide them with a sense of self and object constancy. They have defined the concept of the "psychological parent" as the one person, a biological parent or not, who is relating continuously to the child during his formative years. This concept is suggested as a guiding principle to the courts in custody cases and should override blood-kin considerations.

Expanding on the concepts of the "psychological birth of the infant," as described by Mahler and coworkers, and the "psychological parent," described by Goldstein et al., Sonne (1980) recommends the use of the concept of "psychological family" which endows the child with an internalized family image. All three concepts involve the creation in reality of "images and language which are shared by the child and his parental figures" as well as "abstraction and departure from a literal physical oneness of the child with a biological parent or parents and the departure from direct instinctual gratification between biological parent and child."

Sonne emphasizes the need of the child for two parents who are reasonably appreciative of each other, to provide him with the necessary "rooting" from which to construct his own family image. The concept of a psychological family should be enhanced for the child through education, therapy or extra-familial experiences and should be maintained in the cases of marital disruption. Sonne criticizes particularly courts, in custody and adoption decisions, that prefer a *celebate* or asexual parent to a sexually active parent, therefore interfering with the development of a heterosexual and psychological family model for the child. This may reinforce the transgenerational dyad at the expense of the formation of an adequate psychological family and an internalized family image.

Child-Custody Decisions

Changes in the parenting role and male and female life styles have increased the number of disputed custody cases significantly in the past few years. A comprehensive framework of custody criteria and changing developmental needs of the children is lacking, resulting in confusion among judicial, legal and mental-health professionals as to how to resolve the custody issue. Although the courts acknowledge that reliance on the concept of "parental fitness" in determining child custody is outmoded, they generally fail to evaluate fully parental functioning and the parental capacity for meeting the developmental needs of their children. In one study (McDermott et al., 1978), the court investigators were found to base their recommendations on only the most practical and reality-based criteria. In decreasing order of importance, the deciding criteria were caretaking arrangements and parental availability, parenting skills and commitment, child's wishes, child's adjustment, parents' interpersonal relationships and parents as functioning adults. The criteria of the parent as a functioning adult was a deciding factor in awarding custody in only 23 percent of cases, in comparison to caretaking arrangements, which was the determinant factor in custody in 88 percent of cases. McDermott et al. (1978) recommend the use of mental-health consultants and supplementation of the court investigation by some objective tests or procedure to focus on the emotional and psychological relationship between the parent and child. They have utilized an instrument—Parent-Child Interaction Test—to measure this relationship.

The concept of joint custody as tried first by John and Charlotte Sheedy in 1971 has gained significant support in recent years. Initially, this concept was attacked by the bar, judges and legal scholars as contrary to "the best interest" of the child, the guiding standard in custody decisions. The prevailing view was that a child of divorce needs the stability and security of one home and one custodial parent to make the major decisions in his life (Dullea, 1980). Solnit (1980) views it as important for the child to know that there is one adult who will continue to have the same amount of responsibility and authority for his daily care in one place once the divorce decision has been made. The child needs an anchor, and he considers joint custody as only two half anchors. He particularly views the shuttling between two homes as confusing for preschool-age children.

More recently, the advantages of joint custody have become the focus of parental and professional attention. It has the benefit of maintaining the child's relationship with both parents. The child will be able to receive support from both parents and go back and forth between them when his or her relationship with one parent becomes temporarily and highly conflicted. The maintenance of the relationship with both sets of grandparents, friends and relatives are another advantage of joint custody.

Joint custody is not forbidden in any state, and six states have passed specific legislation facilitating and favoring joint custody. However, it is not appropriate for all divorcing families. Joint custody works best when there is a civilized divorce between the marital partners. The bare minimum requirement for a successful joint custody is the ability on the part of the parents to separate and isolate their marital troubles from their parental roles. The parents should also share the basic belief in the competence of each other as a parent.

The increased risk of the children being used as a spy or weapon is an inherent danger in any joint custody. Gardner (1980) recommends against joint custody when parents appear hostile. He also recommends a trial period of joint custody for cooperative parents, to be reviewed after six months. Beyond that, he sees joint custody as the situation which approximates most closely the traditional home stiuation.

The usual arrangement in joint custody is for the child to have a room and a set of bare necessities in each parent's house. The joint-custodial parents generally reside in the same community, where the child can maintain the same school and friends. Less commonly, the children can remain in the house and the parents can move in and out of the house on a rotation basis to remain with the child. The amount of time spent with each parent can vary from a few days to a few months or even a year. For example, the child may spend a week or part of a week with each parent. Some parents prefer the child to spend six months or a year with them. Of course, the child would then maintain contact with the other parent. Once a child becomes older, he may assume a more decisive role in making the time arrangements according to his own wishes. There can be a variety of financial arrangements for sharing the expenses of the child in cases of joint custody.

Incomplete emotional divorce is common is disrupted families, particularly when the responsibility for joint children does not allow the parents to move away from each other and establish new lives. The lack of such resolutions or mourning for the departed spouse may result in the engagement of the children in the parental conflict, particularly if the parents are unable to separate their marital difficulties from the needs of their children. Resolution of conflicts and completion of mourning for the marriage and the departed spouse are essential in order to minimize the continued fights through the children.

Therapeutic and Preventive Considerations

Therapeutic efforts with families who have undergone recent marital disruption should address themselves to the crisis situation involving the children and the parents. They should attempt to reduce the confusion and tension for everyone involved, clarify the issues for the parents and the children, and delineate the needs of the children as well as find ways for their satisfaction. The social support system of the family should be optimally mobilized, and the tendency toward revival of the old conflicts within the nuclear or extended families should be countered. Using a family-based intervention model, the maintenance of a healthy self, clear gender identity and the family image in the children should be supported. Additional experiential encounters inside and outside the family may be necessary to maintain the child's family image.

Wallerstein and Kelly (1977) have delineated an intervention strategy consisting of six weekly sessions for divorcing families. They specifically recommend intervention to be timed at least one month, but not longer than six months, from the actual separation. Premature intervention captures the family in too much chaos, while intervention after six months may find symptomatic behaviors and parent-child alignments consolidated and strongly defended. They did not make a specific requirement for both parents to participate, but as the technical skills of the team increased, few fathers stayed away. The parents brought in "crowded agendas" in addition to negotiations about the children. Kelly and Wallerstein (1977) have considered their intervention too brief for families who had experienced other recent losses and for families with mentally ill parent members. All the families were adjudged normal at the time of intake. Treatment was considered a success when the parents were able to perceive their childrens' needs as separate from their own.

Sholevar and Sonne (1979) recommend a family-based intervention utilizing the contributions of family-systems theory and the psychoanalytic view of the child's development. Following the conceptual model of "psychological family" and "family image" (Sonne, 1980), they postulate that optimal mental health requires the development of an internalized "family image," and therapeutic intervention should aim at the construction of such an image. A child needs to grow up with a family image of two parents working cooperatively with each other and toward his development so that he may come to his own marriage with some concept of what is necessary for success. In addition, his parents—or heterosexual adults involved—need to have a positive feeling about marriage and family in general in order to transmit this to the child.

In order to establish a stable sense of self, a secure gender identity and an internalized family image in the children, Sholevar and Sonne (1979) recommend a family-based intervention by a heterosexual co-therapy team for divorcing families. This intervention is particularly important for preschool-age children and with families who have suffered previously from mental illness or losses. In addition to its immediate therapeutic effects, such an intervention may have preventive value in preempting future maladaptive behaviors in the children.

The incidence of parental mental illness has been described as higher in divorcing families. Morrison (1974), who studied mental illness related to the incidence of divorce per se, found that parental mental illness was twice as high in divorced parents of child psychiatric outpatients as in married parents. Children of divorce are also disproportionately represented in psychiatric clinics (Kalter, 1977). Briscoe and Smith (1974) have confirmed the increased incidence of mental illness in parents who divorce. As is clear from the above studies, the incidence of mental illness tends to be higher in divorcing families, and the children of divorce are at a higher risk for subsequent mental illness. Therefore, it is essential to recognize the importance of *preventive intervention* at the point of divorce as well as of treating the long-standing deficiencies in divorcing families. One should tailor a treatment program to address possible long-term deficiencies as well as the acute and immediate critical situation. This is particularly important if the custodial parent has the history of mental illness, is socially isolated, is cut off from or involved in a conflicted relationship with his or her family of origin. The absence or limited availability of the noncustodial parent will make such a child particularly at risk for mental illness.

As a preventive measure toward future emotional disorder, a variety of *educational approaches* are springing up throughout the country with the hope of preparing children for the possible divorce of their parents. The goal of such educational efforts is to minimize the shock, trauma and disorganizing effect of marital disruption on the children and to reduce the childrens' tendency to blame themselves for the breakup of their parent's marriage. Such educational efforts are being introduced in schools as well as in other social agencies. It is hoped that by these early educational approaches and sensitizing the health and educational professionals, the ill effects of marital disruption on children can be prevented or at least minimized.

Our current knowledge about the actual impact of family disruption on the developmental process of children, its short- and long-term influences on the children and on their future families, is extremely limited. We also lack knowledge as to the effectiveness of different educational, preventive or therapeutic interventions with children of divorce, particularly those children who are at a higher risk due to socio-economic factors, the presence of mental illness in the parents, only children, etc. Systematic and well-controlled studies for exploration of these issues are essential in providing the necessary insights for effective intervention with this major challenge.

CONCLUSION

The significant increase in family dissolution by divorce and separation and its impact on the development of children have posed a major challenge to the child mental-health profession and the legal system in the 1980s. The impact is particularly hard on children caught in disputed custody battles or reared in families with prior mental illness in the parents.

This chapter examines the impact of different phases of marital disruption on the developmental process of the children according to the child's developmental stage at the time of marital dissolution. It further examines the prevailing issues in child custody as well as the therapetuic and preventive interventions with divorcing families.

ACKNOWLEDGMENT

Collaborative efforts and contributions are acknowledged of John S. Sonne, M.D., Jacquelyn Zavodnick, M.D., Ruth Zager, M.D., Helene Dichter, MED, MFT, and David Brashear, M.D., to this chapter as part of

A Family-Based Intervention with Children of Marital Disruption, a research project of Jefferson Medical College, Thomas Jefferson University.

REFERENCES

Abarnal, A. Shared parenting after separation and divorce. *Am. J. Orthopsychiatr.*, 1979, *49*, 2.

Bernstein, N., and Robey, J.S. The deterioration and management of pediatric difficulties created by divorce. *Pediatr., 38.*

Briscoe, C.W., and Smith, J.B. Psychiatric illness—Marital units and divorce. *J. Ner. & Ment. Disord.*, 1974, *158*, 440–5.

Cline, D.W., and Westman, J.C. The impact of divorce on the family. Child Psychiatr. and Human Dev., 1971, *2*: 1, 78–83.

Cramer, B. Outstanding developmental progress. *Psychoanaly. Study Child*, 1975, *30*, 15–48.

Cytryn, L., and McKnew, D. Affective disorders. In Nopschitz (Ed.), *The basic handbook of child psychiatry*, Vol. II. New York: Basic Books, 1979, pp. 321–340.

Derdeyn, A.P. A consideration of legal issues in child custody contests. *Arch. Gen. Psych.*, 1976, *33*, 165–171.

Dullea, G. N.Y. *Times*, February 3, 1980.

Francke, L.D., Sherman, D., Simons, P.E., Abramson, P., Zabarsky, M., Huck, J., Whitman, L. *Newsweek*, February 11, 1980.

Gardner, R.A. *Psychotherapy with children of divorce.* New York: Jason Aronson, 1976.

Gardner, R.A. In G. Dullea, N.Y. *Times*, February 3, 1980.

Goldstein, J., Freud A., and Solnit, A.J. *Beyond the best interest of the child.* New York: Free Press, 1973.

Grief, J. Father, children and joint custody. *Am. J. Orthopsychiatr.*, 1979, *49.*

Kalter, N. Children of divorce in an outpatient psychiatric population. *Am. J. Orthopsychiatr.*, 1977, *47*: 1, 40–51.

Kelly, J.B., and Wallerstein, J.S. The effect of parental divorce: Experience of the child in early latency. *Am. J. Orthopsychiatr.*, 1976, *46*, 1, 20–32.

Kelly, J.B., and Wallerstein, J.S. Brief interventions with children in divorcing families. *Am. J. Orthopsychiatr.*, 1977, *47*, 23–39.

Longfellow, C. Divorce in context: Its impact on children. In G. Levinger and D.C. Moles (Eds), *Divorce and separation.* New York: Basic Books, 1979.

McDermott, J.F., Jr. Parental divorce in early childhood. *Am. J. Psychiatr.*, 1968, *124*: 10.

McDermott, J.F., Jr. Divorce and its psychiatric sequelae in children. *Arch. Gen. Psychiatr.*, 1970, *23*, 421–427.

McDermott, J.F., Jr., Tseng, W., Chair, W., Fukunaga, C. Child custody decision making; The search for improvement. *J. Am. Acad. Child Psych.*, 1978, *17.*

Morrison, J.R. Parental divorce as a factor in childhood psychiatric illness. *Compr. Psychiatr.*, 1974, *15*, 95–112.

Sholevar, G.P., and Sonne, J.C., in collaboration with Zavodnick, J.M., Dichter, H., Brashear, D., and Zager, R. A family-based intervention with children of marital disruption. Unpub. report, Jefferson Medical College, Thomas Jefferson University, 1979.

Solnit, A.J. In G. Dullea, N.Y. *Times*, February 3, 1980.

Sonne, J.C. On the question of compulsory marriage counseling as a part of divorce proceedings. *Fam. Coord.* 1974, *23*, 303–305.

Sonne, J.C. The psychological family and family image construction in unrooted children. *Fam. Ther.*, 1980, *7*: 3, 255–284.

Sonne, J.C. A family system perspective on custody and adoption. *Int. J. Fam. Ther.*, 1980, *2*: 3, 176–192.

Sonne, J.C., and Swirsky, D. Self-object considerations in marriage and marital therapy. In G.P. Sholevar (Ed.), *The textbook of marriage and marital therapy.* New York: Spectrum Publications, 1981.

Sorosky, A.D. The psychological effects of divorce on adolescents. *Adoles.*, 1977, *12*: 45, 123–136.

Tooley, K. Antisocial behavior and social alienation postdivorce: The man of the house and his mother. *Am. J. Orthopsychiatr.*, 1976, *46*, 33–41.

Wallerstein, J.S., and Kelly, J.B. The effect of parental divorce: The adolescent experience. In E.J. Anthony and Kupernik (Ed.), *The child and his family*, Vol. 3, New York: Wiley, 1973, pp. 479–505.

Wallerstein, J.S., and Kelly, J.B. The effect of parental divorce: Experience of the preschool child in chess of themes. *Annu. Prog. Child Psychiatr. & Child Dev.* 1976, 520–537.

Wallerstein, J.S., and Kelly, J.B. The effect of parental divorce: Experiences of the child in later latency. *Am. J. Orthopsychiatr.*, 1976, *46*; 2, 256–69.

Wallerstein J.S., and Kelly, J.B. Divorce counseling: A community service for families in the midst of divorce. *Am. J. Orthopsychiatr.*, 1977, *47*, 4–22.

Chapter 20

The Contextual Approach to Child-Custody Decisions*

Margaret Cotroneo
Barbara R. Krasner
Ivan Boszormenyi-Nagy

The contextual approach to child-custody decisions is based on an integrative comprehension of personal, familial, communal and clinical factors of interrelatedness. Context conveys the notion that each individual is born into a complex network of past and present relationships which shape the nature of future relationships. A relational network includes (1) the individual's legacy, (2) the resources and limitations endemic to relationships with members of family, peers, friends and the world at large and (3) a connective relationship to the next generation. The context thus includes both what is unique to the person and what (s)he actually and potentially shares in common with others. The contextual approach assumes that individual action or behavior can be most fully comprehended when placed within a person's relational context.

---

*Sections of this chapter have been presented by Margaret Cotroneo at the Yale Law School Child Custody Seminar, April 28, 1979, and published in *Connecticut Bar Journal*, 1979, *53*, 349–355.

The customary term "family system", whose partiality stands on the side of structure and pattern, ignores the dimension of rootedness and its resources. By acknowledging rootedness as the given ground from which all relationships proceed, the contextual approach identifies four dynamic dimensions of interhuman reality. Those dimensions include the concrete facts of existence, the competing needs of individuals, the realm of interpersonal transactions and interpersonal justice born of experienced trust. The contextual approach offers clear and rational guidelines and strategies for short-term and long-term actualization of child-custody decisions.

In child-custody cases, the effort of contextual therapy is to surface the non-negotiable nature of lifelong interlocking commitments between parent and child. Viewed from the perspective of lifelong interlocking commitments, even the non-parenting parent must be considered a potential resource. Beyond the short-term interest of physical and emotional comfort and stability lies the long-term interest of continuity of significant biological relationships. The opportunity to reclaim one's roots is a direct corollary to a person's capacity to view the world as potentially worthy of human trust. Irrevocably cut off from their roots, people often condemn and abandon their legacies, behavior that results in an ever-intensifying and expanding circle of mistrust. Without minimizing inherent limitations in relationships to which one is born, the permanent irretrievable loss of those relationships is potentially confusing, disorienting and undermining to future relationships.

Where do the contextual approach and the best interests of children intersect? In the first instance, in our view, *the best custodial parent is the parent who can most fully tolerate and cooperate in helping children maintain contact with all significant persons in their relational context.* Whenever possible, a custody agreement should provide children with a structure in which they can receive parenting from their biological parents, grandparents, aunts, uncles, other relatives and close friends of the family. Severance from significant relationships is a disorienting event in the life of any child and cannot be ignored. Legal intervention that supports such severance without considering future costs to a child's development and motivation inadvertently distorts the nature of the parent-child relationship in a variety of ways. Some of the distortions and imbalances born of rigid one-sided partiality in legal processes include (1) an unrealistic treatment of the non-custodial parent and siblings as if they were non-contributory or even nonexistent, (2) an assumption that the fit custodial parent is the sole source of family relatedness and the sole object of a child's concern, (3) participation in a process of moral and psychological condemnation of one parent by the other, in which the child becomes a helpless victim, (4) collusion in parental irresponsibility through diverting the issue from accountable parenting to one of faulty and incompetent parenting, (5) providing a structure in which custody of children becomes a battleground for unfinished business in the marriage, (6) implicitly encouraging spiteful, manipulative, blackmailing behavior on the part of children, who soon learn to take advantage of their parents' opposing positions.

In any event, exposure to the fact of divorce is an additional developmental demand for any child. Children who are caught in a web of split loyalties will tend to overinvest themselves in the facts and recriminations of divorce rather than learn to cope with its implications. And it is likely that they will grow up with a view of one or both parents as malevolent or shameful persons, a perspective that inevitably undermines a child's entitlement to self-worth and trustability. Conversely, attempts to bridge the gap caused by the opposing pull of two parents result in the increased capacity of children to invest in their own growth, development and success.

In a parallel vein, being severed from a parenting relationship to one's children also has implications for the lives of the adults. The non-custodial parent is not only stigmatized and demotivated in his or her will to parent by the lack of opportunity to be a contributing parent but is also cut off from a genuine linkage to the future through the companionship of their children.

In addressing the imbalances of a rigid one-sided partiality in legal processes, the contextual approach operates on the following premises:

1. Every child is entitled to be raised to maturity by his or her biological parents. That fundamental right has to be acknowledged regardless of the manifest quality of the parent–child relationship.

2. From the child's side, a bad or distorted relationship to parents is better than no relationship at all.

3. Children are deeply committed to preserving the continuity of their parents' relationship, both to each other and to themselves.

4. Children who are prematurely "used up" by being caught in exploitative aspects of parental behavior tend to replicate that unfinished family business in new relationships unless and until some serious effort is made to face and rework their relationship to their parents.

5. There is no replacement for the loss or deprivation of primary parenting figures. The loss or deprivation can be rebalanced by input from others—stepparents, for example—but the relationship to the primary parent cannot be broken.

6. Children caught in a web of split loyalties to their parents will tend to manifest a diminished capacity for full investment in relationships to colleagues, mates, friends and even their own children.

From our perspective, custody decisions in cases of separation or divorce call for flexibility and balance rather than for fixed or absolute principles. Balance and flexibility, however, are best implemented when the court assumes a strong mandate in protecting the child's access to both biological parents and to all other significant family members. Implicit in such a mandate is the court's continuing jurisdiction in matters which have to do with the long-term best interests of children. Of course courts are limited in the degree to which they can implement decisions regarding close human relationships. Nevertheless, the courts' insistence on balance and flexibility as a framework for shaping decisions can help to limit the "splitting" tendencies of custody determinations in divorce. Thus, it is the courts' guardianship of the continuity of significant relationships rather than its implicit power that becomes the criterion of balanced decisionmaking.

What recommendations are useful in implementing balanced decision-making in custody decisions?

Continuity of Relationship. The view that treats the non-custodial parent, siblings and other family members as peripheral to a child's well-being sets the stage for a myth. In fact, the law can aid or hinder the dynamics and living processes of human relationships. But the law can neither create nor terminate them.

Consequently, judicial decision making should aim at providing the child with an ongoing relationship to both biological parents and with as many members of the child's family of origin as possible. It follows, then, that the best custodial parent is the one who is most able to tolerate and collaborate in maintaining an ongoing relationship to all or as much of the child's family of origin as possible.

Multilateral Advocacy. Children pay a heavy cost for the moral and psychological condemnation of one or both of their parents in a loss of trust in authority that may well be played out against the world. Consequently, the judicial decision-making process should not confirm the moral and psychological condemnation of one parent by the other. Instead, as an adjunct to the adversary process, the court should insist on professional evaluation of the family by an expert experienced and trained as a multilateral advocate. A multilateral advocate is able to identify merit on behalf of all of the relating partners, parents as well as child, and can work toward a resolution which does not advocate for one family member at the cost of the relationship to other family members.

Team parenting. Whenever possible, judicial decision making should provide a framework within which both parents can work toward the goal of team parenting. Team parenting is a long-term process which acknowledges the fact of divorce but raises the possibility that if both parents have the resources to parent, each one should have the opportunity to do so consistently and reliably. Team parenting involves shared decision making as well as shared responsibility. Since it is a resource rather than a pathology-oriented notion, team parenting presumes that even parents who disagree over their adult relationship can learn to collaborate in the parenting of their children.

Pre-divorce family counseling. Early evaluation and intervention in marital breakdown in the form of pre-divorce family counseling can help to reinforce familial capacities to enable, foster and nurture the full expression of a child's potential growth, development and motivation. The trauma of visitation in the early phases of separation too frequently goes unattended as a result of parental confusion over alternatives. The multilateral professional can advocate for both parents as well as for the child and thereby free the child from a sacrificial concern for parental neediness. The problem of parentification, i.e., the inappropriate assignments of a parental role to a child, flows directly from the child's vested interest in keeping his parents together. The child's implicit concern for and attachment to his parents' well-being cannot be addressed effectively by legal attempts to sever the relationship to either parent. The child needs an opportunity to address that concern in an age-appropriate and protected way. From the parents' side, early intervention prevents the possibility that the parent who is rendered peripheral may deplete his emotional and physical resources and be forced to choose his own well-being over relationship to his/her child.

Post-divorce family counseling. Custody agreements can provide a structure within which parents can begin a process of team parenting, but they cannot guarantee that the process itself will take place. Therefore, a prior step to team-parenting agreements would be post-divorce family counseling that can help spouses sort out which conflicts belong to their marriage and which belong to the ongoing parenting of the child. Guiding a family toward post-divorce counseling places the court in a unique position which can guarantee continuous accessibility to both parents in a way which does not overburden the child. Here again, the courts' insistence on the help of a multilateral advocate is at the center of effective implementation of team-parenting agreements.

SUMMARY

More and more the court is being called upon to make decisions on behalf of families that families once made on their own behalf. Frequently, in its decision-making process in custody cases, the court is hampered by adversarial positions when they could be helped by multilateral input. Multilateral input more closely reflects the full reality of a child's relational network and family loyalties. The resultant judicial decisions often reflect a one-sided advocacy that converts children and parents into adversaries. Conversely, as an adjunct to the adversary process, the contextual approach to child-custody decisions offers the view that the needs and interests of children cannot be separated from a concern for their long-term relationship to both parents and to all significant members of their relationship system, however distorted the relationships.

REFERENCES

Boszormenyi-Nagy, I., and Krasner, B. A Contextual approach to psychotherapy: Premises and implications. In Gerald Berenson (Ed.), *Annual review of family therapy.* In press.

Boszormenyi-Nagy, I., and Krasner, B. Trust-based therapy: A contextual approach, *Am. J. Psychiatr.*, 1980, *137*, 767–775.

Boszormenyi-Nagy, I., and Spark, G., *Invisible loyalties: Reciprocity in intergenerational family therapy.* New York: Harper and Row, 1973.

Boszormenyi-Nagy, I., and Spark, G. Child custody litigation in divorce, *Group for the advancement of psychiatry report, committee on the family.* In press.

Colon, F. In search of one's past: An identity trip, *Fam. Proc.*, 1973, *12*, 429–438.

Colon, F. Family ties and child placement, *Fam. Proc.*, 1978, *17*, 289–312.

Cotroneo, M. At the intersection of family systems and legal systems: Child custody decisions in context. Paper, Child Custody Seminar, Yale Law School, New Haven, Conn. April 1979. (Pub. *Conn. Bar J.*, 1979, *53*, 349–355.)

Cotroneo, M., and Krasner, B. A family-based evaluation within the legal system. In *How to handle a child abuse case: A manual for attorneys representing children.* Support Center for Child Advocates and the Committee on Child Abuse, Young Lawyers Section, Philadelphia Bar Association, 1978. (Pub. *Familiendynamik*, Oktober 1979, 355–361.)

Foster, H. Review of *Beyond the best interests of the child, Bull. Am. Acad. Psychiatr. & Law*, 1974, *2*, 46–51.

Nelton, S. After divorce children still need parents, *Phila. Inq.*, July 11–16, 1976 (See Cotroneo, M., July 13, 1976, and Krasner, B., July 15, 1976).

Stierlin, H., *Separating parents and adolescents.* New York: Quadrangle, 1974.

Chapter 21

Neurotic Problems in Marriage

Abraham Freedman

This chapter will discuss the influence of neurotic character and symptoms on marriage. In some cases neurotic factors predominate in marital choice and in sustaining a marriage. At other times the neurotic components of marital choice can interfere with the outcome of a marriage, and the essentials of the choice might make the future marriage have an unhappy or nonviable outcome.

Every neurosis is an anachronism in which current human relationships are entrapped in an attempt to repeat or rework the relationships of the past. In a sense, this is true of all human relationships. We say it is neurotic when the past overwhelms the present or when the conflicts of the past, reenacted in the present, produce maladaptation and symptoms. The cultural form of mate selection is a variable which influences the degree to which neurotic selection can operate. In Western cultures, with the ideal of romantic love, marital choice is ostensibly on the basis of love. Since the feeling of love is itself a conglomerate of many complex factors which are derived from early experiences, marriages based upon love choice must bear within them the sequelae of early traumatic or neurotogenic relationships. However, even in those cultures which have arranged marriages, it is still possible to react to the mate in terms of old experiences, so that neurotic interaction can still be present. For example, witness the disturbed marriages which have occurred in an immigrant population where the marriages were arranged by the parents in the old country. Even in countries where arranged marriages are the norm, there are myths and stories about romantic love. One of the best known is the Chinese willow plate pattern, which shows an irate father pursuing his daughter and her lover across a garden bridge as she runs away from her intended husband.

Yet, there are marital problems in our culture that appear common in our eyes and strange to professionals who come from other lands. I recall a psychiatric case conference in which a severe marital conflict was being described. One of the psychiatric residents was a young Indian woman who still wore a sari in her daily work. She spoke up about the problem and said, "That would not happen in my country. Our families choose whom we marry, and we don't have that kind of trouble." At another conference, a black resident from Mali said about a dispute in a young couple, "In my village, the man and his wife would go to the man's father and tell him about the argument. He would listen and tell them what to do, and they would do it." It is probably true that the imposition of strong social expectations and their acceptance by individuals act to decrease the internal conflict as individuals carry out their social roles. This occurs by enhancement of group superego forces within the personality with concomitant easier suppression of drive forces. This is generally true of more authoritative societies, where there is apt to be more order at the cost of suppression of creativity and initiative. However, conflicts among intrapsychic forces are not erased but shift in their arena and have different expression than in freer societies. Free choice of mating is a part of democratic ideology, and the difficulties that ensue have to be accepted along with its benefits. Moreover, when one studies psychiatric illness transculturally, one finds similar frequencies of mental problems and evidence of neurotic problems affecting marriages. This chapter, which is based upon clinical experience, will deal with neurotic problems in marriage which occur in our society with its free choice of a spouse.

Marriage by choice is always more of an unconscious than a conscious choice. Early relationships to the parents and other important loved ones influence the selection of mates and the interaction with those mates in marriage. Indeed, it is an overpowering truth that the choice of a lifelong partner, one of the most important choices made in a lifetime, a choice that will greatly influence one's future happiness or unhappiness, is determined by forces that are largely outside of one's conscious recognition or control. In arranged marriages, although the choice is to some degree less determined by the participants than in romantic love, the behavior of the spouses with each other will still be determined by unconscious forces resulting from innate nature and past experiences in earlier life.

If one should ask a group of people the question Why do people get married? one would get a variety of reasons which represent realistic and conscious, as well as unconscious, factors. In this chapter we shall mention some of these reasons. We will review genetic and developmental factors which underlie the conscious reasons for getting married, describe the intrapsychic conflicts which result and discuss how these conflicts affect marriages for better or worse.

Falling in love is the most common reason for getting married. What is "falling in love"? It can be a wish to be with another person as often as possible, a wish to be admired, cared for, gratified and generally made to feel happy, as well as a wish to provide the same for the other person. These wishes may or may not be reciprocal. If they are one-sided, they could lead to a bilateral frustration of the demands. People get married for sexual gratification, although more and more in recent years this is available without marriage; but people still like to have the assurance of gratification with a permanent partner. As one man in his late thirties put it, "I could still go to singles bars and get all I wanted, but I was getting tired of the rat race." People get married because their families and society expect it. Despite recent experimentation with various life styles, for most people society is couple and family oriented. The presence of a mate gives a person an ally with whom to face a world that is not always friendly. Such a wish can be severely disappointed when the spouse turns out to be a critical person who seems to join in the barbs from without.

The need to have a permanent companion has evolved in the human species, and only few individuals do not share this wish. It is related to earliest development, when the mother-infant dyad formed the pattern of a close, intimate relationship. There is a developmental push during adolescence to separate from the family of origin. The separation leaves a void, which drives most individuals to seek close companionship with another person. The failure to form a relationship leaves the individual with a feeling of loneliness, which is a complex affect involving painful feelings of loss, a sense of personal imperfection and a constant yearning or seeking. Although marriage is not the only state which can satisfy the yearning and prevent loneliness, it is a cultural pattern which most people hope, consciously or unconsciously, will fulfill the wish for permanent intimacy with another.

People marry to have a family that would repeat the life pattern of their parents. They seek to become adults by having children as their parents had done. People marry for financial reasons, either to be wholly supported or to have a coworker. Two cannot live as cheaply as one, but two incomes can support two together better than two apart. Some unmarried people complain of no happiness in life because there is no goal or need to care for someone else and life seems aimless. Such people, often quite self-centered, might seek marriage later in life. Marriage might be the only way someone can think of to get away from an unhappy family situation. Most people in an uncomfortable situation do not recognize their part in creating it and hope that they would be happier if only the situation were different. The external situation is a conscious perception, but the inner conflicts related to it are unconscious. Of course, the inner conflicts are carried along when one goes to a new situation; and there is a tendency to repeat with others the relationships and sorrows of the past. This often occurs when individuals leave an unhappy home to escape through marriage and reenact with the spouse the old difficulties they had had with parents and siblings. Even if the home situation is indeed intolerable, entering into a marriage mainly for the purpose of escape preempts other factors of marital choice and may lead to an ill-considered marriage. In any case, the child of an unhappy home will have neurotic conflicts which will interfere with future healthy adaptation.

In most people, marriage is a confirmation of sexual identity. Society is apt to wonder about the sexuality of the older unmarried single, but within the individual mind the act of marriage fortifies one's sexual role for oneself and makes one feel more like everybody else of the same sex. The psychosexual identity is further strengthened by the roles of fatherhood or motherhood which usually occur in marriage.

A marriage can be deliberately sought for other goals without the intention of having a loving relationship. I recall an anatomy professor who liked to awaken the class with an epigram. He once said, "For the untalented there are still three routes to success which utilize the major bodily openings: per oram, per anum, and per vaginam. You can charm someone to care for you like a suckling babe, you can kiss the boss's ass or marry his daughter." In cultures where marriages are arranged, family alliances and power can be prime considerations; but even in our culture, a person can feign love in his quest for power. The wish to dominate or to be dominated can be a conscious factor in seeking a mate. A man might say that he is attracted to a girl who seems helpless and needs protection. A woman might say she is looking for a strong man when she really wants a tyrannical master. But here we are getting into the more unconscious factors in marriage, which we shall take up later with a few clinical anecdotes.

The primary focus of psychoanalytic understanding of human behavior is on intrapsychic activity. It is not to be assumed that societal conditions or relations with others are unimportant. The preceding few paragraphs discuss marriage from a sociological point of view; and it is apparent that psychoanalysts would have no argument with this approach, but their particular contribution would be the intrapsychic activity of the individuals concerned. It is possible to observe behavior by looking at the transactions within a family. It is also possible to observe (by the analytic method) the intrapsychic activity of a single person as he contributes to and receives the impact of the transactions. Each person in a marital transaction brings to it a personality which is at that moment the product of his genetic background, his drives, the vicissitudes of his drives and the resultant of his many experiences with his parents, siblings and others. The complex, diverse forces of the psychic apparatus are sometimes successful in achieving biological adaptation, satisfaction and happiness. At other times, the inner forces are intrinsically incompatible and conflictual, and behavior is marked by the symptoms arising from an attempt to compromise the conflicts and an unsuccessful trial at involving other people in the present to solve the conflicts and gain satisfaction. A psychoanalytic study of marriage problems would therefore focus on the vicissitudes of individual development and the manifestations of old patterns and problems as they affect the marriage. To do this completely would need more than one book, certainly not just one chapter. However, we shall proceed to review briefly psychosexual development as we elucidate how early stages of development affect the interaction of two people in a marriage.

If love is generally considered to be the most important factor in marriage, we had better understand the psychology of a state of love. Let us look at love, as we look at all things analytically, as a product of constitutional, developmental and experiential conditions. As we review the psychology of love, we shall try to observe its derivatives as they appear in marriage. The earliest "love" is that of mother and infant. The infant "loves" the mother out of a need for survival. It learns to experience her absence as a threat to survival and develops a dependency which has been termed "anaclitic" love. In a complicated interaction of instinctual behavior and repeated experience, a signal system is developed that enables the infant to communicate his needs to his mother and receive the gratifications that come with her response. One can find some married people who are disappointed when the spouse cannot understand them without the necessity of verbalization. They expect that their needs should be appreciated and promptly satisfied, and they feel hurt and angry when this does not happen. Nurturing behavior by one adult to another might assume a high level of importance, as in the case of a man dissatisfied with his marriage who complained repeatedly that his wife never gave him breakfast in the morning. There are some husbands who talk as if they would starve to death if they were left alone in the house. Not only nutriment but also closeness, skin contact, cuddling and physical availability are important to the infant. In some adult psychopathological states these needs are much more important than genital sexual needs. For example, if one listens to the complaints of a depressed middle-aged woman about her husband, one hears conflicting needs which make sense only if one hears them as the complaints of an infant about her mother. "He is away too much" (in the office earning money for her support and treatment), but "he doesn't buy me the things I want" (he doesn't *give* enough). She does not like to be home alone and cannot find interests for herself without him. She wants to be held and cuddled but resents having sexual intercourse. She has a feeling that he doesn't understand her, by which she means that he doesn't anticipate and satisfy her needs. She complains that he doesn't talk to her enough, but she gets upset if he talks about business, which is usually all that is on his mind when he comes home. She is asking for emotional and noncognitive communication, like the cooing of a mother to her baby. The reaction of the husband is dependent on many factors. In the normal course of development, even male children have some identification with their mothers, and adult males have varying capacities for mothering; but usually the husband does not understand what is happening and might feel angry at the demands put upon him, guilty about not fulfilling them or inadequate as a man. He would develop defensive attitudes and behavior, which cause further marital difficulty.

As the infant develops, he has both a need for closeness with his mother and a need for his own autonomy. Some adults who have not solved the conflicts of this stage carry them into a marriage. Desire for closeness and separateness might not be confluent in the two people of a couple at the same time, and one might have a sense of abandonment or, conversely, a sense of being smothered. An individual who has not solved the problem intrapsychically would not be able to communicate to the spouse what is wanted, because both opposites are needed at the same time.

All children pass through a stage of ambivalence, during which they have loving attitudes when their needs are satisfied and hateful, destructive wishes when they are not. Such a child sees his mother as two different people, according to his own internal state. Some adults retain this mode of relating to others and see the spouse sometimes as a devil and sometimes as an angel. If the spouse cannot adapt to the extreme shifts, he would feel confused and uncertain of being constantly loved. We speak of this phenomenon as "splitting," and it occurs in people who have had disturbed relationships in early childhood. Other forms of ambivalence do not involve splitting, but an individual might not be able to have pure love feelings for another without the admixture of negative feelings. The spouse of such a person would never have the gratification of feeling wholly loved. He might tend to react with complementary ambivalence or might have fantasies of a less ambivalent love from somebody else. (Please note the difficulty of the sexual pronoun and understand that "he" can usually be replaced by "she" in the discussion.)

Around age two, the infant has a developmental push to master his own body and his environment. All mothers are familiar with the battle of wills between herself and her two-year-old. The failure to resolve the conflicts of this stage can result in an endless struggle with the world and especially with the person to whom one is most closely related. The need for power and dominance can be at the base of marital problems when the partner is no more acquiescent than the mother was.

Throughout the preceding discussion, there is a personality characteristic which may be the thread which colors the whole cloth. I refer to a wide range of phenomena which are subsumed under the term "narcissism." Feelings of self-worth, self-satisfaction, self-esteem, and the confidence that one is respected by others are developed in early childhood experiences. One might emerge with a solid base of such feelings about the self, or with a constant need for reinforcement from others, or with a void which can never be filled. (The latter is the theme of Arthur Miller's play, *After the Fall.*) The person with unsatisfactory narcissistic development will be easily injured, and his spouse would always have to be alert to avoid the tender spots and to soothe the hurts. Of course, this capacity has considerable variation. Self-love is the earliest form of love. Love of others evolves from the need to preserve the self. Even the form of love which is valued highest and tends to be most enduring, "mother love," is love for the being which was once part of the self and is intensely narcissistic. In other forms of narcissistic love, one may value in the other what one wishes to be or what one has a fantasy he is. Failure of the spouse to provide narcissistic needs or to live up to a narcissistic overevaluation could be very disappointing.

With the onset of the phallic stage of development and the oedipal phase, narcissism has different content in the two sexes. In the male, narcissism becomes centered on phallic wishes and accomplishments, including power, activity, mastery and conformance to social expectations of masculinity. In the female, physical narcissism is related more to the whole body image and its enhancement by clothes and personal care, by being loved and eventually by motherhood and the narcissistic investment in children. Of course, there is an overlap of these extremes of narcissistic content in both sexes; but the satisfaction of the sex-linked forms of narcissism is sought in marriage, and its frustration by the spouse can cause marital difficulty. For example, a young wife was in a pique for a week because her husband had teasingly said, "You're cute but not as cute as you think you are." There was no sexual intercourse until he apologized. A young husband sought treatment in a state of anxiety because his wife had mentioned that the young man who was painting their house was a "pretty sexy guy." As the interview proceeded, the husband revealed his fear that the wife would find that the painter had a better, more satisfying penis than he had. A woman who tried to find satisfaction for her own need for power in her husband's business success became a carping wife when her husband had to give way constantly to his older brother and father in the family business, even though they lived very comfortably on his ample salary. (In thinking about the examples cited, the reader should remain aware that they are excerpted from clinical cases with complex factors and that a single issue used as an illustration does not imply that the entire problem was that simple.)

The oedipal period of development is reflected in all adult relationships, and unresolved problems from this period appear in the vicissitudes of marriage. The man who as a child had to repress sexual ideas about his mother might still be unable to accept sexuality in his wife if he unconsciously equates her with his mother. He has tried to solve his dilemma by thinking of women as either madonnas or prostitutes. He places his wife on a pedestal and is either totally or partially impotent with her. At best, he cannot express his full sensuality with her but must find another woman to satisfy what he feels are his baser feelings. If his early defense against sexual feelings for his mother was to argue with her to keep her distance, he might continue to do this with his wife; or he might compulsively find work to do which keeps him away from her as much as possible. He might regress to a pre-oedipal situation in his mind, so that he acts as if he were her little boy. Many husbands call their wife "mommy" or a similar name. The woman may or may not accept this role from her husband. The woman who grew up adoring her father might be very happy if she finds a husband sufficiently like him or she might have too much guilt over unconscious incestuous wishes to enjoy sexuality with a man. The woman who never resolved her conflict over attachment either to mother or to father might show this as an inability to relinquish her mother in favor of a close relationship with her husband.

In each sex, the outcome of the oedipal complex is an important factor in determining the gender identity and the relationship to those of the opposite sex. A man who has resolved his oedipal complex satisfactorily and who has identified with a good father image will see himself as a good husband and father. He will have sufficient identification with the mother in the process of relinquishing her as a sexual object so that he can be tender and affectionate rather than purely phallic and aggressive in his relationships with a wife. Neither will his castration complex interfere with his sexual function nor will it make him defensive about his masculinity. His self-assurance as a male will not be threatened by attacks, real or imagined, by his wife upon his masculinity. He will not have to constantly defend masculine prerogatives within the marital relationship.

A woman with a satisfactory outcome of her oedipal complex will be able to transfer to the husband the affection she had once felt toward her father. She will have identified with her mother and have a feeling of worthiness as a female. She will not be jealous of her husband's penis or the masculine position in society. She will also be sufficiently sure of her own worth as a person so that she will be able to pursue her own independent career without being forced to emulate men. She will not have to attack her husband's masculinity to alleviate the narcissistic hurt she suffered in her developmental penis-envy complex. She will be able to identify with her husband and take pleasure in his accomplishments and her own rather than being an envious rival.

When the outcomes of the oedipal complex have not been as satisfactory as described above, there would be a marriage in which the wife would be described as a castrating woman and the husband would constantly regress from his adult masculine role because of castration anxiety. A woman in her forties sought psychiatric treatment with symptoms of neurotic depression. She was feeling unloved by her husband (of the same age) because he was increasingly impotent. As the history was developed, she and her husband had met when they were both schoolteachers. After they married, she soon had children while her husband advanced in his profession and was now a school principal. In her childhood, she had felt deprived because her mother seemed to prefer her older brothers; but this attitude had been preceded by envy of the brothers' masculinity and disgust with her own female genital. She had been a model student, with the feeling that she could intellectually surpass her brothers and gain mental supremacy as a substitute for genital inferiority. Her role of motherhood had interferred with her ability to maintain scholastic and career equality with her husband, and she had never considered accomplishments of motherhood as valuable as other achievements. The husband had been attached to his mother, who with her own problems had tended to infantilize him and had prevented him from having a good relationship and identification with his father. In the marriage, he had suffered early from premature ejaculation. He tended to compensate for his sexual inadequacy by insisting on frequent intercourse. This gave his wife the opportunity to belittle his performance and reject him sexually on the grounds that there was nothing in it for her. Although he was successful professionally, in the home she repeated the family pattern of the dominant wife with the passive husband, which was reminiscent of his childhood situation. The cause of her depression was not really that she felt rejected and unloved by the sexually impotent husband but that she was becoming suspicious that her antagonism to him had injured his masculinity and had caused his impotence, and she was feeling guilty. In general, difficulties in the oedipal period with unsuccessful resolution of oedipal conflicts produce sexual problems in a marriage. Sexual frustration increases neurotic severity in the individual and has a deleterious effect on the whole marital relationship.

The phenomenon of transference is universal. Its restricted meaning in the psychoanalytic situation is the tendency to displace unconsciously upon the analyst wishes, expectations and feelings that were experienced with earlier important people in childhood. In the broader sense, transference is ubiquitous in human relationships. In marriage, there is always a tendency to displace onto the spouse the feelings, wishes, expectations and problems that had been experienced with parents and other important people in the past without being aware of it. The object of the transference is usually not aware of the origin of the behavior (if he is not an analyst) and will react to its current meaning; in other cases, the transference behavior of one person will stimulate the transference behavior of the object. Thus it is common to see marital conflict when each spouse is unknowingly acting as if the partner were someone else.

So far, we have described in general the principle that each phase of development can be reenacted inappropriately in married life and be a source of difficulty. It should not be assumed that there has to be difficulty whenever this occurs, because we sometimes see situations when there is a fitting together of anachronistic behavior in such a way that the needs of both parties are satisfied. It is not possible to make general predictions from a few known facts in the development of a marital pair. There are many variations in life experiences and an infinite number of possible combinations. In a game of chess, each of the pieces can be moved only in a limited way; but a knowledge of each mode of movement cannot be predictive of what will happen in the game before it starts. After the game has gone on for a while, one can observe the positions at any point, and with a knowledge of the style of play and aptitude of the players, one could venture a prediction about the outcome; but even then one could be wrong. Before proceeding to the next part of this chapter, I want to warn again about oversimplification and stress that examples will be given of a particular outcome from a particular set of circumstances in a marriage. This will not imply that people with somewhat similar circumstances should expect the same outcome. Each case used as an example of neurotic interaction in marriage has more variables than can be presented here.

It happens very often that intrapsychic factors which cannot be appreciated by outside observers are operating in a marriage. For example, there was a husband who was always complaining about the treatment he received from his wife. She disrespected him, insulted him in front of company, never gave him credit for his accomplishments, criticized him whenever possible, dominated him to the point that all decisions that affected him were made by her. He complained continually until friends and relatives wondered why he did not separate from her. What they did not know was that this man was very attached to his mother and as a child had always been made to feel guilty when he tried to separate from her. His conscience could not allow him to be happy without his mother, and the message in his marital complaints was directed to his mother. "Look how I suffer! Do not think that I am happy without you!" By suffering in his marriage, he was able to retain his mother's love. In addition, he was repeating with his wife his childhood experiences with his mother; so in a sense, he was not really separated from his mother. His wife had her own reasons for treating her husband this way in their marriage. She had been raised in a family where her brothers were more highly valued than she, and her developmental dissatisfaction with her feminine gender was intensified by the apparent privileges afforded her male siblings. Whether or not the parents actually valued her brothers more than her is not as important as the fact that she felt that they did. Secretly she believed that if she had been a boy she would have surpassed her brothers and would have won her parents' affection. Her unconscious selection for a husband was a man she could dominate and feel superior to. He received the brunt of her secret hostility toward her brothers. As her attacks cut down his masculinity, he became less and less of a satisfactory sexual partner; and many of her criticisms of his incompetence were really complaints about his impotence. This behavior further reduced his sense of adequate masculinity, but he accepted the situation because it fitted his need to demonstrate his unhappiness to his mother; it also fitted his neurotic conflict centered around his oedipal period, which made adult male sexuality a source of anxiety. The highlight of his week was every Sunday morning, when he visited his mother alone for an hour or two and let her know how his wife was abusing him.

Sometimes one sees a marriage which occurred because a set of circumstances fit the actual needs, both in reality and psychologically, of both partners, and the marriage became disharmonious due to a disruption of the original conditions. There was a woman who had had rheumatic heart disease as a child. In addition, there were circumstances in her home which had interfered with the development of herself as a woman. Despite her illness, she was able to finish high school, attend a business college and obtain a fairly responsible position. In her early twenties she had begun to suffer attacks of pulmonary congestion whenever she had a respiratory infection, and she was often sick for days at a time. She had sought consolation for her physically impaired existence by becoming religious. The young peoples' group at the church was headed by the young assistant pastor. He showed much compassion for the sickly young lady. He visited her in her apartment when she was ill, did her shopping, cooked meals for her, cleaned the apartment and nursed her. When she was well, he would telephone every evening after she had returned from work to see if she was all right. She appreciated his care and became fond of him. She was one of a large family, and her mother had never had much time for her except when she was sick. She had felt most loved as a child when she had the initial rheumatic heart disease and during the several relapses.

They married, and her husband went into the field of religious education with a plan to return to school, get a doctorate and have an academic career. She had a strong desire to have a child, and this was accomplished despite the life-threatening risks for her. She was very ill with congestive heart failure after the delivery, and when she and the baby came home, her husband took over the care of the house and the infant. He did everything but nurse the infant, and he would have done that if it were humanly possible. He coddled his wife, allowed her sufficient rest while he cleaned the house, prepared the meals and made the baby's formula and fed him. Her recovery was slow. When the baby was about one year old, open heart surgery was being pioneered in the city where she lived. She underwent an operation for the repair of her damaged heart valves and had a magnificent result after an extremely difficult convalescence. She returned home ready to take her place as the woman of the house. At that point, she told me later, her husband refused to come out of the kitchen. He wanted to continue cooking, cleaning and caring for the baby. With her improved physical strength, her sexual desires increased; and she learned that her husband's interest in her as an adult, healthy woman was not very intense. She became an embittered and carping wife. She found that although he could clean the kitchen, he could not wire a lamp, paint the outside of the house or put up a set of shelves. He resisted all her attempts to take charge of the house and her child, and the son became the center of their struggle for control. She worried that her husband was not a good masculine ideal for the boy. At the same time, she remembered his compassion and tenderness when she had been an invalid and was very guilty over her anger toward her husband.

They tried marital counseling, which degenerated into a parody character-ized by the same bickering and fighting for control that went on every day at home. Each of them was then treated in analytic psychotherapy because it was essential that there be some character change to enable them to adjust to a new set of circumstances. The husband's failure to respond to his wife as a man to a woman had deeply injured her feelings of self-worth. When they were married, he had acted the part of a loving mother with a sickly child. He had deep-seated needs to be motherly, which enabled the relationship to start on that basis, and at that time they were a compatible couple because her physical needs required his motherliness. The life-saving surgery re-moved her physical dependence on him, but of course it did nothing to change his character and the tremendous gratification he received from her appreciation of his caring for her. The restoration of her physical health helped to change her from a child to a woman, and she then needed a man who was not to be found in her husband's character structure.

The case described above is unusual and was selected because the facts and inferences are readily apparent. There are many other marriages in which there are more subtle changes over the years in the needs of one or both spouses and they cannot adapt to a new state of circumstances or changes in the mate. A young man who is unsure of his masculinity might choose a girl who is immature and unthreatening. As he continues to develop, he might resent her childishness and ceaseless dependency. A woman had a sexual conflict that produced a neurosis and a need for treatment. In the course of treatment she resolved her conflicts, came to terms with her sexuality and recognized that her disabling symptoms had been a compromise of her repressed sexual drives and her defenses against them. At this point in her life, she was ready to respond sexually to a man for the first time. She then discovered that the sexual frequency (or shall we say infrequency) of her husband's needs of once or twice a month were formerly satisfactory to her only because her sexual conflicts were thereby not stirred up very often. Now his lack of sexual interest made her feel unwanted, not lovable or lovely. In every other way her husband had been considerate and affectionate. As her history was developed in the psychoanalysis, it was learned that as a teenager and college girl she avoided boys who were "too fast" and was comfortable only with the shy boys or very gentlemanly ones. Unconsciously she had selected a husband who had his own sexual conflicts and who would not make many sexual advances to her. After marriage, she found that her husband suffered from premature ejaculation; so that even if she were aroused, there could be no sexual satisfaction for her. Sometimes the intervals between intercourse were extended into months, and she suspected that her husband was secretly masturbating instead of approaching her sexually. She worried about her attractiveness, had sexual fantasies (unconscious at first, but they emerged in the analysis), anxiety attacks, phobic and depressive symptoms. In the course of treatment, her fantasies became conscious; there were thoughts of marital separation. On the other hand, she liked her husband as a person, he was considerate and was a good provider. She had a strong conscience and sense of justice that would not let her deceive him by having an affair. The husband who was very suitable when she was neurotic became an inadequate male as her neurosis was resolved. She finally threatened to leave if he did not seek treatment for his own sexual conflicts, which were now incompatible with a continued marriage. In this case a marriage was made possible because there were mutual interlocking sexual conflicts. The husband's neurosis had become a character formation (passivity and charm) which caused him no suffering. The wife's neurosis developed severe symptoms. As her neurosis was treated, the original conditions in the marriage no longer existed; and compatibility could be restored only by a resolution of individual sexual conflicts in individual analyses.

Even if sexual conflicts are severe in both parties, a marriage can remain visible if both parties adjust to them and the original situation is not changed. A man in his late fifties was having a routine medical checkup by his physician, and a mild diabetes was discovered. The physician inquired about possible sequelae of diabetes, such as circulatory changes, eyesight difficulties, weight changes and sexual impotence. The patient responded to the question about change in sexual needs and performance by stating that there had been none. The doctor then asked about the frequency of intercourse, and the patient did not understand the question. When the doctor explained further, the patient said, "Oh, that!" He went on to say that when he and his wife were first married they had heard something about that sort of thing. They tried it, and it didn't work. Besides, it was a dirty thing to do; they soon stopped trying it. As far as the physician could ascertain, the couple had been married for over thirty years, lived a quiet, inactive life, were superficially friendly with their neighbors and got along together as any good brother and sister would. They both had either very low sexual drives or severe inhibitions; neither developed a neurosis and they had a lasting, compatible marriage.

In some cases, an obvious neurotic disturbance in both parties can fit compatibly into a marriage. A few years ago there was a popular film, *The Odd Couple*, which portrayed the attempt by two men with differing habits to live together. One was a slob and the other was an immaculate perfectionist. In one, the neurosis took the form of tics, impolite belching and croaking sounds, indecision and ambivalence toward his wife. The other had none of these symptoms, but he was very neat, fussy, fastidious and perfectionistic. In real life I have seen such a heterosexual couple make a satisfactory marriage. The perfectionistic variety of the compulsive character gets a high degree of narcissistic pleasure and self-satisfaction from the very character traits that make her seem prissy to others. This satisfaction is even greater if she lives with a slob, whose vices can constantly be compared with her virtues. (This combination can work in reverse; it is just clumsy to have to say "he or she.") On the other hand, the living situation of the slob is enhanced if he always has a crazy-clean wife to straighten things out for him. The marriage which would seem impossible because of the contrasting habits of the partners actually thrives on her enhanced self-esteem and the fact that his physical needs are better served than if he were doing things for himself. In addition, a truly compulsive person is happiest when there is work and responsibility to relieve a latent sense of guilt. This combination does not always work out. If the slob is too sloppy, the compulsive mate will be unhappy in a situation where no amount of work can keep the place in order. The slob might find that the constant nagging to clean up or to think of not making a mess above all other considerations is too much of an interference with other needs. But ordinarily, when such a marriage occurs and nothing happens to change the original premises, it is likely to endure.

In other cases, there are husbands who demand a perfectionism in housekeeping, which the wife cannot provide. In one case the husband had a perfectionistic mother. He could not stand her strictness when he was a boy, but he had unconsciously identified with her attitudes. Consciously he had chosen a wife who he thought would not nag him like his mother had done, and he selected a woman who would never be able to run a house efficiently. But then his unconscious identification with his mother's attitudes came into play; and although he did not wish to be nagged, he could not stand his wife because she did not have the house cleaned and dinner ready when he came home from work. Sometimes such a marriage is not in trouble until after a baby is born. Every new mother has little time to devote to household tasks other than the care of the new baby, but when she has a compulsive, demanding husband, much unhappiness can result. To this situation is often added the jealousy of the husband over the attention to the baby, which stems from his own infantile problems. Each of such partners will need a thorough understanding of the self and the interaction among his or her own original personality, that of the spouse and the marital situation.

Some of the most tight-fitting marriages occur when both of the partners have similar compulsive characters. There was an older couple who had a seashore home. Their neighbors admired the trim house, the manicured grounds, and the boat with the shiny brass at the dock. The husband spent all his vacation time painting the house, doing minor repairs and polishing the brass on the boat at the dock (it rarely left the dock) when other people were enjoying the beach, boating, fishing and so forth. While he was doing his tasks, his wife would be busy inside vacuuming the carpets (it was the only house in the area with wall-to-wall broadloom), scrubbing the walls and waxing the kitchen floor. They were both always busy working, never idle, never playing, and they had already celebrated their fortieth wedding anniversary. The man was pleased when a neighbor had a little job that he could help fix, and his wife was always ready to help with community-organization cooking. They were a pair of well-adapted compulsive characters, both intra-psychically and to each other.

The related phenomena of sadism and masochism play a part in many human relationships but especially in marriage. Each of these factors has sexual and nonsexual forms. Sadism in the sexual sense is the gain of sexual pleasure or satisfaction by inflicting pain upon the partner. Masochism is a gain of sexual pleasure or satisfaction through suffering. In the nonsexual forms, sadism is the narcissistic pleasure of power and control derived from the ability to make others suffer and comply with demands, and masochism is the necessity to suffer and obey as a condition of life. A sadist has been defined as a person who is kind to a masochist. Sadism and masochism develop from drive sources and early experiences. The retention of these needs in the adult personality is important in understanding neurotic interactions in marriage. Sadism and masochism usually appear together in the same individual, although one may be predominant. In marriages that have a sadomasochistic bind, the partners may alternate in being the persecutor and the victim. In general, sadism is a male sex-linked characteristic, whereas masochism is more likely to be a feminine component; but there is much overlap and either quality can predominate in either sex. However, it is probably true that biologically sadism tends to be a normal or innate component of male sexuality, whereas masochism is a normal female component. A certain quantity of dominance or aggression is physically required to complete the male action in sexual intercourse, whereas the capacity to submit even in the presence of pain would be required for at least the initiation of successful female sexuality and its culmination in childbirth.

A newly married husband came to be treated for sexual impotence. He could be aroused and have an erection until the moment of penetration, but would lose it at the first sign of pain from his virginal wife. Analysis disclosed an unresolved problem with his father with fantasies of murder during his adolescent masturbation. He also had sexually sadistic masturbation fantasies which were conflictual. In the wife, attempt at vaginal penetration stirred up violent masochistic fantasies which were unacceptable and exaggerated her perception of the pain. Only after the analysis of the husband's conflicts over aggression was he able to use enough physical force to have intercourse with his wife. She had also required treatment.

A certain amount of sadomasochistic play is often found in normal sexual relations, such as in teasing and playful biting, slapping, etc. In some marriages when the tendencies to sadism and masochism are stronger, the marriage might be marked by physical fights followed by love-making. Some couples report that the best sexual experiences always follow a severe argument.

Another form of masochism, "moral masochism," exists when there is a need for punishment arising out of guilt (often unconscious), so that pleasure is not allowed to be experienced except in relation to expiatory punishment. Actually, the punishment is often isolated in time from the pleasure, so that the individual remains unaware of the connection. Suffering can also be experienced as a narcissistic satisfaction, making the person feel ennobled; and it might have a cultural value, as in one who "nobly bears his cross."

Sadism and masochism are usually found in combination under most circumstances because one cannot exist without the other. It is possible that a sadist can victimize an object without the other person wishing it, but such a relationship would eventually end by either the death or the escape of the victim. One can really observe this interaction in a marriage that exists for a long time. For example, a couple sought marital counseling after nearly twenty years of marriage. The wife complained that the husband was needlessly cruel, and she was particularly disturbed by the inconstancy of his behavior. Sometimes he would be very tender and sweet to her, and she would expect that they could be happy together. At other times he would degrade her with insults. He would tell her she was stupid, incompetent, unloving; at other times he would berate her for being a sexual animal because she wanted to have intercourse with him. Such tirades would go on for days at a time until she began to believe him and felt horrible about herself. She would become depressed and cry unceasingly. Then her husband would become tender and beg for her forgiveness. On a few occasions she became infuriated and screamed at him, calling him names and expressing wishes that he would go away or die. At such times he became abject and humble. She had the feeling later that he had been trying to produce her angry response and his humiliation. The husband began to drink in the later years of the marriage, would physically abuse her when he was drunk and claim no memory of it when he was sober. He sometimes became sullen and withdrawn, slept in another bedroom and forbade his wife to enter it. She would go into it anyway and tearfully plead with him to tell her what she had done to offend him, but he would threaten to hurt her if she did not leave the room and would sometimes threaten to murder her.

When this couple had seen a marriage counselor, the husband sabotaged the treatment by telling the counselor that nothing was wrong with their marriage, but he was accompanying his wife at her request because she was a hysterical woman who tended to exaggerate their difficulties. After leaving the counselor's office, he bragged to his wife about how clever he was, how he had fooled the counselor and that he could fool anyone she complained to because he was so clever and she was so stupid. He said that he could do anything to her because she was so stupid that nobody would believe her. After failure of marital therapy, the wife threatened to leave him but agreed to wait until he had seen a psychiatrist. In order to hold onto her, he went to a psychiatrist but maintained the same bland, innocent attitude. When the psychiatrist was able to note some discrepancies in his stories, he finally admitted to the truth of his wife's complaints while pleading that he never knew what came over him when he had acted as she described. He admitted to feeling satisfied when he was able to make her cry but said that she should try to understand him and ignore his ugly moods and wait until he felt better.

This man had had a mother who was probably psychotic, and he had identified with her. He had been abused by his mother when he was a child, hated her, and the hate spread to all women. He functioned at a high level in business, but his relationships with men were hampered by a suspiciousness that bordered on paranoia. During the periods when he was not sexually relating to his wife, he masturbated with sadistic fantasies. He broke off treatment when he felt threatened by the emergence of homosexual feelings for the therapist. In the meantime, his wife felt physically threatened, feared for her life and finally separated from him. Her separation was also a factor in his leaving treatment, because he had originally agreed to seek treatment in an attempt to hold her. The wife was seen by another therapist after the separation.

This case raises at least two obvious questions: If he hated women so much, why was he willing to see a psychiatrist in order to get his wife to stay with him? On her part, if she was aware of her suffering from his cruelty and repeatedly experienced frustration of her hopes for a happy marriage, why did she not leave him earlier and why did she not seek treatment for herself before the separation? When she first sought treatment, she said that she was depressed because she felt like a fool for putting up with her husband for twenty years. Even after separation, in the legal hassles that followed, he continued to arouse her hopes and then disappointed her, during which she was willingly victimized and became unhappy. She claimed that she thought she could have a happy marriage because she had a happy childhood in a loving home and could not believe that anyone would want to hurt her. However, as her history developed in the treatment, it was revealed that she had a financially successful father, like her husband, and her father dominated her mother. She was a pretty little girl who would be teased by her father, grandfather, uncles and older brother. She loved their teasing and would always be hugged after she began to cry. Her sexual fantasies were masochistic. In one fantasy, she was a concentration camp inmate who seduced the cruel Nazis to torture her and to have sex with her in order to save her family. Her masochistic fantasies were gratified early in the marriage. It was only when her husband's sadism became a threat to her whole being that the game became too dangerous, and she had to quit to save herself. A sadistically perverted love was the only kind of relationship her husband was capable of, so naturally he tried to keep his cooperative partner. It is also interesting to note that although she was a bright, attractive, charming woman, she had never been interested in a man who was tender and loving without being cruel. In childhood she had enjoyed being hurt by males who loved her, and it took a long time for her to see the differences between their behavior and that of her husband's. She had always unconsciously believed that his cruelty was a sign of love.

In other cases of masochistic wives, the woman is attempting to atone for her past fantasies or actual sexual guilt. A woman who had disgraced her respectable small-town family by a series of sexual escapades during late adolescence married a very religious, paranoid husband who knew all about her but was willing to offer her the Lord's forgiveness. During their marriage, he repeatedly reminded her of her past sins, treated her with cruel disdain and humiliated her in public and in the presence of their children. She suffered nobly and felt she deserved what she got. Unconsciously she was trying to win the pity of her family and thereby regain their love, while she was also trying to come to terms with her own conscience. The husband used cruelty to her as a projection of the punishment he would otherwise have inflicted upon himself for his misanthropy and sexual wishes.

In some marriages one sees different kinds of neuroses which are complementary. One such combination is the compulsive-obsessive husband with the hysterically neurotic wife. The affective isolation of one protects him from the excessive emotional demands of the other. The obsessional neurosis is a method of handling hostility and has an underlying sadistic quality which fits the masochistic orientation of the hysterical woman. There is also a fit of the sexual conflicts and their neurotic outcomes. The obsessional neurotic has a regression from adult genitality and thereby has become less threatening to the hysterical neurotic, whose anxiety is increased by sexual stimulation. The fear of helplessness of the hysterical phobic is calmed by the orderliness and outward control exerted by the obsessional. At the same time, the mutual sexual frustrations imposed by each of the pair upon the other makes it more difficult to solve sexual conflicts if one of them is in analytic treatment. It is therefore frequently necessary that both neuroses receive individual treatment, but one cannot predict whether the marital situation will be enhanced or dissolved during the process. At least it would become clarified.

In summary, neurotic interactions might make a marriage possible and may maintain it. They might cause difficulties which seem impossible on superficial observation but which on a deeper level are seen to be a necessary component of the marriage. An outsider cannot judge the happiness or sorrow of a marriage by his own needs and values. Only deeper understanding of the issues can explain the paradoxes. Changes in a marital situation or in one of the partners can cause serious disharmony when neurosis has been the binder. In this chapter we have reviewed the developmental processes that are active in love and marriage. There are forces related to individual development that determine character formation and the forms of relatedness to other people. We have illustrated some of the possible combinations of neurotic interactions in marriage with a few brief clinical abstracts; but in the cases described there are many other factors which were not pertinent to the purpose of this chapter and which were intentionally omitted.

REFERENCES

Fenichel, O. *The psychoanalytic theory of neurosis.* New York: W. W. Norton, 1945, chaps. I, VIII, IX, X, XX.

Freud, S. *Stand. Ed.* London: Hogarth Press, 1960.
    1910, Vol. 11, *Contributions to the psychology of love,* p. 163.
    1914, Vol. 14, Sec. 2, *On narcissism,* pp. 84–91.
    1916, Vol. 16, *Introductory lectures: Libido theory and narcissism,* p. 412.
    1921, Vol. 18, *Group psychology and the psychology of the ego: Being in love and hypnosis,* p. 111.
    1922, Vol. 18, *Some neurotic mechanisms in jealousy, paranoia, and homosexuality,* p. 221.

Kernberg, O. *Object relations theory and clinical psychoanalysis.* New York: Jason Aronson, 1976, chaps. 2, 3, 7, 8.

Lidz, T. *The person.* New York: Basic Books, 1968, chaps. 13, 14.

Waelder, R. *Psychoanalysis: Observations, theory, applications.* New York: International Universities Press, 1976, Papers 5, 13, 17, 26.

Chapter 22

Spouse Abuse

Susan V. McLeer

INTRODUCTION

Spouse abuse is an emotionally charged issue. Attempts at defining the nature of the problem are immersed in political rhetoric; efforts directed toward achieving clinical objectivity are obscured by the territorial trappings of one's academic or clinical discipline, be it of sociology or psychology, social work or psychiatry. Points of intervention, the definition of the "unit" designated as "the patient," include the individual, the family or society at large. The very structure of society and its institutions, the mode of transmission of societal values and attitudes, is oftentimes designated as the most crucial point for intervention or effecting lasting change.

Spouse abuse in this chapter will refer to the hostile, aggressive interaction between two individuals, usually of the opposite sex, who are intimately involved with each other. This includes the dyad of husband and wife irrespective of whether they are physically living together or not. This includes unmarried lovers. The dyad is usually heterosexual, but abusive relationships are found in homosexual relationships also and must not be overlooked. It is recognized that abuse between intimates falls not only along the quantitative spectrum of mild to severe but also along a qualitative spectrum of emotional to physical abuse. This chapter will focus primarily on the identification and management of physical abuse. While emotional abuse can be severe and result in lasting psychological damage, physical abuse is life-threatening.

THE EXTENT OF THE PROBLEM

Battered Women

It is difficult to determine with accuracy the number of relationships in the United States that involve serious physical abuse. The definition of what constitutes physical abuse is elusive. The occurrence of abuse is underreported, because of shame, guilt and fear. The book *Scream Quietly, the Neighbors Will Hear* (Pizzey, 1974) reflects the pattern of maintaining battering as a family secret. According to FBI statistics, the number of wife beatings reported in the United States is three times that of reported rapes (there is a rape reported every three minutes). Additionally, the FBI estimates that less than 10 percent of the total number of rapes are actually reported (Uniform Crime Reports, 1973). Leghorn has, on the basis of FBI statistics, made a conservative estimate of the frequency of wife beating in this country. At least one woman is beaten by her husband every eighteen seconds. This does not include all the women beaten by lovers, boyfriends and strangers in the street (Leghorn, 1976).

Murray A. Straus has recently completed a large study of the extent of spouse abuse in the United States. A study was made of a nationally representative sample of American families (Straus, 1978), in which 2,143 families were interviewed. In approximately half the cases, the person providing information about the family was a woman, and in half it was a man. Male-female couples ages eighteen to seventy were included. The couples did not have to have children, nor did they have to be legally married. The sample included couples, married and unmarried, with and without children in the same proportion as are found in the United States population. Of the respondents, 3.8 percent reported one or more physical attacks. "Physical attacks" were defined according to a physical-violence index, which was obtained by utilizing the Conflict Tactic Scale (CTS), developed by Straus. These scales provide an indication as to how family members deal with conflict. The physical-violence index of the CTS contains the following eight items (Straus, 1979):

K.   Throwing things at the spouse
L.   Pushing, shoving or grabbing
M.   Slapping
N.   Kicking, biting or hitting with the fist

O.   Hitting or trying to hit with something
P.   Beating up
Q.   Threatening with a knife or gun
R.   Using a knife or gun

Applying an incidence rate of 3.8 percent to the 47 million couples in the United States means that in any one year, approximately 1.78 million wives are beaten by their husbands. If one assumes (which one cannot do) that there is one beating incident per wife, from Dr. Straus' data alone it can be calculated that every 17.6 seconds a woman is beaten by her partner in the United States. The data, however, indicates that among couples in which beatings occur, the beating is not an isolated incident. Dr. Straus' data is outlined in Table I. The distribution curve for this data is clearly skewed,

Table I
Violence Rates per Hundred Marriages, 1975

CTS Violence Item	Incidence Rate for Violence By		Frequency*			
			Mean		Median	
	H	W	H	W	H	W
Wife Beating and Husband Beating (N to R)	3.8	4.6	8.0	8.9	2.4	3.0
Overall Violence Index (K to R)	12.1	11.6	8.8	10.1	2.5	3.0
K. Threw something at spouse	2.8	5.2	5.5	4.5	2.2	2.0
L. Pushed, grabbed, shoved spouse	10.7	8.3	4.2	4.6	2.0	2.1
M. Slapped spouse	5.1	4.6	4.2	3.5	1.6	1.9
N. Kicked, bit or hit with fist	2.4	3.1	4.8	4.6	1.9	2.3
O. Hit or tried to hit with something	2.2	3.0	4.5	7.4	2.0	2.8
P. Beat up spouse	1.1	0.6	5.5	3.9	1.7	1.4
Q. Threatened with a knife or gun	0.4	0.6	4.6	3.1	1.8	2.0
R. Used a knife or gun	0.3	0.2	5.3	1.8	1.5	1.5

*For those who engaged in each act, i.e., omitting those with scores of zero.

SOURCE: Straus, Murray A. Wife beating: Causes, treatment and research needs. In *Battered women: Issues of public policy*. U.S. Commission on Civil Rights, Washington, D.C., January 30–31, 1978.

since in some relationships beatings occurred daily or weekly; hence the median gives a more accurate reflection of statistically normative behavior than the mean. The median frequency per year is 2.4. Using this figure, one can calculate that a wife is beaten every 7.4 seconds in the United States.

Dr. Straus himself regards his data as being a drastic underestimate of the actual incidence of family violence. Several reasons for this were cited:

1. Some individuals may have found domestic violence so much a normal part of family life that it simply was not noteworthy.

2. Other individuals may have been reluctant to admit to violent episodes because of shame, guilt or fear.

3. The nature of the sample was such that only couples living together were investigated. The data collected by Anne Flitcraft at Yale University Hospital[6] suggests that extrication from the legal constraints of marriage does not guarantee an end to the abusive relationship. In fact, it seems that women who are separated or divorced are at an increased risk. Hence, a significant number of beating incidents were not included in the research population.

All of this suggests that spouse abuse—"wife battering"—is a significant clinical problem and that Lisa Leghorn's estimates made back in 1976 are conservative indeed.

Battered Men

The perpetuation of violence in an intimate relationship is not a one-way street. Many early studies have indicated that the man is frequently the victim of violent attacks (Gelles, 1974; Steinmetz, 1977). Folk stories and jokes about the abuse a man receives at the hands of his wife suggest that there might be a germ of truth surrounding the origin of these tales. In Table 1 data collected by Dr. Straus (Straus, 1978) documents that for all violent acts during the survey, there was only a slightly higher incidence for husbands than for wives (12.1 percent versus 11.6 percent). Additionally, women were found to engage in violent episodes somewhat more frequently than their husbands (again, using medians 3.0 times per year for wives as compared to 2.5 times per year for husbands). The summary data suggests that women were more violent than their husbands. However, one needs to look at more specific considerations. Referring again to Table 1, it is obvious that women tended to be "throwers." They threw things at their husbands about twice as often as their husbands threw things at them. Likewise, hitting with an object or kicking tended to be used more by the women than by the men. This is not surprising given the physical strength differential between the sexes. The data does indicate that for half of the violent acts, the rate is higher for husbands and the frequency is higher for husbands in all but two categories.

Dr. Straus, in his presentation to the United States Commission on Civil Rights (1978), rightly pointed out that the rate of violence by wives should not divert attention from the need to focus clinically on the problem of wives as victims. The reasons for this were as follows (Straus, 1978):

1. A validity study carried out in preparation for this research (Bulcroft and Straus, mimeo) shows that underreporting of violence is greater for violence by husbands than it is for violence by wives. This probably is so because the use of physical force is so much a part of the male way of life that it is typically not the dramatic and often traumatic event that the same act of violence is for a woman.

2. Even if one does not take into account this difference in underreporting, the data in Table I shows that husbands have higher rates for the most dangerous and injurious forms of violence (beating up or using a knife or gun).

3. Table I also shows that when violent acts are committed by a husband, they are repeated more often than is the case with wives.

4. These data do not tell us what proportion of the violent acts by wives were in response to blows initiated by husbands. Wolfgang's data on husband-wife homicides (1957–1958) suggests that this is an important factor.

5. The greater physical strength of men makes it more likely that a woman will be seriously injured when beaten up by her husband than the reverse.

6. A disproportionately large number of attacks by husbands seems to occur when the wife is pregnant (Gelles, 1975), thus posing a danger to the as yet unborn child.

7. Women are locked into marriage to a much greater extent than men. Because of a variety of economic and social constraints, they often have no alternative to putting up with beatings by their husbands (Gelles, 1976; Straus, 1976, 1977).

Morbidity and Mortality

The extent of husband-wife battering is alarming. The emotional trauma sustained must be significant. The threat to life and limb is variable. Physical morbidity is greater for women, but mortality due to family violence is significant for both men and women. Of all murders, 25 percent occur in families; 50 percent of these are husband-wife killings. Husbands are the victims almost as often as wives (48 percent compared to 52 percent).[2] These are alarming statistics indeed.

Causal Factors

"When we try to pick out anything by itself, we find it hitched to everything else in the universe" (Muir, 1967). The behavior involved in spouse abuse is unbelievably complex. Individuals must be seen interacting dynamically within their familial, societal and cultural matrix. The theoretical framework provided by the general-systems theorists provides a useful point of departure in analyzing family violence.

GENERAL-SYSTEMS THEORY AND VIOLENCE

A system is a real physical structure composed of interacting subelements which can be localized in space and time and which exhibit coherent characteristic functions or behavior over an extended period of time. A system may itself be a subelement of a larger system, or conversely, the subelements of a system may themselves be systems in interaction with super-elements. Specific properties of systems which are useful in analyzing battering relationships are as follows:

A system is more than the sum of its parts. Interactions among subelements endow a system with properties which its subelements, acting independently, do not have. A corollary is that the dysfunction of any element of the system affects the functional integrity of the whole.

An application specific to spouse abuse would be the difference in the autonomous functioning of individuals (batterer and batteree) versus their violent interaction or functioning within the context of their marital relationship. The super-structure, mainly the societal matrix, can have a stabilizing or disruptive effect on the marital relationship. The family structure, mainly others in the nuclear family (children) and the extended family, constitutes another super-structure impacting on the marital system.

The individual subelements of the marital system include the specific individuals involved with their own biological and psychological resources, which in themselves are subelements to be considered as impacting on the relationship.

Systems are located in space and time. There is a past history; there is a future for any system. Each subelement has a developmental history which affects structural integrity. The larger system as a whole, likewise, is affected by the passage of time.

Systems are designed, or evolve, to perform characteristic functions, to achieve characteristic goals. Disruption in the system's steady state will affect all the subsystems, as self-regulation and return to the steady state is attempted.

There are four major goals within the marital system itself, if it is considered as a relatively closed system:

1. To minimize loneliness and provide for personal affirmation vis-à-vis interpersonal reorientation.
2. To provide sexual pleasuring and gratification.
3. To provide mutual ego support, both adaptive and defensive.
4. To maximize economic advantages through the pooling of individual resources.

Whenever these goals are not being met, whenever one or both partners are stuck rather than moving toward these specific goals, disequilibrium results. In marital systems involving a battering relationship, specific attempts at adaptation and change are initiated, which usually result in an escalation of violence.

Much research on spouse abuse has been directed at delineating structural and functional aspects of society which result in the precipitation and tolerance of intra-familial violence. Von Bertalanffly (1968) has noted that

> we may conceive of a scientific understanding of human society and its laws . . . Such knowledge can teach us not only what human behavior and society have in common with other organizations, but also what is their uniqueness . . . The main tenet will be: man is not only a political animal; he is, before and above all, an individual. The real values of humanity are not those it shares with biological entities, the function of an organism in a community of animals, but those which stem from the individual mind. Human society is not a community of ants or termites, governed by inherited instincts and controlled by the laws of the superordinate hold; it is based upon the achievements of the individual and is doomed if the individual is made a cog in the social machine.

Consequently, in examining social factors which influence the outbreak of marital violence, the significance of the individuals making up the marital dyad must not be lost.

SOCIETY AND ITS IMPACT ON THE MARITAL DYAD

Cultural Theory and Violence

The social system consists of the activities, interactions and sentiments of the group members, together with the mutual relations of these elements during the time the group is active (Homans, 1950). This is true for society at large and for smaller groups, such as the family or even the marital dyad. Clearly, societal attitudes and norms will impact on family systems. These attitudes will affect not only family and individual attitudes but also specific activities and interactions of the family and its individual members. Theoretically, it would seem axiomatic that any effort to inflict bodily harm or to induce fear of bodily harm would be considered aberrant. This does not seem to be the case. Violence seems to be approved of and valued within American society. Social norms have developed which indicate when and under what circumstances violence is to be used. The most widely condoned expression of violence in our society is the physical punishment of children. Not only is physical punishment condoned, but abstinence suggests poor child-rearing practices ("Spare the rod, spoil the child"). A survey by the National Commission on the Causes and Prevention of Violence found that about one third of the population had been spanked frequently as children (almost all at one time) (National Commission on the Causes and Prevention of Violence, 1969). It comes as no surprise that children experiencing physical punishment in their families quickly learn that violence is an effective way of dealing with others.

There have been extensive studies of situations where physical punishment is taken to an extreme, as seen in child abuse. The studies of the abusers have clearly documented that abusing parents more often than not were abused children themselves (Sears et al., 1953). More significantly, Robert Sears and his associates (1953) studied 379 five-year-olds and their mothers. In this study, it was found that the high use of physical punishment increased the child's destructive aggression markedly. Sears places particular emphasis on the exacerbation of the helpless posture for a child when confronted with the physical strength and power of the adult. This in turn results in a buildup of frustration and rage within the child. There is additional evidence that the use of punishment, especially physical punishment, tends to produce a child who is relatively low in internalizing moral standards and controls (Hoffman, 1970; Kohlberg, 1964). This would have implications regarding the societal approval of physical punishment, the family's utilization of physical punishment and the development of the individual with inadequate intrapsychic control mechanisms over impulses, specifically aggressive impulses.

Families have other value systems which are socially transmitted and which encourage the use of violence. It is not uncommon for families to teach children to be tough. This is particularly true for the socialization of little boys. A survey conducted by the National Commission on the Causes and Prevention of Violence (1959) revealed that 70 percent of the 1,176 respondents agreed with the statement "When a boy is growing up it is very important for him to have a few fistfights."

Violence between marital couples appears to also have its roots in societal norms. Women have been treated as property in marriage for centuries, as indicated by the early bartering for wives. Jeannette M. Bond, in her paper *Wife Abuse, Reasons and Remedies*, points out that a husband's right to abuse his wife physically is steeped in the notion that a woman, like a child, is a person in need of control. In 1765, Blackstone noted that as the husband had to answer for her misbehavior, the law thought it reasonable to entrust him with this power of restraining her by domestic chastisement. This was based on the same rationale that a man is allowed to correct his apprentices or children (Sears et al., 1953). More recently (since the 1940's), court decisions have held that the common-law right to beat one's wife no longer exists. In spite of this, Richard Gelles, in his book *The Violent Home* (1974), describes his study of eighty married couples, the majority of which consider violence between married couples normal, routine and generally acceptable. The Harris report (1969), the outcome of the National Commission on the Causes and Prevention of Violence, notes that in a sample of 1,176 people, a fifth of those interviewed approved of slapping one's spouse on appropriate occasions. Straus had suggested that in many instances the marriage license is a hitting license (Straus, 1978).

Once violence between married couples is established, it is transmitted through the generations. Parker and Schumacher found in their study of fifty women that if the mother in the wife's family of origin was a victim of battering, there was a statistically significant probability that the wife would be battered by her husband (Hoffman, 1970). Straus has found that battering husbands frequently had the opportunity to learn this behavior from their fathers (Straus, 1976). Scott further suggests that battered wives are carrying out roles learned from their mothers (Kohlberg, 1964).

THE RESOURCE THEORY AND VIOLENCE

It has been postulated that within American society we have a subculture of violence. Data regarding the distribution of spouse abuse according to social-economic gradients is variable. Richard Gelles, in his early study, found that the incidence of spouse abuse was higher in the lower social-economic group (Gelles, 1974). Levinger, in his study of applicants for divorce (1975), found that among those seeking divorce because of physical abuse, 40 percent were from the working class and 23 percent from the middle class. Erlanger, in a comprehensive review of social-class differences regarding the use of physical punishment (1974), found that there was less use of this technique among the middle class, but that this difference was small indeed. A sizable difference occurred only when the analysis took into account differences within class, such as race, sex, parental ambition, etc. Erlanger suggested that variation within the social class was at least as important as differences between the classes. Goode's work (Goode, 1975) and O'Brien's work (O'Brien, 1975) support the hypothesis that violence is more prevalent in families where the husband fails to possess the achieved skills upon which his superior status as head of the household is based. O'Brien states that violence is most common when the husband-provider is deficient relative to the wife-mother in achieved-status characteristics. Gelles' data confirms this (Gelles, 1974). Goode postulates that social economic status per se has little to do with the etiology of family violence. He points out that while the incidence is a bit higher for those in the lower social-economic group, in fact there are crucial elements that cut across class lines in precipitating the outbreak of violence. He postulates a resource theory of social control: violence is a resource which can be used to achieve desired ends. It tends to be used when other resources are lacking or found to be insufficient. He goes on to point out that people have four major sets of resources by which they move others to serve their ends. These are (1) economic variables, (2) prestige or respect, (3) likability, attractiveness, friendship or love, (4) force and its threat (sometimes called power). The relationship or powerlessness and the outbreak of violence in individuals is described beautifully by Richard Wright in *Native Son* (1969) in a scene where Bigger awaits his execution for murder.

> "Mr. Max, I didn't mean to do what I did. I was trying to do something else. But it seems like I never could. I was always wanting something and I was feeling that nobody would let me have it. So I fought 'em. I thought they was hard and I acted hard." He paused, then wimpered in confession, "But I ain't hard, Mr. Max. I ain't hard even a little bit . . . " He rose to his feet. "But . . . I—I won't be crying none when they take me to that chair, but I'll be—be feeling inside of me like I was crying . . . I'll be feeling and thinking that they didn't see me and I didn't see them . . . "
>
> "I ain't trying to forgive nobody and I ain't asking for nobody to forgive me. I ain't gonna cry. They wouldn't let me live and I killed. Maybe it ain't fair to kill, and I reckon I really didn't want to kill but when I think of why all the killing was, I begin to feel what I wanted, what I am . . . "
>
> "I didn't want to kill!" Bigger shouted. "But what I killed for, I am! It must have been pretty deep in me to make me kill! I must have felt it awfully hard to murder . . . "
>
> "What I killed for must have been good!" Bigger's voice was full of frenzied anguish. "It must have been good! When a man kills, it's for something . . . I didn't know I was really alive in this world until I felt things hard enough to kill for . . . It's the truth, Mr. Max, I can say it now, 'cause I'm gonna die. I know what I'm saying real good and I know how it sounds. I feel all right when I look at it that way . . . "

Additional issues which need consideration regarding the apparent increased incidence of family violence in lower social-economic families are the lack of privacy in lower-class families and the tendency to call in social-control agencies (police) rather than social-support agencies (psychiatrists). Hence there is a difference in reporting of battering incidents.

CONFLICT THEORY AND VIOLENCE

The conflict theory and its relationship to the outbreak of violence are held by many sociologists and philosophers, such as Ibn Khaldern, a medieval social philosopher of the Islamic world, Thomas Hobbes, Karl Marx, Louse Coser, etc. This theoretical position postulates that conflict is a fundamental and often constructive part of social organizations, including families. It should be added that conflict is inherent in all systems and subsystems. It clearly is the nature of behavior and symptom formation set forth by the psychoanalytic theorist.

The conflict theory postulates that violent acts are generally thought to be goal-directed and problem-solving in design, that violence is thought to bring about some needed change in social order (Marx, 1970) or to reaffirm in a ritualistic sense the existing, structurally differentiated status quo (Neiburg, 1970). Conflict is most likely to occur during the decision-making process, particularly if the process of decisions fails to follow rules of hierarchal power. If a member of a subordinate status group fails to concede the decisions of the superior group, the superior group will use coercive means in order to effect the desired change (O'Brien, 1975). The question raised by Simmel (1955) in discussing this issue is that if conflict and violence are endemic in the structure of a social system, why do peace and tranquility prevail? Simmel suggests that the answer lies in the dynamics of the process by which legitimacy and value consensus are learned in early socialization. In fact, he states that the process of learning to accept legitimacy of structure is central to the socialization process. If social structure and hierarchy are challenged, disequilibrium results. Hierarchical status in families is assigned according to two factors—age and sex. Children have less status than any. Women are next to children in the dominance pattern. With the rise in feminism, the dominance pattern, or mating gradient, if you will (Leslie, 1967), is disrupted. Violence then becomes an effort to bring about a shift back toward the old order.

In looking at society and its impact on the marital dyad, we have discussed theories explaining the precipitation of violence within the marital system. These theories have included cultural theory, resource theory and conflict theory as well as a general systems-theory overview. It is relatively obvious that these theoretical positions are not mutually exclusive but, rather, relate to one another in a mosaic fashion.

The Individual and His/Her Impact on the Marital Dyad

Cultural and societal attitudes, sentiments and behavioral patterns are transmitted from one generation to another through child-rearing patterns. To review child development and its relationship to the growth of psychic structure with its consequent impact on the development of interpersonal relationships is not possible in this chapter. The reader is referred elsewhere for this information (Freud, S., 1905, 1915, 1923, 1926; Freud, A., 1966; Erikson, 1950; Mahler et al., 1975; Lewis, 1973). However, inasmuch as the individual is one of the subelements of the marital system, it is crucial to assess individual structure and function in order to adequately understand the battering relationship. While it is understood that on occasion physical blows are exchanged by both husband and wife, boyfriend and girlfriend, there tends to be one individual in the dyad who is more prone to violent outbursts than the other. There tends to be one individual who is more frequently the recipient of physical assault than the other. Hence, for the purpose of analysis, the characteristics of "the batterer" will be discussed and the characteristics of the "victim" will be examined in isolation.

The Batterer

Inflicting bodily harm on another person cannot be justified. The behavior can be understood but cannot be condoned. Provocativeness can be extraordinarily irritating but does not give an individual the right to assault another. The issue facing the clinician is one of understanding the behavior in determining the nature of the individual psychodynamics affecting the marital dyad.

In battering relationships, it is rare for the batterer consciously to plan to beat up his/her spouse at a specific time. Rather, the violence is precipitous in onset, intermittent and recurrent. The behavior is characterized by a loss of impulse control, expressing primitive fear-rage affects. The psychiatric diagnostic spectrum is great, ranging from neurotic, through characterologic, to psychotic disorders. The stresses resulting in loss of control may impact on the individual both from without, the external environment, and from within, the internal environment. The stress clearly overpowers the usual mechanisms used for control and adaptation. Drugs, including alcohol, can temporarily weaken adaptive and defensive mechanisms for control in individuals who are usually able to cope in the absence of such agents. In assessing the individual client, there are two things which must be evaluated:

1. *The nature of the stress.* Mature and psychologically healthy individu-

als with flexible adaptive resources can ultimately be overwhelmed by severe stress. This was particularly seen in concentration camps during World War II.

2. *The strengths, defensive and adaptive, of the individual involved.* Clearly, different individuals have different thresholds of endurance in the face of stress, both from without and from within. The ability to maintain impulse control has much to do with an individual's ability to test reality and differentiate between inner feelings and fantasies and the nature of the outside world, as do the ability to tolerate painful affects, be they anxiety, sadness or anger, and the ability to maintain self-esteem. These strengths and abilities grow out of the mother-child relationship developmentally. The individual, in order to accomplish these three tasks, must have developed a psychic structure with mental representations which allow the individual to see himself/herself clearly as different from others, particularly in respect to the development of a clear self-representation and representation of mother (internal object) (Mahler et al., 1975). The individual must have developed an ability to accept both good and bad in others and in himself or herself. Additionally, internal standards and prohibitions must be realistic and not too severe. Finally and most importantly, the person must have felt loved consistently and loved in return.

There are several diagnostic considerations which must be addressed. The psychotic client demonstrates severe impairments in reality testing, is under tremendous instinctual pressure and has a severe lack of self-esteem as well as confusion over the boundaries between self and others. This individual does not have adequate controls from within and will need help from pharmacological agents (anti-psychotic drugs), from therapists and perhaps from the structure of a psychiatric in-patient unit. The impulse neurotic needs to be recognized in that his or her impulsive acts are a rebellion against overly strict standards and prohibitions (infantile superego). Individual psychoanalytic psychotherapy or psychoanalysis is the treatment of choice. It should be directed at structural change vis-à-vis the development of a more realistic set of standards, prohibitions and expectations in order that internal conflict over needs and restraints be not so severe as to require such a violent rebellion. Such individuals tend to appear overcontrolled except when there is a breakdown in the characterological mechanisms for coping and adaptation. It seems paradoxical, in thinking about spouse abuse, that the precipitation of violent episodes of discontrol could be caused by overcontrol. There are others prone to violent outbursts who do so because of faulty controls from within. The psychotic is at one end of the spectrum, but others with less severe psychopathology can have episodes of impulse discontrol. Monroe (1974) speaks of the impulsive acts as a "short-circuit" between stimulus and response. Under normal conditions there is a lag, or delay, between a stimulus and the subsequent responsive behavior. There are two components to this delay, which is so often absent in the more violent partner in the battering relationship: (1) *Reflective delay*, which refers to "the time necessary for establishing the uniqueness or familiarity of the stimulus by associative connections with past experiences; the time necessary to contemplate alternate courses of action; the time necessary to project into the future and predict the outcome of alternative actions;" and (2) *Choice delay*, which refers to the decision to postpone immediate gratification for long-term rewards (Monroe, 1974). A defect in choice delay is more frequently found in the sociopathic person, who feels that the end justifies the means; the immediate gratification is in ascendency and the long-term consequences are insignificant. The violent outbursts in battering relationships more often than not relate to reflective-delay defects. This behavior is egodystonic in retrospect. The batterer frequently is embarrassed and chagrined. The individual is unable to control himself or herself and needs external means of control. External controls might be as simple as a neighbor being present and inhibiting the violent outburst or may involve legal prohibitions, court orders or actual separation of the marital partners.

Not infrequently a person will be referred who seems to be well adjusted and successful, both socially and professionally. He or she will nonetheless be involved in a battering relationship. On first blush, it is difficult to determine why such a person is having trouble at home. All too often the conclusions will be reached that the spouse is a shrew, hence deserving of the abuse. We must not reach such a conclusion too quickly, for the causes of behavioral differences lie in the intimacy of the marital relationship. The psychoanalytic concepts of transference and transference phenomena are helpful in understanding what evolves. "Transference is the experience of feelings, drives, attitudes, fantasies, and defenses toward a person in the present which are inappropriate to that person and are a repetition, a displacement of reactions originating in regard to significant persons of early childhood" (Greenson, 1967). These feelings evolve in some degree in all intimate relationships. Frequently in the marriage where spouse abuse occurs, these feelings can become quite intense. Yearnings for a close, all-understanding relationship as fantasized in an ideal mother-child relationship are not that uncommon. The subsequent disappointment in the spouse who fails to meet such rigorous criteria in the relationship can result in primitive rage. Clearly in individuals with impulse discontrol, intra-familial violence can result.

The Victim

While much is written about the individual who demonstrates a propensity toward violent behavior, the literature is indeed sparse regarding those who are the recipients of violent attack. Only two articles were found in the literature in which an attempt was made to determine the psychological issues faced by women victims. John Snell and his associates, in the article *The Wife Beater's Wife* (1964), studied twelve families between 1957 and 1962 in which the wife formally reported the husband to the court because of repeated physical assault. There were no controls, nor was the sample randomized. Conclusions regarding those studied were that the wives, for the most part, were aggressive, efficient, masculine and sexually frigid. The husbands were described as shy, sexually ineffectual, reasonably hard-working "mothers' boys." A second study of twenty-two women who lived with violent, alcohol-abusing men was done by Hanks and Rosenbaum (Hanks and Rosenbaum, 1977). This study found that the women involved were not a homogeneous group. They originated from three different family-background types: (1) subtly controlling mother/figurehead father; (2) submissive mother/dictatorial father; (3) disturbed mother/multiple fathers. This paper, while dealing with a small population, is nonetheless a major contributor to the understanding of battered women for several reasons: First, it clearly documents that battered women are a heterogeneous group and cannot be reduced to a simple stereotype, be it that of an aggressive, masculine and frigid woman or of a masochist. Second, while the major thrust of the paper is a delineation of the interactional aspects of the relationship between the battered woman's parents and herself, there is an indirect inference which suggests that the development of sexual identity, vis-à-vis a woman's experience in her own family of origin, is a crucial determinant for her patterns of relating within her own marriage as well as for her own sense of self and her maintenance of self-esteem. A fascinating phenomenon seen by those of us who work with battered women is that more often than not the women have greater feelings of guilt than those men who beat them. As Dr. Gelles noted from his research data (Gelles, 1974), women frequently state that they "deserved to be hit," that they "needed to be hit" or that "husbands are supposed to hit their wives." Psychological issues facing the battered woman and battered man have yet to be clearly delineated and further study is warranted. The likelihood is that further research will document the tremendous heterogeneity of this group.

CLINICAL PRESENTATION OF THE BATTERED-WOMAN SYNDROME

Case 1

Mrs. A is a fifty-six-year-old woman brought to the emergency room by police. She stated that her husband punched her on the left side of her head, in the left eye and on the left jaw. Her vision was unimpaired. She had no headache nor other physical complaints. On examination she had an inch-long cut with bleeding above the left eye and some bruising about the left side of her head.

Mrs. A lives at home with four small children and her husband. There is no phone at home. She has been beaten repeatedly by her husband. He tends to beat her when he is drunk. He has beat her with a milk crate, his fists and a pistol. This has been happening for three and one half years, since they first married. She has called the police several times and has been to this same emergency room on four other occasions. Her husband does not beat the children.

Husband has a previous criminal record (small charges). Mrs. A has had him locked up for the night on several occasions, but has never pressed charges. She stated that she is not afraid to go home.

Case 2

Mrs. G is a twenty-seven-year-old married woman brought to the emergency room by the police after being beaten up by her husband. He beat her with his fists, knocked her down and kicked her in the groin. She sustained multiple cuts and bruises about the head and had a broken nose.

She returned to the emergency room eight days later with a swollen right leg. She had a four-inch-by-two-inch mass in her right thigh that was painful to touch.

Her husband has been beating her for over a year, at least once a week. He frequently is drunk when he beats her. She had been referred to Women Against Abuse on previous occasions. She pressed charges against her husband one month before (charge: assault and harrassment). He was ordered to stay away from her for one to two years.

Her three-month-old child died three months prior to this contact with the emergency room after swallowing a small object at home.

Case 3

Mrs. E is a thirty-eight-year-old married woman brought to the emergency room by the police. Her husband pushed a chair against her neck. She developed local pain and started coughing up blood. She was also beaten and pushed around. Developed pain on touch around bones in her chest.

The husband put the chair against the woman's neck and threatened her, saying she must not call anyone. She subsequently called the police, who arrived in five minutes. They advised her to press charges, stating they could not pick up the husband unless she did so. The police then brought her to the emergency room.

Her husband beats her two to three times a month. He has threatened her repeatedly with a knife (as recently as four days before). He has been doing this for six years, ever since they got married. She has had multiple visits to the emergency room. There are no children involved.

Case 4

Mrs. I is a separated woman referred from one of the medical clinics at a local hospital, where she was being followed for ongoing medical problems. The physician noted that she had bruises all about her body. She had been beaten by her boyfriend, who punches her with his fists frequently (twice a week). He has thrown bricks at her. He has been doing this for over a year. He beats the children (three children). She has had multiple E.R. visits for this same problem.

She went to City Hall one week prior to this incident to press charges—the summons had not been served at this time.

The boyfriend is sober during the beating incidents. He has a criminal record (assault with intent to kill). The patient stated she was afraid to go home.

The husband's probation officer told patient to call the police and that a summons would be served in three weeks. The Emergency Shelter for Women was full. The patient decided to go home; throw boyfriend out of the house; would call the police.

Battered women, because of shame and fear, frequently disguise the true nature of their problem. Consequently, battering relationships go undetected. There are, however, patterns which can be identified that aid in diagnosing the battered-woman syndrome.

Dr. Anne Flitcraft conducted a study in the Yale–New Haven Hospital's emergency department. She studied all those women patients (ages sixteen to ninety-eight years) who presented in the emergency department during December 1975 with evidence of trauma. Five hundred twenty (520) women were in the study. Records were not found for thirty-nine women due to insufficient identification or lost records. Hence, a sample size of 481 women was reflected in the data.

Each trauma episode in a patient's medical record was classified in one of the following categories:

Positive. Inuury was attributed to spouse or boyfriend in the medical record of the event.

Probable. The patient was beaten, kicked, hit, punched, but no personal etiology was noted.

Suggestive. The record etiology of the injury did not seem to adequately account for the injury (i.e., fell down stairs and got two black eyes).

Negative: Nothing in report of the injury would raise suspicion that injury was a result of battering.

The following trends were noted by Dr. Flitcraft:

1. Of all trauma patients 7.2 percent had a positive history for battering. Of these trauma patients, 21.4 percent had a trauma history that was at least suggestive of battering (11.6 percent being either positive or probable batterings).

2. Battered women had more injuries than non-battered women.

Table 2

Category	Sample	Number of Injuries	Percent Total Injuries	Mean Trauma Incident/Patient
Positive	9.6	319	22.5	6.35
Probable	4.8	152	10.7 46.8	6.26 In adult life
Suggestive	10.6	197	13.6	3.08
Negative	75	755	53.2	1.83

3. Most women do not experience many injuries which demand emergencyroom intervention. For sixty percent of the non-battered women December 1975 was their first such injury. This was true for only six percent of battered women.

Table 3

Number of Prior Injuries	Percent of Non-Battered	Percent Battered
None	60%	6%
1	24%	11%
2	9%	16%
3	4%	15%
	97%	48%

Note: In order to include 97 percent of the battered population the table would have to be expanded to twenty prior injuries.

4. A "body map" was developed at Yale, which documented some most interesting patterns.

If the source of injury was work or a household accident, a person's hands or feet were most commonly injured. Deliberate physical assault carried a

different body map of the likely injury. Mainly the hand, face, chest, breast and abdomen were more likely to be involved in battered women while non-battered women demonstrated injury to the forearm, hand, lower leg and feet.

Table 4
Percent Incidents with Injury at Site

Site	Positive	Probable	Suggestive	Neg.	Total
Head	18	15	17	9	9
Face	50	52	22	11	14
Chest/ breast/ abdomen	26	16	9	2	4
Forearm or hand	12	10	22	30	21
Leg or feet	4	7	22	23	17

Note: While these data indicate injury patterns that are suggestive of battering and therefore are important signs in heightening the index of suspicion for the diagnosis of the battered-woman syndrome, one might not be lulled into an abandonment of suspicion solely on the basis of injury location. Simplistically, injuries to the feet do not rule out the diagnosis of battering.

5. Battering tends to escalate in severity over time. One must not, however, consider minor injuries as being unrelated to battering or even as being insignificant. One needs to recognize that without intervention, the severity of the injury to the battered woman will most likely worsen with subsequent events.

6. There is not a correlation between patient's age and the likelihood of being battered.

7. The number of children in the family is not significantly related to battering.

8. There is an increased tendency for pregnant women to be battered.

9. Battering is not confined to legal relationships between husband and wife.

Table 5
Relationship in Positive Case Load

Husband	54
Boyfriend	32
Father	4
Son	4
Brother	1
Father-in-law	1
Uncle	1

10. Extrication from the legal constraints of marriage does not guarantee an end to the abusive relationship. In fact, women who are separated or divorced are at an increased risk.

11. The Yale study finally sounds a macabre note: the risk of battering for women, once married, falls significantly only for the widowed (Flitcraft, 1977).

These patterns have been additionally documented in two unpublished studies conducted by the Research Division of the Section of Emergency Medicine at the Medical College of Pennsylvania. In this work, a retrospective review of all female trauma cases which presented to the emergency department in 1976 documented that 5.6 percent of all cases were positive cases of abused-battered women. Another 10.9 percent were probable cases and 9.2 percent were suggestive cases. This means that actual or suspected abuse was found in 25.7 percent of all female trauma cases. Hence, the health profession must maintain a high index of suspicion for any woman presenting with trauma.

Management and Treatment Consideration

An accurate diagnosis and adequate management hinges on eliciting a good history with specific questions designed to identify the presence of battering in the relationship and to determine the degree of danger present to the woman and her children.

Basic information, such as the client's age, address, marital status and number of children, needs to be obtained. Other necessary questions include the following:

Who lives in the home?
What are the children's ages?
How were you hurt?
Has this happened before?
When did it first happen?
How often does this happen?
How badly have you been hurt in the past?
Was a weapon involved?
What kind?
Are the children in danger?
Have they been hit or hurt by him?
How badly hurt have they been?
Have you ever told anyone about this before? If so, who?
Did you report this to the police? If no, why not?
If yes, which precinct?

What did they say?
Have you ever tried to press charges this time or before?
Does your boyfriend/husband have a criminal record?
Are you afraid to go home?
Where can you go?
Management goals must be divided into acute and long-term plans.

Acute Management

Acute management goals include the following:

1. *Identification of the woman's medical and surgical needs.*
2. *Determination of her emotional status as a result of the acute stress of being battered.* One needs to determine whether the woman is coping with the stress, is hopeful for resolution and is able to identify resources available to her; or, whether the woman is feeling regressed in response to the stress, helpless and unable to identify strengths and resources. Clearly these positions fall at either end of a behavioral spectrum. If the woman is more regressed and feeling hopeless, it is advised not to take over for her but, rather, to talk with her, help her start sorting out issues which need to be faced and help her to identify resources available for adapting to her stressful condition in life.
3. *Determination of the degree of risk to the woman and to her children.* The need for emergency shelter must be assessed. If children are being abused, this needs to be reported to the appropriate social agencies within the community.
4. *Determination of the need for legal information.* The courts and the legal systems are specific resources available to battered women. These means of external control are often necessary when violence can be controlled in no other way. The specific laws regarding intra-familial violence vary from one state to another. There are basically two different legal mechanisms which can be utilized:

1. *Civil procedures.* Different states have developed civil procedures designed to provide protection to those individuals who are the recipient of violent attacks within their own families. The Pennsylvania Protection against Abuse Act (P.L. 1090, No. 218) is exemplary. The act is a civil, not criminal, action. There are no criminal ramifications unless the respondent violates the court order obtained under the act. Generally, the act covers only physical abuse and/or threats of physical abuse, including "menacing gestures." There are no provisions for what is termed "emotional" and/or "mental" abuse. "Family or household members" are protected by this act. This includes those who are lawfully married and living together as well as

persons living together as spouses, including persons of the same sex. Blood relatives (brothers, sisters, parents and children) and relationships by marriage affinity (in-laws) are also protected.

The act provides a mechanism for obtaining protection from abuse vis-à-vis a court order. The court can do one of two things: First, an order can be issued that the defendant refrain from abusing the plaintiff or minor children. Second, if such an order is not adequate, the defendant can be evicted from the household. The act gives explicit power to district justices and municipal court judges to issue emergency orders for protection whenever the court of common pleas is not in session. Such an emergency order will expire automatically on the first day that the court of common pleas resumes regular business. Hence, the formal process for protection must be initiated. Upon violation of a protection order or a court-approved consent agreement, the court may hold the defendant in indirect criminal contempt and punish him in accordance with the law.

2. *Criminal procedures.* A battered woman can choose to utilize a state's criminal laws in obtaining protection against physical abuse. Most criminal statutes utilized for domestic violence are related to charges of assault. There are usually three categories of assault: summary offenses, misdemeanors and felony offenses. Conviction of a criminal charge, unlike that of a civil-law conviction, means that the individual will have a "record." Penalties range from a fine to probation to imprisonment. District judges and district attorneys have the reserved right to use their judgment in determining which charges will be brought against a defendant.

Specific behaviors which are classified as assault and consequently criminal are as follows:

Harrassment. A person commits a summary offense when, with intent to harrass, annoy or alarm another person (1) he strikes, shoves, kicks or otherwise subjects him to physical contact or attempts or threatens to do the same; (2) he follows a person in or about a public place or places; or (3) he engages in a course of conduct or repeatedly commits acts which alarm or seriously annoy such other persons and which serve no legitimate purpose.

Simple assault. A person is guilty of assault if he (1) attempts to cause or intentionally, knowingly or recklessly causes bodily injury to another; (2) negligently causes bodily injury to another with a deadly weapon; or (3) attempts by physical menace to put another in fear of imminent serious bodily injury.

Simple assault is a misdemeanor of the second degree unless committed in a fight or scuffle entered into by mutual consent, in which case it is a misdemeanor of the third degree.

Aggravated assault. A person is guilty of aggravated assault if he (1) attempts to cause serious bodily injury to another or causes an injury intentionally, knowingly or recklessly under circumstances manifesting extreme indifference to the value of human life; (2) attempts to cause or intentionally, knowingly or recklessly causes serious bodily injury to a police officer making or attempting to make a lawful arrest; (3) attempts to cause or intentionally or knowingly causes bodily injury to another with a deadly weapon.

Aggravated assault as described in (1) and (2) above is a felony of the second degree. Aggravated assault as described in (3) and (4) is a misdemeanor of the first degree.

Recklessly endangering another person. A person commits a misdemeanor of the second degree if he recklessly engages in conduct which places or may place another person in danger of death or serious bodily injury.

The specific statutes relating to criminal charges vary from state to state. The reader should familiarize himself/herself with these.

There are two more criminal statutes which are occasionally utilized in domestic violence. These are defiant trespassing and interference with custody of children.

It is difficult for the battered woman to choose which legal route is best. Issues of how much external control is necessary are paramount. Secondary problems which are crucial relate to the mechanisms for implementation. Legal counsel is necessary as well as clinical judgment as to the degree of danger to the woman if she is living with her husband at the time that he is served a summons.

Long-Term Management Issues

The battered-woman syndrome by definition is a chronic recurrent problem. Individuals can stay in shelters only for brief periods of time. Ultimately, decisions have to be made as to whether a woman should remain in the relationship or extricate herself and her children from it. This is not a simple process. The nature of the marital dyad and the individuals who constitute its subelements must be examined and understood. Issues outlined in the section on causal factors need to be identified in order to determine if a man can control his violent behavior by himself or needs help. If control of violent outbursts is not possible, then the woman needs help in extricating herself from the relationship. This is not an easy process. Women frequently are reluctant to leave for many reasons. One reason is pragmatic. Women oftentimes do not have the educational, vocational or financial resources to strike out on their own. Apart from the pragmatics, battered women find leaving emotionally difficult. The violent behavior of the spouse is so often at odds with his non-violent behavior that it is hard for the woman to see the violence as a real and integrated part of her husband's personality. This is particularly true if he is a "nice guy" outside of the home. "Hope springs eternal" when the husband appears considerate and sensitive. The wish is that the violence is a thing of the past. Transference issues make for considerable difficulty for the woman. Feelings from childhood experiences emerge as the woman tries to control an uncontrollable situation. Oftentimes she explains her husband's violence as being due to her own ineptness. If only she would change, he would stop beating her. In such instances, the woman needs help in separating out her feelings and behavior from those of her husband. She needs to have the opportunity to start seeing her husband in a clear, realistic way. She needs to see his shortcomings, his problems of control. These problems need to be seen as his, not hers, in order for her to have a clear sense of herself and to allow her to extricate herself from the battering relationship.

It is hard for the clinician to work with the battered woman. The adhesiveness of the battering relationship is impressive. Behavioral change occurs slowly. Psychological issues which prevent the woman from extricating from such a relationship need further study. The men who batter women are reluctant to seek professional help; hence their problems and needs are poorly understood. Much research is needed to understand and reduce the extremely high incidence of spouse abuse.

REFERENCES

Bulcroft, R., and Straus, M.A. Validity of husband, wife and child reports of intra-family violence and power (mimeograph).

Erlanger, H.S. Social class differences in parents' use of physical punishment. In S.K. Steinmetz and M.A. Straus (Eds.), *Violence in the family.* New York: Dodd, Mead, 1974, pp. 150–158.

Erikson, E.N. *Childhood and society.* New York: W.W. Norton, 1950.

Federal Bureau of Investigation. *Uniform crime reports.* Washington, D.C.: FBI, 1973.

Flitcraft, A. Battered women: An emergency room epidemiology with a description of a clinical syndrome and critique of present therapeutics. Unpub. thesis, Yale Medical School, New Haven, Conn., 1977.

Freud, A. The ego and the mechanisms of defense. Vol. 2: *The writings of Anna Freud.* New York: International University Press, 1966.

Freud, S. *Stand. Ed.* London: Hogarth Press, 1960.
　　1905, Vol. 7, *The essays on the theory of sexuality,* pp. 125–245.
　　1915, Vol. 20, *Instincts and their vicissitudes,* pp. 109–140.
　　1923, Vol. 14, *The ego and the id,* pp. 12–16.
　　1926, Vol. 20, *Inhibitions, symptoms and anxiety,* pp. 77–175.

Gelles, R.T. Abused wives: Why do they stay? *J. Marr. & Fam.,* 1976, *38,* 659–668.

Gelles, R.T. *The violent home: A study of physical aggression between husbands and wives.* Beverly Hills, Ca.: Sage Publications, 1974.

Gelles, R.T. Violence and pregnancy: A note on the extent of the problem and need services. *Fam. Coord.*, 1975, *24*, 81–86.

Goode, W.J. Force and violence in the family. In S.K. Steinmetz and M.A. Straus (Eds.), *Violence in the family.* New York: Dodd, Mead, 1974, pp. 25–43.

Greenson, R.R. *The technique and practice of psychoanalysis.* New York: International Universities Press, 1967.

Hoffman, M.L. Moral development. In P.H. Mussen (Ed.), *Carmichael's manual of child psychology*, 3rd ed. New York: Wiley, 1970, pp. 261–359.

Hanks, S.E., and Rosenbaum, C.P. Battered women: A study of women who live with violent alcohol-abusing men. *Am. J. Orthopsychiatr.*, 1977, *47*, 291–306.

Homans, G.C. *The human group.* New York: Harcourt, Brace, 1950.

Kohlberg, L. Development of moral character and moral ideology. In M.L. Hoffman and L.W. Hoffman (Eds.), *Review of child developmental research.* New York: Russell Sage Foundation, 1964.

Leghorn, L. Speech, Wisconsin Conference on Battered Women, October 2, 1976.

Leslie, G.R. *The family in social context.* New York: Oxford Press, 1967.

Levinger, G. Physical abuse among applicants for divorce. In S.K. Steinmetz and M.A. Straus (Eds.), *Violence in the family.* New York: Dodd, Mead, 1975, pp. 85–88.

Lewis, M. *Clinical aspects of child development.* Philadelphia: Lea and Febiger, 1973.

Mahler, M., Pine, F., and Bergman, A. *The psychological birth of the human infant.* New York: Basic Books, 1975.

Marx, G.T. Issueless riots. *Annals*, 1970, *391*, 21–33.

Monroe, R.R. The problem of impulsivity in personality. In J. Lion (Ed.), *Disturbances in personality disorders: Diagnosis and management.* Baltimore: Williams and Wilkins, 1974.

Muir, J. *The gentle wilderness: The Sierra Nevada.* New York: Sierra Club/Ballantine, 1967.

Neiburg, H.L. Agnostics—Rituals in conflict. *Annals*, 1970, *391*, 56–73.

O'Brien, J.E. Violence in divorce-proned families. In S.K. Steinmetz and M.A. Straus (Eds.), *Violence in the family.* New York: Dodd, Mead, 1975, pp. 65–75.

Pizzey, E. *Scream quietly or the neighbors will hear.* London: If Books, 1974.

Sears, R.R., Whiting, J.W.M., Nowlis, W., and Sears, P.S. Some child-rearing antecedents of aggression and dependency in young children. *Gen. Psychol. Monogr.*, 1953, *47*, 137–236.

Simmel, G. *Conflict and the web of group affiliations.* (Trans. K.H. Wolff and R. Bendix.) Glencoe, Ill.: Free Press, 1955.

Snell, J.E., Rosenwald, R.T., and Robey, A. The wife beater's wife. *Arch. Gen. Psychiatr.*, 1964, *11*, 107–112.

Steele, B.F., and Pollock, C.B. A psychiatric study of parents who abuse infants and small children. In R.E. Helfer and C.H. Kempe (Eds.), *The battered child.* Chicago: Univ. of Chicago Press, 1974.

Steinmetz, S. *The cycle of violence: Assertive, aggressive and abusive family interaction.* New York: Praeger, 1977.

Straus, M.A. Measuring intra-family conflict and violence: The Conflict Tactics (CT) Scale. *J. Marr. & Fam.*, February 1979, 75–88.

Straus, M.A. Sexual inequality, cultural norms and wife beating. *Victimol.*, 1976, *1*, 54–76.

Straus, M.A. Societal morphogenesis and intra-family violence in cross-cultural perspective. In L.L. Adler (Ed.), *Issues on Cross-Cultural Research. Annals of the New York Academy of Science*, New York, 1977, *285*, 719–730.

Straus, M.A. Wife beating: Causes, treatment, and research needs. Battered Women: Issues of Public Policy. Consultation, U.S. Commission on Civil Rights, Washington, D.C., January 30–31, 1978.

To establish justice, to insure domestic tranquility. Final report of the National Commission on the causes and prevention of violence. Award Books, 1969.

Von Bertalanffy, L. *General systems theory.* New York: George Braziller, 1968, pp. 52–53.

Wolfgang, M.E. Victim-precipitated criminal homicide. *J. Crim. Law, Criminol., & Police Sci.,* 1957–58, *48*, 1–11.

Wright, R. *Native son.* New York: Harper and Row, 1969, pp. 388, 391–392.

Chapter 23

The Co-Professional Marriage

Lana P. Fishkin
Ralph E. Fishkin

The two-professional marriage was, until very recently, unusual enough to be regarded as a curiosity and certainly did not warrant a whole chapter in a book. However, as increasing numbers of young women are demanding graduate training and embarking upon high-level careers, we are witnessing the greater prevalence of a special type of marital relationship, that of two highly trained, professionally ambitious partners. The particular stresses and strains on this union, with its unique set of problems to solve, require a flexible, creative approach. More conventional solutions are less applicable, and the partners are often without social and psychological supports for their venture. In this chapter, we will attempt to discuss this issue from an interactional as well as intrapsychic perspective.

First of all, a precise definition is required. After all, current figures indicate that over 50 percent of married women are employed. Unfortunately, a precise definition is difficult, as Rapoport and Rapoport point out in their comprehensive review of the literature on dual-career families (Rapoport and Rapoport, 1978). Their article cites a number of recent papers, both psychological and sociological in their orientation, which discuss issues pertinent to the co-professional couple. Many of these issues will be examined later in this chapter. For our purposes, we wish to restrict the concept of co-professional marriage to that in which both partners are involved in a demanding graduate-level profession in which an interruption or an extended reduction in work-hours means a sacrifice of career ambitions with respect to faculty advancement, opportunities for research, outstanding achievements within the field, etc. For both partners, professional obligations and commitments far exceed the limits of the forty-hour work week. Thus the groundwork is laid for potential marital conflict and role strain, which are generally avoided in more traditional marriages, where role behaviors and expectations are more strictly defined and limited, even if both partners are working. In a two-job marriage, as opposed to a co-professional marriage, the time pressures are greatly reduced, since one or both partners limit their work to the traditional forty-hour work week.

In the more conventional marriage, role specifications for husbands and wives (and mothers and fathers) do not permit much latitude. Wives in general are responsible for managing the household and the associated domestic chores. They become the primary caretakers of any children in the household and are responsible for the additional obligations and duties attendant to rearing children. Their feminine self-concept as essentially full-time wives and mothers is satisfied by this arrangement, unless there is some associated unresolved ambivalence. Their life ambitions generally do not include high-level professional achievement. Husbands in such unions are the primary wage-earners, even if their wives supplement their incomes. It falls to the husbands to pursue professions, if such is their inclination.

There have been numerous attempts to classify marital relationships in recent years. No single classificatory scheme has proved to be comprehensive. In their overview of marital therapy, Berman and Lief (1975) describe several of the existing classifications of marital relationships. These are based upon considerations of power, intimacy, personality style and parental stages. While each of these diagnostic classifications can be variously regarded as relevant to the special problems of the co-professional marriage, the diagnostic classification by parental stage, advanced by Otto Pollak (1965), seems most appropriate. Pollak's classification includes the following stages: (1) before childbearing, (2) early child-rearing, (3) latency and adolescent child-rearing and (4) after the children leave (the "empty nest"). This system appears to have special relevance for the co-professional marriage, since it is in the area of child-rearing that intrapsychic and interpersonal conflict are likely to be most intense. Let us consider in detail each of these states and their implications for the co-professional relationship.

BEFORE CHILDBEARING

Prior to the advent of children, the likelihood is that any relationship problems will be exacerbated by the intense commitment of each partner to his profession. For example, conflicts can occur when both partners are highly competitive, regardless of whether they are in the same or different professions. The disproportionate success of one partner may constitute a narcissistic injury for the other, with subsequent reactions of envy, retaliatory fantasies or depression. To complicate matters further, the more successful partner may experience guilt. It is generally the case that this reaction occurs more commonly when it is the wife who has the greater professional stature. The shared unhappiness of both husband and wife, or their respective defenses against their feelings, can serve to intensify marital discord, particularly if the relationship is tenuous in the first place. The following case illustrates some of these issues: A young childless couple, married since they graduated from college, began to experience substantial marital discord when the wife, a law student, completed her training and went into practice. The husband had been teaching undergraduate courses at a nearby college and was having difficulty completing his doctoral dissertation. As his wife's professional career flourished, he became markedly more distant, critical and antagonistic. He spent increasingly more time away from home and became involved with one of his former students. The wife initially felt guilty about her obviously greater success, including her income, which had doubled. She tried to minimize her professional accomplishments at first, but subsequently felt entitled to them and became aware of her own storehouse of anger and resentment toward her husband. The marital relationship was too troubled to weather this onslaught, and the couple separated.

The above case example illustrates a type of marital-conflict syndrome (Berman, Sacks and Lief, 1975) which is becoming increasingly more common as students marry and subsequently have to confront the rapidly changing situation as they launch their careers. The enhanced professional stature of the wife in this case affected the balance of power between the spouses and contributed to their marital dissatisfaction. The husband, who had married a dependent, subordinate and self-effacing fellow student, was loath to acknowledge his wife's growing success. His behavior became increasingly defensive, regressive and destructive to their relationship.

There are other considerations in the co-professional marriage which confront the couple with potential conflicts. Specifically, there are *two* highly trained, well-educated individuals with definite ideas, opinions, value systems, goals and commitments, which may not be congruent. Obviously, this is less of a problem in the more traditional marriage, in which the husband generally sets the standards, selects the life style, determines where the family will live and with whom they will socialize. These decisions are in the service of his professional advancement.

However, in the co-professional marriage, the clash of value systems can manifest itself in various aspects. For instance, one spouse who is a university-based physician or basic scientist might have a very different professional orientation from his or her clinician spouse. To illustrate how this might create a problem for the couple, consider the case of two married psychiatrists. The husband was involved in biological psychiatric research, since his interest was in determining biochemical causes of emotional illness. His wife was a practicing clinical psychiatrist, pursuing psychoanalytic training. The husband was contemptuous of his wife's involvement in "Freudian psychiatry," sincerely believing that the whole enterprise was misguided. She, feeling denigrated by her husband's attitude, withdrew emotionally from her husband and became reactively critical of her husband's "cold, unfeeling scientific" approach to human suffering. Of course the conflict described above was multiply determined and might not have presented a significant disruption had the relationship been supportive and mutually respectful from the outset.

Another potential source of marital discord unique to the co-professional marriage arises when a geographical change necessary for the career advancement of one partner creates a career disruption for the other partner. Such a problem arose for a young childless couple who had married during college and had pursued different graduate training. The husband, upon completing law school, had taken a position in a prestigious law firm and was anticipating an offer of a partnership in the near future. His wife, who had taken several years longer to finish her doctoral training, was now receiving desirable offers of employment in other cities. Since her field was highly specialized, she was unable to obtain a position in the city where they were currently living. The acute strain which ensued from this untenable situation precipitated the need for marital therapy. Issues concerning competition, power, dominance and dependence emerged in the treatment of this couple.

Being co-professionals can be mutually advantageous, especially if both partners are in the same profession or at similar levels of training. The potential for empathy, support and encouragement is enhanced when professional accomplishments are not threatening to one another. The opportunities for sharing ideas, providing discipline, sustaining enthusiasm, can flourish readily in such an environment. For example, a couple who had finished a psychiatric residency within a year of one another was able to take certification boards in psychiatry in the same year. Preparing for this examination together provided an opportunity for professional and personal sharing on an intense level. Although there was occasional trepidation about what might ensue should only one of the couple pass the examination, the experience was evaluated as positive by both partners. This couple continued to develop together professionally and to share their clinical experiences as well as psychiatric meetings and conferences. Their mutual toleration for one another's demanding schedules and occasional emotional depletion was enhanced by their similar professional orientation. Each partner was ready to provide a mini-consultation for the other, and their conversations ranged over both intimate concerns and theoretical or technical matters. The scope of what they were able to share with each other was far greater than if they had different professions. Since rivalry, competition and envy had never been of much concern to them, each was pleased to see the other grow professionally.

EARLY CHILD REARING

The years of early child rearing present new problems for the co-professional couple. The dramatically accelerated demands made by the addition of a baby creates added pressures for the couple. They must make a consensual, uncoerced decision at the outset that one parent will temporarily reduce his or her professional commitments in order to become the primary caretaker of their child. Generally speaking, it is more appropriate for the wife to assume this responsibility in most marriages, in view of her biological and psychological disposition to motherhood as well as the existing social and cultural sanctions for this role. While the above assertion is undoubtedly controversial in some quarters and may seem to be tainted with sexist discriminatory attitudes, we feel compelled to stand by this premise and will attempt to justify it psychologically, if not politically.

The nine months of gestation forge a psychological bond between the expectant mother and her child. This full-time biological attachment is a unique and unduplicated relationship. It is obvious that the expectant father can participate only vicariously at this time. Delighted observations of the baby's movements in utero add to the excitement and anticipation of both expectant parents, but prior to its birth the baby appears to have a more intense psychological reality for the mother.

Psychoanalytic theory lends further support to and justification for the primary caretaking function of women. Johnson and Johnson (1977) describe an "androcentric model" of feminine identification which is premised upon a reactive devaluation of the mother and which occurs in both sexes. They cite Lerner's (1973) discussion of the mechanism of the devaluation: the affects of fear, envy, rage and shame aroused in the child by his helpless dependency on an all-powerful maternal figure result in a subsequent defensive devaluation of women and a corresponding definition of appropriate "masculine" and "feminine" behavior, which carries over into adult life. Thus, Lerner's conclusion is that "the opprobrious social and cultural depictions of women exist as projections of defensive intrapsychic devaluations, internalized by both males and females during the oedipal resolution." Since the girl's unconscious resolution of the separation from mother consists of her identification with her mother as a devalued object, this dynamic might in part explain the psychological susceptibility of most women to succumb to the demands of others for need satisfaction. This intrapsychic mechanism thus supports the social expectation that the wife will assume primary responsibility for household and child-care activities. It also explains the husband's intrapsychic need to devalue maternal roles for himself as an outgrowth of his earlier identification and dependency conflicts with his mother. Again we see how intrapsychic mechanisms and sociocultural role expectations within both partners conspire to make the strain of role proliferation most keenly felt by the professional woman. There are both internal and external biological, psychological and social justifications for her assumption of the primary responsibility for domestic activities. Since she is already heavily invested in her career, she must choose either to temporarily surrender her professional aspirations entirely or to add another role, generally considered to be full-time, to her repertoire. It is not surprising, therefore, that the concept of "role strain" characterizes the professional mother who is desperately attempting to do a more-than-passable job at home and at work.

Johnson and Johnson have elaborated the concepts of role proliferation and role strain in high-commitment career women. *Role proliferation* refers to an "additive combination of disparate and disassociated roles, each of which requires deep commitment to both role expectations. This constantly poses competitive concerns and demands which are synchronous and continuous in time." They cite an autobiographical case study of twelve successful women which was recently published in the Annals of the New York Academy of Sciences. Virtually all of these women felt that their activities were regarded as deviant by their peers, teachers and superiors, but that their parents, and later their husbands, gave them a great deal of encouragement and support with respect to their professional aspirations. It was important that these women had the capacity to cope emotionally with being regarded as deviant. It was also important that their husbands, in addition to providing support during their training and professional life, chose professions which facilitated a reciprocity and sharing of financial, emotional and caretaking responsibilities. This supportive position is as necessary for the attainment of a harmonious co-professional marriage as it is for the wife to make an uncoerced decision regarding child-rearing responsibilities. Thus, to a greater and lesser extent, both partners are confronted with a degree of role proliferation within the marriage.

It is clear that the years of child rearing pose the greatest strains on the co-professional couple, with maximal role proliferation for both partners. Compromises must be made on professional and domestic fronts to ensure the continuity of these activities for both spouses. It is unlikely that the woman will opt for a full hiatus in her professional involvements, electing to become, even if temporarily, a full-time mother. She will probably reduce her work load to something less than full-time if her occupation permits. In this connection, the concept of "quality time" represents an important and justifiable compromise. Stated simply, it means that the mere duration of time spent with the child is much less significant than the kinds of interactions and activities which occur in that time interval. "Quality time" is a subjective and psychological maternal concept. It indicates the mother's relative lack of ambivalence about the balance of her role commitments.

Of course, that unconflicted state represents an ideal, which is possible to only approximate. The achievement of a comfortable balance between career and domestic responsibilities is a highly individual matter for each couple. The assessment of that amount of "quality time" which is adequate to ensure the proper psychological, social and intellectual development of the child is subjective and complicated. A recurrent process of reevaluation continues, with periodic concerns about whether the child is being short-changed of "quality time."

It should be pointed out that this dilemma is especially intense for the professional mother involved in the field of mental health, in view of the following considerations: First, by virtue of her training, she is intimately involved with theories of child development which stress the importance of the mother-infant bond and warn of the hazards for the child who is faced with early separation from the mother. Second, if she is a sensitive person, one whose own feelings and the feelings of others are readily perceived by her, she will be much more attuned to the conflicts involved. These conflicts are not necessarily neurotic, since they are substantially based in an external reality situation, the resolution of which is complex and difficult, if even possible. Thus, the professional mother feels herself often caught between Scylla and Charybdis in her ongoing effort to strike a relatively harmonious balance.

Some women seem to handle this conflict more easily than others. Women whose own mothers worked and women whose mothers were professionals themselves appear to have less conflict in the pursuit of professional satisfactions. Or, to put it another way, they seem less concerned about deviating from a more conventional sociocultural role, making whatever arrangements necessary for the care of their children with minimal anxiety.

The presence of reliable, competent domestic help obviously makes the integration of professional and domestic activities considerably easier. The professional mother who knows that her children are well cared for and her household is well maintained while she is at work is relieved of a tremendous emotional burden. It has been said only half humorously that the professional mother needs to have a good "wife" at home. While a competent housekeeper can minimize role strain for the professional mother, such a woman is extremely hard to find these days. Having ourselves witnessed the turnover of four housekeepers in one year, we shake our heads in wonderment at the good fortune of Nadelson and Eisenberg (1977) to have found that elusive but saintly being, the superhousekeeper.

In fact, co-professional couples often end up with worse help than their affluent but more conventional married friends. Naïvely, they begin their search for a highly competent "executive" housekeeper, but lack the luxury, in view of their busy schedules, to carefully screen personnel. Feeling harassed and desperate and facing tremendous disruption in their work if there is no housekeeper to care for their children and tend to household chores, they often settle for substandard help. Their demanding professional involvements don't permit them to fully explore community resources and neighbors for baby-sitting, home repair and cleaning services.

In her book *In Defense of Mothering* (Fraiberg, 1977), Selma Fraiberg points out the difficulties for the mother as well as for the child inherent in the use of inadequate day-care facilities or primitive housekeeping personnel. In fact, the poignant examples in her book are unfortunately not isolated or unusual cases. People who glibly advocate the use of such measures may not have examined the realities closely enough.

In view of this somewhat dismal situation, there is a further good argument to be made for the professional mother's reduction in her career activities in order to remain the principal and constant object in her young child's life. She is thus an ongoing buffer against the inevitable losses and disruptions as hired caretakers come and go.

Another set of co-professionals, blessed with twins, found the wife for the first time in her adult life having something in common with her mother, who moved in to help her. Rather than endure a dependent, regressive relationship, she was able to effect a rapprochement with her mother on an adult level, with subsequent enrichment for all concerned. For those lucky enough to have their parents still alive, healthy and desirous of an active role as grandparents, there is an opportunity to satisfy those obligations of "invisible loyalties" (Boszormenyi-Nagy and Spark, 1973) which may not have been fulfilled and, at the same time, to provide children with an opportunity to experience the only unambivalent love relationships that they may ever have.

An obvious way to reduce the extent of role proliferation and disruption for the co-professional couple is to limit the number of children or to have children closely spaced in order to get these most difficult but rewarding years behind them.

Role strains for the professional couple with young children are not limited to the allocation of time and energy among career, chores and children. Husband and wife roles are subjected to acute stress with the advent of a child. Both actual and emotional time and energy must be reapportioned, and those leisurely dinners, during which the day's happenings were shared by both partners, become a fond memory as baby clamors for attention. The intimate relationship may suffer as well, both emotionally and sexually, from the now multiple and intensified demands on both partners. Sexual difficulties, such as inhibition of desire (Johnson, Kaplan and Tusel, 1979; Kaplan, 1977) may occur at this time and represent a situational disturbance. This may be related to the level of fatigue engendered in husband and wife as a result of the various activities which lay claim to their days and part of their nights as well. Such problems obviously may also represent conscious or unconscious conflicts in the couple which, with the additional stress of new family responsibilities, have now become symptomatic.

LATENCY AND ADOLESCENT CHILD REARING

While young children create the most strain on the relationship, raising latency-age and adolescent children can also provide hurdles for the co-professional marital pair. As children get older, they make continued demands for parental attention and compete for precious leisure time, time for the couple to be alone with each other and time that each spouse might wish to devote to professional activities. After all, a professional motivated to excellence in pursuit of a highly demanding career can be expected to put in more than a forty-hour week. Yet one or both must make time for participation with children in their sports, social activities, cultural interests and education. In fact, in missing out on these activities, the parent loses one of the most satisfying and fulfilling experiences in life—seeing one's own offspring grow and develop. This can be especially poignant and conflictual if the professionals realize that their own intellectual and emotional development was enriched by parents who actively and intensively participated in their formative years. Conversely, if the professional parents suffered the real or functional *absence* of either one of their parents, they will inevitably experience guilt as they realize they are repeating the same process with their children.

Nevertheless, co-professional parents of latency and adolescent children find themselves with increasingly greater freedom as their children develop more autonomy. Conventions, scientific meetings both in and out of town and postgraduate professional training become more accessible. Summer vacations with the children in camp give a taste of the freedom long ago surrendered. Books can be read, and the lost art of unhurried conversation can be rediscovered.

AFTER THE CHILDREN LEAVE

After the children leave, the co-professional couple, like all parents, must confront "empty nest" living. A distinct advantage of the co-professional marriage is that each spouse has continued to remain involved in an absorbing, stimulating and challenging career, which can more than fill the void. In addition, each has, ideally, the benefit of a gratifying relationship with an interesting spouse, one who has not stagnated intellectually. There is now even more time for the exploration of separate or shared professional activities and for increased personal involvement with each other. The added income of two working professionals makes for a luxurious life style or for the opportunity to pursue expensive hobbies, provided the couple has not mortgaged all they own to too many money-guzzling universities due to an earlier excessive enthusiasm with child bearing.

In their recent book on dual-career couples, Bryson and Bryson (1978) include a number of papers which address themselves to some of the abovementioned issues. These papers focus on the special problems of the dual-career couple, particularly in the areas of job-seeking, domestic responsibility, the effects of having children, personal values and marital adjustment. These papers attempt to provide some statistical and interview data to document many of the points discussed above. One interesting paper by Pingree et al. in this collection examines the extent to which academic administrators hold attitudes that would be prejudicial to the hiring of a couple, thereby preventing a happy solution to the employment problems of academic dual-career couples.

As can be seen from the foregoing, the issues facing two professionals married to each other can be considerable. That is not to say, however, that all is problem and conflict. There is tremendous satisfaction and fulfillment in both the marital relationship and professional activities that can be achieved by both partners.

What makes some such marriages succeed while others fail? We feel compelled to speculate about this before we close, though our discussion should be seen as such rather than as objective certainty. We hope our guesses will be educated ones.

First of all, flexibility and adaptability are individual character traits important to the success of the co-professional marriage. While this may be true of any successful marriage, the particular stresses involved in a co-professional relationship, as noted above, require the ability to adapt to rapidly changing situations. The punches can be multiple, and the capacity to roll with them a real asset. The Group for the Advancement of Psychiatry monograph (1975) on the educated woman discusses the rapidly changing role conceptions of men and women. Flexibility is required, both from individuals and from their social environments, in order to accommodate to these new roles.

However, we wonder if these characteristics are merely surface phenomena which are related to a more fundamental underlying psychodynamic reality. It seems to us, based on personal observation and clinical experience, that the relative absence of intrapsychic conflict in both partners regarding their multiple roles is a sine qua non for the smooth structuring of their lives and activities. Specifically, to the extent that the wife is unambivalent about her desire to undertake several demanding concurrent roles, to the extent that her husband can unambivalently support her goals and to the extent that they are not conflicted about the measures that need to be taken to make their complicated lives workable, co-professional marriages are viable.

In an atmosphere of trust, openness, affection, and healthy assertiveness, difficulties are more readily and realistically resolved. In this connection, the existence of unconscious interpersonal marital contracts must be acknowledged, at some point, and negotiated. Sager (1976) has discussed this concept extensively, and it has, in our view, particular relevance to the co-professional couple, since there are so many more areas of potential misunderstanding and friction. For example, a co-professional couple who married when the wife was still in training experienced marital difficulties when she began to acquire some professional stature, after her semi-retirement for several years while her children were small. The contract under which they were both operating required that she pursue her profession, the same as her husband's, as an avocation. The husband was unprepared to recognize and accept her marked elevation in professional status, preferring to keep her dependent and nonthreatening. As both partners acknowledged their previously unconscious contractual expectations of the other, hostility escalated, and negotiations failed. Their longstanding difficulties with communication made a separation inevitable. Numerous clinical vignettes similar to the above are provided by Rice (1979) in his comprehensive and practical approach to therapy with dual-career couples. He incorporates the contractual concepts of Sager into his model of interpersonal conflict.

As we have elaborated above, adequate support systems are a necessity. We will mention this only in passing here to underscore how vital they are to ensure the smooth functioning of the partners' lives. Indeed, the opportunity to collaborate on this chapter was variously provided by housekeepers, two sets of grandparents, and of course, by each of us in turn.

Ultimately, the success of the co-professional marriage depends on the degree of congruence in the vision of life shared by the marriage partners. Both must have a high commitment to their own and each other's respective careers at the same time as they have a strong investment in their family life. They must agree that their personal marital relationship and the relationship they are building with their children are just as valuable parts of their master plan as are their professional goals. With these ideals in common, they can encourage each other through smooth or rough waters and provide inspiring, challenging role models for their children. We feel fortunate and privileged to be able to enjoy life at its fullest in our professional and personal lives. Each aspect of our many involvements has enriched and enhanced the others. We could wish for no better for our children.

REFERENCES

Berman, E., and Lief, H. Marital therapy from a psychiatric perspective: an overview. *Am. J. Psychiatr.*, 1975, 132: *6*, 583–592.

Berman, E., Sacks, S., and Lief, H. The two professional marriage: A new conflict syndrome. *J. Sex & Marit. Ther.*, 1975, 1: *3*, 242–253.

Boszormenyi-Nagy, I., and Spark, G. *Invisible Loyalties*. New York: Harper and Row, 1973.

Bryson, J., and Bryson, R. *Dual career couples*. New York: Human Sciences Press, 1978.

Frailberg, S. *Every child's birthright: In defense of mothering*. New York: Basic Books, 1977.

Group for Advancement of Psychiatry. *The educated woman: Prospects and problems*, Report 92. New York: GAP, 1975.

Johnson, F.A.. and Johnson, C.L. Role strain in high commitment career women. *J. Am. Acad. Psychoanal.*, 1977, 134: *10*, 1071–1076.

Johnson, F., Kaplan, E., and Tusel, D. Sexual dysfunction in the two-career family. *Med. Asp. Human Sexual.*, 1979, 13: *1*, 7–16.

Kaplan, H. Hypoactive sexual desire *J. Sex & Marit. Ther.*, 1977, 3: *1*.

Lerner, H. Early origins of envy and devaluation of women: Implications for sex role stereotypes. *Bull. Meninger Clin.*, 1973, *37*, 538–553.

Nadelson, T., and Eisenberg, L. The successful professional woman: On being married to one. *Am. J. Psychiatr.*, 1977, 134: *10*, 1071–1076.

Pollak, O. Sociological and psychoanalytic concepts in family diagnosis. In B.L. Greene (Ed.), *The psychotherapies of marital disharmony*. 1965, pp. 15–26.

Rapoport, P., and Rapoport, R. Dual career families: Progress and prospects. *Marr. & Fam. Rev.*, 1978, 1: *5*.

Rice, D. *Dual-career marriage*. New York: The Free Press, 1979.

Sager, C.J. *Marriage concepts and couple therapy*. New York: Brunner/Mazel, 1976.

Index